AN INTRODUCTION

TO

LITERATURE &

THE FINE ARTS

———————————————

MICHIGAN STATE COLLEGE PRESS

1950

Copyright 1950
By Michigan State College Press
East Lansing
Designed by Charles Pollock
Printed in the
United States of America

ACKNOWLEDGEMENT IS GRATEFULLY MADE to Appleton-Century-Crofts, Inc., for permission to include in this book a quotation from *Poetry of the English Renaissance* by J. William Hebel and Hoyt H. Hudson, copyright, 1929; to Dover Publications, Inc., and Bell & Sons (London) for permission to quote from M. D. Hottinger's translation of *Principles of Art History* by Heinrich Wölfflin; to J. M. Dent & Sons, Ltd. (London), for permission to quote from the Preface of *Nigger of the Narcissus* by Joseph Conrad; to Harcourt, Brace & Co. for permission to quote from Dudley Fitts' and Robert Fitzgerald's translation of the *Antigone* of Sophocles; to Harcourt, Brace & Co. and to Routledge and Kegan Paul (London) for permission to quote from *Practical Criticism* by I. A. Richards, and to Harcourt, Brace & Co. and Faber and Faber (London) for permission to include lines from *Gerontion* by T. S. Eliot; to Alfred A. Knopf, Inc., for permission to quote from André Gide's *Journals;* to Oxford University Press (New York) for permission to quote from *Voltaire* by H. N. Brailsford; to Penguin (London) for permission to quote from E. F. Watling's translation of *Oedipus Rex* by Sophocles; to Simon and Schuster for permission to quote from Igor Stravinsky's *Autobiography;* to Viking Press for permission to quote from *Portrait of the Artist as a Young Man* by James Joyce; to the Yale University Press for permission to quote from *God and Philosophy* by Étienne Gilson, from the *Heavenly City of the Eighteenth-Century Philosophers* by Carl Becker, and from the Abbot Haymo's letter in *Medieval Architecture* by A. K. Porter; and to the University of Chicago Press for the use of a quotation from E. Cassirer's *The Renaissance Philosophy of Man*.

PREFACE

An Introduction to Literature and the Fine Arts is a collaborative study of the arts of literature, of music, and of architecture, sculpture, and painting in the development of the Western tradition. It is an attempt to reinstitute the historical relationships of the arts to each other and to the common substance of culture out of which they severally emerge.

The plan of the work is historical. Its essential unity is not the neutral chronology of art products, but the pervasive, profoundly imperious human attitudes which at one epoch and another in Western history have been sufficient to govern life and conduct among men. Against the background of the classical and medieval traditions, as represented in the art of 5th-century Greece and the age of the French cathedrals, are projected Renaissance and Baroque art, the art of the 18th century and of Romanticism, and the art of the contemporary scene.

The special significance of *An Introduction to Literature and the Fine Arts* does not consist in the merit of the individual items which have been selected for study, but in the scheme by which works from different media of art, and from each of the major historical periods, have been brought together in a single enterprise. By the isolation of the arts from each other in contemporary discourse each of the arts has been historically falsified, and the concrete function of art in human culture has been misconceived. In this work an attempt is made to restore the commonwealth of the humanities, preserving the historical unison in which the human arts comment on and complement each other.

Two alternate programs are included, either of which may be studied separately. These are designated by footnotes to the several titles as Programs A and B. Each program is the equivalent of the other.

Each of the chapters, except the last, is introduced by a general reflection on the cultural predicament in response to which, for the period in question, the arts have arisen. The remaining articles in each chapter consist of analyses of individual works of art and of special tendencies among them.

The last chapter, Chapter VIII, is a systematic statement of musical theory and an analysis of the musical forms which will be encountered.

The execution of the plan has been the charge of a committee in the Department of Literature and Fine Arts of the Basic College at Michigan State College under the chairmanship of Professor Gomer Ll. Jones. Acknowledgements of individual authorship are made in the Contents. The editorial task has been shared by Professor Diether Thimme and in its latter stages by Professor William W. Heist.

J. F. A. T.

East Lansing
August, 1950

CONTENTS

page v *Preface*
xiii *Introduction*

I CLASSICAL ANTIQUITY

1 The Golden Age of Greece (5th Century B. C.)
    JOHN F. A. TAYLOR
10 Greek Tragedy: Sophocles: *King Oedipus* and *Antigone*
    LAWRENCE BABB
18 Greek Architecture: *The Parthenon*
    JOHN F. A. TAYLOR
28 Greek Sculpture: *The Parthenon*
    PAUL V. LOVE

II THE MIDDLE AGES

33 Medieval Christianity
    JOHN F. A. TAYLOR
40 Medieval Architecture and Sculpture: *The Cathedral of Amiens*
    JOHN F. A. TAYLOR
54 Medieval Music: Plainsong
    JOHN M. WARD
    General Observations
56 From the Ordinary of the Mass
        Kyrie Eleison
56   *Agnus Dei*
    From the Proper of the Mass
58   *Pange Lingua*
59   *Jubilate Deo*

III THE RENAISSANCE

61 The Rediscovery of Man, Nature, and the Ancient World
    DIETHER THIMME and JOHN F. A. TAYLOR
    Renaissance Painting and Sculpture
    The Dawn of the Renaissance

68	Giotto di Bondone: *The Arena Chapel*
	PAUL V. LOVE
73	Jan Van Eyck
	CHARLES D. CUTTLER
	The High Renaissance in Italy
78	Leonardo da Vinci
	PAUL V. LOVE
83	Michelangelo Buonarotti: *The Medici Chapel*
	PAUL V. LOVE
89	Titian
	PAUL V. LOVE
	The Renaissance in the North
94	Matthias Grünewald: *The Isenheim Altarpiece*
	HUGO MUNSTERBERG
97	Pieter Bruegel the Elder
	HUGO MUNSTERBERG
	Elizabethan Literature: William Shakespeare
100	The Elizabethan Playhouse
	HARRY R. HOPPE
106	Elizabethan Tragedy: Shakespeare
	Othello and *Antony and Cleopatra*
	LAWRENCE BABB
114	Elizabethan Poetry: Shakespeare: *Sonnets*
	ARTHUR J. M. SMITH
	Renaissance Music
118	Religious Polyphony: Josquin des Prez
	MILTON STEINHARDT
	General Remarks
	The Pange Lingua Mass
119	*Kyrie Eleison*
120	*Agnus Dei*
121	Traits of Renaissance Religious Music
	Sixteenth-century Secular Polyphony
131	The Madrigal
	HANS NATHAN
133	John Wilbye: *Sweet Honey-Sucking Bees*
	MILTON STEINHARDT
136	John Farmer: *Fair Phyllis I Saw Sitting All Alone*
	HANS NATHAN
140	Orlando Gibbons: *The Silver Swan*
	HANS NATHAN

IV THE AGE OF THE BAROQUE

145	Baroque Thought and Expression
	JOHN F. A. TAYLOR
	Baroque Painting and Sculpture
152	Tintoretto
	DAVID LOSHAK
161	El Greco
	DAVID LOSHAK
168	Peter Paul Rubens
	CHARLES D. CUTTLER
172	Gian Lorenzo Bernini
	CHARLES D. CUTTLER
175	Nicolas Poussin
	JESSE J. GARRISON
180	Rembrandt van Rijn
	JESSE J. GARRISON
186	Diego Velasquez
	JESSE J. GARRISON
	Baroque Music: Johann Sebastian Bach
191	General Characteristics of Baroque Music
	HANS NATHAN
194	Johann Sebastian Bach
194	*The Magnificat*
	HANS NATHAN
212	Cantata No. 4: *Christ Lag in Todesbanden*
	HANS NATHAN
	Seventeenth-Century Literature
224	John Donne: *The Sun Rising* and *Batter My Heart*
	ARTHUR J. M. SMITH
228	Andrew Marvell: *To His Coy Mistress*
	ARTHUR J. M. SMITH

V THE EIGHTEENTH CENTURY

231	Classicism and the Enlightenment
	C. DAVID MEAD
	Classical Music: Wolfgang Amadeus Mozart
235	Mozart's Life and Music
	GOMER LL. JONES
236	Mozart: *Pianoforte Quartet in G minor*
	GOMER LL. JONES
249	Mozart: *Clarinet Quintet in A Major*
	GOMER LL. JONES

Eighteenth-Century Literature
260 Thomas Gray: *Elegy Written in a Country Churchyard*
BRANFORD P. MILLAR
263 Voltaire: *Candide*
JOHN A. CLARK

VI THE ROMANTIC AGE

269 Romanticism
JAMES D. RUST

Romantic Music: Ludwig van Beethoven
276 Mozart and Beethoven
GOMER LL. JONES
279 Beethoven: *Violin Concerto in D Major*, Opus 61
LASZLO J. HETENYI
289 Beethoven: *Pianoforte Concerto in G Major*, No. 4, Opus 58
GOMER LL. JONES

Romantic Literature
301 John Keats: *Ode to a Nightingale*
ARTHUR J. M. SMITH
304 Herman Melville: *Billy Budd, Foretopman*
WALLACE B. MOFFETT
308 Romantic Painting: Francisco Goya
PAUL V. LOVE

VII CONTEMPORARY ART

313 The Twentieth Century and Its Antecedents
ADRIAN H. JAFFE

Contemporary Painting and Architecture
320 Impressionism
DAVID LOSHAK
323 Claude Monet
DAVID LOSHAK
328 Pierre Auguste Renoir
DAVID LOSHAK
332 Post-Impressionism: Paul Cézanne
DAVID LOSHAK
340 Pablo Picasso
HUGO MUNSTERBERG
345 Contemporary Architecture: Frank Lloyd Wright and the Internationalists
JOHN F. A. TAYLOR

Contemporary Literature
353   Thomas Stearns Eliot: *Gerontion*
ARTHUR J. M. SMITH
357   James Joyce: *A Portrait of the Artist as a Young Man*
ADRIAN H. JAFFE
362   Joseph Conrad: *Victory*
ARTHUR J. M. SMITH

Contemporary Music
366   Paul Hindemith: *Quintet for Wind Instruments*
JOHN M. WARD
372   Igor Stravinsky: *Octet for Wind Instruments*
JOHN M. WARD

VIII RHYTHM, TONALITY, AND FORM IN MUSIC

Elements
GOMER LL. JONES
381   Rhythm
383   Tonality

Polyphony
JOHN M. WARD
390   The Nature of Polyphony
392   Polyphonic Formal Procedures
395   The Forms of Homophonic Music
GOMER LL. JONES

One-Movement Forms
396   Binary
397   Ternary
399   Simple Episodic
401   Rondo
404   Variation
405   Sonata-Form
409   Sonata-Rondo
410   The Sonata (a Cyclic Form)

INTRODUCTION

EVERY WORK OF ART may be considered in either of two aspects: it is a formal structure; it is a historical revelation.

The interest of the practicing artist is usually an interest in form, an interest in a kind of structure which answers to a special need for expression. His manner of perceiving the merit of his own work, or of the work of any other artist or age, is fundamental to any study of the arts, whether on the part of artist or of historian. For unless a work of art be contemplated as a formal structure responding to some definite need for expression, it cannot be perceived as a work of art at all. Its existence as a work of art—as music or literature or painting or sculpture or architecture—consists primarily in the form or organization which it takes, and unless it be regarded with respect for these formal properties, it remains merely a physical object, a lump of stone, a patch of pigment, a chain of sound—a neutral thing which has not achieved for us the status of a living symbol.

Every work of art exists, therefore, as a kind of formal organization, whether the things organized be shapes, or colors, or lines, or sounds, or words. But it exists also as the vehicle of a human content.

All physical things, living or dead, have a formal structure of one sort or another. The peculiarity of works of art is that their formal structure is deliberately contrived; it is something made. A work of art may or may not be designed for use. It may, as in a building, be linked to the practical purposes of men; it may, as in a lyric poem, be the product of a free and spontaneous activity, fashioned for its own sake. It invariably constitutes an act of expression and carries with it, for the eye or ear which is sensitive to its forms, a meaning.

One of the first observations of the historian of the arts is that the forms of art are not constant. They vary with persons and with places and with times. Each individual work is unique, self-contained, and self-complete, nor is it understood by understanding what art is in general. It can be understood only by grasping the conditions which have made it individually what it is. Heinrich Wölfflin writes:

Ludwig Richter relates in his reminiscences how once, when he was in Tivoli as a young man, he and three friends set out to paint part of the landscape, all four firmly resolved not to deviate from nature by a hair's breadth; and although the subject was the same, and each quite creditably reproduced what his eyes had seen, the result was four totally different pictures, as different from each other as the personalities of the four painters. Whence the narrator drew the conclusion that there is no such thing as objective vision, and that form and color are always apprehended differently according to temperament.[1]

This reminiscence will serve to show what is technically meant by style in the arts.

Richter and his friends "see" differently, according to the evidence of their canvases, only because the Tivoli landscape is not actually what their canvases record. What they have perceived is no doubt the same for each, the patterned colors, the importunate voluminousness of an environing space, the thick creature detail. But their painting transcribes not so much the things seen, as the manner in which they are seen. The landscape is itself artistically neutral. The artistic fact, which is recorded on the canvas, is the kind of transformation which the landscape undergoes in being made a matter for art, in being

[1] H. Wölfflin, *Principles of Art History,* tr. M. D. Hottinger (New York, Holt, 1932), p. 1.

submitted to the formal sense which each artist individually brings to the scene. Style in art is the character in the finished work which makes of it a human document, the record not of an Italian countryside but of a human content.

It is for this reason, because every work of art bears the imprint of a style, that art and history are basically allied. Since there are styles of ages and nations and races as well as of individuals, we are able to say of an artist's work that not merely the man but a nation or an age speaks through it. Michelangelo paints as only Michelangelo paints, but he paints also as a Florentine and a Renaissance Italian. One perceives, on the crusted surface of a vault, no mere depiction of the scenes of the Creation and the Fall of Man, but a manner of depiction, a style charged with an artist's and an age's presence, which one shall know, and find accessible, solely by such means as this.

So, for the critic and historian, every work of art, besides being a thing of grace and beauty, is by its own nature a human record, from which one may gather more accurately than from other relics the intimate life of the past. The most important human records are not those in which men have deliberately sought to represent themselves to posterity, reflective histories which posterity may find reason to dispute. On the contrary, those works are of greatest importance in which, without thought of documenting men or times, an age leaves the unpremeditated traces of its special quality. So it is with the art of the Greek historian Thucydides. Thucydides' *History of the Peloponnesian Wars* is a document of contemporary events, but it is interesting, besides, as the record of a special form of historical sense, of a style of historical compilation and reflection. More in fact is to be learned of Thucydides, and of the intellectual character of Greece, from the art of his work than from the narrative of events it relates. For, later, the narrative may be qualified, the art can never be.

The humanities are properly the study of the forms in which man has left record of himself. The history which is recorded in the styles of art is, however, the history of humanity, not the history of the styles of art. The genius of the humanities consists not in the revelation of a past which is irrevocable, but in enabling us to reflect on possibilities in the human condition which have at one time and another been real, actual, imperiously urgent in men's minds. The persuasion of Greece that knowledge was a sufficient guarantee of goodness, the faith of the Middle Ages that life was a penance of the time-entangled human soul, the enthusiasm of the Renaissance that science and self-mastery were one—each of these, once passionately embraced, has been the effective attitude, the profoundly operative conviction, of men. We both share them and experience a disturbing unease that in some ways they contradict each other, that it is impossible that they should coexist as attitudes to which a man may devoutly commit himself. The sole function of the humanities is to produce the reflection that the culture of a people, whether in the 5th century before Christ or in the 20th century after him, is no accident of grace which can be simply inherited; that it is a thing contrived, made by man; that it is grounded in human decision and can be maintained only by it; that it can be destroyed by default of it.

In each of the chapters which follow, for Greece and the Middle Ages, for the Renaissance, the Baroque, and the Enlightenment, for the 19th and the 20th centuries, the several arts are brought together in concert upon this single theme.

I

CLASSICAL ANTIQUITY

THE GOLDEN AGE OF GREECE (5TH CENTURY B.C.)[1]

I. THE TWO PRIMARY EVENTS in the history of Western man are Greece and Christianity. Of these Greece was the earlier in time and existed, at the beginning of our epoch, as the way of life and thought and expression against which Christianity was forced to compete. The name which the ancients gave to Greece was "Hellas." By its association with a special attitude of mind which belonged to Greek-speaking communities in the ancient world, Hellas has acquired the meaning of a cultural ideal. It is the name neither of a place nor even of a people, but of a form of philosophic suasion, of vital beliefs according to which men have chosen to represent their place in the world and to define the good which they commonly pursue.

The formation of the Greek ideal falls between the 9th and the 4th centuries before Christ. Its culmination alone belongs to the Greek peninsula, where, in the brief hour of Athenian political supremacy, it found its cultural center in Attica. The Homeric poems, which tell of the fall of Troy and the wanderings of Ulysses, reduce to legend the account of a pre-Greek civilization which had already been destroyed when the poems were composed. The destruction is known as the Dorian invasion, the predatory descent of tribes from the north upon Greece and upon the Achaean civilization which it had nurtured. Before the victorious Dorians, in one of the great mass-movements of history, the displaced peoples of Greece fled the peninsula, some to the islands of the Greek archipelago, some to the Ionian shores of Asia Minor which lie on the Aegean seaboard, some to southern Italy and Sicily. There for three centuries their cities grew and sent out colonies. In Greece proper the arts and language of the conquered took captive the Dorian conquerors, so that there was formed a new type, the Dorian Greek or Doric, which claimed the heroic age of Homer's poems as a tradition of its own. By the 6th century B. C. the Mediterranean was studded with Greek-speaking communities—Dorian as well as Ionian—from Sicily and lower Italy to the Bosporos and even to the yonder edges of the Black Sea. The civilization of Greece—Hellas—was produced by these scattered Greek communities, geographically widely dispersed and politically distinct. The earliest Greek philosophers—Thales, Anaximander, Anaximenes—were natives of Miletus in Ionia on the shore of Asia Minor; Empedocles was a native of Sicily; Pythagoras and Parmenides founded their schools at Croton and Elea in southern Italy. Some of the archaic Greek temples, distinguished works by no means provincial in their quality, are to be found at Selinus and Acragas in Sicily and at Paestum, near the modern Naples. Bound together by a common language, nurturing a common poetry and religion, sharing broadly the same artistic and philosophic ideals, these peoples contrived for themselves a self-reliant way of life so various in its application to human issues, so sensitive in its discernment of human virtues, so poised in its preservation of human wholeness, that history, neither then nor now, has exhausted the meaning of their example, and only Christianity has been sufficient to supplant it.

II. The high period of Greek civilization, its Golden Age, belongs to the second half

[1] Programs A and B.

of the 5th century before Christ. Its center and cultural metropolis was the city of Athens, in Greece proper.

The Athens of the Golden Age is an event of culmination. Its foundations in philosophy and science, in drama and poetry, in sculpture and architecture had already been laid. To the century preceding belonged the formation of that attitude of inquiry which Western men have since indelibly associated with rational knowledge: the single date which is known of Thales in the first generation of Greek philosophers and men of science is 585 B. C., the date of an eclipse of the sun which he predicted; Thales is the first historical personality to search for a rational principle of prediction beneath the manifold appearances of the sensible world. To the 6th century belonged also the ritual processions which celebrated to choral chant and phallic dance, in the festivals of Dionysus, the mystery of earth's cycle of fertility; and the choral contests in which, for the prize of a goat's head, Thespis originated the role of the first dramatic actor and formed the medium of drama in which Greece's profoundest poetry was to find its place. To the 7th and 6th centuries belonged the formation of the Doric and Ionic styles of architecture and the beginnings of a sculpture which, informing stone, impregnated nature with an ideal of humanity such as neither nature nor humanity had ever known.

The consequences of these beginnings had been as yet, in these archaic molds, only partially divined, when this free civilization of Greek peoples in the West came into stark opposition with the Empire of Persia. In 500 B. C. the Greek cities on the Ionian coast of Asia Minor revolted against the Persian monarchy which for half a century had drawn tribute from them. The revolt was itself rudely suppressed. But Athens had been induced, in prospect of the calamity, to send a fleet to assist the Ionian Confederacy, and by her act had now exposed not only herself but all of Greece to the revenge of the most powerful force of conquest in the ancient world. Twice, in numbers so great that, if Herodotus is to be believed, rivers were drunk dry at their crossings, the armies and flotillas of Darius and Xerxes descended upon Greece. The victorious battles which Greece fought at Marathon (490 B. C.), and ten years later at Salamis and Plataea, are among the most fateful which are recorded in Western history, for in them it was decided that there should be a separate Europe and a distinctive history of Western man, that the initial act of Europe should be a revolution of the mind rather than the endurance of a despotism.

As the Persian avalanche receded, Athens, having withstood the shock, though her temples had been levelled, her olive orchards felled, and her city fired and left in ruin, was nevertheless at the pinnacle of her fortunes, a democracy supreme in its naval might, unrivalled in its intellectual prowess, the cultural center of the Mediterranean world. Head of the Delian naval league which had formed about her fleets, she controlled its treasury and directed the destiny of a nominal empire. Not without justification could she claim to represent the sentiment of Hellas, of a common Greek culture, which the Persian advance had wakened in the Greek-speaking world.

The period of Athens' reconstruction is known variously as the Golden Age or, taking its name from her most gifted statesman, as the Age of Pericles. On the Acropolis, the ancient hill-city above the town which formed the site of her public worship, great sculptured temples and monumental entrance-ways arose—*Parthenon, Propylaea,* and *Erechtheum,* the handiwork of Pheidias, Ictinos, and Mnesicles. Beneath these buildings, the architectural expression of the communal life, every former activity recommenced. In an amphitheater scooped from the hill and open to the sky, within the conventions of the ancient festival of wine, the tragic actor, masked and buskined, unfolded in the plays of Aeschylus and Sophocles the retribution which befell Agamemnon and the generations of the house of Atreus. In the market place, at banquet table, and at last in prison cell Socrates contended with the Sophists and with himself in discourses on the meaning of

THE GOLDEN AGE OF GREECE 3

the good life, the substance of which is recorded in the *Dialogues* of Plato and in the moral philosophy of Aristotle. To these same generations belongs the foundation of historical inquiry itself, the form of scientific pursuit exhibited in Herodotus' *History of the Persian Wars* and in the tragic history of Thucydides, in which the decline of Athens herself is told.

The Golden Age of Greece represents a precarious political equilibrium which was soon destroyed. Athens and Sparta, the two major city-states of Greece, as opposed in their economic interests as in their social ideals, engaged each other in struggle in a war from which neither was actually to emerge victor. In the aftermath of the Peloponnesian War Hellas was a cultural ideal without political substance. Greece—Athens and Sparta alike—became subject to Alexander of Macedon, whose empire carried Hellenic civilization abroad, as Christianity in quieter conquest was later to be carried abroad from Palestine, to the races of the earth.

III. The dispersion of Greek communities through the Mediterranean Basin was never conducive to any political unity among them. The idea of a nation, of a larger group bound together by community of language and culture into a political unit, is a phenomenon of modern times. Greek antiquity underwent only two forms of group existence —city-state and empire. The latter belongs only to its late stages and to its decline under the military conquest of Alexander and of Rome. The city-state is the basic original form of Greek society, its irreducible unit. A Sparta might exercise an uneasy political supremacy over tributary cities in the Greek Peloponnesus; an Athens after the defeat of the Persians might stand instably at the head of a naval league. But the proper expression of communal life in Greece remained always the individual city-state, geographically isolated and in principle, if not always in fact, politically sovereign in the government of its own people. The existence of these independent communities generated the most extraordinary variety of individual types, it released human energies into every avenue of intellectual and artistic pursuit, it exhibited the whole gamut of political complexions— from the tyranny of a despot, to the rule of few, to the rule of many. To the insularity of her communities, which forbade Greece ever to live equably in a larger political union of her own making, Greece owed her inevitable decline. To these communities she owed also the intense variety of her intellectual life and the humane generality of her cultural ideal.

Within the social and political limits of the city-state Greece created the most generous conception of moral and intellectual freedom which the world has ever known. Greek moral and political theory is dedicated in its entirety to a speculation upon the proper meaning of human individuality in society. If it be the business of the state and society to produce free individuals, what must be the function of the individual in the state, what must be his obligation to society? To have freedom without function, liberty without obligation, is not, in Greek political theory, to gain individuality, but precisely by an irresponsible aspiration to lose it.

In the democratic communities of modern times the unit of primary worth, in whose interest and for whose sake government exists, is the individual. Government is therefore restricted to the performance of a negative function, the function of harmonizing the collisive interests of individual men, of preventing one in the prosecution of his own ends from working injury upon another. The life of the community has become, in consequence, simply a togetherness endured, not an end sought after. For if the community of men is only a means which men use in order to obtain their individual ends, it can generate no positive good from which men shall draw a common sustenance; it can provide no content for human individuality, whereby individuals are made richer by a common good and a common dedication. It can only mollify the abrasive egotisms of individual men, who suffer each other because without each other they cannot live. Every harsh contradiction in contemporary society, its moral desperateness, has been owing to its inability to find some positive sense and value in the togetherness of men, which is not merely the additive value of Jack and Tom. To reconcile the claims of Jack's and Tom's existence-apart as individual men with the claims of their existence-together as a community of men, to preserve each claim as real while limiting both as complementary, is the problem which tragically confronts the civilization of the West. The humane alternative to egotistic individualism in society is not, and never has been, the totalitarian state, which cancels individuality by using men as means. The alternative belongs to the philosophers of Greece—to the *Republic* of Plato and the *Nicomachean Ethics* and *Politics* of Aristotle, in which is formulated the political ideal of humanity so long as humanity remains rooted to earth.

Aristotle writes in the *Nicomachean Ethics* (I, 2):

For even if the end is the same for a single man and for a state, that of the state seems at all events something greater and more complete whether to attain or to preserve; though it is worth while to attain the end merely for one man, it is finer and more godlike to attain it for a nation or for city-states.

The common presupposition of Greek political awareness is that the end for a single man and for the state is one and the same, namely, the good life. The state is therefore the positive extension of the citizen, the human soul "writ large," whose virtue can be nothing else than to guarantee to its citizens the conditions necessary to the highest possible development of their native talents. State and citizen exist in mutual interdependence; neither is a means for the other's use; there is no good which is not for both. To a father who inquired how his son should be educated, a Pythagorean sage replied, that he should be made a citizen of a community with good institutions. The meaning is not that such a community exists, or ever has existed; the meaning is that the community, not the isolated individual, is the unit of human society, within which alone the dignity of a human being can be realized. For apart from the institutional life of a community a man is neither free nor capable of realizing the virtues which it is the destiny of a human being to assume. Man is, in Aristotle's phrase, the "political animal," who is destined to live in social intercourse with others of his kind and to be governed in conformity with a common good. He is free not by detachment from the external demands of society upon him, but precisely by reason of his duties within society, which supply to him the proper content of his existence as an individual. He can be perfect as individual only by being complete as citizen of his kind. The epitaph which was inscribed on the tomb of Leonidas and his Spartan comrades at Thermopylae was: "Go, stranger, and tell the Lacedaemonians that we lie here in obedience to their laws."

IV. In Sophocles' tragedy *Antigone* the division of allegiance which separates Antigone and Creon and sets them in tragic antagonism to each other depends upon a conflict between the laws of man and the unwritten laws of heaven. To Creon, whose human edict she has transgressed, Antigone says:

For it was not Zeus that had published me that edict . . . nor deemed I that thy decrees were of such force, that a mortal could override the unwritten and unfailing statutes of heaven. For their life is not of today or yesterday, but from all time, and no man knows when they were first put forth.

The ideal justice appealed to, which is superior to the pronouncements of custom and use and which must displace custom and temporal authority when they are in disagreement with it, is in Greek thought the concern of philosopher as well as tragedian.

In the dissolution of beliefs which had begun in the Golden Age itself, there were men who no longer credited the unalterableness of the moral law. Greek philosophy is not everywhere affirmative. Its major irritant in the 5th century, the symptom of dissolution against which Socrates reacted, was the teaching of the Sophists, a group of disputants in Athens, variously scrupulous and variously wise, who professed, for a fee, to teach men wisdom. At its worst, Sophistry represents the meaning which the tradition of our language has preserved for the word, a specious dexterity in argument, the cynically empty rhetoric of the market place and the court of law, which professes truth without caring for it. At its best, it is the skeptic germ in Greek philosophy. Protagoras, one of the most distinguished of the group, is the author of the famous doctrine, that "man is the measure of all things." The doctrine is the form under which Greek philosophy gave expression to the theory of moral and intellectual relativism, the theory that the moral law has no objective status in nature; that the values to which men subscribe, their ideas of goodness, of beauty, and even of truth itself, have no authority except the authority of custom, no sanction except the sanction of use; that as customs vary among different peoples and at different times, so also the standards of good and evil, of beauty and ugliness, of truth and falsity must vary; that therefore there can be no significant argument with respect to those matters which, as men live, must matter to them most. To Protagoras, Antigone's appeal to the unwritten laws of heaven is not, as Sophocles believed it, an appeal to a law of God or to a fixed moral law of the universe; it is in reality only a refinement upon written law, reflecting the deeper moral sentiment of a people which is not yet written into custom.

Socrates' whole life of thought is a remonstrance to Protagoras. If man be the measure of what is good, if custom be the arbiter of what is right, with what right does one speak of custom's refining upon itself? If the deeper moral sentiments of a people must decide on good and evil, then by reference to what standard shall one decide which sentiments are deeper, Antigone's or Creon's? The standard cannot be custom itself, since this precisely is what Creon and Antigone represent in its written and unwritten forms. The standard which gives precedence to one part of custom over the other cannot be custom; it must be in some way distinct from custom, superior to it, and therefore superior also to Creon and Antigone. This standard is not relative to custom but independent of it. It can be known, according to Socrates, only by rational insight into the nature of man and of the good after which he ultimately aspires. Goodness, beauty, truth are not man-made. On the contrary, they have an ideal objective existence from which men can err only by ignorance and at cost of degradation.

V. What is the sin of Creon or of Oedipus in the tragedies of Sophocles? The Greeks described it as *hybris,* tragic insolence. *Hybris* is the excess of what in right measure might have been a mark of nobility in either man. What Oedipus and Creon offend against and come to acknowledge as the moral law is a humane sense of proportion. The sense of what is proportionate and just conforms to the old Greek proverb: "Nothing in excess." As formulated by Plato and Aristotle, the proverb goes by the name "the doctrine of the mean."

Aristotle writes:

We often say of good works of art that it is not possible either to take away or to add anything, implying that excess and defect destroy the goodness of works of art, while the mean preserves it; and good artists . . . look to this in their work. (*Nicomachean Ethics,* II, 6)

In the same way, with respect to human action, there is a mean at which man, in acting according to his best nature, aims. Every human virtue is a mean between two extremes, which represent the excess or the deficiency of it. In the government of the passions man's good consists neither in reckless self-indulgence nor in ascetic self-denial. The one is an excess, the other is a deficiency: both are deviations from the mean, which is to employ the passions rightly and in proper measure. Flesh is not of the devil, but of man, whose virtue is temperance, moderation in all things. Similarly, courage is a mean between rashness and

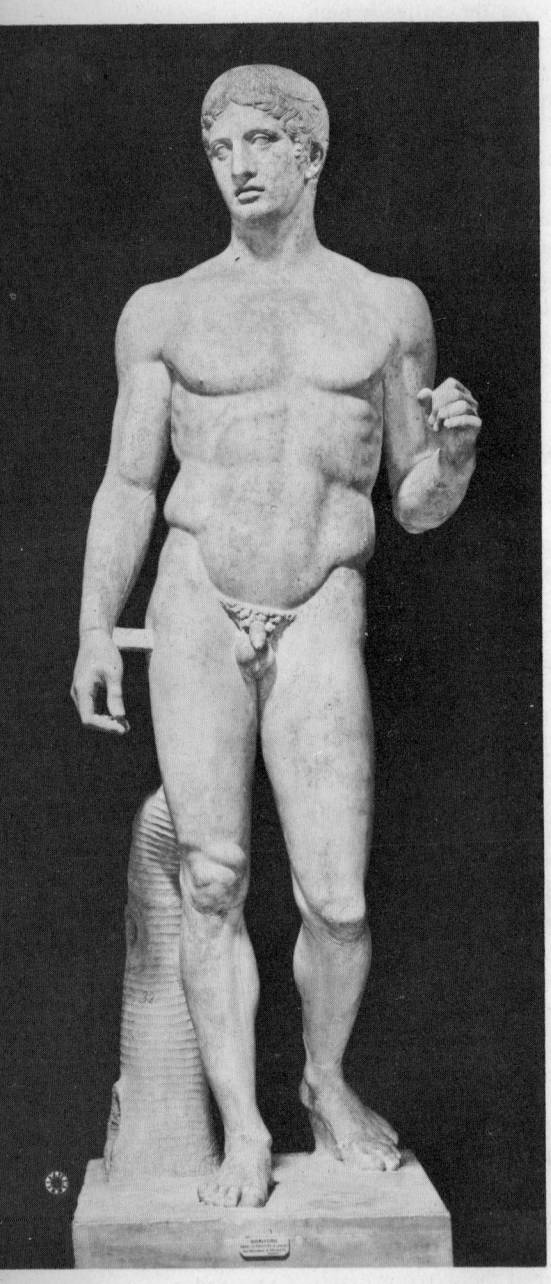

Fig. 1. After Polycleitos, *Spearbearer, ca.* 450 B.C., Museo Nazionale, Naples (*Anderson*)

timidity. It includes a measure of boldness, but also of judgment and circumspection. The mean is everywhere the measure of what is just, proportionate, consistent with the harmony of man's whole nature. The doctrine of the mean is simply an acknowledgement that there are many ways of erring from what is right, there is but one way of performing it. Yet, in human action as in art, this mean is never mathematically calculable. Six pounds is an absolute mean between two and ten, since six exceeds and is exceeded by an equal amount. But in a matter of diet the mean will be relative to persons: six pounds of food may be too little for Milo the Wrestler, too much for Socrates. It is nevertheless true that for any given individual—Milo or Socrates—there exists a certain course of action from which he may deviate only by transgressing what is good for him in his quality as a human being. He shall transgress it only by losing his properly human character which it is his moral destiny to maintain. Man is, in Greek moral theory, the fashioner of his own destiny for good or evil and is bound, in the conception of it, to rely on his own critical faculty of discerning what constitutes the true good. Except as he gives it freely to himself, his destiny is not given to him, either by God, or by fate, or by inheritance, or by custom. The fateful responsibility of humankind is that it can sin against no God, but only against itself.

VI. Greek art is commonly described as "idealist." The description is intended to denote not a characteristic of Greek artists, but a positive property of their works, whether in architecture or sculpture or tragedy. In the representation of human figure or of tragic personage a Greek work of art is invariably the delineation of a type. It seizes the feature whereby the single man exemplifies all men. The particular trait, the idiosyncrasy by which one man is distinguished from another, finds no place in the work. Oedipus exemplifies the type of tragic insolence in man; Antigone the type of human loyalty and dedication to the moral law: in either case it is the tragic circumstance, not the personage, which is specific; the personage is particularized only in the degree which the necessity of the action demands. So, in Polycleitos' *Spearbearer* (Fig. 1), the proportions of the form are the ideal proportions of all men, but the actual proportions of no one. In the *Hegeso Stele* (Fig. 2), gravestone of a dead maiden, the portrait-figure does not exist by its likeness to a particular individual woman; it is woman herself, represented in the characteristic perennial act of women everywhere—a self-adornment plain in its neatness, as it were to say, "As I am enduringly, so also thou art."

In the ideality of any one of these figures may be discerned the substantial presence of a total philosophy, a philosophy so

THE GOLDEN AGE OF GREECE

profoundly operative in Greek thought and expression that no part of either escapes its universal claim. This philosophy was formulated, during the generation which followed Socrates, in the *Dialogues* of Plato. Platonic philosophy is the compendious intellectual expression of the Greek world. The highest achievement of Greek intellect, it is the veritable complement of Greek art.

Greek reflection on the nature of reality is an attempt to find, in the midst of change, some basis of permanent order which is capable of being known. The world revealed to us by the senses is composed of fugitive particular events—colors, shapes, sounds, smells, impressions of touch, spread out in space and passing in time, things which occur "here" and "now," or "then" and "there." Everything which we experience is such a particular, a "this" or a "that," localized somewhere in space and somewhere in time, and its particularity consists precisely in its being somewhere and sometime. Yet this experience, in which things occur and pass in space and time, is no idle parade of impressions, in which the mind is stupefied and bewildered. It is not, as the early Greek philosopher Heraclitus represented it, "all flux," all change, all perishableness, so that one cannot step twice into the same stream. It is the characteristic of an event that it occurs, and retreats irrevocably into the past of the world; with respect to its spatial and temporal position it is absolutely unique. But in the midst of these events which occur but once and are gone there are certain elements which are capable of recurrence, of occurring again, in different parts of space and at different times. Thus, I say of my book *The Dialogues of Plato* that it is the same book which lay on my desk yesterday, that it is the book which Plato wrote, and that it exists in the library of every educated man. What I must mean by *"The Dialogues of Plato"* is not the particular event which is here before me now, but a special arrangement of symbols, a formal order, which is capable of recurring at different places and at different times. The places and times alone are different; the formal order which inhabits them is everywhere the same. The text before me and the text before Plato

Fig. 2. *Hegeso Stele, ca.* 400 B.C., National Museum, Athens (*Alinari*)

are simply particular instances of this one form which is the same for him and for me. In the same way, if I speak of the color "red," or of "circularity," or of "goodness," or of "man," I refer to elements in experience which are capable of occurring not merely once, but many times. Each is capable of being a property which is shared among a variety of events. It is upon these recurrent elements in experience that any knowledge whatever is grounded. If such recurrent elements were not available in experience, the knowledge of one event would give us no information about any other. It is because events are in some respects alike, because in the midst of all differences they are still the same, that we may generalize about them and find in particular events instances of general truths.

These elements which are capable of recurrence Plato calls "Ideas" or "Forms." In a later terminology they are known, in contrast to particulars, as "universals." Thus, in knowing Peter and Paul, I know not merely individuals, but the characteristics which they share in common whereby I call them both alike "men." Peter and Paul are said to be particular instances of the universal "man."

To these universals or ideal forms Plato ascribes a special existence in a realm of pure being.[2] This ideal world has for Plato an eminent reality which the things of the world perceived through the senses only partially and incompletely share, as the reflection of an object in a mirror has only a dependent and incomplete existence in relation to the thing reflected. The descent of these ideal forms into space and time, into what Plato calls "the matrix of becoming," inevitably qualifies and contaminates their purity. In all the many things which are said to be beautiful there is but one Beauty, the ideal form by sharing in which they have their character; and to know this form is to know the degree of reality which these things have.

For he who would proceed aright in this matter should begin in youth to visit beautiful forms; and first, if he be guided by his instructor aright, to love one such form only—out of that he should create fair thoughts; and soon he will of himself perceive that the beauty of one form is akin to the beauty of another; and then if beauty of form in general is his pursuit, how foolish would he be not to recognize that the beauty in every form is one and the same! And when he perceives this he will abate his violent love of the one, and will become a lover of all beautiful forms; in the next stage he will consider that the beauty of the mind is more honorable than the beauty of the outward form. So that if a virtuous soul have but a little comeliness, he will be content to love and tend him, and will search out and bring to the birth thoughts which may improve the young, until he is compelled to contemplate and see the beauty of institutions and laws, and to understand that the beauty of them all is of one family, and that personal beauty is a trifle; and after laws and institutions he will go on to the sciences, that he may see their beauty, being not like a servant in love with the beauty of one youth or man or institution, himself a slave mean and narrow-minded, but drawing towards and contemplating the vast sea of beauty, he will create many fair and noble thoughts and notions in boundless love of wisdom; until on that shore he grows and waxes strong, and at last the vision is revealed to him of a single science, which is the science of beauty everywhere. . . . beauty absolute, separate, simple, and everlasting, which without diminution and without increase, or any change, is imparted to the ever-growing and perishing beauties of all other things. (*Symposium,* 210-11)

The world of particulars in space and time which is experienced through the avenues of sense is not therefore for Plato the real world, but only the distorted and imperfect appearance of it. Reality consists in an order of pure being which is accessible only to rational insight, the realm of ideal forms which are out of time and out of space—perfect, eternal,

---

[2]The exemplary science for Plato was, therefore, mathematics. A geometer's reflections on the properties of the circle do not depend on the existence of this object in space and time. The perfect circle nowhere exists, but may nevertheless be explored as a pure possibility. The proposition "$2 + 2 = 4$" is true in all cases, and may be known to be true prior to all experience, since its truth does not depend upon the special character of the objects added or upon the spatio-temporal existence of any objects whatever.

THE GOLDEN AGE OF GREECE

and incorruptible. For the reality which alone can be known is not the external riot of particulars, but the samenesses among them. In a modern phrase, reality is not in events, but in the order and regularity among events, not in phenomena but in law. To the eye of the philosopher the motley world of sense is but "the moving image of eternity"—the imperfect and perishable reflection wrought by a divine architect according to the plan of an imperishable world of pure forms.

VII. Every age has its fables, in which it has recorded its vision of itself. As modern man finds himself in the tragedy of Faust, who, to have perfect knowledge and perfect power, sold his soul to the devil; as medieval man found himself in the awful presentiment of the Last Judgment, in which the naked human soul was chosen for heaven or damnation, so, in the Greek world, man's perfect self-awareness, his tragic sense of his existence in the world, is recorded in the vision of Er. Slain in battle, the hero Er lay ten days among his fallen comrades in arms. When at last the dead bodies were taken up in a state of corruption, the body of Er was found still perfect without decay. On the twelfth day, as his body was laid on a funeral pyre, the hero awoke and recounted what he had seen in the world of the dead, where souls were prepared for their transmigrations to other lives. There presided the Fates, daughters of Necessity, clothed in white robes and wearing chaplets on their heads—Lachesis, Clotho, and Atropos.

Hear the word of Lachesis, the daughter of Necessity. Mortal souls, behold a new cycle of life and mortality. Your genius will not be allotted to you, but you will choose your genius; and let him who draws the first lot have the first choice, and the life which he chooses shall be his destiny. Virtue is free, and as a man honors or dishonors her he will have more or less of her; the responsibility is with the chooser—God is justified. (*Republic,* 617)

The tale is a commentary on the sense of Justice and responsibility which permeates and sustains Greek tragedy; it is the justification which gives moral meaning to the destiny of Oedipus, whose unwitting murder and unwitting incest are fated yet punishable. Its meaning, removed from the vestments of fable or vision, is the self-sufficiency of man.

In the last of the plays of Sophocles, the *Oedipus at Colonus,* Oedipus, blind wanderer, reflects upon the principle of evil, the source of sin in himself (*hamartia*). Murderer of his father, husband to his mother, brother to his children, he claims fairly to have sinned by no choice of his own, but involuntarily without choice, in ignorance of the identity of the man he has slain or of the woman upon whose body he has begotten his own pollution. Yet even Oedipus regards himself as contaminated by his act. Ignorance of circumstance may permit him to disavow malice; it does nothing to extenuate the guilt which attaches to his act of incest and of parricide. The moral law is binding, the moral order must be preserved, even though he must suffer to preserve its inviolableness. As ignorance exempts no man, knowledge is a part of the obligation by which all men are bound.

One of the most imperious persuasions of the ancient world is the Socratic doctrine that without knowledge, without understanding, without rational reflection, no happiness or virtue is available to man. The doctrine is an expression of a point of view which mankind has not always shared. It represents a type of mentality which is known as "Classical" or "Greek" or "Hellenic." The Christian conception of life as a penance, of knowledge as an egotism, of blessedness as a redemption from sin, is totally alien to it. The Socratic doctrine is a premise of the ideal of a self-sufficient humanity, reflecting upon the sovereign ends which it sets before itself, confident of its own powers of erecting on earth a rational commonwealth of men, under whose good laws and wise institutions each individual, in the simple exercise of citizenship, shall find liberated his highest intellectual and moral capacities. At Delphi, the most revered of Greek sanctuaries, was inscribed the motto: "Know thyself."

The good which men seek must be the object not of any random desire, but of *informed* desire. The aim of all knowledge is therefore self-knowledge, a knowledge of the ends with which the will must be informed if man would realize in himself the virtues appropriate to a human being. Whence Socrates held, "The unexamined life is not worth living." The only legitimate ends for man are those which are willed freely by a rationally informed decision, and therein, in this free choice of what he shall be, consists the dignity of all that is human.

Recommended reading:

Dialogues of Plato, translated by Benjamin Jowett, available in various editions. The most attractive introductions are the *Apology*, the *Crito*, the *Protagoras* and the *Symposium*, in which Plato shows himself artist as well as philosopher. On the theory of ideas: the *Phaedo*, Plato's masterpiece the *Republic*, and the *Timaeus*. The last is difficult but extraordinarily rich.
Aristotle, *Ethica Nicomachea*, tr. W. D. Ross, London, Oxford University Press, 1925, Books I-III: the classic expression of the doctrine of the mean.
G. L. Dickinson, *The Greek View of Life*, 15th ed., New York, Doubleday, 1924.

GREEK TRAGEDY

SOPHOCLES (496–406 B.C.): *King Oedipus*[1] and *Antigone*[2]

I. THE DEVELOPMENT of European drama began in ancient Greece. Various earlier peoples had included in their religious ceremonies certain symbolic, semidramatic representations of significant episodes in the lives of their divinities. It was among the Greeks, however, that imitative action of this kind first became sufficiently dissociated from ritual to permit the development of a drama which was more than merely often-repeated convention. Yet the Greek drama originated in religious ceremonial and through more than a century of its history retained some connection with it.

The beginnings lie in the 6th century B. C. During the annual festivals honoring Dionysus (or Bacchus), god of wine and fertility, it was the custom for choral groups to sing hymns (or *odes*) concerning the gods and heroes of Greek legend, performing stately dances as they sang. Sometimes the leader of the chorus impersonated the god or hero and carried on a semidramatic discourse in song with the chorus itself. Thus the leader of the chorus assumed a dramatic role. It occurred to a 6th-century Athenian poet named Thespis to add an actor to

[1]Program A. [2]Program B.

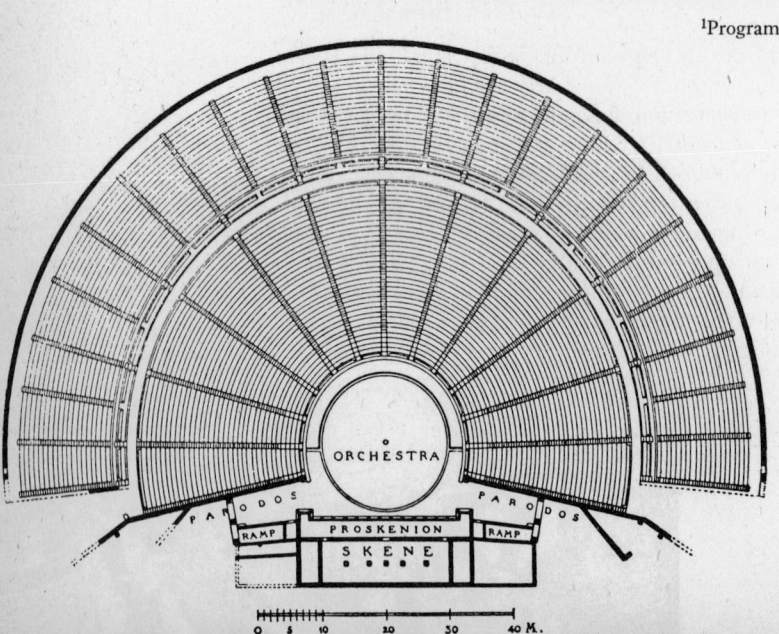

Fig. 3. Plan of Theater, Epidauros, *ca.* 330 B.C. Reproduced with permission from D.S. Robertson's *Handbook of Greek and Roman Architecture* (Cambridge University Press, Cambridge, 1929), p. 165.

GREEK TRAGEDY

the company of performers. The choral ode would now consist of three parts, one for the actor, one for the choral leader, and one for the chorus. An ode of this kind would be a simple play. Early in the 5th century, the tragic dramatist Aeschylus added a second actor, thus greatly increasing the dramatic possibilities, and his younger contemporary Sophocles added a third. (The Greek drama never employed more than three actors. A play might have more than three characters, but no more than three appeared at one time.)

As Greek tragedy evolved thus, there was a parallel development of comic drama. As tragedy originated in the more solemn parts of the ritual, comedy originated in boisterous and orgiastic songs and dances which were a characteristic feature of the Dionysian festivals. Ancient Greek tragedy was invariably and consistently serious in its mood; ancient Greek comedy was consistently hilarious, although it normally had a serious satiric purpose.

The development of Greek drama took place principally in Athens, and it reached its highest point of achievement in 5th-century Athens during the period of Athenian political ascendency under Pericles. The golden age of Athenian drama corresponds with the golden age of Athenian architecture and sculpture, that is, the period of Pheidias and of the construction of the *Parthenon*.

In 5th-century Athens, plays were presented in an open-air theatre built on the south slope of the Acropolis. The auditorium consisted of semicircular rows of seats built concentrically on the hillside so as to take advantage of the slope (Figs. 3, 4).[3] Across the open end of the auditorium stood the *skene,* or actors' building, and between the auditorium and the skene lay a circular space, the *orchestra,* where the chorus performed its dances. In the front of the skene were three large doors, which opened on a colonnaded porch, the *proskenion,* usually one step above the orchestra. The actors usually entered through these doors and usually delivered their lines from the proskenion, although sometimes they descended to the orchestra. From the point of view of the audience, the skene would look much like an imposing public building such as a temple or a palace. For this reason the action of most Greek tragedies takes place in the area just in front of such a building. We should note that the Greek theater had no stage, no curtain, and no artificial lighting (all plays were performed by daylight), and that properties and scenery were simple.

There were two occasions during the year when plays were performed in this theater, the Dionysiac festivals known as the *Linea* (January) and the *Greater Dionysia* (March). The plays performed were offered by various citizen playwrights in competition for prizes. Each competing tragic dramatist presented a series of three tragic plays followed by a short satiric skit. Sometimes the three tragedies constituted a continuous treatment of the same story and might thus be regarded as the three acts of a longer play. In such cases the three related tragedies were known as a *trilogy*. Only one complete trilogy survives, the *Oresteia* of Aeschylus. Of the very large body of drama that was written during the 5th century, all but a very small fraction has been lost. We have works by only three tragic writers, Aeschylus, Sophocles, and Euripides. We have examples of the work of only one comic writer, Aristophanes.

When we read a Greek tragedy we by no means repeat the experience of the spectator who saw the play performed in 5th-century Athens. In performance the effect of the dramatic

---

[3]Athens' theater was rebuilt in Roman times. The illustrations present the theater at Epidauros, which has retained much of its original form.

Fig. 4. Theater, Epidauros, *ca.* 330 B.C. Reproduced with permission from Margarete Bieber, *The History of the Greek and Roman Theater* (Princeton University Press, Princeton, 1939), p. 135, Figure 186.

text was supported and enhanced by the actor's skill in declamation, by instrumental and vocal music, by dancing, by richly colored costumes, and in some degree by scenic effects. In its combination of various arts the Greek drama remotely resembled modern opera. The dramatist himself wrote music as well as text and was responsible for the training of chorus and actors. The actors were elevated on thick-soled shoes; they were enveloped in long-skirted, high-waisted robes of strong colors; they wore tall and elaborate head-dresses. All of these features of costume combined to give an effect of height, dignity, and impressiveness. At the same time, they made impossible for the actor rapid movement and subtle gesture such as we see in the realistic modern theater. The actor's face was entirely covered by a mask. This was shaped so as to aid him in throwing his voice to the farthest benches in a very large theater; at the same time it eliminated facial expression. Naturalistic acting, like that which is in vogue in our own time, was obviously impossible in the Greek theater, but it would in any case have been inappropriate to the solemn and elevated mood of the Greek tragedy and to the heroic or divine nature of the characters. The Greek actor delivered his lines, with instrumental accompaniment, in a majestic and chant-like style. His aim was solemnity and grandeur, not life-likeness.

The singing of the chorus and the measured and stately dances which it performed contributed greatly to the pleasure of the Greek audience. As we have seen, the chorus antedated the actors, and throughout most of the 5th century it remained an essential element in the play. In most Greek tragedies the chorus has a truly dramatic role. It consists of persons who might reasonably be supposed to be present at the scene of the action (often the elders of the city in which the story is laid). It responds to the events enacted—with joy, grief, foreboding, etc.—as typical men or women might be expected to respond, and it expresses its reactions in the choral odes. The dramatist thus has a means of prompting the reactions of the audience. In the odes, furthermore, the chorus frequently offers commentary on the action and thus provides a means by which the dramatist underscores the moral significance of his play. In the Greek originals, the odes are metrically very complex. They include some of the most beautiful poetry which survives from ancient times.

A Greek tragedy follows a very definite pattern of related parts. It begins with a *prologue* in which one or more actors present the opening of the story. As the prologue ends, the chorus enters singing the first of the *choral odes* and takes its place in the orchestra, where it remains throughout the rest of the play. There follows a series of *episodes*—usually four or five—with the chorus singing an ode at the close of each. Sometimes an actor sings responsively with the chorus. The play closes as the chorus, singing its final hymn, leaves the orchestra.

II. A tragedy is a story of struggle. It focuses interest on the fortunes of a central character, the hero, or *protagonist*. This character is thrown into conflict with another person, the *antagonist*, or with forces of greater than human power—sometimes, when the antagonist represents such forces, with both at once. The protagonist is usually defeated. In Sophocles' *King Oedipus* (*Oedipus Rex*) the conflict is between Oedipus, who strives earnestly to escape the fate decreed for him, and the gods, who impose it upon him. If the play has an antagonist, it is Tiresias, who might be considered spokesman for the gods. In Sophocles' *Antigone,* the protagonist is Creon, who opposes his own will and his own scale of values to those of the gods—represented by Antigone, the antagonist—and is disastrously defeated. In each case, the conflict and its outcome illustrate the operation of moral principles which, the playwright believes, have universal validity.

In every conflict which has a decisive outcome, there is a turning point, a point at which someone wins and someone loses. The emotions of the persons involved and of sympathetic spectators naturally would reach their greatest pitch of intensity at this moment. This turn of events is known as the *climax*. In *King Oedipus* the climax is the hero's realization of who he is and what he has done. In *Antigone* the climax is the chastening of Creon by the deaths of his son and wife.

A primary problem in dramatic composition is to present the central conflict so as to arouse the greatest possible emotional response in the spectator. To achieve this end, Sophocles and the other Greek tragic writers present highly unified stories, with the result that there is no diversion of interest from the basic situation and no weakening of the feeling which it evokes. The Greek playwright is stringently selective. Every event enacted or narrated in the play has in one way or another a bearing upon the climactic turn of the plot. In the life of any hero, innumerable events would have occurred which had no connection with the principal conflict. There might be many interesting but irrelevant matters related to the lives of minor characters. All such material, however, is rigidly excluded from Sophoclean tragedy. The choral odes invariably are related to the action in progress, sometimes through offering an explanation of it or a commentary upon it, sometimes through expressing an emotional reaction to it. Everything in the play, moreover, is in harmony with the dominant mood; that is, there is no intrusion of laughter in the midst of tragic seriousness.

Concentration in time is another means of heightening emotional effect. Sophocles, following the method which is normal in Greek tragedy, does not attempt to present on the stage the whole story of Oedipus' struggle against his destiny. To begin at the beginning would involve representing Laius' reception of the oracle which foretold that his son would slay him, the shepherd's bearing the baby to the mountainous wilderness, and many other events. Each incident would of necessity be briefly and lightly treated; the play would seem too thinly spread; the emotional effect would be weak. The Greek playwright therefore represents only a brief span of time, often one day or less. In some cases, for instance in *Oedipus*, the action is continuous; that is, the events represented occupy the same time on the stage that they would occupy in real life. In other cases, the playwright asks the audience to imagine that hours or longer periods have elapsed during the singing of a choral ode between two episodes, as during the ode between the first and second episodes of *Antigone*. The time span of the play necessarily includes the climax. It is consequently only the very end of the story which is actually enacted. Pertinent events which have occurred before the opening of the play are sometimes given in rather formal prologues, are sometimes suggested by references to the past scattered through the dialogue and the choral odes, are sometimes very incompletely supplied, for many of the stories were so familiar to the Athenian audience that the filling in of the past was hardly necessary.

It is worth noting that Greek tragedies usually have not only a concentration of time but also a concentration of place. In most of them the action occurs in a single spot. The reason for this was probably practical rather than aesthetic. Since the Greek theater had no curtain, Greek dramatists depended very little on movable scenery. They usually laid the entire action before a palace or temple so that the skene might serve as a plausible background.

In striving for maximum emotional effect, the Greek tragic poet avoids the mistake of trying to maintain a high emotional pitch throughout the play. If he did so his audience would be weary and insensitive long before the close. A play is much more powerful if it is so designed that, starting from relative calm, it rises to a point of very high intensity. This point naturally should be the climax. Sophocles is particularly skillful in producing an effect of emotional crescendo followed by brief diminuendo. With each episode in a Sophoclean tragedy, the action clearly moves toward the climax. Each successive event in *Oedipus* brings the hero's self-discovery patently nearer and makes it patently more inevitable. In each successive episode of *Antigone* Creon entangles himself more thoroughly through his headstrong defiance of divine law, draws his punishment nearer, and renders it heavier. The spectator's perception of this movement toward catastrophe arouses in him a progressively greater emotional excitement. At the point of greatest intensity comes the climax, and it strikes with overwhelming impact. Thereafter the play moves rapidly to its close—slowly enough, however, to permit the relaxation of the spectator's emotional tension before the end. (*Antigone* closes more abruptly than most Greek tragedies.) In a brief finale the playwright reveals how the catastrophe is to affect the lives of the principal characters and through the chorus emphasizes the moral significance of the play.

There is a finality about the close of a Greek tragedy. The spectator feels that both the calamity and its results have been fully treated, that the verdict is irreversible, that nothing need be added. There is also a serenity of mood. However passionate and tumultuous the play may have been, at the close the emotional excitement has subsided; the spectator leaves the theater in "calm of mind, all passion spent."

These Sophoclean tragedies are rigorous in their unity and firm, simple, and lucid in outline. In their structural perfection, their internal harmony, their unpretentious dignity, they constitute a literary counterpart of the *Parthenon*. They illustrate admirably those qualities which we are accustomed to call *Classical*.

III. The Greek tragedy is essentially religious. It was religious in origin; the occasions of its presentation were religious festivals; it employed as its subject matter stories drawn from a body of legend inseparable in the Greek mind from religion. The religious character of tragedy, then, was appropriate, perhaps inevitable, and it was highly appropriate also that it should concern itself with moral principles. Indeed, a tragedy which did not have ethical significance would have seemed seriously deficient to the ancient Athenian audience.

In both *Oedipus* and *Antigone* Sophocles employs an unusually effective method in dealing with moral issues. Early in each play he raises a moral question: he leaves it suspended, unanswered, through the course of several episodes; near the close he presents a definitive and emphatic solution. The moral idea is, of course, intimately connected with the action of the drama; the turn of events which we have called the climax constitutes the answer to the question raised earlier.

In *Oedipus* Jocasta, attempting to allay the fears of her husband, tells the story of her baby son who was supposedly left to die in the wilderness because the oracle had foretold that he would kill his father and marry his mother. Her purpose is to prove that divine oracles are not infallible. If this is true, the gods do not have the power to see into the future or to control human lives that they are supposed to have. Jocasta believes—at least she says that she believes—that human destiny is ruled only by chance. The chorus, reacting as the playwright wishes his audience to react, is deeply disturbed by Jocasta's blasphemies. Are the gods really as blind and as powerless as Jocasta suggests? Before the end of the play, it becomes evident that Jocasta's story proves exactly the opposite of what she has intended it to prove. The question of the power and infallibility of the gods is settled with a firm finality. The gods are all-knowing and all-powerful.

In *Antigone* a conflict very early arises between two moral principles. Creon, king of Thebes, decrees that the body of Polyneices, because of his treachery to the state, be left unburied. This is a posthumous punishment of the traitor, for, according to ancient Greek belief, to leave a body unburied was to condemn the soul of the dead man to age-long miseries. In spite of its severity, the Athenian spectator would have seen reason and justice in Creon's decree. Patriotic devotion to the state was in ancient Greek eyes an even greater virtue than in our own; the authority of the state was deeply respected; crimes against the state were regarded as particularly heinous. Antigone, however, courageously ignores Creon's decree and performs funeral rites for her brother, obeying the divine ordinance which requires the burial of a dead kinsman. In Creon's eyes she is guilty not only of aiding an enemy of the state but of herself defying and resisting the authority of the state, which is vested in him, and he treats her very harshly. Is Creon, who is motivated by a sense of obligation to the state, in the right? Or is Antigone, who is guided by divine law? The chorus—and presumably the ancient Athenian audience would react likewise—is not immediately able to make up its mind. Even as late as the fourth episode the chorus is inclined to side with Creon. It is indeed a difficult moral question. But as the play proceeds, the error of Creon's course of action becomes more and more clearly manifest to the chorus, to the audience, and to Creon himself. As Creon's calamities overwhelm him, the superiority of divine law to human law is emphatically demonstrated.

Both of these plays drive home another moral idea: the evil of pride. The ancient Greeks, with their distaste for anything immoderate, exaggerated, or disproportioned, regarded inordinate self-esteem as a trait highly unbecoming even to the most illustrious of men. They believed, moreover, that human pride was offensive to the gods. For the proud man ascribes to himself superiorities which only the gods may claim. In comparison with divine attributes, the greatest human power is weakness and the greatest human wisdom is ignorance. Mankind must learn that no man is master of his own fate, that no man may ever win security and stability:

> I cannot say
> Of any condition of human life "This is fixed,
> This is clearly good, or bad." Fate raises up,
> And Fate casts down the happy and unhappy alike:
> No man can foretell his Fate.
> Take the case of Creon:
> Creon was happy once, as I count happiness:
> Victorious in battle, sole governor of the land,
> Fortunate father of children nobly born.
> And now it has all gone from him! Who can say
> That a man is still alive when his life's joy fails?
> He is a walking dead man. Grant him rich,
> Let him live like a king in his great house:
> If his pleasure is gone, I would not give
> So much as the shadow of smoke for all he owns.

Oedipus, in the midst of his pride and power, is abruptly thrown from his eminence to become a blind and polluted creature who must henceforth live miserably apart from his kind. At the close of the play the chorus drives home the moral that in human life there can never be assurance of the continuance of happiness and prosperity:

> Then learn that mortal man must always look to his ending,
> And none can be called happy until that day when he carries
> His happiness down to the grave in peace.

In order that human beings may realize their inferiority and weakness the more keenly, the gods often chastise men in high places and are especially likely to do so if such men become proud and presumptuous. Such chastisement is not likely to fall upon the obscure and humble. Various choral odes in various Greek tragedies are devoted to the idea of the relative safety of those whose station in life is modest. It is through the abasement of the great and illustrious that the gods teach mankind the lesson of humility.

IV. A tragedy is a play presenting a spectacle of suffering which is or seems disproportionate to the deserts of the sufferer. (No definition of tragedy covers every drama which the writer calls a tragedy.) Tragedy deals with the problem of human pain. There would be no problem, obviously, if pain were always retribution for the sins of the person who endured it. But human experience indicates that there is no such clear relationship between man's deserts and his rewards. Evil men often prosper in life; good men often are reduced to misery. Superficially at least, there seems to be no reasonableness or justice in the scheme of things, no logic in moral order.

The major tragic writers, in representing the suffering which even great and good men must sometimes endure, attempt to suggest reasons why such things must be—to reveal, that is, a logic and consistency in the apparent moral chaos which every thoughtful spectator must have observed. Though the tragic dramatist does not always make life look less somber, he may at least render it more intelligible. If the evils of life seem due merely to a capricious and inconsistent fate, they seem very forbidding. We can face them much more courageously and confidently when we understand them.

The dramatic treatment of the problem of human pain involves first of all the presentation of a central character who is on the whole a good and admirable person, a person capable of eliciting the respect and sympathy of the spectator, but who nevertheless suffers greatly. A vicious or contemptible person would be altogether unsuitable for the central role in a tragedy. For one reason, the suffering of such a character would fail to arouse the sympathy of the audience, and the play therefore would have little emotional impact. For another, an evil man's evil fate poses no problem, for it provokes no questioning of the moral scheme of life. On the other hand, the tragic playwright is unlikely to make his hero perfect, for that would be to make him inhuman and, to human spectators, uninteresting.

The protagonist of *King Oedipus* has obvious faults of character. He has an inclination to sudden fits of anger, and in his anger he can be unreasonably and cruelly obstinate. His anger and his obstinacy hasten the approach of his humiliation. He is, moreover, reprehensibly proud of his own achievements and of the eminence which he has reached. Yet Oedipus has evidently been a wise and beneficent ruler. He exhibits a deep and laudable concern for the suffering of his Theban subjects. Clearly he is thoroughly scrupulous; it is through his earnest efforts to avoid the crimes predicted for him that he commits them. At the close of the play he courageously accepts, without hesitation or murmuring, the consequences of his involuntary sins and of the curse which he himself has uttered.

Creon, the protagonist of *Antigone,* is perhaps not so clearly an admirable character as Oedipus. He is hot-headed and obstinate and, worst of all, proud and presumptuous in his exercise of authority. By these traits he hastens his calamity and renders it heavier. Yet he too is a man of high principles, which he attempts to carry out with conscientious energy. His decree concerning the body of Polyneices would seem to the Greek spectators not mere arbitrary cruelty but evidence of praiseworthy concern for the welfare of the state.

In each of these plays a strong and honorable man is humbled by divine will. The playwright tells his audience that human destiny is subject to divine rule and that the gods, sometimes for reasons not altogether clear to human understanding, often choose to inflict misery upon men. It is to the will of the gods, then, that Sophocles attributes the suffering which frequently comes to those who seem to human eyes to deserve a better fate. Perhaps the gods act as they do in order to chasten the unbecoming pride which is characteristic of humanity, singling out men of power and eminence for abasement in order that the lesson may be the more emphatic and dramatic. Yet Sophocles probably does not pretend to offer any confident explanation for the gods' severity. He apparently believes that the human intellect is too limited to understand why the gods dispose of human lives as they do, that it would be presumption in a man to believe that he could comprehend the motives of the divine will. Sophocles seems to counsel the spectator to accept the divine dispensation without questioning, to accept it in fortitude and humility. Only through such an attitude toward life may one achieve serenity of spirit.

> There is no happiness where there is no wisdom:
> No wisdom but in submission to the gods.

In neither *Oedipus* nor *Antigone,* it should be noted, can the catastrophe be satisfactorily explained as due primarily to anything blameworthy in the hero himself—to any weakness or vice in his personality or to any sin which he has committed. Creon's lordly arrogance, to be sure, does involve him the more surely and the more rapidly in disaster. It is not his arrogance, however, which starts the train of events leading to this disaster. It is a conscientious error; and such errors, if we accept Sophocles' opinion concerning the limitations of the human understanding, are for a man hardly avoidable. The tragedy of Oedipus is even more obviously dissociated from his personality. It is true that Oedipus is proud and stubbornly choleric, but the sequence of events which leads to his catastrophic humiliation, although it is hastened and made more dramatic by his pride and his choler, is in no way a consequence of them. In both plays the calamity is imposed by an external agency. This is generally true of Greek tragedy. When the protagonist's suffering is not caused by the gods, it is usually due to the sins of other men against him. Almost always tragedy comes from without.

A modern reader finds it hard to reconcile the fate of Sophocles' characters with his own conception of justice. Oedipus is obviously blameless. Creon appears to be more culpable, for he is obstinate and presumptuous in his infringement of divine law. Yet Creon is guilty of error rather than of sin. The sufferings of Antigone are even more clearly undeserved, for she suffers precisely because she is scrupulous in performing a moral duty. Did Sophocles see injustice in the fates of these innocent or relatively innocent characters? This is a difficult question, for Sophocles is not at all explicit. Aeschylus, his elder contemporary, attempts to find wisdom, justice, and mercy in the divine rule. Euripides, his younger contemporary, who represents the attitudes of a post-Periclean generation, bitterly accuses the gods of petty selfishness and injustice. Sophocles probably does not mean to offer any opinion whatsoever on the question of divine justice. Nor does he seem to lament the divinely ordained miseries of humanity. With a calm objectivity he represents the lot of mankind as he sees it.

V. In drawing his characters, Sophocles does not try to achieve a close resemblance to ordinary men. He presents, for one thing, a greatly simplified version of human nature. Each of his persons is endowed with only a few somewhat obvious character traits. He does not supply such intimate items of information as Shakespeare, for example, includes in his much more complex characterizations. The effect for which Sophocles strives is one of clarity and definiteness.

He strives also for an effect of strength and nobility. For the men and women who appear in his plays are not ordinary people; they are the great personalities of national legend. They are, to be sure, helpless in the hands of divine dispensation. Yet there is nothing contemptible in their helplessness. In comparison with average men they are impressive figures indeed. Some of them exhibit unbecoming pride and arrogance in their prosperity, but in the fortitude and dignity with which they endure calamity, they are heroic. Sophocles gives his audiences no fatuous assurances that life is pleasant or beautiful. He does assure them, however, that human nature at its best has a greatness that approaches the godlike. In this he offers some compensation for the darkness of his picture of life.

Recommended reading:
C. M. Bowra, *Sophoclean Tragedy,* Oxford, The Clarendon Press, 1944.
Prosser Hall Frye, "The Idea of Greek Tragedy," in *Romance and Tragedy,* Boston, Marshall Jones Co., 1922.
Edith Hamilton, *The Great Age of Greek Literature,* New York, W. W. Norton, 1942. (Published also in the Mentor Books series, 1948, under the title *The Greek Way to Western Civilization.*)
Gilbert Norwood, *Greek Tragedy,* Boston, J. W. Luce and Co., 1928.

GREEK ARCHITECTURE

The Parthenon[1]

I. THE BELIEF IN ONE GOD, whose single and exclusive authority commanded men to reject all other idols, is in Western history the distinctive contribution of the Hebrew people. Greece nurtured many gods in her pantheon. Greek popular religion exhibits a tendency by no means peculiar to Greece alone, a tendency to impute personality to natural events and forces. The revolutions of night and day, the cycle of the seasons, the patterns of the stars, the round ocean, earth's fair burgeoning and amber harvest, wind and tempest, every elemental and majestic aspect of the natural world is animated with a will, hostile or beneficent, which worship may excite or placate. The tendency to conceive nature after man's own image, to regard the efficacy of the human will as the image of natural causality, is known as "anthropomorphism." Conjoined with this anthropomorphic tendency of Greek popular religion was the rarest poetic faculty, a plastic imagination which peopled the world with gods, which domesticated nature by finding in nature the reflection of itself, which animated not merely the agencies of its cosmic grandeur, but human art and intelligence and impulse as well. Something of the solemnity of man's existence in the world may be got from the ancient hymn, once ascribed to Homer, the *Hymn to Earth the Mother of All:*

> O universal Mother, who dost keep
> From everlasting thy foundations deep,
> Eldest of things, Great Earth, I sing of thee!
> All shapes that have their dwelling in the sea,
> All things that fly, or on the ground divine
> Live, move, and there are nourished—these are thine;
> These from thy wealth thou dost sustain; from thee
> Fair babes are born, and fruits on every tree
> Hang ripe and large, revered Divinity!
> The life of mortal men beneath thy sway
> Is held; thy power both gives and takes away!
> Happy are they whom thy mild favours nourish;
> All things unstinted round them grow and flourish;
> For them, endures the life-sustaining field
> Its load of harvest, and their cattle yield
> Large increase, and their house with wealth is filled.

[1] Programs A and B.

Fig. 5. Parthenon, Athens, 447-432 B.C. (*Alinari*)

Such honoured dwell in cities fair and free,
The homes of lovely women, prosperously;
Their sons exult in youths' new budding gladness,
And their fresh daughters free from care and sadness,
With bloom-inwoven dance and happy song,
On the soft flowers the meadow-grass among,
Leap round them sporting—such delights by thee
Are given, rich Power, revered Divinity.
Mother of gods, thou wife of starry Heaven,
Farewell! be thou propitious, and be given
A happy life for this brief melody,
Nor thou nor other songs shall unremembered be.

The goddess who was specially revered in the communal worship of the Athenians was Pallas Athena, the virgin goddess of wisdom, who stood guardian over the destiny of the city which bore her name. Her sacred precinct in Athens, the place reserved for her temples and her worship, was the Acropolis. There, in the ancient hill-citadel which rose above the habitations of mortal men, was the fabled site at which Poseidon, god of the sea, in contest with Athena for the guardianship of the city, had struck with fierce trident from the rock a brackish spring, and Athena had brought forth her sacred olive tree. The site is commemorated by a temple known as the *Erechtheum*. The principal temple, in which the image of the victorious goddess was housed, is the *Parthenon* (Fig. 5). Every fourth year, in the Panathenaic festival, a procession was formed in the city below which moved, mounted and afoot, bearing the city's offering up the winding road upon the hill-side, past the *Propylaea,* the monumental gateway to the Acropolis, past the gigantic bronze Pheidian sculpture of *Athena Promachos* visible even to ships at sea, past the *Erechtheum,* to the sanctuary of the goddess. The Panathenaic procession is figured in stone relief on the inner frieze of the *Parthenon*. Mounted youths, charioteers, lowing sacrificial animals, maidens with ceremonial vessels, men bearing olive branches, aged magistrates, converge, above the central doorway of the temple, upon a semicircle of seated gods, who witness in solemnity the presentation of the city's gift to its proper divinity. To serve this communal worship the building was erected. In its execution it became the physical embodiment and ideal expression of the life of Greece.

The *Parthenon* is the work of two architects, Ictinos and Callicrates; the sculptural decoration was under the supervision of Pheidias, who was, besides, general superintendent of the works. The building was constructed between the years 447–432 B.C.

II. The plan[2] of a Greek temple is everywhere basically the same. It consists of an interior walled rectangle which is opened by a portal at one of its narrow ends (Fig. 6). This rectangle, within which was placed the sculptured image of the god, forms the essential core of the building; it is referred to as the temple's cella or naos. The cella walls are penetrated by no windows. The single opening for the admission of light, except for a possible opening reserved in the roof, is the entrance portal. Normally it was prescribed that the plan as a whole be so disposed that the main portal of the temple should face the east, in order that the image of the god within might be struck directly by the rays of the rising sun. The temple-plan is for this reason said to have an easterly orientation in space.

[2]The term "plan" is reserved in architectural discussion to mean "ground plan," that is, the two-dimensional distribution of the spaces which are to be enclosed. The vertical enclosing elements, by which the building becomes a volume, are designated the "elevation" of the building.

Fig. 6. Plan of Greek Temple

At either side of the entrance portal in a normal plan, the lateral walls of the rectangle were extended forward so as to form an exterior porch-space before the cella, known as the pronaos of the temple. A similar exterior porch—the opisthodomus—is normally repeated at the other closed end of the cella. The projecting ends of the side-walls which have been brought forward to form the porch terminate in two rectangular jambs called the antae. It is in relation to these antae that the most characteristic feature of Classical architecture— the upright columns of the Classical orders—originally appear. Constructively, they are the means of support for the stone beam which is to be carried at the height of the cella walls across the porch. The disposition of these columns varies in different temples. In some cases they are simply placed between the projecting side-walls so as to provide intermediate support for a beam whose two ends rest upon the antae. An alternative treatment, exhibited in the small *Temple on the Ilissus,* at Athens (Fig. 6), disposes one column directly before each of the antae of the pronaos. Between these columns, which form the angles of the porch, a beam is run over intermediate supports and returned at either side to the antae. By this means the space of the porches (both pronaos and opisthodomus) is extended and the two main facades of the temple are given the special prominence of a classical portico. Such a disposition, which places a row of columns in front of the antae, causes the temple to be described as prostyle.

The *Parthenon* is executed on the plan of a prostyle temple (Fig. 7). Basically, it simply restates the normal temple-plan. A walled cella at its eastern end houses the cult-image; a pronaos with a prostyle portico monumentalizes its entrance-way. The complication of the plan is occasioned by an added function which has been given to the building and by a desire to augment the impressiveness of its exterior facades. The cella chamber is divided into two unequal parts by a cross wall. The larger part on the east (called the Hecatompedon, because it measured one hundred Attic feet) forms the cella proper, or naos, within which stood Pheidias' great gold and ivory statue of *Athena Parthenos.* The smaller part at the temple's western end served the office of a treasury chamber; it was called the Parthenon, the chamber of the virgin, and from it the temple as a whole takes its name. The two rooms of the cella are not interconnected by a doorway; each is entered by its proper portal, the Hecatompedon through a prostyle portico of six columns on the east, the Parthenon through an identical portico on the west.

In temples of large dimensions the strength of the materials available for construction strictly prescribed the distribution of supports. The interior distance between the side-walls of the cella in the *Parthenon*[3] demanded intermediate uprights to carry the roof. The Hecatompedon was for this reason divided by two rows of Doric columns into three longitudinal aisles. At the end of the room opposite the portal, the two outer aisles turned into each other so as to form an ambulatory passing behind the central sculpture of Athena. Each of these rows of ten columns carried, in elevation, a second superimposed order of columns upon which the roof-beams rested. In the adjacent Parthenon chamber four Ionic columns rose in a single order to the same height.

Except for the specially privileged, the temple interior was a restricted precinct; it was the house of the god to which, normally, only the priesthood had admission. The ritual procession which moved from city to temple came finally to rest not in the temple but before it. There, at the temple's eastern end, before the stepped platform on which the temple as a whole was raised, stood the altar of Athena, where the offerings of the city were accepted into sacerdotal hands. Accordingly, the temple has the character rather of a monument to be contemplated than of a building to be entered. Its major aspect, the aspect which alone was given

---

[3] The physical distance is 65'. In general, except for the understanding of constructive demands, such dimensions are of neutral importance. The important consideration in Classical architecture is a consideration not of physical scale, but of formal proportions. Where dimensions are cited, they are given in order to enable the reader to grasp such proportions as a visual ratio.

GREEK ARCHITECTURE

to the familiar vision of a worshipful populace, is its exterior, the outer shell which is the architectural and sculptural celebration of the deity to whom the building was consecrated. To enhance its exterior, the two-chambered cella of the *Parthenon* was girded with a monumental colonnade, which ran continuously around all four sides, skirting cella-walls and porticoes and providing an exterior covered walk beneath their coffered eaves. The colonnade forms the outermost support for the descending load of the roof that forms the temple's watershed. There are eight columns on each of the end facades (whence the temple is said to be octastyle); seventeen columns occur on each of the sides.

III. Every style of architecture is realized within limits set by the strength of materials used and by a principle of construction. Greek architecture employs the principle of post and lintel. The principle consists simply in the placing of a horizontal member, called the lintel, upon vertical uprights, or posts (Fig. 8). Both the lintel and any superstructure which may be placed upon it are physically gravitating weights; whatever form they may take, their downward pressure must be transmitted through the posts to the earth. The lintel, which spans the space between uprights, must therefore have a strength sufficient to support both its own weight and the weight of any superstructure which it carries without breaking. Stresses of two sorts are at work in it. At its upper edge there is a stress of compression, in which its constituent particles tend to be forced together; at its lower edge there is a stress of tension in which its particles tend to be drawn apart. The I-beams which are employed in contemporary steel construction as the framework of buildings are formed precisely in anticipation of these stresses. The steel beam is in section shaped like the capital letter "I": its upper and lower edges, at which the maximum stresses may be predicted, are reinforced by wide horizontal flanges of steel; the vertical steel web which connects them is comparatively tenuous. In stone construction such forms are impracticable—hence the characteristically massive proportions of stone buildings. Stone will resist enormous stresses of compression; it is poorly resistant to stresses of tension, and, as a lintel, unless properly supported, is liable to fracture. In any structure which employs the post and lintel principle the distance between supports is determined absolutely by the maximum limits of compression and tension which the strength of materials will allow. Within these limits alone the architect is permitted freely to work. It is within these limits that the principle of post and lintel in stone construction has been refined into the Classical orders of architecture.

As the variety among the Classical orders will show, the material conditions which limit the architect's design do not determine what that design shall positively be. Its positive character represents an act of expression, in which the forms respond to a special sense of organization in space, in short, to an intellectual or to a spiritual demand.

IV. Except for the timber rafters of its roof and the iron clamps and dowels that bind its unmortared courses of stone, the *Parthenon* is constructed entirely of Pentelic marble, even to the roof tiles which sheltered its interior.

Its vertical elevation[4] is marked by a three-fold division: it rests upon a base; its visible

[4]For the technical meaning of the term, see p. 19, note 2.

Fig. 7. Plan of Parthenon, Athens, 447–432 B.C.

Fig. 8. Post and Lintel: showing downward transmission of gravitational thrusts through the posts

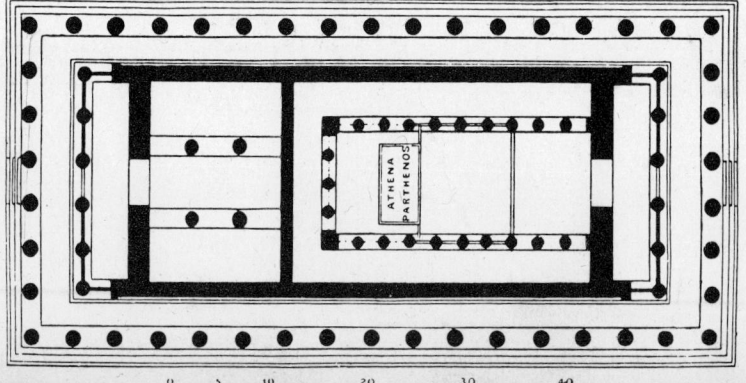
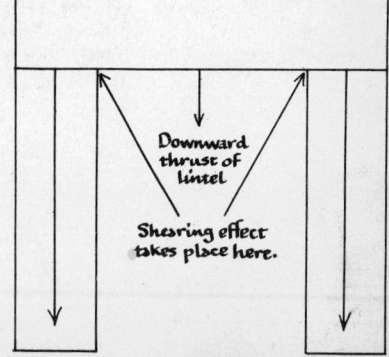

exterior supports are a series of vertical uprights forming a colonnade; its superstructure of horizontal beam and sloping roof is triangulated to a gable at both ends.

Within each of these basic divisions the building is articulated into a set of elementary parts, which have the function of making visually clear the active support and equilibrium of the structure as a whole.

The interrelation of these parts, the organization of vertical and horizontal members, is called an "order" of architecture (Fig. 9). The term "order" includes, specifically, the stepped base, the upright columns, and an entablature, the horizontal members (exclusive of the sloping roof) which the columns hold aloft. A Classical order is not constituted by having these parts alone, but by the system of proportions which exists among them. Greek architecture evolved three distinct orders—the Doric, the Ionic, and the Corinthian; they are distinguished from each other both by their internal proportions and by the detail of the parts which are related. The order employed in the exterior colonnade of the *Parthenon* is the Doric.

The continuous visible base upon which the colonnade of the temple rests is called the stylobate. It consists of three steps, in scale proportioned to the superstructure for which it serves as platform. The steps are too high for easy ascent; at the two ends of the temple, opposite the portals, an intermediate step is placed at each level, giving six risers (Fig. 7).

On the uppermost step of the stylobate rests the colonnade. In the Doric order the individual column is provided with no base molding; it rises directly from the platform which serves as the common unifying base for the colonnade as a whole.

The Doric column is composed of two main members—a vertical shaft and a flared transitional element, known as the capital, which immediately receives the load of the horizontal beams above. In its vertical rise the shaft diminishes in thickness.[5] Though it presents itself visually as a unit, it is actually composite, constructed of marble drums set one upon another and centered by a dowel of cypress wood. The load-surfaces of these drums in the *Parthenon* are ground with such exactitude that the lines of junction are virtually invisible, and the shaft gives the appearance of a monolith. Its outer surface is treated with a series of continuous vertical grooves or channels called flutes, normally twenty in number in the Doric order. The function of the flutes is to diversify the light which falls upon the structural member. In the diffused light of high noon an unfluted column loses its three-dimensionality; it appears simply as a flat strip without appreciable thickness. The concave flutes of the Greek Doric generate a regular variation of lights and shadows upon the shaft for its entire height, preserving in any lighting the coincidence between its apparent and its real shape. The sharp vertical edge formed between adjacent flutes on the shaft is called an arris; these vertical arrises define the linear contour of the shaft as seen against wall or sky.

At the height of the shaft, a few inches beneath the capital, occur three horizontal grooves. These grooves mark the line of division which separates the uppermost drum of the shaft from the marble block out of which the capital is carved. Flutes and arrises, however, are

[5] In the exterior colonnade of the *Parthenon* the shafts diminish in diameter, in a rise of 34′, from about 6′2″ at the base to 4′9¾″ beneath the capitals. The angle columns are thicker; see, below, p. 26.

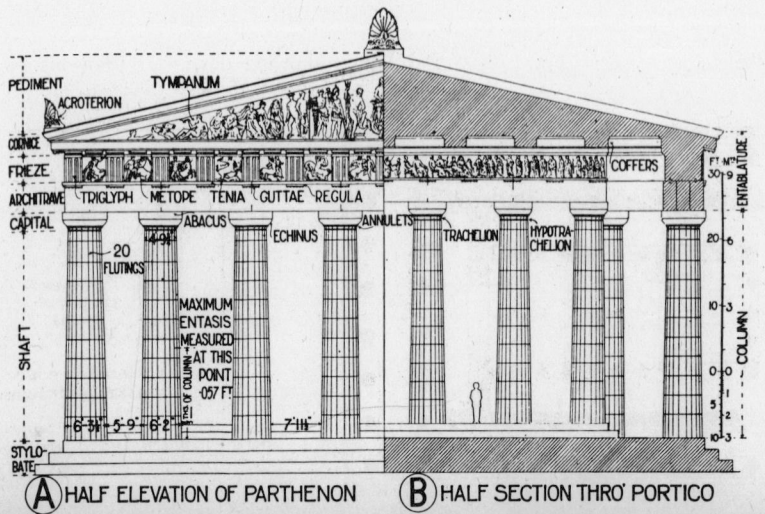

Fig. 9. Elevation and section, Parthenon, Athens, 447–432 B.C. (reproduced by permission from *A History of Architecture on the Comparative Method* by Sir Banister Fletcher [14th edition])

both continued through these grooves and taper off immediately above them. This part of the shaft which is actually attached to the capital is called the necking of the column. The first element of the capital proper is the part which flares outward at the crest of the shaft's vertical rise; it is known traditionally by the name echinus (literally, "sea-urchin"). Upon it rests a square flat slab of marble, the abacus, which forms the upper load-surface of the column. The outward curve in the contour of the echinus returns upon itself just as the echinus receives the abacus-block. Together, abacus and echinus constitute the Doric capital. The architectural function of the capital as a whole is to effect a transition: it mediates between the vertical of the shaft and the stark horizontal of the beam above, which the shaft must carry.

The system of horizontal members which makes a continuous circuit of the temple above the colonnade constitutes the Classical entablature. The entablature consists of three main elements: the architrave, the frieze, and the cornice.

The space between any two columns in the colonnade is designated as an intercolumniation or, more simply, as a bay. The Doric architrave is the plain marble beam which rests directly on the abacus-blocks of the colonnade and spans its bays. It re-establishes the unity of the colonnade, and of the space enclosed, by binding together the series of freestanding supports. Above it is a thin continuous bed-molding of rectangular section, the taenia.

The most remarkable feature of the Doric entablature is the horizontal frieze which rests upon taenia and architrave. It is composed of two alternating elements, known respectively as triglyphs and metopes, which repeat in the temple's upper reaches, like an echo of diminished interval, the measured rhythmic alternation of vertical column and bay in the colonnade below. Structurally, the triglyphs are a series of upright rectangular blocks, rather taller than wide, which take their name from the three vertical channels carved in the outer face of each. There is in fact no entirely satisfactory theory of the origin of the triglyph. It has been conjectured that it represents in stone the decorative treatment originally given to wooden beam-ends when, in the earliest Doric temples, the construction was of brick and timber. The theory is reinforced by the small blocks called regulae which appear directly below the triglyphs underneath the taenia molding. Each regula is carved with six drops, or guttae, which appear to represent the wooden pegs by which, in timber construction, the beams were fastened to the continuous bed-molding. The empty spaces between the triglyphs are almost square; they are screened with flat slabs of stone called metopes. Actually the triglyphs are the structural members of the frieze; the metopes were simply slipped into place between the triglyphs in grooves provided especially for receiving them at either side of the triglyph-blocks. They afford a series of squarish fields for sculptural decoration, the lowest range in the Doric temple at which this form of embellishment was permitted.

A triglyph with its accompanying regula and guttae occurs in the frieze over each column and over each bay. An aesthetic convention which governed the Doric style forbade treating the corner of the temple with a metope; it prescribed that the corner angle should be treated with two adjacent triglyphs. The strict adherence to this convention caused the decline of the Doric order in the ancient world; even in Roman times it was displaced by the Ionic and the Corinthian and by adaptations which the Romans themselves devised. For if the angle triglyphs were placed in adjacence to each other, it was impossible for the Greek or Roman architect to observe a second convention which was considered mandatory with equal rigor, namely, that each triglyph should be directly centered over a column or over a bay. If the first convention was observed, the second could not be, and *vice versa*. The *Parthenon* exhibits the nearest reconciliation which was ever achieved.

Above the frieze and projecting out over it so as to form a protecting eave is the last element of the Classical entablature—the cornice. The repetition of elements begun in the colonnade, and echoed in the frieze, is taken up again, and a second time diminished, at the level of the cornice. On its soffit, or underside, occurs a series of blocks, one over each triglyph

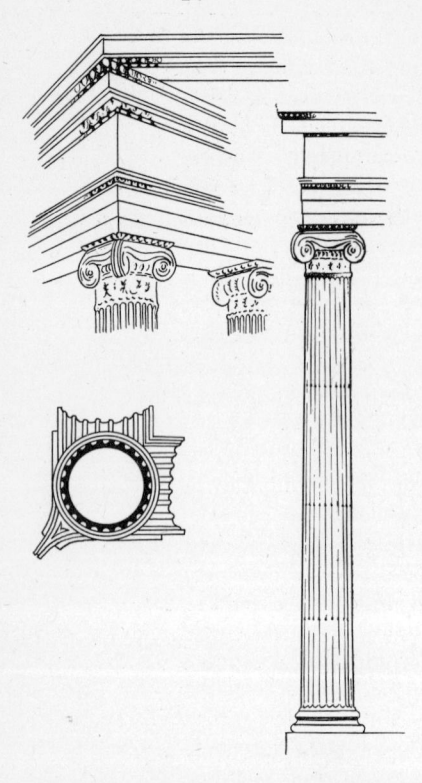

CLASSICAL ANTIQUITY

and one over each metope, sloping slightly downward as if to reflect beneath the cornice the downward inclination of the roof's pitch above. Each is carved with three rows of six guttae. These blocks, which are known as mutules, appear like the triglyphs to translate into stone the motives of timber construction; they appear to represent the plank-ends of the sloping timber roof above.

The triangular gable formed at either end of the temple by the slope of the roof is framed by an upward extension of the cornice called the raking cornice. The cornice itself forms a lofty table upon which the sculptor was free to exercise his art in the round. Freestanding carved figures could be disposed in an elaborate sculptural program against the background of a wall which screened off the interior of the building. The entire complex of the gable, including raking cornice, screen wall and sculptures, is called the pediment of the temple.

V. The columns which carry the roof-beams in the naos of the *Parthenon* are Doric; those of the treasury chamber were Ionic, the second major order of Classical architecture.

The Ionic order is in comparison with the Doric a more attenuated and feminine form (Fig. 10). Its proportions are less massive[6]; its detail is elegant and decorative.

The Ionic order rests, like the Doric, upon a stylobate. Its first difference is the base-molding which occurs between the stylobate and each individual shaft. The base consists of two convex horizontal moldings, separated by a concave molding. The upper convex molding is horizontally fluted. Above it the shaft rises aloft with diminishing diameter. The shaft is fluted (24), but instead of the sharp vertical arris which occurs in the Doric between each pair of adjacent flutes there is a reserved flat strip between flutes known as a fillet. At the height of the shaft there sometimes occurs a horizontal necking-band carved with bead-and-reel and honeysuckle ornament (*anthemion*). The echinus itself is carved with an ornament known as egg-and-dart. It is half-concealed by the overhang of the most conspicuous feature of the Ionic order—the spiral volutes and their connecting cushion of stone which is interposed between the echinus and the thin abacus-block above.

Fig. 10. The Ionic Order (reproduced by permission from *A History of Architecture on the Comparative Method* by Sir Banister Fletcher [14th edition])

[6]It is customary to state the proportions of the several orders in terms of the ratio between the height of the column and its diameter at its base. The Doric columns of the Parthenon are 5½ lower diameters in height; the Ionic columns of the *Erechtheum* (those of the *Parthenon* are not preserved) are 9⅓ diameters (North Porch).

Fig. 11. Corinthian Capital, *ca.* 350 B.C., Museum, Epidauros (*Alinari*)

GREEK ARCHITECTURE

The Ionic capital, unlike the Doric, does not present the same view from every side. The spiral scroll forms of the volutes and the downward curve of the cushion may be seen only on its outer and inner faces. The two sides show only the rounded surface of the cushion as it falls and rolls under so as to form the volutes of the two main faces. Accordingly, for the columns which were placed at the two angles of a portico, a special treatment was necessary. Volutes and cushions were carved on both the outer faces of the capital, the angle volute on each being turned out upon a diagonal so as to be shared by both faces. Since this arrangement gave an unsatisfactory interior junction of the two cushions, the Ionic order was in Roman times displaced by the third Greek order, known as Corinthian. It differs from the Ionic only with respect to its capital, which is of basket form providing four equally satisfactory faces (Fig. 11). Each face is carved with the beautiful natural form of the acanthus leaf, the leaves arranged in two tiers, out of which rise, as from a calyx, volute-forms; the major volute-forms move from the base of the capital diagonally outward toward the angles; the minor volutes, two on each face, meet one another at the middle of each of the four sides of the capital, a floret sprouting upward from their point of junction.

Except for their capitals, the Ionic and Corinthian orders are the same. The columns carry an architrave, unembellished by ornament but divided into three horizontal strips or fasciae, each higher strip projecting beyond the one beneath. Upon the architrave rests a bed-molding which corresponds to the Doric taenia; it is carved with the egg-and-dart motive. A frieze may or may not occur. If it occurs, it is a simple continuous band, normally filled with sculptures. If not, the architrave is surmounted by a range of dentils, a series of projecting rectangular forms which appear to represent beam-ends. The entablature is completed by a decorated cornice which protects the weather-face of the order.

VI. The special quality of the *Parthenon* as sheer architecture consists in the details of its execution. Since the beginning of the 19th century the building has been repeatedly re-examined and subjected to the most rigorous exactitudes of measurement. For it was observed that throughout its total expanse there were actual deviations from the straight lines of profile in which the building appeared to be composed. In appearance the building seems to be a system of verticals and horizontals. In fact it is neither. It is composed upon a system of regularly projected curves: the horizontal plane of its stylobate cannot be defined in two dimensions; its columns taper upward in a line of profile which is subtly curved. The vertical planes of its cella walls, the planes of its entablature, even the axes of its columns, coincide with the direct fall of no plumb-line. The problematic circumstance is that these deviations from actual verticality and horizontality are so systematically regular as to rule out accident or fault of workmanship. Flaws of both sorts exist in the *Parthenon* and may be easily distinguished. The deviations in question must, on the contrary, be assumed to be the deliberate contrivance of the architect; they are the premeditated resources of his craft as an artist. We in fact know from a text of Vitruvius, a commentator of the Roman era, that some of these deviations were prescribed in Classical architectural theory. Their occurrence in the *Parthenon,* moreover, is paralleled, if never quite equalled in sustained delicacy of handling, in other buildings of the ancient world. These "refinements" of the *Parthenon,* as they are called,[7] make of it one of the veritable wonders of the world.

The first of these refinements is exhibited in the stylobate, whose upper rectangular surface is apparently a horizontal defined by two dimensions of length and width. In fact, it is a surface curved broadly upward, as if a carpet, tacked at the four corners, were raised by a draft of air at the middle. The lines of the steps which connect the four corners of the rectangle are neither perfectly horizontal nor straight but rise upward in a broad curve which reaches its crest at the middle of the stylobate on each face of the temple. Since the columns of the exterior

[7] The term is technical, not honorific.

colonnade are all of equal height, this deviation from a straight line in the stylobate translates itself to the entablature, where it affects the horizontality of architrave, frieze, and cornice in the same degree. The rise is barely perceptible—about 2¾ inches in 101 feet of width on the east and west facades, about 4½ inches in the 228 feet of width on the lateral facades. The initial reason for such a deviation is certainly to permit the rainwater to flow from the platform as well as from the cornice table and frieze moldings. But such a material consideration does not sufficiently explain the circumstance observed; in particular, it does not explain the curvature of profile. The rainwater might as easily have been shed, and the execution indescribably simplified, by declining all exposed horizontal surfaces, in step or entablature, outward to a single equal level. This simple and obvious solution is precisely what has not been tried. Some other consideration must therefore have governed the form which was adopted.

The decisive consideration appears to have been this, that a horizontal line extended laterally for any considerable length will appear to a spectator to sag at the middle. Its actual rectilinearity is by an optical illusion distorted. Accordingly, to preserve the mathematical exactitude of a straight line in fact is to lose it in appearance. The problem of the architect was to preserve the appearance of a straight line, and of a horizontal surface, by compensating in physical circumstance for the optical distortion. In effect, by deviating from a straight line in the actual construction of the stylobate, he substitutes a visual for a mathematical rightness.

Similar considerations of visual rightness appear to have determined other deviations in the temple's construction. A column seen against the sky, dark on light, will appear thinner than a column of equal diameter seen against the cella wall, light on dark. Accordingly, to correct this optical illusion, the diameter of the angle columns was measurably thickened; the bay between it and its neighbors was contracted.

Some refinements were made simply for the purpose of imparting a visual clarity to the supporting function of stone. The line of profile which connects the upper circumference with the lower circumference of a column-shaft is not straight, but forms a delicate curve, known as the entasis of the column. An unentasized column remains, despite its Classical details, a physical post, bluntly inert; entasized, it acquires a kind of elastic vitality in the enactment of its supporting function, as if responding to its load. The curve of entasis in the exterior columns of the *Parthenon* is subtle: it deviates from the straight line of diminution by 11⁄16 of an inch in a height of 34 feet. It is regularly subordinated to the column's diminution: every diameter of the column falls within the limit set by its lowest diameter. The result is that the column never assumes the cigar-shape which may be observed in some non-Greek examples of the order.

For the same reason, with a view toward exhibiting the dynamic supporting function of the structural members, the cella walls are given a slight inclination inward. The whole range of columns in the exterior colonnade are similarly inclined (2⅝" in 34'), as if thrusting upward toward a common center upon which each of their axes, if prolonged, would meet.

It is the business of engineering science to build firmly. With that precise undertaking these refinements in the *Parthenon* have nothing to do, since even in their absence the building would stand, and stand securely. Its essential solidity as a structure does not depend upon its appearance. Yet it is exactly in these appearances that its art begins. The point at which engineering becomes art as well as science is the point at which its actualities are made to consist with what appears to an informed and sensitive eye. The authentic appearances of support and load are the surest mark of architectural quality in a building, since in them alone do the stresses of tension and compression in which builders work become visually appreciable and visually declarative. This visual presence is the sole language in which an architect can speak. To guarantee the coincidence of what is real and apparent in building is the common merit of every great style of architecture. An architect may have more to say than this; but unless he says this, he does not speak as architect at all, nor has his building the authentic character of art.

VII. Within the scheme of the Doric order there is room for the widest variations. To know the vitality and freedom of the Classical Doric style as it was forming one must look to examples earlier than the *Parthenon,* to its archaic forerunners, of which some still survive from the 6th century before Christ, beautiful old buildings with a vibrant elastic life in them even in the midst of ruin and decrepitude. Some of the best preserved are at Paestum, the ancient Greek Poseidonia, in Italy, south of Naples. In the weathered massiveness of these ancient orders, unpredictably various in detail, stark in their diminution, their profiles boldly curved, there is a poetry which does not exist by subtlety or reserve. They are the pregnant free essays in which the concept of the perfected Doric had still to be achieved; the potency of the Doric ideal is the more vitally in them because its sense is a problem felt but unresolved. By contrast to them the *Parthenon* is a thing of majestic poise. It exists by balance and restraint, by an ideal of harmoniousness and proportion. From it one may grasp the degree to which the philosophic, the artistic, and the religious ideals of a people are, in the end, ever one and the same.

Greek architecture is composed upon a principle of repetition, which, like the basic pulse of music, rhythmically measures space by reproducing identifiable intervals within it. The thing repeated, which acts as the visual unit of measure, is the architectural order. The significance of any one of the Classical orders of architecture, its function in the design of a building, is to impose this rhythmic measure upon space. It renders space intelligible by providing in it the means by which its limits may be visually assessed.

In enacting this function the Classical orders actually transform the quality of space as it is experienced. Natural space, the space which we experience in an ordinary random act of vision, is experienced simply as the system of relations between things seen. Its regularities are studied by the geometer, who is able intellectually to represent its systematic properties. In geometry this same space which we experience is intellectually mastered. But in ordinary vision the regularities which enable the intellect to master it are rarely appreciable because they are everywhere present. The Classical orders perform the function of making these regularities visually immediate and declarative. They are a visual geometry in space, which give the space of the building a qualitative character never discoverable in natural space. By their means the space of the building is humanized; it becomes, as it were, in contrast to natural space, a man-made thing, a thing calculated and lucid, in which relations, sequences, progressions, even distances, are immediately graspable and predictable. It is this character of the *Parthenon* which is referred to when it is described as having the Classical qualities of clarity, of definition, of orderliness and intellectuality.

The *Parthenon* is the perfected type of Doric architecture. In its proportions, in the balance of its vertical and horizontal accents, in its measured rhythm and essential reserve, the *Parthenon* is the spatial complement of the intellectual ideals of Greece. It serenely transcends its physical condition as a thing of stone and raises itself to the level of a formal art, suffused with the meaning of a total human culture.

Recommended reading:

W. J. Anderson and R. P. Spiers, *The Architecture of Ancient Greece,* new ed., revised by W. B. Dinsmoor, London, Batsford, 1927.

D. S. Robertson, *A Handbook of Greek and Roman Architecture,* 2nd ed., Cambridge, Cambridge University Press, 1945.

Banister Fletcher, *A History of Architecture on the Comparative Method,* 9th ed., London, Batsford, 1931.

GREEK SCULPTURE

The Parthenon[1]

IN CERTAIN PERIODS of history it will be observed that, even though all art forms are practiced, there is one that is dominant and influences all the others. For example, in the 17th century A.D. the thoughts and emotions of the time are best expressed in painting. Architecture and sculpture are subservient to it and, by attempting to conform to its principles, lose some of their intrinsic qualities. In Greece the dominant art is sculpture.

The problem of the sculptor is the organization of a number of related masses which, for their strongest effect, must be kept simple and generalized. It is not his aim to create a naturalistic representation complete with all its accidental details, but rather, by the careful balancing and interrelationship of sizes, masses, lines, and directions, to achieve a formal order. This may be done either by remaining close to the natural form or by moving away from it through abstraction or distortion. A primitive African carving is no less a work of art than a Greek statue, for each is a successful formal organization that expresses the ideal, whether individual or communal, of the sculptor. The medium is solid and tangible; it is (or should be) incapable of the blurrings, obscurings, or maskings that are considered acceptable in painting. This solid presence of sculpture tends to make it occupy space rather than share or penetrate it, although many sculptors have defied these limitations. The Greek sculptor accepted them and worked within them. In this sense Greek sculpture is "nonspatial." It does not assist in activating the space around it; that space remains neutral.

A similar approach to objective and tangible pure forms guided the architect to the end that the Greek temple may be said to have been constructed on sculptural principles. It is conceived as a monument whose planes and masses are magnificently ordered and interrelated. However, the space beyond the building remains neutral, nor is the space of the building itself activated either by the lines or the masses of the building. On the contrary, it is simply measured; the building imposes on the space it occupies a kind of regularity and order whereby it becomes intelligible.

Both sculpture and architecture used a unit of themselves as a standard from which all measurements or relationships were derived. Thus in architecture, a unit such as the diameter or semi-diameter of the column might be taken as a module or measure to regulate the proportions of the building. In sculpture, a unit similarly used might be the head or the finger. This unit gives coherence to the whole. The application of such a system of relative proportions tempers the raw material of the artist and places it under the control of the intellect. It is a complex observation, an intellectual construct, which transforms the first impact of nature on the artist. The Greek mind was of a kind that demanded the imposition of such a system upon nature for the purpose of ordering and arranging it. The Greek therefore always subdued emotion, held it in restraint, and governed it by reason. As the architecture is logical and orderly, so the sculpture is poised, calm, and essentially static. Movement is restricted. The extensions of which the body is capable were never realized in Greek sculpture, inasmuch as movement intensified destroys the equilibrium of the figure. Instability of this sort was abhorrent to the Greek, and, until the breakdown of Greek culture after the 5th century B.C., the figure was generally represented in those moments immediately preceding or immediately following the period of greatest activity. This restriction gave to the figures an aspect of majesty and self-confidence, because only in moments of poise and equilibrium does man appear to be in complete command of himself.

[1] Programs A and B.

GREEK SCULPTURE

These qualities are already apparent in the early work of the Greeks in the Archaic period (625–480 B.C.). As the development of Greek architecture is a history of the refinement and variation upon a theme, so is the development of Greek sculpture. The Greek focused his attention upon man as an isolated entity, not in order to portray him as a particular individual, but rather to raise him to an idealized type who should be the embodiment of all those qualities that contributed to his greatness and made him the self-assured master of his world. The development of Greek sculpture is therefore the intense study of the human organism and the application of that study so as to produce in marble or bronze an ideal organization.

Characteristic of the Archaic period is the standing male nude in Figure 12, carved about 600 B.C. It is one of a series of such works representing youths (*kouroi*), which are commonly known as Apollos. The sculpture is an arrangement of planes that suggest the rotundity of the body without actually reproducing it. The figure, when seen from any position except the front, loses a great deal of the roundness that the front planes suggest and thereby becomes weaker in its effect. Even though it is a free-standing figure in the round (one that can be seen from all sides), in the effect that it produces it is much closer to the type of sculpture known as relief, which is only partially detached from its original stone and has value only in front view. Although the third dimension is used to round the parts and give them projection, Greek sculpture is basically two-dimensional.

In his rigidity, his broad shoulders and narrow waist, his clenched fists, and his posture with the left leg forward but with the weight equally balanced between the two legs, the *Apollo* recalls Egyptian sculpture. The head, however, is more stylized. The face is constructed on a generally flat plane. The eyes are large and bulging because they are carved on the same plane as the forehead instead of being sunk into the eye-cavity. The mouth also is stiff and flat and does not yet curve around the lower face, although some sculptors of this period seem to have attempted to suggest this when they turned up the corners of the mouth, thereby giving the figures what is commonly called the "archaic smile." The hair is conventionally treated as a network of beaded shapes and is carried down to reinforce the neck. The parts of the torso are separated only by grooves or ridges which do not yet take into account the undulation of the muscles. Although the hand remains attached to the thigh, in other parts of the body the Greek sculptor has become more daring than the Egyptian and has begun to free the body members. He has cut through so that both legs are separate and the arms are for the most part detached from the torso.

Fig. 12. *Kouros, ca.* 600 B.C., Metropolitan Museum of Art, New York (courtesy of the Metropolitan Museum of Art)

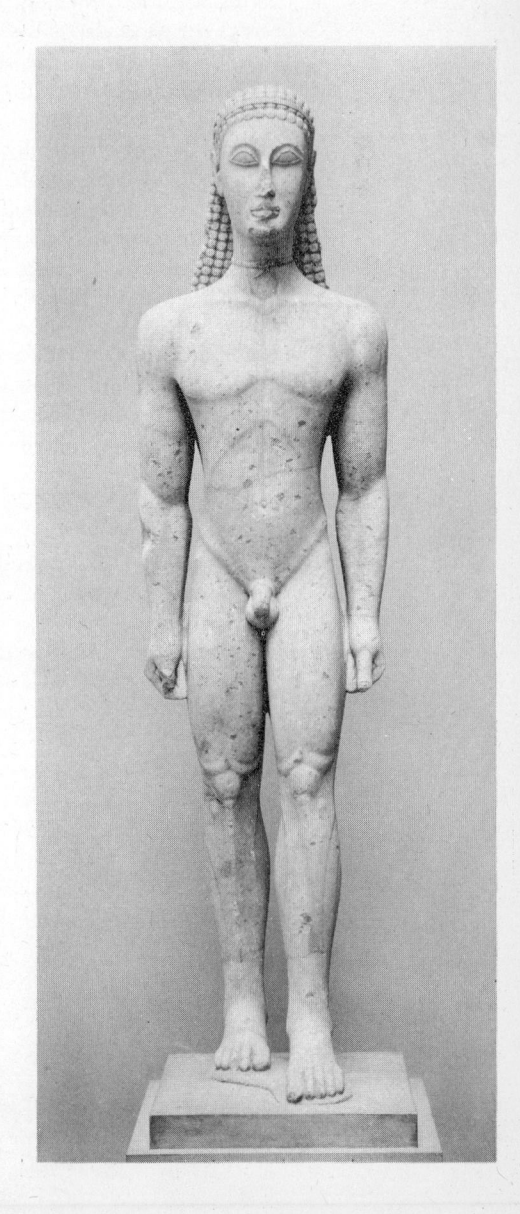

There arises a strong feeling of the interrelationship of the main masses of the body, even though the smaller interior masses are indicated only by lines. It is this articulation and interrelationship of parts which gives vitality to the figure and makes it an organism rather than a collection of additive parts. The alertness of the figure, his squared shoulders, forthright stance, and steady eye, have led certain critics in the 20th century to regard this period of Greek art as stronger and more successful than the later Golden Age. The nature of the stone has been respected; it has not yet begun to lose its firmness in an imitation of softer flesh; its masses have been kept uncomplicated.

The century and three-quarters that elapsed between the *Apollo* and the sculptures of the *Parthenon* was occupied with the slow and steady mastery of anatomy which was to be reflected in the subdivision of the major masses of the body into smaller parts, in the more anatomically correct projection and recession of those parts, and in the easy flow of one mass into another. All of these observations brought the sculptural rendition of the body into closer accord with nature. Never, however, did the sculptor permit his knowledge of the musculature of the body to over-complicate or detract from the total effect of the figure. The developed style represents a balance between knowledge of the actual forms and abstract patterns. From this emerges the distinctive character of Greek art, its idealism which transcends the particular forms of nature. Although more particularized than the Archaic sculpture, the sculpture of the Golden Age (450–400 B.C.) as represented in the *Parthenon* still adheres to the generalization that had characterized the earlier periods.

The adornment of Athens during the first part of the Golden Age was under the direction of Pheidias, a noted sculptor. The conception of the sculpture for the *Parthenon* was undoubtedly his, although he is known to have executed only one of the sculptures himself: the lost ivory and gold statue of *Athena Parthenos* that was placed in the larger of the two rooms in the cella. The importance of the sculptures of the *Parthenon* rests in part in their being some of the few original sculptures of the Golden Age that have come down to us. Much of the work of the period, including that of Pheidias, may be studied only in Roman copies or in coins. Unfortunately, most of the Parthenon sculpture has been removed to the British Museum so that its effectiveness as a part of the temple must be imagined. Its values also have been altered by its being placed on eye level instead of high above on the level of the cornice table. In addition to the main figure of the goddess within the temple, there were three areas that were reserved for sculpture (Fig. 9): first, the pediment, which contained

Fig. 13. *Mt. Olympus* (*Theseus*), from east pediment, Parthenon, *ca.* 438–432 B.C., British Museum, London

Fig. 15. *Contest between Lapith and Centaur,* Parthenon metope, *ca.* 445–438 B.C., British Museum, London

free-standing figures adjusted to the triangular space, second, the metopes, a part of the Doric frieze, which contained battle scenes in high relief; and third, the inner Ionic frieze, which runs around the top of the cella on the exterior and represented a procession of figures and animals in low relief. Of these, the pediment figures were the last to be carved and exhibit a more advanced style than the others.

The eastern pediment represented the birth of Athena. The central figures have long since disappeared but it is known that there were two instead of one as in earlier temples, so that the accent on the main axis in the *Parthenon* is less stressed. It was the custom of the Greek to symbolize such things as time and place through figures. Thus the time of day is symbolized by the horses of the rising sun in the left corner, while, in the right corner, the horses of the moon sink into the sea. A symbol of place occurs in the reclining male nude to the right of and facing the horses of the rising sun (Fig. 13). Although frequently called *Theseus*, he more probably personifies *Mt. Olympus*, the home of the gods. Still further to the right are the three figures, *Demeter, Persephone*, and *Iris*, who are adjusted to the rising slope of the raking cornice by changing positions from seated (*Demeter*) through half-rising to standing (*Iris*). A similar grouping is echoed but not repeated on the right side of the pediment in the figures of the *Three Fates* (Fig. 14). The western pediment represented the contest between Athena and Poseidon for the control of Athens.

The metopes under the projecting cornice were executed by older artists in many instances trained in the earlier tradition, so that the style appears harder and less advanced. The subject matter is derived from mythology and in general represents a contest between barbarism and civilization. The best preserved of the metopes are those which depict the contest between Lapiths and Centaurs: the Lapiths are the human figures, the Centaurs half-man and half-horse (Fig. 15). The two figures are carefully composed within the edges of the stone with lines that connect them and keep the attention focused within the frame. The brilliance of the sun necessitated a strong relief projection for these figures; otherwise, they would have been too much flattened by the light. The diffused light upon the inner Ionic frieze, on the contrary, made such strong projection unnecessary, so that the figures were carved in low relief, projecting not more than an inch and a half from the original stone. This frieze represents the Panathenaic procession which went every fourth year to the Acropolis to present a new robe to the goddess. It is composed of men, women, chariots, horses, sacrificial animals, magistrates, and gods and terminates on the eastern end over the entrance through which the great statue of Athena could be seen. A procession of continuous figures such as this might easily become monotonous. Since a number of sculptors were engaged, of varying talents and training, it might also have become disorganized. It was probably the controlling mind of Pheidias that provided it with its unity and rhythmic flow. By differing intervals between figures, by changes from front to side view, and by the horizontals of the animals' bodies intercepting and crossing the verticals of the figures, an extraordinary variety was achieved. Direction and flow were maintained by subtle curved lines that joined the move-

Fig. 14. *Three Fates,* from east pediment, Parthenon, *ca.* 438–432 B.C., British Museum, London

ment of an arm with the contour of a horse, for example. A certain amount of depth was also indicated in the shallow projection by the overlapping of figures, with an animal now in front of and now behind a figure. Unity and the essential horizontality of the frieze itself were attained by keeping all heads at the same level, whether the figure was seated or standing. The frieze carving projects a little more at the top than at the bottom because, unlike the metopes, it was lighted from below.

The curved line has become of increasing importance in the sculpture of the Golden Age. Frequently a sinuous curve and countercurve overlays the vertical axis of the body. In the Parthenon frieze a mounting and falling curved line plays across the verticals and horizontals of the animals and figures. In such a group as the *Three Fates* from the pediment (Fig. 14), rising and falling curves run across the thighs of the figures and seem to impose a horizontality upon them, although in actuality they form an ascending diagonal. The drapery, it should be noted, is always thin and serves to reveal the structure of the body beneath. Such a figure as the *Mt. Olympus* reveals most of the advances that have been made since the Archaic period (Fig. 13). The pose is freer and more relaxed. The members of the body have been completely freed from the surrounding stone. The incisions and ridges that had marked divisions in the *Apollo* are replaced by swellings and recessions that accurately indicate the minor masses that modulate the surface of the major masses, although the convention of triple horizontal divisions in the torso is still retained. The major masses now flow without interruption one into the other. The figure has been more strongly rounded, and the head has assumed its ovoid shape, with the mouth and eyes following its curvature, the eyes sunk in the head, and the hair close-cropped to outline the skull. Despite the rounding and the greater naturalism, the figure is still conceived from a single point of view and remains closer to two than to three dimensions. The rigidity of the earlier figures has relaxed, the straight line has been replaced by curves which unite the movement or direction of all the parts. This relaxation, coupled with the softer curves of the body and the slight bending of the head, lends greater gravity to the *Mt. Olympus*. He is self-contained but less energetic than the *Apollo:* serene, yet somehow faintly tinged by melancholy. Although part of a group composition in the pediment, he has no relationship with the other figures except a compositional one. Whether it is the isolation and lack of communion with other figures, the outward gaze which intercepts no response, or both of these combined with other aspects that create the emanation of melancholy from the figure, it is most difficult to say. The *Apollo* presents a strong physical presence; the *Mt. Olympus* has added a sense of personality. The inner workings of the human being which go by the name of mind or spirit have been drawn forth and now serve to soften, veil, and, at the same time, enrich the external physical appearance. Figures such as this, which stand at the culmination of a culture, act as the summation of previous developments at the same time that they contain within themselves the germ of that decay which is to fall upon and destroy the culture. As masterly organizations of broad masses mathematically proportioned, they emerge as final statements of the studies begun by the Greeks two centuries earlier. Simultaneously, the faint turning of the body upon its axis, the intangible presence of a personality, and the abstracted, brooding eyes point toward a breakdown of man's belief in his own powers.

Recommended reading:
Gisela Richter, *The Sculpture and Sculptors of the Greeks,* New Haven, Yale University Press, 1946.
Christian Zervos, *L'Art en Grèce,* Paris, Editions "Cahiers d'Art," 1946.
Ernst Buschor, *Die Plastik der Griechen,* Berlin, Rembrandt-Verlag, 1936.
Walter Hege, *Die Akropolis,* Berlin, Deutscher Kunstverlag, 1930.

II

THE MIDDLE AGES

MEDIEVAL CHRISTIANITY[1]

I. EVERY HISTORICAL STYLE of art has an ethical feature. Art is not itself moral, nor is its quality as art to be judged by moral criteria. But the act of expression is nevertheless inevitably a moral act, a consecration to something in which men believe and to which they commit themselves.

The styles of art are therefore as numerous as the possibilities of commitment, and of these possibilities the Classic art of Greece realized but one. Greek art is informed by the conception of a self-sufficient, serene humanity, capable, by the unaided prowess of native faculty, of harmonious development toward a rational ideal. It represents a poised and confident affirmation of the dignity of man, of man who could impute no dignity which was greater than his own; who therefore conceived his gods after his own image, more powerful in degree but identical in kind, perfect in the humane stamp according to which he was himself perfectible; who, doing and suffering in a world in which only excess is punishable, shuns excess not because it offends gods, but because it transgresses the limits of self-control, of what is proportionate, within measure—in short, of what is good for man.

Classic art could maintain itself only so long as man could continue to place such reliance on his own powers. If once this assurance should be disturbed, and he should suspect, tragically, that these powers were finite, that the content of existence, its sense and meaning, were incommensurate with human understanding, Classic art and its ideal humanity must seem an insolent delusion of the spirit.

In the 4th century B.C. a Hebrew poet had already composed, within the compass of an old folk-tale, the tragedy of the man of Uz, whose name was Job. The Book of Job is a Hebrew tragedy. It is, like *Oedipus,* a stark reflection on the problem of evil; like *Oedipus,* it calls into question, and reaffirms, the moral law. But it enjoins a type of reflection for which there is no parallel in the Greek world; it proposes a situation which is essentially repugnant to Greek moral sensitivity. For Job is the tragedy of a just man, a man "perfect and upright, and one that feared God and eschewed evil," who is nevertheless delivered by his own God to Satan, in order that his goodness might be shown. Oedipus offends against the moral law and suffers the retribution therefor; the punishment which he endures is justified by the offense which he discovers himself to have committed. But Job is one who, being righteous, must nevertheless suffer in order to confirm his own righteousness. The tragedy of Job is exactly that he is bound to endure what he cannot understand. When, bereft of his worldly goods, made childless, smitten with sore boils from sole to crown, and sitting among the ashes, he is urged by his wife to "renounce God and die," he answers:

> What? shall we receive good at the hand of God,
> And shall we not receive evil?

The resignation which to the Hebrew poet was a religious acknowledgement of the unsearchable power of God is to the Greek simply the endurance of a natural affliction, or worse, of a moral order which is cruelly capricious and arbitrary. For the endurance of suffering is to the Greek moral awareness never the positive proof of virtue. That the inoffen-

[1] Programs A and B.

sive should suffer without cause is morally repugnant, nor is it consistent with the Greek sense of tragedy. The Book of Job illustrates, therefore, not merely a difference of stress, but literally a contrast of worlds, a difference of moral sphere, in which alone the meaning of Job's suffering can be discerned.

In the *Oedipus* of Sophocles and the Book of Job of the Hebrew Bible are counterposed the two fundamental attitudes whose unreconciled opposition has produced the major tensions in the history of Western culture. The *Oedipus* represents what is referred to as Classical, or Hellenic, antiquity; the Book of Job represents the attitude which is known as Hebraism. At the beginning of our epoch the Hellenic attitude was modified by the Roman; Hebraism for its part underwent the radical and decisive transformation of a sect which carried abroad from Palestine to all the cities of the late-Hellenistic and Roman world the doctrine of a Savior, a Messiah, a Christ, in the person of its founder. So that the two fundamental attitudes which antiquity bequeathed to the Middle Ages, and through them to modern times, are, on the one side, the Classical humanism of Greece and Rome, and on the other, the Christianity which rises out of the Hebrew tradition.

II. In the decline of the ancient world, amidst the dislocations of its communal life which followed on the conquests of Alexander and of Rome, there arose, under the name of Stoicism, the last ethical reflection of antiquity, a philosophic ideal, still Classic in its self-reliance if no longer serene, the ideal of the Stoic sage. As the bonds of society were loosened, the individual man, isolated and estranged from any communal attachments to his contemporaries, turned inward upon himself, forsaking in indifference the world and its goods for the good which he could find only in his inner life. If it were no longer possible for an individual man to control external circumstance, then still, by the inner freedom which was left to him, he might control his own attitude and, claiming to himself an independence of all externals, stand superior to all that could happen to him.

Stoicism was too austere a doctrine to be available to all men. In the social and economic paroxysms of the Roman Empire men enough could be found willing to renounce the world in order to gain it, but few were prepared, in renouncing it, like the Stoic to remain in it, entangled yet free, victimized yet resigned, solitary yet equal. The stern self-reliance of the Stoic sage, in which men found themselves wanting, was not demanded of them in the new religion of Christianity which was to displace it. Christianity offered to all humanity a salvation which Stoicism could offer only to the philosophically wise; it offered for eternity what Stoicism could offer only for a little hour. Like Stoicism it required that the world should be renounced, but it circumscribed the dignity of the unaided human soul. In place of what it regarded as a human egotism it substituted a doctrine of mediation, the doctrine of a Savior God who had made himself man, and had suffered himself to be crucified upon a cross, in order that man might be saved.

The special significance of Christianity as a moral theory is its extension to include all humanity generally. The commandments of the Hebrew Bible were considered a special revelation of God to the Hebrew people, which regarded itself as specially chosen. Christian morality, on the contrary, considers man simply in his character as man; it regards neither race nor caste nor privilege nor political condition. Every human soul, without respect to its social estate in the world, is equal in its nakedness before God; the differences among men belong not to the accidents of nature and society, but to the degrees of moral worth and depravity which men have, whatever their earthly station may be.

Greek moral theory had not this degree of generality. Like the Hebrew, it was restricted to a limited group of men, who alone were regarded as capable of eminent humanity. The group in question was, in Greek society, the class which enjoyed the rights of citizenship in a city-state. The Greek social structure included slavery; Greek society, together with the rest of the ancient world, condoned it. A Greek slave, excluded from the exercise of direction over his own affairs, was simply, in Aristotle's phrase, a "human tool," a thing to be used and therefore without the intrinsic dignity of a human being. In the rigors of the Empire the stiffened structure of Roman society could only serve to widen the gulf between those to whom the consolations of philosophy were available and the masses of the afflicted and the lonely. It was among the voiceless and rejected, the lowly and the destitute, that the promises of Christian salvation were first heard and clung to, even in the face of repression, with a faith which, losing this, had nothing left to believe.

In 313 A.D., in the Edict of Milan, the Emperor Constantine pronounced religious toleration throughout the Empire. Primitive Christianity, the humble doctrine of the one-time Hebrew sect, extended itself in silent conquest through Europe south of the Danube, through Britain, Gaul, and Spain, through Asia Minor and the Mediterranean shores of Africa. The first result of the expansion of the primitive religion was the necessity of stabilizing the doctrines by which the widely dispersed Christian communities were held together. The early communities had been relatively loose-knit, pursuing their faith with an independent earnestness which only the genius of St. Paul had saved from the dissipations of other contemporary mystery cults in the Roman world. Scattered abroad, the integrity of the religion demanded, and got, a centralized institution which was destined in its western branch, under the name of the Catholic Church (the "Universal Church"), to inherit from Rome the empire of the West. The establishment of a centralized Church for Western Christianity imposed upon the religious communities a political as well as a doctrinal unity. It placed the Church and its sacraments in a position of authority intermediate between God and man, and framed for the remainder of the Middle Ages the place which reason and the human arts could aspire to hold in the fabric of medieval faith.

III. It is a characteristic principle of Greek thought, and of all thought which has been directly influenced by it, that knowledge should be valued as an achievement good in itself. That knowledge should in addition have its uses, that it should enable men to control nature or to govern their own destinies, is an incidental feature of its worth. It still forms a legitimate pursuit, even where a use or application cannot be demonstrated. Medieval thought allows no such principle. It subordinates every activity, including the pursuit of knowledge itself, to the one activity to which alone it was willing to accord a value in its own right, namely, the desire for eternal life. The old Latin hymn runs: *Media in vita in morte sumus,* "In the very midst of life we live in the face of death." Immortality is the one good which St. Augustine (d. 430 A.D.), at the beginning of the medieval tradition, affirms as good in its own right. All other goods are merely instrumental, valued not for their own sake but for the sake of immortality, as a tool is valued not for itself but for what it produces. Under these circumstances knowledge and rationality could never become, for medieval thought, self-validating activities. The whole of medieval philosophy is engaged in the task of adjusting to each other the claims of reason and of faith. Knowledge and revelation were counterposed against each other, and it was the business of medieval philosophers to find some way of reconciling the collisions between what constituted truth to the eye of human reason and what constituted faith in the sanctity of God's word revealed. In its extreme form, the opposition between reason and faith issued in the curt dictum of Tertullian, which like a flung gauntlet required reason to abdicate: *Credo quia impossibile, credo quia absurdum,* "I believe because it is impossible and absurd to believe." Its more normal expression, the humility of a gentler religious spirit, is from St. Anselm, who seeks in humility to understand only that which he already believes. In the opening sentence of the *Proslogion* he writes:

I make no attempt, Lord, to penetrate thy depths, for my intellect has no such reach; but I desire to understand some measure of thy truth, which my heart believes and loves. I do not seek to know in order that I may believe; but I believe, that I may know. For I believe this also, that unless I shall have believed, I shall not understand.

The final medieval resolution of the conflict between faith and reason is in the philosophy of St. Thomas Aquinas, for whom reason and faith can present no real contradiction, since faith is to reason not its competitor but its extension and crowning completion, in which it is carried back to God.

IV. Historians of Early Christian architecture have repeatedly observed that its buildings were constructed of pilfered elements. The columns of its arcades, its cornice moldings, the flagstones which paved its naves, were stolen from the temples and public monuments of a forsaken paganism. Even the plan of the church with its central nave and side-aisles and tribune was contrived after the form of a Roman public building, the basilica. One finds the emblem of medieval art in these old buildings, erected in the first generous impulse of a liberated faith, wherein the feet of the faithful moved to holy chant over flagstones whose reverse face, embedded in mortar, was carved with reliefs of Marsyas and Apollo. Of the two main sources from which the art of the Middle Ages rose, only the Greek and Roman afforded any tradition for the visual arts. Hebraic culture transmitted a religion and the prophecy of a Messiah, whose coming conquered an empire. But there existed in Hebrew society no tradition of sculpture or painting, both of which were prohibited in the second of the commandments delivered to Moses from Sinai. The Christianity which was carried abroad to the races of the gentiles was received by men and women who lived in Greek and Roman communities, spoke the Greek and Roman languages, observed Greek and Roman customs, and shared the universal predilection for Greek and Roman art. Christian sculpture and painting is, therefore, the result of infusing the Classic forms of pagan art with Christian meanings.

Under these conditions the borrowed Classical forms underwent a decisive stylistic transformation. A problem therefore exists, to determine in what the difference between Classic and medieval art consists.

The idealism of Greek art resides in the intellectuality of its forms. As the Doric order of architecture is not merely an assemblage of fixed elements, but the scheme of proportions by which they are related, so in the representation of nature Greek art imposes upon natural forms an ideal system of proportional relationships. The operation of this system, which the artist brings to nature, has the effect of eliminating from the represented natural form whatever in it is merely particular, specific, or accidental. The result is that Greek art is a delineation of types. It represents, in whatever subject it elects, the typical rather than the individual feature, as the sculptor Kresilas, in fashioning the portrait of Pericles, represents in fact less the particular individual man than the ideal of the statesman. So, in the representation of the human figure, the Greek artist generalizes the natural form, representing the ideally perfected proportions of the type (Fig. 1). But it is characteristic of Classic art, that where, as in the human body, the natural form has an intrinsic organization of its own, the Greek artist will respect that organization and will resolutely refuse to violate it. The human figure remains, in art as well as in nature, an organization of reciprocally adjusted parts, in which each part, active or passive, carries implications affecting every other. It is the steadfast refusal to violate the form in its natural properties, even while those properties are being generalized, which gives to the Greek representation of the nude its aspect of elastic self-sufficiency. Greek art never, even in its most ideal phase, turns its back on nature; its relationship to nature remains the clue to its distinctive idealism. From the tension between ideal and natural elements in the same form emerges that resilient abstract vitality which is the distinguishing mark of the Classic.

The procedure of the medieval artist is quite the contrary. Medieval art, too, is the generalized representation of types rather than of individuals. Portraiture, if by portraiture is meant the rendering of individual traits, is not a medieval form of art. But the kind of generalization which is produced by the medieval artist is totally opposed to that produced in Classic art. In the very act of generalizing the forms of nature, medieval art transgresses those forms; its abstraction estranges them from their physical meaning (Fig. 27). The organization which belongs to the human figure in its natural estate is systematically distorted as it is schematized and made a matter for art. It is the suppression of the claims of the represented natural form as a physical structure which gives to medieval art its suggestion of otherworldliness, that aspect which is described by the term "transcendental." Medieval art was thereby free to handle meanings which had no existence in Greek art; it was free to represent the spiritual and emotional qualities of man which constituted a reality beyond physical nature. For in the moment that physical nature—this world of space and time, in which things rise and perish—is thought to be illusory, reality must be looked for not in it, but beyond it. The medieval artist, who must perforce choose physical forms to work on, grasps exactly those qualities which abort the physical existence of his subjects. Not the body, the torso of the human nude, but the head, the part whose expression does not depend on total posture, becomes the main vehicle of expression. The eyes widen, stare out intensely beneath arched brows, yet refuse to focus on any specific external stimulus. Their whole sense is inward, enrapt, as if communion had been lost with any outer object which might satisfy their search or allay their need. A Classical figure adjusts itself, as by an inner architecture, to the gravitation of its own weight; a medieval figure makes no physical adjustment and appears preternaturally to float in space, its feet uncompressed by any weight, its limbs responding to no physical necessity. The motivation of the form must be sought elsewhere than in the physical adjustment of its parts. It therefore acquires its meaning not by representation but by suggestion, by evocation of a spiritual world which goes beyond the bounds of nature and is the perfect complement to itself.

V. The otherworldliness of medieval art, its transcendentalism, is reinforced by a formal principle of subordination. The music of plainsong qualifies and heightens the text to which it is written, but in divorcement from its text it has the same kind of sensed incompleteness that belongs to a cathedral sculpture estranged to promiscuous isolation in a museum. Plainsong neither has, nor claims to itself, the sufficiency of absolute music, of music which can exist in its own right, independent of a literary complement. On the contrary, it demands its complement, as the cathedral sculpture demands the context of the cathedral, which alone is the sufficient work of art. Contributory and dependent, the pure melodic line of plainsong imposes no measure of its own; it exists by subordination to the rhythms of the stately prose language with which it is indivorcibly associated, conforming to the irregular accentual pulse of sacred words.

VI. It is one of the features, in some respects it is one of the disabilities, of contemporary art, that it is conceived to be a free activity, that it cannot without loss ally or subordinate itself to any consideration which is extraneous to art. The consequence has been that in modern Europe and America both art and artist have been divorced from society. For an art which loses its function of informing, literally of giving form to, the meanings which men hold or aspire after is socially inconsequent. An art which proposes to itself, in the name of purity, to exclude these meanings is the symptom of profound unease in society itself concerning its own purposes. It has, in the phrase of Michelet, the disinterestedness of the dead. Medieval art has no such freedom. It is committed, from its initial to its final act, to the task of providing expression for meanings which the artist has not himself chosen but which are prescribed for him by the Church. The Church is not only the major patron and beneficiary of the arts; it lays down for the artist the function he is to perform.

The conception of the arts as "fine," as the products of a liberal activity, was precluded by the ascetic ideal of the age. St. Jerome, unable to repress his admiration for the ancient writers, nevertheless reproaches himself for what appears to him the equivocalness of loving Cicero as well as Christ. The justification of the arts consisted for the Middle Ages not in their ability to delight, but in their utility as the instruments of moral and religious instruction, the Bible of the ignorant and unlettered.

To adore a picture is one thing, but to learn through the story of a picture what is to be adored is another. For what writing is to them that can read, a picture is to them who cannot read, but only look, since in it even the ignorant can see what they should follow. (St. Gregory the Great, *Letters,* xiii and cv.)

St. Bernard of Clairvaux, fulminating against the riot of carved ornament which had spread itself in free fancy over the capitals of Romanesque churches, begs his reader, if he will not be moved by the impudence of it, at least to consider the cost! It is the same reluctance to admit the self-sufficiency of art which caused the Church in the 7th century, according to the Venerable Bede, to send a cantor to Britain in order that he might instruct the English choristers in the use of Roman liturgical music. Any art which could not be made consistent with discipline was systematically excluded. As Latin was for the Church, wherever it reached, the unifying language of Christianity, so in music the plainsong, and in representational art the images employed by sculptor and painter, required to be given the authentic purity and singleness of purpose which the Church alone could guarantee. Neither music nor plastic shape was permitted to assume an independent value in the structure of medieval faith. Both were employed because they were found to have a use whereby they could be related either to the order of the Mass or the feasts of the church calendar.

Medieval sculpture and painting are held within a system of fixed conventions which are strictly legislated by the Church. The Decrees of the Second Council of Nicaea read:

The composition of figures is not the invention of painters, but the law and tradition of the Catholic Church, and the ordination and dispensation of our fathers....

Collectively, this system of conventions is called the "iconography" of Christian art, a term which means, literally, a writing in terms of icons, or images, commonly agreed upon. These images serve, by convention, to specify the subject matter which is the occasion for the work of art, as in Greek art a winged female figure indicates a Victory (Niké), a sleeved and trousered figure a barbarian, a dolphin the sea, a figure with club and lion's skin the hero Heracles. In medieval Christian art a similar set of conventions governs the representation of religious subjects. A distinction in the scale of figures separates the human and divine. A halo signifies sanctity, a crossed halo Christ, a dove the Holy Ghost. The saints are identified by fixed attributes: St. Peter by the keys of heaven to which the sacraments of the Church give admission, St. Paul by his baldness and the sword of the church militant, St. Andrew by the distinctive cross of his martyrdom, St. Francis by the stigmata of the Passion of Christ. The four apocalyptic beasts of the Book of Revelation make figurative allusion to the gospels with which they are severally associated: the winged man with Matthew, the ox with Luke, the lion with Mark, the eagle with John. Old Testament subjects are conceived to prefigure those in the New by a rigorous parallelism, as Abraham's sacrifice of Isaac, his son, is the symbol of God's sacrifice of his Son in the Crucifixion. The scenes from the New Testament are filled with such conventional motives, the lily representing the purity of the Virgin in the Annunciation; the ass and the ox the manger in the Nativity; the lamb, its breast pouring forth blood into a chalice, the *Agnus Dei* (Lamb of God), St. John's description of Christ in the Baptism; the skull at the foot of the cross, Golgotha, the Hill of the Skull, scene of the Crucifixion.

The effect of the Church's legislation in such matters was, in the end, not to stifle the vitality of medieval art, but to preserve the symbols of medieval faith. Its system of conventions simply restricts the limits within which the vitality of art must be realized. The medieval artist had neither more nor less freedom than an architect to whom the function of a building is prescribed: the function is never to be overridden, but any design which respects the function remains architecturally possible. Medieval art is, for all of its conventions, an art of inexhaustible variety; by reason of its conventions, it is an art of inexhaustible sense. The real importance of convention in medieval Christian art consisted in enabling that art to sustain its communal significance in medieval society. The modern loss to society in having no longer a common set of symbols is a matter which the anguish of the 20th century, when it does not choose to make a profession of its own impoverishment, is able to assess.

Recommended reading:
Henry Adams, *Mont-Saint-Michel and Chartres,* Boston, Houghton, 1913.
H. O. Taylor, *The Medieval Mind,* 2 vol., N. Y., Macmillan, 1927.
C. H. Haskins, *Renaissance of the Twelfth Century,* Cambridge (Mass.), Harvard University Press, 1927.
E. Mâle, *Religious Art in France, XIII Century,* N. Y., Dutton, 1913.

MEDIEVAL ARCHITECTURE AND SCULPTURE

The Cathedral of Amiens[1]

I. MEDIEVAL ARCHITECTURE is in its primary feature an architecture of interior space; its primary function was not to house a god, but to provide a space for congregation. Within the great screened volume of the cathedral the faithful foregathered to witness, through the mediation of the priest at the altar, the recurrent miracle which is celebrated in the Mass. From this single circumstance the total character of the medieval cathedral is derived.

II. The plan of the cathedral, whatever degree of complication it may come to have in answer to special historical needs, remains always basically the plan of the Early Christian church, which is known as a basilica. Externally, the basilica-form consists of a simple rectangle with a semicircular sanctuary at one end (Fig. 16, plan).

The semicircular space is called the apse; in a church presided over by a bishop it is the space within which the *cathedra,* or bishop's throne, was placed, whence the name cathedral for the building as a whole. Immediately in front of the apse, on the interior of the rectangle, stood the altar before which the rite was performed and toward which it was directed. By a very early tradition in the Church the altar was viewed symbolically as the tomb of Christ. It became therefore customary to place the apse on the eastern end of the church, in order that the altar might be nearest the Holy City, where the actual tomb was located. Medieval churches are for this reason said to have an "orientation" in space.[2] Since the apse lies toward the east, the square end of the rectangular plan, the facade through which the church is normally entered, faces west. The conventional orientation of the medieval church exercises so complete an authority that it continues today to determine the site of church buildings, whenever they lay claim to any architectural distinction.

The rectangular part of the church, into which the communicants were congregated, was divided by colonnades into three, sometimes into five, longitudinal aisles. Of these the central division was the largest, leading directly forward so as to give upon the apse: this division was called the nave of the church. In it, at the end nearest the altar, the Early Christians reserved a space for the clergy who participated in the service by chanting the responses; this space, sometimes enclosed by a parapet, was known as the *schola cantorum,* or choir. From

---

[1]Programs A and B.
[2]*Old St. Peter's,* the basilica which is illustrated (Fig. 16), does not exhibit the normal orientation. The church was consecrated in 326 A.D. during the course of the century in which the convention came to be established. On orientation in Classical architecture see above, p. 19.

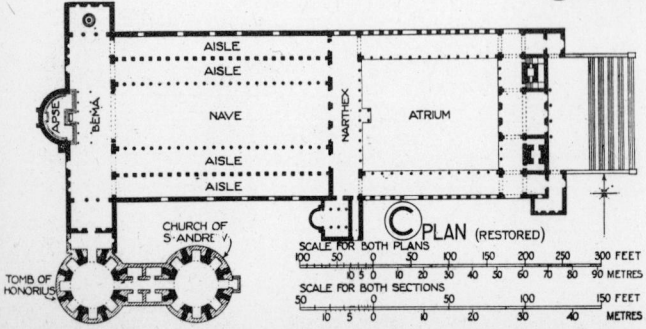

Fig. 16. Old St. Peter's, Rome (reproduced by permission from *A History of Architecture on the Comparative Method* by Sir Banister Fletcher [14th edition])

two pulpits, one at either side of the choir space, the gospel and epistle were read to the congregation, which occupied the western portion of the nave.

In smaller dimension than the nave, flanking it and running for its entire length, were the side-aisles, which provided passages of circulation for persons within the church. Normally a single aisle was disposed at each side of the nave. In the larger metropolitan churches, where congregations were more numerous, the number of side-aisles might be doubled, giving a double row of columns and two open passageways at either side.

Even from Early Christian times the increase in the number of participating clergy made necessary for their special use a provision of additional space near the altar. To accommodate this need, a space was interposed between the nave and the apse, crossing both nave and side-aisles and sometimes projecting beyond the latter so as to give to the over-all plan of the church the form of the letter T. The two projecting arms at north and south are called transepts, and the space at which they traverse the nave the crossing.

At the western end of the nave, immediately within the portals through which the building was entered, was an entrance vestibule, opening into both nave and side-aisles. In the Early Christian Church this vestibule, called the narthex, formed the nearest approach to the altar which was allowed to those who had not yet been admitted to full communion.

Beyond the narthex lay a colonnaded forecourt open to the sky, the so-called atrium of the church, at the waters of whose font, in the middle of the square, the penitents in a symbolic act washed away their sins in the blood of Christ. The function of the atrium was to preserve the insularity of the church itself; only beyond it did monumental portals open out upon the external world. The atrium was a dispensable element of the plan as soon as there no longer existed in medieval society a distinction between those who fell within the pale of the Church and those who fell without. In later Christian architecture its motive is preserved only in the cloister courts of monasteries; its disappearance from the plan of church buildings is the very sign of the extension of the Church's authority through every avenue of medieval life, secular and spiritual.

In elevation[3] the loftiest part of the church is the great central nave, which is raised above the aisles flanking it at either side (Fig. 16, section and interior elevation). Only the transepts equal it in height, giving monumental dignity to the crossing, where, in the Early Church, the altar table stood. The nave is lighted by a range of windows which penetrate its walls above the lean-to roofs of the side-aisles. This upper range of windows, together with the wall spaces between them, is called the clearstory. Below, separating the nave from the side-aisles, a row of columns supported the nave wall. It was variously treated according to the supply of materials which the dismantling of pagan buildings provided. It might carry a normal Classical entablature including architrave, frieze, and cornice molding; it might support an arcade, a series of arches which direct, as by a rhythmic pulse, the movement of the eye toward the altar. Between the nave arcade and the clearstory range of windows occurs a wall space called the triforium; it is formed by the pitch of the roof over the side-aisles and was employed in Early Christian churches as a field for mosaic decoration in the nave. The triforium was at an early date transformed into an arcaded gallery running above the side-aisles and opening at mid-elevation into the nave-space.

The developed medieval church will simply elaborate, in plan and elevation, the form of the Early Christian basilica. The developed style, which is achieved in the 13th century, is called Gothic. Between it and the style of the Early Christians there is first a period of continued disintegration in Classical society, a period known as the Dark Ages, in which the Church alone maintains any bond of continuity with the past. At the end of the 8th century, and again in the 10th, a spiritual quickening occurs in which the sherds of Classical learning are reappropriated and assembled for transmission. Both of these periods are preludes to the

[3]See, above, p. 19, note 2.

emergence, in the 11th and 12th centuries, of a vigorous medieval society, knit together by a Church which has extended the unifying sinews of its authority everywhere. In this period, in which the scattered elements of feudal society are regathered under a single triumphant institution, the Church is assisted by the monasteries, and it is under the hands of the monastic builders that in a great surge of constructive activity all the elements of a new architecture were assembled, "as though," in the words of a contemporary, "the world were throwing off its decrepitude to clothe itself anew in an array of white sanctuaries." The period, as an architectural and artistic phenomenon, is called Romanesque. The term actually denotes a great variety of distinct forms. Gothic, which emerges from it, is the exquisite product of combination. Its essential quality consists less in the invention of new elements than in the use to which elements already available are put. It completes with assurance what the Romanesque had tortuously divined. The *Cathedral of Amiens* is the perfected creation of the medieval world, at once the spiritual setting of its worship, the spatial image of all that it aspired after, and the Bible of its poor.

III. Master Regnault de Cormont, in the third generation of master builders at *Amiens,* directed that an inscription be placed in the labyrinth of the pavement:

In the year of grace 1220 this work was first begun. . . . He who was master builder was called Master Robert and surnamed de Lusarches. Master Thomas de Cormont succeeded him, and afterwards his son Master Regnault, who caused this inscription to be here placed in the year 1288.

The *Cathedral of Amiens* is the product of the 13th century in France. That the names of its architects are known is an exception, since most works of the Middle Ages have been transmitted under the general anonymity of the times, and *Amiens* itself remains still, even with the names of Masters Robert and Thomas and Regnault, of whom nothing else is known, the expression not of them, but of the communal life in which they were spiritually immersed. The cathedral was only one of several which were then abuilding—at Chartres, at Paris, at Reims, and elsewhere, and nothing can be more striking as an historical token than that during this century, the high period of Gothic art in Europe, generations of men should have lavished their energies and their substance on the building of these monuments which, to the end of their own souls' salvation, they dedicated to Notre Dame, Our Lady Mary.

A Norman abbot, Haymo, of St.-Pierre-sur-Dives, in 1145 wrote:

Who ever saw, who ever heard in all former generations, of such a thing, that rulers, princes, potentates, full of the honors and riches of the world, men and women of noble birth, should submit their haughty and puffed-up necks to be bound by straps to carts, and like beasts of burden should drag to the asylum of Christ loads of wine, wheat, oil, mortar, stones, wood, and whatever else is necessary for the maintenance of life or for the construction of the church?

Moreover, it is wonderful to see how, although a thousand or even more men and women are yoked to one cart (so great is the size of the carts and so heavy the load piled upon them), nevertheless the whole company marches along in such silence that no voice, no sound is heard; and unless you saw with your eyes, far from believing that such a multitude was present, you would not think that there was a single person. . . .

There, as the faithful relate, you might see the infirm and those smitten with diverse ailments arise cured from the carts to which they had been harnessed; you might see the dumb open their mouths in the praise of God; you might see those troubled by unclean spirits recover their sanity; you might see the priests, who presided over the various carts of Christ, exhort all to penitence, to confession, to lamentation, and to the leading of a better life; you might see the people themselves prostrate on the ground, lying flat on their bellies, kissing long the dust; you might see old men and young, and boys of tender age, calling on the mother of God and appealing to her with sobs and sighs from the bottom of their hearts, in the voice of confession and praise.

All this is known to be the work of Christ, but after Him, especially of the Virgin. . . . She it was who made famous first the church of Chartres and then ours, both dedicated to herself, by means of so many wonderful miracles, that if I wished to tell what I have seen in a single night, my memory would fail and my tongue be exhausted.

The cult of the carts, which is described by the abbot Haymo, represents a degree of religious fervor which was both temporary and local. It is quite certain that it built no cathedrals. It is nevertheless the profound symbolic act of a people who found in the cathedral, fashioned from hauled mortar and stone and wood, the sublimest expression of medieval faith and of what mattered to them most.

IV. In the plan of the Gothic cathedral the primitive basilican church received an expansion in which, while the original form was preserved it was accommodated to the historical needs of the Church.

The foremost of these needs was to provide a more commodious space for the officiating clergy before the altar, since for this purpose the transepts had long since failed to suffice. Between the transepts and the apse an additional rectangular space was interposed, giving an apparent extension of the nave beyond the crossing (Fig. 17). Into this space the area reserved for the singers (*schola cantorum*) was removed from the nave itself, and from this circumstance the space is called the choir. At *Amiens,* the choir is almost as large as the nave itself. It is by the addition of the choir that the church plan acquires the form of a cross, a form whose symbolic propriety was in all likelihood only noticed after the change had itself occurred.

As the choir forms, in fact, a simple extension of the nave, the side-aisles also were carried forward and sometimes, as at *Amiens,* even doubled beyond the crossing. The extension of the side-aisles around the semicircle of the apse forms a new element known as the ambulatory. It is the initial element of the most beautiful feature of the Gothic plan, the chevet of the cathedral.

The chevet is the result of the popular veneration of the saints in the Middle Ages. The Church claimed to itself alone the capacity to mediate between God and man; between man and the saints no such mediation was required. The Christian Trinity had become, especially as it was made the subject of theological reflection, so formalized that it could function in popular sentiment only as a mystery to be contemplated. The passionate dedication which it had evoked in Early Christianity was therefore reserved for persons less remote, whose unequivocal humanity, in the sympathy of compassion, made them more directly accessible to humankind. The cult of the saints has its primary, as certainly it has its earliest, expression in the glorification of the Virgin, who, Mother of Mercy, was the principal intercessor between God and man. The whole of the Middle Ages lived under the awful expectation of the world's last day, which it represented, in the carved stone of its Romanesque and Gothic portals, as the Last Judgment. If Christ baring his wounds was Savior, he was also Judge, and in the impending act of his day of wrath the scales which Michael held for weighing human souls were the image of a too inflexible justice. The hope of mankind was not in its deserts, which it knew too well to claim, but in the compassion of Mary, the *Mater Dolorosa* crowned Queen of Heaven, who sits intercessor at Christ's right hand. To her, therefore, the medieval

Fig. 17. Title Plan, Amiens Cathedral, 1220–1288 (Reproduced by permission from *A History of Architecture on the Comparative Method* by Sir Banister Fletcher [14th edition])

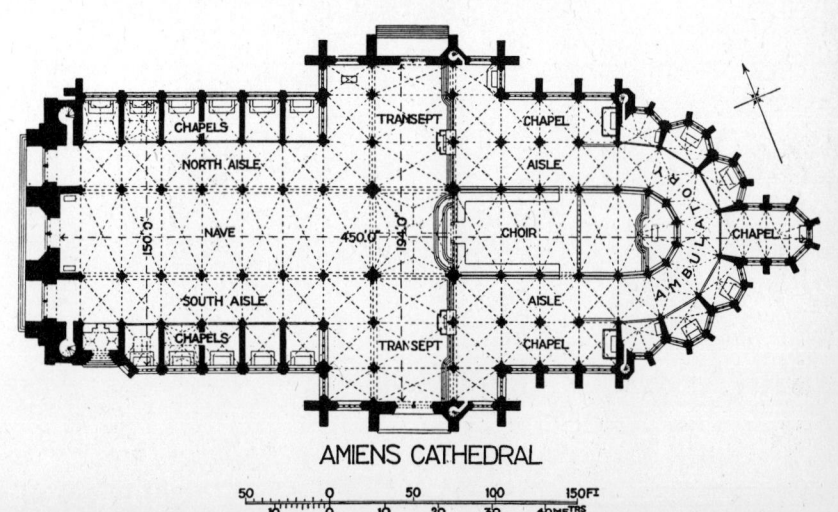

AMIENS CATHEDRAL

cathedral church was normally dedicated. *Paris Cathedral* is known popularly today as *Notre Dame* (Our Lady); the term is equally ascribable to *Amiens* and *Chartres* and *Reims,* each of which is called by the French *Notre Dame.* Under the same motive, that their intercession and their favor might be gained, the lesser saints were venerated. A special altar was required for every saint who was the object of special supplication or whose relics the church possessed. The chevet is a Gothic provision for these altars at the apsidal end of the basilica. It includes the apse with its ambulatory and the series of radiating chapels opening off the ambulatory. Of these the largest is the Virgin's Chapel, which is regularly placed on the main axis of the nave; at either side, radiating from the apse, are minor chapels containing the altars of the lesser saints. At *Amiens,* including the Lady Chapel, there are seven in all.

In elevation the cathedral rises above the town, a composition in verticals, its two great belltowers soaring aloft, the dominant elements of the townscape which spreads beneath their shadow (Fig. 18). The western facade consists of a series of ranges. At the entrance level the three portals are not only splayed, but deeply recessed under covered porches which extend forward to the outer edge of the buttresses massed against the western wall. The porches form the major site of the sculptural program in the cathedral. The arched span of each portal— the so-called tympanum—is filled with carved reliefs above a horizontal stone lintel. At the middle of each doorway, upon the vertical post, or trumeau, which supports the lintel, the master sculptor lavished all the resources of his art: the most famous and most accomplished of all the sculptures of *Amiens* is the figure of Christ, known as the *"Beau Dieu,"* on the trumeau of the central portal (Fig. 29). In the splay of the porch at either side, beneath the series of carved arches which shelter the doorways, stand the jamb-sculptures of the saints who attend upon Christ.

Above the portals is an arcaded gallery penetrating the solidity of the wall mass. It corre-

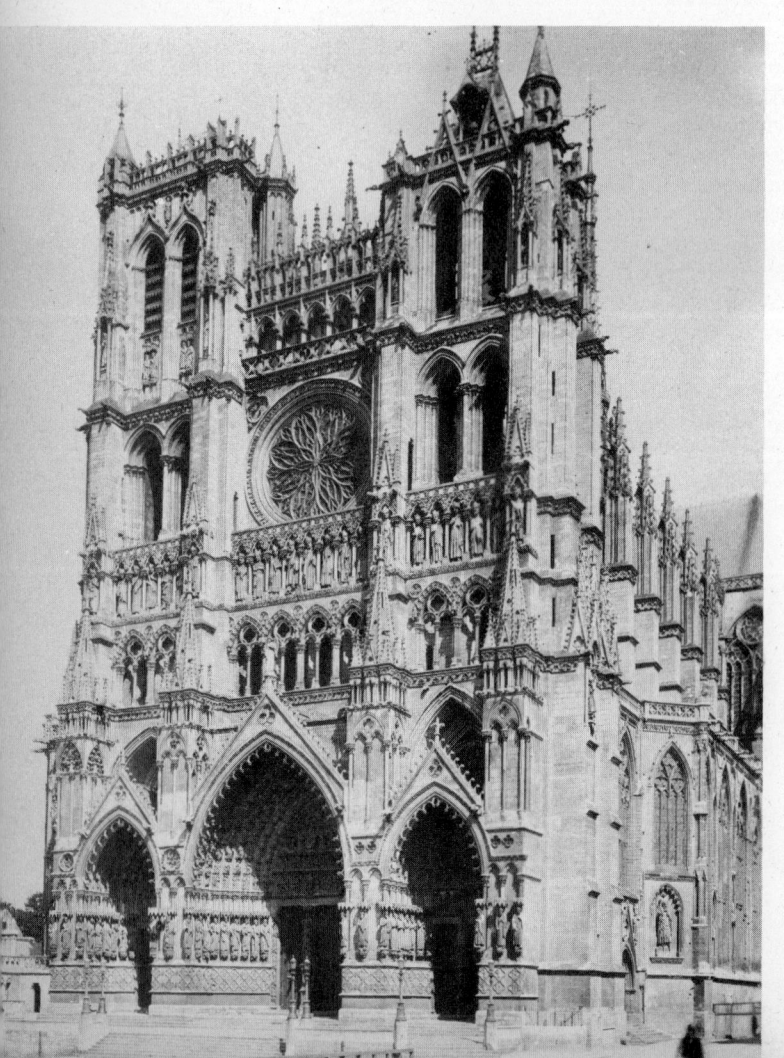

Fig. 18. West facade, Amiens Cathedral, 1220–1288 (*Archives photographiques*)

Fig. 19. The Arch (reproduced through courtesy of Harper & Brothers)

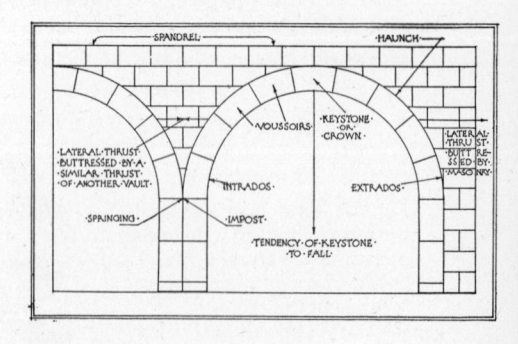

sponds with the triforium on the interior of the church. The gallery is surmounted by a range of arched niches, each of which is occupied by a single sculptured figure—the so-called "gallery of kings." Above it, in the central portion of the facade between the two bell-towers, is a great circular rose-window, which opens at the level of the clearstory into the nave and stains the light of the nave at its western end.

The facade of *Amiens* conforms to a fundamental principle of Gothic architectural design, that the exterior of the building should be a visual declaration of the disposition of interior spaces. Accordingly, the two towers coincide with the portals which give admission to the aisles; the central portal, which is featured both in size and elaboration, opens into the nave. Similarly, in vertical distribution, the exterior design of the elevation repeats the divisions of the interior, the portals coinciding with the nave arcade, the external gallery with the triforium, the rose-window and the sculptured gallery of kings with the clearstory.

V. Greek architecture evolved no concept of interior space. The dramas of Sophocles were performed in an open-air amphitheater; the great Panathenaic procession which wound from the lower city up to the Acropolis came to rest not in the *Parthenon,* whose sanctuary was reserved to the cult-statue, but before an altar erected in the precinct of the temple at its eastern end. The major aspect of the *Parthenon* is therefore its exterior. It has the character of a monument; it commands and orders space without enclosing it. Architecture of interior space is a development of the Romans and of the medieval builders. In both its Roman and medieval examples the development is dependent upon the use of a new constructive principle, the principle of the arch. The principle is very old, though its use prior to Roman times was restricted with but few exceptions to purely utilitarian structures. The Romans invoked the principle architecturally for the purpose of creating an interior space unimpeded by supports.

The arch principle consists in the spanning of a space between supports by means of wedge-shaped elements known as voussoirs (Fig. 19). The span of the arch is composite. No one of its elements is large enough to serve as a lintel. The span between supports has therefore to be crossed by the concerted functioning of many elements, which together do what no one of them could do alone. By the interaction of the voussoirs, the physical forces which, undirected, would destroy the arch are precisely those which sustain it.

The central voussoir, which locks the others into place, is called the keystone or crown of the arch. It can gravitate vertically downward only by displacing the other voussoirs. It is therefore the function of the remaining voussoirs, so long as the arch system is preserved, to transfer beyond themselves the downward thrust of the weight descending from the crown. The descending force of the weight is transformed into lateral thrusts, which the voussoirs transmit to the abutting walls at either side.

The Arabs have a proverb: "The arch never sleeps." The proverb represents the just perception that the existence of a building is, for the period of its endurance, continuously active. Its stability is a matter of calculated balance and counterpoise, suspending the tendency of masses to gravitate earthward by opposing to them either the force of an equal counterthrust or the inertia of massed stone.

At each side, the voussoir which rests directly on the vertical pier is called the springing of the arch. Midway between it and the keystone is the arch's haunch, the point at which, unless provision is made against it, the arch will burst outward under the lateral thrusts transmitted from the crown.

To provide against this active tendency of the arch to destroy itself, some form of buttressing is required as the necessary complement of the arch system. A voussoir transmits the thrust of an arch; a buttress redirects it downward to the earth. The buttressing may be either static or dynamic. It is static if to the thrust at the haunch it opposes the simple inertia of a wall mass (Fig. 19, right). It is dynamic if to the thrust it opposes a counterthrust, as when two arches are placed side by side so that their interior thrusts mutually counteract each other (Fig. 19, left). The wall mass between two such arches, called a spandrel, is the medium through which these counterthrusts are actively and continuously transmitted and thence directed downward through pier to earth.

Since each part of the arch system is the active complement of all the others, the arch does not in fact exist except it be complete, its voussoirs locked by its keystone, and its thrusts absorbed by its buttresses. The construction of an arch out of its elements requires, therefore, the use of a scaffolded wooden form, called centering, which receives and supports the voussoirs until they have been locked and buttressed—in short, until the arch itself has begun to function.

The principle of the arch is the key to medieval construction. The problem of the medieval builders was to provide a shelter over the uninterrupted spaces of their naves. For this purpose it was impossible to employ stone lintels, which were subject to fracture unless intermediate supports were introduced into the nave itself. The Early Christians had employed for the basilica a system of wooden trusses (Fig. 16, section), which satisfied the need but left the roof exposed to the danger of fire, the universal hazard of all medieval structures. The Romanesque and Gothic builders sought a solution, therefore, in an alternative device originated by the Romans, who had extended the use of the arch principle to the construction of vaults.

The first extension of the principle is the barrel vault (Fig. 20, a), which is simply a series of arches set face to face, alternate courses of the masonry serving to tie each arch to its neighbor.

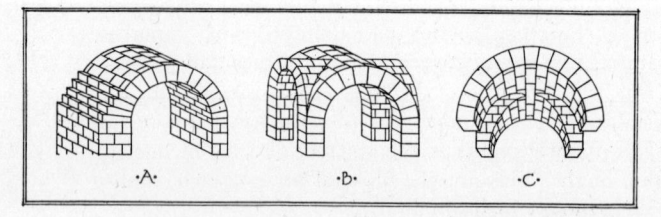

Fig. 20. Barrel and groined vaults (reproduced through courtesy of Harper & Brothers)

The barrel vault must be buttressed for its entire length, since its thrusts outward are continuous for the series of arches which compose it. In consequence, it is costly to build. It is, moreover, like any tunnel, very difficult to light, the more especially as its length increases. Since the vault itself will suffer penetrations only at cost of being weakened, light can be admitted only through the two semicircles, or lunettes, at the ends.

The Romans disposed of these difficulties by causing two barrel vaults of equal height to intersect at right angles (Fig. 20, b,c,). The lines of intersection of the two vaults, called groins, give the name groin vault to the new scheme.

Normally the groin vault realized itself on a square plan. If a hall of some length had to be vaulted, the total space was divided into a series of squares, each of which was covered by an individual groin vault called a bay (Fig. 21). Each bay, a simple groin vault, solved its own lighting problem; two lunettes permitted light to enter in a fall across the axis of the building. Each bay could function therefore as effectively in combination as alone.

The groins in this type of vaulting form arches that spring, in the square plan, from diagonally opposed piers. It is along these groins that the lateral thrusts of the two intersecting barrel vaults meet and redirect each other diagonally outward. The thrusts of a groin vault, channeled along the diagonal groins, are thus no longer continuous but concentrated at the angles. At the junction of two bays the diagonal thrusts which converge upon a single pier will produce a thrust which is transverse to the axis of the bays (Fig. 22).

From this circumstance the Romans, and after them the Gothic builders, evolved a *dis-*

Fig. 21. Baths of Caracalla, Rome, 216 A.D.

continuous system of buttressing. According to this system, the building required to be buttressed only at the intervals at which the thrusts were actively concentrated, that is to say, at the piers. The walls between the piers no longer sustain a function of supporting the vault; they serve merely as screens, separating the interior from exterior space. They may therefore be dispensed with, and in the Gothic period this precisely was the occasion for the development of an art of stained glass. In place of the walls the Gothic builders screened the interiors of their churches with glass and qualified their space with color, wondrous protean lights whose life was as fluctuant and various as the brilliancy of day outside.

Occasionally, in order to save centering, the groin arches were constructed first, two simple arches sprung diagonally from pier to pier and sharing a common keystone. Such arches, providing an armature upon which the vaulting itself might rest, are called ribs. From this mode of construction, which was evolved by the Romans, arose the vault system of Gothic architecture, the ribbed groin vault.

The ribbed vault consists of an armature of six ribs (Fig. 23): the two diagonals coinciding with the groins; two which are sprung across the space to be vaulted and which are therefore called transverse ribs; and two which run the length of the building and are called longitudinal ribs. This armature serves as a kind of permanent centering upon which the vault may be constructed and which thereafter reinforces its weak points.

If the ribbed groin vault realizes itself upon a square plan, it is a matter of simple geometry

Fig. 22. Adjacent bays of a groin vaulted hall. Arrows indicate thrusts from crown of vaults which meet and redirect each other, first along diagonal groins, then in a direction transverse to the axis of the building.

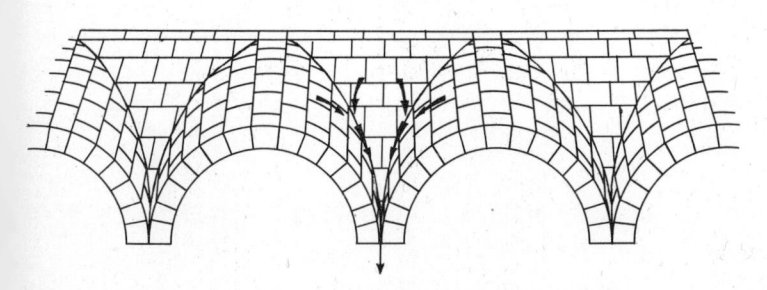

Fig. 23. Groined vaulting with semicircular ribs (reproduced through courtesy of Harper & Brothers)

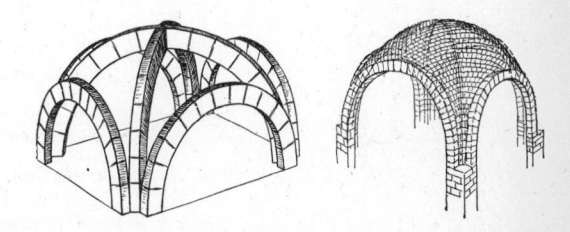

that the semicircular arch which is formed upon the diagonal of the square will be higher than the semicircular arch which is formed upon the side. A ribbed groin vault in which all of the ribs form semicircular arches will therefore have a somewhat domical shape (Fig. 23). The inequality of the rib-crowns complicates the buttressing that is required, for the thrusts are no longer channeled exclusively along the groins, but descend in all directions from the vault crown. The four enclosing arches must therefore be braced against falling outwards.

The pointed arch of Gothic architecture is a form conceived originally not for aesthetic reasons, but in order to solve this structural problem of vaulting. If an arch be pointed, not only is its thrust diminished, but its height is no longer determined by its span. The Gothic builders therefore conceived as their solution of the vault problem the pointing and raising of the ribs on the four sides of the square plan (Fig. 24). By this means, the summit lines of the

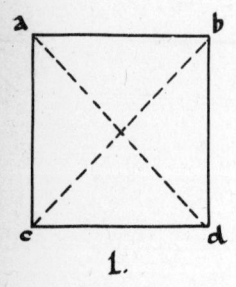

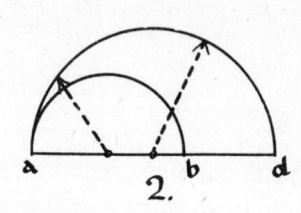

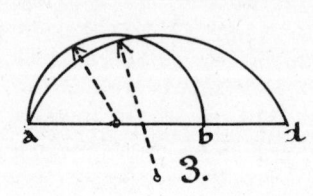

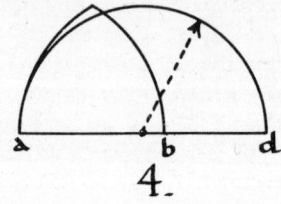

Fig. 24. 1. Plan of ribbed groin vault. 2. Showing relation of crowns with semicircular ribs on side *ab* and diagonal *ad*. 3. The Roman solution: crowns equated by making rib *ad* less than semicircular. Summit line is level but thrust is increased. 4. The Gothic solution: crowns equated by pointing the transverse and longitudinal ribs. Rib *ad* is a semicircle. Thrusts may be further reduced by pointing diagonals as well.

vault were levelled, and the total thrust of the vaulting was concentrated upon the four angles. Having made this advance, however, they discovered themselves no longer to be restricted to a square plan for each bay: any rectangular space might be vaulted, whether square or oblong. Moreover, by a pointing of the diagonals, the vault might be made as lofty as the verticality of Gothic design called for.

The development of the Gothic vault is associated with a peculiar form of buttressing demanded by the plan of the church. The central nave was flanked at either side by aisles which ran continuously for the entire length of the nave itself (Fig. 17). From this plan the church was reared at two distinct levels of elevation (Fig. 25). The loftiest space was the great vaulted nave, which rose above the aisles at either side. Accordingly, any buttress which took the thrusts of the nave vault had necessarily to be so placed that the aisles were not blocked

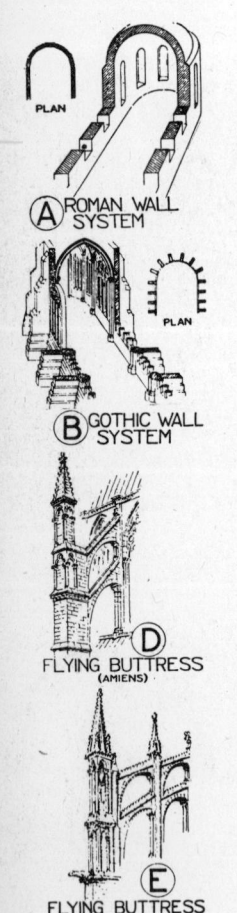

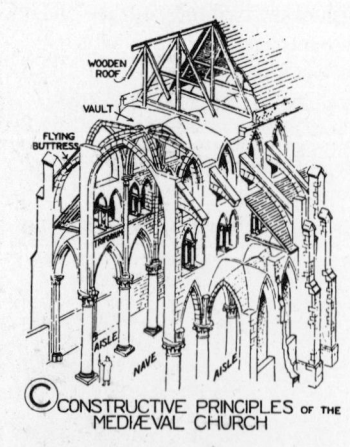

Fig. 25. Title Section, Amiens Cathedral (Reproduced by permission from *A History of Architecture on the Comparative Method* by Sir Banister Fletcher [14th edition])

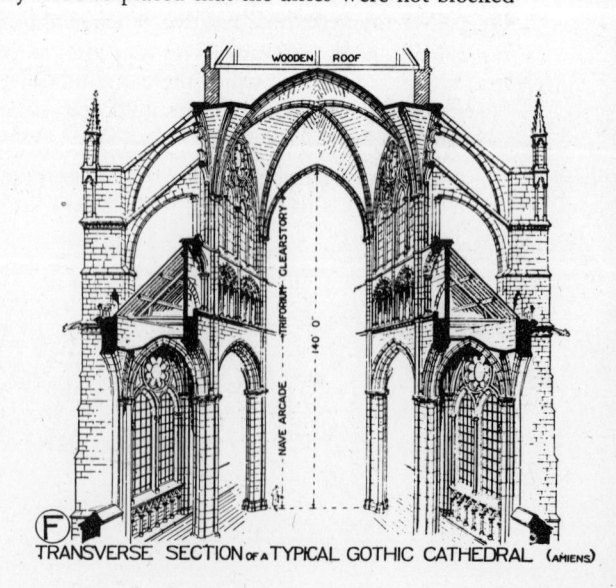

off. This circumstance required that the thrusts, which were concentrated at the piers, be carried over the roof of the aisles to massed stone buttresses beyond. The thrusts are carried by a series of half-arches which span the aisles and connect the vault with the buttress. The buttress, including the connective half-arch, is called a flying buttress. It is the major distinctive motive of a Gothic church as seen from the exterior.

VI. The essential fact of the Protestant Reformation of the 16th century in Europe is the re-establishment of immediacy in the relationship between man and God. No church, no rite, no formalized theology is permitted to infringe the fundamental principle, that the religious consciousness, informed by the Scriptures, which itself alone must interpret according to its lights, is directly in contact with divinity. The consequence is that a Protestant religious service is characteristically directed toward the congregation: a Protestant church is in its primary feature an auditorium. The rite of the medieval Church, and of the Catholic Church today, is precisely the opposite. The priest before the altar is the ordained agent of the Church, and it is through the mediation of the Church alone, through its rite and sacraments, that the individual is placed in relation with God, or that God is accessible to him. Not the congregation, therefore, but the altar, is the center of the Catholic rite. It is the business of architecture in the Middle Ages not merely to permit or preserve, but to prescribe, this concentration.

The interior of the cathedral is organized upon a principle of compulsive focus (Fig. 26). From the vault crowns the ribs are extended downward as shafts, emphasizing by their continuous lines the stark verticality of the interior volume. In accordance with a rule of subordination they are carried to distinct levels of the interior: the longitudinal ribs to the stringcourse beneath the triforium gallery; the diagonal ribs to the level of the pier-capitals in the nave; the heavy transverse ribs to the floor itself, where, in conjunction with the pier, they form the clustered pier of the developed Gothic style.

In isolation an arch is visually static. In the nave arcade, as an element of design, it becomes a factor of directed move-

Fig. 26. Interior, Amiens Cathedral, 1220–1288 (*Archives photographiques*)

ment in space, leading the eye in a measured somber rhythm of repeats, like a pulse of music, toward the apse before which the altar table stands.

The same concentration is sustained by the lighting. The clearstory range of windows high above the nave stains and subdues the lights, and transfigures the space of the cathedral, without claiming to itself the initial response of the observer. The single light which appears to the observer in the direct line of vision upon entering the cathedral comes from the series of lancet windows which surround the apse. To these lights the eye is compulsively drawn, and there held in incorrigible concentration upon the altar, till, reaffirming its own capacity to move, it follows upward again the rib-shafts into the darkling immateriality of the vault-spaces.

VII. The elements of a Classical work of architecture mutually imply one another (Fig. 5). It is possible, from the preservation of only the three angle columns of a Greek temple, to reconstruct it in its original form, to envisage it whole when only its part is known. For the elements of a Classical order are themselves few, and each is subject to use by repetition. As the units of a measuring stick, since they are equal, are therefore predictable, so the rhythmic repetition of the columns in a Doric peristyle, the alternation of triglyph and metope in its frieze, have the effect of reducing the building to something calculable. They are like the rhythmic beat in music; they impose upon space the regularity of a measure.

The special quality of Classical architecture is therefore order, intelligible sequence. Within whatever limits it chooses to operate, it inevitably molds space so as to make it visually measurable, since in measure, in the rule of repetition or progression which man imposes on it, it is alone intelligible.

Medieval architecture is composed upon no such principle. Its space is visually inexhaustible; it is subject to no common unit of measure, visually declared, which regulates its proportions or defines its sequences. The repetition of the arches of the nave arcade has not the effect primarily of measuring the space of the nave, but of imposing on the eye a directed movement toward the apse. Except for the altars in chapel and apse, to every space traversed there exists a felt beyond, indefinite but certified. The lines of contour which in Classical architecture define with exactitude the form are on the exterior of the cathedral dissolved by leaf-motives called crockets, which suppress the clear demarcation of the space of the building from the space beyond.

The whole which results from the multitudinous elements of a Gothic cathedral partakes, nevertheless, of a kind of rationality, albeit a kind of which the Classical world had no awareness. The faith which renounces reason may nevertheless use reason as its servant. As St. Thomas Aquinas, within the rigorousness of the syllogism, ordered the structure of medieval faith, so the cathedral builders by order and subordination imposed on their work of glass and stone the impress of a rational faculty, not one which will demonstrate what faith requires men in humility to believe, but one which will draw forth the consequences of beliefs already held.

The special character of Gothic rationality is declared in its architectural progressions. The lower ranges of the cathedral exist in mass, heavy, resistant, physically inert (Figs. 18, 26). As the eye moves upward, the penetrations are gradually multiplied, and the effect lightened, until in the upper ranges only a skeletal framework remains, or the perforated upper reaches of a bell-tower. The vertical progression from dominant masses to dominant voids carries with it an implication of a space beyond, in which the materiality of stone is sensibly renounced, and the character of space itself is visually palpable and surcharged.

In this progression consists the singular expressive power of the most generally noted characteristic of the Gothic style, namely, its verticality. The towers, the pointed arches and vaults, the rib-shafts—these things of massy stone—appear not to gravitate, but to soar aloft, emancipated from the rule of natural law which governs ineluctably all things of earth. The effect is contrived not by verticality alone, but by the progression which accompanies it. The absence of any such progression in a modern skyscraper makes of its verticality not only a thing earth-born, but irreparably earth-rooted.

Nathaniel Hawthorne gives the impression of the beholder in his description of *Lichfield Cathedral:*

To my uninstructed vision, it seemed the object best worth gazing at in the whole world; and now, after beholding a great many more, I remember it with less prodigal admiration only because others are as magnificent as itself. The traces remaining in my memory represent it as airy rather than massive. A multitude of beautiful shapes appeared to be comprehended within its single outline; it was a kind of kaleidoscopic mystery, so rich a variety of aspects did it assume from each altered point of view, through the presentation of a different face, and the rearrangement of its peaks and pinnacles and ... towers.... Thus it impressed you at every change, as a newly created structure of the passing moment, in which yet you lovingly recognized the half-vanished structure of the instant before, and felt, moreover, a joyful faith in the indestructible existence of all this cloud-like vicissitude. A Gothic cathedral is surely the most wonderful work which mortal man has yet achieved, so vast, so intricate, and so profoundly simple, with such strange, delightful recesses in its grand figure, so difficult to comprehend within one idea, and yet all so consonant that it ultimately draws the beholder and his universe into its harmony. It is the only thing in the world that is vast enough and rich enough.

Not that I felt, or was worthy to feel, an unmingled enjoyment in gazing at this wonder. I could not elevate myself to its spiritual height, any more than I could have climbed from the ground to the summit of one of its pinnacles. Ascending but a little way, I continually fell back and lay in a kind of despair, conscious that a flood of uncomprehended beauty was pouring down upon me, of which I could appropriate only the minutest portion. After a hundred years, incalculably as my higher sympathies might be invigorated by so divine an employment, I should still be a gazer from below and at an awful distance, as yet remotely excluded from the interior mystery. But it was something gained, even to have that painful sense of my own limitations, and that half-smothered yearning to soar beyond them.

VIII. The cathedral is a grand orchestration of the arts, organizing within a single space the work of the sculptor, of the designer in stained glass, of the manuscript illuminator, the poet, the musician. The whole—neither more nor less—is the work of art. No individual sculpture, no stained glass window or chanted song, sustains its full meaning in isolation from the cathedral which supplies its context. Occasionally, in museums, one comes across a jamb-sculpture or a lancet of medieval glass which, divorced from its destined setting, attempts still to make out its existence alone. It gives the impression of an excerpt, which is bereaved of part of its meaning by separation from its intended place. Nothing is so indispensable for the understanding of medieval art as the perception of its sovereign integrity, its essential oneness, which makes each individual art—architecture, sculpture, painting, music, poetry—contributory to a program wider than itself. It is a character which the art of no age has attained in comparable degree either before or since. The principle upon which this character depends is subordination, subordination to a conception and a plan which extends beyond any part and includes it, and from which the part is separable only at cost of ceasing to be what it is. What one experiences as the insufficiency of a medieval sculpture artificially isolated in a museum is not its limited quality as art, but on the contrary its positive feature as part of a larger work of whose presence it has been accidentally deprived. It sensibly demands its complement of architecture and sculpture whereby its measure of individuality may be defined. Of individuality undefined and uncircumscribed it knows nothing and claims nothing.

Gothic sculpture is designed as the adjunct of architecture. It is decorative only in a secondary sense; its primary function is to be the vehicle of a meaning within the limits established by its architectural setting. These limits contract the range of its formal possibilities;

THE MIDDLE AGES

the variety of independent motives which are available in the execution of a free-standing sculpture are eliminated. For, on the one hand, so long as it remains within the authentic limits of the style, a Gothic sculpture is not permitted to disturb the stable forms of the architecture, drawing them, as in certain Romanesque works (Fig. 27), by an irruptive vigor out of their alignment as visible supports; nor, on the other hand, is it permitted, as in a Greek metope (Fig. 15), to preserve inviolate its intrinsic proportions. On the contrary, it conforms itself to the architecture, even at cost of violating its similitude to nature (Fig. 28). It is customary to speak of an emergent naturalism which makes itself visible in Gothic sculpture, a naturalism which indicates, on the part of the Gothic artist, either an awareness of Classical models which we know to have been available to him, or a fresh observation of nature, or both. The new quality of Gothic representation is visibly certified. Formally, however, it is everywhere controlled and held in check by the relation of the sculptural forms to the architecture. The most accomplished Gothic works (Fig. 29) contrive a balance in which both the representation of nature and the quality of architectural sculpture are preserved. In the moment that this balance is disturbed (*Vièrge Dorée*, Amiens, *ca.* 1280), so that the natural predominates over the architectural demand, one observes the destruction of the sculptural ideal of the Middle Ages and the symptom of a redefinition of man's place in the world.

The sculpture of the cathedrals was executed under clerical direction. A general program, formalized by the Church, prescribes to each work its place and to each place its subject. The cathedral becomes, by virtue of its sculptural program, in the

Fig. 27. Isaiah, Souillac, 12th century (*Archives photographiques*)

Fig. 28. *Jamb figures,* central west portal, Chartres Cathedral, *ca.* 1145 (*Archives photographiques*)

Fig. 29. *Beau Dieu,* west portal, Amiens Cathedral, *ca.* 1230 (*Archives photographiques*)

medieval phrase, a *speculum,* a mirror of the world natural, historical, and divine, in which the Middle Ages wrought, in carved stone, both the reflection of the learned and the Bible of the poor. The central image at *Amiens* is the figure of Christ, called by the French *"Beau Dieu,"* which stands in the middle of the central portal on the west facade (Fig. 29). The figure occupies the position of the trumeau, the post supporting the lintel and tympanum of the main portal through which the building is entered. A work of extraordinary reserve, noble in lineaments, majestic and authoritative in dignity, it represents the very type of the medieval ideal—a substantial presence, in the world but not of it. In a draped Classical figure the draperies serve to reveal, and even to reinforce, the structure of the form underneath; in Gothic figure sculpture, which is normally draped, the drapery conceals the physical form, as in the heavy Gothic cascade of folds at the side of the *Beau Dieu.* The head, not the torso, is the major vehicle of spirituality in medieval art. About the *Beau Dieu,* at either side, are disposed the saintly figures who attend upon him (Fig. 30). Thence, the sculptural program expands itself over the facade and into the transepts, representing every aspect of the human destiny —the Labors of the Months, the Liberal Arts, and the history of the world. The history begins with the Creation and the Fall of Man. It relates the prophecies of a Messiah which are given in the Old Testament; the Atonement and Redemption of Mankind which are given, in fulfillment, in the New. It concludes under the awful presentiment of the *Dies Irae,* that day of wrath on which Christ, exposing the wounds which he has suffered for mankind, shall sit Judge over them and mete out the deserts of Elect and Damned.

Recommended reading:
A. K. Porter, *Medieval Architecture,* New Haven, Yale University Press, 1912.
C. H. Moore, *Development and Character of Gothic Architecture,* 2nd ed., New York, Macmillan, 1904.
A. Gardner, *Medieval Sculpture in France,* Cambridge, Cambridge University Press, 1931.
C. R. Morey, *Medieval Art,* New York, Norton, 1942.

Fig. 30. View of central doorway, west facade, Amiens Cathedral, 1220–1288 (*Archives photographiques*)

MEDIEVAL MUSIC

Plainsong[1]

PLAINSONG IS THE SUNG PRAYER of the Catholic Church. It is the oldest art music of western Europe still performed. Its origins, like those of the Church itself, are partly Hebrew and partly Greco-Roman. As the Church, in accumulating traditions and rites, modified and changed those elements which were borrowed from earlier cultures, so music, as servant to ritual, was changed. Within a few centuries the body of plainsong had grown so great and showed such regional differences that codification was needed. This task was undertaken during the pontificate of St. Gregory the Great (*ca.* 540–604 A.D.), after whom the plainsong of the Roman Church has been called "Gregorian chant." Having brought order into its music, the parent Church desired that all churches of Christendom use the same music. To effect this, singers of the Papal Chapel were sent to England, to Germany, and to other parts of Europe, to assist in substituting Gregorian chant for the numerous local "dialect" chants, each of which differed more or less from that used in Rome. Over a period of several centuries almost all of the chant "dialects" disappeared, and only the Roman or Gregorian chant remained.

Like the architects and sculptors of the medieval cathedrals, most of the monks who composed the melodies of the Church are not known by name. Within the frame of medieval culture God and the community, not the individual, were served by art. Thus the goal of the composer of liturgical music was not to be original, but to serve the traditional functions of the Church. Working within such limits, the composer selected a few formulas (*i.e.,* stereotyped musical phrases) appropriate to the text to be set and with them he fashioned a "new" melody. Because of this constant reworking of familiar elements, many Gregorian melodies share only the beauty inherent in the tradition of chant itself. Other chants, composed by more gifted musicians who could transcend the limitations of the formulas, are melodies of the greatest beauty, unique unto themselves.

Gregorian chant is unaccompanied melody[2] sung in Latin. To the uninitiate it may seem curious, strange music. Like authentic folksong, chant presents the listener with a single melodic line. Thus, no matter how many singers perform the chant, they all sing the same melody in unison. Nothing superfluous distracts the ear, so that the mind of the listener (who is, ideally, a worshipper) is free to follow the sacred text; the musical setting is but a heightening, an intensification, of the meaning of the words.

Gregorian chant will probably seem "uneventful" to ears accustomed to more energetic melodies. The *ambitus* or range of chant is small, rarely exceeding an octave, and frequently limited to a fifth or sixth. The melody usually moves stepwise or *conjunctly* from one pitch to the next adjacent pitch, since the purpose of chant is to intensify the quiet contemplation of the divine, and large skips by their very nature create motion and activity. This contrast of sacred and secular can be clearly heard by comparing any chant with such bustling melodies as those which begin Bach's *Brandenburg Concerto No. 3* and Hindemith's *Quintet for Wind Instruments*.[3]

Another element in chant, strange to ears accustomed to major and minor scales,[4] is the

---

[1] Programs A and B.

[2] Not until the 9th century or thereabouts is there evidence that harmony (*i.e.,* the sounding together of two or more different pitches) was known or used in European art music. Even after the "discovery" of harmony, the Church continued to sing its music unaccompanied.

[3] See, below, p. 368, Ex. 99.

[4] See Chapter VIII, pp. 383–90.

use of the ecclesiastical *modes*. The hymn *Pange Lingua,* for example, is in the Phrygian mode. This means that the main body of the melody lies between the tones E and E an octave higher. The *finalis* or final ("home") tone is E and the *tenor* or "reciting" tone (which in this mode is six tones above the *finalis*) is C. All the tones of the melody arrange themselves about these two "pole" tones. Characteristic of several modes, including the Phrygian, is the whole-step from the *finalis* to the next tone below (as may be seen in the last two notes of the *Pange Lingua* melody). This whole-step, which gives the older tonal arrangements their "modal" flavor, is in sharp contrast to the half-step "ti-do," characteristic of both major and minor scales. Peculiar to the Phrygian mode is the half-step from the *finalis* to the next highest tone (as may be seen in the first three notes of the above-mentioned hymn melody).

Most extraordinary for 20th-century ears is the lack of body-rhythm (*i.e.*, basic rhythm or meter) in performances of Gregorian chant. To account for this peculiarity it is necessary to return to the history of chant itself. The medieval manuscripts which preserve these melodies employ a notation which indicates pitch without clearly indicating duration. Thus the melodies are not performed exactly as notated, for this would result in rhythmic monotony; to give life to them the singers must know the unwritten performance tradition. During the Renaissance and the following centuries, this tradition was lost. In the last half-century scholars, trying to recover the older performance practice, have advanced several theories. That most generally accepted and now officially adopted by the Catholic Church is the elaborate theory developed by the monks of the French Benedictine monastery at Solesmes. The manner of performance is referred to as the Solesmes style.

This official Solesmes performance style avoids the single recurring pattern of accented and unaccented beats characteristic of a waltz or march.[5] In its place there is a free mingling of triple (HEAVY-light-light) and duple (HEAVY-light) units, *their sequence depending on the accentuation of the Latin text.* Thus a single line of chant might be composed of the following units: *1* 2, *1* 2 3, *1* 2, *1* 2 3, *1* 2 3, *1* 2, *1* 2, *1* 2 3, etc. In addition to this irregular grouping of small units, the basic pulse, which underlies almost all European art music, is frequently altered by means of a *rubato* or slight slackening of the speed. Stated in the simplest terms: it is impossible to tap one's foot to a Solesmes performance of Gregorian chant.

The various musical characteristics just described combine in a grave, dignified music of the greatest beauty. Gregorian chant is prayer; for this reason it is sung, not played by instruments. It is servant to worship, inducing contemplation in the auditor by avoiding those musical elements which might recall the market square or the tavern on the green. The attitude of the Church towards its music can best be expressed by one of the early Church fathers, St. Augustine, who wrote in his *Confessions:*

How greatly did I weep in Thy hymns and canticles, deeply moved by the voices of Thy sweet-speaking church! The voices flowed into mine ears, and the truth was poured forth into my heart, whence the agitation of my piety overflowed, and my tears ran over, and blessed was I therein.

While there are thousands of different chants, they fall into one or the other of two great divisions: the music of the Mass or the music of the Daily Hours of Divine Service. There are eight occasions during the day when divine service may be held,[6] and for these the music of the Daily Hours provides. Chants for the Mass are divided into the Ordinary and the Proper. The Ordinary consists of settings of texts employed in every Mass; the Proper consists of chants *proper* to the season or saint being commemorated on a particular day. All of the chants to be studied belong either to the Ordinary or to the Proper of the Mass.

The mass is the central ceremony of the Catholic Church, during which the sacrifice of

---

[5] See Chapter VIII, pp. 381–82, for a fuller discussion of meter and rhythm in general.
[6] These are: *Matins,* during the night; *Lauds,* at sunrise; *Prime, ca.* 6 a.m.; *Terce, ca.* 9 a.m.; *Sext* midday; *None, ca.* 3 p.m.; *Vespers* or *Evensong,* at sunset; *Compline,* nightfall. Mass is usually sung after Terce.

Christ on the Cross is commemorated and re-enacted. The Ordinary (or unvarying parts of the Mass) consists of five principal sections:

KYRIE eleison ("Lord, have mercy on us")
GLORIA in excelsis Deo ("Glory be to God in the highest")
CREDO in unum Deum ("I believe in one God")
SANCTUS Sanctus Sanctus ("Holy, holy, holy")
AGNUS DEI qui tollis peccata mundi ("Lamb of God, who takest away the sins of the world")

The capitalized words are those by which the sections are usually called.

1. *Kyrie eleison*.[7] This, the only portion of the Mass with Greek text, consists of three invocations each repeated three times:

Kyrie eleison.	Translation:
Christe eleison.	Lord, have mercy upon us.
Kyrie eleison.	Christ, have mercy upon us.
	Lord, have mercy upon us.

The first line is sung three times to one phrase of music; and the second line three times to a new phrase of music; the first two statements of the third line are set to a variant of the music of the first line, while the last *Kyrie eleison* is sung to a final new phrase of music. In abstract (each letter standing for a *full line* of text together with its musical setting) this chant has the following form:

Kyrie: a a a   Christe: b b b   Kyrie: a a c

Simplified, the form is A B A, or *ternary* form, a type of musical structure found in music of all periods.[8] The last phrase, "c," is a *coda* or "tail-piece," which simply rounds out the form.

This *Kyrie* is in the Dorian mode, with an *ambitus* (range) of an octave plus one note. The main body of the chant lies between the tones D and D an octave higher, with D the *finalis* and A the *tenor*. The melody arranges itself about these two tones. For example: the last tone of each phrase is D, and while, as at the very beginning, the melody hovers and occasionally rests on the *tenor* A, it always falls to the *finalis* D.

Conjunct or stepwise motion prevails, though there are a few skips of a fourth and a fifth. Note in particular how the supplication of the text ("Christ, have mercy on us") seems to be reflected in the music. The leap of a fifth upward to the highest note in the chant gives the music an urgency more pronounced than in the invocations to God the Father. Herein is a possible musical symbolism: man's salvation lies through Christ the Son, therefore the invocation to Him is stronger, more intense.

The use of the melodic formulas, already mentioned, is seen in the occurrence of the notes E-D-C-D-D at the end of each musical phrase of this *Kyrie*. Many Gregorian melodies use the same formula for phrase-endings. In such minute details the music of the Church composer expresses his subservience to tradition.

2. *Agnus Dei*.[9] The last sung portion of the Ordinary of the Mass is the *Agnus Dei*. The Latin text, which in part is John the Baptist's description of Jesus (John I, 29), is as follows:

Agnus Dei, qui tollis peccata mundi: miserere nobis.
Agnus Dei, qui tollis peccata mundi: miserere nobis.
Agnus Dei, qui tollis peccata mundi: dona nobis pacem.

Translation:
Lamb of God, that takest away the sins of the world: have mercy on us.
Lamb of God, that takest away the sins of the world: have mercy on us.
Lamb of God, that takest away the sins of the world: grant us peace.

[7]Program A. The music of the *Kyrie eleison* is printed below, Ex. 1, p. 57.
[8]See Chapter VIII, pp. 397–99.
[9]Program B. The music of the *Agnus Dei* is printed below, Ex. 2, p. 57.

MEDIEVAL MUSIC   57

The first and third lines of text are sung to the same melody; the second line, while beginning and ending like the other two, has another musical setting of the central phrase of the text "qui tollis peccata mundi." In abstract (each letter standing for a *half-line* of text together with its musical setting) this chant has the following form:

Agnus I: a b
Agnus II: a¹ b
Agnus III: a b

This *Agnus Dei* is in the Lydian mode, with an *ambitus* (range) of an octave. The melody lies between the tones F and F an octave higher, with F the *finalis* and C the *tenor*. Unlike other ecclesiastical modes, the Lydian mode has a half-step from the *finalis* to the note below, like the "ti-do" of the major and minor scales: thus the Lydian mode lacks some of the archaic "modal" flavor of melodies in Dorian or Phrygian (*e.g.,* the hymn *Pange Lingua*).

While the melody of this *Agnus Dei* begins with two upward skips of a third, most of the chant proceeds *conjunctly* or stepwise. Note how the melody to the first full line of text rises from F to C and then rises higher to the next *finalis* F, where it hovers for two phrases, and then slowly falls to the original pitch level F. This type of melodic curve is characteristic of Gregorian chant, both in the slow rise and fall and in the placid, supple movement of the melody.

Example 1

Example 2

1. *Pange Lingua*.[10] Mention was made earlier of chant "dialects" which were superseded by the codified Gregorian chant of the Roman Church. In certain instances the conquering Roman music absorbed individual chants which were unique to one of the "dialects." This happened in the case of the hymn *Pange Lingua,* which originally was found only in Gallican or French liturgical chant. The text, one of five by St. Thomas Aquinas, was written at the request of Pope Urban IV on the occasion of the institution of the Feast of Corpus Christi ("The Feast of the Body of Christ") in 1264. The words are as follows:

Pange lingua gloriosi
Corporis mysterium,
Sanguinisque pretiosi,
Quem in mundi pretium
Fructus ventris generosi
Rex effudit gentium.

Translation:
Sing, my tongue, the mystery of the glorious Body and of the precious Blood which the King of Nations, fruit of a noble womb, poured forth for the redemption of the world.

Nobis datus, nobis natus
Ex intacta Virgine,
Et in mundo conversatus,
Sparso verbi semine,
Sui moras incolatus
Miro clausit ordine.

Given to us, born to us of a spotless Virgin, He dwelt in the world, and having sown the seed of the Word, ended that period of his sojourn in wondrous wise.

In supremae nocte coenae,
Recumbens cum fratribus
Observata lege plene
Cibis in legalibus,
Cibum turbae duodenae
Se dat suis manibus.

On the night of the Last Supper, sitting with his brethren, after first fulfilling the Old Law by eating of the food ordained, with his own hands He gives himself as food to the twelve.

Verbum-caro panem verum
Verbo carnem efficit:
Fitque sanguis Christi merum,
Et si sensus deficit,
Ad firmandum cor sincerum
Sola fides sufficit.

The Word-Made-Flesh, by his word, makes the very bread Flesh, and the wine is turned into the Blood of Christ. Even if the senses fail, faith alone suffices to assure the pure heart.

Tantum ergo sacramentum
Veneremur cernui:
Et antiquum documentum
Novo cedat ritui:
Praestet fides supplementum
Sensuum defectui.

Let us, then, with bowed heads, venerate this so great Sacrament; and let the Old Dispensation yield to the New: let faith be supplement to sense, bearing witness where the senses fail.

Genitori, Genitoque
Laus et jubilatio,
Salus, honor, virtus quoque
Sit et benedictio:
Procedenti ab utroque
Compar sit laudatio.

To the Father and to the Son be praise and rejoicing, salvation, honor, power and blessing; and to the Holy Ghost who proceeds out of them be equal praise.

This hymn, which belongs to the Proper of the Mass, is sung three times during the ecclesiastical year: on the Feast of Corpus Christi, on Maundy Thursday (the Thursday of Holy Week), and during the Forty Hours' Adoration. It is a hymn of the Eucharist or Most Blessed Sacrament. This sacrament is the bread and wine which have been transformed by the priest into the Body and Blood of Christ and of which the bread is distributed to the congregation during that part of the Mass called Communion, or the Lord's Supper.

Unlike the text of the *Kyrie* and *Agnus Dei,* that of the hymn *Pange Lingua* is set to a

[10]Programs A and B. The music of the *Pange Lingua* hymn is printed below, Ex. 3, p. 60.

MEDIEVAL MUSIC

metric pattern (trochaic tetrameter) which consists of four trochaic (*i.e.*, HEAVY-light) units per line. While the poem follows this metric pattern throughout, the musical setting is not restricted to a single pattern. Whenever two notes are sung to one syllable the result is a triple unit. As will be seen in the following figure, the metric pattern of the first two lines of music is: *1* 2, *1* 2 3, *1* 2, *1* 2 3 / *1* 2 3, *1* 2, *1* 2, *1* 2 3.

Pan-ge lin-gua glo-ri-o-si / Cor-po-ris my-ste-ri-um,

San-gui-nis-que pre-ti-o-si, / Quem in mun-di pre-ti-um

Fruc-tus ven-tris ge-ne-ro-si / Rex ef-fu-dit Gen-ti-um.

Each of the six lines of the first stanza of St. Thomas' hymn is set to a different phrase of music. Two musical phrases form a larger musical unit or "sentence" set off by a pause (*i.e.*, a rest). In abstract the first stanza of the hymn together with its musical setting follows this plan:

TEXT-LINE: 1 2   3 4   5 6
MUSIC: a b   c d   e f
            ‿‿   ‿‿   ‿‿
             I   II   III

Each succeeding stanza of the hymn is sung to the same melody. As a result the form of the whole hymn is *strophic*.

The Phrygian mode, already discussed above,[11] is used in this chant. Melodic movement is essentially stepwise or *conjunct*; skips of a third occur several times, the larger skip of a fourth twice, while that of the fifth occurs only once, with the expressive fall from A to D at the end of the fourth phrase.

2. *Jubilate Deo*.[12] This chant is the Offertory for the Second Sunday after Epiphany;[13] thus it belongs, not to the Ordinary of the Mass, but to the Proper. It is sung while the priest prepares the bread and wine for Communion. The text is taken from Psalm LXV, verses 1, 2, 16:

Jubilate Deo universa terra: psalmum dicite nomini ejus; venite, et audite, et narrabo vobis, omnes qui timetis Deum, quanta fecit Dominus animae meae. Alleluia.
Translation:
Make a joyful noise unto God, all ye lands: Sing forth the honor of His name: Come and hear, all ye that fear God, and I will declare what He hath done for my soul. Alleluia.

Jubilate is a song of joy, one of the most exuberant in Roman chant. The mode is Dorian (D–D); however, the range of the melody (a twelfth) is so great that the octave-*ambitus* is exceeded and portions of the chant are in the Lydian mode (F–F). The change from one mode to another, which technically is known as *modulation*,[14] necessitates the substitution of one *finalis* or "home" tone for another. For example: on the second occurrence of the word "jubilate" the rise of the melody goes outside the Dorian octave and for the greater part of that which follows the melody is in the Lydian octave. Only at the end ("animae meae, alleluia") does the melody return to the Dorian mode and to the *finalis* D.

[11]See p. 55.
[12]Programs A and B. The music of the *Jubilate Deo* is printed below, Ex. 4, p. 60.
[13]In the Church calendar Epiphany commemorates the coming to Bethlehem of "the Wise Men from the east;" it is the anniversary of the first appearance of Jesus to the Gentiles.
[14]See Chapter VIII, pp. 388–90.

There are two basic styles in Gregorian chant: *syllabic* and *melismatic*. In the first style only one note of music is set to each syllable of text. The hymn *Pange Lingua,* which is largely *syllabic* in character, is an excellent example. *Jubilate Deo* furnishes a fine example of *melismatic* style. The longest *melisma* (forty-three notes to one syllable) occurs on the repetition of the word "jubila . . . te." Note that the exuberance of the melody as it rises higher and higher is consciously held in check by *conjunct* or stepwise movement; there are few skips in the melody.

Recommended reading:
Curt Sachs, *Our Musical Heritage,* New York, Prentice-Hall, 1948, pp. 49-62, 69-72.
W. H. Frere, "Gregorian Music," in *Grove's Dictionary of Music and Musicians,* 3rd ed., New York, Macmillan, 1944, II, 452-454.

Example 3

1. Pan-ge lin-gua glo-ri-o-si Cor-po-ris my-ste-ri-um, San-qui-nis-que pre-ti-o-si, Quem in mun-di pre-ti-um Fruc-tus ven-tris ge-ne-ro-si Rex ef-fu-dit gen-ti-um.

Example 4

Ju-bi-la-te De-o u-ni-ver-sa ter-ra: ju-bi-la-te De-o u-ni-ver-sa ter-ra: psal-mum di-ci-te no-mi-ni e-jus: ve-ni-te et au-di-te, et nar-ra-bo vo-bis, o-mnes qui ti-me-tis De-um, quan-ta fe-cit Do-mi-nus a-ni-mae me-ae, al-le-lu-ia.

III

THE RENAISSANCE

THE REDISCOVERY OF MAN, NATURE, AND THE ANCIENT WORLD[1]

1. AT THE BEGINNING of the 14th century, after an interlude of more than a thousand years, the ideal of the ancient world was once again resumed. In Italy, seat of the ancient empire, the Classical tradition had never in fact been totally extinct. The remains of the Classical world were everywhere present; even in ruin and disuse it was impossible not to feel the imposing reality of the antique residues which existed at every hand—in Roman arenas and baths, in memorial columns, in fragments of porticoes, in sculptured reliefs and tomb sarcophagi, silent testimonies of the grandeur of an ancient society, Italy's own progenitor and titular genius, which only the opening of ancient book was needed to rediscover and affirm. The waning of the Middle Ages was anticipated in the 12th century by the rediscovery of the ancient literatures—Greek as well as Latin—and the rise of universities in which ancient law, medicine, and philosophy were reappropriated. One of the first results was the great medieval synthesis itself—the Gothic cathedral and the theology of St. Thomas Aquinas. By the 14th century the alien presence of antiquity is clearly visible, but its incompatibility with the structure of medieval faith is hardly felt. Dante in the *Divine Comedy* represents the commanding presence of the medieval scheme of thought and expression, yet it is the Latin poet Virgil whom he chooses to guide him through Purgatory and Inferno; and he composes not in the Latin of the Church but in the vernacular, the spoken language of the people, the first great piece of literature in Italian. The painter Giotto represents with sympathetic devotion the life of St. Francis of Assisi and of Christ, yet he reproduces forms whose massive shapes have no precedent in medieval art. The moment of easy coexistence was short. In the 15th century the enthusiasm for ancient art and thought was in full career; it was, moreover, supplied with the resources which an energetic scholarship had assembled and was still in process of assembling. There occurred the momentous transformation which is called by name the Renaissance, a term which suggests, literally, the "rebirth," in which Classical thought and feeling were born again.

The term "Renaissance" is here used to refer to the period which extends from the beginning of the 14th to the end of the 16th century. The importance of this period in modern history is incalculable. In the re-emergence of the Classical ideal the two most powerful traditions which have operated in the formation of Western civilization were counterposed. Once before, in the earliest Christian times, the same opposition had occurred. But in this former instance the collision of the ancient and medieval attitudes had been no meeting of equals. The ancient world was in process of expiring, the medieval in process of being born. The result was a contest between youth and decrepitude, between earnest faith and old fatigue. The ancient world, disenchanted and disillusioned, had no success in preserving even its intellectual authority. The philosophy of Plotinus, the last effort of paganism to reconcile Christian with Classical beliefs, was regarded by both parties as a dissipation. Nor was the authority of the Roman state, which had emptied itself of its last spiritual claim upon men's minds, sufficient to combat the one claim to which men were willing permanently to bind themselves. The singular circumstance of the Renaissance was, on the contrary, the re-emergence of the Classical ideal in a Christian society, a society in which Christianity was still vital. Society found

[1] Programs A and B.

itself divided between two competing ideals, both of which were indispensable to its needs, neither of which it would renounce, the two of which it could not reconcile.

II. On April 26, 1336, in Provence in Southern France, the Italian humanist and poet Petrarch made an ascent of Mount Ventoux. In a famous essay he describes how on reaching the peak he saw before him a magnificent view of the Cevennes Mountains, the Gulf of Lyon, and the River Rhone. As he admired the vast panorama before him he opened a volume of St. Augustine's *Confessions* with the intention of reading whatever might occur to him first.

Where I fixed my eyes first, it was written "and men go to admire the high mountains, the vast floods of the sea, the huge streams of the rivers, the circumference of the ocean, and the revolutions of the stars—and desert themselves." I was stunned, I confess, and closed the book angry with myself that I still admired earthly things.

Petrarch's essay presents a curious mingling of medieval Christianity and Renaissance humanism. The passage in St. Augustine's *Confessions* which struck his eyes and gave rise to his repentance in having admired the beauty of the world is characteristic of medieval Christian thought. It reveals the element of scorn and misgiving which medieval man felt for the world of the senses. If God had created the world, he had created it as a mere transitory stage on which man should prepare himself for the eternal life. Man's soul, not his body, God's Word, not the world, were man's concern. The medieval Christian ideal is spiritual and otherworldly, concerned not with life on earth but with the salvation of the soul in eternal life. Yet this same Petrarch was the devout admirer of Classical Latin authors, and especially of Cicero, whom he regarded as his worldly mentor from the ancient past, to whom, as if to a great contemporary spirit, he addressed letters in his own hand but in an ancient tongue, whose manuscripts he collected and transcribed with a passionate acquisitiveness, the rhythm and cadences of whose Classical Latin he savored for their sound as a child and emulated for their substance as a man. What Petrarch admired in the writings of Cicero was a Classical mentality, a form of cultivated humanity, self-confident, self-assured, and intellectually free. The Christian saint whose *Confessions* could cause him to shut his eyes on Mount Ventoux was not more venerated than the pagan saint who could cause him to open them. Petrarch's life contains within itself, therefore, contradictions which neither he nor any modern man after him has sufficiently resolved.

The return to the sources of ancient thought and feeling had one immediately decisive effect: it readdressed men's minds to the validity of earthly pursuits; it secularized human awareness. Man rediscovered himself, he opened his eyes upon the natural world about him, he reflected upon the condition of society and upon the history of human institutions. To all of these he was related with an actuality and immediacy of which ancient literature was the free record. That the natural world was a legitimate subject for science, that the structure of society and of human institutions in society was a thing open to the shaping powers of will and intellect, that man was, in short, capable of becoming master of his own destiny in the world —these were the premises of a humanistic literature and art. Against the medieval goal of salvation was set the earthly goal of perfecting the mortal life of man by the harmonious development of all his faculties, physical, mental, and spiritual.

III. While these new ideas came to achieve in the end one of the greatest revolutions in Western history, it must be realized that the Renaissance did not take shape in the form of a sudden and radical break with the medieval tradition. It was still possible for the age which rediscovered the ancient world to be profoundly moved by the example of Francis of Assisi, the late-medieval saint in whose expansive sympathy for all created things men believed themselves to have rediscovered the way of Christ himself. For although the new age witnessed the diminishing authority of the Church and the increasing authority of science, it remained still religiously bound and remained strongly under the influence of the fundamental concepts by which the Middle Ages had envisioned the nature and aim of man.

In particular, the Renaissance retained and developed as one of its central ideas the medieval Christian concept of a duality in man's nature. According to this concept man is in part a physical creature allied to the beasts, and in part a spiritual being akin to the angels. The Renaissance, no less than the Middle Ages, took it as man's principal task to free himself from his lower physical nature and to achieve the fullest realization of his spiritual nature.

But while the men of the Renaissance did not question the medieval Christian principle that man should raise himself from the physical to the spiritual sphere of existence, they regarded their own resources as sufficient to the task, learning and rationality as the means, a poised and perfected humanity as the end.

This reinterpretation of the medieval view of the human task was derived from the ancient Classical tradition. Different as were the two traditions under whose joint influence Renaissance culture was formed, they had significant points of contact which enabled the Renaissance to use both as complementary sources of inspiration and guidance. This is particularly true of Plato's theory of ideas, of his distinction between man's lower and higher nature, and of his doctrine that every creature should strive to ascend on a scale leading toward its most perfect and ideal form. Plato's writings, which were rediscovered during the Renaissance, began therefore to enjoy a reputation and authority which made them very nearly rival the Scriptures. The philosophical movement which devoted itself anew to Plotinus' task of creating an idealism out of Christian and Platonic thought, and which flourished mainly in Italy, was called Neo-Platonism.[2] Michelangelo, who, together with most artists of the Italian High Renaissance, was strongly under the influence of this movement, gave symbolic expression to the union of pagan ethics with Christian orthodoxy when he decorated the ceiling of the *Sistine Chapel* with alternating figures of Prophets and Sybils, representations respectively of Biblical and pagan sources of wisdom. The philosopher Marsilius Ficinus referred to Plato as the "Attic Moses"; and Erasmus, regarding Socrates as a pre-Christian saint, wrote: "St. Socrates, pray for us."

IV. The new concept of the aim and nature of man which evolved during the Renaissance is known as Humanism. Drawn from a study of Greek and Latin philosophy and culture, it was essentially an affirmation that human dignity consists in moral and intellectual freedom and is therefore to be won by the free development of human faculty. As an ideal, it was no less austere, it demanded no less vigilance and self-control, than that cherished by any medieval saint: it could be, and often was, joined to a fervently devout and sensitive Christianity.

The religious and austerely idealistic aspect of humanism found one of its finest and most characteristic expressions in the *Oration on the Dignity of Man,* written in 1486 by the great Florentine humanist Pico della Mirandola. Praising man as God's most marvellous creation, he declares man's task in the form of a speech addressed from God to man:

We have made thee neither of heaven nor of earth, neither mortal nor immortal, so that with freedom of choice and with honor, as though the maker and moulder of thyself, thou mayest fashion thyself in whatever shape thou shalt prefer. Thou shalt have the power to degenerate into the lower forms of life, which are brutish. Thou shalt have the power out of thy soul's judgement to be reborn into the higher forms, which are divine....

O supreme generosity of God the father, O highest and most marvellous felicity of man! On man the father conferred the seeds of all kinds and the germs of every way of life. Whatever seeds each man cultivates will grow to maturity and bear in him their own fruit. Who would not admire this chameleon! Or who could more greatly admire ought else whatever...!

[2]See, below, pp. 84–85.

Medieval Christianity maintained an orthodox exclusiveness which did not permit "the germs of every way of life" their sufficient nurture. For this the Renaissance turned to the free-ranging Classical spirit of antiquity. Manuscripts were searched out with avidity, painstakingly transcribed and compared. The enthusiasm for Classical expression and Classical learning was unbounded. Architects and sculptors moved among the Roman ruins to take knowledge from monuments which for a thousand years had stood mutely unobserved. Of an antique sculpture found near Florence, Ghiberti wrote in his *Commentaries:* "The touch only can discover its beauties, which escape the sense of sight in any light." Ciriaco da Ancona, asked why he had journeyed abroad even to Asia Minor and Africa in search of antique remains, laconically answered: "To wake the dead." The essential discovery of humanism consisted simply in this, that by an act of sympathetic imagination a whole world of the spirit could be resuscitated and exhibited as an alternative which men might freely choose. It is from the work of the Renaissance humanists that the "humanities"—philosophy, history, the arts—receive their character and their name *(litterae humaniores)*; it is from the humanistic attitude that arts and letters may be spoken of as in a strict sense "liberal," *i.e.,* emancipative, the resources which free men's minds for the contemplation of humane possibilities other than those which are realized in themselves.

V. No one who reads the dramas of Shakespeare can have failed to reflect on the inexhaustible variety of his personages. Out of tragedy and comedy and historical play emerge the lineaments of men and women so strongly marked in individual trait, so characterful in moral demeanor, as to constitute a series of vivid and memorable portraits. In this array of individual characterizations is the clue to a transformation which the Renaissance brought over the minds of men. For Shakespeare is not alone among Renaissance artists in practicing the art of individual portraiture. From the masters of pictorial art the actual features of a whole throng of Renaissance men and women are preserved. Isabella d'Este, Pope Julius II, Leo X, Baldassare Castiglione, Lorenzo and Giuliano de' Medici, the Emperor Charles V, Pietro Aretino—portraits of them all, prince and publicist, may be found. In the face of his Madonna one may see the mistress of Fra Lippo Lippi. The painter Botticelli, commissioned to paint an Adoration of the Magi which represented the members of the Medici family as witnesses of the holy scene, scruples not to include a portrait of himself as well. Michelangelo represents himself in sculptor's smock as the Prophet Jeremiah on the ceiling of the Sistine Chapel, the private chapel of the Pope in Rome. Leonardo and Titian have left portraits of themselves—two of the shrewdest commentaries of the Renaissance world—in memorial of their name and fame. Dante's features are preserved from the hand of Giotto, Henry VIII's from the hand of Holbein, Erasmus' from Dürer's burin, and Dürer's own from his own hand in a portrait which offers itself as the head of Christ.

The significance of these portraits, apart from their quality as works of art, consists in their indication of a new emphasis in the Renaissance—the discovery of man. They suggest the emergence of the individual man from the general anonymity of medieval communal life. During the Middle Ages the sense of human individuality was circumscribed by the structure of society itself. Individual men were primarily aware of themselves not as individuals, but as members of groups, as belonging to the corporate life of community, Church, or guild. Only within the group was a socially accredited life possible; only within it was an individual distinction aspired after. So that the book of St. Augustine's *Confessions* is the drama of a human soul committing itself to Christian salvation; the philosophy of St. Thomas Aquinas is the magnificent accomplishment not of an individual but of a churchman; and the master-builders of the cathedrals are for the most part known only in their works, and then only as agents of a religious life which the cathedrals represent.

During the course of the Renaissance the structure of medieval society, which defined the place of man in society and guaranteed the character of his contribution to it, was transformed. The names of individual men—of Galileo, of Lorenzo the Magnificent, of Columbus, of Thomas More—each claiming its mark of distinction by its own right rather than by right of membership or allegiance, are the signature of the age in which the spirit of the modern world awakened.

Though the forms of medieval institutions persisted, their authority was no longer operative with the same sovereign exclusiveness. The new individualism is reflected, for example, by the condition of the artist in society. An Italian master practiced his art still as a member of the druggist's guild, from which his pigments were obtained. But the guild was the guarantee only of his monopoly in his art. He set up his own *bottega,* or work-shop, but refused the name of artisan as too little honorable for a craftsman who stipulated to prince and Pope, in written contracts, the fees of a liberal profession. Although the majority of his commissions were still for religious works, he might be, like the painter Perugino, an avowed atheist, or like Leonardo, a man of the new science, or like Michelangelo, a spirit profoundly moved by the need for reconciling Christianity and the Platonism of the ancient world. His patron was no longer necessarily the Church; on the contrary, in the majority of cases he executed commissions let by a wealthy individual or ruling house. The Arena Chapel in Padua, in which Giotto painted the passion of Christ, was dedicated to the Virgin Annunciate by the family of Rinaldo Scrovegni, a wealthy usurer, whom Dante in the *Divine Comedy* placed in Hell. Even when the Church was patron, the motive behind the patronage was apt to be personal and private and worldling, like the motives of Pope Julius II, who in his own lifetime set Michelangelo to creating not a work to the glory of God but a tomb to the glory of himself.

VI. The 16th century is the age of the Protestant Reformation. The authority of the Roman Catholic Church, which for the whole period of the Middle Ages, as the sovereign medieval institution, had held together the fabric of medieval life, was challenged and divided against itself. Medieval Christianity had been constituted upon a principle of mediation, which gave to the Church the sole and exclusive function of interpreting the Scriptures and administering the sacraments to man; the Church claimed to itself a position intermediate between the individual human soul and its God. The significance of the Protestant Reformation was to suspend this principle. Each individual conscience was established as the arbiter of its own faith, which it was required to determine only in accordance with God's revelation of himself in Christ. No church, no sacrament, no priestly ministration, was permitted to intrude itself between man and God. The knowledge of God was not the special perquisite of a church but of the inner light of individual men, assisted and illuminated by the Bible. The Reformation, like all other movements of the Renaissance, is a paradoxical phenomenon. On the one hand, it reflects an intensification of religious feeling resolved on purifying itself by direct contact with its source. On the other hand, it is an expression of Renaissance individualism opposing itself to the communal authority of the Church. Its effect in the subsequent history of Western culture has been to isolate human souls and to atomize the human beliefs by which Christendom was once bound together. But this was known only in the event. In the 16th century the intense religious sentiment leaves its indelible mark on the arts of all peoples among whom the Reformation was embraced. It is the most powerful single factor of the Renaissance in northern Europe.

VII. The emphasis which the new humanism placed upon man and his life on earth was accompanied by an increasing interest and delight in the natural world perceived by the senses. For its consequences in modern times the most important result was the emergence, at the hands of Copernicus, Galileo, and Kepler, of the sciences of nature. Theological speculation based on Christian orthodoxy had reached its final posture in the 13th century in the work of St. Thomas Aquinas. The new experimental sciences of nature came now to claim for themselves the task, hitherto reserved to theology, of explaining the laws which govern physical nature. Their emergence at this time is a signal indication of the new relation in which man stood to the nature he inhabited. The complementary tendency in the arts of sculpture and painting is known by the name of "realism."

Realism itself was not the spontaneous creation of the Renaissance. Its beginnings appear in the late Middle Ages, when, in the 13th century, the arbitrary proportions and abstract forms by which medieval artists had given powerful expression to their spiritual and otherworldly conceptions, were brought more nearly into harmony with the forms of the visible world. But throughout the Gothic Age, the delight in earthly beauty continued to bear the stain of sin; and even the most "humanized" figures of Gothic art remained essentially medieval in character, vessels of an otherworldly beauty and truth.

The characteristic product of Renaissance realism in the art of painting was the theory of perspective. If it be the aim of art to capture a similitude to nature, then the problem exists for the artist, how to render on a two-dimensional plane the three dimensions (height, width, depth) which belong to visual nature. Medieval art professed no positive interest in the representation of natural space; where distinctions of depth in space were required by the demands of subject-matter, these distinctions were rendered by a simple convention of overlapping, the nearer figures blocking off the view of the more remote. But this convention was insufficient to convey the rigorous distinctions which a realist art demanded. If on a two-dimensional surface an artist undertake to represent a third dimension in depth, then this third dimension must be contrived as a visual illusion, and there must be a system according to which the objects in the representational space are related. This system is called "perspective."[3]

The significance of perspective as a cultural phenomenon is precisely that nature is regarded as having a systematic order governed by laws of its own: the representation of nature must therefore conform to natural effects. In fact, Renaissance perspective is, like the medieval convention of overlapping, itself a convention, although a very elaborate one. The realist motive behind its discovery is nevertheless evident enough; it exhibits a spirit willing to subserve itself to observation of the concrete individual appearances of the visible world. The artist felt himself compelled to a careful and minute study of the visible world in order to duplicate as in a mirror the beauty and truth of nature.

Leonardo da Vinci writes in his *Notebooks:*

The mind of the painter must be like unto a mirror which ever takes the color of the object it reflects, and contains as many images as there are objects before it. Therefore realize, O Painter, that thou canst not succeed unless thou art the universal master of imitating by thy art every variety of nature's form. . . . His mind will by this method be like a mirror, reflecting truly every object placed before it, and become, as it were, a second nature.

North of the Alps Albrecht Dürer expresses the same view:

Art standeth firmly fixed in nature, and who so can read her forth thence, he only possesseth her. . . . The more closely thy work abideth in life, so much the better it will appear; and this is true.

The conception of art as an "imitation of nature" lies at the basis of Renaissance realism. By realism is meant not that art is a mere photographic reduplication of things seen, but that nature and life are the productive sources of the forms which the artist's eye discerns. Michelangelo writes in a famous sonnet:

> The best of artists hath no thought to show
> Which the rough stone in its superfluous shell
> Doth not include: to break the marble spell
> Is all the hand that serves the brain can do.

[3] See, below, p. 78.

The function of the sculptor is not to create form, which is eternal, but simply to liberate it from its bed of stone. Even when nature is imitated, she is transformed. Art is never the passive and mechanical effect of natural vision, but an active discernment of the typical and underlying forms which for the man of insight are found to reside in nature and to constitute its truth.

VIII. The differences which separate northern and southern Europe, differences between French, Fleming, Dutch, English, and German on the one side and Italian on the other, existed even in the Middle Ages. They may be seen in the differences which attend the Gothic style of building as it occurs in each of the several parts of the European scene. Such differences are noted when a historian finds it necessary to distinguish French from German Gothic, English from Italian. But during the Middle Ages these real differences of what were in the Renaissance to become national traits were held together and diminished by the common medieval institution of the Church, which spiritually governed all alike. The Renaissance was to release these differences into free and self-conscious expression.

The Renaissance makes its earliest appearance in Italy. Italy had always retained some consciousness of its Classical pagan past and was therefore in some measure predisposed to free itself from the hold which the Middle Ages exercised upon it. Europe north of the Alps presents a contrary situation. The North had never been completely subjected to Classical civilization and showed more reluctance to abandon, even where it was free to do so, the medieval thought and expression which were its authentic product. The specifically Classical Renaissance—Humanism—which had begun in the 14th century in Italy, was therefore in the North postponed; not until the 16th century does it assume major proportions in the countries of northern Europe. The North had, however, meanwhile exhibited an intellectual quickening of its own. From the Netherlands musicians like Josquin des Prez were drawn to all the courts of Europe, and there is a problem in deciding whether the real source of the musical Renaissance was not in fact the North rather than Italy. Italy appears to have been merely the cultural center to which the musical talent of Europe was attracted and on which its tendencies were fused. In the presence of Grünewald's *Isenheim Altarpiece* (Fig. 46) or of Bruegel's *Harvesters* (Fig. 48) one is insistently aware that the Classical humanism of Italy could never have, in the North, the easy tenancy which it gained among the Latin inheritors of the ancient world. The figures who inhabit Bruegel's landscapes are no longer the focus of Creation, nor do they claim under Bruegel's hand even the pre-eminence of central motives to which the landscape is subordinated. They have become part and parcel of a universal nature in which all things have their equal place, as warp to woof in the texture of God's garment, not one thread of which shall break without diminishing all. By the side of Bruegel's human sympathy and his ability to discern the dignity in man's unpremeditated daily act, there co-existed in the North a religious fervor which incontinently transgresses every bond of Classical repose and restraint. Grünewald's strenuous art is an uninterrupted vision of religious earnestness. Its sense is medieval still; its intensity and its means alone belong to the Renaissance. The exaggerated, even the crass, realism which causes the cross to sag from the physical weight of Christ's swollen, lacerated, and infected body is the sheerest affirmation of nature; the differences of scale in the figures, the harsh distortions, the presence of the Baptist, are the sheerest denial of it. Even the color is deliberately dissonant, as if in the struggle between spirit and mortality only suffering remained as the means to grace and redemption. The meaning of such a work is wholly untouched by Classical humanism, which, if it is known at all, is known only to be rejected.

As a general cultural movement the Renaissance transgresses national frontiers. The properties which are held in common between the North and the South—the realism of the Renaissance, its openness to experience, its sense of conquest and discovery, its shrewd self-awareness

—these properties constitute a single massive transformation of the human mind. Yet in each of the countries in which, whether later or earlier, its influence came to be felt, it assumed in addition to its general properties, the character of a special national idiom. It is therefore necessary, in referring to the special regional differences which appear, to speak of the "Renaissance in Germany," the "Renaissance in the Netherlands," the "Italian Renaissance," or "Elizabethan England." Each of these has its unmistakable individual trait, Italy its ideal of Classical balance and restraint, Germany its intense religious mysticism, Flanders its realistic perception of man's place in the all-encompassing texture of nature, England its inexhaustible awareness of the coursing human scene and a language of incomparable richness, whose resources, drawn from the quick idiom of the people, it knew how to command.

Recommended reading:
J. Burckhardt, *Civilization of the Renaissance in Italy,* New York, Oxford University Press, 1944.
J. A. Symonds, *Renaissance in Italy,* New York, Modern Library, 1935.

RENAISSANCE PAINTING AND SCULPTURE
THE DAWN OF THE RENAISSANCE

GIOTTO DI BONDONE (1266–1336): *The Arena Chapel*[1]

THE NECESSITY for light in the interiors of the buildings in northern Europe played its part in the development of the cathedral in France, where the wall appears to have been broken into segments set at right angles to the main axis of the building. The series of openings thus created was filled in large part with stained glass. In the South, however, larger areas of light were not needed; the warm sun of Italy usually led the builders to more enclosed forms in order to retain coolness in the interior. This led to an increased wall area that was adaptable to decoration. The North had found its richest expression in stained glass and sculpture; the South was to find it in painting of monumental proportions.

The most important painter of the late medieval period was Giotto di Bondone. His work is best preserved for us in the series of frescoes that were executed in the early 14th century in the Arena Chapel, Padua, Italy. His importance lies in his ability to give full expression to a new Christian content and in his tentative solutions to problems that were to preoccupy artists in the following centuries. In the former sense, his work may be considered as a culmination of the Gothic period; in the latter, it may be considered as a forerunner of the Italian Renaissance.

The content of Giotto's paintings is inconceivable without St. Francis, who, a century earlier, had preached the brotherhood of man and the humanity of Christ. St. Francis broke down the barriers that medieval theology had erected between God and man and thus enabled man to have an immediate relationship to God. The recognition of the divine in man gave rise to an increasing individualism which was to reach extreme limits in the 15th and 16th centuries. St. Francis's affirmation of the kinship of all earthly things did much to undermine the flat patternism of Byzantine art which had prevailed in Italy for centuries. The new emotionalism could not be stated in medieval Byzantine forms. A new and vigorous world was being slowly revealed; it demanded a greater reality in painting. The divine was

[1]Program B.

no longer remote and abstracted; it had become humanized and needed mass and weight to bring it alive in the known world. The abstract images of the medieval world needed to be changed into more realistic images that could be readily understood.

The gravity and monumentality of the Roman period had already been re-experienced by such artists as Niccolo Pisano, the sculptor. The times awaited an artist who could combine this Roman monumentality with the sincerity and deep emotion of the new concept of Christianity. The problem was for Giotto a difficult one. He found it necessary to mingle and fuse two seeming opposites: the spiritual and the actual, the intangible and the tangible, the universal and the particular. Both in his earlier frescoes on the life of St. Francis at Assisi and in his later ones on the lives of Christ and Mary at Padua, it was necessary that his figures should be involved in scenes from everyday life but, at the same time, retain their heroic stature and their universal significance. The greatness of Giotto lies in his success at combining these opposites. For a moment in the history of the Western world, Christ was to become a majestically presented man, great and noble. Giotto's works expertly balanced the human and the divine, the actual and the universal. But such a balance is precariously held. In giving importance to the human qualities, Giotto was required to accentuate mass and to give a more exact sense of time and place to his scenes. His preoccupation with mass was in accord with the increasing mental bias in Florence. Form in the sense of three-dimensional mass moved into the ascendancy in painting. Art became intellectualized and realistic. As the inquiring mind observed things and reached definition and comprehension of them, the artist was able to depict them with greater and greater fidelity to nature. The type of realism that resulted in the Renaissance was, of course, not synonymous with photography. The realistic object was used to express an idea. The intellect was always in control for the purpose of ordering, composing, and deleting.

Through his tentative beginnings in this direction, Giotto may be called a Renaissance artist. His technical devices were to be explored intensively in the 15th century. He attacked the problems of light and shade, of the rendition of three dimensions on a two-dimensional plane, of the creation of adequate space, and of linear perspective—all problems that were to be pursued unremittingly by later artists, but for quite different purposes. In later Italian painting the limits of realism were probed with the result that the divine vanished. With few exceptions, Renaissance painting, even though perforce it used religious themes, was concerned only with man. No longer could a commentator remark, as one had at the end of the 13th century when Duccio's painting of the *Virgin Enthroned* was completed:

On the day that it was carried to the Duomo the shops were shut; and the Bishop bade a goodly and devout company of priests and friars should go in solemn procession, accompanied by the Nine Magistrates and all the officers of the Commune and all the people; all the most worthy followed close upon the picture, according to their degree, with lights burning in their hands; and then behind them came the women and children with great devotion. And they accompanied the said picture as far as the Duomo, making procession around the Campo as is the use, all the bells sounding joyously for devotion of so noble a picture as is this. And all that day they offered up prayers, with great alms to the poor, praying God and His Mother who is our advocate, that he may defend us in His infinite mercy from all adversity and all evil, and that He may keep us from the hands of traitors and enemies of Siena.

Foremost in Giotto's work is the emphasis upon weight and mass in his figures. Mass requires a space in which to exist—will, in fact, create that space by its very presence. The space, once created, suggests other things to fill it to give the figures a setting. All of these—mass, space, setting—had existed in Roman art but had been slowly pushed aside to make way for a two-dimensional style from the East which seemed best to express the abstract qualities of the Christian religion. The new and different stresses in the Christian religion that had been brought about by St. Francis opened the way for these latent Italian tendencies toward three-dimensional form and narrative. The emphasis upon mass is readily apparent in the *Madonna and Child Enthroned* (Fig. 31). It is suggested by the simplest rendering in light and dark and reinforced by the enclosing triangle with its uninterrupted base. Although enthroned, the Madonna is no longer the Queen of Heaven but an earthly mother; she is moved into the actual world, and her compassion and maternity are dramatized by the simplest means. Her increased size in relation to the other figures is a continuation of the medieval tradition wherein the more important figures were made larger in scale. The dignity, self-possession, and warmth of the figure, however, are new, as is also the unwavering direction of glance of the surrounding figures. At the same time that the Madonna is given weight and substance, the prominence of the Christ Child is maintained. Giotto accomplishes this by the slight tilting and twisting of the Madonna's torso, by the sudden projection of her hand from the dark cloak, by the diagonal shadows in the blouse which oppose the diagonals in the garment of Christ, and by the projection of Christ's head from the enclosing triangular form.

Giotto's qualities may perhaps be best observed in the Arena Chapel. This one-aisled structure includes thirty-seven scenes from the lives of Mary and Christ arranged in three horizontal bands along the side walls. Each scene is separated from the next by a painted, decorative vertical strip or by windows. The technique used in these scenes, in the *Majestas* on the triumphal arch, and in the *Last Judgment* on the entrance wall, is fresco, a painting on wet plaster. After the drawing has been transferred to the wall, a last thin coat of plaster is applied to a part that can be painted in one day. The drawing in this part is restored and the painting proceeds. Powdered pigment mixed with water is used. If the painter is unable to complete the selected part by evening, the unfinished area must be chipped off and plastered afresh on the following day. The painting becomes by the fresco technique as permanent as the wall-surface. Giotto followed this procedure in all parts except the sky, where paint was applied to dried plaster. The paint in the true fresco areas (the figures, rocks, and buildings) has sunk deeply into the plaster and has thus preserved its freshness, whereas that in the sky, because it was applied like a skin over the plaster, has deteriorated and flaked off.

The *Lamentation* (Fig. 32), one of the most powerful scenes in the Arena Chapel, shows, against a deep blue sky, a group of restrained mourners, and more distraught angels lament the Christ whose body has been removed from the cross. The figures are bulky, tangible masses set within a

Fig. 31. Giotto, *Madonna Enthroned, ca.* 1310, Uffizi, Florence (*Alinari*)

shallow, airless space. Better than any other paintings that remain from the period, this and the other frescoes in the series indicate the way toward an accurate rendering of the phenomena of vision. It should be remembered that for many centuries the artist had been more a copyist than an observer and recorder of nature; he had drawn his work from preceding works. Giotto appears to have observed the human figure directly and to have reduced it to the eloquent and essential masses that appear in his paintings. All extraneous detail is removed. Line is used by him to delineate and isolate the basic form with the utmost clarity. Within the form it is used to express the logical relationship of the parts. In the grouping of these masses a second system of lines is observed which knits them together. An ellipse whose lower part is the body of Christ unites the main group; it is carried through the arms of the mourning woman (Mary Magdalen) at his feet and up to the figure with outstretched arms above (St. John), whose direction carries it to the mourning women at the left and thus down to his head. This ellipse is flanked right and left by a vertical block of figures which direct the attention constantly inward. The obviousness of such an arrangement might lead to too great a stability and to monotony; it is of interest to observe that Giotto has varied it by keeping the vertical block of two figures on the right separated from the main movement, and more restrained and quiet, whereas the left vertical block has been incorporated into the ellipse itself. Variations within the central group also point up the subtleties within this apparently simple composition. The three figures—one seated with her back to the spectator, one kneeling, and one bending forward (St. John)—bring in a horizontal accent in the outstretched arm and the back at the same time that they form a straight line that leans slightly to the right. This is a variation of the two vertical blocks and creates a "falling vertical," which Giotto used also on other occasions to express restrained emotion. This falling quality is stabilized by the second seated figure, who, added to the three, creates a triangular form. In contrast to the rendering of natural setting in medieval art, the landscape becomes a functional element in the design; the rock formation, in addition to being a background for the group, runs diagonally downward to the head of Christ. Its movement is repeated in the angels above, whose grouping forms a fan of lines whose focus is Christ.

A minimum amount of shading within these masses completes the illusion of a three-dimensional form. The light is generalized and diffused; it does not come from a particular source. Cast shadow is rarely used. In the use of light and shade, Giotto stresses the points of strain in the drapery, thereby again accentuating the figure's bulk. Frequently, shadowed

Fig. 32. Giotto, *Lamentation, ca.* 1305, Arena Chapel, Padua (*Alinari*)

lines fall from the high-lighted point of strain and cluster in the deeper shadow, as from shoulder to elbow in the seated figure to the extreme left, or from leg to base of spine in the seated figure on the right. These lines follow the natural movement of the body. In earlier Christian painting, the drapery had often been a richly decorated surface, a pattern of arabesques. In Giotto it reveals the body beneath, but it differs from the Classical Greek treatment, which also revealed the body, in that the soft, sensuous curve of the Greek is everywhere abandoned in favor of a straighter line. The result is the appearance of a heavier drapery that marks only the basic structure of the body and not its surface undulations.

The three-dimensional quality of Giotto's figures, whose masses create a feeling of depth, has already been noted. It should be remarked, however, that the arrangement and rendering of the figures still keeps them closer to a sculptured relief than to a free-standing statue. The wall surface is penetrated for only a short distance, whereupon the eye is abruptly stopped by the rock background and the impenetrable deep blue of the sky. All masses are kept close to each other and close to the surface. Movement is permitted only from side to side and never into depth. We consider a fresco most successful when it provides a decoration that does not destroy the character of the surface upon which it is painted. In this sense, Giotto is highly successful; the character of the wall surface is retained throughout.

One further element may be noted in composition. Giotto attempts, in the *Lamentation* and in many other works, to break down the rigidity of a bilateral symmetry, that is, a central mass with balancing features left and right. He replaces it by a decentralized composition—one in which the center of interest is no longer centrally placed, but occurs at the side. The center of interest in the *Lamentation* is the unit composed of the heads of Christ and Mary in the extreme lower left of the picture. It is enclosed within and is part of the ellipse; all major lines and directions of glance lead to it. The picture as a whole is kept in balance, however, by several devices: by the concentration of light in the right half of the picture, by the separation of the two vertical figures on the right, whose verticality is further accented by the tree above, by an interval or break in the ellipse above the arms of Christ which separates the larger mass of figures on the right from the smaller mass on the left, by the tilting to the right of the three central figures, by the construction of a triangle of four figures to the right of center, and even by the spreading of the figures in the right group compared to the concentrating of figures in the left group. Giotto's compositions appear simple and inevitable; actually they are, in many cases, extremely complex organizations.

The figure type most frequently encountered is a massive body with sloping shoulders and a short neck. The head is generalized and repetitive in most instances, although efforts toward individualization will be noted. The eyes are slanted and are derived either from the medieval Byzantine tradition or from similar usage in Gothic sculpture. Emotion is greatly restrained and indrawn. It may reveal itself in no more than the slope of a shoulder, the inclination of a neck, or the sag of a drapery. Movement as well is inhibited, so that the figures appear static, although far from inert or rigid. There is a tremendous energy in them which emerges more in potential than in actual movement. The gestures never move outward into space nor activate the space around the figure. Even the angel in the *Lamentation* with downthrust arms and a grimace upon his face cries within himself. More emotional figures, as in the *Death of St. Francis,* tend toward a falling diagonal position, as though their gravity had been disturbed. This may be an echo of the emotionalism of the Byzantine East; it may be a conflict within Giotto himself between mind and emotion—a doubt nagging at faith.

The restraint in movement and gesture would seem to indicate a feeling of repression in Giotto's figures, but this is not so. The figures find their most energetic release through the eyes. Exactly how Giotto achieves this, by what presence or absence of line and shadow, it is impossible to describe. Nevertheless, the glance may be so intense that the path of its direction becomes almost visible. The eyes do not serve as shields or shutters but rather as infinite wells from the depths of which the spirit of the figure pours. On occasion the interchange of glances between two figures may be illumined by that instantaneous, mutual recognition which occurs at those rare times when the barriers of the eyes are removed.

These things are all clues to the technical devices Giotto employed; their result is something over and beyond them. Baldly described, they do not quite account for the humility, the warm human sympathy, and the profound simplicity of his work, which remains for us today one of the richest and most direct expressions of Christianity. The technical resources are sufficient for the concept to be expressed. They were to be greatly enlarged in the following century, but such enlargement and elaboration will, over a period of time, weaken rather than strengthen the creative artist, who becomes stifled in an excess of riches. It is false to assume that the more realistic work will be the greater one. A deeper space, a more realistic rock, a textured drapery, or a strongly individualized face might give us another work, but it would have caused the loss of all the essential qualities that belong to Giotto.

Recommended reading:
Carlo Carra, *Giotto,* Milan, Collezione Silvana, n.d.
Roger Fry, *Vision and Design,* New York, Peter Smith, 1947, pp. 87-116.

JAN VAN EYCK (?1385—1441)[1]

IN THE PAINTINGS of Jan van Eyck the Gothic world of *Amiens Cathedral* merges with the revived interest in a rational form of expression which had been slowly making its way to the North since Giotto's death in 1337. Jan van Eyck, court painter to the powerful Duke Philip of Burgundy, synthesized Gothic naturalism and feeling for space, light, and color with a new gravity. The combination brings together two essentially contrary points of view. A rational approach has been united with an outlook which stresses values beyond the limits of human knowledge. In the dominance of the latter Jan shows himself to be rooted in the Gothic world of the North.

For this synthesis Jan van Eyck has adopted the use of oil colors. He presents to the viewer a wealth of glowing, minutely observed detail, creating a persuasive pictorial reality permeated with a meaning beyond itself. Each detail in his paintings (Figs. 33 and 34) represents the object not merely for its own sake but for a greater purpose, the revelation of God on earth to whom it owes its existence. Minute treatment of the detail comes from the medieval art of manuscript illumination, in which Jan had worked as a young man. With that art he unites a concern with the things of this world; he brings to panel painting a close observation of the fall of light, and acquaintance with pictorial organization in terms of perspective, a presentation of plasticity and weight in all natural forms, and less elongated proportions in the human figure.

The most famous work of the artist is the *Ghent Altarpiece* in the church of St. Bavon in Ghent. Begun before 1426, the year in which Jan's brother Hubert died, it was com-

[1]Program A.

pleted in 1432. Some scholars attribute part of the work to Hubert and its completion to Jan; others deny Hubert any part. The art-historical problem is a recognition of the complexity of this great work. Dedicated to the Lamb of God, it reproduces in painted form the sculptured altar decorations characteristic of Northern churches of the 13th and 14th centuries. These altarpieces formed impressive backgrounds for the altar cross and other articles placed upon the altar table. As the focal point of the church, the altar's embellishment was felt as a keen necessity. Jan acknowledges the traditional sculptured altar on the exterior (Fig. 33), where some of the scenes are painted in *grisaille,* a monochromatic imitation of stone sculpture.

On the exterior the upper row shows the Annunciation to the Virgin within a typical Flemish interior. Above the annunciating angel Gabriel is the Old Testament prophet Zachariah; above the Virgin the prophet Micah, while over the separate panels representing the room interior are two oracles of the Classic world, the Erithrean and Cumaean Sibyls. Zachariah, Micah, and the Sibyls, according to medieval belief, prophesied the coming of Christ; in these panels their prophesies are lettered on scrolls behind them. These four figures form iconographic links of the Old Testament and the Classic world with the New Testament. The painted niches in the lower zone contain the donor and his wife, Jodocus Vyt and Elisabeth de Borluut, who flank the original patrons of the church, St. John the Baptist and St. John the Evangelist. The saints are conceived as sculptured figures, their drapery falling in large, angular folds. They contrast with the donor and his wife, who, casting soft shadows as they kneel, are treated in color with minute observation of surface detail and visible portrait character. The figures of Gabriel and the Virgin act as a transitional element, their draperies seemingly of stone, their faces of flesh.

Opened only on feast days, the colorful interior (Fig. 34) contrasts with the *grisaille* of the exterior. The interior reveals two rows of painted panels arranged symmetrically about the figure of God the Father on the upper level, and about the Adoration of the Lamb on the lower. God the Father in solemn pose looks directly at the spectator. He is crowned with the triple tiara of the Roman Church, a worldly crown lying at his feet. On each side, in separate panels, are the Virgin Mary and John the Baptist, removed from the spectator by an inner concentration communicated by turning the gaze away from the observer. Flanking these two figures are panels of angels singing and playing musical instruments. The ensemble of the upper row is completed by a nude figure at either end, the first man and woman, Adam and Eve; iconographically they symbolize the fall of man, whose ultimate redemption is promised through the sacrificial Lamb in the lower panels. Large and simply outlined, the central figures are quiet in gesture and glowing in color, the simplicity of outline giving an effect of grandeur to which the details in the ornamentation—jewels, flowers, and

Fig. 33. Van Eyck, *The Ghent Altarpiece,* exterior, ca. 1425–1432, St. Bavon, Ghent (*A.C.L. negative,* Brussels)

brocaded bands—afford a muted contrast. There is a further animating contrast in the varied positions of the heads of the angels. Adam and Eve covering their nudity add a note of severity to the composition. There is a lack of unity in the perspective: the eye of the spectator is placed on a level with the feet of Adam and Eve; in the other panels of the row on a level with the heads. In accordance with medieval practice, God the Father is represented in larger scale than the other figures in order to establish visually his greater importance. A continuation of the sculptural concept seen in the figures of the two saints on the exterior reappears in the isolation in niches of the figures of Adam and Eve, a contrast to the other paintings of the interior, with which they do not appear to be entirely unified.

In contrast to the glorification of God in the upper panels, the lower zone is devoted to the adoration of Christ on earth. The Adoration of the Lamb, central panel of the lower row, is flanked on the left by two panels of Just Judges, and on the right, by two panels of Holy Hermits and Pilgrims led by St. Christopher. The Lamb, symbolic of Christ, stands in a meadow upon an altar surrounded by throngs of worshippers, a subject ultimately inspired by The Revelation of Saint John the Divine. The Biblical texts in question read:

And I looked, and, lo, a Lamb stood on the mount Sion, and with him an hundred forty and four thousand, having his Father's name written in their foreheads. (XIV, 1.)
And he shewed me a pure river of water of life, clear as crystal, proceeding out of the throne of God and of the Lamb. (XXII, 1.)

Into a chalice on the altar flows the blood of the Lamb, symbolic of the blood of Christ which flowed at the time of the Crucifixion when His side was pierced by the lance of the centurion. Kneeling angels hold the Cross, the Column, the Crown of Thorns, and other symbols of the Passion of Christ. Martyrs, Fathers of the Church, Prophets, and Apostles group themselves on both sides of the altar and the Fountain of Life, which stands in the foreground; in the background is seen Jerusalem, the Holy City. A dove, symbolic of the

Fig. 34. Van Eyck, *The Ghent Altarpiece,* interior, *ca.* 1425–1432, St. Bavon, Ghent (*Braun & Cie,* Paris–New York)

Holy Ghost, descends from above; rays radiating from it fall upon the symmetrically arranged groups below. An illusion of reality is created by the careful characterization of the various plant forms and trees (pine, palm, lemon, etc.). The perspective of the panel is, however, inconsistent. The standing figures in the foreground are seen at eye level, as are the figures in the flanking panels; but the observer feels himself to be looking down upon the altar and the fountain with its kneeling prophets. Despite these inconsistencies, the illusion of reality is maintained by the diminution in size of the middleground figures and the lighter color of the farthest part of the background. The semicircular groups of prophets lead the eye into the landscape where the semicircular motif is repeated by the kneeling angels. In contrast to this spatial design in three dimensions, the two-dimensional surface pattern of the panel is based on the continuous repetition of the triangle.

The influence of Italy is seen in the tendency toward monumentality in the figures and in the use of perspective. The inconsistent use of perspective indicates that the clarity and logical organization of the Italian Renaissance has not as yet succeeded in gaining control over the thought and outlook of the Gothic North. Significant is the great difference which exists between North and South in the use of color. The spirit which produced the stained glass of the medieval cathedral appears again in the work of the Flemings. Color is the basis of emotional impact in Flemish 15th-century painting. The transparent oil medium in combination with pure colors of high intensity provides a feeling of depth in color and space. In contrast, the Italians used subdued, mixed colors of low intensity, avoiding the rich sensuous elements which might divert attention from the articulation of the figure. Italy's concentration on the idealized human figure has little echo in the North; the Italian simplification and subordination of details to the main movements of the figure contrasts with the Northern concern for individual differences. To Jan van Eyck infinite variety is a natural concomitant of this concern for individual differences; one detail is no more important than any other, for each is in equal degree revelatory of God's presence. It is this which determines the character and shapes the form of Northern naturalism.

Fig. 35. Van Eyck, *Giovanni Arnolfini and His Wife,* 1434, National Gallery, London (by permission)

A feeling for surface rather than for the underlying structure governs Jan's treatment of light. He models closely from light to dark in gradual stages, using reflected light in the shadows; this, combined with the absence of strong highlights, gives a luminous and atmospheric effect to the whole. Through the treatment of light, space is found to be a major artistic concern; not the closed, cubic space of the Italians, but one unlimited in its flow sideways and into depth, a moving element augmenting the mystic character of his work like the flow of space within the Gothic cathedral. Jan van Eyck concerns himself with the external character, the visual aspect of his world, rather than with its internal structure. Nurtured by the mysticism of the Gothic era, yet aware of the humanizing spirit of Italy, Jan van Eyck sets himself before us as a figure of transition.

In the portrait painted in 1434 representing *Giovanni Arnolfini and His Wife* (Arnolfini was the agent at Bruges of the Medici interests), the luminous, spatial tendencies of the *Ghent Altarpiece* are carried further, as a comparison of this work (Fig. 35) with the figures of Adam and Eve will show. The figures, almost hieratically posed, are shown standing in the room in which they will live; light falls softly about them and reveals a vast complex of detail. All has been fused into a coherent whole by the spatial atmosphere. Again the inwardness of the glance of the figures adds to the air of solemnity and partial withdrawal from the ever-present finite world, a world brought closer to our consciousness by Jan's signature above the mirror in the background, with the words, "Johannes de eyck fuit hic," "Jan van Eyck was here."

Jewel-like in effect, luminous and glowing in color, the works of Jan van Eyck reveal the perfection of a space-development in terms of light and dark, a spatial *chiaroscuro*. Through the close observance and careful portrayal of surfaces in relation to light diffused in space, the painter has realized a unification of spatial and plastic aims. However, these artistic elements in their unique combination are merely factors in the representation of a world which, though material in aspect, is in every detail revelatory of God.

Recommended reading:
Martin Conway, *The Van Eycks and Their Followers,* New York, Dutton, 1921.
Max J. Friedlaender, *Die altniederländische Malerei,* Vol. I, Berlin, Cassirer, 1924.
Leo Van Puyvelde, *The Holy Lamb,* Brussels, Marion, 1947.
W. H. J. Weale and M. W. Brockwell, *The Van Eycks and Their Art,* London, Lane, 1912.

THE HIGH RENAISSANCE IN ITALY

LEONARDO DA VINCI (1452–1519)[1]

THE PROBLEMS that had been suggested in the frescoes of Giotto remained in a state of suspension for the remainder of the 14th century. Among the students and followers of Giotto, there was none of sufficient calibre to comprehend the changes he had effected. In the 15th century, however, the problems were avidly taken up and quickly solved. From the time of Leonardo in the late 15th century until the breaking up of the Renaissance tradition in the 19th century, only color and light awaited further study; even aspects of these had been studied and remarked upon in the voluminous notes of Leonardo da Vinci.

Characteristic of the intellectual activity in the 15th century, particularly in Florence, which was to become the cultural center for Italy as Athens had been for Greece, was the constant effort to measure, describe, and define objects and to formulate rules. The study of perspective in this period may be considered as a corollary of the increasing realism in art. With the aid of the architect Alberti, the science of linear perspective was developed and first applied in the frescoes of Masaccio in the early 15th century. Giotto, among other painters, had been aware of the apparent converging of parallel lines at the horizon but had used a general vanishing area rather than a vanishing point. By the time of Masaccio, it could be stated that all parallel lines in a single plane, when seen at an angle, converge to a single vanishing point on the horizon. That is, when a wall with a row of windows, for example, is seen from directly in front, the horizontal lines of the top and bottom of the windows are parallel. The wall is at right angles to the line of vision. However, when the wall is seen at a lesser angle—that is, when one end of the wall recedes from the spectator—the horizontal lines appear to come together as they recede. If such lines are carried out, they would appear to come together at a single point on the horizon line. This point, in a pictorial representation of space, is known as the vanishing point. This convergence makes the windows appear to decrease in size. In general terms, the purpose of perspective is the rendering of solid objects so that they will appear in the painting as they actually appear in nature when seen from a given position of the spectator.

Simultaneously with the codification of linear perspective, aerial perspective was also studied. Aerial perspective is the apparent blurring or softening of lines and the weakening and neutralizing of color, because of the intervening veils of atmosphere, in objects seen at a distance. For this reason, a distant range of mountains will appear blue or bluish grey.

Through the use of linear and aerial perspective, the space of the painting was increased in depth, although it still remained stage-space with the objects arranged in bands parallel to the picture plane. Movement occurred from side to side; movement backward and forward was not used extensively until the following century. Renaissance space is therefore inert and static; depth is implied but never activated.

At the same time that the artist was studying and recording nature, he felt the necessity of some plan and order to hold the parts and give them significance. Geometry seemed to supply the answer. The art of the Renaissance is primarily an intellectual one and is based upon carefully calculated schemes. Bilateral symmetry—the balancing right and left around a central axis—replaced the off-center balance of earlier periods. Such devices as triangles, circles, and ellipses became important as means of holding the various elements in balance.

[1] Programs A and B

RENAISSANCE PAINTING AND SCULPTURE

The scientific approach for a time suppressed all else. Movement and flow were sacrificed for a static equilibrium. The intellectual stirrings of the 15th century needed a framework, and the Italians attempted to find it in Roman examples. At the opening of the century, the architect Brunellesco thought it necessary, because of his failure to win the competition for the bronze doors for the *Baptistery* in Florence, to devote several years to the study and measurement of examples of Roman architecture in Rome. This pursuit was undoubtedly spurred by the rediscovery of an ancient manuscript on architecture and painting by the Roman theorist Vitruvius. The effort to find the key to the seeming perfection of these remains led to many mathematical and geometrical formulas, to rules for proportion and devices for plotting out the painting surface.

Subject matter also shifted and broadened. In Giotto the god had become humanized; in the Renaissance the human being had become godlike—a creature of vaulting ambition and unlimited power, unshackled by any bonds. Medieval iconography was retained throughout the period, but in most cases there was a transformation in meaning. The sincere religious content of a Giotto was less frequently found. Portraits, battle pieces, and mythological scenes appeared.

Great artists contain but also overleap the period in which they work. Giotto belongs both to the Gothic and the Renaissance worlds. Leonardo da Vinci belongs both to the Renaissance and the following Baroque period. Early Renaissance artists, with some notable exceptions, had been obsessed with one element of painting to the neglect of others. In the field of painting, Leonardo's importance lies in the fact that he was able to encompass all of the diverse experiments that had been made and fuse them in a single work. In this, he is a summation of the Early Renaissance. Simultaneously, he was to delve in the field of psychology and suggest accents and stresses that were to find expression only in subsequent periods. In addition to integrating previous experiments, he made profound observations of his own on perspective, movement, and anatomy. He was also an extraordinary scientist who has left for us in his notebooks studies in astronomy and geology and projects for submarines and airplanes that were to anticipate the entire scientific development in the following centuries. In this he is a characteristic man of the Renaissance—a person of high intelligence who is capable of becoming a master in several fields.

The ability to fuse many detailed parts and hold them in balance is exemplified in the *Madonna of the Rocks* (Fig. 36). The figures are anatomically correct, except in a few parts which may have been completed by a pupil, but the anatomy is felt rather than insisted upon as it had been by certain earlier Renaissance artists who had devoted their

Fig. 36. Leonardo, *Madonna of the Rocks, ca.* 1483–1494, Louvre, Paris (*Alinari*)

time to its study. The triangular grouping of figures, used by earlier artists, is tightened and integrated: the figures in the base angles are closer to each other and in stronger relationship with the apex. In fact, the triangle is given a degree of depth which converts it into a pyramid. The plant forms, such as the clump of violets by the supporting hand of the Christ child, are precisely rendered and yet unobtrusive. They blend into the whole setting and belong to the damp and shadowed grotto in which they appear. Previously, plants had been as accurately drawn but they had usually been scattered promiscuously in any setting. The grotto itself, often used in stage settings and mystery plays of the period, is minutely drawn and opens onto a hazy distance. Through the use of an enveloping shadow, however, its parts are made to take their place in the ensemble; it enhances rather than intrudes upon the foreground group.

The sense of air is strongly present. It comes from the use that Leonardo makes of *chiaroscuro,* the play of light and dark across a surface which models forms and distinguishes one from the other (Fig. 37). In this sense, *chiaroscuro* was used by Giotto. Leonardo employs a greater variety of lights and darks, introduces the secondary or reflected light within the shadow, and achieves a subtler play of lights, half-lights, and deep shadows. To obtain these effects, he was forced to sacrifice light and to use increasingly large areas of dark, thereby accentuating the single source of light. The light areas appear as small spots of high intensity within a monochromatic veil of shadow. It is this increase in the dark over the light areas that distinguishes his *chiaroscuro* from that of Giotto.

In the *Madonna of the Rocks,* the lights appear along two diagonals that cross at the Madonna's head and give a spotty effect to the picture that is not entirely pleasing, although they do achieve a quality that is lacking in earlier work. The greater areas of light in the work of earlier painters allowed the eye of the spectator to wander across the picture and enjoy its parts, which were held together only by mechanical means. In Leonardo, the monochromatic veil which envelops and connects the spots of local color gives increasing plasticity to his figures and a sharper, more compelling focus. His paintings are thus more instantaneously perceived. There are distinct limitations in such a method. His shadows are without color. Because they cover such a large area, they restrict color to small, isolated spots. For this reason, Leonardo's paintings can be studied adequately in black-and-white

Fig. 37. Leonardo, *Madonna of the Rocks,* detail, *ca.* 1483–1494, Louvre, Paris (*Alinari*)

reproductions. This circumstance will explain why such a drawing as that of *St. Anne and the Virgin* may seem more subtle in its modelling and richer in appearance than some of his paintings. The extremes to which he carried this light-dark modelling not only destroy color but also limit the time of day he might wish to depict to twilight. Possibly unintentionally, his *chiaroscuro* also imparts the qualities of mystery and romance to his work.

In addition to this fusing of the parts, there are a number of details which constitute his signature. The arrangement of the background into a dark central panel with openings of light on each side was to be repeated, in variation, in his *St. Jerome* and *Last Supper* (Fig. 38). The idealized and sexless head was also to recur. The hair is wet and crinkly and brushed with metallic highlight lines. The head has a broad forehead, a tapering chin, a slender and sensitive nose, shielded eyes, and a faintly smiling mouth. These things, softened in shadow that plays almost imperceptibly across them, give his figures a tremulous life which was new in painting. They are revealed from the inside; the spirit is brought to the surface and tantalizingly glimpsed behind the mask of the face.

Leonardo was an artist of nuance, of delicate shading whether of tone or of expression. He has said, "Look at the faces of men and women on the streets when evening comes and the weather is bad; how great is the grace and sweetness one sees in them." He expresses this transient quality by accentuating the head and, more particularly, the eyes. This ideal of grace and sweetness is a fragmentation of the figure that is completely unclassical. The wholeness of the human being is sacrificed so that he may express a fleeting psychological overtone. The Greeks expressed the wholeness of man as a self-sufficient individual; the Gothic artists expressed the wholeness of man as a spiritual being. Like Leonardo, the Gothic artist placed the accent upon the heads of the figures, but the effect is totally different. The Gothic head is the seat and center of the spiritual being, whereas in Leonardo it is merely the mirror of a passing emotion.

The restriction of Leonardo to the pursuit of grace and sweetness was to give a sameness to his works, no matter what their subject. The heightening of these qualities could, and sometimes did, lead to an over-sweetness. He became so absorbed in analysis that he was unable to arrive at a successful synthesis. It is probably for this reason that he did so few paintings, and that many of them were left unfinished. Previously it has been stated that Leonardo's importance lies in his ability to fuse the various elements that had been studied by earlier Renaissance artists. The statement that he could not achieve a successful synthesis may thus seem a contradiction. It is not. He did integrate the preceding elements through line and mass; in this sense, he was inextricably bound up in the Florentine bias toward form and structure. The conflict arose when he attempted to float these solid forms in light and air. Both of these elements, in their very essence, dissolve form. They are incompatible with an insistence upon solid form. His works thus become a formal structure overlaid by a new and more dramatic use of light and dark that conflicts with, when it does not destroy, the structure over which it is laid. A solution to this problem will not be found until the time of Rembrandt in the 17th century.

The subtle handling of shadow that has been referred to was due to the new oil medium which had been developed in the north of Europe between the time of Giotto and Leonardo and had quickly been adopted in the south. The earlier media, tempera (a mixture of dry pigment with egg white) and fresco, had been limited as to color and had dried too rapidly to permit the reworking of the surface which would give greater richness to a painting. The possibilities of oil had been experienced by Leonardo in the *Madonna of the Rocks*. When he was confronted with the problem of doing a fresco of the *Last Supper* (Fig. 38), he was no longer content with its limitations. For the sake of a slower drying medium, he experimented with a combination of fresco, tempera, and oil. Unfortunately, his experiment was disastrous and the *Last Supper* began to deteriorate a short time after it was painted.

Nevertheless, the composition and the psychological character of the work were of such a calibre that it remains one of the great paintings of the Renaissance.

Previously the apostles had been strung along the back of the table, with Christ in the center and Judas set alone at the front of the table. Leonardo gave the subject greater compactness by arranging the apostles in groups of three with Christ alone in the center, both psychologically and physically. Christ is the only quiet and resigned figure; his stability is accentuated by the triangular shape which encloses him. Leonardo has gone farther than earlier artists also in concentrating upon a particular moment during the Last Supper: the dramatic moment directly after Christ's statement that one of the group has betrayed him. The figures are no longer static, but now move and react emotionally to the statement. They are held together by an undulating line that sweeps abruptly to the left and right of Christ, and slows and returns at the extremities of the panel. The reaction is strongest in the two inner groups, weakest in the two outer groups, as though some time had elapsed between the two—the inner groups stunned into a physical withdrawal from which they have not recovered, whereas the outer groups have recovered from the shock and have reached a point of discussion.

Leonardo takes the devices of the 15th century and makes them perform a larger and more important function. The perspective not only defines the stage space; all of the lines are made to converge upon the face of Christ. To a degree, this destroys the space-making character of perspective, since the eye, in its effort to move back into space, is invariably brought forward into the frontal plane occupied by Christ. The windows, in addition to being openings, are so placed as to enframe and isolate the Christ. The central one, with its intense light, takes the place of the conventional halo. Shadow is also used in the same functional manner as was perspective. It not only models the figures but serves to separate Judas from the group. This use of shadow may be called psychological as well, insofar as shadow may be ominous and tragic. The undulating line that unites the figures has already been mentioned above. In one instance, the line is used to separate figures. The group of three figures to the right of Christ is held together within a semicircular form so that they become a compact mass. The group to the left repeats this semicircular enclosure but has before it a strongly defined triangle which is Judas. The compactness of the group to the right is absent in the left group; it has been broken into two shapes, one overlapping the other. Furthermore, the triangular form of Judas breaks the plane of the other two figures and moves forward. He is thus isolated by the projection forward, by the triangular shape, and by the massing of shadow. He has broken the rhythm of the grouping.

The intellectual ordering of Leonardo's compositions is frequently weakened by a too abundant use of dramatic gesture. The flickering confusion of arms and hands in the *Last*

Fig. 38. Leonardo, *Last Supper, ca.* 1495–1498, S. Maria delle Grazie, Milan (*Alinari*)

Supper creates a feeling of unrest and tension. The hands in particular are staccato notes that are in conflict with the orderly lines of the composition. Their structural weakness and fluttering movement lessen the power of the emotion that sways the figures.

However one may regard the Renaissance—whether as one of the high points in a steady ascension of Western civilization, or as a brilliant flash that illuminates its slow decline— the widespread influence of Leonardo cannot be contradicted. He made exhaustive observations and attempted to find new significance in them. His *chiaroscuro* and the psychological overtones it evoked were to lead to the great portraits of Rembrandt. His immersion of man in nature, even though only partial, was to lead to profound experiments in spatial relationships. Whether his influence, and that of the Renaissance at large, was eventually to be deleterious cannot be judged until the progress of Western art has been observed through the 19th century.

Recommended reading:
Ludwig Goldscheider, *Leonardo da Vinci,* Phaidon, 1943.
A. E. Popham, *The Drawing of Leonardo da Vinci,* New York, Reynal and Hitchcock, 1945.

MICHELANGELO BUONAROTTI (1475-1564): *The Medici Chapel*[1]

ONE OF THE GREATEST FIGURES in the High Renaissance in Italy was Michelangelo. Like other artists in this period, he was a man of vast ambition and varied interests which, because of their more restricted scope, enabled him to accomplish more during his lifetime than had Leonardo. Although primarily a sculptor, he was also a poet, an architect, and a painter. The core of the *Church of St. Peter's* in Rome was designed by him; he painted the famous frescoes on the ceiling and the end wall of the *Sistine Chapel*. These and other works were, however, conceived in a mind that thought always in terms of solid, tangible, three-dimensional mass. For this reason, we shall consider him only in that medium which was natural to him, sculpture.

The monument that fully expresses the mature style of Michelangelo, as well as the ideals of the High Renaissance, is the unfinished *Medici Chapel* in the Church of San Lorenzo in Florence. That Michelangelo should take upon himself all aspects of this project is characteristic of the Renaissance artist. He proposed to execute not only the sculpture but also the interior architectural setting and the painting. In this he was attempting to perform a task that in previous periods had been the joint effort of a corps of workmen and artists. It is very possible that the concentration of the work of many into one during the Renaissance contributed to the feeling of strain that is apparent in many of the monuments of the late 15th and early 16th centuries and left so many of them unfinished.

As seen today, the *Medici Chapel* has two of its four tombs partially completed; the projected frescoes were never begun. As evidenced here and in all of his work, Michelangelo chose man alone as the vehicle for his expression and poured into the human form all of his energy and wrath. Where Leonardo had been muted, Michelangelo was thunderous. The disquiet in the work of the former increased to torment in the work of the latter. There is

[1] Programs A and B.

a possibility that Michelangelo's own physical smallness and deformity attracted him to the monumental, perfectly-proportioned, and energetic male form, but it does not account completely for the sense of strain and inner conflict that resides within and emanates from his figures. Undoubtedly his personal misfortunes and the many schemes that never reached fruition embittered and antagonized him. The weakened state of the Christian religion during his life, the tendency of the Christian leaders toward self-glorification rather than spiritual growth, and, above all, the collision of the pagan and Christian ideals concerned him.

It was not until the Renaissance that man was able to view the Greek world and its culture as an entity remote in time and as a period which had reached its own conclusions on a completely different basis than had been assumed in the medieval world. Body and soul were one to the Greek artist, but to the medieval artist the body was debased and the soul elevated. The temporal world had value for the latter only in so far as it might be a symbol of divinity. The demands of the flesh were none the less insistent and formed a wedge which was to split asunder the balance that had been reached in the late 12th and the 13th centuries. In the Renaissance a reintegration of these two approaches became necessary. Man had attained a sense of history; he was able to study Greek philosophy and art separately and no longer as modes of expression that must be reinterpreted through Christianity in order to have importance. Such an objective approach was impossible so long as man was held firmly in the grip of medieval belief. When man became increasingly aware of the intrinsic value of himself and the world in which he lived, he turned to the Greeks because they had earlier reached conclusions concerning the temporal world. He had, however, between him and the Greek world, many centuries of inculcation in the Christian faith which could not be easily forgotten. The problem of the High Renaissance—after the field of antiquity had been explored as it had been in the 15th century—was to arrive at a new mode of expression that would incorporate both the pagan and the medieval ideals and yet be different from both. The Christian faith which had bound society together was no longer sufficient. To fill this void, the High Renaissance man attempted to clothe himself in the garments of the gods.

The structure that was erected to absorb these opposing ideals was called Neo-Platonism. Briefly, this philosophy conceived of the universe as divided into four levels of being. The supercelestial realm was the Cosmic Mind. Below it was the celestial realm, the Cosmic Soul, which introduced motion and converted the static ideas of the Cosmic Mind into dynamic causes. These two, in their turn, influenced the third zone, the Realm of Nature or the terrestrial world. The lowest zone was the Realm of Matter which had no life unless it altered itself by uniting with form. The supercelestial realm was passive and contemplative; the celestial realm was active. The perfection of either of these zones reached man in the terrestrial world only in a broken and partial form. Man was therefore always imperfect, even though he strove for perfection. He was always imprisoned and therefore disturbed and in conflict.

The soul of man, according to the Neo-Platonists, was split into two parts, the Lower and the Higher Soul. The former was closely associated with the body and included the physiological functions, the five senses, and the imagination. The Higher Soul, composed of Reason and Mind, will most concern us here, since it was the basis upon which Michelangelo created his figures of *Giuliano* and *Lorenzo* in the *Medici Chapel*. The two faculties, Reason and Mind, stood for the Active and the Contemplative Life. Reason became involved with the demands of the body. Mind was less bound and could communicate directly with the supercelestial realm. Both were required to interact, or Reason would fall before the passions of man's lower nature. At the same time, Mind, because of these demands made upon it, was distracted from its contemplation.

Man's soul was thus conceived as ill at ease in his body. It could find no peace until it could return to its original source. An intuition of this divine source or pre-existence was necessary to enable man to rise above his inner conflict and attain an earthly bliss. His Reason should be directed toward the solution of human problems; he thus led an active life. His Mind should be directed toward the contemplation of eternal truth and beauty; he thus led a contemplative life.

By laying such stress upon the individual, this philosophy was to lead to a retreat from the problems of actual life. It was to fragment society into its individual parts and set them adrift. The ship of faith, symbolized in the nave of the Gothic cathedral, was broken and destroyed. Its congregation was scattered into a sea of individual swimmers. Neo-Platonism and those other aspects of the dignity of man summed up under the term Humanism were to be among the sparks that ignited the world in the 20th century.

In what way does Neo-Platonism find expression in the *Medici Chapel*? At present each of the two tombs has a sarcophagus surmounted by two reclining figures and a statue in a niche above, flanked by smaller niches for which statues were never completed (Figs. 39 and 40). The room is divided horizontally into four zones which were to correspond with the four realms of Neo-Platonism. The empty zone below the sarcophagus was to have represented the Realm of Matter symbolized in two figures of river gods. The second zone, the Realm of Nature, is represented by the reclining figures on the sarcophagus. The seated figures of *Giuliano* and *Lorenzo* move into the celestial zone; they are depicted as embodiments of the souls of these men rather than as portraits of them upon the earth. The narrow strip under the dark-colored entablature and the plastered wall above it were never completed. The latter was to have had frescoes; the former was to have shown the trophies, empty thrones (indicating the presence of a divinity), and unborn children stricken with grief as they become aware of the Realm of Nature to which they must descend when born. Both parts were to illustrate the supercelestial zone.

The *Tomb of Lorenzo* (Fig. 40) represents the Contemplative Life. Lorenzo appears as a pensive figure, introverted, and remote from the activities of life. His temperament is suggested by the helmet which casts his eyes into deep shadow and by the index finger over the mouth as a symbol of silence. Parsimony is associated with this kind of person and is illustrated by the arm that rests firmly upon the money box. Upon the box is a relief of a bat, emblem of melancholy. The legs are crossed, thus rendering the figure immobile. The whole figure is composed within an oval, a form that is closed at all points and accentuates the intro-

Fig. 39. Michelangelo, *Tomb of Giuliano de' Medici*, 1520–34, Medici Chapel, S. Lorenzo, Florence (*Alinari*)

THE RENAISSANCE

verted quality of the figure. It is a form that Michelangelo had used earlier in his frescoes, in the Sistine Chapel, as in the *Delphic Sibyl*, to suggest the contact with the divine intellect experienced by the seers and prophets.

In general, the figure is relaxed and inert. The hand at the mouth is heavy and listless, while that on the thigh is motionless. The outward facing of the palm itself suggests an incapacity for action. The muscles of the torso are soft and smooth. In the figure of *Giuliano,* symbol of the Active Life, the opposite of these qualities is found (Fig. 39). The torso muscles are tense and contracted. The legs are open, indicating the readiness of the figure for instantaneous action. The eyes are alert and unshadowed. Giuliano holds a sceptre and his open right hand holds two coins, indicative of generosity. Although enclosed within an oval, he penetrates its restricting closure at several points: through the fixed glance, the strained neck, the twisted body, the diagonal line of the sceptre.

The attributes of the Active and the Contemplative Life are echoed in the figures below. Coupled with the active figure of *Giuliano* are the more positive aspects of time, the female *Night* and the male *Day*. Both figures twist and writhe in a strained position, one (*Night*) forward and the other (*Day*) backward, thereby imparting a feeling of movement to the whole composition even though the figures are locked and imprisoned. The powerful, masculinized *Night* (Fig. 41) shows no relaxation and no quiet. The forward movement of the elbow is awkward and tense, the eyes do not close, and one arm surrounds a demonic mask that affirms the evil things that consort with darkness. *Day* is a convulsive figure with wrathful eyes (Fig. 42). In each case, it requires tremendous effort for these creatures from the Realm of Nature to act. The terrestrial world to which they belong was, for the Neo-Platonist, the only realm fraught with actual suffering and conditioned by time.

Fig. 40. Michelangelo, *Tomb of Lorenzo de' Medici,* 1520–1534, Medici Chapel, S. Lorenzo, Florence (*Alinari*)

Fig. 41. Michelangelo, *Night,* from tomb of Giuliano de' Medici (*Alinari*)

RENAISSANCE PAINTING AND SCULPTURE

The two more transient aspects of time, *Dawn* and *Twilight,* are reserved for the *Tomb of Lorenzo*. They also convey a feeling of restlessness and pain. The male figure, *Twilight,* feels deep disgust as he views the terrestrial world. The female figure, *Dawn,* is filled with exhaustion. The contemptuous glance of *Twilight* finds its fruition in the uneasy *Night,* as the over-whelming fatigue of *Dawn* finds its fruition in the wrath of *Day*.

The sense of inner conflict that pervades the figures is achieved by *contrapposto* more than by any other means. The nearest English equivalent to the word is "counterposition." *Contrapposto* means the movement of the parts of the body around its axis so that different parts face in different directions, the extreme difference within a single figure being about 90 degrees. Such movement always involves torsion, or twisting, in the torso, often accentuated by an abrupt turn of the head. It is exemplified in the figure of *Night,* for example, where the legs incline inward (toward the wall), the pelvis straightens, and the upper torso turns forward. The movement of the chest is further accentuated by bringing one arm forward and thrusting the other violently backward.

Contrapposto was already apparent in a restrained form in Michelangelo's early statue of *David*. It was to increase in violence in his later work. The quality of strain is caused by the fact that the movement is not permitted to burst outward but always circles in to the body and is always carefully balanced by oppositional movements. This balance is implied in the word *contrapposto* itself, where the counterpositions cancel out any movement in a single direction. Even in such an apparently energetic figure as *Giuliano,* the glance of the eyes and the pointing of the knee to the right are counterbalanced and immobilized by the tilt of the leg and torso to the left. Within this framework, the direction of the head to the right is locked by a shoulder and arm movement to the left and back. In a similar fashion, Giuliano's advancing left arm rests on a retreating left leg, as his retreating right arm is balanced by an advancing right leg. Similar advancing and retreating parts around a turning axis may be observed in the figures of *Night* and *Day*. They are kept within a rigid framework but, because of the movement suggested, the figures attain neither action nor repose.

The figure is strongly separated from his environment through the use both of an en-

Fig. 42. Michelangelo, *Day,* from tomb of Giuliano de' Medici (*Brogi*)

compassing outline and a bulging, convex line which at all points hold the movement in and direct the spectator's eye inward. The isolation of the figure by convex lines is not restricted to Michelangelo but is a characteristic manifestation in the Renaissance. Its stress in this period may be attributed to the insistence upon the individuality of man and his importance over and above anything else. For this reason, he is never incorporated into the landscape and, in the High Renaissance, becomes larger than life—a figure monumentalized. The slow, shallow curve of the convex line in the Golden Age in Greece isolates a figure who is in repose, stabilized within his society. The convex line of the Renaissance attempts to bound a figure totally different in nature from the Greek—a figure at the center of the collision between pagan and Christian thought. The convex line of Michelangelo bulges and strains to the bursting point. The balancing movements become shackles.

The oppositional character of the movements is further expressed in the division of the figure into a tensed and a relaxed half. In the *Giuliano*, the right side of the figure is relaxed, the left side tense; in the *Lorenzo*, this is reversed. While all of these qualities are indicative of the torment that attends man's life on earth as expressed in the Neo-Platonic philosophy, they are also indicative of stresses and strains that go much deeper and color the whole life of the times. The attempt to fuse the Greek and Christian ideals in Neo-Platonism was to be unsuccessful. There is reason to believe that, even while applying Neo-Platonic principles to the *Medici Chapel,* Michelangelo was struggling against the constraints that they imposed. Work on the chapel was interrupted many times. It has been said that the unfinished state of some of the sculpture was due to these interruptions and eventual stoppage. The lower part of the face of *Day*, for example, in the *Tomb of Giuliano,* was never released from the stone, whereas other figures were completely finished and polished. Michelangelo's early figures are smooth and polished throughout. In some of the figures of the *Medici Chapel* there is a contrast between smooth and rough unpolished parts. In this respect it is of interest to note that the treatment of the walls reveals a contrast of light and dark surfaces. Such contrasts are more dramatic and emotional. In view of Michelangelo's later work and the sharp contrasts of light and dark that were to emerge in the following Baroque period, it is possible that an incipient emotionalism may be found in the *Medici Chapel* and that, in some parts at least, the statues were not unfinished but were purposely left with contrasting surfaces.

In a period of intense creative activity, Michelangelo stands as a towering artist who attempted to express the universal man, a creature of dignity and power, a kind of human god. His work is a valiant struggle to achieve the impossible. The scientific methods of the Renaissance continued to grow; capitalism was developing; analysis precluded synthesis. The human being was stranded, bombarded, and slowly disintegrated in a culture all of whose accents were increasingly emptied of human content. It became impossible for the dignity of man to be maintained. The troubled and tense figures of Michelangelo are an early statement of the chaotic conditions that were to become explosive in the 20th century. In following the development of art in the succeeding centuries, it should be kept strongly in mind that the men of the Renaissance, although Italian and removed from us by four centuries, are part of a period that has not yet worked itself out in our time.

Recommended reading:
Ludwig Goldscheider, ed., *The Sculptures of Michelangelo,* New York, Oxford University Press, n.d. (1940?).
La Peinture de Michel'Ange, Paris, Editions Alpina, n.d. (1943?).

TITIAN (1477-1576)[1]

LINE AND MASS organized on a geometrical basis were the means used by the Florentine artist to express the individuality of man. Mass was absolutely necessary to describe the physical being; line sharpened and accentuated the mass; geometric devices gave order to chaotic nature. These formal elements must be recognized and insisted upon inasmuch as they clarify the approach of the Renaissance artist to the world that surrounded him.

Line as a rhythmic, emotional device defining and decorating a two-dimensional object, coupled with rich, vibrant color, sufficed in the medieval period for the expression of divinity. But when man was no longer responsible to a higher divine order but was himself the measure of all things; when he lived in a world which was no longer filled by divine emanations but which had to be mastered; and when power and money took on aspects totally unrealized in the medieval period, the uniqueness of man could be expressed only in the massive, isolated figures that inhabit Renaissance art.

The shattering of that unity which had been provided by the Christian faith was to result in the extinction of communal life. It was replaced by a society in which man, as an individual whose life was in his own hands, could determine his place only by wealth or by the exercise of his wit and enterprise. Thus were set in motion those forces that were to open new continents, add to the fund of human knowledge, stimulate science and invention, sanction ruthlessness, and lead to the dehumanization of the structure of society.

Cast loose from the anchor of Christianity, it was but natural that man should seek out and explore the accomplishments of others who had also believed that man was the fashioner of his own destiny. It is for this reason that the Classical world of Greece and Rome had such a profound influence upon Renaissance thought. The ancient world seemed, to the Renaissance man, to have met nature and conquered it, and to have raised man to heroic stature. From the study of ancient models, clarity and order became paramount in all works of art. In the Early Renaissance, it seemed to have given expression to the new dynamic that was activating Italy. Dynamic? The sculpture of the Golden Age in Greece is poised and static. It should be remembered in this respect that the Classical inspiration for the Renaissance did not come from the Golden Age but rather from the period of decline when the Roman Empire had engulfed Greece. It was the Roman architect Vitruvius whose writings influenced Renaissance architects. It was the delicate Roman ornamental forms that influenced the Renaissance painter and architect, Raphael. It was such late works as *Laocoön and His Sons* that appeared to the Renaissance artist to be the epitome of the Classical style in sculpture. All of these works had been done after the boundaries that had previously isolated the Greek world had been broken, permitting new ideas and new religions to flow in and bringing into question the validity of the concept of man as the master of his own fate. The so-called *Theseus* on the pediment of the *Parthenon* is poised, stabilized, and static; he exists within a space that is negative and inert. The *Laocoön*, on the other hand, is active, twisted, tormented, and dynamic; he exists within a space that is charged, active, and consciously felt as space. It is such dynamic figures as the latter that were to stimulate the Renaissance artist in Florence.

As the Greeks moved into a larger, changing world with uncertain boundaries, they reacted in many ways. Space, and the objects that existed in space, now concerned them. Man could no longer rise above and be distinct from his surroundings; he was a part of

[1] Programs A and B.

them and was influenced by them. In their attempts to cope with this new relationship, the Greek artists moved toward illusionism and atmospheric landscape. In all cases, the strength of the purely Classical figure declined, the line softened, and the concept weakened. In some cases, sensuousness and eroticism entered. Color became of increasing importance.

After the decline of Athens, the centers of Greek culture were to be found in Egypt and Asia Minor. It was here that color, which was characteristic of Eastern expression, began to exert an influence upon the West. Mass or three-dimensional form is the characteristic expression of a people dominated by the intellect; color belongs to emotion. How color was slowly mastered and permitted to encroach upon and smother mass need not delay us here. The point is that it did enter and became the means of expressing a religion that had also come from the East: Christianity.

It has already been remarked that the Renaissance artist in Florence and Rome turned back to the tangible mass of Classical art, evidences of which surrounded him. At the same time, there was one portal in Italy which still provided entrance for Eastern influences: this was Venice, whose maritime commerce was constantly bringing in Eastern products. There was a strong tradition of color here that was to influence the painter Titian; through him and the Venetian school as a whole, it was to move across the face of Europe. Thus, in Italy during the Renaissance, two traditions were established that were to condition European art until the 20th century—the one intellectual, expressed through mass; the other emotional, expressed through color. The Florentine's preoccupation with mass led him to neglect color as an active element in his painting. He used it mainly in a descriptive sense. It was something that was added to beautify the painting; it was never implicit in the structure of the painting itself. The Venetian, on the other hand, gave it at least an equality with line and mass and sometimes made it the primary element. For its fullest effect as a sensuous and emotional device, it was always associated with *chiaroscuro,* that is, spots of glowing and vibrant color set in large areas of rich dark. This playing of lights and darks across a surface is Eastern in its derivation; it is called colorism.

It will be recalled that the tendency toward colorism had been apparent in the work of Leonardo and Michelangelo but had remained unresolved. It was unresolved in Leonardo because the *chiaroscuro* lay like a veil across sharply delineated forms with which it was not united; it was unresolved in Michelangelo because it was kept within the linear contours of his tightly-encased forms. Of the three artists, Titian comes closest to a solution, although, unfortunately, he still felt impelled to retain the mass with its convex boundaries that had been the typical Florentine expression. He was nevertheless acutely aware of the nuances of light and hue, of the presence of color in shadows, and of the value of color as a repeated motive to draw together the different parts of his composition. The line that he uses is still an enclosing and isolating one, but it is greatly softened and blurred so that it becomes less insistent. The *chiaroscuro* thus blends his figures to a greater degree with their setting, or, stated in another way, the sense of a warm, soft, enveloping atmosphere is more immediate in Titian's work than in that of any painter so far considered.

In general, Titian maintains the separation between the figures and their setting that is characteristic of the Italian Renaissance: that is, the figures and setting are arranged in two or more parallel planes with no movement backward and forward to unite them. They are held together solely by *chiaroscuro* and by color. It should be remembered, however, that Titian lived for almost a century; he saw and was touched by the different styles of other painters, and by the changing concepts that were to culminate in the Baroque style in the following century. As man's environment and his place within it were to take on greater importance, so Titian was to experiment with the backward and forward movement of figures—although to such a degree as only to bend, not to destroy or to fuse the parallel planes. He was to turn also, but briefly, to landscape painting. The presentation of landscape for itself was a new subject in European painting. Its presence is indicative of the break-down of the importance of man.

The feeling of unity in Titian's composition is achieved in part by two technical devices that appear for the first time in our study. One of these is Titian's use of a dark reddish underpainting over the whole canvas, which thus influences all colors placed upon it. Paint, it should be remembered, is active for a long time after it has apparently dried. In this way, the reddish ground eventually incorporates itself with the paint placed upon it and gives a warm reddish cast to the entire painting. The second of these is Titian's use of glazes. Oil paint normally is opaque, but it can be diluted until it becomes transparent. When so diluted in oil or some other medium, it is called a glaze. A multitude of such transparent veils can be brushed over the painting, and it is these that contribute to the strong sense of atmosphere and the living quality of the flesh in Titian's work.

The sensuous surfaces which are the result of this type of painting are most successful when they are coupled with sensuous subject matter. They enhance the innumerable recumbent Venuses and the stories from Classical mythology that Titian frequently employed. In themselves, they might also enrich religious themes, but, when coupled with rich materials, luxurious settings, and ample physical forms, they tend to destroy all spirituality. Christ revealing himself to his apostles during the supper at Emmaus after his resurrection thus becomes a rich Venetian fulfilling a social engagement at the luxuriously appointed home of one of his friends. It was not until late in his life that Titian was able to rise above his social position and approach a universal and deeply religious quality in such paintings as his *Christ Crowned with Thorns* (Munich, Pinakothek) or his *Pietà*.

More characteristic are *Sacred and Profane Love* and *Venus and the Lute Player*. Titian was an exponent of that phase of Neo-Platonism which treats of Platonic love. In Michelangelo, the dual nature of man was expressed in the Active and the Contemplative Life, two aspects of man's nature each of which was commendable and desirable. A similar duality is expressed in the work of Titian when he treats of the temporal and the eternal aspects of love. Love, in this sense, is defined as the desire for beauty and is related to the desire for perfection already exemplified in Michelangelo's application of the Neo-Platonic doctrine in the Medici Chapel. Temporal and eternal love were depicted through the clothed and the nude Venus. *Sacred and Profane Love* (Fig. 43) is an illustration of the twin aspects of Venus in Neo-Platonic doctrine. The nude figure symbolizes eternal beauty and holds in her hand a vase of fire symbolizing the love of God; the draped figure symbolizes the tangible but perishable beauty on earth, further symbolized in the bowl of jewels and the flower. The Neo-Platonic belief that love acted as the agent between heaven and earth may be expressed in the Cupid who stirs the water in the fountain. The poetic

Fig. 43. Titian, *Sacred and Profane Love, ca. 1512–1515*, Galleria Borghese, Rome (*Alinari*)

landscape, the broad planes of color, and the precision in the drapery folds reveal Titian's indebtedness to the Venetian painter Giorgione, with whom he studied and worked. Characteristic of Titian is the ample female form with its long, shallow convex lines, its tight torso, its small breasts, its weak hands, and its bland and rather vacuous head.

The recurrence of the nude Venus in other associations would lead one to believe that Titian was disposed toward the sensuous and erotic nude over and above its Neo-Platonic interpretation. In this respect, his continued friendship with Pietro Aretino may be illuminating. Aretino was one of the first yellow journalists, a person who preyed upon the indiscretions of the rich and fattened his purse on scandal. Fortunately, he elected to act as publicity agent for Titian and sing his virtues as a great painter. Characteristic of this phase of Titian's work is his *Venus and the Lute Player* (Fig. 44) with its lush female figure, its rich setting, its glimpse of a poetic landscape, and its contrast of a nude and a clothed figure. The color is richer, but the clarity of drawing is gone. The hands are flaccid; the drapery is wrinkled and mussed. Attention is usually called to the torso of the nude figure by the glance of the clothed companion and by some object held in the hand making a dark accent beside the pale breasts. In other recumbent Venuses, a small lap-dog at the feet of the figure frequently replaces the clothed male figure.

In the *Pietà* (Fig. 45), painted some sixty years after the *Sacred and Profane Love,* Titian has increased his shadow and blurred and sometimes obliterated his line. The brushstrokes are looser and more apparent. The color penetrates and enriches the shadows. The luxurious setting has been forgotten in his concern for colored light and shadow. This dissolu-

Fig. 44. Titian, *Venus and the Lute Player, ca.* 1560, Metropolitan Museum of Art, New York (courtesy of the Metropolitan Museum of Art)

RENAISSANCE PAINTING AND SCULPTURE

tion of the mass in deep color harmonies was to forecast the work of Rembrandt in the following century. Despite his brief excursion into deep space in the manner of Tintoretto, Titian was to return in the *Pietà* to the Renaissance tradition of a closed composition with the figures in a band across the foreground. The diagonal line of the main figures is carefully prevented from suggesting too much motion by placing across it an opposing diagonal composed of the bodies of Christ and the cherub with the torch.

Titian is regarded by many as the most important artist of the Venetian Renaissance. His long life, covering almost a century, carried him across many changes in style, but he was, in many respects, little touched by them. The vigor of movement, the great energy, and the violent diagonal thrusts into space of a Tintoretto were to affect him only briefly during his life. He was to move from the clarity of line and the poetic expression of a Giorgione early in his life to a freer, more impressionistic handling of paint and greater dramatic expression late in his life. The poetic sensibility of his painting influenced by Giorgione was soon to give way to a coarser eroticism that was saved chiefly because of his amazing dexterity with the brush and his magnificent color. This phase of his work sings the nude female. This theme was to be continued in the voluptuous nudes of Rubens, the melancholy nostalgia of Watteau, and the roly-poly peasant glow of Renoir, until it expired in the 20th century. At the close of his life, in such paintings as the *Pietà*, Titian was to paint his most profound masterpieces, in which his extraordinary technique coalesces with a rich and moving content.

Recommended reading:
Charles Ricketts, *Titian,* London, Methuen, 1910.
Giovanni Stepanow, *Tizian,* Leipzig, Fretz and Wasmuth, n.d.
Hans Tietze, *Titian,* London, Phaidon, 1937.

Fig. 45. Titian, *Pietà*, 1573–1576, Accademia, Venice (*Alinari*)

THE RENAISSANCE IN THE NORTH

MATTHIAS GRÜNEWALD (d. 1528): *The Isenheim Altarpiece*[1]

WHILE THE RENAISSANCE in Italy took on a strongly Classical complexion owing to the revival of interest in the ancient art and culture, in the North, where the Gothic tradition was stronger, the Renaissance expressed itself in a different way. A new vision of man and nature makes its appearance here as in Italy. But the interest in the natural world and its appearances, which is common to Renaissance naturalism wherever it occurs, is not in the North idealized and condensed into a Classical style. For the restraint and harmonious balance which normally tempered the naturalism of Italy, the Northern artists substituted a realistic art, emphatic and intense in its emotional impact.

In Germany the Northern genius found its most powerful expression in the works of the great 16th-century master Matthias Grünewald, whose *Isenheim Altarpiece* the American writer Thomas Wolfe called the greatest work ever painted. In it the artist gives expression to the mysticism and religious fanaticism that had arisen in the wake of the Reformation. The *Altarpiece* is in many ways still close to the medieval tradition, especially in its deeply religious and symbolical content. The style employed is usually referred to as Expressionistic: it is characterized by distortion of natural forms and colors for the sake of greater emotional expressiveness.

Little is known about the artist's life and work; only recent scholarship has determined that his true name was Mathis Gothart Neithart. The place of his birth was in all probability the Franconian town of Würzburg; the date is unknown. His life, as far as is known, was spent in southwestern Germany, where he painted numerous religious works, only a few of which have been preserved. He died in 1528, the same year as Albrecht Dürer, the other great German artist of this period.

Grünewald's most important and extensive work, upon which his fame chiefly rests, is the large altarpiece painted between 1510–1515 for the monastery church of the Antonite Order at Isenheim, in Alsace; the work is now in the museum at Colmar. It consists of a series of panels which portray, through the suffering and triumph of Christ and St. Anthony, the struggle and redemption of the human soul. In contrast to the scientific spirit of Leonardo and the Neo-Platonism of Michelangelo, Grünewald here gives expression to the intense Christian faith which, despite the rational and humanistic tendencies of the age, continued to be felt by many of the most profound men of the Renaissance.

The altarpiece is a polyptych, *i.e.*, it is composed of a series of panels so hinged as to open outward from the center, each opening revealing a new triad of representations.

On its outer panels, which were seen on ordinary days, the altarpiece revealed scenes of suffering: in the center the Crucifixion of our Lord; and on the side-panels representations of St. Sebastian, a martyr of the Church, and St. Anthony, the patron saint of the monastery. Tradition has it that the likeness of St. Sebastian is a portrait of the artist. Below, in the predella, the artist represented the scene of the Lamentation over the dead Christ.

On holidays the outer panels were opened, revealing scenes of triumph and joy instead of suffering: in the center the Nativity with a group of angels playing musical instruments

[1]Program B.

in honor of Mary, and on the side-panels the Annunciation and the Resurrection. This series celebrated the incarnation of our Lord and his rising again from the dead.

On the very highest holidays, and especially the feast-day of the patron saint, the inner part of the shrine was opened, revealing wood carvings by Nicolas von Hagenau which represent St. Anthony between St. Jerome and St. Augustine; the side-panels painted by Grünewald, portray two scenes from the life of the patron saint of the church, one showing St. Anthony in conversation with St. Paul the Hermit, the other representing the saint's temptation by a throng of fantastic devils. The predella, which had at the first opening remained unchanged, now shows carvings of Christ surrounded by the twelve apostles.

The most moving of the paintings that make up the Isenheim altar are the two central panels of the outer series, which represent the *Crucifixion of Christ* (Fig. 46). Here Grünewald uses the discoveries of the new realism of the Renaissance but exaggerates and distorts the forms in order to give them greater expressive power. In the very center of the composition is the crucified Christ hanging from the cross. His limbs are elongated; his body is covered with scars to bring out the agony he suffered. His fingers seem virtually to cry out to heaven, and his face is contorted in paroxysms of pain. Blood is shown running from his wounds indicating that Christ shed his blood for our redemption.

Christ's tortured body is illuminated against a simple dark background, a contrast which focuses our attention upon the crucified Lord. He is surrounded by four sacred figures: on the right St. John the Baptist, on the left St. Mary with St. John the Evangelist and Mary Magdalen. St. John the Baptist is represented as a hermit holding the open Bible in one hand and pointing with the other to Christ. Beneath him are the lamb and the chalice, symbols of Christ as the Lamb of God, who is suffering and dying for men. The finger and hand of John are distorted and elongated in order to make them more expressive and to lead the eye inevitably to the central figure; behind the hand there is a Latin inscription reading: *Illum oportet crescere, me autem diminui* ("He must increase, but I must decrease," John III, 30).

The group at the left is particularly expressive. The forms of the mother of Christ and St. John are among the most moving representations of pain which have ever been painted. Mary, dressed like a nun in white, is seen in a swaying position; fainting, she is held up only by St. John, who himself is torn by profound grief at the event which he is witnessing.

Fig. 46. Grünewald, *Crucifixion, Isenheim Altarpiece,* ca. 1510, Museum, Colmar

THE RENAISSANCE

The silent and inward sorrow of Mary, whose eyes are closed, is contrasted with the more overt grief of John. At the foot of the cross is Mary Magdalen kneeling in prayer, her face and gestures expressing her pain at the tragedy she beholds.

The total composition is highly integrated and balanced, Christ in the center forming a vertical axis to which all movements lead: he is flanked by a vertical accent on each side. The forms are distorted in order to intensify the dramatic tension of the scene. Most remarkable is perhaps the wonderful glowing somber color, which is in keeping with the scene portrayed. Grünewald uses color as his main means of artistic expression, as Michelangelo had used line and plastic form. Against a greenish-black background, the body of Christ is painted a ghastly greenish flesh color, while the side figures of St. John the Baptist and the Lamb, and St. John the Evangelist and Mary, are red and white. The color contrasts add to the drama of the scene.

The painting, although characteristic of the Renaissance in its emphasis on realistic detail, treatment of bodily movement and depth in space, is at the same time medieval in spirit. The very size of Christ, who is larger in scale than the surrounding figures, is characteristic of the symbolical nature of Grünewald's art, for he thereby gives expression to the greater spiritual importance of the crucified Lord. Also the presence of St. John the Baptist is symbolical, for he died long before this scene took place and is shown here because he prepared the way for the Messiah. In the same way the presence of the lamb holding the cross and the chalice into which the blood flows are symbols of Christ as the Lamb of God, who dies for our redemption. In this way Grünewald combines medieval symbolism with Renaissance realism and creates a style which is painterly and expressionistic, resembling in some ways already the Baroque style of the subsequent period.

Among the other panels probably the most powerful are those representing the *Resurrection* and the *Temptation of St. Anthony* (Fig. 47). Grünewald reveals himself a great master not only in the excellence of the individual paintings but in their variety as well. Each is adapted in its style to the particular scene represented. The idyllic beauty of the *Nativity,* for example, stands in striking contrast to the horror and agony of the *Crucifixion* and the glory of the *Resurrection*. In the same way the style of the *Temptation* is particularly fitting for that subject matter. For here the dream world of the Northern fairy tales finds vivid expression. The fantastic forms of the strange creatures which are falling upon the unhappy saint seem to come out of some terrible nightmare. It may well be said the Grünewald along with Jerome Bosch became the predecessor of the Surrealist

Fig. 47. Grünewald, *Temptation of St. Anthony, Isenheim Altarpiece, ca.* 1510, Museum, Colmar

painters of our own day. Like the modern artists Grünewald delves deeply into the realm of our imagination and our subconscious.

No greater contrast than that between this fantastic scene and the serene beauty of the Italian masters can be imagined. The struggle between St. Anthony and the horrible monsters of evil who are trying to tempt him is also mirrored in heaven, where devils fight the angels of the Lord who have come to the saint's aid. Towering above the distant mountains, Christ himself is seen in heaven witnessing the struggle of his saint. In this painting Grünewald shows how the patron saint of the church withstood all the wiles of the devil, and he admonishes us not to succumb to temptation but to follow the Redeemer and St. Anthony so that we may have life eternal.

Recommended reading:
F. J. Mather, *Western European Painting of the Renaissance,* New York, Holt, 1939, pp. 260-268.
A. Burkhard, *Matthias Grünewald,* Cambridge, Harvard University Press, 1936.
C. Zervos, *Matthias Grünewald*, Paris, Cahiers d'Art, 1936. (Mainly pictures.)

PIETER BRUEGEL THE ELDER (*ca.* 1525–1569)[1]

IN FLANDERS the outstanding painter of the later Renaissance was the 16th-century master Pieter Bruegel. A pantheist and humanist, Bruegel reflected the climate of opinion prevailing in Renaissance Europe. In this respect he was closer to the Italian masters than Grünewald. However, in spite of a trip to Italy, he shows little Classical influence and turned for artistic inspiration to the late Gothic painting of the 15th-century Dutch painter Bosch, whose fantasies and religious paintings reflect the strange nightmare world of the declining medieval period. The exact date of his birth is not known, but he is believed to have been born around 1525 in the Flemish village of Bruegel. He died in 1569, when only in middle age. His work, although small in quantity, is nevertheless rich and varied, showing the many facets of his remarkable genius.

His fantastic and imaginative side is brought out in his scenes depicting the legends and the folklore of Flanders, as for example in the famous *Triumph of Death*. The late Gothic tradition of masters such as Jerome Bosch lives on in these works, for Bruegel like these earlier artists is giving expression to the world of nightmare and imagination. A wealth of detail is employed in order to give reality to this inner vision; but here no ultimate simplification is attempted, for the weird and horrible appearances of this nightmare world do not demand or permit it.

Among the many genres of Bruegel's work one of the most important is his landscape painting. In fact, his paintings depicting the months of the year are among the first true landscapes in the Western tradition. To medieval man nature had been significant only in so far as it reflected the divine, but to Bruegel the beauty of nature is important for its own sake and for the indwelling presence of God. In these paintings the landscape no longer serves as a mere backdrop to the activity of man: nature herself becomes the true hero and main topic of the paintings; human beings merely form part of the vastness of the cosmos,

[1] Program A.

Fig. 48. Bruegel, *Harvesters* (*July*), 1565, Metropolitan Museum of Art, New York (courtesy of the Metropolitan Museum of Art)

no more important than the trees and animals. Bruegel attempts to portray the totality of the natural world with a wealth of narrative detail, but at the same time he achieves a composition which is integrated and simplified by a clear organization of form and the use of pure, abstract color pattern.

Yet another type of painting which is characteristic of the master appears in his representations of peasant life, which depict the lustiness and vitality of the Flemish peasants from which he had sprung. In his numerous representations of country weddings and dances Bruegel created colorful and animated pictures showing the joys and feasts of simple laborers in the fields. The artist is filled with love and admiration for the vitality and simple strength of these peasants despite an awareness of their crude and uncouth ways. This feeling is best illustrated in his painting of peasants dancing beneath the gallows, which is a glowing tribute to the vitality and joy in life of the peasants even in the face of death.

Perhaps most characteristic of all his works are his moral allegories and his religious paintings, which give profound expression to his view of man and the universe. In the artist's religious paintings, such as the *Adoration of the Magi* and the *Road to Calvary,* Christ is represented as an insignificant part of a large panorama of Flemish life. The artist thereby indicates the wrong sense of values man has who does not understand the true importance of these events. For Christ is born and dies while the Flemish peasants, like the people of Palestine, indifferently go about their own business, unmindful of the great happenings which are taking place. The same idea is also expressed in his allegories, in which man is portrayed as blind and foolish, like the men in the wonderful picture of the *Blind Leading the Blind,* or the farm in the *Fall of Icarus*. For Icarus the dreamer, the idealist, is dying without anyone caring; the farmer continues to plow, the fisherman to fish, the merchantman to travel to a distant port. Bruegel holds a mirror in front of us in which we see our own folly.

Of the works painted by Bruegel there are only two in America, one representing the month of *July,* also known as the *Harvesters,* in the Metropolitan Museum in New York, and the other, called the *Wedding Dance,* in the Detroit Institute of Arts. Both of them are excellent examples of the artist's production in their respective genres.

RENAISSANCE PAINTING AND SCULPTURE

The painting *July* (Fig. 48) represents the vast panorama of the Flemish countryside at harvest time, with peasants eating and resting in the shadow of a large tree, while others cut grain and still others are on their way to and from a distant village. The scene is represented in great detail, showing many aspects of Flemish village life during this time of year. The dominant colors are the yellow and green of the season, which is portrayed in contrast to the white and black of the winter scene in the same series. The composition is organized along diagonal lines which lead the spectator's eye into the distant background, where a haywagon is seen on the road to the distant village, with a church and tiny figures of children playing games. Man is represented as but a tiny part of the vastness and grandeur of nature, in keeping with the pantheistic philosophy characteristic of the artist.

In spite of the complexity of the scene portrayed, Bruegel achieves a remarkable unity in his over-all design. This is achieved by two main devices: one is the clear organization of space along diagonal lines; the other is the use of flat, pattern-like areas of color which gives the forms a simple, abstract quality. It is this last-named device which makes Bruegel's work seem so modern in spite of his Renaissance humanism and realism; it has indeed been the 20th century which has discovered the full greatness of his genius.

In the *Wedding Dance* (Fig. 49) Bruegel portrays the gaiety of the Flemish peasants as they celebrate this occasion. He shows a large number of figures in rhythmic, swirling movement, expressing through them the spirit of the dance. Again a wealth of detail is combined

Fig. 49. Bruegel, *Wedding Dance, ca.* 1565, Detroit Institute of Arts (Collection of The Detroit Institute of Arts)

with a very carefully planned organization of the figures which creates a strong all-over pattern in spite of the complexity of the composition. Similar formal patterns are repeated throughout the design and increase its unity. In addition to his characteristic diagonals there is also a curved movement which leads the eye from the right background around the foreground and back into the center of the scene.

The individual figures are treated with great simplicity. The artist has almost entirely omitted modelling in terms of light and shade for the sake of a colorful pattern of flat areas of colors which preserve the simplicity and unity of the design. Bruegel uses whites, reds, browns, and blacks throughout the picture, which also tends to accentuate the all-over color pattern so characteristic of the artist's work. It is this combination of a wealth of realistic detail and close observation of nature with a highly formal abstract beauty which places Bruegel's paintings among the greatest in the Western Tradition.

Recommended reading:
F. J. Mather, *Western European Painting of the Renaissance,* New York, Holt, 1939, pp. 317-331.
M. Dvorak, *Die Gemälde Pieter Bruegels des alteren,* Vienna, Schroll, 1941. (Mainly pictures.)
G. Glück, *Pieter Bruegel,* New York, Hyperion, 1939.

ELIZABETHAN LITERATURE

WILLIAM SHAKESPEARE (1564–1616)

THE ELIZABETHAN PLAYHOUSE[1]

"THE STAGE in Shakespeare's time," wrote Coleridge nearly 150 years ago, "was a naked room with a blanket for a curtain, but he made it a field for monarchs." Though his final words are as true as ever, we have learned since Coleridge's day that the stage on which Shakespeare's dramas were performed was anything but naked or primitive. Though lacking the resources that electricity can give the modern stage, it possessed a speed and flexibility that the present-day theater is still unable to equal. Above all it more than made up for a relative absence of scenic effects by a design which provided "hooks" on which the spectators' imagination, aided by the magical power of the playwright's language, could drape itself.

There were several theaters in London during Shakespeare's day. We shall confine our attention to the Globe playhouse, where *Othello* and most of the plays of his maturity were performed. This was a wooden frame structure, probably octagonal in form with an outside diameter of about eighty-five feet, each of the eight sides being about thirty-three feet high and thirty-six feet wide. It enclosed an octagonal courtyard about fifty-eight feet across. Though the building proper was roofed, the courtyard, which contained the stage, was open to the sky. Performances were held during daylight, in the afternoon.

Inside the building (facing the courtyard) were three galleries, the lowest about twelve feet high, the second about eleven feet, and the highest about nine feet. Five sections of the galleries and the ground floor of the courtyard (called the "pit") were assigned to the spectators (Fig. 50).

[1]Programs A and B. This account of the Elizabethan theater is greatly indebted to John C. Adams, *The Globe Playhouse* (Harvard University Press, Cambridge, Mass., 1942). The student who is interested in knowing more about the subject should consult this book.

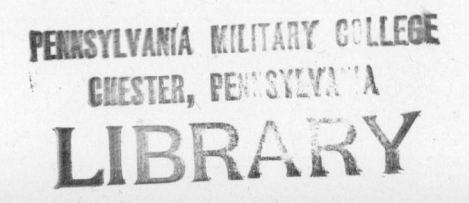

ELIZABETHAN LITERATURE

The pit accommodated standees only; the galleries had three or four tiers of benches arranged bleacher-fashion. The remaining three sections of the octagon were given over to the needs of the actors—the stage proper with its scenic background and, backstage, the dressing rooms and storage space for costumes and properties. The entire area comprised in these three sections was generally called the "tiring house," *tiring* being a contraction of *attiring*. The stage was not the "picture-frame" type that we are nowadays accustomed to and had no large curtain which descended and cut off the audience completely from the players and from the stage. To modern eyes the most conspicuous feature of the stage was the wooden platform, probably four or five feet high, which projected halfway into the pit. Perhaps forty-three feet wide at the rear where it met the scenic wall, it probably tapered to a width of about twenty-four feet at the front, and occupied about one-third of the ground area (Fig. 50A). Surrounding the outer edge of the platform was a low but stout balustrade (perhaps a foot high) which served to protect enrapt actors from tumbling into the pit and to hinder "groundlings" in the pit from clambering onto the stage.

There were two entrances to the theater: the back-stage door, primarily for the actors, situated somewhere in the rear of the sections reserved for the players; and the main entrance, situated in the front directly opposite the stage. This doorway was probably rather narrow, so that the spectators would have to enter in a single file. Standing at the doorway a "gatherer" held out a box in which each spectator dropped a penny (worth perhaps a quarter in present-day purchasing power) or two pennies if a brand-new play was on the boards. This initial payment entitled one to standing room in the pit. If a spectator wished a better location, he paid additional fees for entering the galleries. In all these galleries seats were available on a "first come, first served" basis; those who came too late had to stand in the passageway behind the benches.

Fig. 50. Plan of Globe Theater:
        A. First level
        B. Second level
        C. Third level
(John C. Adams, *The Globe Playhouse*. By permission of Harvard University Press, Cambridge.)

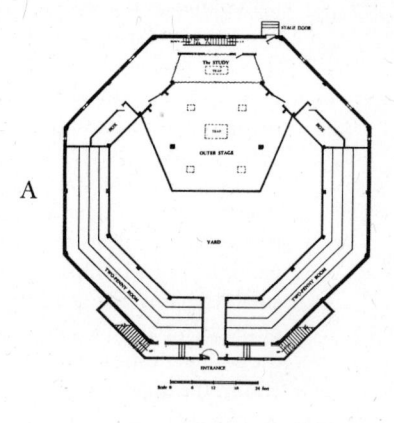

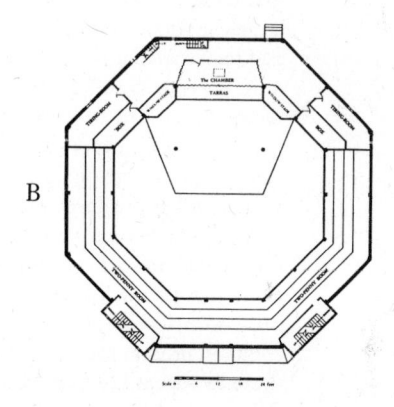

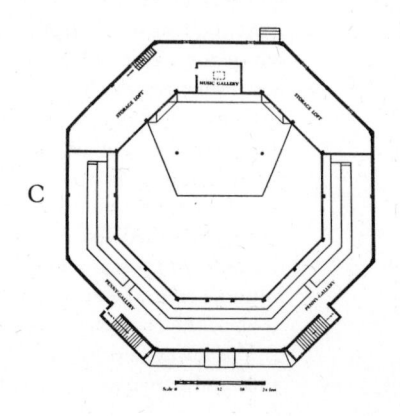

There were two other places where privileged spectators could sit—on the platform stage itself and in boxes adjoining the extreme ends of the first and second galleries. For sixpence a gallant could enter from backstage and ensconce himself on a stool or recline on the floor beside the platform balustrade; for a shilling he could have a seat, probably cushioned, in one of the boxes, commonly called the gentlemen's rooms. Various conjectures have been advanced concerning the total capacity of the playhouse; 2,000 is a moderate estimate.

Looking at the stage, the spectator installed in, say, the first or second gallery would see two stout pillars rising from the platform and supporting a wooden canopy that projected from the roof about halfway over the stage and helped to protect the players from the weather (Fig. 51). Even these pillars could be put to scenic effect; in a forest scene they could in imagination become trees, in a ship scene the masts. The canopy was often called the "heavens," and numerous references in plays of the time suggest that on its underside were painted representations of stars and the planets. Surmounting the heavens was a small house-like structure with a door and a window or two—called the "hut." It was here that the Elizabethan sound effects man most often plied his trade. A cannon ball rolled along an inclined plank betokened thunder or distant gunfire. For nearby cannon fire the real thing was used, small cannons discharged with blank loads. In *Othello* the shots that announced the arrivals of Othello's and Desdemona's ships (II. i) were doubtless fired from such weapons. Most of the trumpet calls (flourish, alarum, sennet, retreat) that figure so prominently in battle scenes and in the appearances of kings or other great personages were sounded from the hut. Here was located also the great bell which roused Othello after Cassio had wounded Montano (II. iii). Occasionally the hut served a more specifically dramatic purpose. There was probably a large trap-door in the floor of the hut opening through the heavens. Through this by a block-and-tackle arrangement in the hut various objects would be lowered and raised, often with quite spectacular effect. In *Antony and Cleopatra* it was probably employed to hoist the dying Antony up to the Monument, *i.e.,* the upper stage, where Cleopatra had taken refuge.

Lowering his eyes to the platform our spectator would also be able to spy trap-doors on that stage: a very large one, perhaps four feet by eight feet, in the center of the platform and four smaller ones, just large enough to permit a man to emerge or descend, in the corners (Fig. 50A). Ladders set up under the stage probably sufficed for actors using the small traps, for instance in scenes where devils or witches pop up here and there. The large trap had some kind of mechanism which could lift small arbors, dragons' heads and even groups of six or eight men into view of the audience. This area under the platform, often called the "cellarage," could on occasion be used for dramatic purposes. The ghost of Hamlet's father was doubtless there to repeat "Swear!" in sepulchral tones as Hamlet charged his companions to secrecy. The music "under the earth" which announced the abandonment of Antony by his patron god Hercules (*Antony and Cleopatra,* IV. iii) was played in the cellarage.

At the rear of the platform the spectator would perceive the scenic wall. The central section was occupied by three recesses, one above the other, each one forming a miniature stage not unlike the modern stage. The topmost recess or stage was relatively small (Fig. 50C), perhaps ten or twelve feet wide, probably constructed like a box with one side knocked out, the open side, toward the stage, being covered by a curtain. A doorway at the back would permit ingress. The commonest use of this stage was to house the musicians in most of the scenes where music is called for. The "music i' th' air" in the scene from *Antony and Cleopatra* mentioned above was probably played there. But on occasion it served more specifically dramatic purposes: a lookout told to post himself on the top of a castle tower, on "yonder hilltop," or in the crow's nest of a ship would probably appear there and report his observations to the characters below.

The lower and middle "inner" stages were, however, fairly large, about twenty-four feet wide and perhaps eight feet deep (Fig. 50A, B). The height of each stage would be the same as the corresponding balcony. Each could be cut off from the view of the audience by a curtain whose two halves opened and closed laterally. The floor of the second stage projected two or three feet over the lower inner stage so that there was space between the curtain and the balustrade to form a balcony. In plays concerned with warfare and sieges this balcony could represent the walls of a city or castle, or in a nautical scene it could represent the bridge or quarter-deck of a ship.

These lower and middle inner stages were not enclosed structures, not boxes with one side broken out, but simply large openings in the tiring house, and their rear walls were really permanent screens shutting off a view of the interior. They were open at the ends and separated from the interior merely by curtains through which actors could enter or depart easily and through which stage hands could easily carry "properties": tables, chairs, benches, thrones, even four-poster beds. In the rear wall of each inner stage was a window which opened on nothingness and a door which led to a stairway between the two levels. Between the window and doorway was probably an opening filled by a curtain (Fig. 50A). It was very likely behind this curtain that Polonius (in *Hamlet*) hid himself to eavesdrop on the talk between Hamlet and the Queen and through which Hamlet stabbed him.

Various names were given to these stages; the commonest were "music room" for the upper, "chamber" for the middle, and "study" for the lower stage. The study often represented just that (Faustus discovered [*i.e.* revealed] in his study, reading a book). It could also represent such places as a cave (like Prospero's cave in *The Tempest*), a pantry or buttery of a large house, a stall or shop on a city street, the tent of a king or general (as in *Richard III* or *Julius Caesar*), a tomb (as in *Romeo and Juliet*), a prison cell, and the like. Action was not rigidly confined to the study; it could flow back and forth between the study and the platform stage. In *Othello,* I. iii probably opened with the "discovery" of the Duke and the senators seated in the study around the council table, but with the arrival of Brabantio, Othello, and their attendants, and later Desdemona, the action doubtless moved out onto the platform. A scene might also begin on the platform and subsequently move toward and into the study. It may be added that the study was the one place where scenery resembling what we are accustomed to today could be set up. It seems likely that when Bottom the Weaver (in *A Midsummer Night's Dream*) retired to the "hawthorne brake," whence he later emerged adorned with an ass's head, he disappeared behind some arrangement of branches which had been set up in the study. References in plays to a character's lying or reclining on "yonder grassy bank" are so frequent as to justify the inference that the study sometimes contained a piece of scenery answering this description.

The chamber on the second level could represent the kind of room to be found on the second floor of a building, perhaps most frequently a bedroom or a dressing room, but also a private room in a tavern and so forth. Pieces of furniture like a bed, table, chairs, or benches, wardrobes, and cupboards could be placed here, though it is doubtful that more elaborate forms of scenery were used. This chamber probably represented the bedroom in which Othello smothered Desdemona, and also, as suggested earlier, the Monument in which Cleopatra took refuge in Acts IV and V of *Antony and Cleopatra*.

Flanking each end of the study were two large strong doors, probably as much as five feet wide and perhaps eight feet high (Figs. 50A and 51). These doors, which were the most frequent means of entering or leaving the stage, had to be large enough to accommodate the passage of soldiers bearing spears or muskets, pallbearers shouldering a coffin, or even, as in Marlowe's *Tamburlaine*, a chariot drawn by defeated kings. Each door was probably provided with a knocker and at least one of them contained a grilled opening or wicket situated at eye-level. The main purpose of the wicket was to enable the prompter to jog the memory of forgetful actors, but it was also frequently used when characters on each side of the door had to speak to one another or when one character had to peer inside a house.

Projecting out over each of the stage doors (and therefore flanking the chamber) was a bay fitted with casement windows, *i.e.,* the kind of window which swings outward door-fashion (Figs. 50B and 51). From such a window as this Romeo bade farewell to Juliet before descending by a rope ladder and fleeing to Mantua. The general effect of this arrangement of doors surmounted by windowed bays was that of a portion of a row of houses on a city street. This possibility was utilized in the opening scene of *Othello* where Iago and Roderigo rouse Brabantio to inform him of his daughter's elopement. Iago and his companion knock at one of the doors ("Here is her father's house") and cry out to Brabantio who opens a window overhead and leans out to identify the disturbers. His undressed state gives Iago an opportunity to twit him on his nakedness ("For shame put on your gown"). Later Brabantio appears at the door below, clad in a dressing gown ("Enter Brabantio, in his nightgown, and servants with torches"). The use of torches confirms numerous suggestions in the dialogue that the time is the dead of night. It is probable also that V. i, the scene in which Roderigo attempts to murder Cassio, was thought of as taking place in the street before Othello's house. According to the text Othello "enters" just after Cassio is wounded, and delivers three short speeches, spoken to himself. Othello probably appeared at one of the windows, as if looking out from a room in his house. It would be incongruous indeed if he appeared on the platform and stalked about while Cassio and Roderigo writhed in

Fig. 51. Reconstruction of the Stage of the Globe Playhouse
(reproduced by permission of Dr. John Cranford Adams)

pain and called for help, whereas it would be entirely comprehensible if he looked down from a window and, hearing only the anguished voices in the darkness, supposed that Iago had accomplished his mission to kill Cassio. The next scene would then open with the withdrawal of the chamber curtain and the revealing of Desdemona in her bed. Othello would enter through the end curtains, as if coming from the adjacent room at whose window he had just been seen.

The general resemblance of the first two levels of the stage to a row of houses does not imply, however, that the dramatist was restricted to such a locale.

> Thus with imagined wing our swift scene flies
> In motion of no less celerity
> Than that of thought. (*Henry V*, Prologue to Act III)

Words, and especially words charged with poetry, could make the stage suggest almost any setting. Duncan enters, declaring "This castle hath a pleasant seat; the air Nimbly and sweetly recommends itself Unto our gentle senses," and immediately in the spectator's imagination he is viewing the entrance to Macbeth's castle. When Benvolio calls out, "He ran this way and leaped this orchard wall," the audience knows that Romeo is lurking under Juliet's window in the Capulets' orchard. On the other hand when, a scene or two earlier in the same play, house servants are seen bustling about and then Capulet enters with his guests and calls out, "A hall! a hall! give room and foot it, girls," the spectator realizes that the stage now represents the great hall of a nobleman's mansion, where they are all about to dance. Thus when the locale is important the dramatist skillfully puts into his characters' mouths the words which tell the audience what it needs to know. On the other hand, when the locality does not matter, the dramatist leaves the scene "unlocalized." These unlocalized scenes have irked many modern editors accustomed to a "set" for every scene and stirred their inventiveness to supply, too often needlessly, place-phrases in brackets: "[A street in Verona]," "[A heath]," etc. The student will find it instructive, especially on re-reading *Othello* or *Antony and Cleopatra,* to keep an eye open for the phrases in the dialogue which locate the scenes and, no less important, those which indicate the time, not only the time of day or night but also the sequence or lapse of time.

Finally, we must bear in mind that a performance itself was anything but a drab spectacle. The actors' costumes were expensive and sumptuous, often gorgeous. The outlay of fifteen or twenty pounds ($75.00 or $100.00) for a costume was not unknown, and that at a time when money had ten to fifteen times its present buying power. The stage and auditorium were handsomely decorated in brilliant colors with much gilt overlay. The astounded comments of foreign visitors testify to the impressiveness of the London theaters of Shakespeare's day. Apart from Italy, the rest of Europe had nothing to equal them until well into the 17th century. And the actors themselves, though their style was doubtless more florid than that of actors today, were highly trained products of long years of apprenticeship (during which, as boys, they played the female roles) and of subsequent years of experience in playing mature parts. They could hold their own against the best actors of today. Altogether, the performance of one of Shakespeare's plays in his own day must have been an eye-filling and ear-filling as well as a mind-filling experience. The actors could have performed Shakespeare's plays before a blanket as a curtain, but they had far more than that.

Recommended reading:
John C. Adams, *The Globe Playhouse,* Cambridge, Harvard University Press, 1942.
Muriel C. Bradbrook, *Elizabethan Stage Conditions,* Cambridge, Cambridge University Press, 1932.
Alfred Harbage, *Shakespeare's Audience,* New York, Columbia University Press, 1941.

Elizabethan Tragedy

SHAKESPEARE: *Othello*[1] and *Antony and Cleopatra*[2]

I. THE SURGE of intellectual and artistic energy which we call the Renaissance reached England late. England was remote from the Italian centers of art and learning and consequently, during the 15th and 16th centuries, lagged somewhat behind continental Europe in cultural development. In England the Renaissance reached its culmination during the reigns of Elizabeth and James I, a time when the Italian Renaissance was in its decline. The artistic achievements of the English Renaissance lay especially in the field of literature. Indeed, the last twenty years of the 16th century and the first twenty of the 17th century constituted a golden age of English letters. The greatest literary accomplishment of the period was in the drama. The leading dramatist, both in tragedy and in comedy, was Shakespeare.

The Greeks produced the first body of great tragedy; the Elizabethans the second. Elizabethan tragedy is in a sense a descendant of Greek tragedy, for it owes much of its character to the example of the Latin tragic writer Seneca, who in turn imitated the Greeks. Yet Elizabethan tragedy is strikingly different from the Greek.

The difference is due in part to the fact that the Elizabethan drama was in no way connected with religious institutions or ceremonies. Indeed, many devout Englishmen of Shakespeare's day regarded the drama as a diabolical form of entertainment. Because of its secular character the Elizabethan drama lacked the atmosphere of pious solemnity that one finds in Greek tragedy and was much less preoccupied with religious and moral questions than the Greek. Yet, because some of the playwrights were thoughtful men and because they addressed themselves to audiences which included thoughtful men, consideration of ethical problems occurs in the Elizabethan drama also, although, to be sure, much less obtrusively than in the Greek.

Elizabethan audiences had a liking for variety in dramatic entertainment. They would have been little pleased by the strict unity of action which is characteristic of Greek tragedy. Elizabethan dramatists consequently are inclined to use two—sometimes three—plots instead of one and to introduce miscellaneous elements—comic interludes, songs, dances, spectacles—which do not advance the action of any plot. This introduction of irrelevancies is made possible by the greater length of the Elizabethan play but is basically due, not to the length of the play, but to the taste of the audience.

Shakespeare's *Othello,* it happens, is much more highly unified than most Elizabethan tragedies. There is very little in it which does not contribute to the forward movement of the action. *Antony and Cleopatra* is exceptional in the opposite respect. It is possibly the most disunified of Shakespeare's plays. Shakespeare represents a soothsayer entertaining Cleopatra's somewhat frivolous attendants (Act I, scene ii); he takes his audience to the borders of Parthia to hear Ventidius moralize on the dangers of succeeding where one's superior has failed (III, i); he devotes a scene to the description of ominous prodigies which portend disaster for Antony (IV, iii); etc. The relationship between Antony and Cleopatra continually competes for the spectator's interest with the contest between Antony and Caesar, which is certainly the main narrative theme. In fact, the entire fifth act, although it is absorbing and deeply moving, is really irrelevant, for the hero dies at the end of the fourth act.

[1]Program A.   [2]Program B.

ELIZABETHAN LITERATURE

The Elizabethan taste for variety results also in an intermingling of moods. Shakespeare's audience would have been disappointed if there were nothing to laugh at in a play, even the most somber of tragedies. Accordingly in *Othello* one finds two low comedy episodes (III, i; III, iv) in which a "clown," that is, a yokelish servant who is cleverer than he appears to be, exchanges quibbling banter with other characters. (These episodes in *Othello* certainly do not represent Shakespearean comedy at its best.) In *Antony and Cleopatra* one has semi-comic scenes, for example, that in which Sextus Pompey entertains the triumvirs on board his flagship (II, vii), and one low comedy episode, in which a countryman brings asps hidden in a basket of figs to Cleopatra. The latter passage, like the episode of the drunken porter in *Macbeth* and the graveyard scene in *Hamlet,* comes at a point of very high dramatic tension, a moment when the audience realizes that tragic events are rapidly developing. In placing these bits of low comedy, Shakespeare seems frequently to follow the principle that comedy is more laughable by contrast with tragedy and tragedy is deepened by contrast with comedy.

Because of the relative length of the Elizabethan play and because of the Elizabethan playgoer's relative indifference to unity and concentration, Shakespeare does not, as the Greek dramatist usually does, confine the action to a narrowly limited span of time. He is inclined to represent the story much more completely than the Greek playwright, and he depends much less therefore on narration of past events. The action of a Shakespearean play sometimes covers a very long time span. The events represented in *Antony and Cleopatra* occurred historically over a period of about ten years. *Othello* is exceptional among Shakespeare's tragedies for its relative concentration in time. The last four acts take place within a period of about thirty-six hours. (The play, however, contains contradictory indications concerning the passage of time.)

The Elizabethan dramatist did not feel the same restrictions in regard to setting that the Greek dramatist felt. The two curtained stages of his theater permitted very rapid shifts from one setting to another.[3] The outer uncurtained stage was available, without benefit of scenery, for use as any locale whatsoever, for the Elizabethan audience was quite accustomed to supplying imaginatively whatever might be lacking in the way of realistic backgrounds. The Elizabethan dramatist is inclined to shift his scene very freely. Shakespeare's *Othello* takes place altogether within the limits of two cities and thus shifts about relatively less than most Elizabethan plays. Yet even in *Othello* we find a wide variety of settings: the street before Brabantio's house, the council chamber of the Venetian senate, the seaport of Cyprus, etc. In *Antony and Cleopatra* Shakespeare moves very rapidly from one part of the ancient Roman world to another. This shifting back and forth across the Mediterranean is perhaps a little confusing (it would have been less so on the stage of the Globe Theater than in a modern theater), yet it achieves an effect which would be impossible if greater unity of setting were observed: the effect of a panoramic view of a great empire and of significant related events taking place in the various parts of it. It is useful also in drawing the contrast between the new and vigorous Roman civilization and the ancient and effete Egyptian culture which it has overcome.

Shakespearean tragedies are, of course, not altogether structureless. Each has its protagonist, and in most of them there is an easily identifiable antagonist. Each of them tells a story of a struggle (as all good drama must). *Othello* concerns a conflict between the hero and Iago (Othello is an unusually passive protagonist, for Iago plays upon him without any effective resistance on his part). *Antony and Cleopatra* concerns a contest between two men of unusual energy and ability for the rule of the Roman Empire. A Shakespearean tragedy has a climax, a turn for the worse in the fortunes of the hero; and this normally comes in the third of the five acts, much farther forward in the play than the climax of the typical Greek tragedy. The climax of *Othello* occurs at some not altogether identifiable point in Act III, scene

[3]See, above, "The Elizabethan Playhouse," pp. 102–05.

iii, the scene in which Iago arouses Othello's suspicions concerning his wife's fidelity. Othello's nature is such that, once the passion of jealousy has taken hold of his mind, he is completely unreasonable; the harm which Iago has done is therefore irreparable; the rest of the play is concerned with the tragic consequences of what has happened in the climactic scene. In *Antony and Cleopatra* the Battle of Actium (III, x) constitutes the climax, and the rest of the play represents the consequences of Antony's folly on that occasion. Normally the hero dies in the final scene of the play.

Although these structural elements are present in an Elizabethan tragedy, it has none of the spare simplicity of Sophocles. The typical Elizabethan play is a rich and varied dramatic feast. It is likely to give an effect of sprawling profusion, to offer a panoramic view of many lives, many places, many events. It is likely to have also something of glamor and magnificence. As often as he can, Shakespeare includes scenes of colorful pageantry with appropriate sound effects. He often introduces the flamboyant and melodramatic. Nothing could be more spectacular, for example, than Othello's manner of committing suicide.

The Elizabethan love of the splendid and opulent—a taste which Elizabethan Englishmen shared with men of the Renaissance period in general—is nowhere more fully illustrated than in the dialogue of Shakespeare's drama. Shakespeare's lines are richly musical and beautifully ornamented with imagery:

>   Now boast thee, death, in thy possession lies
>   A lass unparallel'd. Downy windows, close;
>   And golden Phoebus never be beheld
>   Of eyes again so royal! Your crown's awry.
>   I'll mend it, and then play.   (*AC,* V, ii, 318-22)

>   Not poppy, nor mandragora,
>   Nor all the drowsy syrups of the world,
>   Shall ever medicine thee to that sweet sleep
>   Which thou owedst yesterday.   (*Oth.,* III, iii, 330-33)

In Shakespeare's verse one finds also the largeness, the expansiveness, the love of the gorgeously superlative, which is characteristic of the Renaissance:

>   Farewell the tranquil mind! Farewell content!
>   Farewell the plumed troop, and the big wars
>   That make ambition virtue! O, farewell!
>   Farewell the neighing steed and the shrill trump,
>   The spirit-stirring drum, th' ear-piercing fife,
>   The royal banner, and all quality,
>   Pride, pomp, and circumstance of glorious war.
>   (*Oth.,* III, iii, 348-54)

>   His legs bestrid the ocean: his rear'd arm
>   Crested the world. His voice was propertied
>   As all the tuned spheres.   (*AC,* V, ii, 82-84)

II. In the brave new world which the Renaissance discovered, nothing aroused its interest and enthusiasm more than man himself. The Middle Ages had been relatively indifferent to the physical and psychological characteristics with which man was endowed during his brief stay on earth. A man was a soul to be saved; his earthly life was merely a period of preparation and trial which derived significance only from its relationship with the life hereafter. The physical equipment, the emotions, the intellectual faculties of temporal man—all of which he retained only for the short span of life on earth—could have little value in the eyes of men who thought thus.

The Renaissance, however, was far from indifferent to the temporal nature of man. It discovered that the physical world contained numberless objects of legitimate interest and curiosity and that it offered limitless opportunities for pleasure and achievement. It discovered also that man himself (the microcosm, the "little world") was a most absorbing subject of study and that he was endowed with senses, emotions, and intellectual abilities which enabled him to enjoy the satisfaction of his curiosities, to take advantage of the manifold pleasures of the world, to achieve things beyond the imagination of the Middle Ages. It is probably this Renaissance belief in man's powers and potentialities which beyond anything else characterizes the Renaissance view of life. In the contemplation of human powers and faculties, the Renaissance thinker loses himself in wonder and admiration: "What a piece of work is a man! How noble in reason! How infinite in faculty! In form and moving how express and admirable! In action how like an angel! In apprehension how like a god!" Man is a creature of two worlds, a "great and true *amphibium*," for he has a spiritual as well as a physical nature. He is only a little lower than the angels.

Yet man, although he is richly gifted, is not ideally endowed. If all men were so, there would be no evil and no suffering. Adam in the Garden of Eden possessed the perfectly constituted personality. By his disobedience he sacrificed this ideal temperament, and because of his sin there are imperfections, imbalances, in the personalities of all his descendants. Each man has his peculiar deviations from the ideal norm of character: an excess of this passion, a defect of that, a weakness of intellect or will. Adam's sons therefore are confronted with problems of self-government which Adam before the Fall did not have. They must study human nature and their own individual temperaments so that they may know themselves. With self-knowledge one can shape his character and his life intelligently by compensating for his defects and by mastering his excesses.[4] Thus he may hope to fulfill his duty to himself, the duty of realizing his own potentialities.

The decay and corruption of human nature resulting from the Fall do not condemn man to error and misery. They mean simply that greater effort is required of him in the winning both of temporal happiness and of heavenly salvation. He has still the God-given power to rule his own destiny. The evils in his life are due to his own failures. They are not imposed upon him. On the other hand, if he achieves happiness and success, he may credit himself.

III. One would expect dramatists belonging to a generation thus enthusiastically interested in human nature to devote a large share of their creative energy to the development of the characters in their plays. There are many Elizabethan plays, to be sure, in which the characterization is feeble and uninteresting. At its best, however, Elizabethan drama is a drama of character. Shakespeare's plays are memorable especially for their depiction of human personality and for their revelations concerning the desires, fears, loves, and hatreds which impel men and women to act as they do.

This does not mean that a Shakespearean play presents merely a series of portraits. Static portraits do not make drama. Shakespeare is interested not so much in character as in character in action. His concern with character, moreover, does not mean that his plays are uninteresting as stories. In a Shakespearean drama character and plot are so related that interest in one is necessarily interest in the other.

We have noticed in Sophoclean drama a rigorous unity, a careful shaping of narrative material into a dramatic creation of simple and firm outline, a skillful fitting of one episode to another to form a coherent sequence which, while emotional excitement constantly rises, leads to a climactic reversal of fortune. In comparison, the formal construction (that is, the construction of the action) in most Shakespearean plays is very loose, sometimes careless. A Shakespearean play, however, has a structure of another kind, a structure which might be

[4] See *Othello*, I, iii, 322–337.

called a pattern of character interreactions. For the whole action of the play grows out of the personalities of the men and women involved and out of their influence upon one another.

In *Othello,* for example, Shakespeare is dramatizing a story (taken from an Italian collection of tales) which ends with the hero's killing his young and beautiful wife because of an unfounded suspicion that she has been unfaithful to him. The hero of a tragedy is normally a person of admirable qualities, and Shakespeare makes it clear in the first act that Othello is an honorable man of self-assured dignity, a man who has won a great military reputation through courage and ability as a commander. But Othello must also be a man who is capable of killing a lovely and innocent woman. To bring about this apparently impossible finale, Shakespeare represents Othello as a forthright and honest man incapable of any kind of dissimulation and utterly without subtlety. Since he is himself "of a free and open nature," he does not see subtlety and indirectness in others. He expects others to be like himself, "thinks men honest that but seem to be so." Thus he can "tenderly be led by th' nose As asses are." Because he has spent his life in military action, he is even more poorly equipped to judge women than to judge men. He consequently does not really understand his wife and, without knowing it, is uncertain in his confidence in her. Above all he is a person of very deep and compelling passions which, once they are aroused, completely deprive him of judgment.

To impel this high-minded but naive protagonist into the killing of his innocent wife, Shakespeare creates Iago, a person who is deficient in moral scruples but who has unusual intellectual keenness and consummate skill in influencing other people. This dangerous antagonist has motives, conscious and subconscious, for wishing to injure Othello. Cunningly taking advantage of Othello's ignorance and weaknesses, Iago implants in his mind suspicions concerning his wife's fidelity and thus sets in motion the sequence of events which leads to the catastrophe. The personalities of Othello and Iago are very skillfully fitted together to achieve a dramatic purpose.

There are other elements in this narrative pattern of personalities. Because of her youth and inexperience, Desdemona is innocently unperceptive and trustingly passive. If she were shrewder, more vigorous, more assertive, she might be able to take matters into her own hands and thus deflect the course of events into an altogether different channel. She is also a generous and sympathetic person so that she may plead fervently for the reinstatement of her supposed lover and thus seem to confirm Iago's accusations. Cassio is necessary to the story as the man toward whom Iago directs suspicion. To play this role, he must be young, handsome, well-bred, and gallant; and so that Iago may the more readily use him for his purposes, he must be somewhat easily influenced and somewhat gullible. Emilia, Brabantio, and Roderigo also are given such traits as will fit them for the lesser parts that they must play. To alter the personalities of any of the major characters would be to destroy the whole pattern or to set up a new one. If the play is to reach the conclusion that it does, the characterizations cannot be otherwise than they are.

In *Antony and Cleopatra* Shakespeare is dramatizing material which he has found in Plutarch's *Lives*. The protagonist is an ambitious man of great military and political ability. He is engaged in a contest with a man of somewhat smaller capacity for the control of the Roman Empire. The outcome of this conflict is to be the defeat and death of Antony. Shakespeare prepares for this issue by making it clear, in the first act, that Antony, in spite of his high capabilities, has certain qualities which under the circumstances are grave disadvantages to him. He is adventuresome, impulsive, inclined to undertake the daring and spectacular act. He is loyal, friendly, warmly generous. He is a lover of luxury and pleasure and is inclined to self-indulgence. Most important of all, he is highly susceptible to feminine charm.

His antagonist is Octavius Caesar, who is endowed with just the qualities which should enable him to defeat such a man as Antony. Although he is much younger than Antony, he is not impulsive and adventuresome. He is cool-headed, clear-sighted, shrewd. He unhesitatingly avails himself of every political or military advantage that offers itself with no desire whatever to engage in the spectacular performance and no concern whatever for sportsmanlike generosity or personal attachments. He has little taste for convivial pleasures (note the contrast between Antony and Caesar in Act II, scene vii). Neither pleasure nor sentiment could possibly deflect him from the undeviating pursuit of his ambition.

Yet Caesar would not defeat Antony if there were no Cleopatra. Although she does not realize it, Cleopatra is Caesar's ally. Her fascination plays upon Antony's weakest point and is the cause not only of his military defeat but of his failure in his obligations to the state and to himself. Her influence upon Antony is strengthened by the pleasures which he enjoys in her barbarically luxurious court.

These three personalities form a pattern calculated to produce a certain narrative outcome. Octavia also has a somewhat important place in this pattern. Octavia has an appealing sweetness, a dignity, and a long-suffering devotion to duty, but she lacks the seductive charm necessary to supplant Cleopatra in Antony's affections. Instead of acting as a bond between her husband and brother, she becomes the issue in their final quarrel and furnishes Caesar with the perfect pretext for making war upon Antony. The other very numerous persons of the drama play insignificant roles. In *Antony and Cleopatra* there are many persons, just as there are many events, which contribute little or nothing to the principal action. Even Enobarbus, although we should be reluctant to sacrifice his blithe cynicism and his trenchant commentary on the action, could be taken out of the play without affecting the course of events.

Shakespeare's men and women are warmly human, and one often develops a feeling of intimate acquaintanceship with them. In comparison with them, the persons of Aeschylus and Sophocles seem elevated, remote, sometimes rather forbidding (as they were intended to be). Shakespeare's characterizations are more detailed than those of the Greek tragic writers. The Greeks draw their characters with a few clear lines; motivation is lucid and simple. Shakespeare supplies much more information, and the motivation is sometimes highly complicated. The characterizations of Iago and Cleopatra, especially, are remarkable for their subtlety and complexity—and for the superb skill with which they are done. One of the principal pleasures to be derived from the study of Shakespeare lies in the analysis of such persons.

IV. Earlier in this volume tragedy has been defined as a dramatic spectacle of human suffering which is, or seems, out of proportion with the deserts of the person who endures it. Tragedy depicts the miseries of humanity in those situations in which they seem most unjust and most inexplicable. Tragic dramatists, as was suggested earlier, are seldom content with merely representing the hard conditions of human life; they seek to find order in the apparent moral chaos; they offer explanations for the pain which so unaccountably occurs even in the lives of good and great men.[5]

The Greek tragic writers seem to believe that pain is imposed, even upon persons who apparently are blameless, by external agencies, usually by the gods, whose motives in such matters are not always clear to limited human understanding. The Greeks are highly conscious of man's inferiority to the gods and of his helplessness in their hands. The Renaissance mind, with its fervid belief in human capability, would not be likely to find this view of life satisfying. The Elizabethan is less conscious of man's inferiority to the divine powers than of his kinship with them. He is more conscious of man's strength than of his weakness.

It would seem inevitable that the more thoughtful playwrights of an age so greatly interested in the nature of man and so highly confident of man's powers should look for the causes of man's failures and miseries in human nature itself. If man is regarded as master of

[5]See, above, pp. 15–17.

his own destiny, then he cannot attribute his sufferings to any outside agency; he himself is responsible. He is endowed with such qualities as should enable him to cope with the difficulties and problems of his life. If he fails, he has been in some way wanting in self-knowledge or in self-mastery.

For there are excesses and deficiencies in every man's nature which he must understand and for which he must compensate. These are his most dangerous enemies. It is conceivable that a man might go through life without ever meeting a situation which demanded self-knowledge and self-mastery of him. An avaricious man might conceivably never have a tempting opportunity to steal. But Shakespeare's tragic heroes are not so fortunate. Each one of them is placed in circumstances nicely calculated to search out and play upon his imperfections and thus, unless he makes a strenuous effort of mind and will, to impel him toward disaster.

Othello is deficient in shrewdness, in ability to read the characters and motives of others; he is also a man whose passions are of such power that they can completely extinguish the light of reason. He finds himself in circumstances (Iago is the principal circumstance) which call imperatively for clear judgment and cool self-control. Othello fails. Antony is a generous, impetuous man, a lover of pleasure and a lover of woman. His situation demands that he suppress his characteristic desires and impulses. If he does so, he will become the dominating figure of the entire civilized world; failure to do so will mean catastrophe. Antony is aware of his problem: Cleopatra, he knows is a "serpent of old Nile," "cunning past man's thought." But Antony never makes the effort of will which is so urgently necessary. He consequently fails in his duty to himself and to the Roman state, and his life ends in magnificent ruin.

If there is any one idea which Shakespeare's tragedies convey, it is the idea that there is a close relationship between what a man is and what happens to him. If Brutus, or Macbeth, or Hamlet, or Othello, or Antony were a different man, he would not meet the calamity which he does. Each of these heroes fails in a situation designed to exert pressure upon his weak points. The circumstances, to be sure, are somewhat artificial. In real life, the issues are never quite so clear as in a play; failure is usually relative, not absolute; the reasons for it are usually obscured by a thousand irrelevancies. The playwright simplifies, clarifies, emphasizes. Although his representation of life is by no means photographically realistic, it is essentially true.

The foregoing may give the impression that Shakespeare, by long and arduous pondering on the problems of life, had clearly formulated an ethics and an explanation for human suffering, and that he set out deliberately to disseminate his conclusions through his plays. There is no doubt that Shakespeare was deeply convinced of the truth of the ethical ideas which appear in his plays. He himself, however, did not formulate them, nor was there any necessity for his disseminating them, for they were a part of the mental furniture of every educated spectator in the Globe Theater. Shakespeare simply gave expression to beliefs characteristic of his age and society. As they appear in his plays, these ideas command respect partly for their intrinsic worth and partly for the superb dramatic and poetic form which Shakespeare has given them.

The Elizabethan view of life, we should notice, is much more optimistic than that which we met in Greek tragedy or than that which we should meet if we studied the naturalistic tragedy of recent times. (Shakespeare's *King Lear* and *Troilus and Cressida* are exceptional in their pessimism.) In Elizabethan eyes, man is no helpless victim of external forces which he cannot hope to meet on equal terms. A man's calamities are due to his own misuse of his very great abilities or to his failure to use them. If this is true, it follows that man, by exerting himself to employ his God-given talents as God intended he should, can avoid calamity and win success and happiness. It may be objected that Othello, being credulous, sensitive, and tempestuously passionate, can act in no other way than he does, that Antony, being amorous and impetuous, must of necessity do exactly what he does. This view, however, is a modern view, the product of our biology and psychology. While such deterministic thinking was not unknown in Renaissance Europe, it gained small currency in England.

V. Shakespeare's tragic heroes, although they fail because of their imperfections, are not weak or contemptible persons. Indeed, many of the character traits which underlie their failures are qualities which, if they appear in moderation, are generally respected. Othello and Antony are men of energy, courage, and ability; they have high standards of honorable conduct; they leave finally an impression of heroic poise. One learns to like them and to admire them, for they have a greatness of spirit—a magnanimity, as the Elizabethans would say it.

In the course of this essay, we have noted many contrasts between Greek and Elizabethan drama. We should note also that, in the nature of their tragic heroes, they have an element in common. Both Sophocles and Shakespeare seem to reassure us that human beings can rise above the dreary and contemptible mediocrity that we continually see about us or feel in ourselves. They seem to tell us that, although the conditions of human life are very hard, it is at least possible for men to exhibit integrity and nobility even in the midst of calamitous failure. They renew our faith in our own kind.

Sophocles and Shakespeare could create heroes of this nature because they lived in periods and among peoples which believed in the dignity of man. When one examines the drama of the last seventy-five years, he finds in the work of the abler playwrights few if any persons of such stature. The absence of noble and heroic characters from our drama suggests that our age has little faith in human nature. Certainly there has been some change in humanity's valuation of itself since the advent of modern science.

Recommended reading:
J. C. Adams, *A Life of William Shakespeare,* Boston, Houghton Mifflin, 1923.
A. C. Bradley, *Shakespearean Tragedy,* London, Macmillan, 1904. (Note especially the chapter on "The Substance of Shakespearean Tragedy" and the two chapters on *Othello.*)
Harley Granville-Barker, *Prefaces to Shakespeare,* 2 vols., Princeton, Princeton University Press, 1946-47. (Vol. I contains an essay on *Antony and Cleopatra,* vol. II an essay on *Othello.*)
Theodore Spencer, *Shakespeare and the Nature of Man,* New York, Macmillan, 1942.

Elizabethan Poetry

SHAKESPEARE: *Sonnets*[1]

ELIZABETHAN POETRY had its rise in humanism, the attitude of mind that placed the first value in the study of mankind and nature, and in the art of the Italian Renaissance. Sir Thomas Wyatt (1503–1542) lived in France and Italy and brought back from Italy a love of her lyric poetry and a desire to fashion English poetry on Italian models or on that of antiquity seen through the medium of the Italian Renaissance. He tried (though not with complete success) to introduce a new dignity, elegance, and harmony into English poetry. From Italy he borrowed forms new to England, of which one, the sonnet, was destined to have an immense influence. The sonnet is a short reflective poem that follows a rather strictly limited formal pattern. It consists of fourteen lines, usually iambic pentameter. The Petrarchan or Italian form of the sonnet is made up of two stanzas or paragraphs—an "octave" of eight lines and a "sestet" of six lines. The rhyme scheme of the octave is *abbaabba,* while any combination of two or three rhymes is permitted in the sestet. Wyatt introduced into his sonnets a new style, rich in images, filled with elaborate metaphors in the subtle and elaborate manner of Petrarch. He translated into his own idiom some of the courtly, artificial, sincere, and intense sonnets of the Italian master. Number 104 of these, to quote an example that is characteristic both of the form and substance of Petrarchan love poetry, is entitled *Description of the Contrarious Passions in a Lover.*

> I find no peace, and all my war is done;
> I fear and hope; I burn, and freeze like ice;
> I fly aloft, yet can I not arise;
> And nought I have, and all the world I season.[2]
> That locks nor looseth holdeth me in prison,
> And holds me not, yet can I 'scape no wise;
> Nor lets me live, nor die, at my devise,
> And yet of death it giveth me occasion.
>
> Without eye, I see; without tongue, I plain;
> I wish to perish, yet I ask for health;
> I love another, and thus I hate myself;
> I feed me in sorrow, and laugh in all my pain.
> Lo, thus displeaseth me both death and life,
> And my delight is causer of this strife.

English poets, even when utilizing the form of the Italian sonnet, seem to have found the epigrammatic or summing-up couplet at the end a particularly attractive device, and it was this that became one of the special features of the English sonnet, which was first developed by a younger contemporary of Wyatt, the Earl of Surrey (1517-1547)). This poet established a simpler form of the sonnet, which was to find its finest exponent in Shakespeare. The English sonnet, like the Italian, consists of fourteen lines, but instead of a rhyme scheme distributed through two nearly equal stanzas, it is made up of three quatrains, rhyming *abab, cdcd, efef,* and a climactic couplet, *gg.* Surrey also originated unrhymed ten-syllable lines out of which was to develop blank verse. The theory of blank (unrhymed) verse was typical of the Renaissance desire to return to the spirit of the Greek and Roman classics.

English poetry, indeed, in the last two decades of the 16th century, began to reflect with an

---

[1] Programs A and B.
[2] Seize upon, as a hawk its prey.

energy and brightness caught from the Italian Renaissance the glory and intenseness of the English world. England had broken from the Catholic Church, had established a powerful and brilliant monarchy, and was challenging the power of Spain and her fabulous empire in the New World. England's new self-consciousness expressed itself in a tremendous outburst of poetic energy, and for two generations England was filled with a galaxy of poets whose work reflected the age they lived in, the Renaissance, with its enraptured rediscovery of Classical art and poetry and its delighted absorption in the world of sensuous experience.

Poets like Sir Philip Sidney, Edmund Spenser, Samuel Daniel, Thomas Lodge, Michael Drayton, and, most significant of all, William Shakespeare began using the sequence of a connected series of sonnets as a vehicle of love poetry. Various elements drawn from the chivalrous and courtly love poetry of the Middle Ages, from Platonic philosophizing, from Renaissance art, and from the direct experience of life were combined to produce a kind of grammar of love in ornate and sometimes extravagant verses. Petrarch's great series of love sonnets to Laura were imitated and, in Sidney, Spenser, and Shakespeare, equalled. Usually the Elizabethan sonnet cycles were addressed to a lady who was given a Classical name and eulogized with ingenious and fantastic praise.

The type, illustrated in Wyatt's translation of Petrarch which is quoted above, has been described by J. W. Hebel and H. H. Hudson:

The general Petrarchan conventions of the cruel mistress, golden-haired, and with lilies and roses contending in her cheeks, and the faithful lover, alternately hoping and fearing, at once freezing and burning, are at the basis of most of the cycles, though transcended by the best writers.... There is a continual search for comparisons worthy of the Lady's beauty and grace: the four seasons and the heavenly bodies are under frequent requisition; as are legendary heroes and ladies, gods and goddesses, kings and kingdoms, usages of the law courts, and even the signs of the Zodiac.[3]

But Spenser's and Shakespeare's sonnets are more serious than this. Spenser, who is perhaps the most perfect representative of the earlier Renaissance in England, unites the Christian spirit with Platonic idealism and pagan sensuousness in a way that illustrates the vivifying influence of Classical antiquity upon medieval otherworldliness. Not only in the magnificent and elaborate allegorical poem, *The Faerie Queene,* but in his marriage odes, *Prothalamium* and *Epithalamium,* and his sonnet sequence *Amoretti* (love songs), Spenser blends the spirituality of courtly and Christian chivalry with a pagan delight in sensuous beauty and finds them united most closely in an idealized and yet passionate love. Here are some lines from *Epithalamium,* the ode written in celebration of his own marriage:

> Tell me, ye merchants daughters, did ye see
> So fayre a creature in your towne before,
> So sweet, so lovely, and so mild as she,
> Adornd with beautyes grace and vertues store?
> Her goodly eyes lyke saphyres shining bright,
>   Her forehead yvory white,
> Her cheekes lyke apples which the sun hath rudded,
> Her lips lyke cherryes charming men to byte,
> Her breast like to a bowle of creame uncrudded,
>   Her paps like lyllies budded,
> Her snowie necke lyke to a marble towre,
> And all her body like a pallace fayre,
> Ascending uppe, with many a stately stayre,
> To honors seat and chastities sweet bowre.
> Why stand ye still, ye virgins, in amaze,
>   Upon her so to gaze,
> Whiles ye forget your former lay to sing,
> To which the woods did answer, and your eccho ring....

[3] J. William Hebel and Hoyt H. Hudson, *Poetry of the English Renaissance,* 1509–1660 (New York, Appleton-Century-Crofts, 1940), p. 955.

> Open the temple gates unto my love,
> Open them wide that she may enter in,
> And all the postes adorne as doth behove,
> And all the pillours deck with girlands trim,
> For to receyve this saynt with honor dew,
>   That commeth in to you.
> With trembling steps and humble reverence,
> She commeth in before th' Almighties view:
> Of her, ye virgins, learne obedience,
> When so ye come into those holy places,
>   To humble your proud faces.
> Bring her up to th' high altar, that she may
> The sacred ceremonies there partake,
> The which do endlesse matrimony make;
> And let the roring organs loudly play
> The praises of the Lord in lively notes,
>   The whiles with hollow throates
> The choristers the joyous antheme sing,
> That all the woods may answere, and their eccho ring.

The union of the sensuous and the spiritual, which these verses illustrate, is Spenser's special contribution to the literature of the early Renaissance in England. When one turns to Shakespeare's sonnets and plays after the sonnets and poems of Spenser, one has another view of the poetry of the Renaissance, a view which shows it to be human, dramatic, vivid, and as comprehensive as the mind itself. Shakespeare's is the poetry of psychological realism. His sonnets stand apart from all but a few of the best single sonnets of his contemporaries. His imagery is bolder and more actual, drawn from a wider field of experience and learning, and the emotional depth of the poetry far transcends the merely conventional and literary. Indeed, Shakespeare's style is fantastic, rich, and, above all, dramatic. His imagery is adventurous and various; comparisons to the most familiar things are made in the most surprising connections; and the language varies from the most exalted poetic diction to the most homely and familiar of colloquialisms. Sometimes grammar itself is twisted to convey meaning with a greater intensity or concentration, and new words and new usages are coined with an exuberance of fancy that makes Shakespeare one of the greatest innovators in the history of the English language. The music of Shakespeare's poetry varies too. It can be lyrical, resonant, and mellifluous when the thought or the dramatic situation requires these qualities; and it can be heavy, harsh, sardonic, broken, or dissonant when thought or passion falls into a different mood. What is so striking an indication of Shakespeare's genius as poet and "lord of language" is the psychological realism with which his verse reflects all shades of feeling and thought. It has a mercurial power of combining the most diverse tones and ideas in a poetry that makes use of words and idioms from all levels of speech and images from the most unexpected areas of experience.

It is interesting to see these qualities in the brief compass of the sonnet and to observe how exactly the form of the poem fits the thought and the mood. Let us examine from this point of view the sonnet (LXXIII) beginning, *That time of year thou mayst in me behold*. The thought itself is simple, but the final effect of the poem is to do much more than state this thought with precision: it is to communicate the feelings and attitudes that rise out of the thought and also, perhaps, contribute something to it. The logical structure of the poem is as follows: the same thing is said three times (in a different way each time), and then a consequence of it is stated in the concluding couplet. What is said is merely that "I am growing old and my youth must die. You, beloved, see the signs of this, but it makes you love me all the more."

Each of the three quatrains making up the main part of the sonnet present the idea of age and the approach of an ending in terms of a different image: autumn, the ending of the year in the first; twilight and sunset, the ending of a day, in the second; and the dying of a fire in the third. These images are not in any way original. What gives them validity is their appropriateness, universality, and especially the rich emotional overtones with which the poet's musical language endows them.

The line

> Bare ruined choirs where late the sweet birds sang

is particularly rich in its evocations, even though some of the implications it would leave in the mind of an Elizabethan Englishman may need to be pointed out in a note. The reference, though indirect, is clear: it is to the many cathedrals and churches which with the coming of the Protestant monarchs were stripped of their rich and often beautiful ornaments and hangings.

The reference to "black night, Death's second self," though a commonplace of medieval poetry, serves to suggest, without stating it directly, that it is not only youth which will soon be gone, but life itself, and this is reinforced by the image of the dying fire and the reference to "death-bed."

The line

> Consumed with that which it was nourish'd by,

is a good instance of Shakespeare's concentrated accuracy. The key idea is that it is the richest, most crowded, and intensest life that burns out soonest, and this is suggested perfectly in the image of a fire choked with ashes all the sooner because of the very abundance of the fuel—a thought which gains in intensity and clarity because it is presented thus in terms of a concrete image.

This sonnet is typical of the earlier sonnets in Shakespeare's sequence in that it still contains a good deal of ornate and artificial language, although this is never used to conceal emptiness of meaning. Such a sonnet as *Poor soul, the center of my sinful earth* is a more serious, a more sober, and as far as language and style are concerned, an even more concentrated piece of work.

The poem is addressed to the writer's own soul, his being, the immortal part. "Sinful earth" is the body; "these rebel powers" are the senses. The poet is accepting the Christian view of the sinfulness of the body and its desires; but it is curious to notice how clear an appeal is made to practical economy. The central images are of a tenant (the soul) in "a fading mansion" (the body), who wastes his substance painting the outward walls. Note the language of business in the word "lease"; of a master with a wasteful servant; and of an investor who is advised to buy what is valuable ("terms divine") and to sell what is worthless ("hours of dross"). This is a thoroughly modern, Protestant, and un-medieval appeal to the practical business of worldly living. Shakespeare is definitely a child of the Renaissance.

Recommended reading:

E. K. Chambers and Charles Williams, *A Short Life of Shakespeare,* Oxford, Clarendon Press, 1933, pp. 122-132.

L. C. Knights, "Shakespeare's Sonnets," in *Explorations,* New York, Stewart, 1947.

J. M. Robertson, *The Problems of Shakespeare's Sonnets,* London, 1926.

J. W. Mackail, "Shakespeare's Sonnets," *Lectures on Poetry,* London, 1911.

RENAISSANCE MUSIC

RELIGIOUS POLYPHONY: JOSQUIN DES PREZ (*ca.* 1445–1521)[1]

IN THE HISTORY OF MUSIC the term Renaissance is used to designate the period from *ca.* 1450 to *ca.* 1600. It was during this time that the newly invented art of printing was applied to music, making possible a wide diffusion of a composer's works. The great quantity of early printed collections of both sacred and secular music, the number of composers represented in them, and the quality of the compositions themselves show this to have been one of the richest periods in musical history.

Sacred music in the Renaissance was written to be performed in churches, in the home, and in the private chapels of princes. Rulers vied with each other in securing the services of the best musicians obtainable and even sent agents to foreign countries to engage them. The maintenance of a well-trained choir, conducted by a composer of stature, was considered by most of the rulers more than a religious duty. Such a choir was an ornament to the court, a source of pride, and a token of the cultured taste to which the Renaissance prince aspired.

Nearly all of the composers of this period, even those who were best known for their secular works, were affiliated at some time of their lives with a church or chapel choir. Often they had served a musical apprenticeship as choirboys, in return for which they had received room and board, clothing, and other necessities, as well as education. Their training in music was under the direction of the leader of the choir, who was a master of the craft of music. As a result, most choirboys, when their voices changed and they left the choir, were already skilled singers and usually capable composers. Later they found their greatest opportunities for employment as singers or composers in the court or church choirs. Thus it is not surprising that the greatest part of a Renaissance composer's musical production was religious.

The early life of Josquin des Prez, about whom little is known, probably conformed to the above pattern. He was a native of the Netherlands, that country which, during the Renaissance, was the chief exporter of musical talent to all of Europe. As a young man he went to Italy, the crucible within which the Gothic spirit of northern Europe was "humanized." Here he spent a number of years as a musician at the ducal courts of Florence, Milan, and Ferrara. From 1486 to 1494 he sang in the choir of the Sistine Chapel in Rome. Membership in this group, which provided liturgical music for the Pope himself, was a high honor. Later Josquin apparently served King Louis XII of France.

Josquin (as he is usually called) wrote, among other works, a number of polyphonic masses. These are musical settings for a group of voices of the same texts that have been discussed in connection with the monophonic plainsong mass.[2] In the polyphonic mass, however, these texts are sung to a number of simultaneously sounding melodies. Each of these melodies is called a *voice,* or *voice-part,* because, theoretically at least, it lies within the range of one of the types of the human voice: soprano, alto, tenor, or bass. The voice-parts in polyphony are so contrived that each would sound well if sung alone, yet all of them combine to form a sonorous whole. This is, in essence, what we mean by polyphony: the simultaneous sounding of two or more melodies in such a manner that they retain a certain amount of independence (that is, they can be followed separately by the ear), yet blend together.[3]

One of the results of polyphonic writing is that any specified tone in one voice-part is heard

---

[1] Programs A and B.
[2] *Kyrie, Gloria, Credo, Sanctus, Agnus Dei;* see above, pp. 55–56.
[3] See Chapter VIII, pp. 390–92.

against some other tone in another voice. The pitch relationship between two such tones is called an interval, between three or more, a chord. Intervals are classified as *consonances* if they are agreeable and satisfying to the ear, *dissonances* if they sound harsh or disagreeable.[4] During the Renaissance the consonant intervals (octaves, unisons, thirds, fifths, and sixths) could be used freely, but the dissonant ones (such as seconds, fourths, and sevenths) were to be employed only according to certain rules, designed to render them unobtrusive. Note, for example, the treatment of the dissonance in the following excerpt (Ex. 5) from Josquin's *Pange Lingua Mass* (*Christe eleison,* mm, 24–25). At the beginning of measure 25 the top-

Example 5

most voice forms a dissonance with both of the voices below it. This double dissonance (a fourth and a seventh) is, however, "prepared" and "resolved" in accordance with Renaissance theory. That is, the dissonant tone, F, is introduced as a consonance (a third) in the preceding measure and then, after forming the dissonance, progresses to other consonances (a third and a sixth) by descending one scale step. Such a formation, termed a "suspension," robs the dissonance of much of its harshness.

In writing the *Pange Lingua Mass* Josquin employed a procedure very popular during the 16th century. He chose a pre-existent melody, the *Pange Lingua hymn,* and distributed phrases from it among the voice-parts of each large section of the mass. Furthermore, he presented these phrases, usually, in such a way that the statement of one of them occurs first in one voice and is then repeated successively by the other voices. This repetition of a melodic idea by various voices in turn is called *imitation.*

The Pange Lingua Mass

1. *Kyrie Eleison.*[5] The *Kyrie* of the *Pange Lingua Mass* illustrates the technique just described and at the same time demonstrates the freedom with which Josquin handled it. The over-all form of the *Kyrie* is dictated by the traditional three-fold division of the text.[6] During the course of the three musical sections, each a self-sufficient polyphonic unit, quotations from all six phrases of the *Pange Lingua* hymn appear in successive order. This can be seen most clearly in the beginnings of each of the six entries of the soprano voice.[7] Comparison of these entries with the plainsong phrases from which they are derived shows that the quotations from the hymn tune are but a point of departure. The addition of measured rhythm and the "spinning out" of each phrase has extended the range of expressiveness, so that there results a melodic line, sometimes soaring, as at the beginning of the first *Kyrie eleison,* again gently undulating, as at the *Christe eleison,* or forcefully repetitive as at the conclusion of the second *Kyrie eleison.*

The technique of imitation is apparent in the *Kyrie* from the manner in which each phrase of the hymn is introduced by the several voices in turn. Thus, at the beginning, the first five notes of the tenor voice are repeated (though at different pitch levels) at the entries of the

[4]It should be noted, however, that the conception of consonance and dissonance exists primarily within the mind of the auditor. Hence the degree of dissonance of a specific interval may vary according to the context in which that interval is heard, the manner in which it is sounded, etc. Also the concept of dissonance has varied from one period to another.

[5]Program A. The score of the *Kyrie* of the *Pange Lingua Mass* is printed below, Ex. 7, p. 122.

[6]See, above, p. 56.

[7]In the fifth entry the first note of the corresponding hymn phrase is lacking.

bass, soprano, and alto voices. Josquin liked to use the voices in pairs, so that often two of them enter in close succession, later to be followed by two others, which imitate rather strictly the first two. Each of the three divisions of the *Kyrie* begins in this way. In the first *Kyrie eleison,* for example, the melodic phrases sung by the tenor and bass (first pair) are repeated almost in their entirety by the soprano and alto respectively (second pair).

The prevalence of two-part writing in Josquin's works results in a generally "thin" texture. That is, the interweaving of only two strands of melody obviously sounds less full and rich than that of a greater number. Note, however, that Josquin "thickens" the texture near the end of each of the three divisions of the *Kyrie.* By this means, and also (in the first and third sections) by the use of repetition of short phrases within each voice, he achieves a sense of climax.

2. *Agnus Dei.*[8] The technique of imitation is exemplified at the beginning of the *Agnus Dei.* The opening phrase of the *Pange Lingua* hymn appears first in the alto, then in the bass, tenor, and soprano successively. In addition, the voices are paired, that is, the alto and bass present one version of the hymn phrase, the tenor and soprano another. Such pairing of the voices was a favorite device of Josquin's. Whereas he often presented the pairs successively, as, for example, at measures 74+, here at the beginning they overlap to a great extent. The second phrase of the hymn is presented by the tenor and soprano only (mm. 8 and 11), while the other two voices sing counter-melodies. A counter-melody is one which is played or sung against (*i.e., counter to*) a melody which is the subject of imitation. Then, to conclude the first *Agnus Dei,* Josquin introduces a melodic phrase not derived from the hymn and hence presumably freely invented (m. 17). The tenor and soprano engage in imitation on this phrase, which appears in several variants. As these voices overlap in "close" imitation, the words sung by them, *miserere nobis* ("have mercy upon us"), are, by repetition, given dramatic emphasis.

The second *Agnus Dei* opens with imitation on a brief subject derived from the first phrase of the hymn melody. In introducing this subject the voices are not paired and enter at regular intervals of one and a half measures. After the fourth entry the soprano sings (mm. 32+) a statement in long note-values of the entire first phrase of the hymn. The first five notes of this phrase appear successively, the sixth and seventh pitches follow after a pause of several measures, and the last note of the hymn phrase after a melodic insertion several measures in length. Here Josquin has treated the plainsong phrase as a *cantus firmus.* This term refers to the presentation of a pre-existent melody (such as the *Pange Lingua* hymn) in notes of relatively long time-values by a single voice chosen from the voice complex. In this instance the soprano sings the *cantus firmus* while the other voices engage in imitation on a rapidly moving counter-melody.

At the words *qui tollis* ("that takest away," m. 50) the bass and, later, the tenor sing a melody derived from the second plainsong phrase, while the alto and soprano engage in imitation on a counter-melody. This section tapers off as the voices drop out (mm. 63+), and it is followed by a fresh setting of the same words on a melody derived from the third hymn phrase, appearing in the soprano and then imitated in the tenor. These voices are supported by the bass, moving parallel to each of them in succession.

The fourth plainsong phrase is made the subject of imitation in all the voices, entering in pairs, at the words *dona nobis pacem* ("grant us peace," m. 73). Repetition of these words is set to a new melodic subject (m. 80) derived from the fifth phrase (without the first note) of the plainsong. This subject is imitated in all the voices. The conclusion of the *Agnus Dei* (from m. 87 on) sets the words *dona nobis pacem* once more and with particular attention to good text declamation. That is, the actual accentuation of the Latin words is observed in

---

[8]Program B. The score of the *Agnus Dei* of the *Pange Lingua Mass* is printed below, Ex. 8, p. 126.

the musical setting (*e.g.,* a stressed syllable is set to a longer note than an unstressed syllable). The subject of this concluding section is a six-note phrase (not derived from plainsong) which pervades all the voices.

Traits of Renaissance Religious Music

The *Pange Lingua Mass* illustrates two important aspects of polyphonic music, the treatment of the church modes[10] and of rhythm. In polyphonic compositions the role of the modes is considerably weaker than in plainsong. Although each voice-part of a many-voice work is usually cast in a mode, the frequent addition of sharps or flats tends to destroy the relationships of intervals characteristic of that mode and often creates pitch successions like those of major or minor scales.

Nevertheless, in most 16th-century polyphony a modal flavor is still noticeable to some extent. The *Pange Lingua* hymn, and hence the mass based on it, employs the Phrygian mode, with its tonic, or final, on E. The prominence of this pitch and its neighboring notes, D and F, in certain parts of the mass gives these passages a distinctively Phrygian character. See, for example, the beginning of the *Agnus II*, or the conclusion of the *Kyrie*.

The rhythm of polyphonic music, in contrast to that of plainsong, is based on a regular beat. This pulsation serves a double function. It is a means of keeping the performers together, and it also plays a role in governing the succession of consonance and dissonance. Dissonances do not occur on stressed beats unless they are suspensions, since this would make them too prominent for Renaissance taste. Against this background of a regular beat, however, each voice-part is free in rhythm; that is, its stressed notes usually occur at irregular time intervals (Ex. 6). Much of the charm of polyphonic music results from the interplay of the stresses of the various simultaneously heard melodies.

Example 6

Renaissance music is noted chiefly for the traits of clarity, symmetry, balance, euphony, and restraint. Clarity results from the use of a small number of voice-parts in a polyphonic texture. The parts do not obscure each other; rather, each one may be followed by the ear as a separate melody, even though it is sounding against other voice-parts. Symmetry manifests itself in the frequent division of the four voices into two pairs, also in a liking for balanced structural proportions. The formal plan of the *Kyrie,* for example, is:

Kyrie eleison	*Christe eleison*	*Kyrie eleison*
16 measures	36 measures	18 measures

Symmetry and balance are kindred concepts, the former term relating to the disposition of component parts, the latter to their treatment. Thus when all the voices share equally in the

[9]Programs A and B.
[10]See Chapter VIII, pp. 383–86.

presentation of a melodic idea, as in imitative polyphony, the impression of balance is given. Euphony, or pleasing sound, results from the preponderance of consonances and the careful manner in which dissonances are treated. Restraint, in this music, manifests itself in this same regulation of dissonance and in the preference for relatively few voice-parts (usually three to six). It is also apparent in the smooth flow of the melodic lines, which move predominantly by stepwise progression, that is, along the scale line. Leaps larger than the minor sixth (except for the octave) are rare.

The qualities described above are, in general, more characteristic of the sacred music of the Renaissance than of the secular. They constitute, however, the norm for all music during the greater part of the 15th and 16th centuries.

Recommended reading:
J. R. Milne, "Josquin des Prés," in *Grove's Dictionary of Music and Musicians,* 3rd ed., New York Macmillan, 1947, II, 791-794.
P. H. Lang, *Music in Western Civilization,* New York, Norton, 1941, pp. 194-199.

Example 7

25
, chri - - ste
3
chri - - - - ste
ste
3
30
chri - - - - ste
, chri -
, chri - - ste
35
ste
4
e - - - lei - -
, chri - - - - ste
40
4
e - - - lei

45
e - lei
son e - lei - son e - lei · son
e - lei
son, e - lei - son e -
50
son
e - lei - son
son e - lei - son
lei - son
55
ky - ri - e e - lei - son,
ky - ri - e e - lei - son,
ky - ri - e e - lei -
ky - ri - e
60
ky - ri - e ky - ri - e ky - ri - e e -
ky - ri - e, ky - ri - e, ky - ri - e e -
son, ky - ri - e e - lei -
e - lei - son ky - ri - e e -

Example 8

pec-ca - - - - ta mun - - - - - - - - - - - - - di qui
lis pecca - - - - ta mun-di qui tol - lis pec - ca - - - ta
lis qui tol - - - - lis pec - ca - - - - - ta mun - -
lis qui tol - lis tol - - lis
tol - lis pec-ca - ta mun - di mi - se - re - re no - - - bis mi-se-re
mun - - - di mi - se - re - - re no - - bis mi-se - re
di mi-se-re re no - - - bis mi-se-re re no - - -
pec - - ca - - - - - - - ta mun - - di
re no - - - - bis mi - se - re - re no - - - bis
re no - - - bis mi-se-re-re mi-se-re-re no-bis mi-serere no - bis
bis mi-se-re re no - - - bis mi-se-re-re no - - bis
pec-ca - - ta mun - - - - di mi-se-re-re no - bis
A-gnus de - - - - - i
A - - gnus de - - - - - i
A - - gnus
A - - gnus de - - - - -
15
20
25
30
4 (varied)

35
a - - - gnus de - - - - - i
a - - - - - - gnus de - - - i a - - - - - - - gnus de -
de - - - - i a - - - - gnus de - - - i de
i, a - - - - - - gnus de - - - i , a - - -
40
a - - - - - - - -
- - - i a - - - - - - - - - - - - - - gnus de - - - - -
- - - - i a - - - gnus de - - - - - i
- - gnus de - - - - - - - - - - - i a - - - - gnus
45
- gnus de - - - - - -
- - - - - i a - - - gnus de - - - - - - - - - - - - -
a - - gnus de - - - - - - i a - - - - gnus de - i
de - i a - - - gnus de - i
50
55
i
i qui tol - lis pec - ca - - - ta mun - - - - - - - - - -
qui tol - lis
qui tol - lis pec - - - - ca - - - - - - - - - - - - -
6b
6a

6b
60
qui — tol - - - - lis pec-ca - - - ta mun - - - - - - - - - - -
di — qui — tol - - lis pec - - - ca - -
6a
qui tol - - lis pec - - - ca - - - - - - - - - - - -
ta mun - - - - - di qui — tol - lis pec - -
65
7
di — qui tol - lis pec - - ca -
- - - - - ta qui — tol - - lis pec - ca
ta mun - - - - - - - - - - - - di qui
- - ca - - - ta — mun - - di qui tol - lis pec - -
70
- - ta mun - - - - - - - - - - - di —
- - ta - mun - di — do - - na no - - - - bis
7
8
tol - lis pec - - ca - - - - ta — mun - di do - na
ca - ta mun - - - - - - - - - - - - - - - - - di do -
75
8
do - - na no - - bis pa - - - - - - -
8
do - na no - bis pa - - - - - -
no - bis pa - - - - - - - - - - - - cem
8
na na - bis pa - - - - - - - - cem

80
9
9
85
- cem do - na no - - bis do - na no - - bis pa - -
9
- - - - cem do - na no - - - bis do - - na no - bis
9
9
do - na no - - bis do - na no - - - - - - - bis pa -
9
do - na no - - bis pa - - - cem do - - na no - bis pa -
10
90
- - cem do - na no - bis pa - cem
10
10
pa - - - cem do - na no - bis pa - cem do - - na nobis
cem do - na nobis pa - cem do - na nobis pa - - -
- - cem do - na nobis pa - cem do - - na no - bis pa - cem
10
95
10
do - na no - bis pa - cem do - na
10
pa - cem do - na no - - bis do - na no - bis pa - cem
10
cem do - na nobis pa - cem do - na no - bis
10
do - na no - bis pa - cem dona no - - - bis pa - cem do - na
100
nobis pa - cem
do - na no - - bis pa - - - - cem
10
do - na nobis pa - cem pa - - - cem
nobis pa - cem dona no - bis pa - - cem

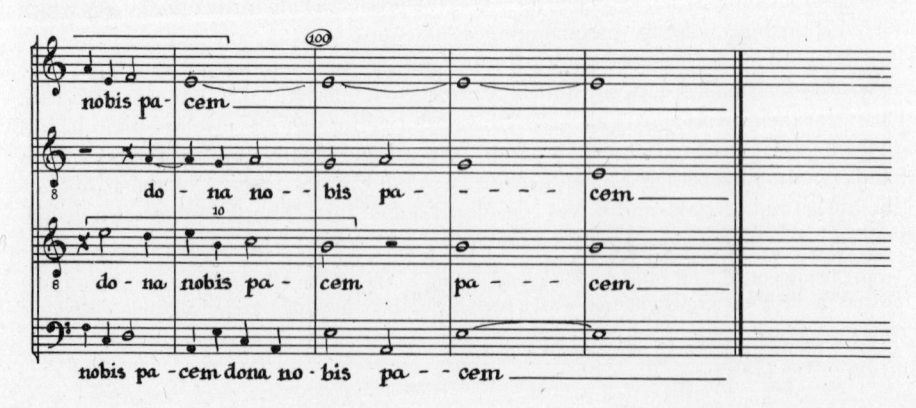

SIXEENTH-CENTURY SECULAR POLYPHONY

The Madrigal[1]

RENAISSANCE COMPOSERS served two strata of society. On the one hand, they composed for the devotional functions of the Church, which, despite the more worldly outlook of the time and its interest in pagan antiquity, had retained much of its spiritual and political power. On the other hand, composers provided music for princely and civic ceremonies as well as for the refined pastimes of the aristocracy and wealthy merchant class. The spirit of the Renaissance thus reveals itself both in secular and sacred music.

Characteristic of 16th-century music is its tendency toward an international style, which asserts itself in the midst of regional differences. In this development, the role of Italy, center of Renaissance culture, was most important. Because it attracted foreign musicians to its courts and chapels, it was in Italy that the various musical styles amalgamated. One consequence of this was the madrigal, the principal secular form of the late Renaissance. It was intensively cultivated in Italy by Flemish and Italian composers for almost a hundred years and, from the 1580's into the second decade of the 17th century, it flourished in England. Although borrowing many of its features from Italy, the English madrigal quickly developed a character of its own.

The growth of a school of English madrigal composers was facilitated not only by a native musical tradition, but also by the attempt to match musically the flavor and value of the contemporary English poetry on which the madrigals were based. Among the best-known English madrigal composers are William Byrd, Thomas Morley, John Wilbye, and Orlando Gibbons. John Farmer, although not so well known, reveals in his madrigals the high degree of craftsmanship which composers of every rank had in common at this time.

The 16th-century madrigal is a vocal composition for several voice-parts (three to six, as a rule) based on a secular text in the vernacular; it is usually of an amorous nature and is sometimes based on a pastoral theme. In the second half of the century it tends to follow, although not rigidly, a structural principle borrowed from sacred music. According to this principle, the text is divided into various sections which determine the formal layout of the music. Each section begins with a motive of its own which is subsequently treated in imitative or non-imitative polyphony, with occasional sections in chordal style. In sonorous, polished verses and poetic images which are often highly contrived, the texts of madrigals deal with unrequited as well as requited love, pastoral themes, and simple philosophical ideas. These poems are apt to be heightened at the end by an epigrammatic point. The predominance of amorous subjects stamps the madrigal as the product of an aristocratic society which considered courtship one of its essential·aesthetic pursuits.

The subtle, subdued style of the madrigal is in tune only with intimate surroundings, since it was written for small groups of musical amateurs who performed it, one singer to each voice-part, for their own enjoyment. It was this sort of performance that John Milton had in mind when, in his *Areopagitica,* he referred to "the airs and madrigalls, that whisper softnes in chambers." In Elizabethan England madrigal singing was a pastime of the aristocracy and the upper middle class, and it was considered one of the accomplishments of a gentleman to be able to take part in a vocal ensemble.

But supper being ended, and Musicke books, according to the custome being brought to the table: the mistress of the house presented mee with a part, earnestly requesting mee to sing. But when after

[1] Programs A and B.

manie excuses, I protested unfainedly that I could not: everie one began to wonder. Yea, some whispered to others, demaunding how I was brought up: so that upon shame of mine ignorance I go nowe to seeke out mine olde frinde master Gnorimus, to make myselfe his scholler. (Morley)

What distinguished the madrigal and secular music in general from sacred music is not merely its more worldly total character but specific details of its composition. First of all, as a highly refined type of musical entertainment, the madrigal follows the principle of diversity. This is stressed by Thomas Morley in his book *A Plaine and Easie Introduction to Practical Musicke:* "The more varietie you shew the better shall you please." Among the means by which variety is achieved are subtleness of harmony as well as variation in the number and in the kind of voices combined for a particular passage. In contrast to sacred music, imitation in the madrigal is less strict, and there is greater use of a syllabic style, *i.e.,* one which sets only one tone to a syllable, than of a melismatic one.[2] The general breakdown of the modes already noticeable in the music of Josquin is equally apparent in the madrigal. The English madrigal which comes at the end of the Renaissance is almost never modal, but in a major or minor tonality.[3]

In the 15th century the structural elements of a vocal composition were more important than its text. In the 16th century, however, particular attention was given to details of the text, especially in the madrigal. Morley writes:

You must ... if you have a grave matter, applie a grave kind of musicke to it, if a merrie subject you must make your musicke also merrie. ... You must then when you would express any word signifying hardnesse, crueltie, bitternesse, and other such like, make the harmonie like unto it, that is, somewhat harsh and hard but yet so it offend not. Likewise, when any of your words shal express complaint, dolor, repentance, sighs, tears, and such like, let your harmonie be sad and doleful. ...

For a light subject, Morley proposed fast moving music, but "if lamentable, the note must go in slow and heavie motions...." Word accent and sentence structure must be respected: short and long syllables are to receive tones of proportionate duration, and rests should not separate the syllables of a word, nor should a sentence be disrupted by a long rest. It must be noted, however, that these suggestions were not always strictly followed in actual composition. Morley also mentions that word images are to be expressed literally in music, and this kind of symbolism, which appears also in sacred music, abounds in madrigals:

... you must have a care that when your matter signifieth ascending, high heaven, and such like, you make your musicke ascend: and by the contrarie, where your dittie speaketh of descending, lowenesse, depth, hell, and others such, you must make your musicke descend. ...

The effort of Renaissance composers to give vivid expression to their texts is paralleled in painting by the attempt to "imitate nature." An active sense of form, color scheme, and design prevented Renaissance painters from creating mere copies of the outer world. Composers, for their part, did not concern themselves with nature in the raw but with nature as transformed by poetry. Thus, by musically symbolizing the sentiment and the images of their texts, they too "imitated nature," but they were sufficiently aware of the demands of their medium to write music which could exist even without reference to its words.

The intimate fusion of word and music was a significant feature of the Renaissance madrigal. Even more characteristic of the age is perhaps an element of repose which, as expressed in the madrigal (with the exception of those that anticipate the effusiveness of Baroque style), prevented sentiment from being too excessive or too personal. This quality was emphasized by Orlando Gibbons in the preface of the collection in which his madrigal *The Silver-Swan* (discussed below) appeared:

It is proportion that beautifies everything, this whole Universe consists of it, and Musicke is measured by it, which I have endeavored to observe in the composition of these few Ayres. ...

[2] See, above, p. 60.
[3] See Chapter VIII, pp. 383–90.

"Proportion" (meaning here an integration of all parts of the composition into a balanced whole) is brought about in madrigals by avoiding dramatic contrasts and by the utter clarity of the polyphonic texture. It is also sustained by stable chords which include dissonances of a mild nature (suspension dissonances), by a melodic style with a preference for narrow range (*ambitus*) and small intervals, and finally by gentle accentuations produced by duration of tone rather than by dynamic stress.

Recommended reading:
Walter Rubsamen, article "Madrigal," *The International Cyclopedia of Music and Musicians,* 1946, pp. 1066-1069.

JOHN WILBYE (1574–1638)

Sweet Honey-Sucking Bees[1]

JOHN WILBYE spent the greater part of his life as resident musician at Hengrave Hall, the estate of a wealthy and music-loving English family. He wrote many madrigals, but little sacred music. During his lifetime two volumes devoted to his works were published, the first in 1598, the second in 1609. "Sweet Honey-Sucking Bees" appears in the latter publication, entitled *The Second Set of Madrigales to 3. 4. 5. and 6. parts apt both for Voyals and Voyces.*[2] The title of this volume indicates what many pictures of the time show, that Renaissance vocal works were often played on instruments as well as sung.

Sweet Honey-Sucking Bees is a musical setting of a poem in two stanzas praising the charms of a certain Melisuaviae.

> *1st part*
> Sweet honey-sucking bees, why do you still
> Surfeit on roses, pinks, and violets,
> As if the choicest nectar lay in them
> Wherewith you store your curious cabinets?
> Ah make your flight to Melisuaviae's lips;
> There may you revel in ambrosian cheer,
> Where smiling roses and sweet lilies sit,
> Keeping their spring-tide graces all the year.
>
> *2nd part*
> Yet, sweet, take heed, all sweets are hard to get;
> Sting not her soft lips, oh beware of that:
> For if one flaming dart come from her eye,
> Was never dart so sharp, ah then you die!

The madrigal consists of two relatively self-sufficient divisions, each setting to music one stanza. For both divisions five voices—two sopranos, alto, tenor, and bass—are employed.

The method of construction is that described above,[3] in which the successive musical sections are based on successive segments of the text. An annotated formal analysis of this madrigal might be made as follows:

[1] Program A.
[2] *Parts*="voice-parts," *apt*="suitable," and *voyals*="viols," a type of stringed instrument played with a bow.
[3] P. 131.

Part one

Section	Text and Remarks	Measures
1	"Sweet honey-sucking bees." Imitation on two themes by four separate combinations of two voice-parts.	1-6
2	"Why do you still surfeit on roses, pinks, and violets." Rapid alternation of paired voices in imitative style on a very short motive, followed by a more chordal setting of the latter part of the text.	6-12
3	"As if the choicest nectar lay in them." A shortened repetition of the music of section one.	12-14
4	"Wherewith you store your curious cabinets." Derived musically from the first part of section two, using the short motive.	14-19
5	"Ah make your flight to Melisuaviae's lips." Imitation, but more of rhythm than of pitches.	19-27
6	"There may you revel in ambrosian cheer." Imitation on a brief theme with much overlapping of voices.	27-33
7	"Where smiling roses and sweet lilies sit." Three voices are arranged in the form of a short duet for the upper voices, supported by the lower one. Non-imitative.	33-36
8	Repetition at a different pitch level of the words and music of section six.	36-40
9	Repetition, one octave lower, of the words and music of section seven.	40-45
10	"Keeping their Spring-tide graces all the year." This segment, forming the culmination of Part I of the madrigal is stressed by (1) the quarter-note pause in all the voices which precedes it, (2) its elaborate internal structure based on shifting accents and variation in the grouping of the voices, and (3) its greater length.	45-71

Part two

Section	Text and Remarks	Measures
1	"Yet sweet take heed, all sweets are hard to get." Formal regularity by means of repetition of two short phrases by voice-blocks. Quasi-chordal texture.	1-7
2	"Sting not her soft lips." Contrast of texture by means of suspension dissonances (see p. 119).	7-14
3	"Oh beware of that." Quickening of the pace by alternation of brief phrases.	14-25
4	"For if one flaming dart come from her eye, was never dart so sharp, ah then you die." Formally divisible into three sub-sections (as punctuated in the text), each lightly contrasted with the others but all sung by the upper three voices.	25-38
5	Repetition of the text and music of section four sung by the lower three voices.	38-51
6	Repetition of the text and music of section five sung one octave higher and by still another group of three voices.	51-64
7	Repetition of the words, "was never dart so sharp." The theme previously associated with these words is presented chiefly in inverted form (that is, in a descending rather than ascending order of pitches).	64-70
8	Repetition of the words, "ah then you die." The theme previously associated with these words is broadened and intensified by the use of notes of greater time-value and by the use of all five voices.	70-93

As can be seen from this analysis, there is within each part of the madrigal much repetition, in some passages of both text and music, in others of music only. It will be noted, for example, that over half of the musical material in Part II is derived from the themes of section 4. Such repetition, however, does not result in monotony, for Wilbye rarely restates a musical section mechanically. Rather, he subjects it to modification, sometimes by means of a change in pitch successions (Part II, section 7) or rhythm (Part II, section 8), often by simply shifting from one combination of voices to another. There results a variegated effect quite in keeping with the light and playful sentiment of the text. This sentiment is enhanced by the predominance in the madrigal of the higher-pitched voices. The bass voice is silent much of the time, and during major portions of both Parts I and II only three voices are employed.

The melodic lines of this madrigal are marked by a generous use of that device called sequence. This is the successive repetition in a single voice-part of a motive which appears each time at a different pitch level, usually one scale step higher or lower (Ex. 9; Part I of the madrigal, soprano, mm. 6–8).

Example 9

Although the general texture of *Sweet Honey-Sucking Bees* is polyphonic rather than chordal, there is not much strict imitation (unmodified repetition of the same theme in *all* voice-parts), and a number of passages (for example, mm. 32–35) display no imitation at all. The chief aim of this music is to mirror the carefree mood of the text. Hence the dependence on simple devices such as repetition and sequence, the employment of piquant rhythms with dotted notes and syllabic setting, and the rapid alternation of voice-groups singing brief melodic phrases.

When a smoothly flowing or a melismatic passage occurs it is usually for a special reason, such as word-painting. The madrigalists rarely missed an opportunity to indulge their pleasure in representing the meaning of a word or phrase by a tonal equivalent. In Part I of *Sweet Honey-Sucking Bees* Wilbye paints a charming picture of the darting bees with his melismas on the word "flight." In Part II (mm. 32+) he introduces a musical pun on the word "sharp." It is not by accident that this word is set in nearly all of its statements, to an F sharp or a B natural.[4] Elsewhere Wilbye employs less literal and more subtle means of expression. Especially noteworthy is the irregular rhythm born of the words "keeping their Spring-tide graces" (Part I, mm. 45+). An amusing touch is provided by the change of pace in Part II (m. 20) on the final statement of "oh beware of that." Finally, one must not neglect to point out Wilbye's use of expressive suspension dissonances at the setting of "ah then you die" (Part II, mm. 33+) and the resulting chord progressions, which bring the madrigal to a full resonant close.

Recommended reading:

E. H. Fellowes, "John Wilbye" in *Grove's Dictionary of Music and Musicians,* 3rd ed., New York, Macmillan, 1947, V, 717-718.

E. H. Fellowes, *The English Madrigal,* London, Oxford University Press, 1925, pp. 109-110.

[4] In 16th-century prints of music the sharp sign did duty as a natural also.

JOHN FARMER (ca. 1565–ca. 1605)

Fair Phyllis I Saw Sitting All Alone[1]

OF THE LIFE OF JOHN FARMER little is actually known. He is believed to have been until 1599 an organist at Christ Church Cathedral in Dublin. He published in that year a collection of madrigals and religious music; he is also the author of a treatise on composition. In his collection of 1599 Farmer included a madrigal to the following lyric:

> Fair Phyllis I saw sitting all alone
> Feeding her flock near to the mountain side:
> The shepherds knew not whither she was gone,
> But after her lover Amyntas hied.[2]
> Up and down he wandered whilst she was missing.
> When he found her, oh then they fell akissing.

The lyric is set for soprano, alto, tenor, and bass. While most of Farmer's madrigals are of a contemplative nature, *Fair Phyllis* is in the character of a brief and amusing anecdote. In its combination of love and pastoral setting, it is inspired by an ancient convention of pastoralism in poetry, a convention which employs the imaginative recollection of a Golden Age in a rural Arcadia, peopled by shepherds and their loves, by nymphs and fauns. The convention originated in Classical antiquity in the *Idylls* of Theocritus and the *Eclogues* of Virgil; in Renaissance England it was preserved in such works as Spenser's *Shepherd's Calendar* and Sir Philip Sidney's *Arcadia*. In Farmer's text, love and nature are rendered in such a straight-forward manner that they never blend into a real idyll. Love remains flirtation, and the pastoral costume a mere disguise. A hymnal type of antique poetry has thus received the playful and slightly frivolous interpretation of a leisurely-living society.

Farmer's work is divided, in typical madrigal style, into segments according to the text. Each segment normally contains a new thought or a new image; each is distinguished by a motive of its own and a special kind of elaboration. Most of the segments end with a cadence, a succession of two chords, which, like punctuation in writing, brings the music to a temporary or final stop.[3] While cadences are usually obscured in madrigals by the overlapping of voices, they are clearly audible in Farmer's composition.

The following scheme divides the text according to the musical segmentation, indicating as well how several of these segments combine into larger *sections*.

Sections		Measures
1	Fair Phyllis I saw sitting all alone	1-3
	Feeding her flock near to the mountain side	4-6
2	The shepherds knew not whither she was gone	6-10
	But after her lover	10-13
	But after her lover Amyntas hied	13-16
3	Up and down he wandered	16-21
	Up and down he wandered	21-26
	Whilst she was missing. When he found her,	26-30
	Oh then they fell akissing.	30-40

Section 1: Measures 1-3 ("Fair Phyllis I saw sitting all alone") and measures 4-6 ("Feeding her flock near to the mountain side") complement each other. What holds them together

---
[1] Program B.
[2] Hied = "hastened."
[3] See Chapter VIII, pp. 386-88.

is the soprano melody: it is a solo in one passage (symbolizing fair Phyllis "sitting all alone") and remains the predominating upper voice in the other. In the symmetry of its two strains, both of almost equal length, and in its melodic type, the soprano melody is similar to a jaunty folk-song (Ex. 10). The rhythmic accentuations of measures 4-6 ("Feeding her

Example 10

flock...") are strengthened by a chordal setting. The two phrases form Section 1, which is sung twice.

Section 2 and the first half of *Section 3* (mm. 6-30) contain much imitation. The fast-moving story of the text is thus matched by the rhythmic excitement of the motives' appearance and disappearance.

Measures 6-10 ("The shepherds knew not whither she was gone") has four entries, with the voices entering two by two (Ex. 11).

Example 11

A little motive is imitated in measures 10-13 ("But after her lover") four times in very quick succession (Ex. 12). This is followed by an imitation in pairs of a new motive in measures 13-16 ("But after her lover Amyntas hied," Ex. 13).

Example 12

Example 13

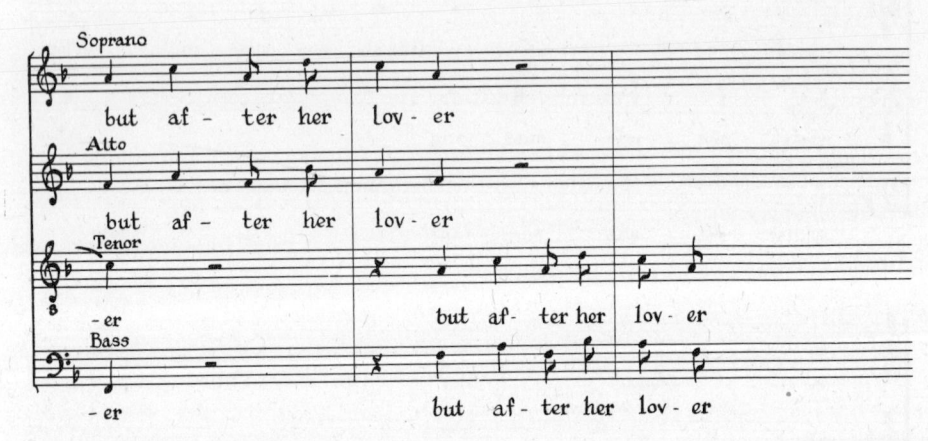

Measures 16-21 and measures 21-26 use the same line of the text: "Up and down he wandered." They are combined by a bass which does not take part in the imitation of the upper voices. Thus the two passages actually belong together. However, they differ in their motives—a device which adds variety to the words they have in common. The image of wandering "up and down" is symbolized here not only by the motives themselves but by their entries at various pitch levels (Ex. 14; the entries of the motives are marked.)

Example 14

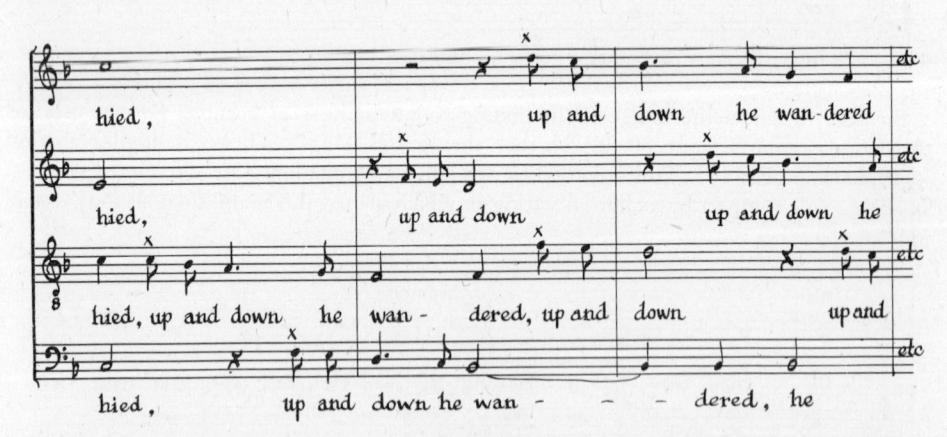

Up to this point Farmer has avoided combining in the same musical segment sentences or parts of sentences which differ in meaning. However, in measures 26-30, in order to isolate and emphasize the conclusion ("Oh then they fell akissing") he joins the *end* of the fifth line of the text ("whilst she was missing") with the *beginning* of the sixth ("When he found her").

The phrase "whilst she was missing. When he found her" is animated by an imitation in pairs, followed by a cadence which combines all four voices. The comparatively long tones of the soprano and bass at the end contrast with the sprightliness of the preceding passage and thus symbolize the conclusion of Amyntas' search (Ex. 15).

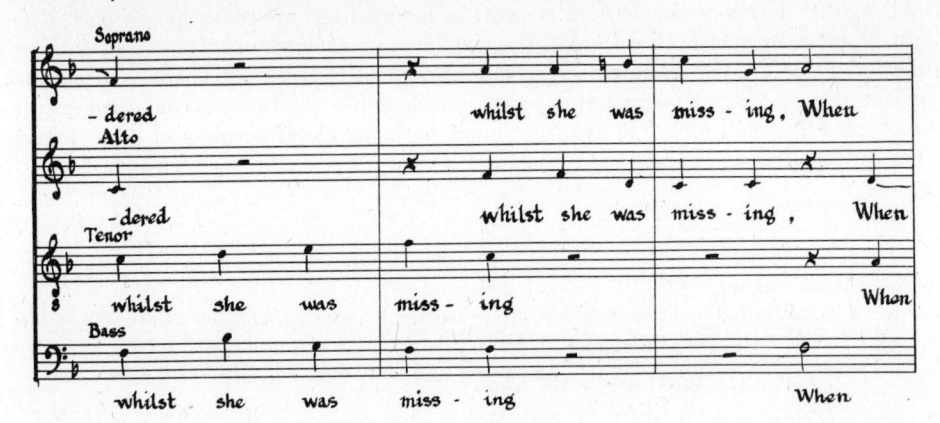

Example 15

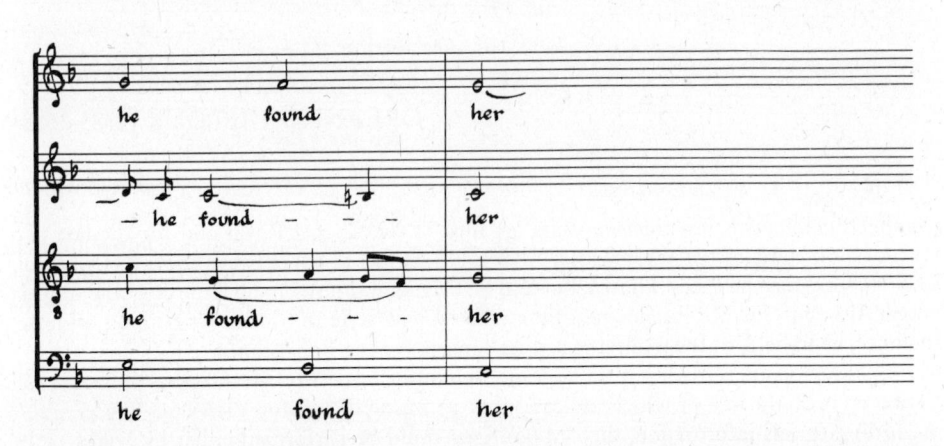

In order to render the image of the kissing couple as lusty as possible, Farmer uses for the end of section 3 (mm. 30-40: "oh then they fell akissing") a heavy dance-like rhythm in triple time (Ex. 16). This is varied by irregular accentuations (see the asterisks in Ex. 16) and made compact by a chordal setting in which at first three, and then all four, voices join.

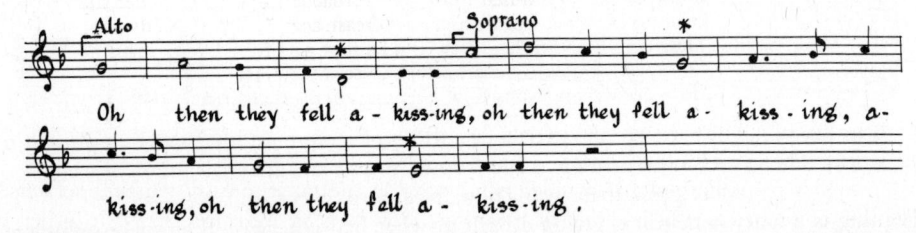

Example 16

The structure of the madrigal is determined by the repetition of some of its sections. Section 1 (mm. 1-3; 4-6) is sung twice, as is section 3 (mm. 26-30; 30-40), although this last repetition is not observed in all renditions. This formal scheme (a repeated opening and ending, enclosing an unrepeated middle section) was derived from a popular type of Italian secular music, the canzonetta. Traces of dance rhythm in Farmer's madrigal may be ascribed to the same influence.

All stylistic devices which Farmer employs in his madrigal are quite appropriate to the light, amorous story of his text. Simplicity, playfulness, and mirth are achieved by thin settings, brief and clearly delimited segmentation, contrast between polyphonic and chordal sections, the symmetry of imitation in pairs, and dance-like rhythm. The motives are curt, sometimes naïve, and even folk-like; the simple harmony consists mainly of a few chords from the tonality of F major.

Recommended reading:
L. McC. L. Dix, revised by E. H. Fellowes, "John Farmer," *Grove's Dictionary of Music and Musicians,* 3rd ed., New York, Macmillan, 1947, II, 201-202.
E. H. Fellowes, *The English Madrigal,* London, Oxford University Press. 1925.

ORLANDO GIBBONS (1583–1625)

The Silver Swan[1]

ORLANDO GIBBONS was for nineteen years organist of the Chapel Royal and for the last two years of his life organist at Westminster Abbey. He composed not only music for the Anglican Church, for which he is best known, but also madrigals and instrumental music of the highest order. Although his life extends to a time when a new style in music was gaining wide acceptance, he upheld, in the main, the artistic concepts of the Renaissance.

The Silver Swan, a madrigal for soprano, two altos, and two basses, opens Gibbons' collection of 1612, the title of which indicates that its music is "apt for Viols and Voyces. . . ."[2] According to this information, the compositions could be performed either by voices or by stringed instruments or by both. This is not surprising, since during the Renaissance the manner of performance was characteristically left to the option of the performer.

Gibbons excelled in setting to music a poetry which combined reflection with a melancholy pensiveness. *The Silver Swan* is an example of this type.

> The silver swan, who living had no note,
> When death approached unlocked her silent throat;
> Leaning her breast against the reedy shore,
> Thus sung her first and last, and sung no more:
> "Farewell, all joys, O death, come close mine eyes;
> More geese than swans now live, more fools than wise."

With exquisite nobility the words describe the death of a swan and her moving farewell to the world. The expression of pathos is interrupted in the last line:

> More geese than swans now live, more fools than wise.

The line is a witty anticlimax, giving a barb to what had otherwise been mere sentiment.

[1] Program B.
[2] Apt="suitable"; viols=a type of stringed instrument played with a bow.

It is the content of such poetry that the madrigal composer undertakes to render musically.

The Silver Swan may be divided into six sections corresponding to the line-divisions of the text. The divisions follow:

Section		Measures
1	The silver swan, who living had no note,	1-4
2	When death approached unlocked her silent throat;	4-7
3	Leaning her breast against the reedy shore,	7-11
4	Thus sung her first and last, and sung no more:	10-14
5	"Farewell all joys, O death come close mine eyes;	14-18
6	More geese than swans now live, more fools than wise."	18-21

The soprano differs from the other voices because of its song-like melodic style and its symmetrical structure (Ex. 17). Its phrases in the several sections, most of which are clearly

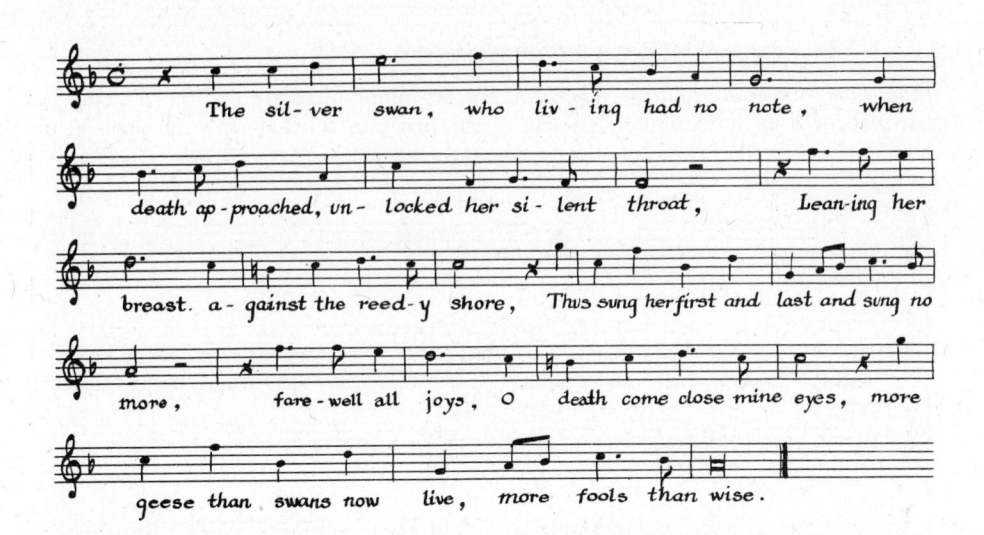

. Example 17

separated from each other by rests, are of almost equal length. The first two phrases complement each other like two parts of a sentence: one ends in suspense, which the other immediately resolves. The fifth and sixth phrases are musically literal repetitions of the third and fourth, both in the soprano and in the total voice-complex.

Because the soprano stands out somewhat from the other voices, the madrigal seems to be similar to a song with chordal accompaniment. However, it will be seen that the chordal character of the music is blended with many polyphonic features. Each voice of the madrigal has been rendered independent in direction and rhythm. In addition to the independence of the voices, which is typical of a polyphonic style, there is a use of imitation.

Imitation occurs mainly where the six sections are joined together; in measures 4, 7-8, 10-11, 14-15, 17-18. It thus serves to break down the regularity of structure imposed upon the composition by the soprano.

Transition from section 1 to section 2: In measure 4 a motive ("When death approached") is developed out of the melodic line of the first bass in measure 3 and appears in quick succession in alto and in first and second bass. It is then taken up, in a modified form, by the soprano at the opening of section 2 (Ex. 18).

Example 18

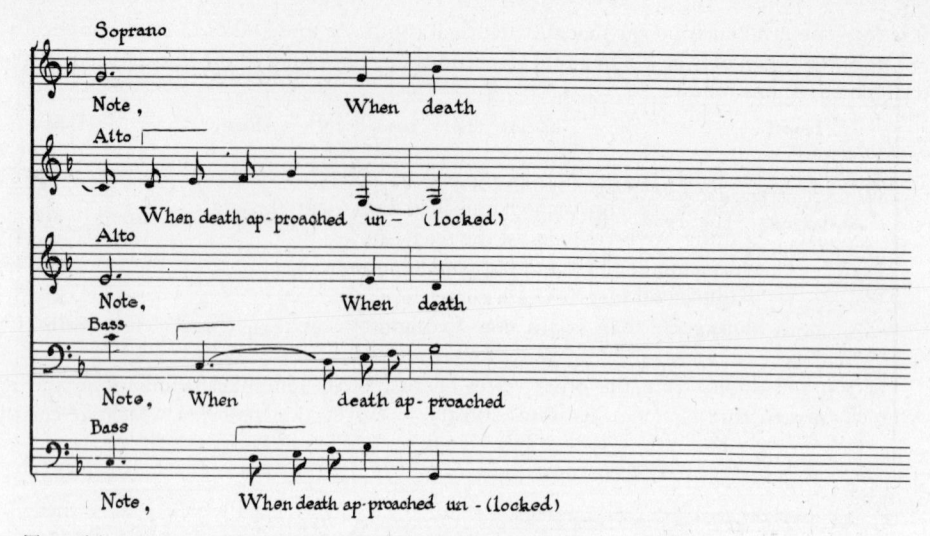

[musical example: Soprano, Alto, Alto, Bass, Bass parts with text "Note, When death ap-proached un-(locked)"]

Transition from section 2 to section 3: At the beginning of measures 7-8 ("Leaning her breast") there is an imitation successively in the first alto coupled with the bass, in the second alto, and finally in section 3 in the soprano (Ex. 19).

Example 19

[musical example: Soprano, Alto, Alto, Bass, Bass parts with text "throat, Leaning her breast against the reedy"]

Transition from section 3 to section 4: This passage is more extended and more elaborate than the previous ones. Through the melodic styles, through dissonance and crowded imitation, it builds up, by degrees, an intensity which finally culminates in the soprano of section 4. The passage opens with a skip in the second bass to the higher octave (m. 9), a melodic interval only sparingly used at this time, and a dissonant chord (m. 10). This is followed by an overlapping imitation of two motives ("Thus sung her first"), the second of which is somewhat varied. One motive (marked *a* in Example 20) appears successively in the first and second bass, while the other (marked *b*), related in direction rather than in intervals to the subsequent phrase of the soprano, turns up successively in the first and second alto (Ex. 20). The intensity generated by all these devices imparts itself to the soprano, which enters in section 4.

Example 20

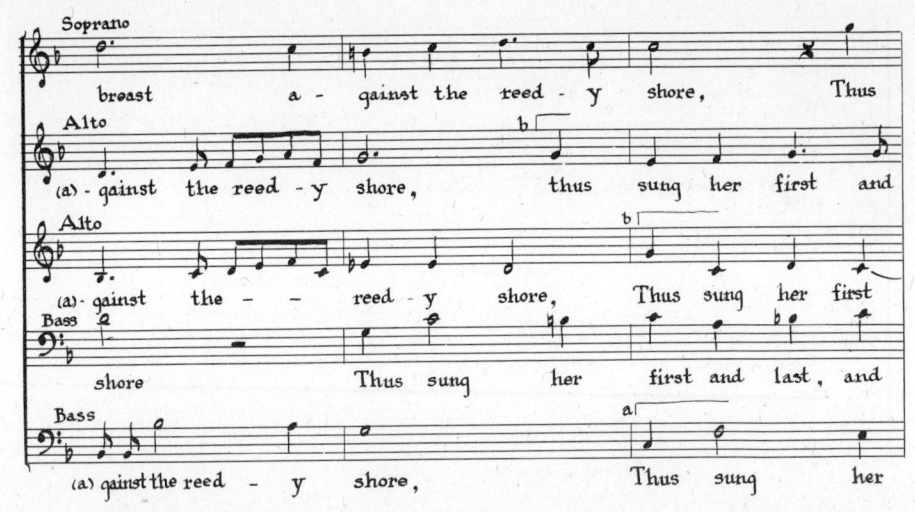

It was mentioned above that sections 5 and 6, involving all voices of the madrigal, repeat literally, though with different words, sections 3 and 4. Although repetitions were not unusual at the time, it was not customary, particularly at the end of compositions, to set the same music to different words. For let us remember that the problem of the composer in setting a text to music is to give a peculiarly musical expression to the substance of the literary work. Normally, a distinction in the intellectual sense of the poem will be matched, as in Farmer's *Fair Phyllis* or Wilbye's *Sweet Honey-sucking Bees,* by an equivalent distinction in the musical sense of the composition. It should therefore be noted that Gibbons' solution is singular: the epigrammatic barb of the last line ("More geese than swans now live, more fools than wise") is projected in deliberate contrast against the melancholy pathos of a musical section which simply repeats the preceding sentiment.

At a first hearing, Gibbons' madrigal might appear quite uncomplicated. It seems to have a merely chordal structure supporting a song-like melody; the harmony, indeed, confines itself to a few triads within F major and to a very small number of dissonances. On further study, however, the simplicity of the madrigal is found to be wholly deceptive, for the music contains a very active polyphonic life to which the harmony adds its own elements of poignancy and, in association with the words, an emotional suggestiveness.

Recommended reading:
E. H. Fellowes, "Orlando Gibbons," *Grove's Dictionary of Music and Musicians,* 3rd ed., New York, Macmillan, 1947, II, 378-381.

IV

THE AGE OF THE BAROQUE

BAROQUE THOUGHT AND EXPRESSION[1]

I. FROM THE CONTRAST of the ancient, medieval, and Renaissance worlds it will have been perceived that a culture is not a natural product, but a human artifact. It is something made, fashioned out of human resource, and as it must be created, so it can be destroyed. Men are not born with it as they are born with the physical attributes of human beings; on the contrary, it is a thing acquired, willed. Men are born into it. It forms the air they breathe in their commerce with each other. No one man has fashioned it, yet each man, as he lives significantly, partakes of it and modifies it. It is the system of thought and expression within which human lives take on meaning, and apart from it they have no distinctively human meaning at all.

In one of its aspects the Renaissance was a wakening of men from dogmatic slumber, a drawing away of a veil which for more than a thousand years had obscured from men's eyes the creative possibilities of human powers and faculties. It was possible to hold the splendid ambition that the world could be mastered by being known. In the intense awareness of new liberty it was believed that man stood, a creature of supple art and infinite ingenuity, in the very morning of the world, reflecting in the fashion of that irregular humorist Pistol,

> Why, then the world's mine oyster
> Which I with sword will open.

In the pride of rebirth even the veneration for the Classical models of the ancient world was abated. The supremacy of the ancients, of Greek science and Roman law, could be disputed even while it was emulated. Francis Bacon sounds the motive (which will be many times repeated) of a long dispute known as the "Quarrel of the Ancients and the Moderns":

Men have been kept back as by a kind of enchantment from progress in the sciences by reverence for antiquity. . . .

As for antiquity, the opinion touching it which men entertain is quite a negligent one, and scarcely consonant with the word itself. For the old age of the world is to be accounted the true antiquity; and this is the attribute of our own times, not of that earlier age of the world in which the ancients lived. . . .

And truly as we look for greater knowledge of human things and a riper judgment in the old man than in the young, because of his experience and of the number and variety of the things which he has seen and heard and thought of; so in like manner from our age, if it but knew its own strength and chose to essay and exert it, much more might fairly be expected than from the ancient times, inasmuch as it is a more advanced age of the world, and stored and stocked with infinite experiments and observations. (*Novum Organum*, lxxxiv)

The critic and biographer Giorgio Vasari, who wrote for Italy the lives of her artists, could reflect that in the art of Michelangelo the moderns had equalled and surpassed the ancients. Vasari's enthusiasm was impermanent. The time would come when men, who knew more of the ancient world than Vasari, would ask why, before a sculpture of Michelangelo (Figs. 39 and 40), it is impossible to know a true Classical serenity or repose, why men should come to reflect upon the human condition as the tortured anguish of *Twilight*

[1] Programs A and B.

or the intellectual immobility of *Dawn?* For in another aspect the Renaissance contained a problem, which only time was needed to expose, "stored and stocked with infinite experiments and observations." The simple fact was that the Middle Ages, which the Renaissance despised, had nurtured a Christianity which the Renaissance could not do without. The Renaissance contained within itself a contradiction. It wished at one and the same time to worship man and God, and bidden to reject its false idol, it was neither equipped nor ready to decide which was false. It wished at one and the same time to exalt the dignity of man, which consisted in intellectual and moral freedom, and to exalt nature, in whose mechanical process, subject to universal law, his freedom appeared only a delusion. It wished by knowledge to make conquest over nature in order that nature might be used for human ends; it was unable to be satisfied with ends which had only the Greek validity of being human. This contradictoriness of Renaissance belief was not experienced by the Renaissance itself. Its separate interests were separately pursued, like the mutually insulated strands of an electric cable which only a rupture will ignite. For the contradictoriness to betray itself, it was necessary that each of the tendencies released by the Renaissance should first be rigorously defined, and this was the task which was undertaken—mainly in the 17th century—by the age known in the history of art as the Baroque.

The term "Baroque" has undergone a variety of usages. Originally, like the term "Gothic," it was employed as an expression of contempt. It referred to the large and exuberant forms of the art of the Catholic Reaction;[2] the term was meant to suggest the license with which the stable and reposeful forms of Classical art had been modified. Its meaning in this restricted sense still frequently occurs, though its derogatory note has been lost. The term has, however, acquired a broader signification, which refers to the entire course of the arts in Europe (including the art of the Catholic Reaction as but one of its phases) from the middle of the 16th century through the first half of the 18th—to the death of Bach in 1750. The dates are too inclusive. When the earliest Baroque tendencies discover themselves in Italy and Spain, the Renaissance in England—Shakespeare's England—had still to be realized. When Bach produced his last Baroque works in Germany, France and England alike were already in the midst of a movement known as Neo-Classicism and the Enlightenment. The Baroque Age is too complex, its distinct voices were too numerous, to provide a perfect consistency for all Europe. Under this extension of the meaning of Baroque, the term includes the broadest variety of tendencies, many of which are in the fiercest opposition to each other. The term "Baroque" must therefore be construed to mean not the least common denominator among these (though one does exist), but in general the cultural predicament of which both these tendencies and their oppositions are part and parcel. In this sense the Baroque refers to the age in which the Renaissance became a philosophical as well as a historical problem. It is the first age which fully deserves the name "modern," since in it the philosophical foundations of the modern natural sciences were formulated, nationalism became both a powerful force and a reflective motive of European society, Protestantism isolated the spiritual destinies of individual men, and the Catholic Church reacted with a Reformation of its own. Yet, even while it is the first, the Baroque is also the last modern age which succeeds in combining the humane learning of the Renaissance, still confident of its own powers, and a scepticism in which, in human affairs, that confidence was eventually to be lost.

II. The ideal of a free science of nature, of science unfettered by dogma, is the product of 17th-century Europe. Historically, it is simply a drawing out of consequences implicit in the Renaissance; it is grounded in the intellectual and moral freedom in which Classical humanism discovered the essential dignity of man. Yet the spirit of free inquiry which regards all truth, humanly arrived at, as partial and open to doubt, is the creation not of the ancient but

[2] See, below, pp. 148–49.

of the modern world. Its special genius consists in the doubt which it turns upon itself and upon its own resources; it makes scepticism the very method of its inquiry.

The philosophy which has governed the development of the modern natural sciences is the work of a 17th-century Frenchman, René Descartes, who perceived that only by imperilling such knowledge as we have can such knowledge as we have be made secure. In his *Meditations* (1640) Descartes chose methodically to suspend judgment over every traditional source of knowledge—over opinion and dogma, over sense-experience and reason—in order that the work of science might be begun from a foundation which it was impossible to doubt. Upon such a foundation, could it be discovered, one might proceed by a series of inferences, each clear and distinct in the light of reason, to resurrect the whole system of science, eliminating from it the parts which have no rightful place in the structure of rational knowledge, which are inconsequent or ungrounded, which only tradition or authority or opinion supplies. Such was the meaning of Descartes' celebrated proposition—*Cogito, ergo sum* (I think, therefore I am). The knowledge of one's own existence is the foundation stone of all knowledge; it is insusceptible to doubt, since in the very act of doubting it one thinks, and the existence which is doubted is reaffirmed. As the ancient philosopher Archimedes boasted that given a point outside the cosmos he could move the world, so Descartes claimed that from the sole certainty of his own existence he could regain it.

In the *Novum Organum* (1620), the most eloquent statement of the program of the new science, Francis Bacon proposed that the whole work of understanding was to be commenced afresh; reason and sense-experience were to be allied in a common pursuit in which each should complement and correct the other, the one supplying method to the putting of questions to nature, the other supplying the channel through which alone nature might give her own answers. Neither reason nor experience, taken separately, is a sufficient resource for true science; only by reasoning from what we have empirically observed of nature can we gain a science of the order which is in nature.

For man is but the servant and interpreter of nature: what he does and what he knows is only what he has observed of nature's order in fact or in thought; beyond this he knows nothing and can do nothing. For the chain of causes cannot by any force be loosed or broken, nor can nature be commanded except by being obeyed. (*The Great Instauration*)

But from this it follows that the truths of science are inescapably tentative; there can exist no truths which may be regarded as final or unalterable. Every truth is as limited and partial as the experience upon which it rests, and as experience is enlarged, so accepted truths must be modified to accommodate it. Every accepted truth is therefore perpetually suspect, naked in its own evidence, systematically and deliberately doubted in order that man might preserve, in the very moment of commanding nature, the measure of his ignorance within her.

III. By an irony of history the spirit of free science arose in the very age in which Europe's cultural divisions became fixed and absolute. For the science of the modern world is, and has ever been, a corporate enterprise, maintained by a community of scholars dedicated in singleness of mind to a common end. Scattered abroad in all places and nations, bound together by no government and indeed by no law except the law of a method commonly adhered to, its members have fashioned, in the very midst of the national differences which have divided Europe into politically opposed and rancorous powers, an ideal commonwealth, a commonwealth which has guaranteed to each individual worker in science's name the fullest exploitation of a free talent. The institution of the sciences has had an uninterrupted history from the latter half of the 16th century to the present day. The pre-eminence of the natural sciences in contemporary culture depends on this single circumstance, that the continuity and consistency of their development has been matched in no other phase of the development of modern Europe and America. In philosophy, in art, in politics, in ethics, in religion—in short in every attempt to understand the nature and purposes of man—the history of modern Europe is a record of corrosive irresolution and of crisis, lighted only now and again, erratically, by a vision of humanity which can at once bind men and preserve them free.

In the 16th and 17th centuries Europe was doubly divided. Both politically and religiously, its camps were drawn. Politically, it was composed of national groups—Spanish, French, Dutch, Flemish, English, German, Italian—each speaking its special idiom of language and aware of its separate identity. Even when, as in the empire of Charles V, its groups were bound together under an absolutist government, the ferment of nationalisms stirred and murmured in perilous constraint, which under a weaker monarch—under Philip II—must loose upon Europe, in Holland, the eruptive vigor of a republican ideal. Elsewhere, in England, in France, in Spain itself, nationality was openly declared. It is in the 17th century that the several national types acquire the distinctive traits whereby men are accustomed to speak of the rational lucidity of the French mind, the sensitivity to experience and precedent of the English, the mystic introversion of the German, and so on. Italy, numbed under Spanish authority, was no longer the center of Western culture. The stage of Western culture was the whole of Europe. It had become complex and many-voiced; it included a whole set of competing currents and counter-currents, variously opposed and combined, no one of which was paramount, each of which was now for the first time authoritative and mature. These collisions of impulse, even though they marked the separations and divisions among the peoples of Europe, had nevertheless a real and positive value. They contained the rich variety of creative energies which the Renaissance had released and which now were come to full growth. The times were suffused with the most abrupt contrasts and oppositions—the rationalism of Descartes, the empiricism of Bacon; the monarchist philosophy of Hobbes, the democratic philosophy of Locke; the religious intensity of El Greco even in a landscape, the sheer vital animal sensuality of Rubens even in a religious piece; the rich organ sonorousness and elevation of Milton, the cleanly wantonness of Herrick; the elegance and sophistication of Couperin, the wit and precision of Scarlatti; Bach's impassioned sense of the personal meaning of the religious mysteries, his stricken consciousness of sin, his exaltation in the promise of redemption, Handel's large assurance, his incomparable "Yes," which admits no doubt as it suffers from none; the detached naturalist vision of Velasquez, which sought without judgment the innocence of a recording eye; the expansive sympathy of Rembrandt, which discovered dignity and eloquence in the simplest human act of simple men and women.

IV. Religiously, Europe was divided between Catholic and Protestant. The separation of powers, political and religious, which in contemporary society divides church from state, was in the 16th century still undefined. Philip II of Spain regarded himself as the temporal executor of a Catholic Europe; Henry VIII, in separating England from the spiritual dominion of the Pope in Rome, sought to make the throne of England serve in the place of the Chair of St. Peter; the Pope himself, even while the Council of Trent defined his absolute authority in spiritual matters, had still to learn that more was to be gained in an absolutist Europe by the arts of diplomacy than by martial arms. The separation of church and state was involved by implication in William of Orange's proclamation to the insurgent Netherlands of a religious toleration which would permit Protestant and Catholic to exist peaceably side by side. But this was as yet the voice of a Europe struggling to be born. For the time, the religious issues which vexed the day everywhere carried with them portentous political consequences. Challenged and shaken, its eminence disputed, its paganism condemned, its authority suspect, its flock deserting, the Catholic Church reacted against the Protestant heresy by seeking to reform itself from within. Against the Reformation it launched the Counter Reformation; against Lutheranism and its spawn of sects it convened a Church Council, the only corporate person whose enactments could bind the Pope, or elevate him. The Council of Trent was terminated, and its articles ratified by Papal Bull, in 1563. Its result was to reassert the absolute authority of the Pope in the Catholic Church and to render permanent and irreconcilable the Church's opposition to the doctrines of Protestant Christianity. The sequel to its decisions in the 16th and 17th centuries is known as the Catholic Reaction or the Counter Reformation.

The two religious groups which carried into execution the policy of a revived and militant Catholicism were the Order of St. Dominic and the Society of Jesus. The Dominican Order was given the task of suppressing heresy in a Europe which Protestantism had split apart; its efficient instruments were the Holy Office of the Inquisition and the Index of Prohibited Books. By the one, heresy was sought out, tried, and condignly punished; by the other, the printed book which disseminated heretical views was eliminated and destroyed under the operation of a system whose rigors reduced Venice, once the book-mart of the world, to a minor stall. The Society of Jesus was founded as the militant arm of the Church by St. Ignatius Loyola. Formed on the plan of a military brotherhood, it exacted of its members, besides the normal vows of chastity and poverty, a vow of obedience, abject and unquestioning, to the directions of the General of the Order, who was himself committed to executing, by whatever means the occasion offered, the purposes of the See of Rome. In the latter half of the 16th century the Jesuit Order was one of the most powerful formative influences in Europe. It took to itself the work of education within the Church and the task of winning back, in a precariously divided Europe, those former faithful who had been spurred by Protestantism to religious doubt and dissidence. By every means of persuasion available to its uses, it poured into the intellectual forms of orthodoxy the insistent immediacy of things sensed. The Christian mysteries were celebrated in churches which for the first time since the Gothic age set all the arts in a single grand orchestration to the greater glory of God (*Ad Maiorem Dei Gloriam,* the motto of the Order). In the eloquent union of architecture, sculpture, and painting every means was employed to quicken the awareness of the great religious facts of Catholic Christianity. The most abstract doctrines of theology received a dramatically sensuous expression. Not the human drama, the announcement of the betrayal of the Son of Man, but the sacrament, the Eucharistic presence, the breaking of bread and the pouring of wine in which Christ's Body and Blood were miraculously renewed, became the represented motive of the Last Supper (Figs. 38 and 53). Who indeed could fail to believe who was permitted to observe, shaped by Bernini's art (Fig. 63), the holy ecstasy of Santa Teresa of Avila, bride of Heaven, in her mystic trance? Who, if he but believed a little, would pause to reflect that her union with Heaven was as sensual as it was mystic, or that the angel which held the arrow above her breast was a pagan hermaphrodite? The union of the intellectual and the emotional aspects of religion, of the abstract and the concrete, of the rational and the sensuous, is the primary quality of Catholic Baroque art. John Donne, the eloquent and learned Dean of St. Paul's, educated once by Jesuits, will bear the indelible imprint even in a Protestant sermon:

A covetous person, who is now truly converted to God, he will exercise a spiritual covetousness still, he will desire to have him all, he will have good security, the seal and assurance of the Holy Ghost; . . . he will gain every way at Gods hand, he will have wages of God, for he will be his servant; he will have a portion from God, for he will be his Son; he will have a reversion, he will be sure that his name is in the book of life; he will have pawns, the seals of the Sacraments, nay, he will have a present possession. . . .

So will a voluptuous man, who is turned to God, find plenty and deliciousness enough in him, to feed his soul, as with marrow, and with fatness, as David expresses it; and so an angry and passionate man, will find zeal enough in the house of God to eat him up. (Sermon No. 21: "Sanctified Passions")

V. Beyond the pale of the Catholic Church, in countries where Protestantism was firmly rooted, the situation of the arts was radically altered. One of the accompaniments of the Protestant revolt in the Netherlands was iconoclasm, the breaking of images which for centuries had adorned the interiors of Catholic churches. In scenes of riotous violence the ancient images of saint and Madonna, the representations of Christ's, Birth and Ministry and Passion, were destroyed, and the churches which held them desecrated. The acts of destruction were short-lived, but profoundly symptomatic. The Protestants professed an inwardness of religious sentiment which had no need of the material accessories of worship.[3] Their churches, originally the open fields outside the town, were plain places of congregation into which one came not to be visually moved, but to hear a man of faith preach and to sing hymns in order that the Lord might be magnified. Protestantism chose to reject the symbol for the idea, the image for the substance, of belief. But in destroying the symbol it destroyed also the means of holding its thought and faith fixed. Some of the intensest religious poetry and music in the world—indeed some of the most profoundly felt religious painting—is the work of Protestant artists. But its tendency is toward lyric utterance; its spirit is intimate, highly personalized, prayerful, as if from the innermost privacies of the individual human soul. The primary effect of Protestantism had been to throw each individual back upon his own inner light; illumination, if it should come at all, must needs come from within. For the time, men—all men—stood near enough to the traditional symbols of the common faith so that the destruction of a Madonna panel, the knocking down of a crucifix, did not yet imperil the community of belief. Milton in the loneliness of his own stature could still write for his world an epic poem on the Fall of Man with a view to justifying the ways of God to men. Rembrandt could forsake the old themes of Catholic art in order to paint the parables of Christ or scenes from the Old Testament without fear that his meaning might escape his spectator. Bach could compose, alongside of his Protestant cantatas, a Mass commissioned by a princely patron who was Catholic. While meanings were so nearly the same, the sameness of the symbol which preserved their identity could have no importance.

Yet, as the bonds which had so long held Western thought in unity were loosened, as feeling was secularized, as the core of a common faith was dissolved and men discovered themselves in a mutual isolation, the loss of a symbol which nothing else supplied was to become a source of incalculable anguish and desolation. This proud reason, the searching beacon of sciences, dignified as *lumen naturale,* the natural light, which only God's grace was needed to kindle into reverence of himself, was even then suspected, if left untouched by grace, to be no guarantee that men should be united in their beliefs and affirmations. For it had still to be discovered that reason was neutral as between good and evil, that, as Blaise Pascal wrote, "the heart has reasons of which reason itself knows nothing," that the neutrality of reason, whatever else it offered, was not sufficient to cause men positively to believe in anything, but only to reject the contradictoriness of beliefs which, for reasons having nothing to do with head or intellect, men choose to entertain at one and the same time. The vanity of reason, its tragic insolence in human life, which disturbed the meditations of Pascal, had not yet discovered that in itself lay one of the possible sources of the human predicament. Donne's "captiv'd reason" was still for most men God's "viceroy" in man, weak because entangled in sense, untrue because misused by passion, obscure because the heart was closed to it by pride. So long as the emancipated reason was believed capable of sustaining those common ideals which constitute the bond of society and man, the common symbols of society were dispensable. So, for the time, spared the consequences and the responsibilities of its new-won freedom, which only time would disclose, modern Europe entered upon its last grand epoch.

---

[3] Calvin wrote: "Men should not paint or carve anything but such as can be seen with the eye; so that God's majesty, which is too exalted for human sight, may not be corrupted by fantasies which have no true agreement therewith."

VI. The intensity of Baroque art is incompatible with the stable Classic forms of the Renaissance. It is nevertheless, in point of craft, an art of rigorous discipline. Its emotional effects are intellectually governed, even as its intellectual meanings are emotionally suffused. Donne writes:

> Then as th' earths inward narrow crooked lanes
> Do purge sea waters fretful salt away,
>   I thought, if I could draw my paines,
> Through rimes vexation, I should them allay.
> Grief brought to numbers cannot be so fierce,
> For, he tames it, that fetters it in verse.

Donne's religious poetry unites the means of a worldling—learned, intricate, profane—with the sincerity of a dedicated spirit. The character of Baroque thought and feeling demands for its expression this conjunction of opposites—a working in terms of contrasts. In a Classical use of metaphor a point of similarity is noted between things otherwise dissimilar, as when the ancient Latin poet Horace compares man, once dead, to ashes and a shade. The initial image gains concreteness and vivid presence by the evocations which are brought to it from an alien domain; but the point of comparison is everywhere positive, as it were a new discovery in which human mortality, ashes wanting warmth, and shadows wanting light are given a parallel exploration. A Baroque use of metaphor has, on the contrary, a premeditated harshness, as in Donne's comparison of his surrendered soul to a woman ravished. It makes a comparison, it deliberately maintains it in a profane and unclaimed territory. The metaphor works by fascination as well as by aptness. The contrariety of the things compared demands to be attended to, so that it becomes a positive element in the comparison, and the image wars upon itself. The vividness of a Baroque metaphor is never explained by the intricate associations which have produced it; its intricacy is felt only because the images associated jar against, as well as complement, each other. The dissonance is preserved and exploited as one of the means of expression.

VII. As in philosophy the doctrines of theology were subordinated to the sciences of nature, so in Baroque art the content of expression was secularized.

The doors of Protestant churches had been closed upon the visual arts. Painter and sculptor, divorced from service to the institution which for more than a thousand years had been the major patron of the arts, were left to discover for themselves a new place in secular society. A Rubens or a Bernini might still sustain the splendid tradition of Catholic religious art, designing altarpiece or cathedral throne for the ancient Church; the Protestant artist was deflected into the busy, teeming currents of the social scene. If Rembrandt paints a religious piece, it is commissioned for the private devotions of a Dutch household; it no longer has the character of a public monument and may therefore become intimate, introspective, personalized, in the manner of a soliloquy.

Yet all artists alike—Protestant and Catholic—will portray, in addition to religious subjects, the secular world about them. The Baroque Age is the age of landscape and portraiture. Holland dedicates a whole generation of genre artists to painting the familiar jostling scene of its everyday life—its low-lying farmlands laced with canals, its pastures and woodlands and the trundling clouds which the wind sweeps over its enclosing seas, its thatched sunlit hamlets, its country feasts and urban demimonde, its fish stalls and butcher shops, its cups and saucers and wine decanters, peeled fruits, its beggars, brawlers, and bibbers, the old men of its ghetto, its burghers and their plump well-laced ladies, its military clubs, and the syndics of its guilds. Every aspect of its life has been portrayed with a gentle and genial sympathy and unerring craft. Rembrandt's series of self-portraits—etched and painted—is one of the richest autobiographies and most merciless psychological studies in the world. A thousand extraordinary personalities come radiantly alive, sensitized by the brush of such artists as El Greco and Velasquez, Hals and Rembrandt, Rubens and Van Dyke. The most disturbing portrait of all is the one which Poussin has left of himself—ravaged with an inner struggle which the structured serenity of his canvases has austerely excluded. These portraits no longer represent, like Renaissance portraits, the discovery of man. Man, in the 17th century, no longer needs discovery. Only his needs remain to be discovered, and the discovery of these will prove the hardest quest of all.

Recommended reading:
J. A. Symonds, *Renaissance in Italy,* New York, Modern Library, 1935.
H. Höffding, *A History of Modern Philosophy,* tr. B. E. Meyer, London, Macmillan, 1924.
H. Wölfflin, *Principles of Art History,* 7th ed., tr. M. D. Hottinger, London, Bell, 1932.
M. F. Bukofzer, *Music in the Baroque Era,* New York, Norton, 1947.

BAROQUE PAINTING AND SCULPTURE

TINTORETTO (1518–1594)[1]

"THE DRAWING of Michelangelo and the color of Titian." This was the motto that Tintoretto is reputed to have written on the wall of his studio. Such a combination was in fact impossible for any artist to attain, but that Tintoretto should have aspired to achieve it is revealing of the new attitude taken by artists in the second half of the 16th century. Their great predecessors of the High Renaissance seemed to have arrived at the ultimate perfection of art, and all that was left was to strive to imitate and combine their various excellences. Such an eclectic attitude betokens a lack of faith in the capacity of the individual to work out his own artistic destiny, a willingness to submit to authority entirely foreign to Renaissance ideology.

Without a doubt many complex factors contributed to this renunciation of the proud, springtime faith of the Renaissance in the omnipotence of the human individual. In ever-increasing measure the Italian peninsula became dominated by the backward, semi-feudal power of Spain. The flowering of intellectual and material commerce was thwarted by the advent of social, political, and economic reaction. And a new spirit of religious orthodoxy came into being, partly as a natural consequence of the pessimism engendered by loss of faith in the human and material world, but also actively fostered by the Catholic Church in its efforts to stunt the menacing spread of the Protestant Reformation. Once again the individual was forced to bow to authority—the authority of the Church, the authority of the court, and, so pervasive had become the habit of submission, even to the authority of the great Renaissance painters, notwithstanding their expression of ideals ill in keeping with the spirit of the new age.

This was the era that gave birth to the complex of artistic styles known as the Baroque. But at first the dissolution of the Renaissance spirit attendant upon the new conditions mentioned above manifested itself in a bewildering variety of ways, frequently dependent upon local artistic traditions and shifting political circumstances in the numerous principalities and city-states into which Italy was at this time divided. These heterogeneous styles which marked the transition between the Renaissance and the Baroque are generally grouped together under the name "Mannerism" (like "Baroque" itself, originally a term of oppro-

[1] Program B.

brium.)² But beyond saying that by and large the art of this period exhibits a feeling of profound nervousness and unrest, and a love of the complex and the irrational, it is hard to define its qualities in any general way. Chaos rather than homogeneity almost inevitably follows the collapse of a dominant cultural ideology. Consequently it is next to impossible to single out any one artist as being characteristic of the period; we are, in fact, confronted with the paradox of an age when individualism was depreciated showing greater stylistic variation than the preceding era during which it was exalted. It is generally agreed, however, that the painter Tintoretto was the greatest Italian artist of this time, the second half of the 16th century, and he as much as anyone foreshadowed the future development of the Baroque.

Jacopo Robusti was born in Venice in 1518. Being the son of a dyer, he received the nickname of Il Tintoretto ("the little dyer"), and it is by this sobriquet that he has survived in history. Practically his whole uneventful life was passed in his native city, where he died in 1594, leaving his workshop and unfinished paintings in the care of his son Domenico. Little more is known of his life than that he lived quietly and in moderate affluence, the head of a devoted family. Unlike Titian, he did not associate with noblemen and men of letters. Of his personal character it can be said that he was unquestionably a devout Catholic. He is reputed to have been unpopular with fellow artists on account of his somewhat unfair practices in the matter of obtaining commissions, but since on many occasions he showed himself willing to work for exceedingly modest remuneration, his dubious business ethics should be attributed to an all-consuming passion for exercising his craft rather than to undue acquisitiveness.

For a very short time he was a pupil of Titian, who is said to have expelled him because he was jealous of the young man's talents. Who his other masters were is not known, and whatever his personal relations with Titian, there can be no doubt that he was deeply influenced by the older man, who since the death of Giorgione had become the presiding power in the molding of Venetian Renaissance style. None of Tintoretto's earliest works evince any significant departure from the general direction of this style, until the year 1548, when he painted a large canvas of the *Miracle of St. Mark*.³ Here for the first time he reveals that stormy dramatic power in the treatment of religious themes that was to be his greatest contribution to the formation of the Baroque. The picture caused a sensation, for nothing like it had been seen before in Venice. Unprecedented forcefulness in the contrast of light and shade produces an effect of dramatic immediacy without parallel in the Renaissance. A continuity of movement seems to catch up all the individual figures with the fervor of its emotional momentum, while the figure of St. Mark, violently foreshortened, swoops down from heaven with an inward rush so compelling that it draws the spectator with it and breaks down the barriers separating him from a direct emotional participation in the action of the drama. The rich color of Titian is retained, and the twisted, foreshortened figures are strongly reminiscent of Michelangelo, especially of such late paintings as the *Last Judgment* and the *Conversion of St. Paul;* but the impetuous breadth of handling and the vehemence of *chiaroscuro,* the staccato pulse of lights and darks over the surface, are to be found in neither of these predecessors.

It is eminently appropriate that Tintoretto's new style should first have manifested itself in the painting of a miracle, for the new spirit of religiosity set a premium on the painting of subjects which emphasized the supernatural or theological aspects of the faith, while discouraging those in which the human interest predominated. Thus if we examine the whole of Tintoretto's vast output we shall find scarcely a single representation of the "Madonna

---

²Mannerist tendencies are already to be found in the later works of many painters of the High Renaissance period, *e.g.,* Michelangelo, Raphael, Pontormo, Correggio.

³More accurately entitled the *Miracle of the Slave;* it was one of several miracles of St. Mark painted by Tintoretto.

and Child" or the "Holy Family," subjects so beloved by the Renaissance masters and so well in conformity with their humanistic leanings.

Unlike Titian, who travelled considerably and did much work for non-Venetian clients, Tintoretto was essentially a local, Venetian phenomenon, and to this day nearly all of his important works are still located in his native city. Again unlike Titian, he was not patronized by princes and nobles, but worked a great deal for the Venetian *scuole*. These *scuole* were associations or confraternities of merchants organized on a religious basis, each being dedicated to a different saint and each specializing in a different kind of charitable work. They were also mutual-aid societies, and had something of the esoteric exclusiveness of freemasonry. Although they had been in existence long before the 16th century, it was during this period that they attained their maximum wealth and power. Probably their growth was due to the increase of religious sentiment. The Venetian Republic had long been a stronghold of secular tendencies, for besides being far more independent of papal authority than the rest of Italy, it had a history of continuous prosperity, based on a far-flung commercial empire, stretching back for hundreds of years. But in the course of the 16th century the material fortunes of Venice declined steadily, so that although the Republic retained its independence, it was not entirely unreceptive to the mood of religious zeal then spreading throughout the Catholic world.

It was for one of the organizations described above, the Scuola di San Rocco, that Tintoretto executed the greatest undertaking of his life. Working intermittently over a period of twenty-four years, from 1564 to 1588, he decorated the walls and ceilings of the three main halls of the Scuola with a long cycle of gigantic paintings representing scenes from the Bible, including both Old and New Testaments. Although essentially mural decorations, these pictures are painted in oil, on canvas, since the fresco technique was not suited to the dampness of the Venetian climate.

As a whole the series may be said to illustrate the gamut of Tintoretto's extraordinary emotional range. Only one example can be examined here, the *Christ before Pilate* (1566) in the hall known as the Sala dell' Albergo (Fig. 52). This is the scene in which Christ is brought to trial before Pilate, the governor of the Holy Land, who yields to the will of the priests in sentencing him to be crucified. Tintoretto shows us the moment, described in the book of Matthew (XXVII, 24), when Pilate hypocritically washes his hands, in token of disclaiming responsibility for the judgment. Christ stands before him draped in a white robe, which, in virtue of its striking silhouette against the sombre tones of the other figures, establishes him as the focal point of the composition. This contrast is enhanced by the diagonal rays of light that filter through the columns behind Pilate's throne and spotlight the figure of Christ. By the use of light in this dramatic fashion Tintoretto originates one of the fundamental pictorial instruments of the Baroque style. Not merely the figure of Christ, but the whole painting, is conceived in terms of a balanced orchestration of lights and darks. Herein lies one of the major stylistic distinctions between Tintoretto and Titian. For in the latter, except in his very late works, color always reigns supreme. But Tintoretto was less concerned with the sensual aspects of his art, and color would have been a poor instrument for conveying his peculiar synthesis of dramatic and spiritual intensity. For this purpose only strong *chiaroscuro* would suffice. Therefore, although his color is rich in the sense that it is broad and painterly, it has not the intensity of saturation to be found in Titian, but is invariably subordinated to a pattern of light values. It is this subordination which gives Tintoretto's color its somewhat monochrome aspect.

The diagonal direction in which the light rays fall provides for the entire composition a dominant accent, re-echoed in the steps of the throne, the perspective of the architecture, and the disposition of the foreground figures. Such a diagonal emphasis is another typically Baroque feature anticipated by Tintoretto. It endues the design with a dynamic quality, a feeling of tension and unrest, markedly at variance with the harmonious feelings imparted by the more symmetrical, more obviously geometric and rational patterns of design favored by the Renaissance masters.

Something of a similar change is to be found if we consider the treatment of space. The space in a Renaissance picture is harmonious and clear. It furnishes a rational and commodious matrix for the disposition of the various figures and objects. But in Tintoretto, although a realistic perspective is used, even emphasized, there seems to be something cramped and troubled, something almost irrational, about the space. One element contributing to this effect is the fact that the vanishing point towards which the lines of the architecture converge in perspective lies *outside* the picture space, not within it, as was usual during the Renaissance. This imparts a shut-in quality to the composition. It rouses feelings of troubled ambiguity, for while we are confronted with a realistic space conforming to the rules of perspective, by the omission of the vanishing point we are at the same time denied the rational justification for the validity of such rules. Again, the free, capacious flow of the space, a normal quality in Renaissance painting, seems inhibited by the crowding of architecture and figures. As our eye attempts to pass obliquely into the depth of the picture on the upper left, its attention is constantly arrested by the groups of figures to the lower right. These figures seem to be arranged in two chains or screens, the first consisting of the Moor on the right and the scribe who crouches at the foot of Pilate's throne, the second of Pilate himself, Christ, and the soldier on the extreme left. The flat, chain-like pattern formed by this grouping is so insistent, and in such extravagant contrast to the deep space on the left, that we are able to perceive neither the one nor the other as a discrete entity. Space and figures, in fact, though preserving their realistic identities, have become interdependent. What in the Renaissance is described as *space* should in Tintoretto more accurately be referred to as *atmosphere*.

If one examines the figures alone a similar interdependence of parts will be discovered. It is not the expression on the face which determines the individual's psychological state, nor is it even the gesture of the hands; it is the position and movement of the entire figure; the awe-struck Moor, the impassioned scribe, the calm Christ, the cruel soldier, and the weak Pilate, who turns away both from Christ and from his hypocritical hand-washing. All expression seems to depend upon movement, to an even greater extent than in Michelangelo,

Fig. 52. Tintoretto, *Christ Before Pilate*, 1566, Scuola di San Rocco, Venice (*Alinari*)

from whom these twisted poses were ultimately derived. For here the movement of each figure is not independent but integrated with the structure of the entire picture.

The figure of Christ merits special attention. The face is almost a blank—nothing about it suggests either the character of the man or the meaning of the picture. If the white-clad figure be considered as a whole, however, certain interesting qualities emerge, such as the extreme elongation of the body and the slightly swaying posture that assumes the form of an S-curve. This form has about it an almost Gothic quality of spiritual attenuation, and since during the early period of the Counter Reformation there existed strong factors encouraging a return to a medieval way of thought, the resemblance is certainly no accident.

But if the figure as a whole expresses the supernal character of Christ, it still tells us nothing of the tragic drama enacted on this occasion. Only in the relations of the figure to the forms of the rest of the painting can its full significance emerge—in its whiteness as against the darker shades of the other figures, in its cool resignation as against their rabid emotions, in its wraith-like fragility against the menacing crowd and the frowning architecture. The columns of the latter reinforce the verticality of the figure of Christ, emphasizing its opposition to the crouching attitudes of the remaining figures, and without the echoing curve of the arch above, Christ's back would not express the tragedy that it does.

In sum, this picture demonstrates that in Tintoretto's world, though individual man retains his dignity, and even assumes the guise of heroism, he no longer commands through the power of his own reason, but must subserve, equally with the rest of nature, designs that transcend his understanding.

One further quality distinguishing both *Christ before Pilate* and all the other paintings in the Scuola di San Rocco must be remarked upon. This is the great breadth and speed with which they are executed. We shall look in vain at the details of these pictures for superbly executed "passages" of painting, such as abound in the works of the Renaissance masters. Everything seems to be roughed in with unprecedented breadth, as though the artist were working at a feverish pace. Many details seem of quite inferior quality, and even those that impress do so by reason of their sheer bravura and vitality.

There are several circumstances to account for this quality. It must be remembered that no previous series of oil paintings by a single artist approaches the magnitude of the Scuola di San Rocco (*Christ before Pilate* measures 18' x 13' and is by no means the largest of the sixty-odd paintings that compose the series). Assistants from the master's workshop unquestionably had a hand in executing many of the canvases. Again, the halls of the Scuola being dimly lit, fastidious execution would have been wasted. And in dealing with subjects that obviously aroused deep personal convictions, it was not in the nature of Tintoretto's genius to halt the rapid flow of his inspiration.

Besides these special reasons, however, it must be remembered that in the period following the Renaissance speed of execution was considered a positive virtue in art, since without it the artist could not obtain the desired effects of grace, boldness, and effortless inspiration. Such ideals were quite different from the quality of "beauty" prized during the Renaissance. For beauty was held to be something that could be produced by carefully adhering to correct rules of harmony and proportion, a quality dependent on the judgment of the mind. But the "grace" beloved by the artists of the later-16th century was something much more irrational, a kind of facile inspiration, a spontaneous elegance; ultimately an indefinable quality dependent on the judgment not of the mind, but of the eye. Hence, whereas the ideals of the Renaissance encouraged slow and methodical execution, those of the later 16th century encouraged speed and facility.

Perhaps the peak of Tintoretto's achievement as a religious painter is to be found not in the Scuola di San Rocco but in the church of San Giorgio Maggiore. Here is his painting of the *Last Supper,* completed in 1594, the year of his death (Fig. 53). It is the last and greatest of his many versions of this subject.

Fig. 53. Tintoretto, *Last Supper*, 1592–1594, San Giorgio Maggiore, Venice (*Alinari*)

The general stylistic qualities of the work are similar to those revealed in *Christ before Pilate* and other of the San Rocco masterpieces. But in the *Last Supper* of San Giorgio these qualities are intensified to a pitch hitherto unattained, in conformity not only with the nature of the subject but also with the heightened religious susceptibilities and conceptual powers of the master's last years. Never before or since has the instrument of *chiaroscuro* been used with more bewitching dramatic effect. Light and shadow have now lost all touch with the laws of nature, for they have become purely agencies of the supernatural, and the pattern formed by their disposition is as miraculous as the spiritual drama they reveal.

To gauge the gap that separates the late Tintoretto from the art of the High Renaissance, one can do no better than compare briefly the *Last Supper* of San Giorgio—"this divine hallucination," as it has aptly been called—with the famous *Last Supper* of Leonardo da Vinci (Fig. 38). The crucial distinction rests in the subject matter itself. Whereas Leonardo shows us the scene of the Lord's Supper at its most pregnant psychological moment—that at which Christ announces his impending betrayal—Tintoretto chooses rather the moment of greatest religious import, that of the actual institution of the Eucharist, when Christ breaks the bread, saying "Take, eat; this is my body." Thus where Leonardo shows us a great human drama, Tintoretto offers instead a great drama of the spirit; and in so doing each respectively typifies the spirit of his age.

All formal differences are related to this essential difference in content. In Leonardo the table is set parallel to the picture plane, with the diners placed behind it, so that it serves both as a stable basis for the composition and as a proscenium, a psychical barrier separating the action of the drama from the world of the spectator. But in Tintoretto the table is set obliquely, imparting a diagonal accent to the whole composition, and irresistibly drawing the spectator into the depths of the picture-space, wherein he can do nothing other than participate *personally* in the solemn miracle unfolded in his presence. This same picture-space in Leonardo seems rational and finite, because it is clearly defined by the perspective of the architecture. There is ample space in the Tintoretto painting also, yet it is anything but rational. There seems, in fact, no end to the murky depths of this thaumaturgic cavern, with its ghostly bevy of angels revealed by the light emanating from Christ. The whole scene writhes and flickers in the thrall of this miraculous effulgence, the heads of the disciples glowing against the dark background like moons basking in the reflected glory of their sun, the lamp in the foreground flaming as though animated by the breath of a great unknown wind. Compared with this turbulence, Leonardo's vision appears sober indeed, for though it contains action and drama a-plenty, the individual movements are balanced to form a static unity, and the drama is enacted under natural and human auspices.

Again, Leonardo's figures behave independently. Each reacts to the situation in accordance with the traits of his individual personality. Their faces and gestures are full of expression. Tintoretto's figures, on the other hand, even including that of Christ himself, are devoid of individual expression. All are caught in the toil of a pervasive religious experience, which robs them both of their emotional autonomy and of the kinetic autonomy in which it would naturally be reflected.

Yet despite this spiritual authority, physical reality asserts itself vehemently in Tintoretto's painting. The room in which the Supper is held, for all the atmospheric vagueness of its space, is conceived unequivocally as the interior of a humble Italian inn. It is far more sharply individuated than the somewhat "abstract" apartment in which Leonardo sets his scene. Moreover, Tintoretto's figures are far from phantoms; on the contrary, they are weighty, even sculptural, in their proud poses. This is especially true of the innkeeper and servant in the foreground, who, together with the cat peering inquisitively into the basket of viands, form one of those elegant chains or screens of figures that Tintoretto sometimes draws across the foregrounds of his pictures. Indeed, in contradistinction to Leonardo, who prunes out all that is irrelevant to the subject matter, Tintoretto places astonishing emphasis on such extraneous appurtenances. The picture abounds in all manner of genre details, like the cat, the servants, the flagons of wine, the fruit, the cutlery, etc., and seemingly the artist takes a positive delight in asserting their corporeal reality.

It is not hard to see how Tintoretto came by this preoccupation. Behind 16th-century Venice stood a commercial tradition of over 500 years, in the course of which had been molded a practical, materialist mentality that no papal vicissitude or religious revival could wholly wipe out. Hence one cannot look for asceticism in Tintoretto, who for all his spiritual fervor is still a Venetian, and therefore one to whom no reality can be meaningful when divorced from artifacts—the stuff and essence of Venetian life.

The *Last Supper* of San Giorgio may best be described as a unity of opposites, as a dynamic interplay between the natural and the supernatural. Perhaps only by being placed in tense opposition to the sensual world could the realm of the spirit have been evoked with such dramatic cogency.

In addition to his output as a religious artist, Tintoretto painted a large number of portraits and mythological subjects. A few words should be said concerning the latter, since they display qualities at variance with the treatment of similar themes during the High Renaissance. We may take as an example the beautiful *Bacchus and Ariadne* (Fig. 54), one of the series of four mythological paintings executed in 1577 for the Ducal Palace. Ariadne, abandoned on the island of Naxos by her former lover, is rescued by the wine-god Bacchus, who emerges from the sea and offers her a ring in token of betrothal. Overhead hovers the goddess Venus, who completes the union while investing Ariadne with a crown of stars.

So languidly buoyant, so instinct with lyrical grace are these massive figures that they appear to float rather than move. Especially is this true of the remarkably foreshortened figure of Venus, who glides through the air as though it were some dense submarine domain. The entire figure composition seems to rotate majestically like a great wheel, of which the axis is formed by the hands meeting in the centre of the painting, and the spokes by the delicately curving bodies and limbs, their silhouettes tracing an exquisite filigree against the distant background of sea and sky.

BAROQUE PAINTING AND SCULPTURE

Obviously this arabesque is reminiscent of the "chains" of figures already noted in connection with Tintoretto's religious works. There is, however, this difference, that here the chain of nudes does not merely serve as a screen for a composition in space; it constitutes the entire figure composition. The design of the picture is restricted to a surface pattern, and notwithstanding Venus' foreshortening and Bacchus' forward movement, there is little sense of depth. The background is essentially a backdrop, a kind of remote dream world that, though harmonizing with the emotional atmosphere of the action, bears no tangible relation to it. The figure-pattern seems to fill the entire area of the painting, thereby enduing it with a pronounced decorative quality seldom to be found in the art of the High Renaissance.

To appreciate fully these and other qualities in the *Bacchus and Ariadne* one must remember that it was commissioned by the state, which was an important patron of the arts in Venice. The type of art favored by the state reflected the characteristic Venetian love of pageantry, in itself a reflection of a long tradition of internal peace and material prosperity. But the state was also aware of the necessity for preserving the political solidarity upon which depended the retention of such prosperity. For this reason painting was often employed as an instrument of political propaganda. This was the case with the series of mythological paintings to which the *Bacchus and Ariadne* belongs. Together they constitute an allegory of the wisdom and glory of the Venetian Republic. In the present instance Ariadne denotes Venice, while Bacchus symbolizes the sea from which he emerges. Just as Ariadne is crowned by divinity in virtue of her marriage to Bacchus, so Venice is favored by the gods in virtue of her union with the sea, whence derives the trade that is the source of her commercial wealth.

Allegories of this sort could not possibly inspire a man like Tintoretto in the same way as religious subjects. In the latter he gives vent to all the fire of personal conviction, and paints in a very fury of creativity. The *Bacchus and Ariadne* is executed far more meticulously. One senses that the artist is here, so to speak, on his best behavior, realising that he now acts in an official capacity, and thereby invites comparison with his great contemporary, Veronese, the undisputed master of Venetian pageant-painting. Hence it is hardly surprising that no

Fig. 54. Tintoretto, *Bacchus and Ariadne*, 1577, Ducal Palace, Venice (*Alinari*)

Baroque *chiaroscuro,* no dramatic diagonal vistas, are to be found in this picture, whose flat, decorative composition and silvery tones induce something of the same calm resplendence to be found in the official art of Veronese.

This formal, allegorical treatment of mythology illustrates well the changed attitude towards Classicism typical of the early Counter Reformation period. If the reformers could have had their way, every vestige of Classicism would have been eliminated from an art solely devoted to the Christian religion. But this was not possible, since Classicism by now was too deeply bedded in the Italian consciousness to be eradicated. Mythological art was therefore permitted in order to slake Romantic feelings about the antique, and indeed, mythology in itself was harmless enough to the Church, *provided it was divested of its essentially humanist content.* That such is partly the case in this picture may be appreciated by comparing it with the mythological works of Titian, for instance with the older master's version of the same subject in the National Gallery at London. Titian's *Bacchus and Ariadne* is no decorative allegory; it is the full-blooded evocation of a way of life and thought, conveyed with all the creative abandon, the power and the conviction, that in Tintoretto we find only in religious works. What Titian *experiences* in Classical humanism, Tintoretto can only observe from afar.

Yet observe it he does, and in this respect he is poles removed from the numerous painters elsewhere in Italy who at this time were engaged in weaving twisted Michelangelesque nudes into sterile allegories. The *Bacchus and Ariadne* has about it a certain warm, nostalgic poetry, a kind of gentle and melancholy Romanticism, not to be found elsewhere at this time. Especially may this be observed in the face and figure of Bacchus. Even the political meaning of the work is conveyed in terms of human feelings rather than of materialistic symbols.

Such qualities would indicate that the spirit of the Renaissance lingered on in Venice long after it had departed from the rest of Italy. For though Venice in the 16th century was impoverished and humiliated, it was never dominated by Spain or by the Church as was the rest of the peninsula. Thus many Renaissance traits survive, though in a more sober, reflective guise. Despite its ingenious decorativeness, despite the ambiguity of its space, the presence of these qualities lifts *Bacchus and Ariadne* above the servile coldness and neurotic mannerism of court art as practiced in other parts of Italy during the later-16th century.

It will be realised from the foregoing account that the art of Tintoretto is of a complex nature. Sententious apophthegms by which it may fairly be summarized do not readily present themselves. On the one hand, it is affected by a sensualism and a survival of Renaissance humanism, both peculiar to Venice; on the other, by the artist's profound religious sentiments and his predilection for an irrational, decorative grace, both typical of the new age of the Counter Reformation. Out of the perpetual conflict between these disparate elements are born many of the stylistic qualities associated with the Baroque.

But Tintoretto is not a fully Baroque painter, because in him the sensual and the spiritual are never completely fused. They are always separate entities, sometimes existing peacefully side by side, but frequently at odds with each other. On such occasions his art rises to the level of heroic drama, its religious values of greater compulsion than those of the Baroque proper because it is by strife, and not by compromise or rhetoric, that they assert themselves.

Recommended reading:
Hans Tietze, *Tintoretto,* London, Phaidon Press, 1948.
E. M. Phillipps, *Tintoretto,* London, Methuen, 1911.

EL GRECO (1541-1614)[1]

IF TINTORETTO, who spent his whole life in Venice, can be considered an insular personality who nevertheless encompassed many diverse trends in his art, El Greco, a generation younger, shows exactly the reverse characteristics. Though cosmopolitan in training and experience, his art reflects but one dominant trend. It is the narrowest, the purest, and the most intense artistic expression of the Counter Reformation to be found in the second half of the 16th century. The stronghold of this movement was in Spain, most powerful of Catholic countries and home of the greatest instruments of Catholic propaganda—the Inquisition, the Jesuit Order, and the great mystical saints, Teresa of Avila and John of the Cross. Thus towards Spain El Greco inevitably gravitated, Greek though he was by birth and Italian by training, and through his art he conveyed the spirit of his adopted land more perfectly than any of his contemporaries.

El Greco's real name was Domenikos Theotokopoulos, "El Greco," meaning "The Greek," being the name by which he came to be known in Spain. He was born at or near Candia, on the island of Crete, in or about the year 1541. At this time Crete was a dependency of Venice, and it was to Venice that El Greco came as a young man in order to further his artistic studies, which had probably already commenced either on his native island or on the Greek mainland. While in Venice he is reported to have been a disciple of Titian, but the evidence of his early work would make it appear more likely that he actually studied with Tintoretto or a member of the Bassano family. At all events, in 1570 he left Venice and came to Rome, where he was befriended by the miniature painter Giulio Clovio. Here he encountered the work of Michelangelo, which, though he professed to dislike it, must have made an impression upon him. There is interesting evidence that at this time El Greco's sympathy with Tridentine ideals, the ideals of the Council of Trent, was already pronounced, for when Pope Pius V ordered draperies to be painted over some of the nude figures in Michelangelo's *Last Judgment* El Greco volunteered to replace it with an entirely new fresco, more "modest and decent, and no less well painted than the other."

Exactly when, or under what circumstances, El Greco left Rome and travelled to Spain, we do not know. All that can be said with certainty is that by the year 1577 he had arrived and established himself in the city of Toledo. The most vigorous ecclesiastical center in Spain, perhaps in all Europe, Toledo was at this time a veritable seed-bed of monasticism and fanatical religiosity, more fervently Catholic than Rome itself. Here El Greco found his true spiritual home, and here he continued to live until his death in 1614.

Except for involvement in a few lawsuits connected with his work, his life in Toledo was passed fairly uneventfully. Throughout this long period he seems to have lived with a woman named Jeronima de las Cuebas, though it is not known whether they were ever married. Their son, Jorge Manuel Theotocopuli, was born in 1578. He too became a painter, assisting in his father's workshop, as was customary during the 16th century.

An inventory of his effects, compiled at the time of his death, sheds considerable light on El Greco's manner of living. The books then in his possession indicate wide literary interests, Classical as well as Christian. As regards material circumstances, he appears to have subsisted in a typically Spanish fashion; a kind of genteel poverty coated with a veneer of extravagant luxury. Such a life accurately reflected the condition of the country as a whole, for Spain's superstructure of glory and gold was by then beginning to totter on its crumbling economic foundations.

[1] Program A.

El Greco's early works, containing little more than a compound of sundry elements picked up in Venice and Rome, reveal only slight hints of the striking originality characteristic of his mature art. Not until after his arrival at Toledo did the essential qualities of his style begin to emerge. To the decade following this event belong the three most celebrated of his religious masterpieces: the *Espolio* (Despoiling of Christ, 1579) in Toledo Cathedral, the *Martyrdom of St. Maurice* (ca. 1581) in the Escorial, and the *Burial of Count Orgaz* (1586).

It is generally agreed that the last-named work is El Greco's greatest (Fig. 55). It still stands in the church of Santo Tomé at Toledo, for which it was originally painted. The subject derives from a legend concerning the Count of Orgaz, a 15th-century nobleman of unusual piety who especially reverenced Saints Augustine and Stephen and who bequeathed an annuity to the church of Santo Tomé, where he was buried. At the time of his interment the two favorite saints miraculously descended from heaven and took over the task of lowering the dead Count into his grave, thereby honoring him in reward for the good works he had performed during his lifetime. This is the scene disclosed in El Greco's picture. The Count's body rests in the arms of the two saints, who are flanked by priests and monks. Behind appears a crowd of noblemen, friends of the dead man. The officiating priest, standing on the right with his back to the spectator, looks up toward heaven, where he sees a vision of Christ presiding over a great multitude of saints and cherubim. An angel, who forms a connecting link between the lower and upper parts of the composition, flies swiftly upwards, bearing the soul of the Count—a muffled shape of somewhat embryonic aspect—on whose behalf John the Baptist intercedes with the Lord. The figure of the Virgin Mary on the left balances that of St. John the Baptist.

Few subjects could be better adapted than a miracle story of this kind to expressing the purest ideals of the Counter Reformation. Count Orgaz is the perfect exemplar of the all-important moral—that those who stay faithful to the Church (and, incidentally, resist the Protestant heresy) will receive their due rewards in heaven. Never, perhaps, have these rewards been more vividly dramatized than by the hand of El Greco in this painting.

Possibly "dramatized" is not the most accurate description. Certainly there is about this picture little of the specifically dramatic quality that we find in Tintoretto. The latter, irrational though he frequently is, conceives his scenes objectively, in terms of the dramatic interplay between natural and supernatural forces. But in looking at the *Burial of Count Orgaz* one cannot help feeling that El Greco's vision is essentially subjective; that just as only the priest in the painting can see the heavenly host above, so only could El Greco himself undergo the particular religious experience embodied in the complete image. Being an intuitive personal experience, it is therefore mystical, and hence similar in character to those of the great 16th-century saints who spearheaded the Counter Reformation. There is no real drama here, because there is no conflict between the natural and the supernatural. El Greco simply eliminates the natural and gives free play to his imagination of the supernatural. In pictorial terms, the latter can only be conceived in the language of nature, but El Greco so transforms and distorts this language that its supernatural significance emerges unmistakably.

Speaking more technically, therefore, one may say that as a painter El Greco is *expressionistic* rather than dramatic, and it is now possible to examine briefly the formidable technical apparatus whereby he transforms the world of nature into a world of the mind. The *Burial of Count Orgaz* is above all else a dazzling pattern of lights and darks. It is not a dramatic pattern, associated with the identity and nature of the objects whose forms it defines, such as is still the case in the art of Tintoretto. Rather is it practically independent of the subject matter in regard to the emotional effect which it produces. As in all abstract designs, it is the quality of the design which conditions its emotional impact, and the *Burial of Count Orgaz* owes much of its effectiveness to the exact emotional equivalence of the *chiaroscuro* pattern, considered as a separate entity, to the religious meaning or content of the work.

Fig. 55. El Greco, *Burial of Count Orgaz*, 1586, Santo Tomé, Toledo (*Anderson*)

The only respect, perhaps, in which this remarkable light-pattern appears directly relevant to the content is the way in which it forces our gaze upward, ultimately focalizing our attention on what is by far the brightest object of all, the figure of Christ at the top of the picture. The stooping forms of the saints, the figure of the angel, and the great cloud formations that meet at an angle near the center, all constitute arrowheads of light leading to the resplendent Christ. Aside from this, the *chiaroscuro* achieves its results through the extraordinary complexity of its pattern in conjunction with the sharpness of its modulations. The light itself seems drawn out into long, tenuous strands; now soft and wavy, as in the clouds, now sharp and zigzag, as in the figure of the Baptist. These various qualities combine to produce a singularly unearthly effect, flickering in its rhythms and charged with an almost galvanic vibrancy. In some places, as on the diaphanous robe of the priest, the configurations of light seem so arbitrary that one experiences the same sensation of eeriness as when looking at the negative of a photograph, and for the same reason. Of the two elements whose opposition constitutes *chiaroscuro,* light always predominates, never shadow, as is sometimes the case with other great masters of the art, like Tintoretto, Caravaggio, and Rembrandt. For shadow is essentially an instrument for the portrayal of drama and can play only a negative role in the conveying of a mystical vision.

Partly as a result of these qualities of lighting, the individual figures are weird, almost ghostly in aspect. The handling is broad and painterly—a legacy of Venetian training—but tends to be lighter and smoother than that of the great Venetians, with none of their rich feeling for substance. This monotonous uniformity of texture further contributes to the dehumanized effect. Color is brilliant but strangely unrealistic, the selection of hues seemingly determined by emotional rather than rational considerations. The figures tend to be elongated—sometimes, as in the case of John the Baptist, to the point of emaciation. Their ascetic appearance is enhanced by expressions of swooning ecstasy on their faces, the eyes bulging from cavernous sockets. The tapering hands twitch with nervously exaggerated gestures.

Most of these expressionistic devices, it will be noted, are more prominent in the upper half of the painting than in the lower, and in this way El Greco effects a distinction between the kingdoms of heaven and earth. But the difference is one of degree only.

In Tintoretto's religious pictures the element of space had already assumed a somewhat irrational character. El Greco, however, goes further, and in the *Burial of Count Orgaz* would seem intent upon an almost complete devaluation of the space factor. We feel that there is no real background in this painting. The entire complex figure composition presses forward towards the front plane of the picture, even bursting beyond it in the figure of the Baptist. Once again, the irrational quality is more marked in the upper half of the picture, where the separate figures (or groups of figures in the case of the saintly host) appear to exist in private spaces of their own, between which can be detected no appreciable continuity. In the terrestrial half of the work there is a more rational extension, but one's efforts to grasp at a sense of depth are entirely frustrated by the impenetrable wall of faces, almost menacing in their monomaniacal devoutness, belonging to the aristocratic mourners. The dramatic diagonal vistas of Tintoretto are wholly lacking, for the spectator is not given the option of participating in the world of the picture. On the contrary, it is as though this world were striving to burst forth from its bounds in order to invade that of the spectator. Certainly the crowding of these flickering forms produces sensations of tension of a nature analogous to claustrophobia.

It has often been supposed, with a good deal of reason, that the religious fervor and expressionistic distortions of nature to be found in El Greco may owe something to his origin in a Byzantine culture. There is indeed a kind of quasi-Oriental austerity in his work that can be accounted for only by his known contact with Orthodox as well as Catholic civilization. The elongation of the figures, for instance, was a Byzantine as well as a Gothic device for enhancing their spiritual aspect. Specific resemblances in design and iconography have been detected between certain of El Greco's paintings, including the *Burial of Count Orgaz,* and the famous Byzantine wall paintings in the monasteries of Mount Athos.

Notwithstanding such resemblances, the spirit of El Greco's art is far closer to the land of his adoption than to that of his birth. Essentially it is an ecstatic personal mysticism, reflecting the conscious and determined struggle of the Catholic Church to tighten its spiritual discipline in order to withstand the double threat of Reformation and Renaissance. It is not the spirit of unquestioned authority, of universal hieratic symbolism, that informs the

BAROQUE PAINTING AND SCULPTURE

art of the Byzantine world. And it must be remembered that most of the expressionist elements in El Greco's style were anticipated by one or other of the early Mannerist painters in Italy, such as Pontormo, Parmigianino, and Beccafumi. We have already seen how a gothicizing elongation occasionally intrudes even in the relatively humanistic art of Tintoretto. Consequently it is unjustifiable to assume that his Byzantine heritage did any more than strengthen El Greco's disposition to employ such distortions in expressing the Tridentine spirit of the West during his own age.

Once El Greco had created the basic elements of his personal style, which had already matured by 1586, the date of *Count Orgaz*, they remained with him for the rest of his life. His later works manifest no significant change of manner. They do, however, evince a progressive exaggeration of those qualities already noted. The practice of elongating figures becomes habitual, and is pushed to such extremes as to banish all vestiges of naturalism. The sense of movement increases, though it is still movement largely confined to planes parallel and close to the picture surface. Flickering patterns of light and dark become ever more nervous and agitated, facial expressions ever more ecstatic. Some of these late works are extremely impressive, like the *Descent of the Holy Ghost* in the Prado, Madrid, and the *Assumption of the Virgin* in the Museo de San Vincente, Toledo, both dating from the period 1604-1614. But, generally speaking, what in the earlier paintings was convincing in its intensity often descends to little more than a formula in the later; the exaggeration of style tends to become a mannerism.

That El Greco's art was motivated by a quite unusual singleness of purpose is attested by the fact that many of the stylistic traits of his religious paintings are discoverable in only lesser degree in his portraits, of which there remain a considerable number. Among the finest of these is the portrait of *Cardinal Fernando Niño de Guevara*, painted about 1600, in the Metropolitan Museum, New York (Fig. 56). El Greco shows us the Cardinal seated, in a three-quarter position; a pose which obviously derives from a longstanding Italian tradition in the portraiture of ecclesiastical dignitaries. Raphael's famous portrait of *Pope Julius II* may well have served as the model. But there is no further resemblance between the benign humanist Pope and the austere Cardinal of a later day, unless indeed it be the fact that El Greco has succeeded almost as well as Raphael in exposing the essence of his sitter's character. To an astonishing degree he has succeeded in bringing out the expressive qualities of Guevara's face, in making us aware of mingled strength and sensitivity, of high intellectual refinement, perhaps even of an underlying relentless zeal befitting, prophetically, the office of Grand Inquisitor, which he later assumed.

If El Greco's treatment of the face, and of the nervous, tapering hands, shows insight into his sitter's private personality, his handling of the work as a whole is equally appropriate to the Cardinal's cultural significance. Most of the general properties of style observed in the *Burial of Count Orgaz* are here also, insomuch as they could be adapted to portraiture. The figure is noticeably elongated, and seems pressed into the foreground, as if the room had not space enough to contain it. Much of this effect is contributed by the oblique setting of the floor tiles, the boundary lines of which converge to the left, at a point beyond the picture. Since the lines of the chair, reinforced by the Cardinal's forearms, converge on a second vanishing point lying far to the right of the picture, the Cardinal himself seems to be pushed forward in virtue of being situated at the confluence of the two dominant sets of parallel lines in perspective. The very large areas of color into which the painting is divided impart a flatness to the design, yet because some of these areas—the brown screen on the right and the white surplice of the Cardinal—are divided into elaborate reticulated patterns, there is equally present a quality of nervous excitement. The whole color scheme is dominated by the rose madder of the Cardinal's robe, another factor which tends to crowd his figure into the foreground. The psychological effect of this color is interesting. It is far removed from the

THE AGE OF THE BAROQUE

Fig. 56. El Greco, *Cardinal Guevara, ca.* 1600, Metropolitan Museum of Art, New York (courtesy of the Metropolitan Museum of Art)

warm, friendly shades of red that would have been preferred during the Renaissance. Instead, its cold brilliance has a biting, acidulous effect, in perfect consonance with the mood of the subject and all that he represents.

El Greco's ability to transmit this intense if monotonous mood extended even to the painting of landscape. The *View of Toledo* in the Metropolitan Museum (Fig. 57), painted about 1600, has been called, erroneously, the first pure landscape in the history of European painting, but it is a sufficiently remarkable work even without the distinction of originality. One may wonder, knowing the character of El Greco's art, how he could show an interest in nature for its own sake, and the answer is that he does not. This is a picture of Toledo. Therefore it is not really a *landscape* at all in the ordinary sense, but essentially a *religious* picture, like everything else the artist painted during his maturity. The city is seen from across the river Tagus, a grim fortress of the Church perched on a rock. Moonlight flickers through the shifting clouds above, providing a typical pattern of *chiaroscuro*. But the stark deadness of the landscape itself, and the frigid glints of light on the buildings, suggest rather a scene of pitch blackness suddenly illuminated by a flash of lightning. Certainly no other familiar phenomenon could parallel a vision of nature so alien to normal human experience and at the same time charged with so electrical a mood.

BAROQUE PAINTING AND SCULPTURE

We have seen that in the complex art of Tintoretto there appeared some of the qualities that have come to be known as Baroque. El Greco shows us others—in the ecstatic quality of his religious emotionalism and in his complete fusion of the separate components of a picture into one indivisible whole, one pattern, one mood, one movement. On the other hand, he no more than Tintoretto can be considered a fully Baroque artist, for he is lacking in precisely those qualities which Tintoretto applied to the creation of a militantly religious art—the human, the sensual, and the dramatic. In the Venetian we find the sensual and the spiritual in conflict, in the Spaniard a mystic expression of the pure spirit. Only in the full Baroque, above all in the person of Rubens, do we find a harmonious union of the two.

Essentially, the differences between El Greco and Rubens correspond to those which divided the Council of Trent and the Counter Reformation in general. While El Greco can to some extent be identified with the attitude of the Dominicans, with those who looked back toward the Middle Ages and sought to encourage rigid dogma and ascetic spirituality, Rubens, with his fleshy females in ecstasy, represented the new ideas of the Jesuits, who strove to make religion more palatable by utilizing human weaknesses instead of merely castigating them. Inevitably the Jesuits triumphed, as the art of Rubens has triumphed in popularity over that of El Greco[2]—that is, until the present century, during which a new trend toward dehumanization has invaded the arts, making possible a new appreciation of the power and originality of El Greco's painting, if not of the ardor which underlaid it.

Fig. 57. El Greco, *View of Toledo,* ca. 1600, Metropolitan Museum of Art, New York (courtesy of the Metropolitan Museum of Art)

Recommended reading:
Frank Rutter, *El Greco,* New York, Weyhe, 1930.
Ludwig Goldscheider, *El Greco,* London, Phaidon, 1938.

---

[2] Federigo Barocci (1526-1612), who worked for Pope Pius IV, the supporter of the Jesuits, anticipated the future direction of Catholic Baroque painting more clearly than either Tintoretto or El Greco.

PETER PAUL RUBENS (1577–1640)[1]

SPONTANEOUS, EMOTIONAL, full of the vigor of life itself, the art of Peter Paul Rubens overwhelms the senses by its sheer vitality. Possessing an amazing vigor of conception and execution—over a thousand paintings are from his hand—Rubens established the dominant direction of 17th-century Flemish painting.

Rubens transplanted from Italy to the North the tradition of monumental figure painting, enriching that tradition by a productive and inventive genius. The human figure predominates in the work of Rubens. A large, heroic, monumental type is created, whose gestures and movements are used for the rendering of both Christian and pagan subjects. These forms express the nature of a man who delighted in extolling as a positive and simple force the principle of life itself.

Rubens' paintings appeared at a time when the southern Netherlands were undergoing a period of revived religious activity. Under the leadership of the Jesuit Order churches were being built and decorated throughout Flanders. As a result the country experienced the rise of an extremely active group of painters at a time when commercial prosperity was on the decline. The culture in which Rubens developed was Roman Catholic, courtly, and learned. His training fitted him perfectly for the prominent position within it which he created for himself.

Born in Siegen, Westphalia, in 1577, Peter Paul Rubens was the son of a Flemish jurist who had fled the excesses of the Counter Reformation in Antwerp. The family lived in Cologne until 1589 and then returned to Antwerp, where Rubens spent two years in a private school learning Latin and Greek. Rubens passed several years as a page at the court of Princess Margaret de Ligne; he left court life to enter in succession the studios of several minor masters, terminating his apprenticeship under a Roman-trained painter and humanist, Otto van Veen. Rubens stayed with van Veen until 1600, when he departed for Italy to begin his "wander years." He visited Venice, Florence, Rome, and finally Mantua, where he was employed as court painter to the Duke. In 1603 he was sent as artist-envoy to Spain, where, besides delivering some prize horses and pictures, he made the acquaintance of the court officials who later figured among his patrons. In Italy again, he probably spent most of his time in Rome in the circle of humanist scholars, of which his brother Philip was a member, and in a careful study of the great paintings and Classical remains of Italy. These years enabled Rubens to assimilate the monumental tradition of Italian figure painting and to develop a concept of the antique based on detailed archaeological studies. His return to Antwerp was occasioned in 1608 by the illness of his mother. Appointed court painter to the Archduke Albert in the following year, Rubens began to create the works which were soon to establish his position as an artist of major stature. To satisfy the great demand for his works, Rubens gradually built up a large workshop which employed many specialists in a system of mass production. Painter-specialists executed the parts in many paintings—hands, heads, animals, still life, or landscape—while Rubens himself set the general design and corrected the final version with his own sure touch.

The art of Ruben's early period is characterized by a strong plastic style with great violence and extreme contrasts in movement, both in the figures and in the use of light and dark. The early style is somewhat hardened by the comparatively sharp delineation of the edges. An example of this more sculpturesque style is the *Descent from the Cross* (Fig. 58), a work painted for the cathedral at Antwerp and still hanging in the transept. This work was ex-

[1] Program B.

Fig. 58. Rubens, *Descent from the Cross,* 1611–1614, Cathedral, Antwerp (*Braun & Cie,* Paris–New York)

ecuted between the years 1611 and 1614. The composition is one of extreme complexity. Upon a violent centripetal movement are superimposed diagonals which meet in the figure of Christ. A spatial spiral which starts in the lower left-hand corner dominates the formal organization, a spiral echoed in the figures at the lower right. Despite these dominant movements, the composition is somewhat lacking in clarity.

Rubens' beautiful, heroically proportioned forms are represented in the prime of physical vigor. Such idealization recalls the work of Michelangelo. However, these forms move in a manner never found in the work of the Italian master; stronger *contrapposto* and an emotional gesturing break with the concept of the closed outline and the self-contained figure characteristic of the Renaissance. Rubens' figures are caught up in a mass movement and surrender part of their independence to further the total message. This message is reinforced by the strong use of light and dark; the main light is concentrated upon the beautiful body of Christ. By an emphasis upon those elements of the body which evoke an emotional and sensuous response—gesturing arms, elegantly poised hands, large liquid eyes, and full lips —the heroic nude of Michelangelo's art appears in new guise. Bound together in a sensuous medium of color and light, Rubens' figures are caught up in a turbulent, continuously evolving centripetal mass. As they reach out to span the space which separates them from each other, these forms become parts of a strong rhythm which overwhelms the vigor of their individual existence. The man on the left arm of the cross, who reaches downward with a gesture terminating in a rather elegantly poised hand, and the grimacing man on the right, who holds the winding sheet in his teeth, show this characteristic emphasis. Yet instead of achieving existence as additive elements, elements which though part of a larger whole still have an existence of their own, they subject themselves to the dominating flow of movement which grows in intensity like the swift flow of a river fed by many tributaries.

In its highly sensuous color, in its concentration upon emotive elements, in its movement both of design and light, this early work of Rubens presents the basic characteristics of his style and outlook. The sensuousness of the surfaces and the variety of the textures, which appeal to the emotions rather than to the intellect, produce here, as in the sculpture of Bernini, an art universally acceptable and understandable.

Rubens' fame grew rapidly, resulting in the reception of large commissions for decorative paintings, one of which was given to him in 1622 by Marie de Médicis. This commission called for the decoration of the ceilings of the Palais de Luxembourg in Paris, for which he executed twenty large paintings, assisted by his pupils. In these works Rubens succeeded in giving grandeur and impressive dignity to events from the life of the queen, events which in actuality were either sordid or humdrum. The banker's daughter whom Henri IV had married for her money appears in scenes from her life which interweave, in masterful fashion, allegory, delightful fantasy, and the reality of actual persons and events. Typical of the series is the canvas of *Henri IV Presented with the Portrait of Marie de Médicis* (Fig. 59). Henri

Fig. 59. Rubens, *Henri IV Presented with the Portrait of Marie de Médici,* 1622–1625, Louvre. Paris (*Alinari*)

BAROQUE PAINTING AND SCULPTURE   171

IV dressed in gleaming armor strides forward to gaze at the portrait of the future queen, which is held by two flying figures. The Classical figure of Minerva, the goddess of the arts of war and peace, looks over the shoulder of the resplendent king, as Jupiter and Juno, king and queen of the gods, also the gods of marriage, seated on a low cloud, overlook the scene. Their attributes fill the surrounding space—the eagle of Jupiter, the peacocks of Juno. Below, two charming cupids play with the war gear of the entranced king. A distant landscape adds to the sumptuous character of the whole. Both the surface and spatial designs are based on a spiral that begins in the lower left-hand corner of the canvas and leads the eye up and around

Fig. 60. Rubens, *Judgment of Paris*, 1638–1639, Prado, Madrid (*Anderson*)

to terminate in the portrait of the queen, who looks directly at the spectator. The portrait by its contrast with the allegorical setting creates a tension between the world of reality and fantasy. Portrait, landscape, allegory, actuality—all are combined into a coherent whole by Ruben's mastery and genius of invention. What a shame that the subject of the series was not equal to the master! The gestures are less violent, the movements softer and more graceful, the forms more elegant, yet less posed, than in his early works; the light is softer and less forced, the glance a more significant and thereby a more unifying element, and the ideal forms more exuberant. The rhythm of the composition catches all up in its supple flow without the violent tangential movements of the earlier paintings.

This softer, more supple rhythm of composition develops further in the late works of the master. In the *Judgment of Paris* (Fig. 60), painted in the last years of the artist's life (between 1638 and 1639), the forms are woven into a rhythm that turns the figures into a garland of beautiful female forms as Paris debates whether to award the prize for the greatest beauty to Juno, Venus, or Minerva. The work is subtly unified through the movements of the bodies and the psychological effect of the glance of the actors. Pulsations of physical movement carry the eye from one figure to the next in long, sweeping rhythms which impart the feeling of an inner radiance and life. Arranged in a semicircle, the open end toward the spectator, the group is closed at each end, by Paris and Mercury at the left, Juno and her peacock at the right. The direction of the glance creates a spatial center around which the figures are arranged. The shallow space with its lighter figures at the right is balanced by the darker figures of the two men and the movement into a spacious landscape. There is a commentary on feminine vanity in the reactions of the goddesses to the temptation of the golden apple held out by Mercury.

Rubens' late style presents the characteristics which have been noted in his early works, now achieved with a greater subtlety and profundity, and, if that were possible, a greater feeling for the qualities of life itself. The change that has come about in his color is as significant as the softening in the forms; the earlier almost strident colors are replaced by soft, pearly, iridescent pinks and carnations in the flesh tones. A luminous atmosphere envelops the ideal and luxuriant nudes which people his canvases.

The emphasis upon the sensuous appeal of forms and colors, the dramatic movements of those forms in the revelation of a heightened emotionalism, the subordination of naturalistic elements to a grandiose pictorial scheme—these are the Baroque characteristics of the art of Rubens. His unique quality is the vital and positive feeling of life which he reveals in his canvases.

Recommended reading:
Rubens, Phaidon ed., New York, Oxford University Press, 1939.
Jakob Burckhardt, *Rubens,* Vienna, Phaidon, 1938.
Jan-Albert Goris and Julius Held, *Rubens in America,* New York, Pantheon, 1947.

GIAN LORENZO BERNINI (1598–1680)[1]

A MAJOR CHARACTERISTIC of Baroque art, epitomized in works executed for the Jesuit Order, is the fusion of the arts. Architecture, sculpture, painting, and drama merge to produce a concerted whole which disregards the previously established boundaries of the separate arts. Gian Lorenzo Bernini, sculptor and architect, perfects this new concept in his treatment of stone and bronze. "I have been reproached," Bernini once said, "with what is my best quality. I render marble as supple as wax, and I have united in my works the resources of painting and sculpture." Here in sum is Bernini's attitude toward his medium, his basic concept of organization, and a suggestion of the form his work will take.

The great tradition of Florentine sculpture of the Renaissance had fallen into decay: even Michelangelo, except for the two late Pietàs, had abandoned the medium after 1534. Bernini frees it from the morass into which it had fallen, and revives it to make it one of the most significant manifestations of Italian Baroque art. Bernini's work presents an epilogue to certain tendencies, the prologue to which is seen in Michelangelo's tense, twisting, turning figures in the Medici Chapel in Florence. Previously stagnant, mannered, without self-assurance, through the work of Bernini the art of sculpture joins with architecture and painting to present the ideals of an age unified by the Church Militant in its outlook and approach to life. The Roman Catholic Church, shaken to its foundations by the Protestant Reformation, had re-established its position through the great proselytizing efforts of the Counter Reformation.

Bernini both acts in the currents of his time and is acted upon by them. Partaking of the new spirit of confidence and self-assurance that was to be found in a rejuvenated Rome, he transforms the concept of naturalism in the art of sculpture. This new naturalism depends upon stronger contrasts of light and dark, achieved by a more forceful modeling of the material; it depends upon more vigorous movements in the figure, upon a greater freedom in in their organization, and a new sensuality of surface.

[1]Program A.

BAROQUE PAINTING AND SCULPTURE

At the age of twenty-two Bernini reveals himself in full command of his medium in the group of *Apollo and Daphne* (Fig. 61). Exuberant forms, full, fleshy, and exciting in their movement, present a striking contrast to the somewhat gloomy, always tense figures of Michelangelo. The composition takes the shape of a loosely knit spiral. Space flows between the delicately poised figures to give the sense of a moment seized in time. Surfaces gleam and flow as the eye travels over the figures. The feeling of surface is paramount in the work of this sculptor, and no element in the whole acts against this concentration upon the subtle changes and transitions in the direction of the surface planes. This flow of surface lends conviction to the transformation of Daphne into a laurel tree, a transformation which has already begun as we can see in the arms, hair, and lower portions of the body of the fleeing girl.

Bernini's work recalls Greek art in its capacity to suggest motion by the selection of a single moment in the midst of strong action. This suggestion of motion, the spiral movement, and the flow of light over the smooth surfaces create a painterly illusion of reality which subtly contrasts with the actual immobility of the marble figures. Urged by the flow of light and form, we identify ourselves with the suggestion of continuous action, even though we are visually aware of only a single moment. In the identification of the viewer with the thing seen is found a dominant characteristic of Italian Baroque art. This same identification

Fig. 61. Bernini, *Apollo and Daphne*, 1620, Galleria Borghese, Rome (*Alinari*)

Fig. 62. Bernini, *Cardinal Scipione Borghese*, 1632, Galleria Borghese, Rome (*Alinari*)

is part of the proselytizing efforts of the Counter Reformation, in which the observer was encouraged to feel a union with the mystic rites celebrated before him, through the elaboration and emphasis upon the attendant pageantry. This emphasis in the religious life exerted such a pervasive influence that it became a part of the Italian Baroque attitude and makes itself known even here in a non-religious representation.

The new naturalism is also evident in Bernini's portrait sculpture. The bust of *Cardinal Scipione Borghese* of 1632 (Fig. 62) again bears witness to the sculptor's ability to vitalize the surface. Poised and confident, the Cardinal with his biretta slightly cocked, gives evidence of the stability which the church and its adherents had again come to feel as a result of the propagandizing movements of the Counter Reformation. Bernini has achieved a highly mobile and fluid expression of an inner vitality by contrasts within the face. The rather full cheeks, the smooth planes of the forehead and cap contrast with the sharper modeling of eyes, nose, mouth, and beard. Though agitated in detail, the robe is dominated by the large movement of the main folds.

In 1647 Bernini executed for a Venetian family an altarpiece in the church of Santa Maria della Vittoria in Rome. This altarpiece (Fig. 63), the most famous of Bernini's works in sculpture, fills a shallow chapel, the pseudo-transept to the left of the high altar. The work represents the *Ecstasy of Santa Teresa,* a nun and mystic of Avila whose heart in a vision was pierced by the arrow of Divine Love brought to her by an angel. This subject has been intentionally treated by Bernini as though the drama were acted upon a stage before the spectator. On either side of this chapel are representations in low relief of the donors, the Cornaro family. These show the members of the family in stage boxes as they engage in conversation or turn to the stage as though present at an actual performance. This character of theatricality is further borne out by the architectural forms themselves. Welling out between the columns placed at either side, the forms assume a curve suitable for a stage proscenium. The profuse decoration of the architecture and the lavish use of richly veined marbles all contribute to the luxuriance and sensuousness of the spectacle.

No less theatrical are the protagonists themselves. Unaware of the world, overcome by the rapture of her vision, Santa Teresa lies on a cloud, half reclining, half erect. One arm and one foot without conscious volition hang limply, emerging as pathetic notes from the overwhelming mass of heavy, agitated drapery which envelops the saint. With head thrown back, eyes closed, mouth half open and nostrils expanded, the saint experiences in the most physical of terms the full rapture of the moment.

In dynamic contrast to the utterly relaxed figure of Santa

Fig. 63. Bernini, *Ecstasy of Santa Teresa,* 1647, Santa Maria della Vittoria, Rome (*Alinari*)

Teresa is the poised angelic figure bearing the arrow of Divine Love with which seemingly the heart of the saint has already been pierced. The angel forms a contrast to the diagonal movement in the figure of the saint. The flamelike character of the angel's garment contrasts with the heavy drapery of the saint; the smile of the angel with the enraptured face of the recipient; a supple flow in the locks of hair on the head of the angel with the saint's heavy hood; and the nude upper body of the angel with the heavily robed figure opposite. Nor do the contrasts end here. Low relief modeling in the angel's dress counters the extreme depth of the folds which catch light and form deep shadows in the drapery of the saint. A unification of movement is given by a common direction in the folds of the angel's garment, again a foil to the movements and countermovements found in the robe of Santa Teresa.

These dynamic contrasts create a feeling of tremendous vitality and continuous movement in the two figures, a feeling enhanced by the gilt stucco rays behind the group and by the light which is concentrated upon it through the yellow, glass-covered skylight in the vault above.

Art and nature, imagination and reality, are here fused into one. Naturalistic to the point of bringing actual light into the design, emphatic in its emotionalism to a highly physical degree, conceived and executed as a theatrical performance, engulfing the spectator in the violence and power of its presentation, Bernini's *Ecstasy of Santa Teresa* distils the very essence of Italian Baroque Art.

Recommended reading:
T. H. Fokker, *Roman Baroque Art,* 2 vols., London, Oxford University Press, 1938. Vol. I contains text, Vol. II plates.

NICOLAS POUSSIN (1594–1665)[1]

FRANCE, in the persons of Nicolas Poussin and Claude Lorrain, made a major contribution to the rich painting of the 17th century. Though these men spent almost their whole lives in Rome, they none the less must be considered French rather than Italian. Poussin, the greater of the two, has often been called the father of French painting.

Poussin's painting may, at first acquaintance, seem to be almost wholly unrewarding. No major painting is so devoid of originality, novelty or "picturesqueness" as his. His subjects are stereotypes, themes as old as the Old Testament, the ancient Greek myths, and the Christian legend. Not once is his work enlivened by spontaneous flashes of recognition, those rich observations of life that give so much verve and pungency to men like Rembrandt or Bruegel. In fact, it is a little surprising to observe that Poussin's life-span almost exactly parallels Rembrandt's, so far apart are they in their artistic point of view. But if the qualities so richly abounding in men like Rembrandt are not to be found in Poussin's work, it would be less than reasonable to assume that the latter is deficient in powers of observation and execution—in short that he does not come up to the mark. The artistic points of view of each must be taken into account, not the assumption of *better* and *worse* which usually springs to mind when two artists are compared. Our taste—of liking one thing more or less than another—is a very unreliable guide. If we were to depend upon it wholly, we would

[1]Program B.

never have any new experience—never learn of the large world beyond our necessarily limited horizon.

The point of view, the assumptions underlying Rembrandt's painting, are well revealed in his *The Return of the Prodigal Son* (Fig. 68). Here he treats of a subject inherently rich in dramatic overtones of feeling: the humiliation of the son, the tumultuous love of the father. These are the psychological components which the artist accepts as the essential subject-matter of his painting. The feelings of the principal characters extend to, or are reflected by, the companions of the old man, and even the light and color of the stage exemplify, in their tension, the brooding somberness of the occasion. We as viewers of the painting are likely to be stirred by an expression of deep feeling as we encounter a dramatization of sentiment parallel to some extraordinary experience of our own. For we too know what it is like to be flooded with conflicting emotions that render us mute. We scarcely need to know the familiar Biblical legend to take in fully the import of the painting.

Now, if we examine another Biblical subject as seen through the eyes of Poussin, very fundamental differences in point of view will be apparent. In the *Meeting of Eleazar and Rebecca* (Fig. 64) the artist takes the story of how Eleazar, the servant of Jacob, journeys to

Fig. 64. Poussin, *Meeting of Eleazar and Rebecca*, ca. 1648, Louvre, Paris (*Alinari*)

Rebecca's land to see if she is an appropriate woman for marriage with his master. Poussin gives the minimum of clues to his narrative and one would find it difficult to know what was happening without previous knowledge of the legend. No one would guess, for instance, that the Bible story has for its characters primitive migratory people living in tents in the desert. What we see is something very different: stately draped women in a green Italian landscape with fountains and palaces. Furthermore there is scarcely a hint of the psychological give-and-take necessarily involved when a man makes discreet observations of this nature, or when a stranger is subject to the glances of curious or hostile peasant women. From Rembrandt's point of view everything is wrong in the picture. But Poussin's point of view is as old as art itself; it is a view which belongs to the ancient Greeks and to the Renaissance masters. It was to the Graeco-Roman and Renaissance principle that Poussin swore allegiance. He adopted the Classical view early in life when he made elaborate studies of Raphael's designs. Throughout his life he read the Greek writers, though he could not have known very much about Greek painting or sculpture except as their forms filtered through the ancient Roman and Renaissance masters.

This view is sometimes called *Classic* as opposed to *Realistic* or *Romantic*. It is based securely enough upon the idea that a work of art should embody truth rather than likeness to nature. By "truth" is meant the universal qualities as opposed to the actual characteristic ones. The Greek sculptor, in making a portrait of Pericles, aimed at presenting the moral and spiritual qualities of the statesman instead of the individual line of his subject's nose, the slant of his eye, etc. The result was a highly generalized portrait in which abstract qualities of formal order prevail. So, when Poussin relates the legend of Eleazar and Rebecca, he is motivated by a theory that specifically excluded any diverting play-acting in his characters and all "local color" that he might have observed from the people he saw every day. What he aimed at was a plausible, lucid, and dignified action befitting one of the grand legends of antiquity. It is not surprising, then, to find Poussin's characters, like those in a Greek tragedy, bland and statuesque. As persons they were no more individualized than their Classically draped ideal bodies. All the figures assume attitudes like Greek sculptures: in fact, many of his figures are borrowed ones—some from Roman painting or statues, some from Raphael or even Titian. He is careful to eliminate from his work any fragment that might in itself be provocative or stimulating to a vagrant imagination, lest the grand harmony of his conception suffer some inadvertent disruption. Many observers have felt, and still do, that this austerity of Poussin's is authentic enough, but that it results in aridity and a kind of bleak perfection. This is true enough when one is looking only for the qualities which Poussin has seemed to exclude. But with more patience and perception one will find in the dense amber of his Classic style the richest treasures. His flowing design and subtle color afford an unrivalled delight to the eye, as apparently static figures converge and dissolve in the space patterns of his composition. Behind the placid features of his actors lurk subtle clues to basic human impulses of love or cruelty or courage. In his broad and generalized statement of things and persons may be read more than what is explicitly stated. It is like a grand mansion constructed according to the most humane and generous plans opening to view undreamed-of perspectives of the spirit. Through this capacity to envisage a world real but unseen, Classic art exerts its hold upon the imagination, sustaining the impulses of infinitely varied epochs and personalities.

The *Eleazar and Rebecca* is a good many things. Not least, it is a decorative pattern of color and movement, like a dance opulent and splendid in its variety. Just as we accept the artificialities and the conventions of a ballet, so we may those of this painting: indeed it is most like a grave and stately dance. But it is a dance weighted with the dignity of its Biblical theme, enriched with the thought of love, the radiance of flowers, and the splendor of the landscape. If the women carry urns for water, it is not only to conform to the legend of Rebecca at the well, but to introduce pleasing variations of shapes echoing the curves of the women's thighs and arms. As the many-shaped water jars are spaced at intervals, so reds and blues in their variations appear and reappear at intervals like a statement in music of a theme followed by its variations. The palaces in the distance divide and balance the spaces and give accent to the groups of women in the foreground. In this closely knit, harmoniously balanced composition may be found the wholeness, harmony, and radiance which St. Thomas gave as the requisites of art.

Schooled in the exacting tradition of Classic art, Poussin gave to his forms greater solidity than either Velasquez or Rembrandt. He retained in his work much of the stable structure associated with Renaissance figure painting. A consummate master of composition, he brings his figures into harmony with the landscape, to which he imparts the same structural lucidity. Upon the chaotic disorder of the landscape, he imposes a grand harmonic order best seen in his celebrated *St. Matthew and the Angel* (Fig. 65). While suggesting vast spaces, he holds every form in severest obedience to a great architectural plan in which pyramidal shapes emerge, interlocking with others to form a logical organic whole. The gross design may be indicated by drawing lines diagonally from the opposite angles of the picture to form a large cross. It will be observed that this simple plan approximates the general scheme of the painting. Everything is related to it: the banking of the trees right and left, the position of the saint and the angel who themselves make a small pyramid, the ruined building on the horizon line effecting a pyramid with its organic relation to others. While the principle of structure here as in his other works is derived from Classic sources, the effect is wholly Baroque. No Renaissance painter, and certainly no ancient artist, ever achieved anything like the landscapes of Poussin. The atmosphere becomes tangible like a thin liquid, making dense and palpable the stable forms about which it flows. The 17th century brought with it the greatest of landscape painters, and none surpasses Poussin.

Like Velasquez and Rembrandt, he was a luminist, for whom light had its own unique values. Only an original painting or one of the best collotype reproductions will reveal his steady light, which gives a jewel-like luster to all it touches. Notable in this respect is the *Triumph of Galatea* (Fig. 66), a painting inspired by Raphael's fresco of the same subject, which Poussin saw while living in Rome. A comparison of the two works will reveal Poussin's debt to the earlier master and also indicate how thoroughly Baroque is his style despite his Classical inclinations. Against a seascape a splendid array of mythological inhabitants of the deep advance to the shore amid trumpet sounds and a cascade of flowers. Seldom in painting has the female nude been presented with such exquisite beauty, richness, and warmth. Poussin here has drawn much from the art of Titian, adapting the Venetian's color to his own purpose.

Like all prolific painters, he varies much in the quality of his work; but more notable is the great range of expression which he attains despite the severity of his Classic style. With

Fig. 65. Poussin, *St. Matthew and the Angel,* ca. 1645–1650, Kaiser-Friedrich Museum, Berlin (*Braun & Cie.* Paris–New York)

Fig. 66. Poussin, *Triumph of Galatea, ca.* 1640, Philadelphia Museum of Art (by permission)

a style which excludes illustrational elements and Romantic dramatization—in short, a highly abstract manner—he nevertheless imparts to his work enormous depth of feeling suggestive of other Baroque masters of mood like Donne and Milton. His characteristic poetical feeling emerges in all of his great works. The thought of death touches the shepherds who pause before a lonely monument with the inscription: *Et in Arcadia Ego* ("I too dwelled once in Arcady"). Here Poussin introduces the same disturbing poignancy found in Donne's lines: "Therefore never send to inquire for whom the bell tolls. It tolls for thee." Or in his *Deluge* one finds an almost unbearable statement of desolation, of waste and anguish. These tragic comments on man's mortality must be balanced against the many hymns to physical and spiritual ecstasy such as the *Holy Family, The Kingdom of Flora,* and the *Eleazar and Rebecca.* Without once touching directly upon the specifically concrete, Poussin by indirection brings us face to face with the realities of our inner lives. Perhaps better than any painter of his time he realized that man grasps the great truths of life through the instrument of parable and symbol. He realized that nature was the raw material of the artist, who must transpose it, refine it, endow it with the life that form, and only form, could give. If he was a formalist, it was not because of a pedantic love for neatness and precision, but because he knew that only through a relentless self-discipline expressed in compression, in unity, and in intensity (all form-given qualities) could the artist break down the barriers of chaos and confusion.

The success of his method is proved by the enormous authority his work has exerted for three hundred years. Not only were men like David, Ingres, Corot, and Cézanne profoundly guided by his art, but also the men of our time, the abstractionists, are finding in it abundant clues in their struggle to penetrate the world of appearances.

Recommended reading:
Roger Fry, *Characteristics of French Art,* New York, Macmillan, 1939, pp. 21–41.
Esther Sutro, *Nicolas Poussin,* London, Medici Soc., 1923.
André Gide, *Poussin,* Au Divan, n.p., n.d.

REMBRANDT VAN RIJN (1606–1669)[1]

LIKE THE RENAISSANCE PERIOD, the Baroque age witnessed a vast outpouring of art of all kinds, and in painting there emerged masters who in scope and power are the equals of the Renaissance giants. It is notable that the great painters of the 17th century are non-Italians: men from France, Holland, Spain, or Flanders. These men—Rubens, Poussin, Rembrandt, Velasquez, and El Greco—developed their art with an intimate knowledge of the great works of their Renaissance predecessors. The older masters were held in the highest esteem, though the style of the early 16th century had long since been dissipated. To enlarge their vision, these Northern Baroque artists either journeyed to Italy the better to study the works of Renaissance masters or, like Rembrandt, bought their works for their private collections.

Yet, despite this admiration for the painting of the Renaissance, the Baroque artists formulated styles in sharp contrast to it. Rembrandt, perhaps the most profound exponent of the Baroque style, was least inclined to imitate the older masters, but at the same time he was the most assiduous in taking from them whatever might enrich his own work.

As a Dutchman and a Protestant his feelings were less inclined to flow in the channels prescribed by tradition, especially since Dutch Protestantism had no use for churchly decoration. But the absence of ecclesiastical patronage did not prevent him from creating what is perhaps the richest body of religious art ever created by a single master. Though his patrons were the well-to-do merchants and officials of busy Amsterdam, interested in seeing themselves dramatized in grandiose portraits, he nevertheless found the opportunity to paint and etch the great Biblical legends. In content, spirit, and style they declare the new point of view of the artist and his age over that of his Renaissance forebears.

The difference may be seen when Rembrandt's *Carpenter's Family* (Fig. 67) is placed beside Raphael's *Alba Madonna*. The Renaissance work will, by contrast, emerge with renewed majesty and severe beauty, but at the same time it will be noted that, with Rembrandt, painting has found a new objective and a new content. The majesty of Raphael's Madonna is transformed in Rembrandt's treatment. For him warmth and tenderness pervade a drama of homely intimacy. A Dutch mother with her tiny child sits musing before an open fire on the pavement at dusk, while the foster father, the carpenter Joseph, works at his calling. The figures are small and are enveloped in the pulsating light and space of the portico. Perhaps it is this expression of the creeping light, the densely woven pattern of golden light from fire, window, and trees, that gives the dramatic intensity to the simple action. The intangibles of space penetrated by light meant nothing to Raphael, who concentrated all his energies in defining mass through eloquent lines and contours. Masses and solids are for Rembrandt interpenetrated by light; space is a matter of moving shadows rather than measured separation of solids.

The Renaissance masters had conceived of the Madonna as embodying all that was noble, restrained, and aristocratic. So, for Leonardo and Michelangelo, the Virgin is above all gracious and queenly and often touched by melancholy. Rubens, as a Catholic, is inclined to maintain this tradition, but Rembrandt, the Protestant miller's son, reflects a somber realism in harmony with the spirit of his democratic middle-class Holland. If his Biblical subjects show less of the outward signs of grandeur, they nevertheless reveal unsuspected depths of tenderness and poignancy. In the mystical appearance of Christ revealing Himself to His disciples in the *Supper at Emmaus* (Louvre) the physical and the intangible are so perfectly equated and interrelated that there is no separation possible. All reality is sustained in the waves of light and color which unite two worlds of our being. To speak of "realism" here is

[1] Programs A and B.

Fig. 67. Rembrandt, *Carpenter's Family*, 1646, Gallery, Cassel

to demand a broad redefinition of just what is real, what is illusion, what are truths and untruths. Rembrandt found his own answers to these persistent questions—answers which are of necessity deeply personal, in accordance with his religious views. They are inward-seeking, generous, Christian, and of the utmost grandeur.

How far Rembrandt was to carry this drama of the inner life may be seen in his late work, *The Return of the Prodigal Son* (Fig. 68). At first glance it will reveal little to the beholder, the figures being only partially revealed, the action restrained and unspectacular. Like all

Fig. 68. Rembrandt, *The Return of the Prodigal Son*, 1668, Hermitage, Leningrad (*Braun & Cie,* Paris–New York)

supreme works of the mind, it requires more than a casual glance to be rewarding. It requires our participation of imagination and insight to encompass the crushing pity of the clumsy action. We may miss the heroic, grandiose acting which is so often associated with pictorial drama. By its omission Rembrandt reveals a supreme knowledge of stagecraft and of emotional truth in underplaying an incident which could so easily be destroyed by overt statement. The prodigal son, clad in the humiliation of his rags and broken shoes, falls in selfless humility before his mute father. No eloquent gesture or false note of elaboration intervenes between us and the full impact of the moment. We are not asked to view the setting nor a single detail of figure or garments. But we do note the dumbness of grief and suffering and their impact upon the father's friends, hushed and embarrassed by the sudden turn of events. A figure is discerned poking his head out of a door, his curiosity aroused by the sudden quiet. Such penetration of the psychic life, such revelation of emotion, had never appeared in art before, and Rembrandt is its supreme exponent. Pictorially the *Prodigal Son* is "unrealistic" when compared with the artist's more analytical works of twenty years earlier, like the *Anatomy Lesson* or the famous *Night Watch*. The body of Rembrandt's painting and etching is, among other things, a magnificent revelation of ever-increasing refinement, of progressive deepening and enrichment. While one may justly be enthralled by the decoration, the brilliance, of the earlier work (just as his own people were impressed by them), it is in the late works like the *Good Samaritan* (1648) the *Syndics of the Cloth Guild* (1662), and the *Return of the Prodigal Son* (*ca.* 1668) that the enormous perceptions of the artist come most fully into view.

We know that the artist's own people became negligent, even forgetful of these late works, because they were not showy and "brilliantly" executed. But we find that they confirm our own convictions that art is essentially not a matter of clever entertainment or skillful reproduction of the material world, and least of all a beautiful sermon on the elevated or high-toned life. Rembrandt, to a degree reached by few others, asserts through his art that *realm of being* which we cannot know directly but which requires nourishment through what Henry James called "the beautiful circuit of thought and desire." If the ends or objectives of Rembrandt's art cannot be defined, it is because they are hidden in the intricate maze of human aspiration. In gradually removing from his paintings and etchings the outward delineations of things, of jewels and rich fabrics—all that was most cherished by the taste of his time—he was not rejecting beauty and splendor but transforming *things* into *essences of things*. In this transformation (in many ways similar to that of Velasquez) there took place the renovation of his style, the creation of the *golden light* which encompasses all and illuminates the world. This method, developed over the decades of his career, was to remove Rembrandt from the esteem of his contemporaries, and at the same time it was to lift him to that small circle of men who have found their way to the core of human experience. Many have given brief glimpses of it, but he sustained his vision and suffused it with the steady light of his humanity.

While the Greek sculptors and architects, and to a large degree the artists of the Renaissance, found satisfaction in bounded planes, strict line definition, measured space derived from intellectual processes, the Baroque masters (and specifically Rembrandt) asserted the demands of the individual to probe that *realm of being* beyond the safe grounds of intellectual commonality. In other words, Rembrandt, like every great intellect, recognized that what the mind knows and can grasp, measure, and define is but a particle of reality; that beyond our poor equipment for knowing there lie infinite fields of being toward which man is constantly drawn with enormous and tragic curiosity. Beyond the known are the spaces penetrable only by the will and desire. This is only another way of saying that the individualism inherent in Renaissance thought made a Rembrandt inevitable and that his personalized and intimate and emotion-laden art was but an extension of that of Leonardo and Titian.

BAROQUE PAINTING AND SCULPTURE

It was only natural that this great Dutch master should have many pupils and imitators, but passion and poetic imagination cannot be imitated—only emulated. He has in the past three hundred years been a living demonstration of the capacity of man to penetrate the world of appearances, not by denying them but by *abstracting* them. That is to say, he as an artist recognized that material reality, the common appearance of the world, offers nothing in itself to the artist, nothing but an opportunity to endow inert facts with life. The verb *to abstract* means to withdraw or separate one or more elements from the many of a totality. The whole art activity is largely one of abstraction in this sense, of taking words or colors or shapes out of their everyday context and recombining them in a vital art context.

The term *abstract* has come to be associated with the non-realistic art or non-objective art of our time just because the contemporary artists have so fully honored the practice of the old masters in recording a new point of view. To convey his thought and feeling, Rembrandt, as we have seen, was compelled more and more to abstraction. And paradoxically enough, the greater his abstraction the profounder became the revelation of reality. His feeling for expression through non-imitative design made etching on copper very attractive to him.

In the etching process a needle is used to scratch lines in a film of wax spread over a metal plate. When a plate so treated is submerged in an acid bath the exposed portions of the cop-

Fig. 69. Rembrandt, *Jacob Haaring,* etching, National Gallery of Art, Washington, D.C. (Rosenwald Collection)

per are eroded by the acid; the portions which remain covered by the wax film are unaffected. The system of lines in the drawing is thus transferred to the surface of the plate, which is then said to have been "bitten" or etched; the drawing is preserved as a system of troughs eroded out of the smooth surface of the plate. The wax is removed and the plate is inked. The smooth surface is then wiped free of ink so that ink remains only in the troughs. Under pressure against spongy paper the plate transmits its image to make a number of prints, each the reverse image of the original drawing. An etching is by its very nature highly abstract, since black and white alone can never even approach a simulation of nature as painting can. In some three hundred etchings Rembrandt established himself as a major prophet of a medium little used up to his time. No one has ever approached him in versatility or profundity with an etcher's needle. As in his paintings he here applied himself to all pictorial fields—portraiture, landscape, the representation of Biblical, genre, and mythological subjects. All his etchings, save a dozen or so, were made independently of any painting of the same subject, suggesting how he differentiated between the peculiar artistic problems involved in the two fields of expression. In his etchings, as well as in his drawings (which comprise another major body of work), Rembrandt was more free to express his most intimate life than in the paintings which were often commissioned and of a generally public nature.

The expectation, so often unfulfilled, that a portrait should flatter its subject created friction between Rembrandt and his public, but this could not be the case with the etchings made often wholly for the master's own satisfaction. In the portrait of *Jacob Haaring* (Fig. 69) is found one of the artist's supreme creations in graphic art and in portraiture. Between the two extremes of the black ink and the white of the paper the artist makes the most subtle of pictorial dramas involving velvet blacks made tremulous by the outer and inner room light. But the free wash of light assumes a sombre vitality, seeming to have its origin less in its physical source of windows than in some inner presence of the brooding old man. The geometry of the design shows the work to be of Rembrandt's later life. The pictorial elements are controlled by the most subtle and monumental form. Rising from the base of the paper, the figure culminates in the head to form a densely composed pyramid. Horizontal and vertical accents declare the basic structure of room and figure in a design so lucid as to recall those of Greek and Renaissance masters. Here is the fruit of the master's long and penetrating concern for the imposing concentration of Italian Renaissance art, and proof, too, of his will to endow his own Baroque language with monumental grandeur. In such works as this, thought alone prevails. The incidentals of costume, setting, or action are suggested but relegated to the periphery of consciousness only; the realm of inner being remains. Here, in portraiture, the master occupies a solitary position in his own age and in any.

The briefest examination of 17th-century painting will reveal that because of the great shift in point of view this was the epoch in which landscape came into prominence as a subject regarded for its own sake. Rembrandt, like every other artist of his time, explored this subject—in painting, drawing, and etching. While landscapes form a rather small proportion of his work as such, it may also be said that every work of Rembrandt is a kind of landscape, the essentials of which—*space* and *light*—prevail to the most extraordinary degree. In this he is no innovator, for space and light are basic to the Baroque vision. He simply took from Dutch, German, Italian, and Flemish examples what he needed and created a formidable personal style which was in many ways a synthesis of many lesser styles. This is, perhaps, what every supreme master unconsciously does: he brings into harmony the scattered, wayward notes to form a mighty union.

Landscape in artistic rendering had been since Greek times merely the stage upon which human action took place. Increasingly, in Christian painting, it had emerged during the Middle Ages and the Renaissance, but not until the Age of Rembrandt does it appear as an independent subject for painters. Though the landscapes of Bruegel seem an exception,

BAROQUE PAINTING AND SCULPTURE   185

Bruegel by no means excluded human figures as do the Baroque masters, nor did he subordinate them to the moods and vagaries of light, rain, and wind playing upon forest and plain. Perhaps it would be more exact to say that Baroque masters projected themselves into the landscape, finding in it clues to their intimate sensibilities. If we may judge by the great variations found in Rembrandt's landscapes, this is indeed the case. In some two hundred and fifty drawings, besides his paintings and etchings, he shows himself to be constantly alert to the boundless possibilities it offered for expression. In these works, as always, it is light which is his chief concern. In the celebrated etching *Three Trees* the moist and fertile Dutch countryside emerges fresh from the obscuring veil of a rainstorm. In the *Skating Scene* the slate-grey light reflected from the ice and winter sky proclaims the chill of winter. In the silhouetting of architecture against the brooding light, he created in *The Mill* a monumentality unsurpassed in the history of landscape art. Perhaps most characteristic of the Dutch genius for landscape (which Rembrandt shared with many another) is his *Landscape with Stone Bridge* (Fig. 70). The firm union of buildings, trees, and the remote town, indicated by a church spire, is effected by a horizontal accent in the bridge and its continuing roadway.

Fig. 70. Rembrandt, *Landscape with Stone Bridge, ca.* 1637, Rijksmuseum, Amsterdam (by permission)

Countering this stabilizing accent, a sudden light breaks from the disrupted clouds to make the trees blossom with olive and gold. In all its tones and overtones the human touch is everywhere manifest. Even were there visible no solitary boatman, the painting would still be eloquent of a world of nature made animate and human. His Dutch painting anticipates in sentiment the Romantic poetry of Wordsworth and the Romantic landscape painting of the 19th century. While many of his countrymen were enormously gifted in taste, technical brilliance, and pictorial invention, they are not unjustly called, for all their abundant gifts, the Little Masters. It is doubtful if many of Rembrandt's contemporaries shared his feelings. Most of them certainly preferred (even as today) the more explicit genre painting of domestic drama, handsome costumes, and lively anecdote.

Rembrandt's magnificence was such that he could by-pass conventional ideas of beauty and create his own concept of a somber and tragic reality. This was not to displace Classical or medieval ideas of the beautiful but to enrich them by placing them in a just position in the human landscape. No greater tribute can be made to an artist than to recognize the area of human experience which he encompasses. The area Rembrandt elucidated is a vast one. His light illuminates what came before him and what has come after.

Recommended reading:
Abraham Bredius, *The Paintings of Rembrandt,* Vienna, Phaidon, 1936.
Arthur Hind, *Rembrandt,* Cambridge, Harvard University Press, 1932.

DIEGO VELASQUEZ (1599–1660)[1]

CONTEMPLATING THE COOL and deliberate paintings of Velasquez, one may well wonder what this Spaniard has in common with other Baroque masters. In the very years when the grandiose rhetoric of Bernini and Rubens was winning the praises of all Europe, Velasquez was working in the relative obscurity of court painter to Philip IV. Neither the artist nor his royal patron seemed to share the general enthusiasm for the strenuous and dramatic modes current in the 17th century. Yet in his own way Velasquez was to make a profound contribution to the many-faceted Baroque style. Study, travel, and the sure support of the monarch gave his efforts a singleness of purpose, a progressive development toward lucidity and breadth which carried his style from a local one to universality. As a privileged and able administrator in the palace of Philip IV for thirty-eight years, his opportunities for artistic growth were enormous, and he made full use of them. The appointment as court painter meant that he was free from the social pressures that brought Rembrandt to economic bankruptcy when he abandoned his popular realistic style. Furthermore, his position at court meant he was released from any special obligation to the Church, an obligation which was assumed by the more popular painting of Murillo.

Even in his earliest works he proves that his style is to be on an entirely different plane from that of his great Italian predecessors in the Renaissance. Though he did paint some conventional religious and Classical themes, it was always to transform them by his atmospheric treatment. Those familiar subjects of Greek myths and Christian legends seem to have been convenient exercises through which he could refine and clarify his method. Even his royal

[1] Program A.

portraits have something of the look of magnificent still lifes. His biographer Antonio Palomino wrote:

Aware that Titian, Dürer, Raphael and others held an advantage over him and that their reputation had increased after their deaths, he availed himself of his fanciful inventive genius and began to paint rough and homely pieces with great pretension and with odd lighting and coloring. Some remonstrated with him because he did not paint with delicacy and beauty subjects of a more serious nature so as to emulate Raphael of Urbino. He vindicated himself elegantly, saying: "I would rather be the first in this coarse stuff than the second in nicety."[2]

So, against his tutors' advice, the young Velasquez gave his energies to the "coarse stuff" of street musicians, drinkers, peasant women preparing meals or carrying water jars. Such themes were not uncommon in Spanish and Italian painting of the time, but no painter had lavished upon these "rough and homely" pieces the concentration and energy which Velasquez gave them. At first they were treated in the prevailing dense and dark manner, but gradually the paintings began to take on luminosity and depth. Complexity of light, the infinite variation of texture, the relation of shape to shape, and the enveloping atmosphere were not only observed but incorporated deliberately and schematically in the execution of his mythologies, portraits, and sacred subjects.

His paintings, while nominally called "realistic," are so not because of their factual recording of nature (a simple matter in itself) as much as for a wholly plausible life of their own, which gives them the immediacy of common visual experience. His effects are like happy accidents as he contrives, by arrangements of light, color and space, to screen out irrelevant, obscuring, or confusing distractions. From the process emerges a unity attained ordinarily by the automatic screening process of our mind. It is as though he were constantly pushing his subject away, from a near view to a far view, allowing air and light to modify appearances as they may. When one closely examines a small area of a late Velasquez canvas, it is not to see perfectly formed objects but large formless masses. The exact opposite is true with respect to Renaissance painting. Velasquez sought nothing else—not the exuberance of Rubens, the somber reflections of Rembrandt, nor the religious sentiments of his Spanish contemporaries like Murillo or Zurbaran. While not exactly an inventive painter, Velasquez was yet capable, on occasion, of extraordinary dramatic invention. In the *Surrender at Breda* (Fig. 71), painted in mid-career, after 1634, is found perhaps the most plausible delineation of an historical episode ever made in painting. Some years earlier there had occurred at Breda in Holland a notable victory for Spanish arms, ending in the surrender of the Dutch forces to Spinola, the Spanish general. Velasquez wished to present this victory in full, almost epic contours, and at the same time to bring into focus the meeting of the opposing generals. The encounter takes place between the armies drawn up in characteristic attitudes of victory and defeat. In the distance stretches, thinly veiled, the atmospheric landscape—a countryside spotted by the pall of burning villages. The subject involved the portrayal of personalities, of whom there are many, landscape, and dramatic incident. Both in its largeness of conception and in its physical size it is something like the majestic *Night Watch* Rembrandt painted seven years later in Amsterdam. Each master in his characteristic way brings to his respective work enormous pow-

---

[2]Antonio Palomino, *Museo pictorico y escala optica,* Madrid, 1724 (passage tr. M. Soria).

Fig. 71. Velasquez, *Surrender at Breda,* 1634–1635, Prado, Madrid (*Anderson*)

ers. Velasquez, observing consistently the laws of his atmospheric art, is more direct and coherent, and consequently more inherently decorative.

In bringing before us the swarming armies, the vast array of arms and uniforms, the sweep of the setting, the artist suggests everything by explicitly defining nothing, yet the illusion in detail is established unfailingly. The short lances randomly held by the Dutch and the tall ones proudly massed by the Spanish suggest the thousands of unseen troops. It is hard to imagine a more unwieldly theme than this, and only a very great talent consciously pursuing a plan appropriate to the subject could hope to contain the thousands of details within the bounds of pictorial plausibility. In viewing the work, one should hold in mind the countless swarm of conventional historical paintings with their insistent masses of tedious detail. Then one may well note the artistry which brings everything to view in its inevitable order. His devices for obtaining this lucidity are obvious but effective, like the foreshortened horse at the right which conducts our eye into space and at the same time screens out the complex forms of half an army. At the extreme right appears one of the few known portraits of the artist. The repetition of the vertical lances suggestive of the vast armies gives simple accents to stabilize the over-all pictorial composition. The great sweeping scene is a pictorial and dramatic prelude to the action of the principal figures, who give meaning and point to the rest. Most impressive is the noble generosity of Spinola, who accepts with gravity and dignity the honorable surrender of his opponent, Justin of Nassau.

The virtues of the *Surrender at Breda* are those of intelligence and taste, those of a master wholly confident of his method. It is these qualities clarified and intensified that emerge in the monumental paintings of the late years, *The Maids of Honor* (Fig. 72) and *The Tapestry Weavers*. Few single paintings have inspired the admiration universally accorded the former work, which has been called with reason the "Theology of Painting." Though obviously an elaborately composed or set piece, it has all the effect of absolute spontaneity. This is partly the result of having before us a portrait of the artist (at the left), which serves to depersonalize the point of view. In effect, the observer rather than the artist becomes the painter, and becomes in addition *the King,* by assuming the position ordinarily taken by the artist in front of the object being presented. This is one of the "secrets" of a great and complex Baroque invention comparable to those found in Donne's poetry and in the fantastic ceiling decorations of Baroque churches in Italy of the same period. The active participation of the viewer seems an anticipation of those demands made by 20th-century masters who require not so much the passive acceptance of the viewer as his positive participation in following the flow of forces set up by the artist.

The realist works within the limits of the familiar, the known, and the unexpected, in contriving his patterns of space and energy. In the sense that he scrupulously excluded from his pictures all that lay outside of visual truths, Velasquez was an almost absolute realist. His was a monastic and self-effacing quest for a pictorial vision unobstructed by ideas, sentiment, or convention. When he makes a portrait like the *Innocent X* (Fig. 73) he proceeds as though saying to himself, "I did not create this man, and I do not judge him, but I perceive him as anyone may." A method so pursued might (and often does) result in a dehumanized and mechanical contraption without vitality, a kind of dead-pan photography. But Velasquez suffuses everything with the quickening invention of interplay of light and air, and of textures that absorb light and in turn yield light. Refraining from literal representation, he translates all into its visual equivalent, never losing sight of the unconscious predilection of the human eye to organize, to eliminate, and to subordinate. His paintings are deceiving only in that they appear to be unstudied transcriptions. Anyone who has attempted to draw the simplest object will at once recognize the intelligence and learning requisite to his unsurpassed lucidity.

The detached impersonality of this type of painting is most readily grasped when a portrait like the *Innocent X* is compared with the intensely penetrating characterizations found in El

BAROQUE PAINTING AND SCULPTURE

Greco's *Cardinal Guevara* (Fig. 56) or Goya's *Queen Maria Luisa*. The latter two give us strong leading clues to their models by stressing telling features, like the way the Cardinal holds his hands and head, or the undue grossness of the Queen's neck—in short, pointing up essential physical features to indicate their subject's dominant characteristics. Velasquez must have felt that this kind of character analysis might be accomplished indirectly and more effectively by creating in effect the atmosphere they breathed and the impact of their physical presence with that atmosphere. It has often been noted that painters are inclined to produce self-portraits, no matter whose features they set out to paint. For instance, the identities of some of Rembrandt's portraits are in question because they look so much like the artist. Rubens always seems to have produced in his portraits fragments of his own turbulent energy. Perhaps Velasquez alone made the surest approach to the ideal portrait in remaining uninvolved with judgments of character and refraining from vivid dramatizations. In general, his art is notably free from the brilliant display common to most Baroque work.

But the direction of Velasquez' art is similar to that of other Baroque masters in that he begins in his early life with the construction of solid, tangible material forms and toward the end of his career discovers the fluid nature of the solids as they are penetrated by light and as they flow together in the enveloping space. In the Renaissance the *cage of space*, enclosing all material forms, was realized through geometry. The 17th-century masters were to abolish this cage-like space, recreating it by other means which were visual rather than mathematical. The object and its surrounding space were distinct entities for the Renaissance painter; in the Baroque age they became interacting equals in a visual drama. This transformation becomes apparent in the comparison of any Renaissance painting with any Baroque painting. Then it will be seen how the firm contours of the former melt into tonal values in the Baroque work. To employ blurred images is not to produce faint or indefinite forms but to incorporate new values of reality—the realities of time, space, movement, that the 17th century (the great age of science) was exploring in all fields of human endeavor.

Velasquez brought to a classic perfection a type of painting that has come to be known as impressionistic. The term "Impressionistic" is commonly applied to the painters in the second half of the 19th century who developed systematically (largely following the Spaniard's methods) a style based upon *visual* appearances.[3] This is the kind of painting most people in our time, and for several hundred years before us, have accepted as fundamental and natural. But in the whole history of pictorial art (painting and sculpture) the impres-

[3] See, below, pp. 320–32.

Fig. 72. Velasquez, *The Maids of Honor*, 1656, Prado, Madrid (*Anderson*)

Fig. 73. Velasquez, *Innocent X*, 1650, Palazzo Doria Pamphili, Rome (*Anderson*)

sionistic mode has occupied but a relatively small place. Most Oriental and medieval art is non-impressionistic. Even Renaissance art is so only to a limited degree, and the art of our day is fundamentally non-impressionistic. The very fact that art has fluctuated between images suggested by the eye's vision and those prompted by the mind indicates the infinitely vast range of artistic expression. No art work belongs wholly to the one field or the other. Even the supremely tonal and therefore visual-sided *Maids of Honor* (Fig. 72) owes its vitality to the rhythmic design of rectangular planes (door, easel, ceiling, and floor) each of which defines a unit of the organically enclosed space. While the atmospheric style of this artist is foreign to the style of our day, his mastery of the abstract design is recognized as valid in all art including our own. The style that Velasquez exemplified was to persist for over two hundred years with only nominal variations. It was discarded in part or whole by later painters like Blake and David, who sought the energy of line and mass. Late in the 19th century the style was abandoned as new energies sought expression in activated colors and strong linear designs. Styles change when old forms lose their powers to energize, to shock, and when they no longer enlarge the sense of life. If the style of Velasquez has been abandoned in the 20th century, it is not because it was an inadequate style. In its time it fulfilled its function and opened avenues for succeeding generations. But each generation must create its own way of expressing itself, and the vitality of the age is directly in proportion to the energy it reveals in creating an effective artistic language with which to speak.

The century of Velasquez was undoubtedly the last great epoch of pictorial art. Since the 17th century there has been both fertility of invention and opulence of production in painting, but none of it has attained the high plateau of the Baroque. The latter-day painters have, to a large degree, explored the terrain first sighted by their predecessors. Velasquez attained his eminence by making himself a virtuoso of vision. He is the discoverer of visual reality, and it is only incidental that subsequent painters were to carry his methods to the sphere of "open-air painting" two hundred years later. While Rembrandt declared the majesty of his inner vision, Velasquez made his conquest of external vision. Though neither of these visions can exist without interpenetration of the other, the two extremes are the poles between which the artist works, much as our own being moves in the nexus of body and soul.

By his austerity Velasquez brought to a logical solution one aspect of pictorial vision inherent in all representational art—the part which vision plays in painting. His conclusions were not reached as a physicist might reach them, through analysis, but through the warm and human application of his entire faculties, moral, intellectual, and spiritual.

Recommended reading:
Enrique Lafuente, ed., *The Paintings and Drawings of Velasquez,* London, Phaidon, 1943.
Juan Allende-Salazar, ed., *Velazquez: des Meisters Gemälde,* Stuttgart, Berlin, and Leipzig, n.d. "Klassiker der Kunst," Vol. 6.

BAROQUE MUSIC

JOHANN SEBASTIAN BACH

General Characteristics of Baroque Music[1]

THE PERIOD AROUND 1600 was momentous in the history of music. It was then that a new musical style, which had been gradually developing over more than half a century, was accepted by most composers. The Baroque style in music lasted until about 1750. Of the numerous composers of the time we mention only a few of the greatest. Among the early ones are Claudio Monteverdi and Heinrich Schütz; to those of the second half of the 17th century belong Henry Purcell and Jean-Baptiste Lully. The final phase of the Baroque is represented by Johann Sebastian Bach and George Frederick Handel.

Baroque music abandoned the refinement and reserve which characterize the major trends of Renaissance music. It preferred a more down-to-earth idiom and a bolder expressiveness; it acquired undisguised sweep and passion. The Baroque composer endeavored to stir and stun his audience rather than to delight and edify it with subtlety. However, in spite of its poignancy, Baroque music, except in very early works, did not become formless or sentimental. There were two elements which counterbalanced its emotionalism. One was the tendency towards rhetorical artifice and largeness of effect, which lent rigor to Baroque exuberance. An example of this constrained intensity is opera, one of the products of the time in Italy, with its "oversized" emotions and the formalized rhetorical gestures of its singers. Another element which held emotionalism in bounds was an emphasis on lucidity of texture. This emphasis exhibits itself in polyphony and well-balanced organization of form, probably as a consequence of the rationalism of the period, which made itself felt especially after the middle of the 17th century.

Harmony. The main value of polyphonic Renaissance music lay in the expressiveness of the melodic lines of the composition. Each line was an entity in itself by virtue of its intervals, direction, and rhythmic flow. Chords were produced by tones simultaneously sounded in different melodic lines, but their progressions, except in cadences, were held together mainly by the melodic lines which ran through them.

In Baroque music, chords no longer depend for their existence on the association of independent melodic lines; within the newly established system of tonality they acquire a coherence of their own. It has already been mentioned that the church modes were in the 16th century gradually yielding to the tonalities of major and minor. These tonalities were adopted definitively during the latter half of the 17th century. Their adoption entailed (1) the use of the tones of the major and the minor scales, and (2) the use of triads based on these tones with an increasing emphasis on the triads on I, IV, and V. All other triads were soon relegated to acting as substitutes for these three, so that the harmony of major and minor almost amounted to an enlarged authentic cadence. As a consequence, any composition or section of a composition had a particularly conspicuous and firm center—the tonic (the tone and the triad); moreover, all of its chords tended towards this tonic. Thus they showed a direction and coherence which they lacked, if dissociated from the melodic lines, in Renaissance music.

With the establishment of tonality, it became possible in a single composition to shift from one tonality to another. This process is called modulation.[2] Modulation involves a change from one tonic to another and from one set of tones and chords to another set of tones and

---
[1] Programs A and B.
[2] See Chapter VIII, pp. 388–90.

chords—a novel procedure in music, roughly comparable to a movement in space from one plane to another.

The Baroque and Renaissance epochs differ nowhere more strongly than in their use of dissonances. Baroque composers no longer confined themselves to suspension dissonances which were mild because they were "prepared."[3] In addition, they made use of the bolder and spicier kind of unprepared dissonances, chords whose dissonant tone is not tied over from a preceding consonance and therefore enters unprepared. It must be noted that dissonances in Baroque music were by necessity more poignant than in Renaissance music because of the heavier accentuation that fell on them.[4]

Melody. Baroque composers no longer felt themselves bound to the "vocal" melodic idiom of the Renaissance; instead of small and easily singable intervals, they ventured to write considerably larger ones if the dramatic character of the music called for them. Moreover, they developed a characteristically instrumental style—a style unknown to the Renaissance. By exploiting the peculiarities of a specific instrument, this style allowed for successive wide skips and jagged melodic lines. The instrumental music of the late Baroque, which influenced vocal music, owed much of its exuberance to often repeated motives and single tones, performed with vigor and speed.

The change from a melodic (linear) to a chordal (vertical) conception, around 1600, led to a differentiation in style between the bass and the other voices, which had not existed in Renaissance music. Angular, accentuated intervals make of the bass a firm, heavy foundation for the superstructure in a Baroque composition. The weight of the bass is also increased by a special manner of performance. The bass line is usually played by a low string instrument (a *viola da gamba*[5] or a 'cello) doubled by the lower register of a keyboard instrument, either a harpsichord[6] or, as frequently happened in church music, by an organ. In the higher registers the keyboard-player played chords indicated by figures in the score. A bass of this kind was called a *basso continuo* or *thorough-bass,* because it had few or no rests and therefore seemed to be continuous. Practically all types of Baroque music, except solo-compositions for harpsichord and organ, are distinguished by a *basso continuo*.

Rhythm. In contrast to the light flow of much Renaissance music, Baroque rhythm is always of a more muscular nature. Large and strongly accentuated intervals, repeated tones and motives, sharp and frequent dissonances create stresses of considerable weight and consequently vigorous motion. Moreover, meter,[7] which during the Renaissance had been conspicuous only in dance music and in the secular music fashioned after it, becomes generally accepted in the 17th century, so that its own accentuations are added to those of the other elements of a composition. Much of late Baroque music is particularly stirring because of a steady pulsation of regular beats created, for example, by continuous sixteenth notes.[8]

Dynamics. Only mild dynamic changes existed in Renaissance music. Variations in volume were produced by an increase and decrease in the number of voices. Baroque musicians also employ this device, but, in addition, make use of the dynamic contrast between loud (*forte*) and soft (*piano*) passages. The contrast always appears with startling suddenness, as in the transition from Movement 3 to Movement 4 in Bach's *Magnificat*. It is especially conspicuous if applied to a passage which is repeated. The passage then appears first in *forte* and, immediately afterwards, in *piano*.

[3]See, above, pp. 118–19 and Chapter VIII, p. 390.
[4]See *Rhythm*, below.
[5]An early string-instrument similar to a 'cello though more restrained in tone.
[6]The harpsichord is in appearance similar to a modern grand piano. Its strings, however, are plucked by quills instead of being hit by hammers.
[7]See Chapter VIII, "Basic Rhythm," pp. 381–82.
[8]See Bach's *Magnificat,* Movement No. 4; and *Cantata No. 4, "Christ Lag in Todesbanden,"* Verse III (Violins I and II)

Texture. Tonal harmony was first developed in a homophonic style, a style in which one voice predominates while the others serve merely as an accompaniment; but from the middle of the 17th century, tonal harmony was combined with polyphony. It should be emphasized again that Baroque polyphony differs from Renaissance polyphony in respect to its chord progressions, which are independent of the voices of the composition. Late Baroque composers like Handel and Bach command a wide range of textures ranging from simple homophony to strict polyphony. A favorite Baroque arrangement may be called semi-homophonic: it consists of two upper voices which compete with each other, both supported by a *basso continuo*.

Formal Procedures. Baroque music favored considerably bolder contrasts than Renaissance music. In addition to sudden dynamic contrasts, it employed a type of contrast which can be summarized under the name "*concertato* style." By "*concertato* style" is meant the alternation and interplay of two opposing sonorous bodies. For example, a comparatively large ensemble is set against a small one (often consisting of three players, occasionally only of one)[9]; or, in the arrangement of two upper voices, one voice moves alongside another in a spirit of competitive virtuosity.[10]

The form which seemed especially to meet the demands of Baroque composers was the *variation-form*. One type of variation which composers cultivated consisted of working transformations on a melody or theme such as a chorale or Protestant hymn.[11] Another type is based on the literal repetition of a bass motive, while the voices on top of it undergo constant changes; the bass is then called a *basso ostinato*.[12]

One formal procedure which is related to the principle of the variation-form is the recurrence of an initial motive or pattern of motives, with harmonic and slight melodic changes, throughout an entire movement or through large sections of it.[13] Another is the use of a recurrent instrumental section, the *ritornello*, within a vocal composition. The *ritornello* appears at the opening of the work, alternates with vocal sections in the middle, and reappears at the end. This procedure was often combined with the employment of a recurrent initial pattern.[14]

Other formal procedures, such as the *da capo aria*, binary and ternary forms, and the fugue, are discussed below in connection with the works in which they occur.[15]

[9]See passages in the *Magnificat*, Movement No. 7.
[10]See *Magnificat*, Movement No. 3 (Oboe d'amore and Soprano I) and *Cantata No. 4, "Christ Lag in Todesbanden,"* Verse VI (Soprano and Tenor).
[11]See *Magnificat*, Movement No. 10 and *Cantata No. 4, "Christ Lag in Todesbanden,"* especially Verses No. I, III, and IV.
[12]See *Magnificat*, Movement No. 7 and *Cantata No. 4, "Christ Lag in Todesbanden,"* Verse III.
[13]See *Magnificat* (all movements, except the fugue in Movement No. 11, where the episodes change the above principle somewhat) and *Cantata No. 4, "Christ Lag in Todesbanden,"* Verses No. II, III, and VI.
[14]See *Magnificat*, Movements No. 2, 6, 8, and 9, and *Cantata No. 4, "Christ Lag in Todesbanden,"* Verses No. II, III, and VI.
[15]A general analysis of these forms is given in Chapter VIII: *Da Capo Aria*, p. 401; Binary Form, pp. 396–97; Ternary Form, pp. 397–99; the Fugue, pp. 394–95.

Recommended reading:
Manfred F. Bukofzer, *Music in the Baroque Era,* New York, W. W. Norton, 1947. (Read especially Chapters I, X, XI, and XII.)

JOHANN SEBASTIAN BACH (1685–1750)[1]

THERE EXIST many controversial subjects in the musical world, but the value of Bach's music is not one of them. Bach's numerous works, with few exceptions, are now recognized as sources of profoundest aesthetic enjoyment and moral edification.

They are indeed marvels of organic structure, of a structure in which melody, harmony, and form are welded into complete unity. In all of his greatest works, the details, bold by themselves and wisely distributed, sum up into what is considered one of the highest qualities of art: the sublime. Even the simpler, down-to-earth works of Bach contain an element of the same dignity and intellectual rigor.

Bach's output is so vast that it takes a life-time to acquire an intimate knowledge of it. However, an acquaintance with the following works should belong to the intellectual equipment of everybody: the *48 Preludes and Fugues of the Well-Tempered Clavier,* the *B-minor Mass,* the *Passions* according to St. Matthew and St. John, and the *Brandenburg Concertos.*

Bach was mainly active as a church organist, choir director, and church composer, though at times he performed also in the capacity of violinist and orchestral conductor at princely courts.

He was born in Eisenach, a little town in central Germany, in 1685. He held important positions at the court of Weimar (1708-17), at the court of Coethen (1717-23), and finally at the Lutheran churches of St. Thomas and St. Nicholas in Leipzig. In Leipzig he stayed from 1723 until his death in 1750.

Bach was a deeply religious man. Such ideas as sin, crucifixion, resurrection, and redemption were to him not merely traditional Christian imagery, but vivid inner experiences which he expressed in musical terms of extraordinary concreteness and intensity. The spirit of his Protestantism shows in his work in a certain sturdy confidence and natural strength blended with pious devotion—traditional elements of Protestant church music since the time of Luther.

Although Bach never left Germany, he was well acquainted with the music of his contemporaries, especially with such Italian and French composers as Vivaldi and François Couperin. His idiom is late Baroque in its grandeur and festive splendor, and in its intellectuality. However, since he had also absorbed the music of the early Baroque which included traces of Renaissance style, his work represents not only the Baroque in its entirety but its preparatory stages as well.

The Magnificat[2]

The words of the *Magnificat* are part of the Visitation scene described in the Gospel of St. Luke (I:46-55). They were spoken to Elizabeth, mother of St. John the Baptist, after the archangel Gabriel had announced to the Virgin Mary: "And behold, thou shalt conceive in thy womb, and bring forth a son, and shall call his name Jesus." These are Mary's words:

[1] Programs A and B.
[2] Program A.

BAROQUE MUSIC

Magnificat anima mea Dominum,	My soul doth magnify the Lord,
Et exultavit spiritus meus in Deo salutari meo.	And my Spirit hath rejoiced in God my Saviour.
Quia respexit humilitatem ancillae suae;	For he hath regarded the low estate of his handmaiden;
Ecce enim ex hoc beatam me dicent omnes generationes.	For, behold, from henceforth all generations shall call me blessed.
Quia fecit mihi magna qui potens est;	For he that is mighty hath done to me great things;
Et sanctum nomen eius.	And holy is his name.
Et misericordia a progenie in progenies	And his mercy is from generation to generation
Timentibus eum.	On them that fear him.
Fecit potentiam in brachio suo;	He hath shewed strength with his arm;
Dispersit superbos mente cordis sui.	He hath scattered the proud in the imagination of their hearts.
Deposuit potentes de sede,	He hath put down the mighty from their seats,
Et exaltavit humiles.	And exalted them of low degree.
Esurientes implevit bonis;	He hath filled the hungry with good things;
Et divites dimisit inanes.	And the rich he hath sent empty away.
Suscepit Israel puerum suum,	He hath given help to his servant Israel,
Recordatus misericordiae suae,	In remembrance of his mercy,
Sicut locutus est ad patres nostros, Abraham et semini eius in saecula.	As he spake to our fathers, to Abraham, and to his seed forever.

This text, for many centuries sung in plain chant, is a very old part of the Vespers (evening services) of the Catholic liturgy. It is always followed by the so-called Lesser Doxology which reads:

Gloria Patri, et Filio, et Spiritui Sancto.	Glory be to the Father, and to the Son, and to the Holy Ghost.
Sicut erat in principio, et nunc, et semper, et in saecula saeculorum. Amen.	As it was in the beginning, is now, and ever shall be, world without end. Amen.

From the 15th century composers set the text of the *Magnificat* in polyphonic style, frequently using the original plain chant melody as a *cantus firmus*.[3] Later, the same text was set to music by Protestant church composers. Bach composed his *Magnificat* in 1723. A long and a short version of this work are in existence, both destined for the service on Christmas Eve. It is the second, more popular version which will be analyzed.

Movement No. 1

Text: Magnificat anima mea Dominum.
   My soul doth magnify the Lord.

Scoring: Soprano I, Soprano II, Alto, Tenor, Bass; Violin I, Violin II, Viola; 3 Trumpets; Kettledrums; 2 Flutes, 2 Oboes; *Basso Continuo*.

The movement divides itself into three sections: an orchestral introduction, a choral section, and an orchestral conclusion.

Section I (mm. 1-31): Orchestral Introduction.

The orchestral introduction is not as polyphonic as it appears in the score. When it is performed, its harmony, its motion, and the festive sound of the instruments prove to be its main characteristics. Its voices are unified by a recurrent rhythmical pattern of sixteenth notes combined with eighth notes (m. 1). Within this rhythmic pattern appear two motives

[3]See, above, p. 120.

(marked *a* and *b* in Example 21), the latter of which finally establishes itself at the end of Section I.

The orchestration is based on four distinct groups of instruments: strings, oboes, flutes, and high trumpets. Although in this combination the shrill, metallic sound of the high trumpets predominates, all instrumental parts are lively within the group to which they belong. This type of orchestration, which sets instrumental groups against each other, differs fundamentally from the type of orchestration which characterizes music after Bach's time. During the period between 1750 and 1900 the groups of wind and stringed instruments are blended. Their separateness in Bach's orchestration is a typical Baroque feature of the *Magnificat*.

Section II (mm. 31-75): Magnificat anima mea dominum.

This section, the core of the movement in which chorus and orchestra are combined, is cast in a kind of ternary scheme, *i.e.,* a part at the beginning is repeated, sometimes slightly varied, after a differing middle part.[4] According to this scheme the choral section of Movement No. 1 can be divided thus:

A	Magnificat anima mea Dominum	measures 31–45
B	Magnificat	" 45–61
A²	Magnificat anima mea Dominum	" 61–75

Bach uses for the opening of Part A a structural pattern strongly marked by the rhythm of the word "Magnificat" (Ex. 21):

Example 21

[4]See Chapter VIII, pp. 397–99.

BAROQUE MUSIC

There are interlocked entries of two small groups (Soprano I and II; Alto and Tenor), each with the motive *a,* which soon unite into chords. These chords, associated with the word "Magnificat," are like joyful acclamations. The same pattern appears in measures 35–37, only rearranged, substituting motive *b* for motive *a.*

This opening is followed by a dense polyphonic context in which all five voices of the chorus are kept active (mm. 37–45). Against the florid lines of the outer voices is set the rhythm of the three middle voices, animated by imitation and hardened by the accentuations of the initial word. Finally, on the words "anima mea," the outer voices force the others into an almost synchronized motion which is concluded on "Dominum." The whole of Part A wavers between polyphonic and homophonic emphasis, the latter occurring in the opening and closing passages. It was evidently Bach's intention to make the text stand out as clearly as possible through this device.

The structural and melodic pattern of A^2 (mm. 61–75) is fundamentally the same as that of A except for a rearrangement of the voices and for differences in key.

Although Part B is similar in style to A and A^2, it differs from them in the following features. While A and A^2 modulate but little, and only to related major keys, B modulates both more often and more suddenly, touching on minor keys. The voices are frequently united in chords on the rhythm of the single word "Magnificat." The part is made livelier by the quick successive entries of two variants of motive *b,* twice alternating with each other (Ex. 22).

Example 22

Section III (mm. 75–90): Orchestral conclusion.

An abbreviated version of Section I, identical with measures 17–31.

The character of the entire movement is one of festiveness and grandeur—typical elements of late Baroque music.

Movement No. 2

Text: Et exultavit spiritus meus in Deo salutari meo.

    And my spirit hath rejoiced in God my Saviour.

Scoring: Soprano II; Violin I, Violin II, Viola; *Basso Continuo.*

After the powerful exultation of the first movement religious emotion is now compressed into a more intimate language—a *cantabile* (*i.e.,* singing) style in the melody and the warm timbre of the string ensemble.

Since Violin I predominates over the strings, we are faced with a typical Baroque arrangement—two upper voices (here, Violin I and the Soprano) and a *basso continuo.*

There are in this movement eight brief sections, each concluding with an authentic cadence. The entire musical material is stated in the instrumental introduction (Ex. 23). The rest of the movement, with the exception of Section IV, consists of restatements and variations of Section I.

Example 23

Section I (mm. 1–13): Instrumental Introduction.
Section II (mm. 13–21): Et exultavit spiritus meus.
The section consists of a vocal passage and of a purely instrumental one. It restates Section I—the Soprano slightly varying the main melody—but leaves measures 5–8 unused.
Section III (mm. 21–36): Et exultavit spiritus meus.
The Soprano is combined with the string ensemble. Section I is restated by the strings. Repetitions of several of its phrases expand the section. The Soprano is a variant of the upper melody during the first nine measures (21–29), but then branches out into a new expressive melodic line which imparts intensity to the word "exultavit" (Ex. 24).

Example 24

Section IV (mm. 36–51): In Deo salutari meo.
A continuation of Section III, this section takes up the new melismatic passage developed towards the end of Section III and spins it out into a long, jubilant melodic line. It thus deviates from the pattern of Section I. Because of the sparseness of the instrumental accompaniment, the solo voice is prominent.
Section V (mm. 51–59): Instrumental Interlude.
A purely instrumental repetition of Section I in a minor key. The first four measures of Section I are omitted.
Section VI (mm. 59–71): Et exultavit spiritus meus in Deo salutari meo.
The accompaniment is even sparser than in Section IV, with the result that attention is focused on the solo voice. The opening is fashioned after that of Section I, but from measure 63 on Bach uses the motive that originated in III and was elaborated in IV.
Section VII (mm. 71–81): In Deo salutari meo.
The accompaniment to the Soprano, which consists again (as in III) of the full string ensemble, repeats Section I literally, but omits its first four measures. The Soprano doubles, with slight changes, the first violin, though deviating from it from measure 76 on and finally going its own way unaccompanied.
Section VIII (mm. 81–92): Instrumental Conclusion.
Identical with Section I. The literal repetition of the instrumental introduction at the end is frequent in Bach's vocal compositions (see Movements No. 5, 6, 8, and 9). The principle of stating and varying the same pattern of motives over and over again appears in all movements of the *Magnificat*.

Movement No. 3

Text: Quia respexit humilitatem ancillae suae;
       Ecce enim ex hoc beatam me dicent ... [*Movement No. 4:* omnes generationes.]
      For he hath regarded the low estate of his handmaiden;
       For, behold, from henceforth shall call me blessed ... [*Movement No. 4:* all generations.]

BAROQUE MUSIC

Scoring: Soprano I; Oboe d'amore:[5] *Basso Continuo.*

Measures 1–5: Instrumental introduction for oboe d'amore and *basso continuo.*
This section becomes the pattern for the entire movement. Although the melody is very coherent, two motives (marked *a* and *b* in Example 25) can be distinguished.

Example 25

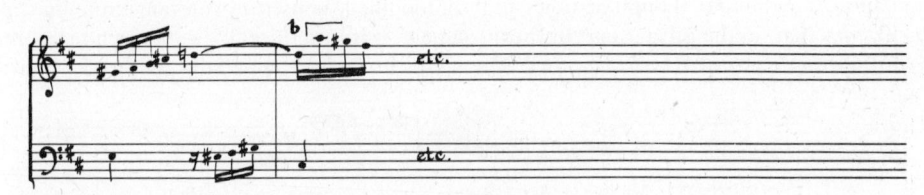

Measures 6–9: Quia respexit humilitatem ancillae suae.

The soprano enters in a melodic line which consists of variants of motives *a* and *b*. The vocal phrases, separated by rests, are bridged by the oboe d'amore which uses the same motives as before, though in a different order.

Shortly before the end of the soprano melody (m. 9), the oboe d'amore begins a variant of measures 1–5. It continues into measure 10 without the soprano, and extends into measure 11, where the soprano re-enters.

Measures 11–14: Quia respexit humilitatem ancillae suae.

In the principle of its structure, this passage is similar to measures 6–9. The key has changed.

Measures 15–18: Instrumental Interlude.

The oboe d'amore varies motive *b*.

Measures 18–25: Ecce enim ex hoc beatam me dicent . . .

In keeping with the word "ecce" ("behold"), there is a new, firm motive in the soprano (mm. 18–19). The energy of this word is supported by the imitation of a brief variant of motive *a* in the *basso continuo* and the oboe d'amore. This imitation leads to a full repetition of the instrumental introduction (m. 1–5) as an accompaniment to the soprano part.

The movement is imbued with a highly personal religious transport, at once intense and restrained. In its restraint it confirms the idea of humility which the text summarizes in the words "the lowliness of his handmaiden." Several elements contribute to the emotional intensity of the music. Among them are the coherent and rich flow of the oboe d'amore melody, its minor and augmented seconds,[6] the dissonant harmony, the minor mode, and finally the penetrating and melancholy tone of the oboe d'amore itself.

The movement has no ending. Instead, its last chord (the tonic within the authentic cadence of F sharp minor) along with the last syllable of the text ("dicent") becomes the beginning of the next movement ("omnes generationes"). Here then is a contrast between an

---

[5]*Oboe d'amore:* an instrument of the oboe family, though sweeter in tone, invented *ca.* 1720 and obsolete by the end of the 18th century.

[6]The size of an augmented second is three half tones, for example, A-sharp to G read downwards (m. 2).

introspective solo and a thundering chorus—a contrast which, in its overpowering force and suddenness, is frequent in late Baroque music.

Movement No. 4

Text: ... omnes generationes (... all generations).

Scoring: Soprano I, Soprano II, Alto, Tenor, Bass; 2 Flutes, 2 Oboes; Violin I, Violin II, Viola; *Basso Continuo*.

This is a thirteen-voiced composition, but, in the main, the instruments double the chorus. We are faced, in effect, with a polyphonic texture of five voices.

The polyphony of the movement feeds itself on one principal motive which is associated with the words "omnes, omnes generationes." It consists of tone repetitions at the beginning and melismas at the end, the one supporting the vigorous declamation of the word "omnes," the other spinning out the syllables of "generationes" in a melodic line which symbolizes jubilation. The motive, though at times slightly modified, is used in constant imitations in such a way that, in the greater part of the movement, it is introduced twice in each measure, each time on an accented beat (Ex. 26). The words of the text, especially the first two, are

Example 26

therefore clearly audible at all times, so that it seems as if Bach meant to din them into the ears of his audience. Since the motive extends over two measures, we often find the syllabic beginning of the motive accompanied, above or below, by the melismatic ending of the same motive in another voice.

The movement is divided roughly into three sections:

Section I (mm. 1–10): Frequent repetition of the thematic pattern described above (Ex. 26), modulating from F sharp minor to A major.

Section II (mm. 10–21): Similar to Section I except for a modulation from A major to C sharp minor.

Section III (mm. 21–27): The same motive as in Sections I and II is used at the beginning and the end, but the whole section is rendered climactic in a special manner. It begins (mm. 21–22) with a *stretto, i.e.,* a quick succession of entries, starting in the Bass and running through all the voices up to the Soprano. The excitement thus created is supplemented by the participating motive itself; its rhythmic vigor has been increased by the substitution of two sixteenth notes for the two eighth notes of its opening. The five voices, hurriedly overlapping end in a sustained chord (m. 24). This is followed by two predominantly homophonic passages, both of which have a shortened version of the principal motive in the highest voice. Thus, at the very conclusion of the movement, the words "omnes, omnes generationes" are thundered forth like a final summing up of what has been said and sung before.

Movement No. 5

Text: Quia fecit mihi magna qui potens est;
        Et sanctum nomen eius.

      For he that is mighty hath done to me great things;
      And holy is his name.

Scoring: Bass; *Basso Continuo*.

The movement is dominated by the *basso continuo,* whose wide, angular intervals and determined rhythm suggest the confidence and sturdy belief in the Lord expressed by the words. The melodic line is of strong individuality (Ex. 27). The *basso continuo* has the special char-

Example 27

acter of a *basso ostinato:* it consists of a single motive which is reiterated throughout the movement. This *ostinato* motive is established in measures 1–5 and is thereafter repeated seven times, though its repetitions involve changes of pitch and even of melody: in measures 21–24 the beginning of the motive is omitted; its beginning is expanded in measures 24–30. The bass voice follows the instrumental *ostinato,* sometimes repeating it literally, sometimes embellishing it.

Measures 1–5: This is not merely a thin bass line as the score seems to indicate (Ex. 27); the *basso continuo* is performed, according to custom, by a low string instrument and a harpsichord to add the chords.

Measures 5–8: Quia fecit mihi magna.

The first eight tones of the motive (to which another tone is added) are sung by the Bass, but continued by the *basso continuo*.

Measures 9–13: Quia fecit mihi magna qui potens est.

The beginning is identical with the preceding passage. However, while the *basso continuo* performs the rest of the *ostinato* motive, the melodic line of the vocal Bass becomes independent, although in its direction it tends to follow the intervals of the *basso continuo*.

Measures 13–17: Quia fecit mihi magna qui potens est.

The *basso continuo* begins the fourth repetition of the *ostinato* motive, whereupon (m. 14), the Bass imitates its first eight tones, but then continues its own way.

Measures 17–24: Et sanctum nomen eius.

The Bass becomes now a highly expressive counterpart to the *basso continuo,* thus imparting special significance to the text. With its coherent melodic line, it ties together the ending of the fifth and the (clipped) beginning of the sixth recurrence of the instrumental *ostinato* motive.

Measures 24–30: Quia fecit mihi magna qui potens est;
                     Et sanctum nomen eius.

The vocal Bass has a melodic line of its own, although it is slightly more dependent in rhythm and direction on the *ostinato* motive than in the preceding passage.

Measures 30–34: This purely instrumental passage literally repeats the beginning (mm. 1–5)—Bach's usual device to insure balance in vocal compositions.

Movement No. 6

Text: Et misericordia a progenie in progenies
       Timentibus eum.

And his mercy is from generation to generation
On them that fear him.

Scoring: Alto, Tenor; Violin I, Violin II, doubled by 2 Flutes, and Viola; *Basso Continuo.*

The rocking rhythm in 12/8 time and the character of its melody stamp this movement a *Pastorale.* The term *Pastorale* was often used by Baroque composers for music which suggested both the solemn and idyllic atmosphere of Christmas. In the *Magnificat,* which was written for Christmas, the *Pastorale* is quite appropriate. Its meaning is directed, however, not to the shepherds of the Nativity, but to the idea of divine mercy ("misericordia"). It is mainly the *basso continuo* and the harmony which lend the movement an element of introspection; the scoring supports rather its idyllic character. Notice the subdued, intimate sound of muted strings (marked in the score *"con sordino"*) and silvery flutes in combination with the mellow vocal timbres of Alto and Tenor.

The orchestral introduction is called a *ritornello* because it recurs between vocal sections. It provides the main pattern for the entire movement. As is customary, the *ritornello* is repeated literally at the end.

The *basso continuo* has a recurrent *ostinato* motive which is sometimes slightly varied, although it always retains its characteristic octave leaps.

Section 1 (mm. 1–4): *Ritornello* (Ex. 28).

Example 28

Section 2 (mm. 4–8): Et misericordia a progenie in progenies: Alto and Tenor.

The parts of Alto and Tenor are almost identical with those of the two violins of Section 1, except that their position is reversed. What was formerly the higher voice (the first violin) becomes now the lower one, sung by the Tenor.

Section 3 (mm. 8–11): *Ritornello.*

Identical with Section 1, except for slight melodic changes because of a modulation towards the end.

Section 4 (mm. 11–15): Et misericordia a progenie in progenies: Alto and Tenor with Violins (doubled by Flutes) and Violas.

Aside from a new key, the vocal parts are those of Section 1. The instruments do not add much to the polyphonic life of the passage. Their main function is to increase the richness of the harmony. This section leads into the thinly set . . .

Section 5 (mm. 15–18): Timentibus eum: Alto and Tenor with Instrumental Interlude.

In successive entries of the Tenor and Alto a brief variant of the opening of Section 1 is

BAROQUE MUSIC

used. This pattern of motives (with changes in pitch) is repeated by the instruments, and then resumed by Alto and Tenor, with the difference that in these two latter passages the entry of the higher voices precedes that of the lower ones.

Section 6 (mm. 18–20): *Ritornello*.

Section 7 (mm. 20–25): Et misericordia a progenie in progenies.

Identical with Section 4, except for differences in key.

Section 8 (mm. 24–27): Timentibus eum.

Identical with Section 5. In order to intensify the words "timentibus eum" ("on them that fear him"), six more measures (27–32) are appended. They are almost identical with Section 4, differing only in that the Alto and Tenor fill in the harmony, while the instruments play, simultaneously, the music of the *ritornello*.

At the end (mm. 30 and 31), our attention is again drawn to the Alto and Tenor, which appear unaccompanied. By means of a chromatic style (*i.e.,* one employing half tones even if they do not fit into a given tonality: notice F natural and B flat within E minor), they not only throw the words "timentibus eum" into relief but lend them a more somber shading.

The formal layout of the movement, which is based on the varied repetition of an initial pattern as well as on the alternation of vocal and instrumental sections, is tightened by the close relation of Sections 4 and 5 to Sections 7 and 8.

Movement No. 7

Text: Fecit potentiam in brachio suo;
       Dispersit superbos mente cordis sui.

       He hath shewed strength with his arm;
       He hath scattered the proud in the imagination of their hearts.

Scoring: Soprano I, Soprano II, Alto, Tenor, Bass; Violin I, Violin II, Viola; 3 Trumpets; Kettledrums; 2 Flutes (in unison); 2 Oboes; *Basso Continuo*.

The delicate effects of Movement No. 6 are now contrasted with the expression of almost ecstatic exultation. To this end the full vocal and orchestral resources of the score are em-

Example 29

ployed. The structure as well as the motives of the movement are inspired by the image of God's power and his scornful dispersion of the proud.

The movement divides itself into two sections, the first in brisk tempo, the second (marked *adagio*) brief and solemn.

Section I (mm. 1-28): Fecit potentiam in brachio suo; Dispersit superbos.

The character of this section is determined by chordal acclamations on the words "Fecit potentiam." The rhythm of its vigorous motive follows exactly that of the words (Ex. 29, motive *a*). Into its homophonic and syllabic texture, another more lively and more melismatic motive associated with the same words is inserted (motive *b*), extending beyond the homophonic setting from which it emerged. In addition to the two interlocked motives, *a* and *b*, there is a contrast between a group of large volume and one of smaller volume, a favorite Baroque device which found its main application in the *Concerto Grosso* (compare Bach's *Brandenburg Concertos*).

The pattern established in measures 1-4 is repeated six times throughout Section I. During the first four repetitions, a new motive is added, each time, to the group of small volume, until motives *b, c, d,* and *e* appear simultaneously (see Ex. 29). The following diagram scheme shows the composition of the pattern in its first and second appearances:

	Large group	Small group
Measures 1-4	a _____	
		b _____
Measures 5-8	a _____	
		b _____
		c _____

By gradually increasing the number of motives in the group of smaller volume, Bach works towards a climax. To the same end he also employs the almost regularly ascending entries of motive *b:* the motive appears first in the Tenor (m. 1), proceeds successively to Alto (m. 5), Soprano II (m. 9), Bass (m. 13), Soprano I (m. 17), and finally shifts to the high trumpets and the flutes (m. 21). At this point the climax is reached. The acclamations on motive *a* are now sung by all five voices, the initial thematic pattern is expanded, and the whole passage is enforced by the full orchestra, which so far has played only intermittently. The word "Dispersit" ("He hath scattered"), which has been appearing more and more often in the previous smaller groups, is now repeated constantly in measures 23-24, as well as in the appended four measures, where it is chiefly associated with motive *e* and its permutations. Dramatic excitement, which has been all along kept up by a *basso ostinato,* culminates on the word "superbos" ("the proud"), presented chordally. Whereupon, follows . . .

Section II (mm. 29-35): Mente cordis sui.

Its long sustained chords, combining chorus and orchestra, do not support the image of those who are "proud in the imagination of their hearts" but rather the might of the Omnipotent.

Movement No. 8

Text: Deposuit potentes de sede,
    Et exaltavit humiles.

He hath put down the mighty from their seats,
And exalted them of low degree.

Scoring: Tenor; Violin I and II (in unison); *Basso Continuo.*

Bach continues in this movement to symbolize the power of the Lord, but with concentrated means. He avoids full orchestra and chorus and confines himself to a very small number of performers: a tenor, two violins playing the same part, and a *basso continuo.*

BAROQUE MUSIC

Bach does not give musical expression to details of the text as he did in the previous movement. Except for a passage towards the end, he writes music which conveys the idea of the text only in general.

The movement employs a *ritornello* which alternates with vocal sections. In the *ritornello* occurs the pattern from which the rest of the movement is derived. The movement is divided into five sections:

Section I (mm. 1–14). *Ritornello.*

The upper melody, played by the violins, consists of separate phrases which are energetic and resolute in rhythm and direction. Although some of the phrases are separated by rests, they are all welded into a continuous melodic line by means of a coherent harmony and the complementary rhythm of the *basso continuo* (Ex. 30).

Example 30

Section II (mm. 14–28): Deposuit potentes de sede; Et exaltavit humiles: Tenor with Violins.

This section is identical with Section I except that the upper melody is taken over by the Tenor, while the violins are used only for accompaniment. Changes occur in measures 23–25, where parts of the main melodic line shift to the violins and the Tenor develops a melody of its own.

Section III (mm. 27–35): *Ritornello*

A condensed version of Section I.

Section IV (mm. 34–54): Deposuit potentes de sede; Et exaltavit humiles: Tenor with Violins.

Another variant of Section I. The distribution of the upper melody between the Tenor and the violins is in principle, if not in exact detail, like that of Section II. However, from about measure 46 on, the section is extended, and the words "et exaltavit humiles" are sung twice. Here the violins continue with motives from the upper melody of the *ritornello,* while the Tenor spins out its melodic line. This extension is not only the musical climax of the movement, but the final intensification of its principal thought.

Section V (mm. 53–67): *Ritornello*

Identical with Section I.

Movement No. 9

Text: Esurientes implevit bonis;
   Et divites dimisit inanes.

   He hath filled the hungry with good things;
   And the rich he hath sent empty away.

Scoring: Alto; 2 Flutes; *Basso Continuo.*

206   THE AGE OF THE BAROQUE

In its details of structure, the movement is identical with Movement No. 8: it is divided into five sections; an initial *ritornello* sets the pattern of motives for the entire movement; vocal and instrumental sections alternate; and the *ritornello* is repeated at the end.

In spite of its close structural kinship with the preceding movement, Movement No. 9 is quite different in character. It has nothing of the highly charged intensity of Movement No. 8. Its mood is more cheerful and relaxed; in quite simple terms it illustrates the idea of the Lord's compassion.

Section I (mm. 1–8): *Ritornello*

The *ritornello* establishes the style of the entire movement. Its instrumentation, consisting of two flutes in high registers and the *pizzicato* (plucked) tones of the *basso continuo,* is light and lucid. In measures 1–4 and again in measure 7, the flutes play a dance-like melody in parallel sixths and thirds. This is a popular type of harmony still known in our own time. Thus a homophonic texture is produced, interrupted, however, by the imitation of a new, scale-like motive (Ex. 31).

Example 31

Section II (mm. 8–17): Esurientes implevit bonis; Et divites dimisit inanes: Alto (with flutes).

This section is patterned after Section I, although the upper melody, formerly played by the violins, shifts to the Alto. The Alto varies the last two measures of the *ritornello* with a melodic line of its own.

Section III (mm. 17–20): *Ritornello*

The *ritornello* is condensed, using only measures 1–4.

Section IV (mm. 21–36): Esurientes implevit bonis; Et divites dimisit inanes: Alto (with flutes).

Patterned after Section I, this section in measures 23–31 expands the third and fourth measures of the *ritornello* by long melismas on the words "bonis" ("good things") and "implevit" ("he hath filled"). The flutes, in the vocal section, add motives from the *ritornello* to the Alto part.

Section V (mm. 36–42): *Ritornello*

Identical with Section I.

Movement No. 10

Text: Suscepit Israel puerum suum,
Recordatus misericordiae suae.

He hath given help to his servant Israel,
In remembrance of his mercy.

Scoring: Soprano I, Soprano II, Alto; 2 Oboes (in unison); *Basso Continuo.*

This movement is a chorale arrangement—one of Bach's favorite types of composition. Its chief element is a chorale, a Protestant hymn, which is embedded in the polyphonic context of additional voices.

Chorales originated in the early 16th century. They were created by Martin Luther and his musical advisers to promote the active participation of the congregation in the service. Many of the tunes to which Protestant texts were adapted were borrowed from secular music and from Gregorian Chant; others were composed by Luther's followers in the 16th and 17th centuries. Protestant musicians soon based their own liturgical compositions on these chorales, thus utilizing a principle which had been familiar to composers in the Catholic Church since the Middle Ages. A representative example of such a use of sacred melody (in this case, Gregorian Chant) in a Renaissance work destined for the Catholic liturgy is Josquin's mass *"Pange Lingua."*[7]

The chorale in Bach's Movement No. 10 is played by two oboes in unison (Ex. 32). Although only the tune was heard, Bach's congregation must have immediately associated it

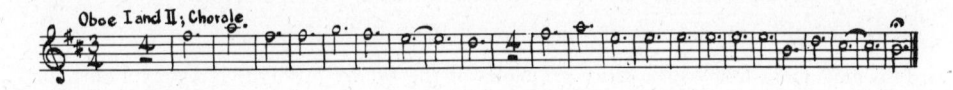

Example 32

with its text, which reads:

"Meine Seel' erhebt den Herren
Und mein Geist freuet sich Gottes, meines Heilands."

This is the German version of the first two lines of the *Magnificat,* which are used in Movements No. 1 and 2. The chorale, hovering in long sustained tones over the other voices, carries with it an element of spiritual tranquillity and becomes the symbol of an unshakable religious truth. The movement consists of two sections, each containing one of the two phrases of the chorale. Section 1 runs from measure 1 to 18, of which the first four and last four measures are without the chorale; Section 2 runs from measure 18 to 37.

The *basso continuo* remains constant, with the exception of only a few passages, throughout the movement. Its *ostinato* motive consists of three repeated tones which change their pitch at the beginning of each measure, usually moving stepwise in a descending or ascending direction.

On top of the metronomic motion of the *basso continuo,* there are three voices—two Sopranos and one Alto. The following recurrent rhythmic pattern lends uniformity to the vocal group of Section 1 (Ex. 33). The pattern is melodically articulated by a simple

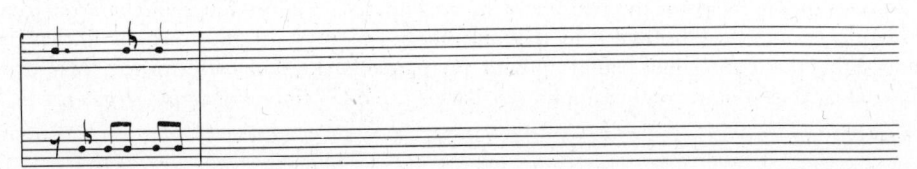

Example 33

[7] See, above, pp. 118–30.

motive which is hardly more than a straight line moving upwards and downwards. It is used in imitative polyphony.

Section 2 has a slightly greater rhythmic variableness. Inspired by the words "recordatus misericordiae suae," its motive, also employed imitatively, has larger intervals at the beginning and, subsequently, a more sinuous line. The ending of this motive recurs frequently in measures 30–37, emphasizing the word "misericordiae" ("mercy") with which it is associated. The same idea is further reinforced by half-tone progressions of the *ostinato* motive of the *basso continuo* in measures 18–24 and 27–31.

More relevant than any motives and their polyphonic treatment is the harmonic texture resulting from the interplay of the three vocal lines and the *basso continuo*. Bach spiced the harmony with many dissonances which appear usually on the third beat. The four voices are crowded into such a narrow space that the second Soprano occasionally crosses the first, and the *basso continuo* goes above the Alto. However, close spacing of the voices and the dissonances do not result in harshness, but in an effect of delicacy and warmth. This effect owes its existence to the flowing motion of the melodic lines, colored by the light timbre of female voices, and to chords which contain occasional parallel thirds and sixths and only unaccented dissonances. The high register of the 'cello partaking in the *basso continuo* adds to the lucidity of the texture.

Movement No. 11

Text: Sicut locutus est ad patres nostros, Abraham et semini eius in saecula.

As he spake to our fathers, to Abraham, and to his seed forever.

Scoring: Soprano I, Soprano II, Alto, Tenor, Bass; *Basso Continuo*.

This movement follows the strict principles of the *fugue*.[8] A fugue is a polyphonic composition, usually of two to five voices. It consists of one main theme, called the Subject. This Subject is introduced at the very beginning by one voice alone, and then successively by the others. One voice presents it in the original key; the next, five tones higher; the third, again in the original key; the fourth, five tones higher; and so forth. In addition to the Subject, there is generally a subsidiary theme, the Counter-Subject. The Counter-Subject appears in the first voice as soon as the Subject is taken over by the second voice, and subsequently in the second voice when the Subject shifts to the third, and so forth. The opening of the fugue in which Subject and Counter-Subject are introduced, is called the Exposition. It usually ends with an authentic cadence, but there is no pause, as a rule, because the voices provide for the continuity of the onward motion.

After the Exposition is completed, the Subject (and often the Counter-Subject, too) is restated several times throughout the fugue, the last time, traditionally, towards the end. In between the appearances of the Subject, there are Episodes, that is, sections which are animated by the imitation of new motives derived from the Counter-Subject or even from the Subject. The Episodes are distinguished by their forward motion rather than by their melodic design. They are closely linked with the passages featuring the Subject.

It is evident that the small number of the structural principles of a fugue leaves the composer ample room for the free use of his imagination. Fugues range in character from playfulness and even brilliance to thoughtfulness and mystical introversion. It may be added that the fugue is not bound up with any particular kind of performance: there exist instrumental as well as vocal examples (*cf.* Bach's *Little G Minor Fugue for Organ*).

---

[8] See Chapter VIII, pp. 394–95.

BAROQUE MUSIC

The following scheme outlines the structure of Movement No. 11:

	Measures
Exposition	1–17
Episode I	17–21
Subject entry	21–25
Subject entry	25–29
Subject entry	29–33
Subject entry	33–37
Episode II	37–45
Subject entry	45–49

Exposition (mm. 1–17):

Bach employs five voices but, contrary to the usual practice, introduces only four of them in the Exposition. The Soprano I, omitted in the Exposition, first appears in measure 21.

Example 34 is the Exposition of the fugue. The Subject and the Counter-Subject are

Example 34

marked, as are two additional motives *a* (mm. 9–13) and *b* (mm. 13–17), which do not belong to the conventional elements of a fugue.

The Subject of Movement No. 11 is of an uncomplicated nature—vigorous and even robust. Its accentuations are chiefly determined by the regularity of the meter. In its first two measures it consists of nothing but an embellished straight line leading from D to the higher A. At this point its flow is stemmed by large, sturdy intervals which make the very last tone of the Subject a conclusive ending—an unconventional feature, since a fugue-subject is usually rendered as continuous as possible. The Counter-Subject has the same square-cut design as the Subject.

A recurrent pattern of motives, established in measures 9–13, dominates the greater part of the fugue. It includes not only the normal Subject and Counter-Subject, but motive *a* as well. Even the manner in which these three motives are combined remains the same in each occurrence of the pattern; only the positions of the motives change. In combination with the three motives just mentioned, there are always one or two additional lines; in most cases one of the added lines is motive *b* or a part of it. The three-motive pattern appears six times in the fugue: in measures 9–13, 13–17, 21–25, 25–29, 29–33, and 33–37. There is only one variant (mm. 25–29), where only the last four tones of motive *a* are used. In the final appearance of the Subject near the end of the fugue (mm. 45–49), the pattern is for the first time incomplete: it includes the Subject, the Counter-Subject, and, instead of motive *a,* merely its last two words "in saecula."

The frequent repetition of the same pattern of motives is unusual in a fugue. Bach resorted to it for textual and dramatic reasons rather than for musical ones. The three motives are each time associated with the same words: the Subject with "sicut locutus est ad patres nostros," the Counter-Subject with "Abraham et semini eius in saecula," and motive *a* (which is only once performed instrumentally) with "sicut locutus est in saecula." The reiteration of these motives suggests, therefore, an emphasis on the text, and it is this emphasis which has given this fugue its peculiar form. The words "in saecula" ("forever") stand out in high relief because they are sung with the Counter-Subject and motive *a* simultaneously at the cadences, which are specially marked passages. The words come even more distinctly to the fore towards the end of the fugue (mm. 42–49), where they are sung first by four voices, and then completely synchronized rhythmically by five voices as the grand conclusion (mm. 49–53).

It is the touchstone of a good fugue that there be agreement in character between the Subject and the fugue as a whole. The simplicity of the Subject is complemented by the following features as the fugue unfolds. Although cadences in a fugue are usually hidden by the voices, they are clearly marked in this movement. Its polyphony is simplified through the influence of the meter on the rhythm of all voices, so that it does not come as a surprise when, towards the end, the voices are rhythmically synchronized. The polyphony is also simplified by the recurrence of the initial pattern of motives (Subject, Counter-Subject, and motives *a* and *b*) throughout the fugue. The harmony is confined mainly to D major; when deviations occur (for example, to the related A major), they are quickly channelled back to the initial tonality.

There are only two Episodes in this fugue. They are closely related to the sections featuring the Subject.

Episode I (mm. 17–21): The episode consists of the Counter-Subject, motives *a* and *b,* and an additional line.

Episode II (mm. 37–45): A shortened version of the Counter-Subject in Soprano I has impressed its rhythm on most of the other voices. The result is a chordal texture which is modified, in the first five measures, by an imitation of the Counter-Subject in Soprano I and the Bass.

BAROQUE MUSIC

Movement No. 12

Text: Gloria Patri, gloria Filio, gloria et Spiritui Sancto.
Sicut erat in principio, et nunc, et semper, et in saecula saeculorum. Amen.

Glory be to the Father, glory to the Son, and glory to the Holy Ghost.

As it was in the beginning, is now, and ever shall be, world without end. Amen.

Scoring: Soprano I, Soprano II, Alto, Tenor, Bass; Violin I, Violin II, Viola; 2 Trumpets; Kettledrums; 2 Flutes; 2 Oboes; *Basso Continuo.*

This movement consists of two sections which follow the divisions of the text: one runs from measure 1 to 19 ("Gloria Patri, gloria Filio, gloria et Spiritui Sancto"), the other from measure 20 to 42 ("Sicut erat in principio, et nunc, et semper, et in saecula saeculorum"). These sections are clearly separated from each other by two distinct styles.

Section I (mm. 1–19): Gloria Patri, Gloria Filio, Gloria et Spiritui Sancto.

When Bach sings of the glory of God, he often does so with means which are impressive for their sheer strength and volume. This section is dominated by several powerful chords of the chorus in combination with the orchestra. Each of these chords (with the exception of the one opening the movement) is preceded by the tumultuous motion of all five voices that enter in quick succession. The intensity of these build-ups is increased by a *pedal, i.e.,* a long tone in the bass (in this case, the *basso continuo*) sustained against the changing chord progressions on top of it (Ex. 35). In its brilliance Section I is of an introductory character; its final cadence is inconclusive.

Example 35

Section II (mm. 20–42): Sicut erat in principio, et nunc, et semper, et in saecula saeculorum, Amen.

This section is closely related to Movement No. 1. It was Bach's intention to conclude his *Magnificat* with exactly the same sentiment of joy and ecstatic praise with which he opened it. In fact, Section II consists throughout of elements borrowed from the first movement.

Measures 20–22: Instrumental Introduction.

Reference to motive *a* of Movement No. 1 (Ex. 21).

Measures 22–24: Choral Section.

Interlocked entries of two choral groups with motive *b* of Movement No. 1 (Ex. 21). The treatment of the motive corresponds to the occurrence in measures 35–37 of the first movement.

Measures 24–26: Instrumental Passage.

Similar to the Instrumental Introduction.

Measures 26–42: Choral Section (with brief instrumental passages).

Motive *b* (Ex. 21) is several times restated in a semi-homophonic style. At the end chorus and orchestra combine in a grand conclusion of the movement, the instrumental parts corresponding to the orchestral conclusion of the first movement.

Recommended reading:

Hans T. David and Arthur Mendel, edd., *The Bach Reader,* New York, W. W. Norton, 1945.

Manfred F. Bukofzer, "Fusion of National Styles: Bach," Ch. VIII of *Music in the Baroque Era,* New York, W. W. Norton, 1947.

CANTATA NO. 4: *Christ Lag in Todesbanden*[1]

FROM THE HAND OF BACH about 200 cantatas, destined for liturgical use in the Lutheran church, have been preserved. *Cantata No. 4* (*Christ Lay in the Bonds of Death*) was probably composed about 1724, in Leipzig, a short time after Bach had been installed as the musical director of the Church of St. Thomas.

A Baroque church cantata was a work for voices (usually both choral and solo) and instruments. At some point in the rendition the cantata was interrupted to make place for a sermon, after which it was continued. Many of Bach's cantatas concluded with a simple hymn in which the congregation joined.

These hymns, or "chorales," as they are called, were created by Martin Luther and his musical advisers to promote the active participation of the congregation in the service. Many of the tunes to which Protestant texts were adapted were borrowed from secular music and from Gregorian Chant; others were composed by Luther's followers in the 16th and 17th centuries.

Inspired by the example of Catholic church composers, who for centuries had embedded melodies of Gregorian Chant in their polyphonic compositions, Protestant composers utilized the chorale in the same manner. Bach's works are studded with these chorales. They appear both in his organ works and in his cantatas.

The text of the chorale *Christ Lag in Todesbanden* was written by Luther himself. Destined for Easter, its seven stanzas appropriately speak of Christ's sacrifice on the Cross, his Resurrection, and the salvation he thus brought to mankind. The mood of the text moves between the two poles of mystic rapture and sorrow on the one hand and of earthly jubilation on the other. Bach used all of its seven stanzas, or verses, and made an independent musical composition (based on the chorale melody) out of each.

The hymn-tune itself consists of two sections, the first of which is repeated (Ex. 36). Its structural scheme (a-a-b) is frequent in chorale-tunes of the 16th and 17th centuries. The melody divides itself into eight phrases—a division which Bach retained in most of the movements of the cantata.

[1]Program B.

Example 36

In its treatment of the chorale, the cantata is related to chorale variations for organ—a type of composition cultivated by German Protestant composers of the 17th and early 18th centuries. In these variations, the chorale itself is usually left intact, but in each movement it is associated with new voices and set into new thematic relations. This is the formal principle which Bach adopted for *Cantata No. 4*. It is noteworthy that this is the only Bach cantata which has the chorale in all of its movements; his other chorale-based cantatas have the chorale only at the end, or only in some of the movements.

Sinfonia.

Scoring: Violin I, Violin II; Viola I, Viola II; *Basso Continuo.*

The term *sinfonia* has no connection with what we now call a symphony. In the Baroque era it designated brief instrumental compositions in operas and cantatas.

Bach's *sinfonia* consists of only fourteen measures, cast in free form. Its consistency depends solely on the meaningful progression of chords and voices. Predominantly homophonic, it has an expressive upper voice (Violin I) and *basso continuo;* the middle voices (Violin II and Violas) are subordinate. However, from about measure 7 on, the middle voices become more lively and soon (m. 10) lead to imitations in which all voices, except the *basso continuo,* participate. This new emphasis on the independence of voices, complemented by an upward striving of the upper voice and an intensified harmony, results in a climax shortly before the end (mm. 12–13). Here Bach uses a favorite device which he will repeat at the end of Verse V. At the moment of greatest intensity, he thins out the texture and channels the accumulated energy into a single melodic line, whereupon the succeeding final cadence, uniting again all voices, resolves the unexpected suspense. The entire second half of the *sinfonia* can be likened to a *crescendo*. It is based, however, on melody, rhythm, harmony, and texture, and not, as a later time would have preferred, on dynamics (*i.e.,* on an increase in volume of sound).

In its brevity and free form, the *sinfonia* is merely an introduction to the subsequent movements of the cantata. Its atmosphere of sorrow and solemnity anticipates emotional qualities which will be articulated later on, and sets the mood for the opening lines of Verse I, which speak of Christ in the tomb. It is also anticipatory in its treatment of the chorale. Only parts of the chorale are quoted, and their identity is obscured by the new melodic lines into which they are inserted. In measures 1 and 2 the half-tone interval of the opening of the chorale appears several times in the bass and the first violin; in measures 3–4 the violin, imitated by the bass, makes two attempts to get the first chorale-line started; finally, in measures 5–7, the entire first phrase is quoted (Violin I).

Verse I.

Scoring: Soprano, Alto, Tenor, Bass; Violin I and II, Viola I and II; Cornetto;[2] Trombone I, II, and III; *Basso Continuo.*

[2] An old wind instrument made of wood, which is not related to the modern brass instrument of similar name. A modern brass instrument is used in the Shaw recording.

Christ lag in Todesbanden	Christ lay in the bonds of Death
Für unser Sünd' gegeben.	For our sins sacrificed.
Er ist wieder erstanden	He is again arisen
Und hat uns bracht das Leben.	And has brought us life.
Des wir sollen fröhlich sein,	So let us be joyful,
Gott loben, und ihm dankbar sein,	Praise God, and be grateful to Him,
Und singen Hallelujah.	And sing Hallelujah.
Hallelujah.	Hallelujah.

There are fewer independent voices than the score indicates, since the wind instruments *double* (*i.e.,* duplicate) the choral parts, and the *basso continuo* for the most part doubles the vocal Bass. The core of the movement consists of the four voices of the chorus. Only the two violins add motives of their own; but they, too, double choral parts towards the end of the verse. It must be noted, however, that by reason of its polyphonic structure and its expansiveness the movement is both intricate and powerful. This is as it should be. For not only does Verse I constitute the actual opening of a deeply religious work, but its text gives the plot of the entire work in outline, beginning with the image of Christ's entombment and ending with His Resurrection.

The choral ensemble, which is the mainstay of the movement, consists of two elements: the Soprano on the one hand, and the Alto, Tenor, and Bass on the other. The Soprano sings the chorale tune but separates its eight phrases by rests. The long tones of the tune and its calm, even rhythm contribute to symbolizing a religious belief, strong and unshakable.

Alto, Tenor, and Bass are engaged in a double role. First of all, they are active within a polyphonic context below each chorale phrase. Though using the text of the chorale phrase, they employ, in imitations, a completely new motive each time. This motive serves to throw into relief the main idea or image of the text. The juxtaposition of the chorale and of imitations based on an illustrative motive is comparable to a sermon which gives a quotation from the Bible and an exegesis of its meaning.

Alto, Tenor, and Bass, which continue even when the Soprano is silent, have a second function of linking the separate phrases of the chorale. In a manner reminiscent of 16th-century chorale arrangements, they anticipate not only the text of the next chorale phrase but its motives as well. Details of the structure of the movement will appear in the following outline.

Measures 1–8: Soprano: Chorale phrase I ("Christ lag in Todesbanden").

Alto, Tenor, Bass: There is no one illustrative motive, except for the winding motive towards the end of the passage (see especially the Bass, mm. 5–8) which refers to Christ's "bonds" (Ex. 37).

Example 37

Measures 8–13: Soprano: Chorale phrase II ("Für unser Sünd' gegeben").

Alto, Tenor, Bass: The half-tone intervals of the motive (Ex. 38) emphasize the feeling of pain and remorse which pervades the idea of "unser Sünd' " ("our sins"). The motive is also used in inversion, *i.e.,* with reversed intervals.

Example 38

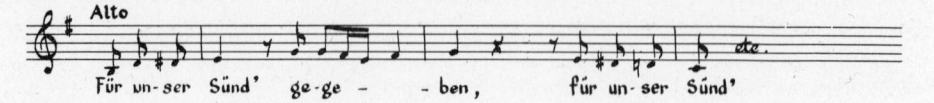

Measures 13–19: Alto, Tenor, Bass use the next chorale phrase as well as a new motive inspired by the words "Er ist wieder erstanden" ("He is again arisen").

Measures 19–24: Soprano: Chorale phrase III ("Er ist wieder erstanden").

Alto, Tenor, Bass: The motive refers, in its affirmative character, to the words "Er ist wieder erstanden." Note that it is not identical with the previous motive (mm. 13–19) associated with the same words, and that it is related to the chorale phrase.

Measures 24–30: Alto, Tenor, Bass use the next chorale phrase as well as its illustrative motive.

Measures 30–35: Soprano: Chorale phrase IV ("Und hat uns bracht das Leben").

Alto, Tenor, Bass use a motive whose animation matches the meaning of the word "Leben" ("life").

Measures 36–38: A brief instrumental passage which continues what was previously an accompaniment to the chorus.

Measures 38–42: Alto, Tenor, Bass use the next chorale phrase as well as its illustrative motive.

Measures 43–46: Soprano: Chorale phrase V ("Des wir sollen fröhlich sein").

Alto, Tenor, Bass: The lively motive refers to the word "fröhlich" ("joyful").

Measures 46–48: A brief instrumental passage which continues the previous accompaniment.

Measures 48–53: Alto, Tenor, Bass use the next chorale phrase and its illustrative motive.

Measures 53–58: Soprano: Chorale phrase VI ("Gott loben und ihm dankbar sein").

Alto, Tenor, Bass: A jubilant motive emphasizes the words "Gott loben."

Measures 58–64: Alto, Tenor, Bass use the next chorale phrase and its illustrative motive.

Measures 64–68: Soprano: Chorale phrase VII ("Und singen Hallelujah"). The chorale appears now in quarter notes instead of in half notes, the momentum of the movement having so increased that it pulls the Soprano into its more active rhythm, and thereby prepares the subsequent *alla breve* section.

Alto, Tenor, Bass use a motive associated with the word "Hallelujah" which is related to the chorale phrase.

Measures 68–94 (Alla Breve): The over-all character of the section is of unrestrained jubilation. This feeling is generated by the exuberant rhythm of the "Hallelujah" motive (a syncopated form of the final chorale phrase), restated in numerous and breathless imitations, and by a fast tempo (*alla breve* indicates a tempo twice as fast as before) and the unusual length of the section. The structure of the previous sections, in which a calm chorale phrase was underpinned by the lively imitations of an illustrative motive, is abandoned here. The Soprano is no longer contrasted with the other voices but takes part in their polyphonic activities. In the process two motives are employed: chorale phrase VIII ("Hallelujah"), appearing for the first time in the Tenor of measures 68–69, and a new "Hallelujah" motive.

Verse II.
Scoring: Soprano, doubled by Cornetto;[3] Alto, doubled by Trombone;[3] *Basso Continuo.*

Den Tod niemand zwingen kunnt	Death no one could subdue
Bei allen Menschenkindern;	Of all the children of men;
Das macht alles unser Sünd',	This is all because of our sin—
Kein Unschuld war zu finden.	No guiltlessness was to be found.
Davon kam der Tod sobald,	Therefore Death came so soon,
Und nahm über uns Gewalt,	And conquered us,
Hielt uns in seinem Reich gefangen.	Held us in his realm imprisoned.
Hallelujah.	Hallelujah.

[3] Not in the Shaw recording.

Luther's text described Death as something powerful, destructive, and inescapable, which comes over mankind as the just punishment for its sins. Bach's setting emphasizes the hopeless, doomed condition of man, before Christ came to save him from Death. The chorale phrases acquire a quality of weariness, through repetitions of the opening notes and extensions within the phrase. In spite of the emotional intensity of the text, the music is cast in the rigorous structure of two upper voices and a *basso continuo*—a favorite arrangement of the Baroque. The eight divisions of the chorale tune establish the divisions in the movement. The Soprano sings the chorale phrase, while the Alto usually imitates the beginning of each phrase and then continues on its own way. Below the two voices, there is a characteristic *basso continuo*. Its stealthy motion caused by frequent octave leaps and the recurrence, with occasional modifications, of a single motive (the first four tones of the bass) give it the general character of a *basso ostinato* or "recurring bass." It symbolizes the implacable nature, the inexorable tread, of Death. The pattern of the two voices and their bass is established in the first eight measures of the movement (Ex. 39), after which it appears eight times more.

The sections are linked by *ritornellos, i.e.,* instrumental passages which are identical with or similar to the instrumental opening.

Example 39

Measures 1–3: Ritornello.
Measures 3–8: Chorale phrase I ("Den Tod niemand zwingen kunnt"). Note how the words *den Tod* ("death") are emphasized; note also the expressive extension on *niemand* ("no one").
Measures 8–9: Ritornello.
Measures 9–13: Chorale phrase II ("Bei allen Menschenkindern").
Measures 13–15: Ritornello.
Measures 15–20: Chorale phrase III ("Das macht alles unser Sünd' ").
Measures 20–21: Ritornello.
Measures 21–25: Chorale phrase IV ("Kein Unschuld war zu finden").
Measures 25–26: Ritornello.
Measures 27–31: Chorale phrase V ("Davon kam der Tod sobald"). Again note the repetitions of *der Tod* ("Death").
Measures 31–32: Ritornello.
Measures 32–36: Chorale phrase VI ("Und nahm über uns Gewalt"). Expressive treatment of *über* ("over") in the Alto.
Measures 36–38: Ritornello.
Measures 38–43: Chorale phrase VII ("Hielt uns in seinem Reich gefangen"). At the word *gefangen* ("imprisoned," "held fast") Bach writes a long-held dissonance—F sharp and E—which "imprisons" or "ensnares" the voices for five beats, thereby illustrating in sound the idea of the word sung.
Measures 43–52: Chorale phrase VIII ("Hallelujah"). This section is expanded by means of imitations among the two upper voices. It is noteworthy that the "Hallelujah" has lost its original meaning. A dragging rhythm and dissonant harmony have transformed it into a pathetic lamentation.

Verse III.
Scoring: Tenor; Violin I and II (playing in unison); *Basso Continuo*.

Jesus Christus, Gottes Sohn	Jesus Christ, God's son,
An unser Statt ist kommen,	Has come to take our place,
Und hat die Sünde weggetan,	And has cancelled our sins,
Damit dem Tod genommen	Thus taking from Death
All' sein Recht und sein' Gewalt;	All his authority and his power;
Da bleibet nichts denn Tod'sgestalt;	There remains nothing but the semblance of Death;
Den Stach'l hat er verloren.	His sting he has lost.
Hallelujah.	Hallelujah.

This movement is related in structure to Verse II. It too consists of two upper voices (the violins, playing in unison, and the Tenor), supported by a *basso continuo*. The eight phrases of the chorale tune are preserved; they are linked by *ritornellos*. However, in contradistinction to Verse II, it is not the two upper voices which form a group, but the highest and the lowest voice, the violins and the *basso continuo*. While they move on almost continuously, they repeat an initial statement (mm. 1–5) throughout the Verse, literally (or only slightly varied) in the *ritornellos,* modified when accompanying the chorale tune. The first seven measures of the verse set the pattern for the entire movement (Ex. 40). The text, expressing jubilation in Christ's victory over Death, is matched by the exuberant motive and the muscular rhythm of the instrumental parts, by simple harmony, and by the unadorned original version of the chorale in the Tenor voice. There are, however, two passages whose intense imagery induced Bach to change somewhat the initial thematic pattern. These are described below.

Example 40

Measures 1–5: Ritornello.

Measures 5–7: Chorale phrase I ("Jesus Christus, Gottes Sohn").

Measures 7–8: Ritornello.

Measures 8–10: Chorale phrase II ("An unser Statt ist kommen").

Measures 10–14: Ritornello.

Measures 14–16: Chorale phrase III ("Und hat die Sünde weggetan").

Measures 16–18: Ritornello.

Measures 18–20: Chorale phrase IV ("Damit dem Tod genommen").

Measures 20–22: Ritornello.

Measures 23–24: Chorale phrase V ("All' sein Recht und sein' Gewalt").

Measures 24–25: Ritornello. In order to anticipate a change in the thematic pattern and a change in expression, the *basso continuo* abandons its solid, angular style by borrowing, though in varied form, the violin figure.

Measures 25–28: Chorale phrase VI ("Da bleibet nichts denn Tod'sgestalt"). In order to emphasize the significance of the word "Tod'sgestalt" ("the semblance of Death"), the tempo is abruptly changed to *adagio* (slow), the chorale phrase acquires an expressive melodic turn, and imitations among the three voices are introduced.

Measures 28–30 (Allegro): Ritornello. This returns to the original tempo (*allegro*: fast).

Measures 30–32: Chorale phrase VII ("Den Stach'l hat er verloren").

Measures 32–34: Ritornello.

Measures 34–38: A variant of chorale phrase VIII ("Hallelujah"). Bach matches the jubilant implications of the text by transforming the chorale phrase into a lively motive and repeating it in imitations among the three voices.

Measures 38–42: Ritornello, a literal repetition of the opening of the movement.

Verse IV.
Scoring: Soprano, Alto, Tenor, Bass; *Basso Continuo.*

Es war ein wunderlicher Krieg.	It was a wondrous battle,
Da Tod und Leben rungen;	When Death and Life wrestled;
Das Leben behielt den Sieg,	Life gained the victory,
Es hat den Tod verschlungen,	It has swallowed up Death.
Die Schrift hat verkündiget das,	The scripture has declared
Wie ein Tod den andern frass,	How one death[4] devoured the other;
Ein Spott aus dem Tod ist worden.	Death itself has become a mockery.
Hallelujah.	Hallelujah.

The structure of this movement, based on the chorale tune and illustrative motives within the polyphonic context of three additional voices, is obviously related to that of Verse I. However, in keeping with the character of the text, it is considerably less complex. There is, first of all, no orchestral accompaniment. In fact, the four voices stand alone except for the vocal Bass, which is doubled by the *basso continuo*. Moreover, a number of sections are repeated literally, in contrast to the ever-changing texture of Verse I.

The chorale tune, which is carried by the Alto, appears unadorned and in its original quarter notes. The down-to-earth style of the movement is mainly supported by the illustrative motives which follow very closely the homespun and tangible images of the text. Particularly the second half of the Verse (from about measure 24 on) is shot through with the most lively scenes, so lively, in fact, that they seem to be a part of a stage action. There is first a solemn Biblical prophecy, the viciousness and confusion of a battle with death, until death has been "swallowed up," then shouts of ridicule and laughter, and finally pealing Hallelujahs.

Observe that in this verse alone the chorale is presented (in the Alto voice) in a key five tones higher than the original key of E minor. The accompanying voices, however, constantly bring the music back to the basic key of E minor by avoiding the expected cadences in the other key. The resulting clash of tonalities conveys in sound the idea of conflict, with which the words are concerned.

Measures 1–5: Soprano, Tenor, Bass: Using the next two chorale phrases.

Measures 5–7: Alto: Chorale phrase I ("Es war ein wunderlicher Krieg").

Soprano, Tenor, Bass: Their motive refers to the word "Krieg" (battle).

Measures 7–9: Soprano, Tenor, Bass: Using the illustrative motive of the next chorale phrase.

Measures 9–12: Alto: Chorale phrase II ("Da Tod und Leben rungen").

Soprano, Tenor, Bass: Their motive is inspired by the image of the wrestling of death with life.

Measures 12–16: Soprano, Tenor, Bass: Identical with measures 1–5, but anticipating the text of the two next chorale phrases.

Measures 16–18: Alto: Chorale phrase III ("Das Leben behielt den Sieg").

Soprano, Tenor, Bass: Identical with measures 5–7.

Measures 18–21: Soprano, Tenor, Bass: Identical with measures 7-9, but anticipating the text of the next chorale phrase.

Measures 21–24: Alto: Chorale phrase IV ("Es hat den Tod verschlungen").

Measures 24–26: Soprano, Tenor, Bass: Using the next chorale phrase, but in an embellished form.

Measures 27–29: Alto: Chorale phrase V ("Die Schrift hat verkündiget das").

Soprano, Tenor, Bass: Using the motive of measures 24–26.

Measures 29–31: Soprano, Tenor, Bass: Using the next chorale phrase. The idea of "swallowing up" is symbolized by hurried imitations, the one "engulfing" the other.

[4]*I.e.*, the death of Christ.

Measures 31–35: Alto: Chorale phrase VI ("Wie ein Tod den andern frass").

Soprano, Tenor, Bass: Their motive is very brief, merely adding to the agitation of the scene. However, as soon as the chorale phrase has ended (m. 33), the three voices acquire a more specific symbolization. By means of hasty imitations and a rapid thinning out of the texture so that only two tones of one voice remain, the image of devouring and its results are suggested. Here (m. 34) the *basso continuo* becomes independent for the first and last time in this movement. It repeats, several times, the accentuated half-tone interval F sharp-E sharp, and thus adds a touch of aggressiveness and obstinacy to the image of the battle.

Measures 35–38: Alto: Chorale phrase VII ("Ein Spott aus dem Tod ist worden").

Soprano, Tenor, Bass: Using a motive which is at first identical with the (inverted) first two tones of the chorale phrase. The motive is associated with the words "ein Spott" ("a mockery").

Measures 37–38: Soprano, Tenor, Bass: The highest voice uses the motive of the next chorale phrase.

Measures 39–44: Alto: Chorale phrase VIII (Hallelujah").

Soprano, Tenor, Bass: Each voice has a Hallelujah motive of its own which is constantly repeated, though with changing pitches.

In Verse IV the dramatic conflicts of the *Cantata* find their resolution. Christ's Resurrection has brought salvation to mankind. The feeling of anguish has given way to joyous exultation. It is likely that at this point a sermon followed, after which the performance of the music was resumed.

Verse V
Scoring: Bass; Violin I and II, Viola I and II; *Basso Continuo.*

Hier ist das rechte Osterlamm,	Here is the true Easter Lamb,
Davon Gott hat geboten,	Which God has offered us,
Das ist hoch an des Kreuzes Stamm	High on the Cross's stem
In heisser Lieb gebraten,	In burning love consumed.[5]
Das Blut zeichnet unser Tür,	The blood marks our door;
Das hält der Glaub' dem Tode für;	This is what Faith opposes to Death;
Der Würger kann uns nicht mehr schaden.	The Strangler can hurt us no longer.
Hallelujah.	Hallelujah.

This verse is cast in the form of a bass aria (an aria is a vocal solo composition in an opera or a cantata) with instrumental accompaniment. Since this accompaniment is not merely a simple harmonic support, we have to consider three rather than two elements—a vocal Bass, the *basso continuo,* and the first violin. The other instruments are fill-in middle voices. As soon as a phrase of the chorale is sung by the Bass, it is immediately imitated by the first violin; the most essential element of the movement thus receives a double statement. The *basso continuo* is a typical example of its kind, but it is shaped in this as in all other movements in accordance with the character of the text. In the greater part of the movement, it is fluent and expressive. The *basso continuo* is associated with the chorale by occasionally anticipating the first notes of a chorale phrase (Ex. 41).

After the triumphant mood of the previous movement, Bach now expresses deep grief over Christ's death on the Cross, which mankind must remember as the price paid for the salva-

---

[5]Luther actually uses the strong pictorial image "roasted," referring of course to the preparation of the traditional Easter lamb eaten by the Jews on the feast of Passover. The next line refers to the origin of the Passover feast; the blood of the lamb, sprinkled on the lintel and doorposts of the Jews' dwelling-places in Egypt, was a sign to the Angel of Death to "pass over" those houses when visiting destruction upon Pharoah's Egyptians (see Exodus, Ch. 12).

Example 41

tion of its life. No wonder then that the chorale does not appear in its original form. It is changed in rhythm by the adoption of triple meter instead of the original duple meter; there are also other rhythmic and, above all, melodic modifications which will be discussed below. All these changes, which are accomplished with the greatest economy of means, serve to throw into relief particular images of the text without upsetting the initial thematic pattern.

Measures 1–10: Chorale phrase I ("Hier ist das rechte Osterlamm"). The opening is anticipated by the *basso continuo,* an expressive, descending chromatic line.[6] The chorale phrase, five tones lower than usual, is imitated in its original key by the first violin, as it continues into a new melodic line.

Measures 10–18: Chorale phrase II ("Davon hat Gott geboten"). As it is spun out, the chorale phrase is imitated by the first violin.

Measures 18–30: Chorale phrase III ("Das ist hoch an des Kreuzes Stamm"). Except for an additional accompaniment of the violins and violas in the first seven measures and a few subsequent minor changes in the middle voices, the chorale phrase and its continuation are almost identical with measures 1–10. There is, however, one noteworthy difference—the intensely expressive treatment of the word *Kreuz* ("Cross"), which Bach loads with pathos by using a melodic extension in the voice part and poignant dissonances in the harmony.

Measures 30–38: Chorale phrase IV ("In heisser Lieb' gebraten") and its continuation are practically identical with measures 10–18.

Measures 38–54: Chorale phrase V ("Das Blut zeichnet unser Tür"). In order to intensify the religious imagery of the text, and to mark the change from thoughts of the Crucifixion to those of the redemption it brought, Bach modifies his previous structural procedure. The opening tones of the chorale tune appear in imitations in the *basso continuo,* the vocal Bass, the first violin, and again in the vocal Bass, where the chorale phrase is completed. Thus the word "Blut" ("Blood"), with which the opening tones are associated, is several times repeated. The chorale phrase itself (mm. 41–45) is expanded and varied by wide intervals which perhaps support the image of the "spreading" of the blood "on our door." Bach strengthens

[6] An almost identical bass line, repeated over and over, underlies the *Crucifixus* of Bach's *Mass in B Minor.* ("He was crucified for us also, under Pontius Pilate.")

this image still further by using the characteristic ending of the chorale phrase in an instrumental interlude (Violin I, mm. 45–50). As a climax of the passage, the chorale phrase in its original form (Violin I) appears simultaneously with a second form of the chorale phrase, a variant of measures 41–45 (vocal Bass).

Measures 54–70: Chorale phrase VI ("Das hält der Glaub' dem Tode für"), imitated by the first violin. When the chorale phrase is spun out, an unusually large skip downwards (an octave and a half) underlines the unexpected and frightening aspects of death ("Tode"). A brief instrumental cadence concludes the passage decisively as though to close the door on Death once for all.

Measures 70–85: Chorale phrase VII ("Der Würger kann uns nicht") and chorale phrase VIII ("nicht mehr schaden") follow in succession. Note that the latter phrase repeats previous words instead of using the word "Hallelujah" as in all other movements. The word "Würger" ("strangler") is emphasized by a very long tone in the vocal Bass, and excitement is added by a sixteenth-note figuration in the first violin. In conclusion, the first violin imitates chorale phrase VII, while the vocal Bass sings a new "Hallelujah" motive.

Measures 85–95: This section is an addition to the movement which serves to deepen the spirit of final jubilation. Its main characteristic is a canonic imitation (*i.e.,* a literal imitation of a melodic line of considerable length) between the first violin and the vocal Bass (measures 85–92). The firm intervals of the melodic line and the zestful forward motion of the imitation match the meaning of the "Hallelujahs" with which they are associated; the joy of the Redemption is so great as to demand the full range of the voice to express it at the end, where Bach writes an exceptionally wide vocal progression covering two octaves (from high to low E).

Verse VI
Scoring: Soprano; Tenor; *Basso Continuo.*

So feiern wir das hohe Fest	Thus we celebrate the holy feast,
Mit Herzensfreud' und Wonne,	With heart's joy and rapture,
Das uns der Herre scheinen lässt;	Which the Lord has made to shine for us;
Er ist selber die Sonne,	He himself is the Sun,
Der durch seiner Gnaden Glanz	Who with the splendor of his grace
Erleuchtet unser Herzen ganz;	Wholly illumines our hearts;
Der Sünden Nacht ist verschwunden.	Sin's night has vanished.
Hallelujah.	Hallelujah.

In this movement Bach returns to an arrangement of two upper voices and a *basso continuo* and to the use of a *ritornello*. The chorale is divided into four segments, in each of which two of its phrases are sounded in succession. Soprano and Tenor share in carrying the phrases of each of the four segments. The beginning of each segment is loosened up by an imitation by one of the two upper voices, while its ending is animated by jubilant melismas in triplets (*i.e.,* three notes played in a time previously allotted to two) into which the chorale melody is spun out (Ex. 42). The *basso continuo* adds to the dance-like rhythm with the energy of its dotted notes (short-*long*-short-*long* etc.), which recurs throughout the movement. The whole effect is that of a festive dance, such as the Psalmist spoke of when he wrote: "Praise the Lord with stringed instruments and dancing." This musical treatment of course derives from the idea of the "high feast" or "festival" introduced in line 1 of the text.

Measure 1: Brief *Ritornello.*

Measures 1–8: Chorale phrase I ("So feiern wir das hohe Fest") appears first in the Soprano but shifts then to the Tenor, which subsequently sings chorale phrase II ("Mit Herzensfreud' und Wonne"). Both voices finally unite in melismas in parallel motion (see Ex. 42).

Measures 8–15: Chorale phrase III ("Das uns der Herre scheinen lässt") is first sung by

Example 42

the Tenor but is then taken over by the Soprano, which continues with Chorale phrase IV ("Er selber ist die Sonne"). Note that the entire passage is identical with measures 1–8 except that the two upper voices have exchanged their melodic lines. Two melodic lines which are constructed in such a way that the higher can become the lower and the lower can become the higher are written in what is called "double counterpoint."

Measures 15–17: Ritornello, identical with the *basso continuo* in measures 1–3.

Measures 18–25: Chorale phrase V ("Der durch seiner Gnaden Glanz") ending in a melisma in triplets. Before the Tenor joins the melismas of the Soprano, it imitates the opening of the Soprano. This is followed by Chorale phrase VI ("Erleuchtet unser Herzen ganz") in the Tenor, whose concluding melismas are joined by the Soprano.

Measures 25–28: Ritornello, using at the beginning, the melodic line of the *basso continuo* of measures 1–2.

Measures 28–41: Chorale phrase VII ("Der Sünden Nacht ist verschwunden") in the Soprano, imitated by the Tenor. The concluding melismas are sung in imitations instead of in parallel motion as before. After this appears Chorale phrase VIII ("Hallelujah") in the Soprano, but it is so modified that it is hardly distinguishable from previous concluding melismas. The phrase is repeated several times and imitated, each time, by the Tenor.

Measures 41–43: Instrumental ending or *Ritornello*.

Verse VII
Scoring: Identical with Verse I.

Wir essen und leben wohl	We eat and thrive
Im rechten Osterfladen,	On the true Easter bread;
Der alte Sauerteig nicht soll sein	The old leaven shall not stand
Bei dem Wort der Gnaden.	With the Word of Grace.
Christus will die Koste sein	Christ will be our food,
Und speisen die Seel' allein,	And He alone shall nourish the soul;
Der Glaub will keins andern leben.	By no other means shall Faith live.
Hallelujah.	Hallelujah.

Here the chorale appears in a form to which Bach resorted time and again for the end of his cantatas. The chorale is sung by the Soprano and supported by Alto, Tenor, and Bass. (The voices are doubled by instruments so that all of the performers of Verse I are assembled again.) Although Verse VII is a homophonic setting, usable for congregational singing, its middle voices have their meaningful direction and flow. According to the text, which reaffirms the Christian's faith in the one Savior, the chorale is given out in all its original simplicity and sturdiness (see Ex. 36), while the lower voices confirm this quality. Only in the final "Hallelujah" do the lower parts introduce more intense lines, which add to the fullhearted joyfulness of the conclusion.

Recommended reading:
Hans T. David and Arthur Mendel, edd., *The Bach Reader,* New York, W. W. Norton, 1945.
Manfred F. Bukofzer, "Fusion of National Styles: Bach," Ch. VIII of *Music in the Baroque Era,* New York, W. W. Norton, 1947.

SEVENTEENTH-CENTURY LITERATURE

JOHN DONNE (1572–1631)

The Sun Rising and *Batter My Heart*[1]

JOHN DONNE dealt the death blow to the artificial love poetry written by the Elizabethan followers of the Italian poet Petrarch and led the way to a new poetry that was at once realistic and intellectual. His secular poems—witty and erudite love poems, written for the most part before 1600—were circulated in manuscript among the wits and men of learning at the court of James I and Charles I. Donne was roughly of the same generation as Shakespeare, Ben Jonson, and the dramatists of the Mermaid Tavern, but he was not, like them, a man of the people, the son of a yeoman or a bricklayer, but a representative of the gentry. He was a Catholic by birth, educated at the university, trained for the law and the Church, and closely attached to the Court. His poetry awakened interest and was read and imitated because of its intensely vivid psychological realism and because of the boldness and accuracy with which a poetic style had been created out of words and phrases from all levels of usage and from apparently the most incongruous sources. He was a man whose instinct compelled him to bring the whole of experience into his verse and to choose the most direct and what, for his learned and fantastic mind, was the most natural form of expression. His poetic style, therefore, presents a striking contrast to the honeyed smoothness of Spenser or the magnificent rhetoric of Milton. He is colloquial, elevated, slangy, rhetorical, erudite, familiar—all in the same brief poem; and he takes his language from the court and the camp, from the jargon of the law, from the study, and from the market place.

This curious combination of qualities, it is interesting to note, can be found alike in his youthful "profane" love poems and in the passionate religious poems of his later life. This can be made clear by a detailed examination of a characteristic example of each group.

The Sun Rising is, in the first place, intended to be an amusing, witty, "clever" poem. It is light verse, but it is also, as we shall see, intensely serious—a good demonstration of the fact that seriousness has nothing to do with solemnity and can be accompanied by a good deal of

[1] Programs A and B.

levity. The poem, of course, is addressed to a somewhat sophisticated audience—sophisticated not so much with respect to manners and morals as with respect to literary convention. The poet is reacting against the artificiality and absurdity of the fashionable love poetry of courtly chivalry in which the conceit of the beloved's eyes outshining the sun had long become a tedious cliche. Donne laughs at the hyperboles (the fantastic exaggerations) of the courtly poetry by pretending to accept them. He piles hyperbole on hyperbole and praises his mistress in terms that only the most extravagant follower of Petrarch would have dared.[2]

But the poem is not intended to be literary satire or literary criticism. It is a genuine and deeply felt expression of the poet's sense of the beauty and perfection of his loved one. Its final purpose is to express the poet's sense of happiness and completeness in the possession of his mistress. *She* is so all-perfect, all-lovely, all-complete that she, and she alone, makes the fantastic hyperboles of the Petrarchan poets sober truth.

From the first line we must be aware that the *tone* of the poem and the changes and developments of the tone are of the first importance. The poem begins with a ranting, swashbuckling, arrogant address to the sun. Like many of Donne's poems this one begins suddenly, with sharp, surprising colloquial exclamation:

> Busy old fool, unruly Sun. . . .

Why this tone? And why the contempt so harshly expressed all through this first stanza—"saucy pedantic wretch," "court-huntsmen," "country-ants"?

The reason is that in the happy and complete possession of his mistress the poet feels that he possesses, rules, and controls the whole world, and therefore is superior to the sun itself. The lover complaining against the sun at morning for ending a night of happiness was, of course, one of the traditional themes of courtly love poetry, but Donne treats it familiarly, colloquially, and irreverently. One of the most concentrated paradoxes of the poem is the application in the first line of the epithet "unruly" to the sun. The sun is actually the standard of order, regulation, and law; but order, rule, and law in the field of nature, of society, of business, and of the court threaten the interests and pleasures of love. So the poet-lover rails against them all. Love transcends time, and the lovers cannot help regarding the sun, which makes time, as a wretch and a busybody to be scorned and triumphed over.

In the second stanza the poet, still ranting and swaggering, proceeds to develop the thought of the present good fortune that makes him superior to the world-dominating sun. And he does so in terms that also manage to pay exquisite compliments to his mistress. The setting of the scene, only implied in the first stanza, is now made specific. The girl sums up in herself all the riches and perfume of the Orient and the West; she is the glory of the whole world, concentrated, epitomized, and here in one bed laid.

One of the strangest and most powerful effects of the poem is the progressive softening of the tone until the outrageous and amusing hyperboles of the opening stanza and the air of extravagant enthusiasm with which they are delivered modulate, in the final stanza, into a hushed and serious (though still fantastic and half-playful) expression of the happiness and trust of a completely satisfied devotion.

The Sun Rising is characteristic of Donne's youthful secular love poetry. It is lighter in texture but not essentially different in method from the deeply felt and sometimes terror-stricken religious poems of his maturity and old age.

A fine example of these is the "Holy Sonnet" (XIV) *Batter My Heart, Three Personed God*. It is an impassioned plea addressed directly to God Himself. In a series of bold images the poet compares his heart to an old pot or pan, himself to a town usurped by treason, and himself, finally, to a girl betrothed against her will to her lover's enemy. The speaker in this poem (Donne himself, though not only Donne but any repentant, God-desiring man)

[2]See, above, pp. 114–15.

appeals to God to intervene violently—this is explicit in the first and last images, implicit in the second.

The sonnet illustrates certain aspects of the two great Christian traditions that had shaped Donne's mind. It is Protestant in the immediacy and intensity with which it makes its appeal directly to God, but the subtlety and argumentative skill with which the appeal to God is developed suggests the legalistic rhetoric of the Jesuits. Donne, it must be remembered, came of a Catholic family and had his first training from a Jesuit tutor. He was deeply read in the theological controversies between the Catholics and Protestants. When this poem was written, probably about 1617 or 1618, Donne was already one of the leading preachers of the Established Church of England; in 1621 he was made Dean of St. Paul's Cathedral.

The conflict between good and evil, which is the central theme of the poem, is made dramatic and given intensity both by the imagery and by the structural development. The external form of the poem is that of an Italian sonnet, divided into two parts, the first eight lines (called an *octave*) connected by use of a single pair of rhymes, the last six (or *sestet*) similarly forming a unit of structure and content, though the final couplet, not regular in the Italian sonnet, is a legacy of the Shakespearean form. Closer examination reveals, however, that not merely the final couplet but the essential form of the whole poem is Shakespearean, consisting of three quatrains and a final couplet, though the couplet here is perhaps more closely linked in thought to the final quatrain than is quite usual. Moreover, the structure of the poem is highly complex, the external form and the imagery not always progressing harmoniously but weaving, as it were, a close-textured counterpoint upon the main theme. Thus the first quatrain and the third are bound by the violence explicitly demanded, while the second and third are related by the notion of usurpation. The first and second quatrains are connected, despite the abrupt shift of both terms of the image (the thing compared and the thing to which it is compared), by the external form. The plan of the whole is one of steadily rising emotion, as the images reach successively higher pitches of personal urgency.

In the first quatrain the central image is drawn from the most homely field of experience, domestic life. God, figured as a tinker, ineffectually trying to mend and polish some worn-out vessel (the speaker's heart), is urged to melt it down and make a new one. The very homeliness of the image, applied to God, is shocking, almost blasphemous. The controlling image in the second quatrain is of a town (the whole being) which has been usurped by rebel powers (the senses), so that its true governor, Reason, God's viceroy, is held captive and powerless, or has even been corrupted itself to rebel against God. Here the imagery is of war and politics; it is vivid and interesting because war and politics are so close to men's practical experience. In medieval and Renaissance thinking such imagery is especially effective because of the close connection between man's duty to obey God and his duty to obey the king, God's viceroy.

In the third quatrain the image changes to a more personal one, but one that is nevertheless closely related to that of the second. The rightful ruler forcing his way into a rebel town is analogous to the lover overcoming with force both the guardians and the scruples of his beloved, kidnapping her and fulfilling against resistance what is, or ought to be, her hidden and deepest desire. The couplet concludes the poem with two stunning paradoxes, that freedom can be found only in thralldom and chastity only in ravishment. These daring paradoxes are the measure of the intensity and seriousness of the poet's feeling. Consider the contrasts among the images of the three quatrains. The first is separated from the others by its impersonality and lack of moral tone. The heart of the speaker is simply an old pot, to be melted down and recast. There is no question of right or wrong involved, but mere utility. In the second it is Reason that is held captive, and it is the enemies of law and justice who are laboring to keep out the rightful ruler. In the last it is right, or at least legality, and chastity that are represented as fighting to keep out the ravisher. What the poet actually says is this: "Unless, O God, you destroy my heart, it can never be made whole; unless you come with the force of a righteously angry prince and relieve a betrayed town, or with the violence of a ravisher, you will never take full possession of me." The first is homely and practical; the second grave, political, ethical, and serious; the last personal, knowing, worldly-wise. There is a surprising air of the morally dubious, or even the blasphemous, about it. What is the purpose of this contrast?

The answer lies in the concluding couplet. The whole poem rests upon a paradox, first stated materially, then politically, and at last personally. Just as to be destroyed completely is the only way to be made new, so to be enthralled (enslaved) by God is the only true freedom, and to be ravished (abducted, possessed utterly) is the only true chastity. Mystics and religious poets, *e.g.,* Solomon, St. John of the Cross, Richard Crashaw, have sometimes compared the union with God to the union of lovers in the flesh, and the paradoxical, half-blasphemous nature of the comparison gives a note of sincerity and intensity that could not otherwise be obtained. Unless human life is known and valued, the spiritual life and joy that transcends it cannot be known and valued either.

The unification of experiences drawn from superficially different levels of value is characteristic of Donne's poetic method, a poetic method so prevalent in the 16th and 17th centuries as to give its name, metaphysical poetry, to the work of a school of poets.

In an essay which has become a classic,[3] Mr. T. S. Eliot has defined some of the common elements in the style of these poets. They employ, he writes, "a device which is sometimes considered characteristically 'metaphysical'; the elaboration (contrasted with the condensation) of a figure of speech to the furthest stage to which ingenuity can carry it." This intellectual and emotional expansion of a figure was called in the 16th and 17th centuries a *conceit*. The term is associated with *concept,* an idea, a mental image as distinguished from a perception, a sense-impression. In Donne's conceits we find, Mr. Eliot points out, "instead of the mere explication of the content of a comparison, a development by rapid association of thought which requires considerable agility on the part of the reader." Both the poems we have been considering afford illustrations of this method, but the critic chooses a stanza from *A Valediction: Of Weeping* in which Donne, starting from the idea of his mistress' face reflected in his tears at parting, develops it as follows:

>On a round ball
>A workman that hath copies by, can lay
>An Europe, Afrique, and an Asia,
>And quickly make that, which was nothing, *All,*
>So doth each tear,
>Which thee doth wear,
>A globe, yea world by that impression grow,
>Till thy tears mixt with mine do overflow
>This world, by waters sent from thee, my heaven dissolved so.

Here the rapid associations of thought move from the empty globe, zero, nothing, to the mapmaker's globe, the whole world (what she is to him), then to the deluge that dissolves the world.

The wit of such poetry as this was aptly described by Dr. Samuel Johnson in his *Life of Cowley* as "a kind of *discordia concors;* a combination of dissimilar images, or discovery of occult resemblances in things apparently unlike." While the great 18th-century critic could not admire the fantastic hyperboles and strained comparisons that the metaphysical poets frequently achieved, he did not fail to recognize their special kind of merit. "Great labour, directed by great abilities," he wrote, "is never wholly lost: if they frequently threw away their wit upon false conceits, they likewise sometimes struck out unexpected truth; if their conceits were far-fetched, they were often worth the carriage. To write on their plan, it was

[3] "The Metaphysical Poets" in *Selected Essays*.

at least necessary to read and think. No man could be born a metaphysical poet, nor assume the dignity of a writer by descriptions borrowed from descriptions, by imitations borrowed from imitations, by traditional imagery, and hereditary similes, by readiness of rhyme and volubility of syllables."

Recommended reading:

T. S. Eliot, "The Metaphysical Poets," in *Selected Essays,* London, Faber, 1932; also in *Homage to John Dryden,* London, The Hogarth Press, 1927.
H. W. Garrod, *John Donne: Poetry and Prose,* Oxford, Clarendon Press, 1936.
H. J. C. Grierson, *Metaphysical Lyrics and Poems of the Seventeenth Century,* Oxford, Clarendon Press, 1921.
H. J. C. Grierson, "The Poetry of Donne," in *The Poems of John Donne,* Oxford, Clarendon Press, 1912, vol. 2, pp. v–lv.
Theodore Spencer, *A Garland for John Donne,* Cambridge, Harvard University Press, 1932.
E. M. W. Tillyard, *The Elizabethan World Picture,* London, Chatto and Windus, 1945.

ANDREW MARVELL (1621–1678)

To His Coy Mistress[1]

ANDREW MARVELL's famous poem *To His Coy Mistress* is an example of metaphysical poetry, a poem which combines (at least in its middle section) the seriousness and intensity of *Batter My Heart* with the wit and anti-Romanticism of *The Sun Rising*.

This poem takes one of the great commonplace themes of lyrical poetry—a theme found in Classical Greek and Latin poetry as well as in such Eastern poetry as that of Omar Khayyam—the theme of *carpe diem,* live for today, and develops it with a freshness and frankness that gives universal and timeless immediacy to the poem and lifts it above such elegant and graceful treatments of the theme as Herrick's *Corinna's Going a-Maying* or *To the Virgins, to Make Much of Time* or Campion's *Vivamus mea Lesbia*. It should be noted that some lines at the end of *To His Coy Mistress* (lines 38–40) are a translation of the same passage by the Latin poet Catullus which is used elsewhere by Campion, Herrick, and Ben Jonson. It may be interesting to place these passages side by side. Thomas Campion phrases it thus:

> My sweetest Lesbia, let us live and love;
> And though the sager sort our deeds reprove,
> Let us not weigh them. Heaven's great lamps do dive
> Into their west, and straight again revive;
> But, soon as once set is our little light,
> Then must we sleep one ever-during night.

Ben Jonson is more terse:

> Come, my Celia, let us prove,
> While we may, the sports of love;
> Time will not be ours for ever:
> He at length our good will sever.
> Spend not then his gifts in vain:
> Suns that set, may rise again;
> But if once we lose this light,
> 'Tis with us perpetual night.

[1] Programs A and B.

SEVENTEENTH-CENTURY LITERATURE

Herrick is more lyrical:

> Our life is short, and our days run
> As fast away as doth the sun.
> And, as a vapor or a drop of rain,
> Once lost, can ne'er be found again,
> So when or you or I are made
> A fable, song or fleeting shade,
> All love, all liking, all delight
> Lies drowned with us in endless night.

Marvell develops this theme much more richly, more fantastically, and though there is a witty elaborateness of illustration, the final effect, because of the concentration of the theme and the compactness of the versification and syntax, is the Classical one of conciseness and intensity.

Marvell's poem, like so many of Donne's, is a witty and somewhat sceptical criticism of the Petrarchan tradition of chivalrous love poetry. The lover from whose point of view these lines are presented is represented as a clever, intelligent, and devoted worshipper of his mistress, but since he knows that youth and loveliness are at the mercy of quickly passing time, he is anxious to bring the period of courtly admiration to its consummation in complete union. He knows too, however, that the lady must be flattered and cajoled, that her pride must be overcome and her "quaint" honor appeased. He sets himself in the opening section (the first twenty lines) to do just this, and at the same time to impress her with his cleverness and sophistication. The tone is light, gay, and knowledgeable, with the refined worldliness of a Mercutio.

The reader should perceive the skillful and almost colloquial modulations of rhythm in the handling of the octosyllabic couplets and the skill with which the imagination is made to fly over vast geographical distances (from the banks of the river Humber in north England, where the poet and his lady are presumed to live, to the side of the Indian Ganges) and to comprehend age-long epochs of time (from "ten years before the Flood" till "the conversion of the Jews"). This mixture of wit and condescension is sweetened with outrageous but charming flattery in which the exaggerations of Petrarchan love poetry are carried to an absurdity, and yet all this is done with such an air of sincerity and conviction that the girl must have been without the vanity of woman if she could resist it.

However, the poet is taking no chances. Wit, cleverness, and a gay lightness of tone are only one sort of persuasion. Sincerity, intensity, and realism are appropriate now. At line 20 the middle section begins, and the change in tone is remarkable. Marvell here rises to the height of his theme and gives us one of the most resonant and majestic statements of the Triumph of Death in English literature. But what makes the bitterness and intensity of these lines so remarkable is what we have already noticed in Donne's *Holy Sonnet XIV*. Their sincerity is vindicated and their intensity achieved by a kind of moral paradox. Acutely aware of what death and time destroy, the lover brushes aside all pretense and all merely conventional rectitude. Honor is "quaint"; love is lust, and virginity is wasted if it is to be preserved for the worms. The entry of horrible images of the grave's corruption into what started out as a witty and elegant piece of fooling testifies to the intense seriousness and reality of the experience the poem presents, and is, furthermore, a characteristically Baroque element in 17th-century poetry, which strove to weld together by force experience and feeling of the most diverse sorts. Shakespeare's *Hamlet* is an instance of it on a grand scale. This peculiar kind of sensibility has been described by Mr. T. S. Eliot as a "combination of positive and negative emotions: an intensely strong attraction toward beauty and an equally intense fascination by the ugliness which is contrasted with it and which destroys it."[2]

[2]*Selected Essays*, p. 20.

Poems like the two sonnets of Shakespeare and the pieces by Donne and Marvell which we have been discussing are not only the products of remarkably self-conscious and highly developed personalities, but they represent a way of thinking and feeling that is characteristic of the age in which they were written. The metaphysical conceits, the subtle and erudite comparisons, the fine and witty distinctions are the result of vigorous, intricate minds coming to grips with problems posed by the break-up of the medieval world-order under the impact of Renaissance science. Metaphysical poems like those of Donne—and like some of Shakespeare's and Marvell's before and after Donne—are poems which are sensuous and intellectual at one and the same time. In them ideas and the logical or fantastic development of ideas are always accompanied by emotion. They are generated by emotion and in turn generate other emotions. In the most successful poems of this period thought, feeling, and sensation are fused into one expression of sensibility.

Recommended reading:
H. J. C. Grierson, *Metaphysical Lyrics and Poems of the Seventeenth Century,* Oxford, Clarendon Press, 1921.
T. S. Eliot, "Andrew Marvell," in *Selected Essays,* London, Faber, 1932; also in *Homage to John Dryden,* London, Hogarth, 1927.
V. Sackville-West, *Andrew Marvell,* London, Hogarth Press, 1929.

V

THE EIGHTEENTH CENTURY

CLASSICISM AND THE ENLIGHTENMENT[1]

THE CULTURE OF THE 18TH CENTURY was in many ways a continuation of the artistic and intellectual life which prevailed during the Renaissance. Curiosity about the universe, typified in Renaissance times by the bold plan of Francis Bacon to study all existing sciences, was exemplified by Isaac Newton's discoveries in the laws of physics or Benjamin Franklin's numerous experiments with electricity. The Renaissance worship of Classical antiquity was paralleled in the 18th century by the conscious effort to follow the precepts of the ancient Greek and Roman philosophers and artists. The intellectual skepticism of the Renaissance had its counterpart in the 18th-century antagonism toward traditional views of religious and social institutions.

In order to realize the dominant spirit of the 18th century it is necessary to consider also the ways in which it differed from the Renaissance world. The Renaissance, with its insatiable curiosity, its vigor, its golden dreams, had brought to the discovery of its brave new world a glowing mood of youthful enthusiasm. It was impatient with restrictions; its impetuous spirit broke out in lyrical song, in experimentation with new ideas and forms in art. The 18th century, on the other hand, admired convention and restraint. For emotion and enthusiasm it substituted dignity, decorum, and common sense. Distrusting private judgments and original views, it relied upon authority, reason, and a studied air of detachment in its appraisal of man and society.

The Enlightenment, as the intellectual product of the century was often called, provided one of Western man's most notable adventures in the quest of happiness and the good life. Beginning with the idea that man should recognize his limitations and confine his activities to what was possible and useful, the age held the optimistic belief that man could live in harmony with his universe if he would follow the dictates of his reason. The words *reason* and *universal* were common in the 18th-century vocabulary. Reason—a mixture of common sense, emotion, and taste, rather than what is commonly called intellect—was assumed to be a faculty identical in all men. If this was a valid belief, it followed that an idea or concept which appealed to the light of reason must be right or true. Thus the universality of a concept was taken as a standard of truth.

So the 18th century sought a universal point of view toward life. The least common denominator among men was reason; in this respect all men were alike. Since the purpose of nature was to make men uniform, as the children of a common mother, to live "according to nature" meant to live according to reason. Faith in reason and belief in the uniformity of men were fundamental ideas in the philosophy of the Enlightenment. Their application to religious and social institutions and to art molded the pattern of 18th-century culture.

The Enlightenment envisioned a better society, a reasonable society which would produce better men. It was apparent to philosophers and artists that man's unwillingness to live "according to nature" had fostered much folly in the world. Such literary works as Voltaire's *Candide* and Swift's *Gulliver's Travels* satirized human folly and made it abundantly clear that man would not achieve a satisfying life until he had freed himself from superstition, intolerance, and the abuses of Church and State. The oppressive regime of Louis XV of France

[1] Programs A and B.

or George I of England hardly measured up to the ideals of men of reason like Voltaire or Swift.

By applying rational principles to life and art, the Enlightenment sought for universal standards which would be immutable and perduring. One of the most interesting and influential experiments of the age was the search for a universal religion, a "religion of nature." Since diversity of opinion was considered to be evidence of error, it was felt that there could be only one true religion. The various creeds and dogmas of the churches were viewed with suspicion, as these creeds contained many interpretations and accounts of miracles that could not be verified by every man's reason. Since universality was the test of truth, it followed logically that the truths of religion were those beliefs which had been common to all mankind. Deism, the rational religion of the Enlightenment, professed to be a religion which all men could understand and verify; or, as Swift declared satirically, it contained "nothing which cannot be presently comprehended by the weakest noddle."

The belief that God in the beginning gave men a true and perfect religion, which had been altered and confused by countless generations of men, led to a search for the religion of Adam. Men in early times were in the best position to know universal truth because they were uncorrupted by the accretion of prejudice, tradition, and arbitrary doctrine. By surveying historical religions, the deists arrived at a core of beliefs which were common to all creeds. Because of their universality, these beliefs were thought to represent original truth. The universe was looked upon by the deists as a huge machine operating according to harmonious laws. Behind the machine was a benevolent Creator who performed his will through unchanging law rather than through divine intervention in the affairs of men. The natural laws of the universe were designed to afford man happiness, and he could have a satisfying existence if he adjusted his life to them by the right use of his reason. Thus for the study of theology the deist substituted the study of natural science in order that he might know more about the universe. For conventional worship through prayer, thorough-going deists like Voltaire or Thomas Paine, or men like Benjamin Franklin, who was moderately attracted by the deistic views, substituted a practical morality of doing good to their fellow men. Although deism did not penetrate to all levels of society, the deistic view of the universe was characteristic of the 18th century's practical, realistic approach to human problems.

The same rational principles which underlay the 18th-century view of religious and social institutions produced the age of Neo-Classicism in art. Here, too, the emphasis was on uniformity. The artist wished to appeal to the reason which is common to all men rather than to reveal his individual feelings and emotions. He was to imitate nature in its characteristic aspects, and the merits of his work would be tested by its conformity with general truths. "The business of the poet," declared a famous passage in Samuel Johnson's *Rasselas,* "is to examine, not the individual, but the species; to remark general properties and large appearances; he does not number the streaks of the tulip, or describe the different shades in the verdure of the forest." According to the Neo-Classic view, art should portray, not what is strange or little known, but what is familiar to all men. This is the meaning of Pope's familiar line,

                    True Wit is Nature to advantage dressed.

In other words, true wit is universal knowledge expressed in an effective way.

In his quest for models of art, the Neo-Classicist turned to the Classical art of Greece and Rome. Not only did these models have universal appeal, but they emphasized good taste, perfection of form, reason, and wit. In Classical architecture or poetry were the dignity, the elevation of purpose, the formal structure admired by the artists of the Neo-Classical age. Here were balance, symmetry, and urbane simplicity. Here was a sane and rational approach to social problems and to art. The period of Queen Anne's reign in England was commonly called the "Augustan Age" because the artists of the time felt that they were accomplishing for the English nation what Virgil, Horace, and the Roman architects and sculptors had accomplished for Rome during the days of the Emperor Augustus.

The Neo-Classical literary creed was admirably expressed in Pope's *Essay on Criticism* and in *L'Art Poétique* by the French critic Boileau. Both of these works stem from Horace's *Ars Poetica*. The influence of the Classical standards of Horace, Aristotle, and other ancient writers and critics gave some special characteristics to 18th-century literature. The ideal of uniformity, which directed the literary artist to make himself understood and appreciated by all men, placed a restriction on the expression of personal emotion. The literature of the period was marked by restraint. The lyrical impulse of the Renaissance was smothered by the Neo-Classicist's exercise of decorum and detachment. The emphasis on correctness and form led to widespread use in poetry of the heroic couplet, which consisted of two rhyming lines of iambic pentameter verse. The couplets of Dryden, Pope, and Goldsmith had a neatness and smoothness approaching perfection. Among the favorite verse types of the Neo-Classicists were the ode and the verse essay. The odes of Dryden and Gray, modeled after the Classical poems of Pindar and Horace, were given a studied balance, symmetry, and finish. Verse essays such as Pope's *Essay on Man* were rational arguments or explanations dealing with some aspect of life or art.

The concern with man and society and the frequent failure or unwillingness of man to measure up to rational standards of conduct promoted the growth of literature that was didactic and satiric. Voltaire in France, Samuel Johnson in England, and Franklin in America were among the prominent writers who sat in judgment on the failure of mankind to live by the pure light of reason. The satiric spirit was expressed in prose exposition and drama as well as in poetry. Taking as their models the Classical authors, the prose writers of the Enlightenment aimed at directness and clarity. The finished correctness of Addison and Steele, the simplicity of Franklin, the brilliant swiftness of Voltaire, the polished wit in the plays of Molière and Sheridan provided notable examples of effective prose.

The standards which guided the course of literature were paralleled by Classical influences in architecture, sculpture, painting, and the practical arts. A leader of taste in the Classical revival was J. J. Winckelmann, a German archaeologist whose influence as a critic stimulated the study of art as a historical discipline: His great book, *The History of Ancient Art* (1764), supported the Classical theories that art should imitate nature modified by conformity to an ideal, and that the highest beauty is marked by an absence of individuality. Winckelmann had a large following among painters and sculptors of the time.

Interest in Classical architecture was especially widespread in the second half of the 18th century, after the excavations of the buried Roman cities of Herculaneum and Pompeii. Europeans admired and imitated the graceful, fine proportions of ancient Roman buildings. The tasteful elegance of Neo-Classical art was typified by the order and simplicity of Georgian architecture, the symmetrical patterns of the gardens at the Palace of Versailles, and the restraint of the Louis XVI manner in architecture. In England the Adam style of architecture, with its uniform detail and regular design, reflected the enthusiasm for Roman art. In America the leading figure in the Classical revival was Thomas Jefferson. When asked to draw up plans for the Virginia State Capitol in Richmond, he designed a modified form of the *Maison Carrée* in Nîmes. The profound effect on him of this example of Roman architecture, which he saw during an European visit from 1784 to 1789, is suggested by his remark that he gazed "whole hours at the *Maison Quarrée*, like a lover at his mistress." The importation of the Adam style into America provided another sidelight on our cultural beginnings. English builders who immigrated to America brought with them their builders' handbooks, featuring adaptations of Greek and Roman design. Since some of these immigrants settled in the West, it was not uncommon in the early 19th century to find an Adam house or a public building of Greek-temple design in the rude villages cut out of the wilderness.

The Enlightenment's theory of *"la belle nature,"* of nature idealized, was impressed upon art by the rigorous doctrines of the academies, which flourished for nearly a century. The French Academy, founded under Louis XIV in 1648, taught that painting was based on the principles of geometry and that the end of art was nobility of mind. Having as its purpose the advancement of the fine arts, the Academy forced upon artists the Classical theories of the ancients, especially as these were portrayed through the techniques of the French painter Poussin. Some artists, like the landscape painter Claude Lorrain, fled Paris to escape the stifling conditions of academicism. Poussin himself passed the major part of his productive career in Rome, where he was able to work among actual examples of Classical art. English taste belatedly imitated the refinements of the French court. The Royal Academy of Arts, established in London in 1768, was the center of Classical influence. The *Discourses* of Sir Joshua Reynolds, presented to students of the Academy at the annual prize-giving, provided the authentic statement of academic theories of painting as they were taught in England. "I would chiefly recommend," declared Reynolds, "that an implicit obedience to the Rules of Art, as established by the practice of the great Masters, should be exacted from the young students." It was against such rigid ideals of the Enlightenment that 19th-century Romantic art was to revolt.

The ideal of Classical art can also be seen in the music of the age. Bach's sons and Gluck, Haydn and Mozart, produced compositions characterized by refinement, orderliness, structural and spiritual balance, fluency, grace, and restraint. The sonata, which developed out of Baroque instrumental forms, was given its Classical stamp by Haydn and Mozart. The triumph over the limits imposed by rigid musical forms is nowhere more complete than in the fine craftsmanship and sublime ecstasy of Mozart's symphonies and chamber works. By fusing perfect form with genius and imagination they rise above the Neo-Classical standard of uniformity, which in the work of minor poets, painters, and composers produced "mere mechanic art."

This personal emotional quality, which mingled with the formal beauties of the *Clarinet Quintet* by Mozart, an opera by Gluck, or an *Embarkation for Cythera* by Watteau, was characteristic of the compromise which the greatest of the 18th-century artists made with the narrow critical standards of Neo-Classical art. Throughout the century there was an undercurrent of reaction against excessive formalism. The conflict between convention and spontaneous feeling was to culminate in the individualism and imagination of 19th-century Romanticism.

The weakening of the Classical mold in literature was marked by the emergence of sentimentalism in novels such as Samuel Richardson's *Pamela* or in the writings of Goethe in Germany. Sympathy for the common man, who was much neglected in Neo-Classical writing, was expressed in Goldsmith's *The Deserted Village,* a poem describing the natural goodness of man and his sentimental happiness in a rural environment when uncorrupted by the evils of the city. The influence of Rousseau and other thinkers who taught the doctrine that man is innately good and perfectible aided in shifting the emphasis in literature from its formal characteristics to the spontaneous feelings of the artist and his characters. The more tempestuous human emotions were caught up in the Gothic revival, which produced, in such novels as Horace Walpole's *The Castle of Otranto,* all the morbid horrors of talking skeletons pursuing innocent heroines in the shadows of ruined castles. These tales were to culminate in the early 19th century in Mary Shelley's *Frankenstein.* The Romantic sentimentality and picturesqueness of the medieval Gothic appeared in architecture as well as in literature. A famous example of Gothic building was *Strawberry Hill,* which Horace Walpole constructed with the aim of giving architectural expression to the melancholy mysteries of *The Castle of Otranto.*

Despite the superficial glitter of 18-century life, with its coffee houses and the elegance of costume and manners of its town and country society, despite the artificial and somewhat oppressive conventions that controlled its art, the age came nearer than any other to living according to its standards. It calmly appraised the nature of mankind and faced realistically the problem of human happiness. Perhaps the ultimate failure of the Enlightenment to find the good life lay in its extravagant claims for the importance of reason. Where life and art are concerned, the heart also has its uses.

Recommended reading:
Carl L. Becker, *The Heavenly City of the Eighteenth Century Philosophers,* New Haven, Yale University Press, 1932.
Arthur O. Lovejoy, "The Parallel of Deism and Classicism," *Modern Philology,* XXIX (1932), 281-299.
Preserved Smith, *A History of Modern Culture,* II, *The Enlightenment, 1687-1776,* New York, Henry Holt, 1934.

CLASSICAL MUSIC

WOLFGANG AMADEUS MOZART (1756–91)

Mozart's Life and Music.[1] Mozart was born in 1756, in the Austrian city of Salzburg. The son of a court musician of established repute, he was surrounded with musical influences and artistic conditions such as few composers have enjoyed in infancy. His precocious genius was recognized, and his musical studies directed, by an intelligent father who gave him solid training in the techniques of his art. Together with an elder sister who was also a child prodigy (though she never developed into anything more), the six-year-old Mozart was taken on the first of several musical tours through the courts and principal cities of Europe, winning universal acclaim from the nobility and gentry in whose hands, at that time, the future of an artist lay. The courtly influences brought to bear on his impressionable, retentive mind, the contacts with Italian opera and the Italian style in general, and the facility of his triumphs, were all important in the development of his genius. Unfortunately, his adult years brought few of the worldly rewards his childhood successes had promised. His only significant court appointment (as concertmaster to the Archbishop of Salzburg) was made so unendurable by the churlishness of his patron that he at last rebelled and quit the Archbishop's service. Envy, intrigue, and sheer bad luck prevented his securing any other permanent official position, and the last ten years of his life were spent in harrowing struggles against poverty, domestic worries, and ill-health. He died in 1791, at the age of thirty-five, and was buried in a pauper's grave.

This is the man whose music, so far from bemoaning "the slings and arrows of outrageous fortune," is recognized as a supreme embodiment of that sweet reasonableness which goes by the name of Classicism in the arts. It is well to know how much of Mozart's style is a product of the age into which he was born; but it is even better to understand how much more is the creation of his own Elysian spirit. The forms, the manner, the diction he employed were a refinement of the musical language of the day—a language molded in part by

[1] Programs A and B.

the Italians, in part by the North Germans (the so-called Mannheim school), and in part by his elder contemporary and friend Joseph Haydn (the other great Classical master). This language was the tonal expression of the ideals of the Age of Reason; balance, restraint, formal perfection, grace, elegance, choiceness of means, smoothness of line—these, and many more, are "signs of the times" which Mozart exhibited along with other 18th-century Classicists. But the inward felicity, the lark-like freedom, the high ecstasy and golden glow of Mozart's greatest moments—these are the attributes of his own serene essence, which we can explain neither by a period-formula nor by a facile psychology of "escapism." His melodic genius is unique, even for an age to which the *bel canto* or singing style was dear. Mozart is the supreme melodist of music, the peerless songster

> That from heaven, or near it,
> Pourest thy full heart
> In profuse strains of unpremeditated art.

The two chamber-music[2] works considered below belong to the last and bitterest years of Mozart's life. If in one of them—the *Pianoforte Quartet in G Minor*—a certain melancholy appears in the opening movement, observe that it is *transmuted* suffering, not repining, and that it is followed by a serene slow movement and the happiest of *finales*. The other work—the *Clarinet Quintet*—is altogether unworldly. None can describe the purity of this music, or its felicity—the airy elevation, the clean, cool sunlight, "the singing and the gold." To our generation, nurtured by a century of Romanticism and racked by a half-century of war, the music of Mozart comes as a reminder that art need not be the mirror of our fate, but that it is always the prerogative of a free-born spirit to soar to the height, which is its home.

Classical Forms. The Classical period (the latter half of the 18th century, in this case) is the period in which the forms of homophonic music were clarified and fixed. The favorite *instrumental* form was the *sonata,* a "cyclic" or multi-movement form which patterned its individual movements after one or another of several smaller forms. Our study of the two works by Mozart (and the two later ones by Beethoven) will entail recognition and understanding of the sonata scheme together with its component forms. The introduction to the article *Homophonic Forms* on page 395 should be read first, and then the section on *The Sonata* (pp. 410-13). The notes on particular *One-Movement Forms* (page 396 ff.) should be read as these forms occur in the Mozart (and later the Beethoven) works; page-references are given at the head of each movement discussed below.[3]

The analyses that follow will assume parallel or advance reading of the material above referred to.

Mozart: Pianoforte Quartet in G Minor[4]

A pianoforte quartet is a sonata for violin, viola, 'cello, and piano. Mozart wrote two such quartets, of which the *G Minor* is by far the greater. It was published in 1786 (five years before Mozart's death), and is therefore a late work, representing the composer's maturest

[2]*Chamber-music,* as the very name implies, is music intended to be performed in the intimate atmosphere of a room, as opposed to orchestral, operatic, or church music, intended for large halls.

[3]Before reading on *Sonata-form* (pp.405-9), however, the section on *Ternary Form* (pp. 397-99) should be studied, since the first-named form is an expansion of the second.

[4]Program A.

CLASSICAL MUSIC

genius. Its first movement shares with the *G Minor Symphony* and the *G Minor String Quintet* (both later productions) a certain somber mood which Mozart evidently associated with this particular tonality; but unlike those tragic masterpieces, the quartet frees itself early from the dark domain, and continues and ends in a glow of sunshine. Indeed, even the first movement is melancholy rather than tragic; whatever suffering it may have represented has undergone the alchemy of Mozart's true spirit and emerges refined and sublimated.

Throughout the quartet, the piano is pitted against the strings in a manner somewhat reminiscent of the Baroque *concerto* style.[5] There are frequent sharp contrasts of instrumentation (as in the opening bars), and the device of presenting a theme twice—first in the piano and then in the strings, or *vice versa*—is much exploited. To some extent this handling of strings and piano as *antithetical* tonal bodies is inherent in the combination, for the percussive piano can never really blend with the singing strings (or with any other instrument, for that matter). There is, however, no *subordination* of one tonal body to the other. The piano has, perhaps, a slight edge in virtuosity (it has, on the whole, the most "showy" part), but the thematic material is impartially distributed, and the total effect is chamber-music of the highest order. Everywhere the song-like tunes flow forth, a running river of pure Mozartean melody.

FIRST MOVEMENT
Tempo: *Allegro* (fast)
Key: G minor
Form: Sonata-form (pp. 405–9)

Exposition: measures 1–99.

I. *First subject,* in G minor (tonic key): measures 1–16. This bold and clearly-defined theme splits up into two exact halves (mm. 1–8, mm. 9–16). The first half (Ex. 43) contains the essential proposition, to wit: (a) a stern, concentrated statement delivered *forte* (loud) by the four instruments in octaves, answered by (b) a contrasting response in the piano alone, *forte* but graceful, ending with a sudden *piano* (soft) cadence-chord which is delicately ornamented by a trill[6] and *staccato* (detached) notes. This dramatic statement-and-answer pat-

Example 43

tern is then repeated. It is a favorite "opening gambit" of Mozart's—one which introduces us immediately to the Classicist's sense of balance and proportion (the bold element being at once confronted by its opposite; contrast the opening bars of Beethoven's *Fifth Symphony*). At measure 9, the unreconciled antitheses of the first eight bars find a natural resolution in the *harmonized* antitheses of the second half of the theme, where strings and piano first quietly complement each other (mm. 9–12; the piano's motive derives from its opening notes

---

[5] A *concerto* is a composition for orchestra with a solo instrument (or solo instruments), in which the soloist is naturally "set off" as protagonist against the orchestra. This quartet recalls the concerto-style of Bach's day rather than that of Mozart's or Beethoven's.

[6] A *trill* is an ornament consisting of the rapid alternation of two neighboring tones (the main or melodic note, and the note above it).

above, in measure 2) and then join in forceful unison (actually, *octaves*—mm. 13-16) to mark the end of the first subject. This "end" is merely a rhetorical question (a half-cadence followed by rests), to which the composer supplies his own answer in what follows.

Transition: measures 17-22. Three separated statements of I(a) in three keys—the first and third quiet, the middle one loud—show us the assertive chief character in process of transformation. The first key is a sudden major of the tonic, G; the third, also major, brings us into position for continuing in the regular second-subject key (the *relative major, i.e.,* the major key whose tonic is the third note of the original minor scale). The transition is extremely short and square-cut; its insistence on I(a) does not lead us off to something new, as transitions generally do. These two points may partly account for the "irregular" opening of the second subject.

II. *Second subject,* in B flat *major* (relative major): measures 23-99. This contains three themes, plus a closing theme and a codetta.

(1) *First theme* (mm. 23-57). Contrary to the usual procedure, Mozart continues, in this first section of the second subject, his treatment of the first-subject theme, I(a). He now shows it, in a sunny major tonality, altogether transformed in character (Ex. 44). Its teeth have

Example 44

been drawn; its sting is gone; instead of domineering, it dances. There are three obvious subsections:

Measures 23-32, where the piano sings and elaborates the tune, the strings quietly accompanying. The signs *sf* and *sfp* indicate sudden single accents within the prevailing *piano* (soft) dynamic range; *sf=sforzando,* which literally means "enforcing."

Measures 32-45, where the strings take over, giving the I(a) motive a new twist (octave leap and delicately ornamented ending—see conclusion of quotation under Example 44), the piano meanwhile supplying a feathery accompaniment, which later breaks into scales and arpeggios.[7] This is a delightful passage, marked by *imitations* in the strings (violin and 'cello, then violin and viola) and a *crescendo*[8] from soft to loud (m. 36) for the brilliant dialogue of the second half (mm. 37+).

Measures 45-57, which start off, softly, as a modified repetition of the preceding eight bars (this time with the "dialogue" in the piano), but soon bring in new matter (*forte*) the bent of which is cadential—*i.e.,* aiming toward and making much of the authentic cadence whereon this whole first theme of the second subject ends. The scales, trills, and arpeggios of bars 55-56 indicate a joyful conclusion of this part of the business; I(a) may now be considered suitably tamed, and more melodious, more typically "second-subject" themes can hereafter receive their proper hearing.

(2) *Second theme* (mm. 57-65). A true "second-subject" idea (Ex. 45), in every way contrasting with the bold first subject; smooth, serene, tuneful, continuous (no basic antitheses

Example 45

---

[7]*Arpeggio* (from *arpa*=harp): "broken" chords, *i.e.,* patterns consisting of chord-notes played in succession, instead of simultaneously.

[8]*Crescendo*=loudening; the opposed term *diminuendo*=softening.

CLASSICAL MUSIC

here); structurally square-cut (two four-bar phrases, one in the piano alone, the other in the strings as well—the typical Mozartean double statement) but having within these contours the most delightful rhythmic irregularity, accentuated by dynamic contrasts (*sf* and *p*) and phrasing (smooth segments indicated by curved lines over the notes, detached or *staccato* passages by dots over the notes). This tune is "felt" not according to the metrical accents (as represented by the bar-lines) but according to the irregular stresses marked by the composer; counting in beats, and starting with the first note of the theme (in the middle of a measure), we feel:

ONE-two-three-four-one-TWO-three-one-two-three-ONE (etc.)

Mozart's articulation (*phrasing*)—the way he enunciates or pronounces his musical "words" —is always most precise; one must carefully observe the dots, curved lines, rests, etc., which indicate this in the score, otherwise one misses the elegance of his language.

(3) *Third theme* (mm. 65–88). This is a busier theme, with energetic elements (the viola part at the beginning and the *forte* passages later), but still essentially light and airy (Ex. 46). Again there are obvious sub-sections, this time two in number:

Example 46

Measures 65–74, played by the strings alone, ending with a definite authentic cadence. Dynamic contrasts (*p* and *f*) are typically clear.

Measures 74–88, a repetition in the piano; note the imitation of the opening line by the violin (mm. 74–78). From measure 79 on we have new material of a cadential nature; observe the continued antithesis of strings against piano, and the imitations in violin, piano, and viola at measures 84–86. The cadence-bars (mm. 87–88) are embellished with triple-trills which recall the end of the first theme of the second subject (*cf.* mm. 56–57), and the sensation of concluding a definite section of the movement is even more marked.

Closing theme (mm. 88–96). Over a long, sustained tonic note (called a *pedal*) in the 'cello, first the violin and then the piano reiterate a two-bar falling phrase (Ex. 47; it occurs four times in all) which is little more than an authentic cadence (V–I) in disguise. Its pur-

Example 47

pose is to *confirm the end* of the second subject in the contrasted key (B flat major). The detail represented by (first) the piano's and (later) the violin's delicate octave-leap comments is significant, as it refers back to measures 2, 6, 10, and 12 of the first subject, and therefore subtly reminds us of the original proposition.

Codetta (mm. 96–98): An insouciant fragment (Ex. 48), adding another pair of undis-

Example 48

guised authentic cadences and leaving no doubt about the light-hearted mood in which the Exposition ends.

Link (Ex. 48). Measures 98 and 99 contain a simple modulation back to G minor, for the usual repeat of the Exposition. Since this particular Exposition is quite long, the repeat here is generally not made. The link is so constructed that it also leads on into the Development section. If the movement were performed as indicated by the composer, the link would be two measures long the first time, and seven measures long the second time. As *we* hear the movement (*without repeat*), we have simply the seven-bar link, which modulates from B flat major to a full authentic cadence in C minor (mm. 105–106). The rich, low-placed, sustained string chords are off-set by the nervous, pressing piano part, in which the two-note falling figure is derived from measure 2 of the first subject. In this link the atmosphere darkens, and we are prepared for the poignant note struck at the opening of the Development.

Development: measures 104–141.

Taking the first two notes of the first-subject theme (a), and lengthening them to twice their original value, Mozart continues with completely new material (mm. 104–111) which to all intents and purposes makes this a new theme (Ex. 49). The scale-passage in measure

Example 49

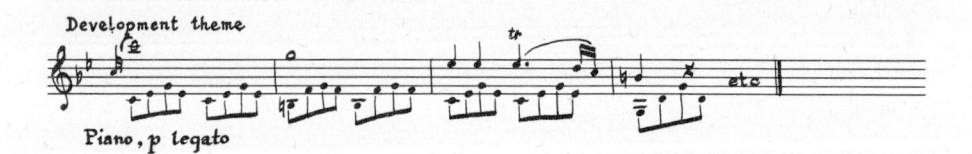

108 does, it is true, recall the somewhat similar *downward* scale in part (b) of the first subject (*cf.* m. 3); but the total effect of these eight bars of piano music is rather a turning away from the main theme than a development of it. Since the next 22 bars—the body of the Development section—consist of further treatment of the new material (so that we do not get back to the forceful first-subject motive until measure 134, where the Recapitulation is already in sight), it is apparent that Mozart is "playing down" the sterner elements of his drama, and adding to the lyrical. His whole bent as a composer is in this direction; for though he does on occasion write as cogent, as closely-reasoned a development of his Expositional themes as Beethoven or Brahms, he is far more likely to follow the procedure shown here, and add to the melodious lines of his Exposition still others in the Development, avoiding discussion of the earlier themes or giving them only oblique references.

In the present case it is possible to argue that the preservation of the first two notes of the first subject, and their frequent repetition throughout the Development, is in fact a "working" of I(a). Certainly we hear enough of the interval of the falling fourth which these two notes outline; it occurs mechanically every two bars between measure 112 (where the strings join the piano) and measure 127. But it is equally apparent that not this interval alone, but rather the whole first phrase (*i.e.,* Ex. 49) of the expressive piano melody introduced in measure 104, is being "worked" in the passage referred to; following which (mm. 126–133, and thereafter) the rising scale-passage of measure 108 is developed in the strings (and later in the piano). Note that Mozart leans heavily upon the somewhat perfunctory device of *sequence* in this Development—*i.e.,* the "chain-repetition," at a higher or lower tonal level, of a set pattern of melody or harmony or both. This takes us through various keys (the key-relationships of a Development section being not prescribed, a composer is at liberty to wander as far afield, *tonally,* as he wishes), and brings us ultimately to the dominant key (D minor) of our original tonic (G minor), where a firm final cadence (mm. 132–133) marks the end of the Development section proper.

Link (mm. 134-141). The mood, which at the opening of the Development was poignant but lyrical, has by this time darkened again; the stern, low-'cello entry in measure 130, and the dramatic color of the next two bars, prepare us for trouble ahead. Sure enough, in measure 134 the bold I(a) motive reappears, emphasized by the up-rushing scales in the piano. Repeated several times in a descending progression which aims at the tonic (G minor) of the opening of the Recapitulation, this motive with its accompanying scale-passage is forged into a *link* of the type often found at this point in a sonata-form movement. Its function is to *build up into* the opening of the Recapitulation—to propel us forward to it—and thereby emphasize the structurally vital point of *return to the beginning*. Links of this kind commonly use first-subject material (as here), and are often based on a *dominant pedal*—*i.e.,* a repeated or sustained V of the I to which we are returning (see below, *Second* and *Third Movements*). Instead of a pedal we have in the present case a compelling chord-progression, which "accelerates" harmonically as it approaches the G minor tonic chord of measure 141. The essential bass line is: E flat (mm. 134-135); D (mm. 136-137); C (m. 138); B flat (m. 139); A and D (m. 140); leading to G (m. 141).

Recapitulation: measures 141-224.

I. *First subject,* in G minor (tonic key): measures 141-148. The first subject is cut down to its first and more essential half, the second half (original mm. 9-16) being omitted entirely. Instead of a definite cadence and a break (as in m. 16), an *interrupted* (or *deceptive*) cadence occurs in measures 147-148, giving rise to a new transition.

Transition: measures 148-152. In place of the original three statements of I(a) which led to a different key (mm. 17-22), Mozart now fashions an entirely new transition out of the little piano cadence-pattern of measures 144 and 148 (original mm. 4 and 8), and makes this new transition lead to the second subject *in the tonic key*. Some such rewriting is always found at this point in the Recapitulation; for were the second subject to appear (as it does in the Exposition) in the *contrasted* key, the whole movement would end in a different tonality from that in which it started. Usually, the necessary alteration of the transition takes the form of a *different manipulation* of the *same* material as was used in the Expositional transition (see *Second Movement,* Recapitulation). In the present case, Mozart achieves the desired result (the avoidance of modulation) by subtler means, and makes the first subject merge with the second subject in the smoothest manner conceivable.

II. *Second subject,* in G *minor* (tonic key): measures 152-223. As before, this contains three themes, plus the closing theme and codetta.

(1) *First theme* (mm. 152-178). This is compressed, by the omission of its original first subsection (original mm. 23-32). From the fact that the first subject, the transition, and the opening of the second subject are all shortened in the Recapitulation, we may gather that Mozart is aware of the somewhat unusual length of his original Exposition, and desires to avoid prolixity in his restatement of it. The second and third subsections (of the first theme of the second subject) now become the only ones; they are restated (mm. 152-165 and mm. 165-178) with little structural variation, but with the tremendous *difference of character* which comes from changing an originally major passage into minor. This is of course true of the whole second subject, the themes of which were originally in B flat *major* and are now restated in G *minor*. The effect is to darken the atmosphere, and make the end of the movement melancholy instead of warm.

(2) *Second theme* (mm. 178-186). This is the one which suffers most from the change into minor. Its originally serene and smiling face is now downcast; and to add to the pathos Mozart makes the violin, when the strings enter in measure 182, describe a poignant, upward-searching gesture, exquisitely expressive of the change of mood. The fetching rhythmic imbalance is preserved, within the square-cut contours of the theme.

(3) *Third theme* (mm. 186-212). Restated almost exactly (in the minor tonic key). As before, there are two subsections (mm. 186-197, mm. 197-212), the first in strings alone, the second with piano.

Closing theme (mm. 212–220). Exact restatement (in minor).
Codetta (mm. 220–222). Exact restatement (in minor).

Link (mm. 222–223). Mozart uses the same link as at the end of the Exposition, this time leading to a repeat of the whole Development and Recapitulation. (The double-bar and repeat-signs in measure 223 refer us back to measure 100, where the corresponding signs will be found). This arrangement for a repeat is a purely conventional gesture, harking back to the days when sonata-form was evolving from simple ternary form, and, like it, repeated both the "A" and the "B–A²" sections of the movement. It is doubtful whether Mozart himself would actually make the long repeat here indicated, and it is certain that no modern performers do. The link, therefore, is to be regarded in practice as a link into the coda, which begins in measure 224.

Coda (mm. 224–251). As is often the case, the coda—a kind of "peroration" to the movement—concerns itself with the first-subject theme, which after all is the basis of the whole argument. Starting with a repeat of the opening bars, this coda introduces at measure 229 a magnificent, declamatory intensification of the piano's reply, by heightening the familiar upward leap to a new and unexpected note, whose urgency is immediately counterbalanced by the quiet passage that follows. Here (mm. 231–239) we see an effective end-of-movement device, which is associated more with Beethoven's name than with Mozart's, *viz.,* a sudden modulation away from the home key—a purposeful confusion of tonalities at precisely the place where settling in the tonic key is looked for—and a subsequent return to the home key with increased dramatic effect. The modulation to E flat major at measure 231 is accompanied by a sudden drop in dynamics (*forte* to *piano*); deep, rich 'cello tones appear, and the same piano cadence-pattern of four notes as formed the new transition in the Recapitulation (*cf.* mm. 148–152) is used with a calming, stroking effect. For a moment we are beguiled into believing that the sharpness of I(a) is past; and it is just this moment that lends dramatic intensity to the inexorable return in measures 236–239, where the stepwise-moving 'cello line and the big *crescendo* to *fortissimo* (the only *ff* in the movement) force us back to the tonic key to face the inevitable. There is no escaping the final dominance of I(a). In measures 239–247 it is declaimed, in octaves, by the strings—an "open" and awe-inspiring sound—to a distraught accompaniment of broken chords in the piano; and at measure 247 all four instruments join to end the movement in forceful unison (actually, *octaves*), concurring finally in the ruthless motive. Note that 18th-century *allegro* movements close without *rallentando* (slowing); the style calls for a flourish at the end, not a pulling up of the horses.

SECOND MOVEMENT
Tempo: *Andante* (rather slow)
Key: B flat major
Form: Sonata-form (pp. 405–9), *abridged* by the omission of the Development section.

Mozart's slow movements are among the loveliest in all music, for here he gives full rein to his lyrical genius, adding melody to gracious melody until the whole movement sings. The mood, in all but a few exceptional cases, is unclouded and serene, the atmosphere golden; one moves in an ideal world, far beyond the storm of life. To describe this music merely as Classical—which it is, stylistically—would be to state only a half-truth. It is Mozart's "new creation"—the unique product of a rare and godlike spirit.

Exposition: measures 1–70.

I. *First subject,* in B flat major (tonic key): measures 1–19. After the conclusion of the preceding movement, the ecstatic melody (Ex. 50) that opens the *Andante* falls on the ear "like dew upon the mown grass." Quietly, simply, and with gracious gestures the line un-

CLASSICAL MUSIC

Example 50

folds itself, its flowing curves delicately adorned with embellishments known as *turns* (∾).[9] Started by the piano, it is continued and completed by the whole group; the strings enter with rich, warm, low-placed tones, and, after an interrupted cadence in measures 15–16, take over the spiralling cadence-pattern from the piano for the final cadence in measures 18–19. Sharp contrasts of intensity (*p* and *f*) point up the expressive elements in the theme, and the same antitheses of instrumentation as we have observed before play their part, here and throughout the movement.

Transition: measures 19–35. Continuing the thirty-second-note movement of the cadence-pattern of the first subject, the transition unwinds a long, smooth skein, first in the piano and then in the violin, to a simple accompaniment consisting, at the beginning, of cadences in the tonic key (Ex. 51). At bar 26, with a modulation out of the key, a new element appears

Example 51

—the fragmented, arching melody delivered *forte* by the piano (and similarly accompanied), which leads us to a cadence wherefrom the second subject may take off easily and smoothly in the dominant key. This melodic fragment is sufficiently important in the scheme of the movement to warrant our calling it *the transition theme* (Ex. 51, latter part), while the thirty-second-note pattern may conveniently be called *the transition accompaniment*. Note the little piano-link, with its grace-notes (the small-type ornaments), which makes the actual connection with the second-subject theme.

II. *Second subject,* in F major (dominant key): measures 35–70. This contains one main theme, a closing theme, and a codetta.

Main theme (mm. 35–50). Another exquisitely-turned melody, typically divided between piano and strings (Ex. 52). The first phrase, which rises in widening curves in the violin and

Example 52

[9] A *turn* is an ornament consisting of the main melodic note, the note next above it, the main note, the note next below it, and the main note to end. The turn on G in measure 3 of this movement is played: G-A-G-F sharp-G.

viola, rests on a quiet 'cello *pedal;* the *fp* markings represent not sharp accents but sighs—ecstatic suspirations from a full heart. The answering phrase in the piano wonderfully complements this aspiring line with warmer tones, similarly punctuated with stresses.[10] In the second half of the theme the instrumentation is reversed—the piano plays the rhyme to phrase 1, the strings reply with the rhyme to phrase 2, ending now with a graceful authentic cadence so characteristic of Mozart as to be almost a trade-mark. The whole theme is a perfect example of the poised, balanced symmetry achieved by the Classical artist even in his expressions of "feeling."

Closing theme (mm. 51–66). Reverting to the transition theme and its running accompaniment, Mozart lingers over the arching melodic fragment (Ex. 53), which evidently

Example 53

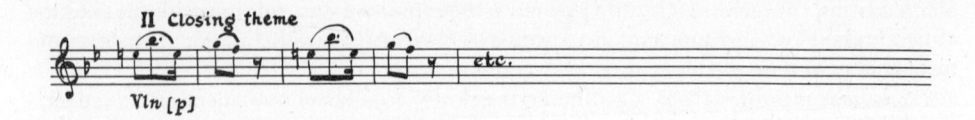

pleases him greatly, since he not only brings it back but presents it in two versions, first with the violin as soloist (mm. 50–58) and then in the piano (mm. 59–66). The long held notes (*pedals*) in viola and violin add a new dimension to the texture; they "float in time and space," heightening the ecstatic overtones of the music. Harmonically the theme is a series of authentic cadences (with one brief color-point of modulation) confirming the tonality of the second subject; which is why we call it a "closing" theme.

Codetta (mm. 66–70). Merely a rounding-off of the closing theme, and hence of the whole Exposition. There is a *pedal* in the 'cello, the running accompaniment in the piano bass, and light cadence-chords in the upper piano and upper strings. It is a twice-told formula (mm. 68–70 = mm. 66–68) signifying conclusion.

Link (mm. 70–75). Instead of working out a Development section, which would now follow in the usual scheme of sonata-form, the composer *abridges* or compresses the form by writing a short link that takes us directly back to the tonic key of B flat for the Recapitulation. Such a curtailment of the full scheme is quite common when sonata-form is used in slow movements. There are two obvious reasons. First, the tempo being slow, a full sonata-form with Development could run to undue length; secondly, the lyrical nature of the themes in the Exposition makes them unsuitable for development or argument. As is often the case, the link is constructed over a *pedal* on the dominant (F) of the tonic key (B flat), to which we are returning. The first phrases in the piano appear to be connected with the little piano link in measures 33–35; the ending anticipates the opening notes of the first-subject theme (like an artist making trial brush-strokes over the canvas before painting in the line). Note the expansive *crescendo* to *forte,* followed by a sudden *piano*.

Recapitulation: measures 75–149.

I. *First subject,* in B flat major (tonic key): measures 75–93. There are some variations in the accompaniment (piano bass and 'cello), but the theme is otherwise restated exactly.

Transition: measures 93–107. By the simplest possible means (the omission of one modulatory phrase—*cf.* measures 102–105 with measures 28–33) Mozart arranges for the end of the transition to lead not to the dominant key (as in the Exposition) but to a continuation in the tonic key. With this important exception, there is no change.

[10]The notation of dynamics being what it is—at best a highly complicated *approximation* to the nuances of emotion—we must avoid, in such cases as the present, the crude assumption that *f* means merely "loud," *sf* merely "accented," and so forth. These signs take their significance from the context—even, be it noted, in Classical music. The *forte* of the second chord in bar 40 here is a far different *forte* from that in—*e.g.*—bar 1 of the first movement. This needs emphasizing, since there is an all-too-common assumption that Classical music is either loud or soft, with no gradations of intensity between.

II. *Second subject,* in *B flat major* (tonic key): measures 107–149. This is restated almost exactly.

Main theme (mm. 107–122). Exact restatement, except for the difference of *register* in the two halves of the theme—the first half low and rich, the second half up an octave.

Closing theme (mm. 123–144). Except for differences in instrumentation, the first eight bars restate the corresponding eight bars of the Exposition exactly. The repeat in the piano (starting in measure 131) is also exact up to its expected cadence in measure 138, at which point an *interrupted* cadence leads to a three-bar extension (mm. 138–140) which in turn is interrupted (mm. 140–141) for a final four-bar extension leading to the long-delayed authentic cadence in measures 143–144. The closing theme is thus built up, to add weight to the end of the movement.

Coda (mm. 144–149). An exact restatement of the Expositional codetta, with the addition of two very soft tonic chords that float away into thin air. Normally in a sonata-form movement this section is treated with more circumstance,[11] the avoidance of which here may be attributed to the same reasons as dictated the omission of a Development section. The necessary "weight" has already been provided in the expanded closing theme; Mozart can therefore let the actual ending evaporate, thus adding a masterly final touch to an altogether ethereal movement.

THIRD MOVEMENT
Tempo: *Allegro* (fast; two beats to the bar)
Key: G major
Form: Sonata-rondo (pp. 409–10)

This *finale*[12] is in the cheerful key of G major—the *parallel* or *tonic major* of the key of the first movement.[13] It is a carefree, swinging movement, chock-full of the most catchy tunes one could imagine; taken in conjunction with the *Andante,* it leaves no doubt as to the predominantly sanguine mood of the quartet as a whole. The form (marked *Rondo* by the composer) is actually a hybrid known as *sonata-rondo*—a cross between an older, simpler rondo form (see p. 401) and sonata-form. In this particular example, the basic divergencies from sonata-form are three:

 a. The Exposition contains a first subject, a transition, a second subject (in the dominant key), *and the first subject again.*
 b. Instead of a Development there is an entirely new and contrasting section—the *Episode.*
 c. The Recapitulation *begins with the transition,* follows with the second subject (in the tonic key), and *closes with the first subject.*

Points (a) and (b) are regular in sonata-rondo form; point (c) is somewhat irregular.

Exposition: measures 1–169.

I. *First subject,* in G major (tonic key): measures 1–43. A joyous melody in simple *binary form* (see p. 396), with the familiar Mozartean double-statement in piano and then strings

---

[11]See *First Movement,* above.

[12]The quartet being in three movements, there is no *minuet-and-trio*—the common third movement of a four-movement sonata. The student should make a point of playing at least one work which does include this most typical Classical form. The minuet from the *Clarinet Quintet* by Mozart is described in detail in this work (pp. 249–59). It happens to contain not one but two trios, and is therefore somewhat unusual; but its style and content are eminently minuet-like, and will serve as perfect examples of a kind of writing with which Mozart's name is constantly associated.

[13]This is a fairly common procedure in sonatas written in a minor key, when the composer wishes to end the whole cycle on a bright note. The *Fifth Symphony* by Beethoven is a familiar case in point. We might observe, in passing, that the Mozart quartet can only technically be regarded as "in G minor," since both the second and final movements are in major keys.

Example 54

(Ex. 54). The first part (A) ends with an authentic cadence in the home key (m. 16); the second part (B), after being presented complete in the piano (mm. 16–26), is repeated by the strings (mm. 26–31), the piano entering for some amusing back-chat towards the end. A busy little codetta (Ex. 54, end), delivered in *forte* octaves by the whole group and followed by a complete break, marks this subject off as a clear-cut, self-contained unit. Particularly notice the *phrasing* (the disposition of slurred and detached notes) which gives to the themes of this movement their springy character and superb articulation.

Transition: measures 44–70. This is in two clearly-defined sections (Ex. 55). The first half (mm. 44–59) is squarely in the tonic key until its final bars, which modulate; the second

Example 55

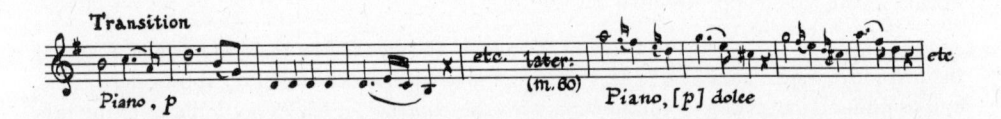

half (mm. 60–70) is just as squarely in the dominant key (where we are going, for the second subject) and derives its new-sounding melody from the cadence-patterns of the first half. The piano, taking the lead throughout, breaks into energetic and showy arpeggios at the close, emphasizing another distinct section-ending which this time points forward like a sign-post to the coming second-subject theme.

II. *Second subject,* in D major (dominant key): measures 71–131. A prodigal subject, offering no less than three themes (an unusual number in sonata-rondo form, though not in sonata-form), of which the first two are hardly separable and the third is distinctly a closing theme.

(1) *First theme* (mm. 71–87). Joined to the end of the transition by a little scale, this melody is of the delightful "nursery-rhyme" type which no one but Mozart could have penned (Ex. 56). Its beguiling innocence ("Twinkle, twinkle, little star") is off-set by sophis-

Example 56

ticated phrasing (Rúm *tee*-úm *tee*-úm *tee*-úm); this gives an effect of subtle syncopation. The theme is presented first by strings and then by piano; the latter extends it and brings it to a half-cadence in bar 87. This is hardly an ending, especially as a link (over a dominant *pedal*)

CLASSICAL MUSIC

carries on the sense and merges with the next theme at measure 93. We separate out two themes simply to clarify what follows.

(2) *Second theme* (mm. 93–111). Busy-work in the strings alone (Ex. 57) emerges out of

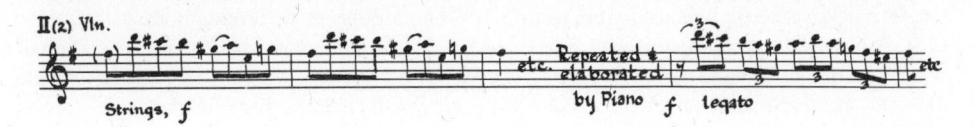

Example 57

the preceding link and leads to a cheery trilled cadence in measures 100–101. The piano seizes upon the idea and elaborates it brilliantly (mm. 101–111, Ex. 57), capping its display with a rocket-like up-rush of notes at the end. It is all very jolly and high-spirited. The scale-passage is so rapid as to be almost a *glissando* (the swooping effect one gets from drawing one's finger swiftly over the white keys of a piano, or the strings of a harp).

Closing theme (mm. 111–131). After the fireworks, another quiet, simple tune (Ex. 58) confirms the end of the second subject, its harmonies being cadential. Twice-stated as usual,

Example 58

it is extended the second time by repetitions of the final cadence (mm. 127–131). Note the warm string-writing (the violin and viola each playing two notes simultaneously) which accompanies the slightly varied repeat in the piano.

Link (mm. 131–135). Were this movement in sonata-form, the point now reached (end of second subject) would also be the end of the Exposition. In sonata-rondo form, however, we now go back to the tonic key for *another statement of the first subject,* which is included analytically in the Exposition. The key-change from dominant to tonic is negotiated here by a *link* of the type we have seen before in previous movements. As usual, it is based on a dominant *pedal* (implied rather than explicit, in this case). It halts on a fat dominant-seventh chord (D–F sharp–A–C) in G major, followed by a break which is lengthened by a pause-mark (⌒). This conventional device effectively points up the coming theme.

I. *First subject,* in G major (tonic key): measures 136–169. This is restated exactly, up to the point where the strings take over and repeat part B (mm. 161+). Instead of ending as before, with an authentic cadence and codetta in the tonic key, Mozart rewrites the repeat and makes it modulate away to the key of E minor (the *relative minor*), where a *half-*cadence leaves the strings in the air, and precipitates the opening of the Episode.

Episode: measures 170–217.

The function of this part of the movement is to supply contrast; it is thus diametrically opposed to the Development of sonata-form, which treats themes previously heard. A new theme, with a new character, in a new key (E minor), is introduced and exploited; not until the later stages, when the composer prepares the way for a return to the Recapitulation, do we hear references to Expositional material. The episode theme (Ex. 59) is based on sharp an-

Example 59

titheses of motives and instrumentation; it reminds one of the first subject of the *first* movement, with its bold announcing motive (a) immediately offset by its opposite—the quiet, rather plaintive motive (b)—and the initial double statement of this dramatic proposition. (As was mentioned in the previous case, the procedure is common in Mozart, and embodies the Classical sense of balance-by-opposition.) What follows is a development *of this new idea.* A busy piano accompaniment appears in bar 179; a somewhat mechanical alteration of octave strings and piano (mm. 178–187) is relieved by the smooth chordal writing of bars 187–193, at which point (m. 193) a repeat is started, with reversed instrumentation (*cf.* mm. 193–200 with mm. 170–177). In the foregoing section, the bold motive (a) was driven home; in this section motive (b) is developed, again by mechanical sequences and strict alternations of instruments (mm. 200–208). This section, moreover, modulates away from E minor, and begins a round-about journey back to the tonic key of G major. Preparing for a return of the first subject in the Recapitulation, the composer introduces at measure 208 ('cello) the opening figure of that subject, and drives it home in a forceful octave-passage accompanied again by piano busy-work. This brings us to a cadence on the dominant of G major (m. 217), where the Episode ends.

Link (mm. 217–225). A piano *cadenza* (solo passage), based on an implied dominant *pedal* (D in the bass), very cleverly negotiates the change from the bustling Episode to the quiet theme that follows. The line is made to *slow down* (triplets followed by duplets followed by quarter notes followed by a half note held over) and *change its character* (brilliance followed by smoothness followed by delicacy followed by lyricism) with a skill so effortless as to be unnoticeable, except by its calming result.

Recapitulation: measures 225–342.

Transition, in G major (tonic key): measures 225–250. Having carefully prepared (in the later stages of the Episode) for a return of the first subject, Mozart now withholds it, and starts the Recapitulation irregularly with the transition theme. Why does he do this? Partly, no doubt, to compress a movement which is by this time running to length (*cf.* Recapitulation of first movement); partly because the first subject has already been brought to mind at the end of the Episode, and may therefore be "taken as read"; partly because, in the typical Rondo spirit, Mozart is playing a little joke on the listener, by leading up to what doesn't happen. He could not have pulled this off except for the fact that the transition theme is so well-defined, and thus can undertake admirably the important role of "leader of the Recapitulation." (Look back at the Exposition, and observe that even there the transition makes *a new start,* following the complete break at the end of the first subject; it is already a "leading" theme.)

As in sonata-form, the transition now has to be rewritten, to bring the second subject in *in the tonic key.* This is done by concentrating on the first half (the original second half in the dominant key being dropped), turning it into the minor in mock-pathetic fashion (mm. 233–236), toying with its cadence-pattern (mm. 237–240), and working it round to a half-cadence in the tonic key (mm. 241–242). Following this, the motive of the second-subject theme is introduced (mm. 242+) and made to lead smoothly, over a dominant *pedal,* into the second subject proper.

II. *Second subject,* in *G major* (tonic key): measures 250–311. This is restated exactly, up to its final bars.

(1) *First theme* (mm. 250–266), and link (mm. 266–272).

(2) *Second theme* (mm. 272–289), with the same piano elaboration of the idea first stated by the strings.

Closing theme (mm. 289–311). The cadential repetitions at the end of this (mm. 305–311) are now used to modulate away to the dominant key, giving rise to yet another link over (and in this case *under*) a dominant *pedal.*

Link (mm. 311–322). The piano holds a long trill on the dominant (D), while the strings, modulating back to the tonic key, prepare for the coming first-subject theme by playing around with its opening motive. The trill eases down chromatically into the first notes of the theme proper, which are neatly incorporated as grace-notes (printed in small type) at the end of the trill.

I. *First subject,* in G major (tonic key): measures 322–342. This final statement of the main subject is cut in half. The "A" part is exactly restated; the "B" part is omitted entirely, and we jump from the end of "A" to the codetta (mm. 337–342). A prize example of an *interrupted cadence* at the end (mm. 341–342) precipitates the coda.

Coda (mm. 342–360): With a sudden plunge into a remote key (E flat major—*cf.* coda of first movement) the composer upsets the tonal apple-cart, for the express purpose of making a final return to the home key (mm. 348–351) the more telling. For an instant, when he is mulling over his first-subject figure in the foreign key, one has the sensation of suspended animation or loss of direction; this is of course a contrived hesitancy, the cheerful outcome of which is the whoop and halloo that burst forth when the tonic key is regained (mm. 351–355, *fortissimo*). The final cadence-repetitions (mm. 355–360) show the first-subject motive kicking up its heels in fine fettle, and galloping to the winning-post at full speed.

Recommended reading:
Alfred Einstein, *Mozart, His Character, His Work,* New York, Oxford University Press, 1945.
W. J. Turner, *Mozart, the Man and His Works,* New York, Tudor Publishing Company, 1938.

Mozart: Clarinet Quintet in A Major[1]

This work for clarinet, two violins, viola, and 'cello was written in 1789, two years before Mozart's death, at the request of a clarinetist attached to the court of Vienna (whose gratitude for the inestimable gift is not recorded). The clarinet was a new-comer in Mozart's day, just beginning to take its place alongside flutes, oboes, and bassoons as a regular member of the woodwind family. With the incredible sureness that characterized all his musical acts, Mozart seized at once upon the clarinet's essential features—its sensuous tone (with the great variance between the low, dark *chalumeau* register and the clear, lyrical upper register), its agility at leaps and arpeggios,[2] its powers of *diminuendo* (softening) and *crescendo* (loudening)—and wrote for it, here and in other late works, music that still ranks as a model in the literature of the instrument.

The clarinet here used is the *clarinet in A;* the written notes are therefore a minor third (three semitones) higher than the actual sounding notes, and the key-signature of the clarinet part denotes a (*written*) key three semitones higher than the *actual* key. The clarinet is, in other words, a "transposing" instrument; and students unaccustomed to transposing should simply follow the *patterns* of the clarinet-part while listening to the recording. In the examples below, any quotation from the clarinet part will give the actual sounding notes.

Throughout the quintet, note how wonderfully the five instruments are blended. The clarinet is not treated as "the soloist," nor the string quartet as "the accompaniment." The-

[1]Program B.
[2]*Arpeggio* (from *arpa*=harp): "broken" chords, *i.e.,* patterns consisting of chord-notes played in succession, instead of simultaneously.

matic material is evenly distributed, and the texture "close-woven," in the finest chamber-music manner. Everywhere the stream of pure Mozartean melody flows on.

FIRST MOVEMENT
Tempo: *Allegro* (fast)
Key: A major
Form: Sonata-form (pp. 405–9)

Exposition: measures 1–79.

I. *First subject,* in A major (tonic key): measures 1–26. Three elements appear in this graceful theme: (a) the opening tune in the first violin, starting with the highest note and dipping to the lowest; (b) the clarinet's contrasting comment on this, in the form of an arpeggio up and down (like the play of a fountain); and when these have been repeated with a slight elaboration, (c) the later clarinet line—starting in measure 19 with a grace-note[3]—which rises more smoothly and, after a series of undulating curves, sinks chromatically to rest in measure 26. Example 60 shows these three elements, all of which will be used later. The first subject cannot be said to "end," since the *half*-cadence in measure 26 is followed immediately by a transition based on (c). The effect is one of fine continuity, the first subject merging with what follows.

Example 60

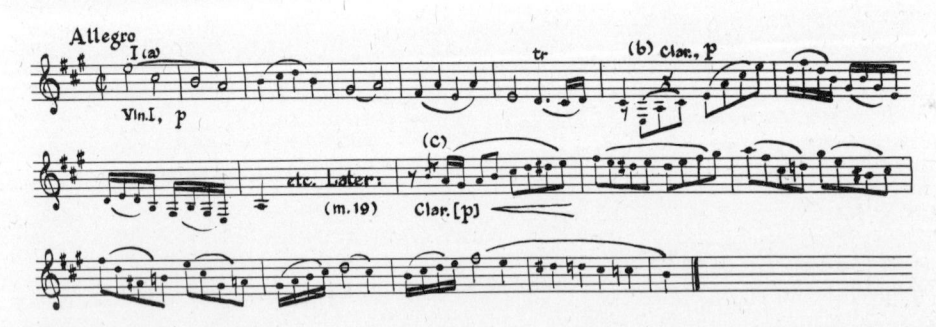

Transition: measures 26–41. Using I(c)—first the undulating part and then the opening, with the grace-note elaborated—the music passes over to the key of the dominant, and confirms its arrival there by cadence-repetitions and flourishes (mm. 35–41). Two bars of *forte* (loud) followed by a complete break point up the end of the transition and the entrance of a new theme.

II. *Second subject,* in E major (dominant key): measures 42–79. This contains one main theme, with a closing theme and a codetta.

(1) The *main theme* (mm. 42–65) is presented first as a violin solo (mm. 42–49, Ex. 61) accompanied by held chords in the second violin and viola, and plucked notes (*pizzicato*) in

Example 61

[3]*Grace-notes* are ornaments added to a basic melodic line. In many cases they are printed (as here) in small type.

CLASSICAL MUSIC

the 'cello. This creates a wonderfully warm, serene atmosphere, in which the first violin sings its aspiring melody in segments first marked off by rests and then linked into a cadence-pattern. In measure 49 the clarinet enters to repeat the theme, whereupon a shadow falls; major suddenly becomes minor (m. 50), and the clarinet reworks (instead of literally repeating) the theme, to a throbbing accompaniment of syncopated chords *pianissimo* (very soft) in the strings. The minor mood is short-lived, however; after only four bars the key changes to a sunny C major (mm. 54–57), and thence (with a *crescendo* to *forte*) back to E major (m. 61), which is achieved with a burst of energy and high spirits indicative of a joyful arrival. Note the cheery triple-trill[4] at the cadence (mm. 64–65).

(2) There follows a *closing theme* (mm. 65–75, Ex. 62), again started in the first violin and then handed over to the clarinet. We call this a "closing theme" because, though new, it has a definite feeling of *confirming the end* of the second subject, not of *carrying it on*. Even when, on its repetition (mm. 69–75), the tune is extended by the clarinet, it still uses cadential harmonies and revolves around the tonic center of E major.

Example 62

Overlapping the cadence-chord of the closing theme, a *codetta* (mm. 75–79) reverts back to the theme of the first subject (as codettas often do) and rounds off the Exposition with a reminder and a flourish. The Exposition is marked for repeat (with double-bar and repeat-signs), but the repetition at this point is generally not made.

Note the uncommon quietude, warmth, and serenity of this Exposition. All the themes are marked *piano;* the word *dolce* (sweetly) is added to two of them; and there are no more than 11 bars out of 79 marked *forte* (with a few more in which *crescendi* occur). Note further that all themes begin in the strings and are then either repeated or else completed by the clarinet. The strings-clarinet sequence is a peculiarity of this Exposition; the repetition of themes as such is not. Mozart loves to present his ideas twice over, either in exact repetition or with elaborations; and with such perfect melodies as he pours forth, who could possibly object?

Development: measures 80–118.

The Development begins quietly, first with an expressive change from E major to E minor (m. 81), and then with a modulation to C major, which has the same effect of expansive sunniness as was commented on above (*cf.* mm. 54–57). Here (m. 83) the first subject theme is presented, with a reversal of the instrumentation of measures 1–9; *i.e.,* the clarinet sings (a) and the first violin answers (*forte*) with (b). This arpeggio motive (b) is then energetically tossed around among the four strings (mm. 91–99), the music changing key several times. In measure 99 the clarinet joins in and, to measure 111, plays arpeggios up and down in eighth notes while the strings occupy themselves with held chords and the *descending,* sixteenth-note part of (b). This section, in other words, develops I(b) by taking its slower and faster elements and playing them simultaneously in different tone-colors. The dynamic range is quiet, with sudden accents on the first note of every bar (*fp*=*forte-piano,* loud-soft). Chord-changes occur every two bars, producing modulations which lead us, by measure 111, back to the dominant chord (V) of our home key (A major). Measures 111–115 confirm this point of arrival, using once again the complete (b) motive, overlapping itself in viola, second violin, and first violin. This marks the end of the Development proper, which is, on the whole, a rather simple one, leaning heavily on the

[4] A *trill* is an ornament consisting of the rapid alternation of two neighboring notes (the main or melodic note, and the note above it).

mechanical device of *sequence, i.e.,* the "chain-repetition," at various tonal levels, of a particular pattern of notes and chords. Mozart does not choose to break up and juggle around the wonderful tunes of the Exposition; they are so perfect at their first appearance that further manipulation would be both dangerous and unnecessary. He therefore—quite typically—seizes on a non-melodic (non-"tuney") motive, and plays around with that, in a none too strenuous or extensive fashion. In a movement of this particular character anything more involved would have been out of place. One does not look for "argument" in an idyll.

Link. The Development is connected with the Recapitulation by a short link (mm. 115–118), in which the lower strings sound the dominant note (E) that resolves onto the tonic (A) of the first chord of the Recapitulation, while the clarinet holds the same note right into the first subject, thereby producing the smoothest possible conjunction, and emphasizing the critical point of return by building up into it.

Recapitulation and Coda: measures 118–197.

I. *First subject,* in A major (tonic key): measures 118–132. Here the clarinet is given the opening melody (a)—note its fanciful flight in bar 122—and the first violin answers with the arpeggio figure (b). Part (c) then enters in the clarinet (the original intervening bars being now omitted) and is modified at the end to lead to a cadence in the *subdominant* key. The first subject is thus *compressed* in the Recapitulation as compared with its initial form (15 bars as against 26), and the transition is made to begin at a different tonal level from that of the Expositional transition.

Transition: measures 132–147. Starting *outside* the tonic key, the music works round to the dominant chord *in* the tonic key, using the same material as in the Exposition, *viz.,* I(c). The point of arrival at the dominant chord (m. 144) is confirmed in the same manner as before (*cf.* m. 35), but with more extended busy-work in the clarinet.

II. *Second subject,* in *A major* (tonic key): measures 148–about 178.

(1) The *main theme* (mm. 148–169) starts out as in the Exposition, but now *in the tonic key.* When the clarinet enters (m. 155) with the minor version, the music is substantially altered as compared with the corresponding section in the Exposition (contrast mm. 49+ and mm. 155+). The tonality now remains minor for eleven bars, until, just as a cadence is being made in A *minor* (mm. 165–166), a sudden interruption (m. 167) takes us swiftly back to A *major,* where the real cadence occurs (mm. 168–169). There is this time no *forte* conclusion, and the triple-trills are omitted (contrast the end of this main theme in the Exposition, mm. 58–65). Rewriting of this kind (here and in the first subject) is not called for by the necessities of sonata-form, nor is it always found. The only *necessity* is a modification of the original transition in some way, to make the second subject enter, in the Recapitulation, in the tonic key. Any other rewriting must be attributed to the composer's creative fertility, which shows him variants of his themes as he restates them. In the present instance the fact that these themes were not developed at all in the Development section may have something to do with their variation in the Recapitulation.

(2) The *closing theme* (mm. 169–about 178) is first presented as in the Exposition (but of course *in the tonic key*), and then, on its repeat, elaborated into a coda.

Coda: about measure 178 to measure 197. This grows out of the closing theme in such a way as to make determination of its exact starting-point artificial and unnecessary. The four-note rising figure of the closing theme is seized on and "worked," first in the clarinet, then in the first violin, then in the 'cello. In measure 185 the clarinet breaks into the same kind of arpeggio figuration as appeared in the Development (*cf.* mm. 99+); and after this (m. 189) the high-spirited scale-passages which originally ended the main theme of the second subject (and were omitted in the Recapitulation) make their appearance, together with a chuckling bar of descending chromatic triplets (m. 191) and the aforementioned triple-trills (mm. 192–193). The whole movement ends (mm. 193–197) with a reproduction of the Expositional codetta, which itself is a reminder of the first subject theme; so "the beginning and the end are one." Note that 18th-century *allegro* movements close without *rallentando* (slowing); the style calls for a final flourish, not a pulling up of the horses.

SECOND MOVEMENT

Tempo: *Larghetto* (rather slow)
Key: D major
Form: Expanded ternary (pp. 397–99)

This movement is one of the loveliest in all Mozart. Its mood is ecstatic, in the true sense of the word ecstasy; for if ever an artist "stood outside of" himself—if ever a spirit achieved perfect, disimpassioned stillness—it is here. The whole movement is a song; its serene melodies are presented with the utmost simplicity. The form is ternary, expanded to accommodate two themes in Part A, and without sectional repeats. The strings are muted throughout (*con sordino*).

Part A: measures 1–30, in D major (tonic key).

(1) The *first theme* (mm. 1–20, Ex. 63) is a clarinet solo, in the clear, lyrical register of the instrument. Bars 16–17 show an interrupted cadence, marked by the plunge of the clarinet to its lowest notes, after which it returns to the upper air for the real cadence.

Example 63

(2) The *second theme* (mm. 20–30, Ex. 64) is a solo for the first violin, against which the clarinet plays a graceful commentary. The ∽ signs in this section indicate ornamentations known as *turns*.[5] In both themes (1) and (2)—and indeed throughout the movement—the lower strings have an accompanimental role; the clarinet and first violin divide the honors of the melody.

Example 64

Part B: measures 30–45, in A major (dominant key).

This continues theme (2) and develops it slightly, modulating to the dominant key (m. 32) and coming to a full close there (m. 45) after a striking interrupted cadence in measure 40. The expressive held chords in bars 34–37 are worthy of note.

A *link* (mm. 45–51), based on the same held-chord pattern, modulates back to the tonic key, the strings dropping out on the only *forte* chord in the whole movement (m. 49) and leaving the clarinet to execute a little *cadenza* (solo passage) which demonstrates to a nicety its powers of controlled *diminuendo*. The link is constructed over an *implied* dominant (A) of the tonic key (D) to which we are returning.

[5] A *turn* is an ornament consisting of the main melodic note, the note next above it, the main note, the note next below it, and the main note to end.

Part A²: measures 51–80, in D major (tonic key).

This repeats Part A exactly, except for the very slight elaboration of the violin part in measures 77–80 (triplet figurations).

Coda: measures 80–85 (Ex. 65). The clarinet adds a little epilogue in the form of a

Example 65

descending chromatic line, which creates an effect of sinking into blissful rest. The triplet figurations just referred to are continued as a murmuring accompaniment, and the whole coda is based on a held tonic note (*pedal*) in the 'cello. Again observe the clarinet in its lowest register at the end.

THIRD MOVEMENT: *Menuetto* (Minuet)

Tempo: not marked, but actually *allegretto* or *allegro* (somewhat fast, or fast)
Key: A major
Form: Minuet with two trios (*cf.* pp. 401–4)

Here we have an example of a comparatively rare procedure. The usual minuet-and-trio, which is a simple episodic form,[6] here acquires an additional trio, which turns it into a *rondo* as far as the form is concerned (I–II–I–III–I). To avoid confusion with the typical rondo *character,* let us call this movement exactly what it is—a *minuet with two trios;* the important thing being to note the characteristics of the minuet dance as preserved by the Classical masters in the third movements of their four-movement sonatas. These characteristics are:

(1) Triple time, with fairly even weight on all three beats of the bar (which distinguishes the minuet from the waltz). (2) Moderately fast tempo—faster than the courtly dance of Mozart's day, but still not *very* fast. (3) Clear, sectionalized form, with internal repeats. (4) *Generally* (there are exceptions) a happy mood, with graceful melodies and a certain delicacy or refinement of character.

All these points are illustrated to perfection by the present case.

MINUET: measures 1–32. Ternary form, in A major (tonic key).

Part A: measures 1–8. A warm, smiling melody in the clarinet (Ex. 66), exquisitely articulated (*phrased*), full of gracious curves, reaching a climax in the fifth bar and floating down to a typically Mozartean cadence in the tonic key. The section is repeated (see

Example 66

point 3 above). Mozart's "enunciation"—the way he pronounces his musical "words"—is always most precise; one must carefully observe the dots, curved lines, rests, etc. which indicate this in the score, otherwise one misses the elegance of his language. (*Senza sordino* means "without mute.")

[6]See pp. 399–400.

Part B: measures 9–20. Develops measures 3–4 of "A" slightly, in viola and 'cello, and adds a new smooth line in the first violin. Modulation to the dominant key (mm. 13+) leads to an interrupted cadence in measures 15–16, the clarinet taking over and repeating the violin line, bringing it to an authentic cadence in the dominant key in measure 20.

Link: measures 21–25. Modulates back to the tonic key over the typical *dominant pedal* (which we have seen twice before in links, in movements 1 and 2). Here the pedal is *figurated;* instead of a held note in the bass the 'cello and viola ornament the dominant note E in trill fashion, taking their cue from the violin pattern in the first bars of "B." The clarinet holds an upper dominant pedal right into "A²" (but note how neatly it joins in the "trilling" in the bar immediately preceding "A²"), while violins I and II build up to the point of return with the figure derived from measures 3–4 of "A" which was also used at the beginning of "B."

Part A²: measures 25–32. An exact restatement of "A," since that ended with a cadence in the tonic key.

"B"–"A²" are repeated together (see point 3 above).

TRIO I: measures 33–73. Ternary form, in *A minor* (parallel or tonic minor). The *episodic*—i.e., contrasting—nature of this trio is discernible in the following particulars:

(1) The clarinet is silent throughout. (2) The tonality is minor. (3) The theme is not a continuous song-like melody, as in the minuet, but a disjunct, fragmentary one, based upon a two-note, sighing fall ornamented with pathetic "leaning-notes," which are sometimes written as grace-notes (m. 34) and at other times incorporated in the melody (m. 36), the effects being the same. (4) The texture is more polyphonic than in the minuet; the two-note motive is imitated freely in all parts, directly and by contrary motion. (5) The character of the trio is, as a result of this, melancholy or nostalgic, as contrasted with the golden glow of the minuet.

Part A: measures 33–48. Starting in A minor with the sighing figure just referred to (Ex. 67), after four bars the music passes over to the *relative major* key (C major), confirming

Example 67

its arrival there by accented, syncopated cadence-chords (*fp=forte-piano*) in measures 39–40. A repetition of these in another key (mm. 43–44) only serves to make the final cadence in C major doubly sure. Note that this cadence (mm. 47–48) is the same one as occurred at the end of Part A (and A²) of the minuet. The identity of voice-writing cannot be accidental; we therefore assume that Mozart, by this detail, intends a "cross-reference" between trio and minuet. There is the usual repeat of Part A.

Part B: measures 49–56. Develops the two-note figure slightly, and modulates back to a half-cadence in A minor (m. 53), confirming this with the *forte-piano* chords. A melodic link in the first violin leads smoothly into "A²."

Part A²: measures 57–73. This is rewritten, with an intriguing *canon* (exact imitation) between first violin and viola in measures 57–64. The original modulation to C major is now avoided, and the cadence in bars 63–64 is in A minor. The same procedure is followed thereafter; the *forte-piano* chords first confirm the cadence, then supply a lovely color-point outside the key, which makes the final cadence in A minor all the more expressive.

"B"–"A²" are repeated together, in the usual way.

MINUET REPEATED, without sectional repeats (as indicated by the Italian words at the end of Trio I). Were the whole movement to end with this repeat, we should have a perfectly regular minuet-and-trio (*i.e.,* simple episodic) form, such as occurs over and over again in sonatas. The addition of a second trio to this particular movement may perhaps be attributed to Mozart's desire to give the clarinet a further showing, in view of its silence in Trio I. More probably, the second trio is a spontaneous gesture, arising out of the lavish geniality of Mozart's mood here.

TRIO II: measures 74–124. Ternary form, in A major (tonic key). Here we have to note not only the episodic nature of the trio—*i.e.,* how it contrasts with the minuet—but also how it contrasts with Trio I. The easiest way to do this is by constructing a table of comparisons and contrasts, thus:

	Minuet	*Trio I*	*Trio II*
Key	A major	A minor	A major
Theme	Easily singable	Not very singable	Half-and-half; "swingable," with some purely instrumental passages.
Texture	Essentially homophonic	Polyphonic	Decidedly homophonic.
Character	Warm, serene.	Melancholy	Gay, playful, waltz-like.
Clarinet's role	Soloist—lyrical.	Silent	Soloist—virtuoso.

Part A: measures 74–85. To a definite waltz accompaniment, the clarinet plays a swinging, care-free melody (Ex. 68), the course of which is interrupted in bars 79–81 by the

Example 68

strings' amusing mimicry; whereupon the clarinet executes a little solo-passage and rounds the section off with—again—the cadence-phrase from the minuet. The solo-passage displays the instrument's facility at arpeggio-work, and its tonal variety. The use of the same cadence-phrase *for the third time* leaves no doubt as to Mozart's intention of "cross-reference" between both trios and the minuet. There is the usual repeat of Part A.

Part B: measures 86–101. This whole section, and the link which follows it, is constructed over a dominant *pedal* (E), which becomes tonic pedal in E major (m. 94) by a modulation to that key (the dominant). The modulation consists of nothing but repetitions of the authentic cadence in E major (V–I, six times), during which the clarinet deftly slips its tune to the waiting first violin, the latter already having a stake in it from the opening bars of Part B and the "mimicry" of Part A. The by-play between these two instruments is most subtle and delightful.

Link: measures 101–108. Still over (or "under," if we must be literal) a dominant *pedal* E, this modulates back to the tonic key, the upper strings building a "dominant seventh" chord (E–G sharp–B–D) and the 'cello taking a flight with the theme, from the bottom to the top of the normal 'cello range.

Part A²: measures 109–124. This is extended slightly by further by-play between clarinet and strings. The little solo-passage (m. 116) is interrupted by the strings' butting in (*rf = rinforzando, i.e.,* sharply accented), so the clarinet has another go at it, a step higher; this also is interrupted. Finally, with another step up, the clarinet "comes out on top," and ends the game with the same gracious cadence as ended Part A.

"B"–"A²" are repeated together, in the usual way.

MINUET REPEATED, without sectional repeats. This ends the movement. Note that both trios are longer than the minuet. This is one obvious but none the less real reason for the fact that *three* hearings of the minuet do not seem tedious.

FOURTH MOVEMENT

Tempo: *Allegretto con Variazioni* (rather fast, with variations)
Key: A major

Form: Variation form (pp. 404–5)

The theme of this set of variations (mm. 1–16, and Ex. 69) is engagingly simple; it sounds like the tune of a nursery-rhyme, with its square-cut form, its cadences every two bars, its pat antitheses of instrumentation, and its sprightly melody.

The form is basically *binary*.[7] Each part contains two four-bar phrases; the second phrase of Part B repeats the *second* phrase of Part A by a common kind of thematic unification,[8] as shown in the following scheme:

$$\|: \quad \text{PART A—8 bars} \quad :\|: \quad \text{PART B—8 bars} \quad :\|$$
$$a - 4 \text{ bars}; a^1 - 4 \text{ bars} \qquad b - 4 \text{ bars}; a^1 - 4 \text{ bars}$$

The scheme also shows, however, that a^1 is a simple variant of a; consequently, the repetition of a^1 after the contrasting b phrase sounds remarkably like a return *to the beginning*.[9] There is about this binary theme, therefore, a certain *"ternary*-ness" which leads one to describe the form as a hybrid.

Example 69

The *form* of all the variations (except the final one) is the same as the theme's, and sectional repeats are marked in each case.

Variation I: measures 17–32. Clearly the clarinet's solo. It adds a new melody to the original, the latter (in "A" and "Ba^1") appearing in the strings with only slight changes. In measure 19 the clarinet breaks into high-stepping arpeggios; the leaps become wider in measures 23–24, and thereafter in Part B. Here is an excellent illustration of Mozart's sure handling of the new instrument, for this kind of agility is "pure clarinet." The rather humorous effect of these particular acrobatics is the result of emphasizing the difference of tone-color between lower and upper clarinet registers by taking single-note, off-the-beat "pokes" at the lower extremity while maintaining a suave nonchalance up above.

[7]See pp. 396–97.
[8]*Cf.* the first example of *Binary Form* on page 396, and see Note 4 in its accompanying text.
[9]This is quite common in Mozart and other Classical writers; see the Minuet (only) of the Minuet-and-Trio quoted under *Episodic Form* on page 401.

Variation II: measures 33–48. Equally clearly the first violin's turn. To a dancing triplet accompaniment in the second violin and viola (the 'cello meanwhile "walking delicately" in the bass), the solo violin sings another new melody, of lark-like freshness, against which the clarinet in both a^1 phrases supplies a smooth counterpoint, (counter-melody). The connection with the theme here is purely structural and harmonic; the same phrase-structure and the same sequence of chords are maintained, but the actual melody of the theme is *replaced* by the new one. Always observe Mozart's precise *phrasing,* indicated by dots, curved lines, and rests; note also his introduction of *forte* markings (*f* and *fp*) for the first time in the movement. By such details, no less than by the obvious changes, is *variation* of a theme achieved.

Variation III: measures 49–64, *in A minor*. The viola's variation. The significant mood-change that comes with the change of tonality from major to minor is emphasized by replacing melody or tunefulness by an obsessive *figuration* (*i.e.,* the working of a *figure* or *motive*) in the viola, the effect of which is dark and drone-like. The viola part is, in fact, little more than a figurated *pedal* on the note E; the *grace-notes* (printed in small type) sound in this context like pathetic little sobs, or "breaks in the voice." As before, the connection with the theme is structural and harmonic only. The first phrase of Part B supplies contrast, but no lightening of mood; the touching, descending chromatic scales in the first violin outbalance its ascending arpeggios. The clarinet's role, in both a^1 phrases, is purely accompanimental; its low-placed notes, however, add further dark color to an already dusky tonal atmosphere. Noteworthy (at the ends of both Parts A and B) is the manner in which the viola draws out its doleful strain to the last eighth note of the cadence-bar—a masterstroke of sentiment.

Variation IV: measures 65–80. Clarinet and first violin share the honors here. The change back to A major, and the burst of activity with which the variation opens (and continues), make it clear that the preceding variation was merely a mock-serious interlude, not to be taken too much to heart. The original theme-melody bounces back in the strings, just as sprightly as ever, and around this the clarinet sports with the liveliest arpeggios, followed in a^1 by the violin with flashing scale-passages. In Part B this order is reversed—the violin embellishes the *b* phrase, now with arpeggio-work, and the clarinet takes over the final a^1 phrase, in the same manner as at the opening. The whole variation is extremely busy; the fast sixteenth-note patterns, introduced here for the first time in the movement, are actually somewhat facile; but used at this point in the sequence—after a doleful variation and before the most lyrical one of all—they provide just the "relief" or contrast that is needed. Equally conscious is the use of the theme-melody here, practically unaltered; it comes after *two* variations in which it was suppressed, and before the one variation in which the melodic material is farthest removed from that of the theme. It serves, therefore, to keep us "on the beam" at precisely the point where such a reminder is most necessary.

Link: measures 81–84. A four-bar passage, starting with bold, loud chords in the strings and arpeggios low in the clarinet, leads to a sustained, soft chord of the dominant seventh (E–G sharp–B–D), which prepares us for some important change ahead. The effect is to set off the slow, expressive *Variation V* from all that have come before—to "point it up" and focus attention on it. Since *Variation V* is also *followed* by a link (see below), it is apparent that Mozart takes care to approach and quit this lyrical moment with delicacy.

Variation V (*Adagio*=slow): measures 85–100. First violin and clarinet again to the fore, but this time as melodists, not as technicians. In slow tempo, to an accompaniment quietly subordinate, the violin unwinds a free and rhapsodic line whose connection with the melody of the theme is rather sensed than heard. The clarinet takes over for the a^1

phrase, and in its clear upper register elaborates even more freely on the original. Reversing the sequence in Part B, the clarinet takes phrase b and the violin phrase a^1 (the latter in a different version from what it sang at the opening—phrase a—so that in this variation there is less of the "ternary feeling" we spoke of above, and the essential "binary feeling" is more marked). Here Mozart gives rein to his pure melodic genius, just as he does time and time again in the slow, expressive second movements of his sonatas, quartets, and symphonies (see this very quintet's second movement as an example). The connection with the theme is maintained by the phrase-structure and chordal sequence, which we have by now heard sufficiently often to be able to recognize even in slow tempo. The melody is spontaneous and almost completely free (though careful scrutiny will still disclose subtle references to essential patterns in the original melody). All in all, this variation is probably the finest in the set, especially when one considers the naïveté of the idea proposed in the theme, and realizes what expressiveness is here drawn out of it.

Link: measures 100–105. A sweetly-simple clarinet phrase, lifting to an effortless climax (on A) and falling again to a dominant chord (on E) embellished by a held dissonance (F sharp) in the solo instrument. The blissful contentment of a line like this, after the lyrical tenderness of the preceding variation, lulls us into a mood of reverie which serves as a foil (contrast) to the concluding variation now about to begin.

Variation VI, or *Coda* (*Allegro*=fast): measures 106–141. Whether this should be labelled "Variation VI with coda," or whether the whole thing should not rather be called "Coda based on the theme," is a point hardly worth settling. It is obvious that the marking *allegro* (instead of the *allegretto* of the theme and first four variations) indicates a final flourish, and equally obvious that this section "cuts loose" from the theme and adds a lot of new "end-matter" to round off the whole movement. But the interesting structural feature is the maintenance of the *binary pattern* in measures 106–121, with Part A strictly adhering to the theme (mm. 106–113) and *a new "B" part* continuing the melodic pattern of Part A (mm. 114–121, repeated in mm. 122–129). We have, in other words, a coda which, for its first 24 bars, represents *the theme re-worked,* and re-worked in such a way as to make no doubt of its "binary-ness"; for instead of a digressing b phrase and a return to a^1 we now have the whole "B" part given over to development of the idea of "A." From measure 130 on we have characteristic coda-feeling, reinforced by the tonic *pedal* (the long held A) in the 'cello, and the concluding cadence-repetitions.

The variation begins quietly, with a new clarinet counterpoint, and then (m. 110) bursts into an energetic *forte,* the 'cello supplying a busy bass to the a^1 phrase. There is no sectional repeat. The quiet "B" part develops the opening measures of "A" first over a *pedal* in the viola (mm. 114–117; note the two sudden *forte* points) and then more freely (mm. 118–121) in rich, colorful, descending chromatic chords, sustained. Mozart likes this new "B" part well enough to repeat it, with another version of the chromatic descent. The eight bars that follow again show his favorite trick of saying a good thing twice; in measures 130–133 the clarinet has the theme, and in measures 134–137 the first violin repeats it exactly (but with different phrasing and accompaniment). The unaffected, "nursery-rhyme" quality of the tune is more than ever apparent here, where the long 'cello *pedal* and the smooth inner voices impart to the music a sweet, childlike repose, eminently befitting the end of such a work as this. As an 18th-century composer, Mozart delivers his very last words with an air, *forte;* but he manages to inject the quiet note even into the formal cadences of the last four bars.

Recommended reading:
Alfred Einstein, *Mozart, His Character, His Work,* New York, Oxford University Press 1945.
W. J. Turner, *Mozart, the Man and His Works,* New York, Tudor Publishing Company, 1938.

EIGHTEENTH-CENTURY LITERATURE

THOMAS GRAY (1716–1771)

Elegy Written in a Country Churchyard[1]

GRAY'S ELEGY (1750) is probably the best-known poem in our language, and quite possibly the best-liked. This is not surprising, for it is certainly one of our most lucid poems, and its moralizing is as easily within the reach of the average man as its imagery is familiar and pleasing to him. Its sophistication is not of the worldly sort of Voltaire or his English contemporaries of the Enlightenment, who were so proud of their circumspection and knowledge of the world and how to behave in it. Yet it has a sophistication which has caused it to be admired by such diverse critics of poetry as Gray's contemporary Samuel Johnson and our own contemporary I. A. Richards. The former wrote in his *Life* of Gray:

In the character of his *Elegy* I rejoice to concur with the common reader; for by the common sense of readers uncorrupted with literary prejudices, after all the refinements of subtlety and the dogmatism of learning, must be finally decided all claim to poetical honors. The *Churchyard* abounds with images which find a mirror in every mind, and with sentiments to which every bosom returns an echo.

Richards praises Gray for his perfect manner, his sense of proportion in dealing with his subject:

Gray's *Elegy*, indeed, might stand as a supreme instance to show how powerful an exquisitely adjusted tone may be. It would be difficult to maintain that the thought in this poem is either striking or original, or that its feeling is exceptional. It embodies a sequence of reflections and attitudes that under similar conditions arise readily in any contemplative mind. Their character as commonplaces, needless to say, does not make them any less important, and the *Elegy* may usefully remind us that boldness and originality are not necessities for great poetry. . . . Gray, without overstressing any point, composes a long address, perfectly accommodating his familiar feelings towards the subject and his awareness of the inevitable triteness of the only possible reflections, to the discriminating attention of his audience.[2]

Both of these critics point to important characteristics of the poem: the lack of originality of thought, and the fittingness of its language. The commonness of the thought is, of course, deliberate on Gray's part. The melancholy theme of the limitations on life this side of the grave was Gray's frequent meditation and personal preoccupation. Probably the poem was inspired by the death of Richard West, a friend whose loss was strongly felt by the shy, lonely Gray. Yet the poem is a quite impersonal elegy, for Gray, in overcoming his grief for West and in reconciling himself to other frustrations, saw himself in a position common with countless other men and saw his own problem as one which hung over all of mankind. He schooled himself to accept the conditions of mortality, and he carefully set out to pattern for himself a workable and agreeable existence within the actual conditions as he saw them. His was no romantic agony. However deeply his own grief was felt, he was able to look at it in perspective, to ask himself what the accumulated wisdom of man has to offer on the common lot of man, and finally to endure that lot with Christian Stoicism.

This is the mood in which he addresses his *Hymn to Adversity:*

[1] Programs A and B.
[2] I. A. Richards, *Practical Criticism* (N. Y.: Harcourt, Brace, 1929), pp. 206 f.

> Daughter of Jove, relentless power,
> Thou tamer of the human breast,
> Whose iron scourge and torturing hour
> The bad affright, afflict the best!
> Bound in thy adamantine chain
> The proud are taught to taste of pain,
> And purple tyrants vainly groan
> With pangs unfelt before, unpitied and alone.

To this poem he attached a motto from Aeschylus' *Agamemnon*: "Zeus it is who has led mortals to wisdom by establishing it as a fixed law that knowledge comes by suffering."

Or again in his *Ode on a Distant Prospect of Eton College,* to which is prefixed a remark by an ancient Greek writer of comedy to the effect that to be a man is in itself sufficient claim for misery, he thinks of what may lie ahead of the careless youth of the schoolboys:

> To each his sufferings: all are men,
> Condemned alike to groan,
> The tender for another's pain;
> The unfeeling for his own.
> Yet ah, why should they know their fate?
> Since sorrow never comes too late,
> And happiness too swiftly flies.
> Thought would destroy their paradise.
> No more; where ignorance is bliss,
> 'Tis folly to be wise.

At about the same time that these lines and the *Elegy* were being written, Samuel Johnson, in imitation of the ancient Roman satirist Juvenal, wrote *The Vanity of Human Wishes,* which began:

> Let Observation, with extensive view,
> Survey mankind, from China to Peru;
> Remark each anxious toil, each eager strife,
> And watch the busy scenes of crowded life;
> Then say how hope and fear, desire and hate
> O'erspread with snares the clouded maze of fate,
> Where wavering man, betrayed by venturous pride
> To tread the dreary paths without a guide,
> As treacherous phantoms in the mist delude,
> Shuns fancied ills or chases airy good;
> How rarely Reason guides the stubborn choice,
> Rules the bold hand, or prompts the suppliant voice;
> How nations sink, by darling schemes oppressed,
> When Vengeance listens to the fool's request.
> Fate wings with every wish the afflictive dart,
> Each gift of nature, and each grace of art;
> With fatal heat impetuous courage glows,
> With fatal sweetness elocution flows,
> Impeachment stops the speaker's powerful breath,
> And restless fire precipitates on death.

Gray, like Johnson and other contemporaries, felt that the duty of the poet was not to anatomize his private feelings but to bring an extensive study and observation of mankind —its nature and its history—to bear on particular problems and thus to see those problems in their broadest, most universal scope, not in their confinement to one isolated and perhaps atypical person. In this fashion one understands and masters his passions. And so in the *Elegy* an established literary habit sets the tone of closely restrained and controlled sentiment. Gray "gave to misery (all he had) *a* tear," not torrents of them. He saves the poem from excessive sentimental pathos by lamenting the fate of other obscure men besides himself, by sensing his identity—his common humanity—with them, and by revealing with clarity the character of their mutual fate. His is a lament for potential energies not realized (nor able to be under the conditions which life imposes on most men), along with the compensatory feeling that the small, quiet life may be a good and satisfactory one after all.

This frame of mind accounts for Gray's desire not to say new and startling things but to characterize a widely felt mood and to record the perennially durable consolations, the generalized thoughts, which would be appropriate over a wide range of men and experience. And for this purpose he was fortunate in having at hand in the common poetic language of his time a highly polished, dignified, and exact diction of just the kind necessary to lend clarity and a certain impersonal majesty to familiar thoughts.

Especially useful for Gray were the conventions of a sharply restrictive imagery. Gray's own temper was not what we would call creative, and certainly not spontaneous. He worked over the *Elegy* for at least six years. What he wanted was not a suggestive, expansive language but one which confined his meaning to precise, limpid figures. He was as fastidious in his love of nature and as precise in his observations of it as he was meticulous in his search for exact shades of moral implication; and it is surely one of the great accomplishments of this poem that he matches so perfectly the quiet resignation of traditional meditative wisdom with the familiar restfulness of the end of a rural day. It is true that there is some of the fashionable imagery of the contemporary "graveyard school"—hence the moping owl in its secret bower in the ivy-mantled tower. But more characteristic are the finely adjectived, epithetical phrases, the neatly turned miniature descriptions: "the breezy call of incense-breathing morn"; "the cock's shrill clarion, or the echoing horn" (a line which reminds us that we must not underrate Gray's verbal subtlety—observe how unobtrusively the echoing horn echoes); "the boast of heraldry, the pomp of power"; the "mute, inglorious Milton." Or the personifications with their cold formality as they mingle with rhetorical circumlocutions:

> Knowledge to their eyes her ample page
> Rich with the spoils of time did ne'er unroll.

There is a simple and forceful directness here. The thoughts are not intellectually abstruse—even the figures of speech add not complexity but an immediate clarity. There is no intense psychological awareness, nor any of the metaphorical complexities that go with it. But as a recent literary historian has said,

> The poem is compact of what Tennyson called "divine truisms," and these are universally, if decorously, affecting. Among poems embodying the noble ideal of
>
> > What oft was thought but ne'er so well expressed,
>
> this *Elegy* must always rank high. Persons with an aversion to reflective commonplaces in poetry may, as T. S. Eliot has done, question the subtlety of the *Churchyard;* but critics who admit *both* clarity and subtlety as merits will be content with the noble and finished transparency of this poem. Its achievement is, of its very nature, the opposite of facile: *"divine* truisms" are not so easily come by![3]

Gray believed in these truisms, which came to him as a religious Englishman in the Age of Enlightenment. He would not carry his enlightenment to the point of rational skepticism such as he saw in some of his contemporaries, and he characteristically remarked:

> Atheism is a vile dish, though all the cooks of France combine to make new sauces to it. As to the soul, perhaps they have none on the Continent; but I do think we have such things in England. Shakespeare, for example, I believe, had several to his share. As to the Jews—though they do not eat pork—I like them, because they are better Christians than Voltaire.

---

[3]George Sherburn, in *A Literary History of England,* ed. Albert C. Baugh (N.Y.: Appleton-Century-Crofts, 1948), p. 1014.

Voltaire, we might say, taught men much about how (and how not) to get along in the world. Gray has something to say on how to come to terms with the world and get along with yourself. If Gray was melancholy, it was perhaps, as David Cecil has suggested, because he "never committed the blasphemy of thinking human existence adequate to satisfy the aspirations of the soul."

Recommended reading:
Thomas Gray, *Correspondence,* ed. Paget Toynbee and Leonard Whibley, 3 vols., Oxford, Oxford University Press, 1935.
Lord David Cecil, "Thomas Gray," in *Two Quiet Lives,* New York, Bobbs-Merrill, 1948.

VOLTAIRE (1694–1778): *Candide*[1]

I. "THE COMMON SENSE of the eighteenth century, its grasp of the obvious demands of human nature," says Alfred North Whitehead, "acted on the world like a bath of moral cleansing. Voltaire must have the credit, that he hated injustice, he hated cruelty, he hated senseless repression, and he hated hocus-pocus. Furthermore, when he saw them, he knew them. In these supreme virtues, he was typical of his century, on its better side." There is much truth in Professor Whitehead's generous tribute to Voltaire; and, up to a point, anyway, one will find ample, richly detailed confirmation of it in Voltaire's *Candide* (1759). We also, however, have to agree with Professor Whitehead when he adds: "But if men cannot live on bread alone, still less can they do so on disinfectants." And *Candide,* in a sense, is a disinfectant, an Eldorado story soaked in Lysol. Unlike Voltaire's poem on the Lisbon earthquake of 1755, which came as near to being an anguished cry from the heart as anything he ever wrote, *Candide* was a dry, clinical mock, composed after he had recovered his rationalistic aplomb and was his cold, grinning self again.

But first, a few background words about his poem, *The Lisbon Earthquake* (1756). In it he was reacting—sadly, despairingly, almost groaningly—against the teachings and philosophizings of men like Leibniz and Pope, who, in their different ways, had given wide currency to the notion that this is the best of all possible worlds, and that whatever is, is right.

In the *Théodicée* of Leibniz, his attempt to justify the ways of God to men, from which so many vulgarized, watered-down versions of philosophical optimism derived in the 18th century, God is an absolutely perfect being. "As such," Professor Gilson says, "the God of Leibniz is also to be an infinitely generous God; and because, morally speaking at least, he can hardly refrain from communicating his own perfection, he has to create. Now a perfect God can create only the best possible world. Among the infinite series of possible worlds, the best one obviously will be the one wherein the highest conceivable richness of effects will be achieved by the simplest possible means. As Leibniz himself says, this is what the mathematicians call a problem of *maximum* and *minimum*. Such problems are susceptible of but one solution. Consequently, the best possible world is exactly the one we are in. A most gratifying certitude indeed, at least so long as it lasts, and Voltaire was to see that it did not outlive the earthquake of Lisbon."

"The metaphysical difficulty, however," Professor Gilson observes, "was not there; it rather lay in the fact that Leibniz pretended to make us accept as the supreme Being a God

[1] Programs A and B.

who was but a nature. As a matter of fact, the God of the Monadology was but the Good of Plato, solving the problem of which world to create, by means of the infinitesimal calculus recently discovered by Leibniz."

In many essential respects, this was the God whom Voltaire, following the Lisbon disaster, rather suddenly began to find so capricious, so pitiless, even somewhat unscrupulous. How closely Voltaire's Deity substantially resembled Leibniz's may be seen by comparing Professor Gilson's following description of the God of the Deists with the description given above of the God of Leibniz: ". . . this ghost of the Christian God has been attended by the ghost of Christian religion: a vague feeling of religiosity, a sort of trusting familiarity with some supremely good fellow to whom other good fellows can hopefully apply when they are in trouble: *le Dieu des bons gens*. As an object of pure philosophical speculation, he was little more than a myth whose death sentence had been irrevocably passed by Spinoza. Having forgotten, together with 'Him who is,' the true meaning of the problem of existence, Fontenelle, Voltaire, Rousseau, and so many others with them had naturally to fall back upon the most superficial interpretation of the problem of final causes. God then became the 'watchmaker' of Fontenelle and of Voltaire, the supreme engineer of the huge machine which this world is. In short, God became again what he had already been in the *Timaeus* of Plato: a Demiurge, the only difference being that this time, before beginning to arrange his world, the Demiurge had consulted Newton. Just like the Demiurge of Plato, the God of the Deists was but a philosophical myth." In other words, Voltaire, before he could very logically reproach the God of Leibniz, was under the embarrassing necessity of complaining of his own. And, to a degree, and for a time, he did, since he questioned not only the philosophical optimism of Pope and Leibniz, but the fundamental deistic belief in a benevolent universe as well.

But to have one's faith in the Watchmaker severely shaken is one thing; to embrace the God of Abraham, of Isaac, and of Jacob is another. In the Lisbon poem, although Voltaire defended the doctrine of original sin and counselled resignation, he refrained from subscribing to the doctrine of immortality. His trust in the rationality of the universe had been dealt a rude blow, but he still believed in Progress, in man's redemption through the exercise of his own unaided will and intelligence. Reason was still the God of Voltaire.

Shortly after the appearance of Voltaire's poem on the Lisbon disaster, Rousseau sent a long letter to the author, in which he accused him of writing against Providence; of denying the immortality of the soul; of blaming God when he ought to be blaming man; and of being almost indecently ill at ease about the state of the world, whimpering blasphemies because of the sufferings of the poor and unfortunate, while enjoying the comforts and luxuries of a king. And, characteristically enough, Rousseau pictured himself in striking contrast as "an obscure man, poor, and tormented by an incurable malady," who found the world good. "You enjoy life, but I hope, and hope embellishes everything."

Voltaire politely acknowledged Rousseau's taunting letter, and thanked him for the interest he had shown in the poem. Two years later, he replied to Rousseau, but not in kind. Instead of dispatching a long letter, he concocted for Rousseau's benefit (and posterity's amusement) a burlesque tale. That, briefly, is the history of how *Candide* came to be written. The rest is literature.

II. By pretty general consent, *Candide,* if we except the wonderful *Letters,* is, despite its theological fade-outs, metaphysical blowholes, and ethical sentimentalities (concerning which a little more later), Voltaire's masterpiece. Today his plays, once the chief stock-in-trade of his literary reputation, go unread and are practically forgotten. His histories are still readable, but not widely read. His *Philosophical Dictionary* is eminently readable, and continues a general favorite, especially among lovers of witty prose, and in those circles where Bob Ingersoll is highly regarded as a theologian, or George Bernard Shaw as a philosopher.

But, as H. N. Brailsford puts it, "*Candide* lives on, and one may read it in any civilized tongue, in rich editions illustrated by great artists, or in paper covers sold for a few pence." Mr. Brailsford, like the rest of us, is not at all sure just what *Candide* should be called. Is it a tale, a satire, or a philosophical romance? "It is all of these things," he says, "but also it is the most perfect model of written prose, in the language that is of all European tongues the best adapted for this art. You will not lay it down, if once you take it up, and as the years crowd upon you, you will find that you can read it over and over again. It is like a quartette of Mozart's: so light it seems, so graceful, so easy, that one supposes that none of its beauties can escape an attentive ear at the first playing, yet repetition is discovery."

One of Voltaire's distinguished countrymen, however, found repetition slightly less rewarding. In 1922, André Gide noted in his *Journal:* "At La Bastide I reread some pages of *Candide*. Simplicity of style amazes me, and I can admire it, only by reason of the complexity of the relations involved. It is not difficult to state simple things simply. Voltaire begins by simplifying his thought; he makes the game too easy for himself."

Twelve years later, Gide has this entry in his *Journal:* ". . . I am saturating myself with Voltaire's *Contes* . . . and do not succeed, any more than I did before, in setting *Candide* far above the others. I even wonder if it is not to the slight naughty bits in it that *Candide* owes its remarkable fame. The satire in it often falls a bit short and in it Voltaire's laugh seems to me more a grin than elsewhere. He writes *Candide* to amuse himself; and while amusing himself he amuses. But one is aware also that he wants to prove something without one's being very well aware what, nor whom he is attacking. To show that man is innumerably unhappy on this earth, there is no need for so much wit. Religion teaches us this too; Voltaire knows this very well and at times it embarrasses him. If he were to return among us today (1934), how upset he would be to have so little overcome many things that he either was attacking badly or else was wrong to attack; and to have played into the hands of so many fools!"

III. Putting *Candide* aside for the moment, let us look at certain general aspects of the spiritual and intellectual climate out of which writers like Voltaire and books like *Candide* issued. Voltaire was one of a group of thinkers who were known collectively as the *Philosophes,* the Philosophers. To their number belonged Montesquieu and Voltaire and Rousseau, Diderot and Helvétius and Baron d'Holbach, Turgot and Quesnay and Condorcet, to mention only the best known. Professor Becker tells us that there is "one not unimportant point about the philosophers that ought, in simple fairness to them, to be noted in passing, especially since few writers take the trouble to mention it: the Philosophers were not philosophers. I mean to say they were not professors of philosophy whose business it was to publish, every so often, systematic and stillborn treatises on epistemology and the like subjects. . . . for the most part the Philosophers were men of letters, writers of books intended to be read and designed to spread abroad new ideas or to shed new light on old ones. I need only mention that Voltaire wrote plays, histories, tales, and an ABC of Newtonian physics for ladies and gentlemen unblessed with a knowledge of mathematics; . . . that Rousseau, in defense of the thesis that art is injurious to mankind, employed a high degree of art in the writing of political propaganda and didactic romances. . . ."

Professor Carl Becker summarizes the cardinal tenets in the credo of the *Philosophes:* ". . . at every turn the *Philosophes* betray their debt to medieval thought without being aware of it. They denounced Christian philosophy, but rather too much, after the manner of those who are but half emancipated from the 'superstitions' they scorn. They had put off the fear of God, but maintained a respectful attitude toward the Deity. They ridiculed the idea that the universe had been created in six days, but still believed it to be a beautifully articulated machine designed by the Supreme Being according to a rational plan as an abiding place for mankind. The Garden of Eden was for them a myth, no doubt, but they looked enviously back to the golden age of Roman virtue, or across the waters to the unspoiled innocence of an Arcadian civilization that flourished in Pennsylvania. They renounced the authority of church and Bible, but exhibited a naive faith in the authority of nature and reason. They scorned metaphysics, but were proud to be called philosophers. They dismantled heaven, somewhat prematurely it seems, since they retained their faith in the immortality of the soul. They courageously discussed atheism, but not before the servants. They defended toleration valiantly, but could with difficulty tolerate priests. They denied that miracles ever happened, but believed in the perfectibility of the human race. We feel that these Philosophers were at once too credulous and too skeptical. They were the victims of common sense."

IV. Reading Professor Becker on the *Philosophes,* and thinking particularly of Voltaire, we began wondering why someone doesn't do, or, if it has already been done, re-do for our confused and atom-haunted world of the mid-fifties a book on Voltaire carrying the subtitle, *"ou la Naïveté."* For, despite all his cleverness, ingenuity, and wit, despite all his intellectual astuteness, despite all his shrewdly planned and consummately executed forays in defense of freedom, justice, and tolerance, despite all his brilliant literary gifts and accomplishments, he was, in many crucial respects, a very "innocent" person. When Professor Torrey tells us that Voltaire could not bring himself to the Church, but fondly hoped that the Church would come to him, we sense innocence, not sophistication, in such an expectation. When we learn from the same source that Voltaire "liked too well such stories as that of the Swiss captain who prayed 'May God, if there is one, save my soul, if I have one,'" we may be amused, but not for very long. And when Voltaire tells Condorcet that "I am tired of hearing it repeated that twelve men were enough to establish Christianity. I want to show them that one will be enough to destroy it," we are neither amused nor impressed. Most of us haven't lived through the present era of totalitarian dictatorships for nothing. Belsen and Buchenwald are not yet entirely forgotten. Even *Reich*-Christians and panzer-moralists, so numerous and so vocal between 1939 and 1945, have their uses, we feel, in the kind of world we are living in today.

When Voltaire bought the seigneury of Ferney, a parish church and a curé went with the purchase. One can hardly imagine Voltaire's acquiring a commissar in this way. There were no Ferneys in Hitler's Germany, and, we may be sure, there are none in Stalin's Russia. If Voltaire were living today, he most certainly would have his work cut out for him. Such a tremendous, such an overwhelming job, in fact, that he might even have to call in the Pope to share the burdens with him.

The crimes committed in God's name are, as we are learning the hard way, often exceeded in their barbarity only by those crimes committed in the name of Man, or Humanity, or Brotherhood, or Classlessness, or Progress, or Science. At times, however, it is not the crimes committed in the name of these latter-day deities, but the superstitious worship accorded them, which is so disturbing and so puzzling. "I will say, in the spirit of the wise Locke: Philosophy consists in stopping when the torch of physical science fails us." Thus speaks Voltaire. "Why D'Alembert is different from a cow, I cannot quite understand. But some day science will explain." Thus speaks Diderot. To put as much faith in Science (or Reason) as Voltaire and his fellow *Philosophes* did is to commit the rather simple-minded sin of sins against the ever-amazing complexity of life and the eternal mystery of human personality. To take such things as Progress and the Perfectibility of Man on trust is the credulousness to end all credulousness.

And in connection with the Idea of Progress, when Voltaire, at the end of *Candide,* talked about cultivating one's garden, he was not thinking of five acres and independence, *à la Thoreau,* but of 5,000 acres and community progress, *à la Faust.* He was thinking of his little kingdom of Ferney, and the benevolent, humanitarian despotism he exercised over its inhabitants, not of a shack on a Walden Pond, with the opportunity it would have afforded of meditating on the possibility "that there is nothing, not even crime, more opposed to poetry, to philosophy, ay, to life itself, than this incessant business." You may make the world a better place to live in by clearing the forests, draining the swamps, etc., Faustian fashion, but a man is hardly fulfilling his end, living according to his nature, when he concentrates all his energies, directs all his aims to the conquest of physical nature. To do that is to live like a lumberman, or an engineer, or a sewage-disposal expert, not like a man.

Moreover, Voltaire was not only naive about such matters as Science, Progress, and the like, but also about God. Throughout *Candide,* one frequently gathers the impression that God was a decided disappointment to Voltaire; that the world, which could be such a fine and pleasant place, was being managed very carelessly and very highhandedly—a sort of potential *Mardi gras* gone sour, and quite unnecessarily so, too. Voltaire, who did not suffer rivals gladly, often seems unable to tolerate the idea of God's being a person, while at the same time he could never quite rest easy at the thought of His being merely a thing. If God is a person, then He is shockingly callous and irresponsible; if God is only a thing, then He is woefully, disgracefully inefficient.

At times, Voltaire seems to want to have his Leibnizian sweet cakes, and yet not have to eat them, too. He wanted his deism, but he wanted it fed to him, as it were, intravenously. The Lisbon earthquake knocked the props, at least the psychological ones, out from under Voltaire's deism along with everybody else's, but it is not exactly easy to infer as much from a reading of *Candide,* and through no oversight on Voltaire's part, either.

V. It might be well to treat briefly of a matter that is really basic to the understanding of Voltaire's many writings on religion and philosophy, not to mention certain of his tales like *Candide.* We allude, of course, to the battlecry, *"Écrasez l'infâme."* A number of Voltaire's biographers, among them H. N. Brailsford, have, in the opinion of Voltaire's latest editor, Mr. Ben Ray Redman, come closer to what Voltaire actually meant by the phrase than most of his earlier ones, but they too, Mr. Redman feels, fall far short of telling the whole truth. "Whether one likes it or not," says Mr. Redman, "—and multitudes have disliked it, with all their being—Voltaire's meaning is clear beyond argument. When he said, *Écrasez l'infâme,* he meant that Christianity must be wiped out root and branch; the whole structure— not only the Roman Catholic hierarchy with the Pope at its head, but the belief in Biblical revelation and 'the Christ-worshipping superstition' (solace of millions) upon which Christianity was based, without which it would be nothing. To tear down the superstructure only, while leaving the foundations unassailed, would be an act of half-heartedness and folly."

After calling attention to Voltaire's limitations as a philosopher, historian, poet, dramatist, scientist, and naturalist, and deploring, among other things, Voltaire's undemocratic contempt for "the people," and "the ugly vein of anti-Semitism which runs through much of his writing," Mr. Redman tells us that the key to Voltaire's greatness is to be found in the fact that in so many important and influential ways he was the most brilliant, potent, and seductive instrument of his century, the most representative man of the so-called Age of the Enlightenment. And whether or not we can agree with Mr. Redman "that for those of us who are incapable of finding supernatural solace, the rationalism of Voltaire—with all its limitations—must remain the best hope and the best instrument that man has on earth," we can certainly agree with him when he says, as thousands of critics have said before him and as millions of readers will echo after him, that *Candide* is a masterpiece.

It might not be wholly out of place to observe that *Candide* was written, of course, to be read, not studied. Wordsworth, we know, was terribly bored by it, but then, he didn't write it. Hawthorne fell asleep over it, but then, he didn't have to worry about passing an examination on it. Besides, he took sin and the problem of good and evil in the world seriously, just as seriously, in all truth, as Wordsworth took himself and his poetry.

Like the characters in most of Shaw's plays or Peacock's novels, Pangloss, Cunegonde, and the others are drawn, one might say, to the argument rather than to the life. They are not, like even the characters in a tenth-rate piece of fiction, especially shadow-casting, nor were they meant to be. They were not created, they were "made"—and out of sawdust. The people in *Candide* are merely puppets, and any resemblance to flesh-and-blood persons, living or dead, is strictly malicious and purely incidental. And the book itself, in tone and structure, if not in theme and intention, is little more than a Ruthless Rhyme writ large.

Recommended reading:
H. N. Brailsford, *Voltaire,* New York, Oxford University Press, 1935.
A. O. Lovejoy, *The Great Chain of Being,* Cambridge, Harvard University Press, 1936.
N. L. Torrey, *The Spirit of Voltaire,* New York, Columbia University Press, 1938.
John Morley, *Diderot and the Encyclopaedists,* New York, Scribner and Welford, 1878.

VI

THE ROMANTIC AGE

ROMANTICISM[1]

I. THE AGE OF ENLIGHTENMENT was dominated by the conviction that the universe is capable of rational explanation. All nature, including human nature, and all the affairs of mankind were thought to be governed by laws and regulations which could be discovered by observation and the rational intellect. This philosophy left little opportunity for originality; it exalted man's logical powers at the expense (sometimes almost the exclusion) of his emotional nature.

Within this intellectual structure of logic, order, regularity, law, common sense, distrust of emotion, lived the typical man of the Enlightenment. But there were men, even in the 18th century, who could not freely move within this imposing edifice—beautiful, orderly, symmetrical, and tasteful as it was. These were the writers, thinkers, musicians, and artists to whom we attach the name "pre-Romantic." There came a time when this dissatisfaction with the structure of things became so acute that the leaders of action and thought decided to destroy utterly the old building, to raze it to the ground, and to build anew. This rejection of the moral, social, and intellectual premises of the 18th century resulted in the cataclysm of the French Revolution, which shattered the framework of French society and released a host of ideas to plague the tyrants of the world for generations.

This intellectual change we call by the name of the Romantic Movement. Romanticism is such a many-sided, complex, sometimes contradictory state of mind that no one individual ever comprehended within himself all its traits; but there are several clearly distinguishable features, the possession of one or more of which will classify a man as partly or wholly Romantic. Several of the more important of these are an impatience with the rules and restraints of Classical thought and art; a deep, abiding sense of the mystery of the universe; a fascination with the remote in time and space; an emphasis on the emotional and imaginative rather than the rational aspects of our nature; a subjective, individual approach to the problems of life; an interest in, and appreciation of, the beauty of nature; and a faith in the dignity and worth of the common man. Each of these traits is a reaction against the corresponding opposite quality in the thought and practice of 18th-century Classicism. Through each of these, moreover, there runs a spirit of revolt, of protest against existing conditions and institutions.

II. An impatience with the rules and restraints of Classical art and thought may be considered in a sense as the most important of all the qualities of Romanticism, its most pervasive and inclusive feature. The Romantic in theory desired freedom above all things. He did not want to be restrained in any way—in his art, in his profession, or in his private life. The Romantic poets, men like Wordsworth, Coleridge, Keats, Hugo, and Schiller, were in conscious and deliberate reaction against what they regarded as the stultifying effects of the poetic doctrines of the 18th century. They did not believe that by studying the proper models of Classical antiquity one could deduce the final rules of poetic composition, application of which would guarantee the quality of art. They regarded themselves as perfectly capable of making their own rules, and furthermore, they proved that they were. In reaction against the Neo-Classical admiration for the writers of the Augustan Age in Rome and the near-worship of

[1] Programs A and B.

Homer, they turned to a study of the older English writers: Shakespeare, Spenser, Milton, and a host of their contemporaries and predecessors. They resurrected the relics of medieval literature and admired the apparent lawlessness and freedom of medieval art. They believed that the Middle Ages and the Renaissance had not been burdened and hampered by the artificial restraints which seemed characteristic of the Neo-Classicism of the 18th century. The Romantic painters—in England, Turner; in France, Delacroix and Géricault; in Spain, Goya—also turned to a study of the Renaissance and Baroque masters in their revolt against the threadbare Classicism of the academic painters. These men, drawing upon the examples of the past, made their own rules. And in music, too, the great Romantic composers rebelled against a narrow formalism which restricted and hampered them. Some of these men—Beethoven, Schubert, and Brahms—retained the musical forms of their predecessors, but by their genius so infused them with Romantic ideas and fervor that the forms live in a way that the world had never dreamed possible. Other composers of the same age (or a little later) found the traditional forms completely unsuitable to their purposes and devised their own; such were Berlioz, Liszt, and, in particular, Wagner.

III. The Romantic is filled with awe and wonder at the mystery of the universe in which he finds himself. He reacts, sometimes violently, against the complacent satisfaction of the deist that the world is a perfectly designed and finished machine. The typical Romantic does not believe that everything can be explained; he is impressed with the mystery, not the clarity, with the confusion and variety rather than the order and unity of the universe and its inhabitants. Carlyle constantly harps upon the necessity for men to cultivate a sense of wonder at the profound mystery of creation. His works echo with such phrases as "encircled with the mystery of Existence" or "the unfathomable, all-pervading domain of mystery." So it is natural that the Romantic writers and philosophers emphasized the importance of the spiritual and the ideal at the expense of the material and actual. They were strongly attracted to the transcendental idealism of the German philosopher Kant, who provided a philosophical framework for Romanticism.

Many Romantics were, and are (for Romanticism is still a force in the world), mystics. For such people, the spiritual or ideal world is so much more real than what the average person regards as reality, that they regard the fleeting moments which they spend in that spiritual realm—the so-called mystical trance—as the times when they are in contact with the truth. These moments of insight, inspiration, or elevation are referred to often by Wordsworth, as, for instance, in *Lines Written a Few Miles above Tintern Abbey:*

>   that blessed mood,
> In which the burthen of the mystery,
> In which the heavy and the weary weight
> Of all this unintelligible world,
> Is lightened:—that serene and blessed mood,
> In which the affections gently lead us on,—
> Until, the breath of this corporeal frame
> And even the motion of our human blood
> Almost suspended, we are laid asleep
> In body, and become a living soul:
> While with an eye made quiet by the power
> Of harmony, and the deep power of joy,
> We see into the life of things.

Such experiences are also mentioned by Tennyson and Shelley, but less frequently. They are an almost constant factor in the life of William Blake.

It is not surprising, therefore, that this sense of the impenetrable mystery of the world combined with the Romantics' distrust of the rational processes of the intellect to make most of them anti-scientific. They believed that the inmost recesses of truth could not be reached by reason but only by intuition and imagination. Hence, Keats's statement in *Lamia:*

> Do not all charms fly
> At the mere touch of cold philosophy?[2]
> There was an awful rainbow once in Heaven:
> We know her woof, her texture; she is given
> In the dull catalogue of common things.
> Philosophy will clip an Angel's wings,
> Conquer all mysteries by rule and line,
> Empty the haunted air and gnoméd mine—
> Unweave a rainbow, as it erewhile made
> The tender-personed Lamia melt into a shade.

Keats believed, like other Romantics, that it was impossible to discover the secrets of the world, and that, consequently, it was best merely to observe with awe and wonder the marvelous manifestations of beauty, power, and intelligence with which mankind is surrounded.

IV. The Romantic is fascinated by the far-away and the long-ago. He turns naturally and eagerly to the remote in time and space. In his search for happiness or perfection, he looks backward to the Middle Ages or to some other time which he thinks of as "golden," or he looks forward to the far-distant future when all will be well with man. Like Miniver Cheevy, who ". . . loved the days of old when swords were bright and steeds were prancing," other Romantics turned to the past—the Middle Ages or Greek antiquity—for relief from the tedium and harshness of life. Some of the principal masterpieces of Romantic literature, Keats's *Eve of St. Agnes,* Coleridge's *Christabel,* Scott's *Ivanhoe,* are products of this tendency to find satisfaction in the past. Even political and social critics turned their eyes to the medieval world and found there cures for the social and economic evils of the 19th century. So Carlyle, Ruskin, and William Morris preached the gospel of feudalism and handicrafts as the panacea for the evils of industrialism. Another aspect of Romantic medievalism is the revival of Gothic, and afterwards of Romanesque, architecture. All over Europe, England, and the United States began to appear buildings in imitation of the Gothic style. In England commissions were let for the construction of Gothic *ruins,* and eminent architects offered their services to supply the need! In music, the most familiar example of medievalism is the use by Wagner of stories from medieval romance, *Tristan and Isolde, Parsifal,* and the cycle of Germanic legends in the *Ring of the Nibelungs.*

Another manifestation of the interest in the past is to be seen in the revival of the folk-ballad and other folk art. The attitude of the Neo-Classic age, with notable exceptions such as Joseph Addison, had been that the ballads were vulgar productions, not worthy the attention of a cultivated man. Even Bishop Percy, who in 1765 published his famous collection of ballads and other ancient poetry, apologized for issuing such a book and made various "improvements" to bring the old poetry more in accord with the "enlightened taste" of the time. Some years later (1814–1817) Sir Walter Scott greatly enriched the storehouse of ballad literature with his collection of Scottish songs, preserving many that would otherwise have been lost. The same phenomenon is observable in other countries affected by the stirrings of Romanticism, especially in Germany, where various scholars and poets collected and edited folk literature. Many of the Romantic composers turned to the folk music of their countries for themes. Examples that come immediately to mind are Liszt's use of Hungarian gypsy tunes and Moussorgsky's similar use of Russian folk music. This whole revival of folk art, moreover, is closely linked with the rising tide of nationalism in Europe, which is by many scholars considered another of the results of Romanticism.

[2]*I.e.,* science.

The far-away proved attractive as well as the long-ago; evidence of this attraction may be found in many places, particularly in such works as Coleridge's *Rime of the Ancient Mariner* and *Kubla Khan,* where, combined with other Romantic features, the lure of far-distant places in the Pacific and the Orient is most obvious.

V. The Romantic emphasized the emotional and imaginative rather than the rational aspects of life. It has been indicated how the scientific rationalism of the 18th century denied the validity and worth of the emotions. The reaction was inevitable. The emotional side of human nature cannot indefinitely be stifled, and when the reaction came during the latter half of the 18th and continued throughout the 19th century, it sometimes resulted in excesses of emotion, in mawkish sentimentality. The feelings usurped the former place of the intellect; the truth became what one *felt* to be true; it was wrong to deny one's feelings; one must at all costs do what one *felt* to be right. Thus Tennyson was able to say in all sincerity:

> If e'er when faith had fall'n asleep
> I heard a voice "believe no more"
> And heard an ever-breaking shore
> That tumbled in the Godless deep;
>
> A voice within the breast would melt
> The freezing reason's colder part,
> And like a man in wrath the heart
> Stood up and answer'd "I have felt."

Thus, feeling or intuition had come to be accepted as the surest, indeed, the only, avenue to spiritual truth.

During the Romantic movement the imagination resumed the place it had held during former ages as the vital element in artistic, especially literary, creation. To Keats, for example, imagination is almost synonymous with intuition; it was not only the means by which men created beauty but was also the avenue to truth. In one of his letters occurs this statement of his belief:

I am certain of nothing but the holiness of the heart's affections, and the truth of the imagination. What the imagination seizes as beauty must be truth—whether it existed before or not. . . . The imagination may be compared to Adam's dream,—he awoke and found it truth. . . .

This idea received its ultimate expression in the *Ode on a Grecian Urn:*

> "Beauty is truth, truth beauty,"—that is all
> Ye know on earth, and all ye need to know.

Wordsworth, in his *Preface to the Second Edition of the Lyrical Ballads,* speaks of imagination as the power which elevates mere reality into poetry. Speaking of his intentions in the *Lyrical Ballads,* he says:

The principal object, then, proposed in these poems was to choose incidents and situations from common life, and to relate or describe them throughout, as far as was possible, in a selection of language really used by men, and at the same time, to throw over them a certain coloring of imagination, whereby ordinary things should be presented to the mind in an unusual aspect. . . .

All the Romantic writers emphasized the importance of the imagination; they considered it mankind's link with the divine. They always connected it with the emotions. Both the Romantics and the Classicists conceived of imagination and reason as almost direct opposites. The latter thought that the emotions and the imagination actually interfered with the search for truth, which could be perceived only by reason, while the former believed truth, at least spiritual truth, could be discovered only by intuition, which can be defined as a blend of emotion and imagination or, from another point of view, as a superior kind of reason. The Romantic point of view is well expressed by Shelley in the opening sentences of his essay, *A Defence of Poetry:*

According to one mode of regarding those two classes of mental action, which are called reason and imagination, the former may be considered as mind contemplating the relations borne by one thought to another, however produced; and the latter, as mind acting upon those thoughts so as to colour them with its own light, and composing from them as from elements, other thoughts, each containing within itself the principle of its own integrity. The one is . . . the principle of synthesis and has for its object those forms which are common to universal nature and existence itself; and the other is . . . the principle of analysis, and its action regards the relations of things, simply as relations; considering thoughts, not in their integral unity, but as the algebraical representations which conduct to certain general results. Reason is the enumeration of quantities already known; imagination is the perception of the value of those quantities, both separately and as a whole. Reason respects the differences, and imagination the similitudes of things. Reason is to the imagination as the instrument to the agent, as the body to the spirit, as the shadow to the substance.

Poetry, in a general sense, may be defined to be "the expression of the imagination . . . ."

VI. The Romantic is an egotist. He has a highly subjective, individual approach to the problems of life. He is interested in himself and his own reactions to the varying phenomena of existence. The poetry, music, and plastic art of the Romantics reveal the inmost thought and feeling of the artists. Much of the pleasure and value to be derived from Romantic art is the result of the contact which we have with unique personalities who did not hesitate to display themselves to the world. Byron became an international figure whose every action and passion was reflected in his verse and whose career, consequently, was watched by breathless thousands throughout Europe. Wordsworth's most important poem is an autobiographical study on which he lavished the effort of over fifty years. *The Prelude* is the record of the influences which had made him a poet, and in this poem he reveals himself more fully than almost any other man of modern times. Autobiography became one of the principal forms of composition for the writers of the Romantic movement. Almost everyone wrote some kind of autobiography, sometimes covering his identity with an easily pierced disguise, sometimes not trying to hide himself at all.

Classicism is social and gregarious; Romanticism is unsocial (sometimes even anti-social) and solitary. The Classic writer deals with society and the problems of the individual as a unit of society; the Romantic tells of the wanderers, the lonely and solitary ones, haunted and outcast—Coleridge's ancient mariner "alone on a wide, wide sea"; Byron's Childe Harold visiting the mountain fastnesses of the Balkans, and later, self-exiled, a tortured but defiant spirit viewing the battlefield of Waterloo, the beauty of the Alps, and the awesome ruins of Rome; and Shelley's Alastor, a shadowy, frail, tragic figure fleeing from the world and perishing utterly alone. The Romantics ransacked the libraries of legend and myth, seizing upon those figures who symbolized for them the individual carrying on alone, often, like Prometheus, benefactors of mankind punished by tyrants and suffering in solitude. As Shelley used Prometheus, Byron sympathetically treated the figure of Cain, the first murderer and outcast, both artists transferring their own indignation against society to their heroes and speaking through them their messages of independence and scorn of conventional society. Wagner used the legend of the Flying Dutchman for one of his operas, and other Romantic composers wrote songs about wanderers and exiles.

VII. Classicism is urban, Romanticism is rural. The characteristic productions of the Classical mind are of and for organized society, congregated in cities—London, Paris, Vienna. There is about them the glare of candlelight and the sounds and odors of palace and hall. The Romantic cannot breathe the air of cities and courts; he escapes to the fields and forests as soon as possible. "God made the country and man made the town," says Cowper, whose sympathetic treatment of nature heralded the Romantic movement. For an interest in, and love of, nature is another of the hallmarks of Romanticism. Wordsworth writes some of his best poetry about nature and his own relations and reactions to her from childhood to manhood. He thus summarizes his attitudes toward nature in *Lines Composed a Few Miles above Tintern Abbey:*

>   And so I dare to hope,
> Though changed, no doubt, from what I was when first
> I came among these hills; when like a roe
> I bounded o'er the mountains, by the sides
> Of the deep rivers, and the lonely streams,
> Wherever nature led: more like a man
> Flying from something that he dreads than one
> Who sought the thing he loved. For nature then
> (The coarser pleasures of my boyish days,
> And their glad animal movements all gone by)
> To me was all in all.—I cannot paint
> What then I was. The sounding cataract
> Haunted me like a passion: the tall rock,
> The mountain, and the deep and gloomy wood,
> Their colors and their forms, were then to me
> An appetite; a feeling and a love,
> That had no need of a remoter charm,
> By thought supplied, nor any interest
> Unborrowed from the eye.—That time is past
> And all its aching joys are now no more,
> And all its dizzy raptures. Not for this
> Faint I, nor mourn nor murmur; other gifts
> Have followed; for such loss, I would believe,
> Abundant recompense. For I have learned
> To look on nature, not as in the hour
> Of thoughtless youth; but hearing oftentimes
> The still, sad music of humanity,
> Nor harsh, nor grating, though of ample power
> To chasten and subdue.

Keats uses the beautiful colors and patterns of nature, the sights, sounds, and smells of wood, field, and stream. For instance, in the *Ode to Autumn:*

> Season of mists and mellow fruitfulness,
>   Close bosom-friend of the maturing sun;
> Conspiring with him how to load and bless
>   With fruit the vines that round the thatch-eaves run;
> To bend with apples the mossed cottage-trees,
>   And fill all fruit with ripeness to the core;
>   To swell the gourd, and plump the hazel shells
>   With a sweet kernel; to set budding more,
> And still more, later flowers for the bees,
> Until they think warm days will never cease,
>   For Summer has o'er-brimmed their clammy cells.

Beethoven, after walking through the country near Vienna, composes the *Pastoral Symphony;* Constable and Turner paint landscapes revealing the breath-taking beauty and mystic power of the English countryside. To the Romantics, however, Nature is not merely the visible garment of God, but is often conceived as God Himself; the Creator is not separate from the created. Nature, therefore, is a source of spiritual strength, of wisdom, and of moral value. Wordsworth says,

> One impulse from a vernal wood
> May teach you more of man,
> Of moral evil and of good,
> Than all the sages can.

Very early in the 18th century the doctrine had been developed by the Earl of Shaftesbury in his *Characteristics* (1711) that man is by nature good, not evil. Man, he said, was naturally good, naturally desired that which conduced to the welfare of society. If one does what is good for himself, it will be good for society, and vice versa. The natural impulses of every human being are toward the good; his instinctive sympathies will lead him to activity which is both moral and productive of his own and others' happiness. How then explain the undoubted evil to be seen on all sides? That, was the reply, is the result of outside influences playing on the individual, of environment, in short. Provide man with the correct environment and he will be able to follow his spontaneous, instinctive impulses to perfection and happiness. This simple and optimistic belief came to be widely held during the 18th century.

No one stated the doctrine of natural goodness more strongly or more effectively than the French philosopher and man of letters, Jean-Jacques Rousseau (1712–1778). In his novels and philosophical works he constantly emphasized that man had been born free and good but everywhere lived in chains and misery, enslaved and corrupted by the institutions of state and church which he had created to protect and help him. Salvation, therefore, lay in a return to nature, a revulsion from the "artificialities" of civilization. Not everyone, it was realized, could escape to an unspoiled primitive environment such as the wilderness of North America or a beautiful tropic isle in the South Sea. Some means had to be devised to safeguard man's freedom in society and to give him the opportunity to develop his natural capacities. The enslaving and corrupting institutions must be utterly destroyed and replaced by a new government directly responsible to the people, from whom its power derived. Furthermore, the government should be only strong enough to protect the people and provide necessary services. The result of these inflammatory ideas was the holocaust of the French Revolution, from which idealistic and optimistic people everywhere expected something very like the Millennium to result. Of course it did not, but the ideas flung abroad by this epochal event took root in men's minds and affected the course of history all over the world.

Men also looked backward in time to more primitive eras, such as those of the ancient world and of the Middle Ages, for their ideal of perfection. Therefore, when a Scottish schoolmaster, James Macpherson, came forward with his prose-poem *Fingal* (1762), which he claimed he had translated from an ancient Gaelic poem by a poet named Ossian, a thrill of exultant satisfaction passed through Western Europe. For *Fingal* revealed that primitive men had possessed those virtues which the philosophers had claimed for them. And curiously, the revelation that Ossian had never existed, that the whole thing was a fraud, did not particularly dampen the enthusiasm. A few years later Robert Burns was hailed as a wonderful example of what nature could do for her children if she were given the chance, for he was thought to be an uneducated ploughboy.

VIII. Another result of primitivism and the doctrine of natural goodness was the appearance of the common man in art and poetry. In the *Preface to the Second Edition of the Lyrical Ballads* (1800) Wordsworth says that he had chosen as the subjects of his poetry "humble and rustic life" because the emotions of such people are simpler and purer, because they "speak a plainer and more emphatic language," and because "in that condition the passions of men are incorporated with the beautiful and permanent forms of nature." He was not the first man to do this, however, for the common man had appeared in Gray's *Elegy Written in a Country Churchyard* (1751) and also had been presented even more sympathetically in Goldsmith's *Deserted Village* (1770). In painting, Millet reveals the new interest in the common peasant and laborer in such pictures as *The Angelus* and *The Gleaners*. Goya's series of bitter paintings and prints dealing with the war against Napoleon in Spain reveal a heart-breaking compassion for the miseries of combatant and noncombatant (Fig. 75). And Daumier's cartoons and paintings reveal a man not only capable of seeing through the sham and pretense of society but also capable of the most intense sympathy for, and understanding of, the poor and unfortunate.

IX. The Romantic Movement covered a long period of time. Its beginning can be traced far back into the 18th century; Shaftesbury's *Characteristics* of 1711 is an important document in the movement. Though the 18th century in all countries was predominantly Neo-Classical, there existed many men who were imbued with the qualities of Romanticism and who, consciously or unconsciously, prepared the way for full-fledged Romanticism. The peak of Romantic feeling and expression was reached at different times in different countries, but the movement came to its climax during the first third of the 19th century. Though it continued throughout the rest of that century, it gradually declined into the decadence of the nineties and the early years of the 20th century. Certain features of the movement, however, are still influential. In its complexity, diversity, and many-sideness, Romanticism was all things to all people, and many were the quarrels among its adherents as to which were the true prophets. The most important feature of Romanticism is the re-emergence of the spirit, of the intangible, intuitive side of man's nature, the recognition that there is that about humanity which is not satisfied with bread alone.

Recommended reading:
Ernest Bernbaum, *Guide through the Romantic Movement,* New York, 1949.
Alfred Einstein, *Music in the Romantic Era,* New York, W. W. Norton, 1947.
Hoxie N. Fairchild, *The Noble Savage,* New York, 1928.
Hoxie N. Fairchild, *The Romantic Quest,* New York, 1931.

ROMANTIC MUSIC

LUDWIG VAN BEETHOVEN (1770–1827)

Mozart and Beethoven.[1]

The music of Mozart, as we have seen, represents a Classical style signalized by great refinement, orderliness, perfect proportion, structural and spiritual balance, fluency, grace, and restraint. When we play a movement like the *Larghetto* of the *Clarinet Quintet,* or the *Andante* of the *G Minor Piano Quartet,* we are in contact with a spirit in which all conflicts have been resolved, all passions sublimated; a golden serenity, like sunshine in high places, pervades the music, and we seem to be in an altogether ideal world.

Yet the external world in which Mozart lived was racked by unrest, and violent remedies were even then being applied to it. A period of upheaval in the intellectual, social, and political spheres was bound to produce a corresponding revolution in the arts; and it was the good fortune of the art of music that a man of consummate greatness—one of the very few giants—was at hand to give expression to the spirit of "the new humanity." In Beethoven we find, not poised perfection, but titanic energy and heroic strife, combined with profound human sympathy and poetic imagination. A new orderliness, arising not from the acceptance of set forms but from a balancing of extremes, a harnessing of forces in conflict—this, together with a prodigious intellectual grip which enabled him to develop his ideas with unprece-

[1] Programs A and B.

dented power, constitutes the chief distinction of Beethoven's style. Because his favorite vehicle of expression was the Classical sonata, and because his expansion of that form—his pouring into it a new, intense, highly personal content—initiates a whole century of individualistic, "subjective" music, Beethoven stands like a colossus with feet firmly planted in two musical worlds, a synthesis of the intellectual and the emotional—a "Classico-Romantic."

Ludwig van Beethoven was born in 1770 at Bonn on the Rhine. The *van* in his name (not the German *von*) indicates that his forebears were of Flemish stock[2]—a fact worth mentioning only because it throws light on his tenacious, independent character. This independence he was forced to develop early; for though (like Mozart) he was the son of a court musician, his father was incompetent and intemperate, and while still in his teens Beethoven had to shoulder the burden of supporting the family. His musical genius, far less spectacular than Mozart's, developed slowly but surely. At the age of twelve he was given a semi-official position at the court of the Electoral Archbishop of Cologne, who resided at Bonn; thus he began (but did not continue) his career under the same 18th-century system of patronage that had proven so disastrous to Mozart. In Beethoven's case it was a help, for the Elector eventually decided to send him to Vienna to study with Haydn, whose interest had already been gained by a youthful composition submitted to his judgment. The assistance of well-to-do friends of good social standing secured for Beethoven an entrée into the musical world of Vienna, which he was soon astounding with his powerful piano-extemporizations and, in due course, his compositions. He arrived there in his twenty-second year and remained until his death in 1827; living erratically, but not penuriously; owing service to no man, but accepting, as a "free-lance" artist, commissions and favors from the aristocracy whose employ he scorned; acclaimed by all as the greatest composer of his time, but isolated (from his thirtieth year on) in a world of deepening silence, due to his progressive deafness. This calamity—the most terrible that could befall any musician—produced a spiritual crisis from which emerged the Beethoven we know: the man of iron will and profound feeling, the hero and the poet, the challenger of fate and the searching philosopher.

The two works selected for study in this volume—the *Violin Concerto* and the *Fourth Pianoforte Concerto*—belong to the great "middle period" of Beethoven's creative life, the period of maturity and masterhood. They were chosen to represent the poetic side of his genius rather than the heroic, and that for three reasons:

a. Since this is the only 19th-century music included in our study it has seemed desirable to choose works which exemplify the most typical of Romantic trends—the predominance of feeling over pure, abstract form.

b. By thus selecting, we exhibit in the sharpest possible way the contrast between Mozart's style and Beethoven's.

c. The Beethoven of the *Fifth Symphony* ("Beethoven the Thunderer"), though hardly less typical of the Romantic spirit in his terrific energy and dramatic power, is perhaps by this time something of a stock figure, at least to the layman. We propose to concentrate on "Beethoven the Poet," hoping to correct the picture to some extent.

As was said before, Beethoven is a *Classico*-Romantic, who did not reject but expanded Classical forms. His preoccupation with design and logic in music is as great as his intensity of feeling; in fact, his *architectonic* sense—his ability to rear vast structures of sound as stable and well-proportioned as cathedrals of stone—is one of the marvels of his genius. In this he differs from many of his Romantic successors. What he shares with them (or they with him, for he showed them the way) is his readiness to "bend the form to suit the content"—to mold an accepted design to the requirements of particular inspirations, or to create new forms for special purposes. In this his music differed from the pure Classical style, to which he otherwise owed so much.

[2] The *van*, incidentally, is not an indication of noble birth—unlike its German and French (*de*) counterparts. *Cf.* Van Gogh.

The Concerto.

The Classical concerto was largely a creation of Mozart's. His extensive use of the form defined its character as a virtuoso piece (*i.e.,* as a vehicle for brilliance on the part of an instrumental soloist, supported by orchestra), and established its structure as a variety of the ubiquitous Classical *sonata*. Its movements are always three in number—fast, slow, fast. The opening movement is in an adaptation of sonata-form, described below; the second is a typical *andante* or *adagio* (slow-ish or slow) movement, simpler in structure; the third is generally some kind of rondo. In the first and often in the last movement allowance is made for a *cadenza* by the soloist—a more or less extensive passage (usually corresponding to the *coda* of non-concerto forms) in which the orchestra drops out, and the unaccompanied soloist displays his technical and inventive powers. In Mozart's day these cadenzas were not written by the composer, but extemporized by the performer. Beethoven, in his first four piano concertos, accepted the convention and left blanks in the score at the appropriate points. Evidently dissatisfied with the empty displays of virtuosity which had come to be the rule, he later supplied his own cadenzas for these four concertos, and in the fifth incorporated the virtuoso-sections in the score. For the violin concerto he wrote no cadenzas.[3]

The chief structural distinction between the concerto and the regular sonata is in the organization of the first movement. As established by Mozart (and retained by Beethoven), the Exposition of this sonata-form movement was presented in two versions, first by the orchestra alone and then with the soloist in the leading role (accompanied by the orchestra). The orchestral Exposition is *in and around the tonic key throughout,* and shows a certain sketchiness in regard to the presentation of themes; it is, as it were, a "preview" of what is to come, but not a completely organized Exposition. With the entrance of the soloist the material is reworked and elaborated, the regular key-relationship of first and second subjects established, and the full complement of themes introduced, in their proper sequence. The *double Exposition,* as it is called, is a unique feature of the form; thereafter soloist and orchestra collaborate in working out the movement, not alternately but in concert (except for the cadenza). Nor is the initial procedure followed in the other movements, which do indeed contain many short sections for soloist or orchestra alone, but nothing comparable to the double Exposition of the first movement.

Beethoven's treatment of the solo instrument is technically more varied than Mozart's. This is in part due to the constant advance in instrumental virtuosity, and (in the case of the piano works) to the development of genuine pianoforte-playing as distinct from 18th-century harpsichord- or clavichord-playing. But it is equally due to the characteristic Romantic urge for *expression,* which led Beethoven to explore all the resources of the instrument in his search for greater (and subtler) varieties of effect. He uses the higher register of the violin more extensively than Mozart did; in the piano, the sustaining pedal enabled him to produce floods of sound, or to blur outlines, in a typically Romantic manner. There are even instances in the *Fourth Piano Concerto* of what, since Debussy, we would call Impressionistic writing, utilizing special pedal-techniques. In Beethoven, so close is the union of color, form, and expression that it is difficult to separate one from another.

As to the orchestral forces used in the two concertos we shall study, their model is the Classical orchestra of *late* Mozart or *late* Haydn. The woodwind choir consists of flutes,[4] oboes, clarinets, and bassoons in pairs; the brass choir, of French horns and trumpets, likewise in pairs; the percussion, of two timpani (kettledrums) playing the tonic and dominant

---

[3] Those most often played are by the great 19th-century violinist Joachim.
[4] One flute only, in the *Fourth Piano Concerto*.

ROMANTIC MUSIC

notes of the key; the string choir, of first violins, second violins, violas, 'cellos, and double-basses. Beethoven later expanded this orchestra (already in the *Third Symphony* he had added a third French horn) until it became the "standard" symphony orchestra of the first half of the 19th century, with four horns, three trombones, three timpani, and such extra instruments as piccolo and double-bassoon. But at this stage, and in these solo-works, the orchestral ensemble is kept at Classical strength, of which the instrumentation given above is the maximum (not used in every movement).

Violin Concerto in D major, Opus 61.[1]

This work, written in 1806, is Beethoven's only concerto for violin. It is generally regarded as one of the truly great compositions in this medium by virtue of its grand scope, lyrical intensity, and emotional power. It belongs with the *Fifth Symphony,* the *G Major Piano Concerto,* and other masterworks of Beethoven's rich "middle period," a period which shows the composer as a Romantic artist with the Classicist's genius for formal organization.

FIRST MOVEMENT
Tempo: *Allegro ma non troppo* (fast, but not too fast)
Key: D Major
Form: Sonata-form (pp. 405–9), with double Exposition

First Exposition: measures 1–87.
I. *First subject,* in D major (tonic key): measures 1–27. This consists of two distinct themes, plus a special motto (a).
(1) *First theme* (mm. 1–17). The theme is a musical sentence in two phrases (Ex. 70), played by the woodwinds and accompanied by the motto in the timpani. Repetition of the motto leads to the second theme.

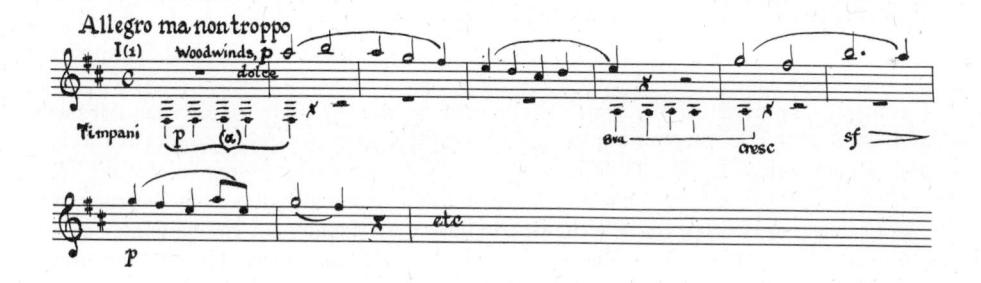

Example 70

(2) *Second theme* (mm. 18–27). A short melody in clarinet and bassoon, accompanied by strings (Ex. 71).

Example 71

[1]Program A.

In characteristically Beethovenian fashion, both themes are somewhat fragmentary in nature. Notice, particularly, how short the actual material in the second theme is—merely two measures, three times repeated and slightly extended at the end. The motto is similarly brief—a simple rhythmic figure, insignificant by itself, meaningful only in the treatment it receives. Beethoven frequently used such mottoes. The famed opening of the *Fifth Symphony* and the first theme of the *Seventh Symphony* are of the same basic type.

Transition: measures 28–42. After the first subject there is a sudden shift in tonality (from D to B flat major) and dynamics (from *pianissimo* to *fortissimo*) as the full orchestra begins the transition. In sharp contrast with the first subject, the material in this transition (Ex. 72) is chordal rather than linear (melodic) in construction, angular and dramatic in character, featuring *sforzandi* (sudden loud bursts of sound). The treatment of tonality is of special interest here. The material itself is modulatory in nature. Having begun in a remote key (B flat), it must now return to D major, since in the *first* Exposition of a concerto *both subjects are in the tonic key*. Such unexpected introductions of strange keys and consequent modulations back to the tonic are often used by Beethoven to create tension and movement (as here), or, in other contexts, for striking poetic effects.

Example 72

II. *Second subject,* in D major (tonic key): measures 42–87. This subject contains one main theme, a link, and a codetta, *all in the tonic key*.

Main theme (mm. 43–64). The main theme is probably the most singable melody of the movement (Ex. 73). Integration with the first subject is achieved by a constant reiteration of

Example 73

the motto. The melody itself starts in the woodwinds, with the motto accompanying it in the violins and timpani. Here again Beethoven's characteristic treatment of material becomes apparent. In addition to a simple statement of the theme, an immediate development is undertaken. The melody is passed around from instrument to instrument, the motto shifting correspondingly in the accompaniment. In its second appearance, furthermore, the theme is changed to the minor and is enriched by an agile, constantly moving figuration in violas and 'cellos.

Link (mm. 65–76). This link is still another treatment of the ubiquitous motto, here developed over a *pedal* in the French horns. A gradual *crescendo* leads to a climax, preparing the entrance of the codetta.

Codetta (mm. 77–87). This codetta (Ex. 74) is still another of Beethoven's fragmentary themes. The brief melody moves from violins to 'cellos and woodwinds, ending not, as might be expected, on the tonic chord, but on a sharply accented dominant. There is no sense of

Example 74

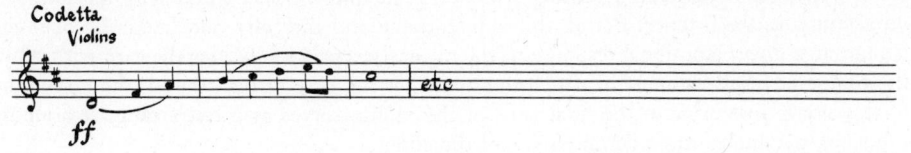

Codetta
Violins
ff

finality, as in the case of an authentic cadence, but a sense of expectation, a focusing of attention on that which is to follow. It is in this spotlight that the composer introduces the solo violin.

The violin enters (mm. 89–100) in one of the most dramatic introductions of concerto literature. Taking its cue from the orchestra, it first elaborates on the dominant chord, then, with increasing agility, leads back to the tonic to prepare a second Exposition and a reappraisal of all that has gone before.

Second Exposition: measures 101–222.

I. *First subject,* in D major (tonic key): measures 101–125. It is clear from the very first measures that the solo violin is not going to be brought into competition with the massed strings of the orchestra. Not only would this place the soloist at an undue disadvantage—pitting one violin against the combined tone of several dozen others—but it would also be contrary to Beethoven's customary practice, which is to develop material constantly and to avoid mere restatement.

(1) *First theme* (mm. 101–117). While the woodwinds state the theme, the violin engages in a lively dialogue with the orchestra. This treatment emphasizes various aspects of the theme (such as its harmonic structure); it is, therefore, a discussion or elaboration of the material previously presented. It represents a certain stage of organic growth in the development of the theme when compared with the statement in the first Exposition.

(2) *Second theme* (mm. 118–125). This theme is left entirely to the orchestra, which presents the material in slightly modified form. The ending is altered from the original presentation so that the theme now leads more directly to the subsequent transition.

Transition: measures 126–143. This section is *not* based on the material found in the transition of the first Exposition. Instead of the dramatic break which started the earlier transition, this section grows gradually from the last theme of the first subject, thereby providing a smooth flow, an obliteration of boundaries between sections. The actual material is a reasonably elaborate development of the second theme by the solo violin, gradually modifying the theme to prepare a modulation to the dominant key. It is a regular transition, such as might be expected in a symphonic work by Beethoven.

II. *Second subject,* in A major (dominant key): measures 143–223.

Main theme (mm. 144–165). It is interesting to note that the composer, after first stating the theme in the major, immediately shifts to the minor mode, exactly as he did in the first Exposition. Beethoven seems to stress the different possibilities contained in the melody by changing its surroundings. The motto is omitted; in its place is a trill by the solo violin and later an ornamental elaboration of the theme. This changed treatment, therefore, retains the interesting shift in mode from the first Exposition, but avoids any mechanical restatement, adding to the element of variety.

Link (mm. 166–177). The link contains no major change from its original form, except for the changed tonality.

Codetta (mm. 178–223). This statement of the codetta is considerably elaborated with *arpeggios* and rapid passage-work in the solo part, culminating in a series of ascending trills. The motto enters under the trills and is heard again just prior to the final section of rapid scale ornaments. The codetta, as it appears in this second Exposition, is another example of Beethoven's masterful handling of material. Its long extension builds up tension, even uncertainty, in the listener. But all this is intentional and carefully calculated. All of it contributes to a *direct* emotional response to the musical experience. Notice the care with which the composer limits the part in which the listener is not sure of his ground; the appearance of the motto, just prior to the final runs of the violin, serves as a restraining, re-orienting influence, re-establishing a definite sense of direction.

Development: measures 224–359.

Measures 224–283. The section which now follows is hard to fit into any specific part of the sonata-form. It is little more than an orchestral repetition of a major part of the *first* Exposition. This is particularly unusual in the case of Beethoven, who was a supreme master when it came to developing material. The chordal transition (mm. 224–237) and the entire second subject (mm. 238–283) appear without intensive figure-development, almost exactly as stated in the first Exposition. For this reason some analysts refuse to classify this section as part of the Development—some conductors even omit it! In our analysis it is, none the less, assigned to the Development.[2]

Measures 284–329. Development in the more generally accepted sense begins with the re-entry of the solo violin (m. 284). It enters in a manner similar to its first appearance, then takes up the first theme of the first subject (mm. 300–329), this time in B minor. In addition to the change to the minor, the theme now is developed in all its component parts. The elaboration and repetition of motives which Beethoven undertakes represents a thorough exploitation of the possibilities contained in the theme. After the initial statement the violin engages in further ornamentation, while the bassoon plays the second half of the theme in a series of variants; through it all the strings sound the rhythmic motto. The balance between unity and variety is maintained with masterful certainty. The examination of theme fragments, here provided by the bassoon, creates constantly shifting interest and is balanced with meticulous care by the unifying violin line and, above all, by the stubborn reiteration of the motto.

Episode: measures 330–356. This section is a departure from conventional sonata-form, a departure, however, which is not unusual in Beethoven's works. It is an *episode, i.e.,* a section introducing new material.[3] The melody belongs to the violin alone, which subjects it to constant rhythmic changes. Throughout the episode repetition of the motto in the orchestra binds this new theme to other parts of the movement. The episode is spun out, its ending melting gradually into the final section of the Development.

Link: measures 357–364. The link leading back to the Recapitulation is primarily a series of *arpeggios* for the solo violin, over a dominant *pedal* held by the entire string section of the orchestra. A final series of fragments from the motto concludes the Development.

Recapitulation: measures 365–496.

I. *First subject,* in D Major (tonic key): measures 365–385.

(1) *First theme* (mm. 365–381). This theme is now presented with all the resources of the full orchestra. The sharp rhythmic figure of the motto is sounded *fortissimo* at the outset,

---

[2]The disputed section is certainly not part of the second Exposition. The key relationships differ (the beginning is in the key of F and the end eventually reaches C major), and the interplay of solo and orchestra, characteristic of a second Exposition, is conspicuously absent. Functionally speaking, this part serves to give additional emphasis and a sense of completion to the involved double Exposition. If all of this is called part of the Development, one takes cognizance of the fact that the Development is an area in which the composer can treat his material pretty much as he pleases. It is a "discussion" of his themes (see Chapter VIII: *Sonata-Form,* p. 405) and if he feels the need for a relatively simple restatement of his themes, there is no reason why he should not so state them. That Beethoven should do this on such a scale is simply additional evidence of the fact that he placed the demands of expression above meticulous observance of formal patterns.

[3]See Chapter VIII: *Sonata-Form;* notes on "Development Section," p. 407.

and several times during this passage the composer admonishes the players: *Sempre fortissimo* (always very loud). The total effect is one of triumph, a truly climactic restatement of the theme.

(2) *Second theme* (mm. 382–385). A shortened version of the theme is presented at this time. Only the section corresponding to measures 122–125 of the second Exposition is heard. By this device Beethoven not only achieves a further intensification through compression, but also emphasizes the close similarity between the theme and the subsequent transition.

Transition: measures 386–417. The transition of the Recapitulation is very similar in character to the one found in the second Exposition. Again it is the solo violin which starts the proceedings, and again there is a quality of thematic development about this section. Just as in the second Exposition, the border line between the last theme of the first subject and the transition is bridged by the violin, which presents an elaboration of the second theme of the first subject. The major difference between the present version and the one in the second Exposition is one thoroughly expected: this transition does not modulate to the dominant key but ends in the tonic key of the movement.

II. *Second subject,* in *D major* (tonic key): measures 418–496. The recapitulation of this subject is perfectly regular in terms of the second Exposition.

Main theme (mm. 418–439).
Link (mm. 440–451).
Codetta (mm. 452–496).

These all appear without major change, except for their presentation *in the tonic key*.

Coda: measures 497–535. The same dramatic transition which first appeared in the first Exposition at measure 28, and which later started the Development, now begins the coda. This time it is heard in B flat. It begins a section which is considerably more than a brief ending tacked onto a movement. Beethoven's codas usually are parts of considerable size and importance devoted to a final discussion of themes; they are practically second Development sections both in length and character. The coda of the movement we are discussing belongs among the characteristic Beethoven examples. It is considerably longer than a mere indication of measures would reveal, since a *free cadenza* is included for the soloist.

Such cadenzas are improvisatory sections for the solo instrument (quite customary in the Classical concerto) in which the virtuoso is at liberty to display his imagination and technical proficiency. Beethoven, according to custom, did not compose cadenzas for this Concerto—since in performance they were to be improvised by the virtuoso. The cadenzas written for this work by the 19th-century violinist Joachim have become classics of their kind. At their worst, cadenzas are no more than musical acrobatics; at their best (as in case of the Joachim cadenzas), they present an ornate and technically intricate development of themes from the movement. Such a development, of course, should always be integrated in style and content with the composition as a whole.

The cadenza ends with a long trill, the orchestra rejoins the soloist, and Beethoven leads to still another discussion of the melodious main theme of the second subject. A brief reference to the codetta and a short *crescendo* to the final cadence bring the movement to a close.

SECOND MOVEMENT
Tempo: *Larghetto* (rather slow)
Key: G Major
Form: Variation-form (pp. 404–5), freely applied

The second movement of this Concerto contrasts sharply with the first. It has been called an example of "sublime inaction" (Tovey). Indeed, there is very little that actually "happens" in this movement. It depends for its effect on a uniformity of mood and an absence of conflict of any kind. Beethoven occasionally resorted to this type of middle movement (*cf.* "*Appassionata*" *Piano Sonata,* second movement; *Ninth Symphony,* third movement) to provide a relaxation of tension between two highly active movements. Such "inactivity" is a positive feature of design. Not only is it desirable by way of contrast, but in itself it becomes a vehicle for lyric expression in a direct and, therefore, Romantic vein.

The design of this movement is a liberally interpreted theme-and-variation form, with some modifications in applying the form to the matter in hand. The theme and its variations account for only part of the structure, which also contains a number of episodes. There is, furthermore, little of the formalized, sectional treatment commonly associated with Classical variation-forms.

Theme: measures 1–10. The theme is a single melody in two phrases (Ex. 75). It is played by the muted strings of the orchestra. The use of this color and the nature of the theme itself

Example 75

(particularly the halting rhythmic figure of the opening bars, and the expressive modulation in measures 3–4) establishes a reticent, wistful mood which is to be maintained throughout the movement. *Pianissimo* (very soft) dynamics and slight but frequent dynamic shadings help reinforce the poetic atmosphere.

Variation I: measures 10–20. The melody is redistributed between strings and woodwinds, the solo providing an ornamental counter-melody in sixteenth notes. This counter-melody and the change in tone color characterize the variation.

Variation II: measures 20–30. Here the theme is played by the bassoon, supported by low strings. There still is no change in the melodic line, but now the solo part becomes more elaborate, with short figures in sixteenth and thirty-second notes.

Variation III: measures 30–40. This variation is for orchestra alone. The theme is more fully scored than before, and fragments from it are echoed by the wind instruments. In this variation we find a good example of Beethoven's characteristic "block orchestration" (mm. 31–36). The instruments are treated in groups, rather than singly, so that the contrast between woodwind and string instruments *as groups* is exploited. Though such orchestration is built on Classical models, the sonorities produced are unmistakably Beethoven's own.

Link: measures 40–44. A brief connecting link for solo violin, thinly accompanied, leads to the first episode.

Episode I: measures 45–55. The regular treatment of variation-form is here interrupted

Example 76

ROMANTIC MUSIC   285

by the appearance of an episode. It is a *cantabile* (singable) theme, voiced on the warmest strings of the solo violin (Ex. 76). The fact that it remains in the tonic key is further evidence of the "static" quality of the movement as a whole. The melody gradually fades into some trills which, like so many trills in this *Concerto,* instead of coming to a stop, are dissolved into a link-like extension (mm. 52–55).

Variation IV: measures 55–65. Without a break, emerging from the extension of the episode, rather than abruptly starting, the fourth variation appears. This time the theme is played *pizzicato* (plucked) by the strings, while the solo violin adds a freely ornamented version of the theme. Notice how the exclusive use of string color contributes to the uniformity of mood.

Episode II: measures 65–71. A second episode is now introduced by Beethoven for additional variety (Ex. 77). Here again the role of a thematic fragment becomes important as

Example 77

a unifying device. The new material might easily destroy the intangible "inactivity" of the movement. To sustain its mood, Beethoven uses throughout the episode a constantly repeated figure, drawn from the rhythm of the original theme and serving as a reminder of it. He also remains in the tonic key.

Episode I (repeated): measures 71–79. Here the melody heard before appears in a more highly ornamented version in the solo violin, contrasting with an accompaniment in clarinet and bassoon.

Episode II (repeated): measures 79–87. This version of the second episode contains references not only to the theme but, in the solo part, to the first variation as well. Such treatment assures a very gradual re-establishment of the atmosphere of the basic theme of the movement.

The introduction of episodes in this section (mm. 45–87) breaks the strictness of variation-form and creates something of an "Episodic" feeling in the movement. This intermingling of forms is one of the ways in which Beethoven transcends the restrictions of Classical design. (A particularly striking example occurs in the slow movement of his *Seventh Symphony*.)

Coda: measures 87–91. A *pianissimo* reference to the opening figure of the theme begins the coda. Next a *fortissimo* statement of the first two bars (the only *fortissimo* in the movement) modulates to the dominant of D major and terminates the movement in mid-air. A brief cadenza, and the violin plunges directly into the closing Rondo.

THIRD MOVEMENT
Tempo: *Allegro* (fast)
Key: D Major
Form: Sonata-rondo (pp. 409–10)

The form of this movement, marked *Rondo* by the composer, is actually a hybrid known as *sonata-rondo*—a further extension of the episodic principle, showing, however, certain strong similarities to sonata-form. In comparing this example of the form with the description of sonata-rondo in Chapter VIII, only one divergence must be noted: this movement contains a *cadenza* as part of the coda. Such a divergence, however, is customarily found in the application of the form to a concerto movement and is therefore not at all unusual. In other respects it closely parallels the outline furnished on page 409.

[4]See Beethoven's Italian direction ("Start the Rondo at once") at the end of the second movement.

Exposition: measures 1–126.

I. *First subject,* in D major (tonic key); measures 1–43. This subject (Ex. 78), which follows immediately after completion of the second movement,[4] is a ternary form,[5] with the repeats written out. *Part A* (mm. 1–8) is stated by the solo violin, accompanied only by the 'cellos of the orchestra. This part is *not* repeated—in contrast to what one might expect in a ternary form. *Part B* (mm. 9–10) is extremely short and is played by soloist and orchestra. *Part A²* (mm. 11–18) is again mainly a section for the soloist, accompanied, however, by the upper strings. The usual repeat of "B" and "A²" (mm. 19–20 and 21–28) is assigned to the full orchestra. The end of this repeat of "A²" is extended, and leads to a simple codetta (mm. 31–45) distinguished by a new melody.

Example 78

The entire first subject is a perfect illustration of Beethoven's genius for taking insignificant material and making it meaningful through the way in which he presents it. Both "A" and "B" of the subject are hardly more than chord outlines: "A" based on the tonic, "B" on the dominant. Similarly, the codetta is merely a part of the D major scale, made rhythmically interesting and embellished by a few ornaments. Yet it is from this first subject that the greater part of the movement is constructed.

Characteristic of Beethoven is also the way in which he connects the first subject to the transition. The cadence pattern (V–I, V–I, V–I) in the bass line is extended by the composer in the upper strings and then assigned to the solo violin at the beginning of the transition.

Transition: measures 45–58. The device just mentioned makes it almost impossible to state where the extension of the codetta ends and the transition starts. Actually, the entire passage is a continuous flow—another example of Beethoven's skill in covering up the dividing point between sections of his design. The solo violin and the woodwinds are the principal instruments in this transition, the main function of which is one of modulation and connection. Once the dominant key is established, we are ready for the second subject.

II. *Second subject,* in A major (dominant key): measures 58–92.

This subject contains two themes.

(1) *First theme* (mm. 58–68). The theme is a strongly rhythmic idea (Ex. 79), similar in mood, though not in actual material, to the first subject. It is presented by the full orchestra alternating with the solo violin.

Example 79

(2) *Second theme* (mm. 68–92). This is a considerably more ornate musical idea (Ex. 80)

[5]See Chapter VIII: *Ternary Form,* pp. 397–99.

ROMANTIC MUSIC

Example 80

featuring mainly the soloist. Considerable extension follows the theme itself. This extension serves to connect the theme with the subsequent recurrence of the first subject. Notice particularly how after measure 80 Beethoven introduces a figure from the first subject, thereby anticipating its return and again providing a smooth progression from part to part of the design.

I. *First subject*, in D major (tonic key): measures 92–126. The return of the first subject —a characteristic feature of sonata-rondo form—is quite regular. The one major modification is the omission of the codetta. Its place is now taken by an extension of the theme, again used as a bridge to the subsequent section.

III. *Episode*, in G minor (subdominant minor key): measures 126–173.

The episode is rather interesting in design. The theme itself (Ex. 81) is in binary form. *Part A* is stated by the solo (mm. 126–134), then repeated by the bassoon (mm. 134–142). *Part B* is also first presented by the solo violin (mm. 142–150) and then repeated by the bassoon (mm. 150–158). The whole theme is without doubt the most lyrical idea in the movement. As if to prolong this lyrical mood, Beethoven next engages in a development of the theme (mm. 158–167), gradually modulating to the tonic key (D major). The final section of the episode is once more link-like in character, based on the first subject and preparing the Recapitulation.

Example 81

Recapitulation: measures 173–278.

I. *First subject*, in D major (tonic key): measures 173–217. The restatement of this subject is quite exact (*cf*. mm. 1–45), including even the codetta.

Transition: measures 217–234. The transition is changed somewhat from the one in the Exposition, but the change is no greater than one might expect. Since the two subjects now both return in the tonic, the transition must prepare a return of the second subject in the tonic key.

II. *Second subject*, in D major (tonic key): measures 234–278.

(1) *First theme* (mm. 234–242). There is no change, except in key, from the version heard in measures 58–68.

(2) *Second theme* (mm. 242–278). The theme itself is not changed; its extension, however, now culminates in a series of trills for the soloist and a *fortissimo* preparation of an inconclusive cadence, which introduces the cadenza.

Coda: measures 278–359.

The coda starts with a *free cadenza* for the soloist. The end of the cadenza is joined to a long trill (13 measures!) for the soloist, under which the strings introduce the motive of the first subject. Beethoven provides a startling shift in tonality—to A flat major, a key extremely remote from the tonic key of D major. The shift to such a remote key is one of Beethoven's favorite end-of-movement devices. It enables him to compose a long and satisfying return to the tonic key, thereby giving a sense of "arrival" when the original tonality is finally re-established. It is in just this manner that he uses the device in the present instance. The first subject not having been restated at *the end* of the Recapitulation, Beethoven develops it extensively in the coda. Several times the orchestra seems ready to conclude the movement, but each time the violin interrupts with scale passages and *arpeggios,* until, after a last ascending treatment of the theme, the *Concerto* comes to a close.

It has been said earlier that in Beethoven's style Classical and Romantic characteristics mingle. On the basis of the evidence in this Concerto it is easy to see that the predominant trait of *Classical* heritage is one of *design* and *formal control.* Beethoven's choice of the sonata for practically all of his major works is in itself Classical. The application of traditional designs within the sonata is Classical also. Above all, the *economy of means,* the utilizing of all the material in a structural way and not merely for momentary effect, is an evidence of restraint irrevocably associated with the Classicist.

On the other hand, even in the interpretation of form Beethoven is different from 18th-century composers. The growth in the dimensions of a composition, the invasion of free developing techniques into sections like the Exposition of a sonata-form, the evolving organic treatment of design, the obliteration of sharp boundaries between sections,—all these point to a new, Romantic approach to traditional form.

The nature of thematic material is, of course, intimately allied to the treatment of design. Beethoven's organic development presupposes material which is suitable for such treatment. His themes are rarely self-contained, complete in themselves; they are, rather, musical *figures* which gain meaning only in expansion and discussion. This treatment also necessitates a new scheme of harmonies and tonal relationships. Greater liberality in the introduction of dissonances, more frequent and more radical modulations, and a heightened chromaticism characterize this departure from Classical models. The same boldness is found also in the tremendous dynamic contrasts of Beethoven's style. The frequent *sforzandi,* the long *crescendi* show a dynamic range far in excess of that found in the music of Haydn and Mozart. All these characteristics must be regarded as *Romantic* in nature.

And yet, all these are but means. The end result of Beethoven's techniques reveals an intensity of emotion and, above all, an immediacy of expression which set him apart from his predecessors. In Beethoven this immediacy is still tempered and controlled by the Classical (formal) considerations mentioned above. In many of the later Romantic composers the restraint was greatly diminished. Along with harmonic experimentation, along with the radical modification of structural principles, came an increasing tendency toward emotional abandon. The emphasis on direct emotion produced, at its best, music of striking power (as in the writings of Berlioz, Wagner, or Moussorgsky) or of genuine lyricism (as in the works of Schubert, Chopin, or Schumann). At its worst, however, the inherent freedom of the style led to posturing and self-exhibition, where dramatic intensity became bombast and lyricism cheap sentimentality.

Recommended reading:
Donald Francis Tovey, *Beethoven,* New York, Oxford University Press, 1945.
Donald Francis Tovey, *Essays in Musical Analysis,* Vols. I and II, *Symphonies,* Vol. III *Concertos,* pp. 3–26, 87–95, London, Oxford University Press, 1936.

Pianoforte Concerto in G Major, No. 4, Opus 58[1]

Of the five piano concertos Beethoven wrote, the first three are in varying degrees imitative of Mozart, though showing the gradual evolution of a new style. The fifth (the so-called *Emperor*) is a brilliant and noble work, often regarded as Beethoven's greatest concerto. The fourth, composed in 1805–6, is "the cloud-piercing peak" of the range; it ranks with the *Third Symphony* (*Eroica*) as a supreme revelation of the Beethoven that came through the fire, the spirit that rebounded from the crisis of 1802, when realization of the incurability of his deafness drove him to despair. As in the *Eroica* he manifests his strength of soul, so in the *Fourth Piano Concerto* he reveals a testament of beauty, by which, no less than by declarations of power, his spirit lives.

FIRST MOVEMENT
Tempo: *Allegro moderato* (moderately fast)
Key: G major
Form: Sonata-form (pp. 405–9), with double Exposition

First Exposition: measures 1–74.

This orchestral Exposition (the piano is silent after the first five bars) presents a kind of "preview" of the thematic material of the movement, in and around the tonic key. Since it is designedly incomplete, we shall describe it in general terms, without assigning the themes to their proper positions within subject-areas.

Beginning: measures 1–28. The main theme of the movement is introduced by the soloist, unaccompanied, in a tradition-breaking phrase which establishes the mood of the whole composition (Ex. 82). The four-note motive (figure) on which it is based (· · · —) is a

Example 82

kind of spiritualized *Fifth Symphony* motive, as calm and inward here as it is stern and powerful there (note the vital difference of *phrasing*). The theme is marked *piano, dolce*—quiet and sweet; in the third bar a *sforzando* indicates an intensification no greater than a sigh, followed by a *diminuendo;* in the fourth bar a feathery scale-passage floats upwards to the high note; and in the fifth the half-cadence is followed by a pregnant silence, the offspring of which is the exquisitely sensitive entry of the orchestra in a remote key (*pianissimo*) in bar 6. The strings, using the same motive, bring the music back to the tonic key by smooth modulations, and after another suspiration in the tenth measure, complete the initial sentence with an authentic cadence in bar 14. This first statement alone represents a completely new, Romantic spirit in music; it introduces us at once to several peculiarly Beethovenian characteristics (motive-based themes, detailed and expressive dynamics, thought-filled silences leading to tonalities rich and strange, obscurations of key and swift returns home by imaginative modulations). There follows a brief development of the motive

[1] Program B.

in the tonic key, leading to a first climax and an insistence on a half-cadence in measures 23–28, where the forceful Beethovenian *stretto* or "piling up" technique should be noted. Observe also the dissolving of the cadence into what comes next.

Middle: measures 29–59. A new theme (Ex. 83) appears in a minor tonality. Like the main theme, it is based on a motive—this time a springier, more active one punctuated by

Example 83

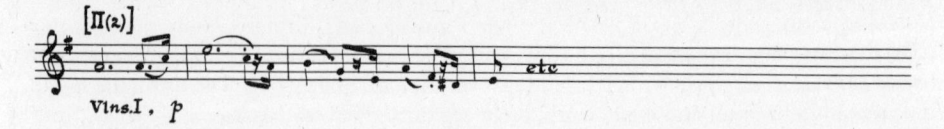

rests, but equally sensitive. Its mood is wistful; in the repetitions of the four-bar phrase it outlines, the most imaginative key-changes and major-minor oscillations occur, taking us by measure 40 far away from the tonic. This is only a brief excursion, however, for we return home in the following bars (by use of the main motive) and build up to a bold, heroic statement (mm. 50–59) which, though obviously related to the preceding theme, is different enough in character to be accounted a new one (Ex. 84). This marks the second and more emphatic climax, after which there is a tapering off.

Example 84

End: measures 60–74. A closing theme based on a scale-motive (Ex. 85) indicates the approaching end of the first Exposition and re-establishes the sensitive mood of the beginning. It is followed in bars 68–74 by a codetta (Ex. 86) which reverts to the main theme and is based on a tonic *pedal* (G), signifying conclusion.

Example 85

Example 86

Beethoven's treatment of the important juncture now reached—the point at which the soloist enters to re-present the Expositional material—is as masterly as it is typical of his mature style. In Mozart the first Exposition generally ends with an unequivocal, clear-cut authentic cadence, often followed by a break. Here, although there is no doubt about the "end-feeling" of the codetta, the actual entry of the soloist is made to *emerge* from the dissonant, inconclusive orchestral chords immediately preceding it—chords which are not resolved onto the expected tonic until five measures later. The whole first piano phrase is therefore poised on an unstable harmony, which gives it not an incipient but a continuing quality, and wonderfully connects the two Expositions. This "hiding of the seams," this fusing of the sections of originally clear-cut Classical forms, is one of the most characteristic Beethovenian traits; it was evident in the *merging of themes* already referred to, and we shall note it repeatedly throughout the work.

Second Exposition: measures 74–192.

Here the soloist, accompanied by the orchestra (which now takes second place, though always a significant one), elaborates on the ideas previously introduced and assigns the themes to their proper positions in subject-areas. We therefore analyze as for a regular sonata-form Exposition.

I. *First subject,* in G major (tonic key): measures 74–97. Beginning quietly with the four-note motive which first appeared in bar 1 and recurred in the codetta, the piano completely recasts the original opening, giving to measures 74–89 the sense of a continuation rather than of a new beginning. In addition to the formal reason for this (the merging of the two Expositions), there is undoubtedly the fact that Beethoven's fine poetic instinct forbade his repeating measures 1–14, with their striking musical imagery, in exact or even in modified form. There are subtle references, in the four-note chordal patterns of measures 83–85, to the main motive (particularly its *phrasing*); but not until measure 89, after an authentic cadence corresponding to the one in bar 14, do we actually take up the original first subject (*cf.* mm. 14–18), and then only briefly. In measure 97 the theme dissolves in a cascade of arpeggios, which may be taken as the beginning of the transition.

Transition: measures 97–119. We cannot fix the exact point at which the first subject ends and the transition begins, since Beethoven has purposely obscured it (the "fusing" technique again). What is clear is that up to bar 97, and for a few measures more, we are squarely in the tonic key, but that by bar 100 we are on our way out of the tonic key. The arpeggios soon give place to a smooth, flowing line (mm. 101+; note the persistence of the main motive in the orchestra) which takes us, by a sudden modulation and dynamic drop in bar 105, way off to the tonal horizons that Beethoven loved, where we hear "the horns of elfland faintly blowing" an echo of the opening phrase of the movement, high and clear in the piano. Quickly returning in a surge of scales, trills, and arpeggios, we reach in measures 110–111 the cadence that marks the take-off point for a second subject in the dominant key. This cadence is emphasized by several repetitions, featuring fast solo work (mm. 111–114), after which connection is made with the second-subject theme both by the rapid piano link that swells and fades and by the forward-leaning orchestral chords in measures 116–118.

II. *Second subject,* in D major (dominant key): measures 119–192. This contains three themes, a closing theme, and a codetta.

(1) *First theme* (mm. 119–134). A completely new melody, withheld until now, reveals itself as the true main theme of the second subject (Ex. 87). Presented in the warm lower

Example 87

register of the strings, it is a typically Beethovenian concentrated idea of only four bars' length, ending with an expressive modulation intensified by *sforzandi*. It is immediately worked over by the piano in a piquant, motive-based, ornamented version which emphasizes the dissonant neighboring-notes adjacent to the real melody-notes, the orchestral woodwinds meanwhile playing the latter in the background. Following this is a contrasting virtuoso-passage in the piano (with the first-subject motive again in the orchestra) which leads, by the same kind of fast finger-work as was seen at the end of the transition, to the next theme. Note the orchestral *crescendo* to sudden *piano* (mm. 132–134)—a common dynamic effect in Beethoven.

(2) *Second theme* (mm. 134–157). With a sudden change to D *minor,* the theme we first met as Example 83 appears in the violins. From this point on, the second Exposition follows

the course of the first Exposition closely, the orchestra presenting the thematic material and the piano a running commentary around it. This time, of course, the music is in (and around) the *dominant* key. The wistful, "gone-away" quality of the second theme is now heightened by the *pianissimo* filigree-work of the soloist in measures 142–145; the recurrence of the first-subject motive in the orchestra (mm. 145–157) produces a gradual animation in the piano patterns, and a dynamic build-up accompanied by sharp, off-beat *sforzandi* in measures 152–157. A flood of sound (mm. 155–157) marks the return to D major and the entry of the next theme.

(3) *Third theme* (mm. 157–180). This, originally a bold, upstanding theme (Ex. 84), is transformed by new dynamic markings into something pliant and feelingful. The piano not only overlays its opening phrases with a wash of arpeggios, scales, and trills, but also gives at measure 170 a highly poeticized version of its own, marked *dolce e con espressione* (sweetly and expressively), which is all the more significant for being the soloist's exit line. The suppressed energy of the orchestra is released at measure 174, and the Exposition is completed as before—by the orchestra alone.

Closing theme (mm. 180–188). As in the first Exposition, except for the change of key (*dominant* here) and some details of orchestration.

Codetta (mm. 188–192). As in the first Exposition, but without the dissonant ending—in fact, without any ending; for the codetta is interrupted by the re-entry of the piano, which again effects a fine formal fusion, this time of the end of the second Exposition and the beginning of the Development.

Development: measures 192–253.

Beethoven is a supreme master of thematic development. The number of changes he can ring on the same few notes, the new lights he throws on apparently simple ideas, the unsuspected implications he elicits therefrom—in short, his resources of musical invention, are limitless. Even when (as in the present instance) the temper of the music is extremely Romantic, he never loses himself in vague vaporizings, but derives his poetic effects directly from motives or "germ-ideas" already announced. We have seen how, in the Expository sections, the motive that appeared in bar 1 underlies the whole structure; in the Development it is everywhere perceptible, either in the orchestral background or interwoven with the texture of the piano part.

Measures 192–231. With one of those imaginative tonal shifts that take us clear to the realm of fantasy, the piano, using the main motive, gently contradicts the D-major chords of the Expositional codetta, and climbs by the same patterns as it used before (at the opening of the second Exposition) to a *pianissimo* pinnacle, from which droop exquisite veils of sound like the slow spray of a waterfall (mm. 196–204; Ex. 88). These dream-like filaments are, in cold analytical language, developed from the falling chord-patterns of measures

Example 88

82–84; each floating curve breaks delicately on the main motive at the base. The orchestra, which first supplies a breathing harmonic background to the piano, takes over the triplet pattern at measure 204 (violins, 'cellos) and combines it with the main motive (woodwinds), while the soloist—in a thoroughly Beethovenian compensatory contrast—bursts into vigorous arpeggios, rising against the orchestra's downward drift. Several measures of this lead to a reference (mm. 216–218) to the fast finger-work of the transition (*cf.* mm. 111+, and the later passage 131-134) and the opening notes of the first theme of the second subject (mm. 219-221; *cf.* m. 119), but these are only passing reminders; the accumulating energy of the music is such that nothing short of a piano-full of arpeggios in step-wise ascent (mm. 222-227) and a furious climax of chromatic scales and trills (mm. 227-230) can support it. Everywhere are strong dynamic markings, indicative of the intensity with which Beethoven conceives his music. Observe the extremes of mood passed through; the balancing of these extremes—the compensating of one by another—is a basic law of Beethoven's expression, which distinguishes him at once from Mozart and from most of his Romantic successors.

Measures 231-239. The key-changes of the foregoing section (far more daring than Mozart's) have led us to one of the tonalities most remote from G major, *viz.*, C sharp minor. In the eight measures now following Beethoven returns to the home key. First comes a *pianissimo* reaction to the stormy mood of the preceding bars; the falling, stroking patterns here (mm. 231-235) are an echo of the closing theme of the Exposition, and are accompanied by the main motive (*pizzicato, i.e.,* plucked) in the 'cellos and basses. The "lift" in measures 223-234 is sheer poetry. The ensuing bars (235-239) enliven the mood, without breaking the stillness, by piano arpeggios as light-fingered as the others, a while back, were rampageous. The main motive persists in the woodwinds; and the horns, which have been silent all through the Development, make of this motive a "horn-call" (m. 238) that ushers in the tonality of G major.

Measures 239-253. This, the conclusion of the Development, corresponds to the *link* which often occurs at this point in sonata-form movements. A forward urge is perceptible in the music, accentuated by imitative writing in the orchestra (which takes its cue from the piano-part of measures 239-243) and a *pedal* on the dominant (D) in bars 245-249. A masterstroke is the suppression of the dynamic level (*sempre pianissimo*=very soft all the time) until, in measures 249-250, a tremendous, fast *crescendo* hurls us into the loudest possible climax, and releases the Recapitulation.

Recapitulation: measures 253-346.

I. *First subject,* in G major (tonic key): measures 253-275. After a rest of two bars to marshal its forces, the piano enters *fortissimo, sforzando* (loudest possible, and then accented) with a triumphant declamation of the main theme, varied. The exuberance is quickly suppressed, and after three measures gives way to quiet (*p*), sweet (*dolce*) ornamentation of the original phrase ending. The orchestral response (mm. 258-266) is wondrously enhanced by high, *pianissimo* solo-work that hangs on the air like gossamer. After the cadence in measure 266, the continuation of the first subject is as in the second Exposition until, at bar 272, a bold modulation takes us to a remote key (E flat major). Again, we cannot say where this subject ends and the transition begins, so closely are the two connected.

Transition: measures 275-286. Just as, in the transition of the second Exposition (mm. 105+), a piano melody high in the air took us suddenly to a far tonal horizon, so here a similar effect is wrought by means of another new-sounding theme in E flat major (mm. 275-281, Ex. 89). It is not actually a new theme, being based on the main four-note motive

Example 89

(which, incidentally, appears in longer notes in the orchestral background) and on the "shape" of the first piano phrase of the first subject; but its ecstatic melody and rich pianistic accompaniment make an exquisitely fresh appeal to the ear, and lift us momentarily into a new world of imagination. The passage works round to a half-cadence in the tonic key in measures 280-281; this cadence is confirmed, and connection made with the second-subject theme *in the tonic key,* by the same kind of solo-work as occurred at the end of the former transition (*cf*. mm. 281–286 with mm. 111–119; note the differences as well as the similarities).

II. *Second subject,* in *G major* (tonic key): measures 286-346. This is substantially the same as in the second Exposition, but now *in the home key.* The first three themes are as before; the closing theme and codetta are omitted.

1. *First theme* (mm. 286-301). Restated exactly.
2. *Second theme* (mm. 301-324). Starts in G minor, ends in G major.
3. *Third theme* (mm. 324-346). The orchestral completion of this theme (mm. 341-346) is made to work round to an emphatic but inconclusive cadence, marked by a held chord (⌒), which releases the *cadenza.* The procedure is conventional—a pulling up of the horses, an "all clear" for the soloist; Beethoven took it over from 18th-century concerto-writers along with the convention of an extemporized cadenza. At measure 346, therefore, we leave the score for a considerable time, returning to the same measure at the soloist's final trill, which Beethoven has indicated by a stylized held note and trill sign.

Cadenza. Formally this corresponds to the *coda* of regular sonata-form movements. Since the cadenza we hear is Beethoven's own (written independently, at a later date), it has a real structural function, and is far more than a mere display of pianism. In it the composer says his final words about his main themes, drawing them together and impressing them, in parting, on the listener's mind. Since he never ceases to *develop* them, they appear in still new lights; note, for instance, the animation, the urgency, and in a few places the imperiousness of the main motive here. In addition to this first-subject idea (naturally the chief feature throughout) we hear references to the first theme of the second subject, now lightened in character, and to the third theme of the second subject—the one with the octave leap—which is still inward and tender. The cadenza ends with a long trill (on A, the note written as a guide to the performer in measure 346), broken for a final *pianissimo* link immediately before the orchestra re-enters.

Coda: measures 347-370. Here again we see Beethoven molding the received form to his own expressive purposes. In the typical Classical concerto, the cadenza comes to a full, brilliant authentic cadence on which the soloist ends; it is followed by a bold orchestral coda, as brief as possible. Here the cadenza merges with the coda in the subtlest, most expressive manner, and the movement is completed by soloist and orchestra together. The composer harks back to the third theme of the second subject (which was interrupted for the cadenza) and re-presents it in the gentlest, most sensitively ornamented version of all (mm. 347-356); the orchestra slips in unobtrusively and hovers in the background, with woodwinds supplying a quiet framework for the soloist's exquisite tracery. At measure 356 the codetta-patterns from the original Exposition return (*cf*. mm. 68+; they are, of course, based on the main motive), and a tonic *pedal* (G) sets in, which marks the "home stretch." A *crescendo* beginning at bar 363, and a swirl of scales accompanied by the main motive, lead to the *fortissimo* arpeggios and forceful, short chords that clinch the close. This typical end-of-movement brilliance is delayed until the last four bars, so that the poetic mood is preserved, to all intents and purposes, right up to the end.

SECOND MOVEMENT
Tempo: *Andante con moto* (slow but moving)
Key: E minor
Form: Its own (no set form).

A movement unusually short, and remarkable in many ways. For pure Romantic sensitivity, imagination and poetic feeling it would be hard to match, either in Beethoven's

ROMANTIC MUSIC

works (and we do not forget the first movement of this very concerto) or in the works of his successors; the refined sentiment, the restrained but deep emotion, are of a quality rare indeed in 19th-century music. For philosophical insight—a term which seems a little heavy for so imaginative a movement— this *Andante* stands alone; not even in his last quartets, where Beethoven stretches the bounds of music in an effort to express philosophical values, does he deliver so clear a spiritual judgment, which words can only approximate in such phrases as "the supremacy of gentleness over force," "the triumph of love over hate," or "the victory of the ideal over the actual." For technical experimentation (the simultaneous use of both piano pedals), and for at least one passage of sheer Impressionism (mm. 55-61), the movement is no less remarkable; we generally associate this kind of "atmosphere"-writing with composers of much later date. Finally, for its formal organization, its masterly manipulation of one simple structural principle—direct antithesis or opposition—this *Andante* is unique. Never was there a clearer instance of the Romantic *dominance of form by content,* for here there is no typable form, no preconceived pattern which the composer used as a framework for his ideas; there is simply the form that this particular expression demanded, and which, by the very nature of the case, no other movement in all music assumes.

There are two characters in the action, played by string orchestra and piano respectively (Ex. 90). The strings—loud, harsh, abrupt (*sempre staccato*=short notes all the time)—

Example 90

are in forceful unison (actually, *octaves*) throughout; the piano—quiet, tender, lyrical (*molto cantabile*=very singing tone; *molto espressivo*=very expresive)—uses harmonies of affecting simplicity, and plays with the soft pedal down all through the movement (see Beethoven's footnote in the score). There is little doubt, at the beginning, as to which character is dominant. The orchestral theme has energy, power, imperiousness, rugged individualism, and the force of inflexibility; it not only sticks to its own one idea, but has no qualms about butting in on other people's (see measure 26, and the following bars). The piano melody, on the other hand, is totally lacking in drive; its nature is meditative, rhapsodic, sensitive, gentle, and dreaming.

Yet with the unfolding of the movement it appears that "the race is not to the swift, nor the battle to the strong." The piano, without raising its voice (note all the *pianissimo* signs) but by lifting up its heart (see measures 28-47), completely subdues the other theme; when the latter is quite overcome (m. 47), then and then only does the piano bring forth its treasures, in a passage unparalleled for poetic beauty and intensity (mm. 47-64). At the beginning of the trills in measure 55, Beethoven marks an impassioned *crescendo* to *fortissimo,* to be accompanied by a gradual lifting of the soft pedal; at the end of the long trill on C a *diminuendo* to *pianissimo* is to be accompanied by a gradual depressing of the same pedal. During the trill (though this detail is not expressly marked) the sustaining pedal is used to produce strange, "modern"-sounding surges of tone from the chromatic scale-passages, which swell like full, deep sighs. This amazing *cadenza* can be related to the rest of the piano's quiet role only when it is understood as the overflowing of a heart surcharged with emotion—one which, for all its restraint and tenderness, has wells of power that the Powerful know not of.

By the end of the movement (measures 64-72 are, formally, a coda) the orchestral theme has become a mere murmuring in the bass; the *ppp* marking (rare in Beethoven) calls for the quietest possible playing, right on the edge of nothing. Long notes and expressive harmony appear for the first and only time in the orchestra, completing the transformation of its original character; the bold theme is not only overcome but—more wonderful yet—converted ("And the lion shall lie down with the lamb"). To this consummation the piano, in one of the most unforgettable endings in music, adds its heart-felt benediction, poised on the air in a long-held dissonance of exquisite pathos, resolving into silence.

THIRD MOVEMENT
Tempo: *Vivace* (lively)
Key: G major
Form: Sonata-rondo (pp. 409–10)

To avoid ruining the sensitive close of the *Andante* by end-of-movement relaxation, Beethoven instructs the performers to go right on to the *Rondo* (see the Italian footnote in the score, at the end of the slow movement), and so arranges its opening that the new mood, new tempo, new key, and new theme are felt as consequences of what comes before, not merely as successors. A *finale,* especially if it is a rondo, generally begins with a will, and almost always in the key which is its tonal center; here the movement begins with a whisper (*pianissimo*) and in the "wrong" key (C major, the subdominant of G; see Example 91 below). The final E of the slow movement is made the pivot, as it were, on which the tonality turns; it is the chief melodic note of the first four bars of the new movement, and from it (m.5) we descend—by a pattern skillfully derived from the *Andante* (*cf*. mm. 1 and 26-27 of the latter)—to the "right" key of G major, which a sprightly cadence confirms (mm. 9-10; *cf*. mm. 4½-5 of the *Andante*). This wonderful beginning does more than establish a connection between movements; by its imaginative mood it serves notice that we are to hear no run-of-the-mill rondo, but one which, for all its jollity, preserves in many details the poetic flavor of the whole composition.[2]

The form (marked *Rondo* by the composer) is actually a hybrid known as *sonata-rondo* —a cross between an older, simpler rondo form (see p. 401) and sonata-form. In this particular example, the basic divergencies from sonata-form are three:
   a. The Exposition contains a first subject, a transition, a second subject (in the dominant key), *and the first subject again.*
   b. The Recapitulation *begins with the second subject* (in the tonic key), follows with a "false return" of the first subject in a remote key, and *ends with the true first subject* in the tonic key.
   c. Since this is a concerto movement, the Coda is arranged to accommodate a *cadenza,* which occurs during its course (not at its beginning, as in the first movement).

Point (a) is regular, in sonata-rondo form; point (c) is regular, in concerto movements of any form; point (b) is irregular, both in sonata-form and in sonata-rondo form.

---

[2] It deserves mention, if only in a footnote, that all three movements of this concerto begin with a single chord, followed by a motive of four or three notes, thus: — ··· — (first movement); — · — · — (second movement); — ·· — (third movement); and that the first themes are all based on this essentially identical motive. (It actually goes further; *all* themes in all three movements begin with a held note followed by shorter notes, the significant exception being the piano melody in the slow movement). The only other outstanding case of such *inter*-movement thematic integration in Beethoven (*intra*-movement integration is, of course, the rule) occurs in the famous *Fifth Symphony,* which Beethoven was writing at the same time as this *Concerto,* and which is riddled with the very same motive (not preceded by the held note). The fascinating thing, however, is not the basic identity of the patterns, but the totally different characters they assume, as in the different movements of this *Concerto.*

ROMANTIC MUSIC

Exposition: measures 1–200.

I. *First subject,* "in" G major (tonic key): measures 1-41. The main theme consists of two related but contrasting phrases (Ex. 91), the one composed of *staccato* (detached) notes, the

Example 91

other of *legato* (smooth, joined) notes, all based on the same three-note motive. Each phrase is introduced by the orchestra and repeated by the piano. It is a jaunty theme, with delightful tonal vacillations between three keys (C major—G major in the first phrase, G major—D major in the second). An amusing skittering at measures 29-31, where the cadence-notes of the second phrase are mimicked in double-quick time, lets loose the full vigor of the theme, thus far suppressed. For the first time in the concerto trumpets and kettledrums join the orchestral forces; so the change from the *pianissimo* string opening to the sudden *fortissimo* of bar 32 is extreme. Were there any doubt about the humorous nature of the shock, the off-beat bass line of measures 32-40 (marked by *sforzandi*) would dispel it. The interrupted cadence in measures 40-41 is, of course, no ending at all; as usual, Beethoven merges first subject and transition.

Transition: measures 41-80. The distinguishing feature is the octave-leap motive (Ex. 92) which is tossed back and forth between orchestra and soloist—a game of catch enlivened

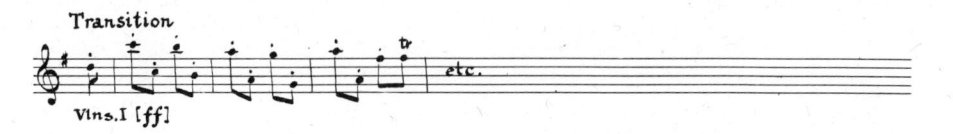

Example 92

by the players' sudden halts in the very act of cadencing. The piano eventually gets the ball (m. 60) and dashes way up the line to a position where the pace can safely slow down and the melody level off (mm. 68+). We have long since arrived at the dominant key (D major); harmonically, measures 57-79 are an elaborate dwelling on the dominant chord of that key. Psychologically, however, the smoothing of the rhythm in measures 68-79—the turning of bustling sixteenth notes into eighth-note triplet patterns, *legato*—is a preparation for the atmospheric second-subject theme. Observe how the line rises step-wise and hesitates on the brink of the coming melody.

II. *Second subject,* in D major (dominant key): measures 80-124. This contains one theme and a kind of codetta.

Main theme (mm. 80-110). A marvelous contrast, illustrating at once the imaginative element in the rondo and Beethoven's technical inventiveness, already commented on in the slow movement. The melody (Ex. 93) is high and floating (*soft, sweet*), accompanied by a

Example 93

single line in the left hand of the piano and by a *pedal* or drone low in the 'cellos—a wide spacing that lets plenty of "air" into the texture. The technical innovation is the direction Beethoven gives to the pianist, to put the sustaining pedal down at the beginning of the melody *and keep it down all through*. This produces an atmospheric "humming" or resonance suggestive of height and space—the kind of thing one hears when voices are raised in a vast cathedral. It is a daring, Impressionistic touch, taking us clean away from the typical rondo mood. When the orchestra begins the repeat of the piano melody (after a curious cadence in measures 92-95) its harmonies are still open-sounding, but they become warmer bar by bar, with lovely imitations among the voices, until the ending is rich and colorful.

Codetta (mm. 110-124). The brilliant arpeggios that follow (Ex. 94) have all the feeling of a "rounding-off" or key-confirming passage. We are suddenly back in rondo vein, with

Example 94

off-beat accents in the orchestra adding a touch of humor to the proceedings. Instead of coming to a definite end, however, the codetta turns into a link.

Link (mm. 124–160). With a drop in dynamics (m. 124) and a changing of the D major tonic chord into minor (m. 130), the music modulates to the dominant chord of *C major* (m. 132), which is dwelt on for the next 28 bars. The piano irons out its figurations, first from sixteenths to triplet eighths, then from these *fortissimo*, detached, to the same *piano*, smooth, then from arpeggio patterns to scale-patterns, and finally from eighths to quarter notes. The arpeggios of measures 142–151 recall the melodic line of bars 3–4 of the first subject, and the orchestra delivers the three-note motive of that subject both *piano* and *forte;* thus the link prepares us for the return of the main theme. The sweeping piano scale-passage in the pause-bar (m. 159) makes the actual connection with the coming theme—a connection, incidentally, difficult to achieve in performance, due to the non-metrical rapidity of the scale.

I. *First subject,* "in" G major (tonic key): measures 160-200. This is restated exactly. As before, the point we choose as the "end" is no ending at all; the music flows uninterruptedly on into the Development section.

Development: measures 200–272.

Continuing with the same material as formed the transition in the Exposition (*i.e.,* the octave-leap motive, tossed around between orchestra and soloist), the music now modulates to the key of E flat major, in which (at measure 216) a development of first-subject material begins. The arpeggio of bars 3-4 of the first subject, and the descending motives of bars 5-6, form the basis of the Development; they alternate in *legato* and *staccato* orchestral sections (mm. 216-224 and 224-228)—a pattern which is somewhat mechanically repeated, twice, in different keys. The piano simply fills in the *legato* sections with brilliant arpeggio busywork, and rests during the *staccato* sections. The third time over, however, it appropriates the *staccato* figure (mm. 248-251), carries it upward, and makes it lead into a new, smooth triplet version of the descending motives (Ex. 95). This, extended and repeated in various

Example 95

keys (mm. 252-272), leads to a cadence on the dominant of G major, which marks the end of the Development proper. Note the quiet background in the orchestra; strings *pizzicato* (plucked) give the arpeggio pattern, while woodwinds *pianissimo* keep reminding us of the basic three-note motive.

Link (mm. 272-299). A rampageous solo passage, over a *pedal* on the dominant (D) of G major, hooks on to the similar solo-passage from the Expositional transition (*cf.* mm. 280+ and mm. 61+), which naturally leads to the same "smoothing-out" section as occurred there, and so to the *second subject* again, but this time *in the tonic key*. It is probable that what led Beethoven (by his "law of compensation") to begin the Recapitulation irregularly with the contrasting second subject was the extensive use of first-subject material in the Development.

Recapitulation: measures 299-443.

II. *Second subject,* in *G major* (tonic key): measures 299-343. This is restated exactly, but now in the home key.

Main theme (mm. 299-329). The atmospheric theme, as before.

Codetta (mm. 329-343). The "rounding-off" arpeggios, leading without break to the same kind of link as before (*cf.* mm. 124+).

Link (mm. 343-369). With the same drop in dynamics and the same changing of the tonic chord (of G major) into minor, the music modulates to *E flat major* (m. 351), and dwells on the tonic chord of that key for twenty bars, again ironing out the solo figurations and bringing back first-subject motives in piano and orchestra (mm. 361-369).

Pseudo-I. False return of first subject, "in" B flat major: measures 369-382. Under a ceiling of piano arpeggios (*pianissimo*) based on bars 3-4 of the first subject, the divided violas and one 'cello bring in a smooth, singing version of that subject in the "wrong" keys of E flat—B flat (Ex. 96); a masterly touch, showing how even the crisp main theme can be influenced

Example 96

by the Romantic mood that dominates the composition. The color-combination of low strings in close position is bold; they produce a warm, throaty, contralto effect, emphasized by the particular foreign tonality chosen. The repetitions of the cadence-pattern at the end merge with what follows.

Link (mm. 383-416). By exploiting the cadence-pattern still further, first delicately with a piano-arpeggio embroidery (mm. 383-390) and then forcefully with the full orchestra (mm. 391+), the composer works round to a cadence on the dominant chord of *C major* (mm. 401-402) and dwells on this chord long enough for the tonality to become settled in the old groove. The soloist reiterates the arpeggio motive of bars 3-4 of the first subject, ending with a delightful G one note higher than all the preceding F's, and with the same kind of non-metrical, rapid scale-connection as occurred before at a similar formal juncture (m. 159).

I. *First subject,* "in" G major (tonic key): measures 416-443. The true main theme—still further varied by the broken solo-patterns and plucked-string accompaniment—returns in the "right" keys of C major—G major. Full orchestra takes over the repeat of the first phrase (m. 426); the second phrase (original mm. 21+) is omitted entirely, which expedites the final portion of the movement. Part of what we have called "the transition" appears (mm. 435-443) only to round off the theme and lead to a clear authentic cadence in the tonic key (mm. 442-443). All that follows this cadence is coda.

Coda (mm. 443–600, and unprinted *cadenza*). A burst of brilliant arpeggios (Ex. 97) such as would lead one to expect a conventional ending (these arpeggios are, in fact, derived from

Example 97

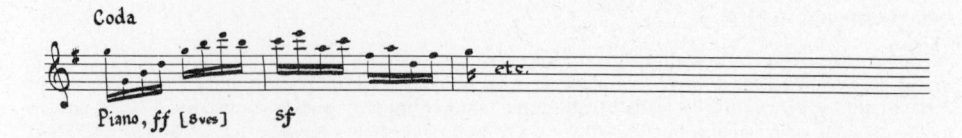

the cadence-confirming patterns of measures 110+ and 329+, which we have called *codettas*) is unexpectedly smoothed out in measures 450-459, and made to modulate to the extremely remote key of F sharp major—the furthest possible tonal distance from the tonic key of G major. There, at bar 459 (Ex. 98), occurs one of the typical Beethovenian coda-surprises—the

Example 98

introduction of the atmospheric second-subject theme, and the imaginative return, by a simple device (mm. 463-467), to C major—G major. Having returned home, the composer has the whole orchestra sing the second-subject tune; first the 'cellos (mm. 475+), then—overlapping them—the violins (mm. 479+), then—overlapping the violins—the woodwinds (mm. 483+). This *stretto* or cumulative section, to which the piano adds momentum by reiterating the little scale first introduced in measure 466, leads to a full-orchestral statement (mm. 487+; melody in bass) that works round to the inconclusive cadence and held chord conventionally associated with cadenzas (mm. 497-499).

Cadenza. Beethoven directs, in Italian: "Let the cadenza be short"; and the cadenza he himself wrote is just that, in contrast to the far more developed one in the first movement. Here he begins by poking fun at the pompous, stylized cadence of measures 497-499, and follows with references to the tuneful second-subject theme and its codetta-arpeggios. Note the omission of first-subject material. Two sharp *sforzando* breaks mark the "end," which again is no ending at all (*cf.* first-movement cadenza and conclusion).

We continue the coda at measure 500. Brilliant trills again mislead us into expecting a conventional close. Instead we get another smoothing-out of the rhythm and, at measure 520, the same lyrical version of the first-subject theme as occurred in the violas at the "false entry" in measures 369–382 (Ex. 96 above). This is stated twice, over a tonic *pedal* (mm. 520–529 and mm. 530–546), the piano lightly embroidering the theme, which fades out in cadence-repetitions at the end. No doubt about the mood here, nor about the Romantic flavor of the little solo line that follows (mm. 546–553). At measure 554 a tempo-change to *presto* (extremely fast) marks the beginning of the final stretch. A *crescendo* to *fortissimo* leads to the last trumpeting of the main theme (m. 568), with a new and furious bass of triplet figurations, still thematically derived. Before the movement finishes there is room for one more imaginative touch—the cadence-repetitions of measures 578–594, with their *pianissimo* "horn-calls" and high piano filigree-work; as in the first movement, this delays the final bold repetitions of the tonic chord until the very last bars. The *Concerto* ends with an impulsive flinging-out of the arms (piano chords, measures 598–600)—a gesture embracing the whole wide world ("O ye millions, I embrace you" is a line from the composer's *Ninth Symphony*); such a gesture as Beethoven the Poet, Beethoven the Seer, may well indulge in at the conclusion of a testament so universal.

Recommended reading:
Donald Francis Tovey, *Beethoven,* New York, Oxford University Press, 1945.
Donald Francis Tovey, *Essays in Musical Analysis,* Vol. III, *Concertos,* London, Oxford University Press, 1936.

ROMANTIC LITERATURE

JOHN KEATS (1795–1821): *Ode to a Nightingale*[1]

CLASSICAL ART, whether in the music of Haydn and Mozart, the painting of Raphael and Poussin, or the poetry of Pope and Gray, is an art that stresses order and wholeness, that tends to be impersonal and objective, and that demonstrates clearly the artist's control of his medium, his subject-matter, and himself. The qualities sought after are balance, harmony, simplicity, clarity of thought, and elegance of expression. Such art subordinates detail to design and seeks to present truth in its general, abstract, and universal aspect. It centers its interest upon the human, not the divine or the demoniacal. It concerns itself with what is normal, not with what is eccentric—with the "representative" man. It stresses social norms, values restraint, and speaks with the voice of reason and society. Intelligence, urbanity, wit, and detachment are the characteristics of the Classical artist. He is self-assured and self-controlled, and he can afford to be so because he is certain of an audience that shares and understands his point of view about all that matters—man, society, God, and nature. The Classic concern with form does not mean neglect of subject matter; it means only that subject matter is the common property of society, not the expression of individual ideas or peculiar feelings.

The theme of Gray's *Elegy* (1750) is generalized and traditional. It subdues personal feeling to reflection and is meditation on the common lot of humanity. But to the traditional theme of rural retirement and obscurity the poet adds a refined and tender pathos. This is prevented from becoming what would seem to the Classical poet too intense and too narrowly individual by the conventional imagery of pastoral poetry and by the somewhat elegant and artificial poetic diction. ("The language of poetry is never the language of the age," wrote

[1]Programs A and B.

Gray.) But above all, it is the theme itself which keeps the poem impersonal, general, and comparatively calm. This theme is the common lot of human life and the leveling of all in the common grave. To protest too violently against what is inevitable is folly; to seek to be individual, personal, or original would simply be impudent.

In John Keats' *Ode to a Nightingale,* it is possible to see what happened to the short-lived Classicism of 18th-century English literature under the impact of the new Romantic attitude towards nature, towards the past, and towards the worth of individual freedom. How different is the theme, the attitude, and the method in the *Ode* written some sixty years after the *Elegy!*

Under the impact of the break-up of the fine balance between intellect and feeling which is the essence of true Classicism, a change began to occur. When sentiment became confused with sentimentality and reason became dogmatic, certain individuals came to realize forcibly how much had been left out to achieve the Neo-Classic order. For these, the ideal and method of the artist were changing, and he tried now to express whatever was most individual, most imaginative, most free. He developed a sympathetic interest in the relics of medieval chivalry or the primitive simplicity of balladry, and he responded with intense emotion to all the aspects of nature that the 18th century sought to ignore or tame—the majestic, the vast, and the elemental.

The artist was no longer looked upon as the calm, superior, impersonal craftsman who shapes in a spirit of high-minded detachment the common ideas and feelings of society into perfect and lasting form. Instead, he was to be an explorer, seeking to express as intensely as possible his own reactions to whatever was new, strange, and unfamiliar in nature. The change in the sense in which the word "nature" was used is significant. In the 18th century it generally meant either "human nature" or "the world of objective reality and fact"; in the 19th it more often meant the vast world of natural phenomena (mountains, oceans, rivers, forests, winds, waves, tempests, sun, stars, moon, etc.), before which man might react emotionally or, by harmonizing himself with it, grow godlike.

But the Romantic movement was more than an expansion of interest into a more emotional and freer concept of man and the universe. It was also a new vision of the worth of the individual and a recognition of a universal right to freedom in the political and economic structure of society. The French Revolution, the American War of Independence, the poetry of Burns, the writings of Rousseau, Paine, and Franklin are all a part of it.

Further, the rise of the middle classes, the growth of cities, and the mechanization of society which resulted from the Industrial Revolution at the end of the 18th century placed the individual, and particularly the artist, in a new and uncertain position. Dryden, Pope, and even Gray, could feel that they spoke to an attentive audience which made up the best and most influential elements of the national life. But after the Industrial Revolution, a polite, sophisticated, and classically trained audience was no longer available, and the poet became more and more the spokesman of his own lonely reveries, seeking what consolation he could find by dwelling with ever-increasing intensity on his inner experience. The melancholy of Gray's *Elegy* is tender, resigned, and relieved by a kind of rational calm which recognizes that if the narrow life of the poor often thwarts genius, it more often prevents great crime. Keats' melancholy is close to despair. It is intensely subjective, and its chief source (though not its only one) is the poet's sense of isolation.

Keats' *Ode* begins with an impassioned and almost physical statement of the poet's mood:

> My heart aches and a drowsy numbness pains
> My sense, as though of hemlock I had drunk....

We then learn what induced this feeling—the nightingale singing in the richly scented summer woodland. And we learn also that it is *excess of happiness* that is responsible for the poet's anguish. Pleasure too intense is pain. The Classic references to *Lethe,* the river of forgetfulness from which the dead must drink, and *dryad,* a wood spirit, here the nightingale, are in keeping with the reference to the hemlock, the drug used to kill Socrates.

How can the poet, he asks himself, enter into the happy world where the nightingale dwells? He suggests the cool, fragrant, intoxicating wine of Provence—a province in the south of France associated with the troubadours and medieval love poetry. This is a happier and more enticing draught than the hemlock of the previous stanza. But the poet's desire is to escape from the limitations and frustrations of the world of fact in which the poet's waking life is spent.

The third stanza makes clear why he wishes to escape—or what he wishes to escape from. Again it is Time (as in Donne's *The Sun Rising* and Marvell's *To His Coy Mistress*) that is the destroyer of youth and beauty and the corrupter of love. But the tone is much more intense than in the brilliant and witty poems of the 17th century, for it is of his own approaching death and wasted youth that Keats is thinking. He knew at the time the poem was composed that he was touched with consumption.

The poet rejects escape through the medium of opiates or wine. "Bacchus and his pards" refers to the god of wine, followed by his train of revellers and his sacred leopards. Instead it is with the aid of poetry, *i.e.,* the creative imagination, the emotions, and the senses, that he will escape into the world of eternal happiness and beauty, of which we should now realize the bird has become the symbol. Note here the Romantic distrust of intellect and reason: "the dull brain perplexes and retards"; "to think," the previous stanza had told us, "is to be full of sorrow."

In the fourth stanza comes a sudden magical change:

> Already with thee! Tender is the night. . . .

The tone is one of surprise. The spell has worked. The poet is transported from the world of sick thought and numbing pain into the eternal, ever-youthful world of the imagination. All is a Midsummer Night's dream of rich and exquisite music, which is presented in the rest of this stanza and in the next with an intensity and precision that perfectly realize the aim of the artist to endow the world of imagination with reality.

The beautiful but almost purely descriptive fifth stanza gives way to a deeply emotional and intensely personal development in the sixth. Here is the expression of perfect ecstasy; but how is it to be retained? How can the inevitable relapse that terminates it be escaped? Is there no way to thwart the ebbing back of the sorrows of the sick world of reality? Only one way suggests itself, and it has suggested itself before: to die at the moment of intensest ecstasy—

> To cease upon the midnight with no pain.

Indeed, in the mood of excitement that the bird has induced, death itself is a sensuous experience—

> Now more than ever seems it *rich* to die.

In the seventh—the most famous and wonderful stanza—the bird as a symbol of eternal, superhuman beauty and as a liberator of the heart into the faery land of the imagination is presented with the greatest directness and in ringing tones that are sharply contrasted to the yearning desperation of the stanza before.

But suddenly, almost unconsciously, at the height of his excitement the poet has stumbled on a word—the word "forlorn"—and the vision so magically and intensely presented in the lines that begin "already with thee!" (line 35) collapses like a bubble. The poet is left forsaken with no resource but his own lonely and inadequate self. The total experience the poem presents is not the ecstatic vision of its central section with its *seeming* escape into the eternal reality of the imagination, but the melancholy and disillusioned awakening to the fact that "the fancy (he does not call it imagination, which to him was man's highest faculty for perceiving truth) cannot cheat so well as she is famed to do." But with what skill the song of the bird fading in the distance is equated to the gradual fading away of the happy vision and the return of the harsh world where but to think is to be full of sorrow!

Here in this marvelous poem Keats has imposed on feelings of the most Romantic wildness a Classical perfection of form that is unrivalled among the productions of the Classical ages.

Recommended reading:
John Keats, *Complete Poems and Selected Letters,* ed. C. D. Thorpe, New York, Odyssey Press, 1935.
J. Middleton Murry, *Keats and Shakespeare,* New York, Oxford University Press, 1930.
M. R. Ridley, *Keats' Craftsmanship,* Oxford, Clarendon Press, 1933.
J. Douglas Bush, *Mythology and the Romantic Tradition in English Poetry,* Cambridge, Harvard University Press, 1937.

HERMAN MELVILLE (1819–1891): *Billy Budd, Foretopman*[1]

MORE THAN A QUARTER CENTURY after the obscure death of Herman Melville (1819–91), an old family trunk yielded a packet of some 340 pages of yellowed paper, covered with his "incredibly crabbed" pencil scrawl, and blurred and slashed with revisions, insertions, and variant readings. The exciting manuscripts, when laboriously deciphered, proved to contain the novel *Billy Budd,* completed but a few months before the author's death, but still in the process of receiving the reworking of a conscious artist who was always dissatisfied with his imperfect work. The illegibility of this posthumous work was so great that the transcription and printing of *Billy Budd* has always remained an uncertain and perplexing problem. But the obvious excellence of even imperfect texts has been evidence enough to refute the common assertion that the great writer had exhausted his creative powers some forty years earlier in the monumental achievement of *Moby Dick.* Artistically, *Billy Budd* can stand comparison with Melville's best, which may well mean with the best in American fiction.

The book has many points of significant contact with the world in which its author lived. The common explanation of the paradoxes in the career of a provocative writer that he was at odds with his age, that he was behind or in advance of his times, is rarely very satisfying or convincing. In the case of Herman Melville, although his voice was often raised in vehement protest, even a casual reader must feel that he was peculiarly responsive to the influences of the cultural milieu of his world as well as dependent on his actual personal experiences in that world. His first writing was done in the main current of 19th-century Romanticism and his early books were shaped by the literary temper of that movement. *Typee* (1846) and *Omoo* (1847) were successes, somewhat scandalous successes it is true, largely because of their conforming to the Romantic tastes of those times. These early romances contained most of the standard ingredients: the enchantment and beauty of strange and remote places and peoples; a scorn of conventional decorum and a willingness to invade forbidden terri-

[1] Programs A and B.

tories; the approved preferences for the intuitive goodness of native innocence over the dubious advances of sophistication and even of Christian civilization; a delight, in *Typee* and *Mardi* at least, in amorous interludes more ecstatic and idyllic than were conventional in the fiction of that genteel era; a stylistic exuberance and lushness that defied all the disciplines of restraint; and a habit of paralleling didactic analogies—aesthetic, philosophical, and psychological—to everything in nature. In Melville's works there are numerous statements in which he decries concern with the formal tyranny of Classical or rational decorum, with finished firmness of design, either in life or in literature, or with a picture of the universe closed in by the tight, neat laws of rule, intellect, or logic as the inexorable terms of man's destiny. With him, life is a dubious battle, but the struggle is of man against man, not man against the gods, and although fate may well play an ironic part in that destiny, man's choices, free or otherwise, always are vital factors in the outcome. One statement of such literary conviction is found in Chapter 29 of *Billy Budd:*

The symmetry of form attainable in pure fiction cannot so readily be achieved in a narration essentially having less to do with fable than with fact. Truth uncompromisingly told will always have its ragged edges; hence the conclusion is apt to be less finished than an architectural finial.

One must remember, however, that much as he protested against the curbs of form, Herman Melville as a careful artist could never be really indifferent to symmetry, and that in *Billy Budd* in particular his draughtsmanship was sure, perhaps surer than he himself realized.

There are in *Billy Budd* surviving vestiges of Melville's early Romantic manner, but there is more massive evidence, in this final inventory, of the last stage of a gradual regression from many of the pleasant Romantic assumptions of his earlier years. A comparison with *Typee* shows how far these modifications had carried him to this last rounding out of his view of the meaning of life. It is, of course, impossible to say how much these changes were due to the impact of the rising realism of the second half of the century, how much to his increased reading of Shakespeare and other dramatists, and how much to his own deepening awareness of the mystical tragedy of human existence, confirmed and validated for him by the ambiguities and frustrations of his own life. Whatever the causes, the darkening of the tone in successive books shows him moving deeper and deeper into despair and farther from the "pleasurable melancholy" of the Romantic view of man and nature. Even the innate liberalism of his temper, which made him peculiarly responsive to mystical concepts of the brotherhood of man, had not been encouraged by his auditing of the lasting fruits of contemporary reforms and reformers or of the records of revolution. Gradually, optimistic idealism had become circumscribed by a realistic sense of human limitations—a dawning conviction that lofty aims are not a safe substitute for good earthy common sense. Starbuck, the splendid first mate in *Moby Dick,* is doomed by the inevitable "incompetence of mere unaided virtue and right mindedness"; *Pierre* points up the folly of a person who presumes to conduct earthly affairs by the absolutes of "Heavenly Wisdom"; and Billy Budd is a pure sacrifice, a Christ-like martyr, to the grim, earthy necessity of things as they are, albeit with triumphant affirmation rather than denial of the eternal reality of the Heavenly, the abstract and absolute values.

Although he asserted, perhaps a bit proudly, that a "whaleboat was his Yale and Harvard College," one must never forget that in any search for the key to Herman Melville's relationship to the thought and literary fashions of his day, reading looms large. Few American writers give evidence of a more voracious appetite for books or of more immediate response to reading. Judged alone from the evidence of literary allusions in his novels, it seems clear that he was not a great reader of prose fiction, but delved for truths and techniques in the Bible, the philosophers, the poets, and particularly in Shakespeare and other dramatists. Thus it is not surprising that the books of Melville often bear less resemblance structurally to the novel than to other literary genres: *Typee* and *Omoo* are rather conventional travel books; *Mardi,* a strange philosophical allegory in the form of a travel book; *Moby Dick,* a great epic, owing much of its power to added elements of dramatic techniques; and *Billy Budd* is a tragedy as stark in effect and simple in structure as a Greek tragedy. As in the Greek tragedies, the problem of Billy Budd is a moral one, the impact on an individual man of the universal dualism of good and evil, which must be allowed its full scope of horror to evoke the purging pity and compassion of the beholder. Aristotle's prescription for tragedy, "an imitation of an action that is complete, and whole and of a certain magnitude" unified by confining the action to one major calamity, is applicable here.

Unity in a Classical tragedy compels limitation. In *Billy Budd,* the stage on which three remarkable men face the inexorable tragic facts of life and death is the isolated one of the scrubbed decks of a man-of-war, the action is limited to the outer and inner life of one particular ship and is focussed on the career of an individual sailor, with a crew of average men to fulfill the functions of a chorus where common men comment on men and events not at all commonplace. The three leading characters, all doomed men, are all of heroic stature; whether for exalted good or monstrous evil, they are never petty, squalid, or vulgar. Billy, the symbol of unlettered, natural goodness, is high-born, handsome, and universally loved as much for his charm of person as for his innocent Adam-like virtue, but impressive for great physical strength as well as for the calm courage of natural rectitude. Claggart, a truly masterful piece of portraiture, becomes the terrifying symbol of evil, depravity as natural as is good in the dark mysteries of existence; his malignity appears utterly without motive to readers of normal human compassion, but it has the inexorable logic of his own dark, twisted necessity. Captain Vere, the unwilling arbiter in this clash of good and evil, has the heroic virtue of Billy Budd, but his role is complicated by the knowledge of good and evil of a civilized man educated in the ways of men and books, a knowledge which ladens him with the grim responsibility of decision in the awful dilemma of heart and head, spirit and law, heavenly good and mundane duty—a responsibility he is too manly to try to evade.

In tragedy, death rather than the happy ending is fate's decree, and here each of the three main characters meets his death. Claggart's death, early in the story, is sudden, violent, and but slightly freighted with significance; the calm and tragic death of Billy is presented not as defeat but as a triumphant declaration that the beauty and dignity of a man's soul are above the whims of fate; Captain Vere, alone aware of the tragic ironies at play, lives on for a time with the bitter memory of his austere decision until he is killed by a musket-ball in a sea engagement. The demands of dramatic unity are strengthened by Billy's last words to the upright judge who has sentenced him, "God bless you, Captain Vere," and by the death-bed words, inexplicable to the attendant, of Captain Vere's murmured "Billy Budd, Billy Budd."

The basis for the plots of Melville's earlier sea stories had been actual voyages in his own youth. Here the story has as background the alleged abuses and advocated reforms in the British Navy after the great mutiny in the Nore in 1797. *White Jacket* (1850) has been concerned with similar issues in the American Navy. The actual incidents of *Billy Budd,* however, parallel rather closely widely publicized accounts of the execution of three seamen of the brig *Somers* by Captain Alexander Sidell Mackenzie. James Fenimore Cooper, among others, had been completely convinced of the innocence of the executed men and had penned a violent attack on the Captain and on the scandal of naval discipline. It has also been pointed out that a cousin of Herman Melville had been a lieutenant on board the *Somers,* and this may well have been his point of contact with the facts and emotional tensions of those controversial events.

In Melville's fictional use of these actual events, the literary craftsmanship is sure. The alternation between swift action and expository comment is skillfully balanced. One feels that the writer has worked outward from living characters toward incident and moral conclusions rather than making use of characters to exemplify his philosophical abstractions. Space in the story is about equally divided among the three characters—Billy, Claggart, and Vere. As is usual with Melville, characters are first presented with great care to picture realistically the physical appearance, but physical details soon become merely the outer evidence of the more significant inner realities of psychology, intellect, and passion. Each of the three men illustrates in his own way the eternal ambivalence of appearance and reality, the physical and the spiritual, the external and internal aspects of the age-old problem of good and evil. Some readers contend that Captain Vere is the real, responsible hero of the tragedy, for he alone has the intellectual stature to lift him above the mere pathos of a weaker character to whom things happen; others feel that Billy Budd, possessed of the Christian might of the meek, not only supplies the technical unity of contact with all other characters, but that he alone lives on indefinitely in the memory and hearts of the crew as well as in the more concrete immortality of legend and ballad. Actually, in the Christian concept of tragedy there is nothing in humility and passive power antithetical to tragic heroism.

The prose in *Billy Budd*, unlike most of Melville's, is lucid and quiet, with a sense of inward peace and acceptance. The exclamatory rhetoric, the fire, violence, and passion of his early books, has become restrained and chastened by the dignity of a philosophical acceptance in place of the heightened colors of passionate and zealous rejection, but without loss in real power. Here one feels that the focus on universal aspects of the moral issue gains from the method without sacrifice of credibility of the characters as actual human beings.

Although it is possible and even profitable to view *Billy Budd* as an artistic achievement apart from the whole body of Melville's work, its real significance emerges when it is examined as the keystone in the never-completed arch of his lifetime of agonized brooding over the dark and inscrutable mystery of life. The earlier books chart the course of the ethical quest of an honest skeptic who was essentially a deeply religious man in the high sense of that term. Successive books, each more serious and less hopeful than its predecessors, failed to record satisfying or affirmative answers—only more ambiguities demanding of a sincere man of good will compromises, rejections, and ultimately despair. This sense of the external ambivalence of good and evil in the nature of things, an awareness conditioned to some degree by Calvinistic upbringing and association, had found many symbols: land and sea, order and chaos, the ideal and the real, the inner and the outer, heavenly wisdom and earthly wisdom, tranquillity and struggle, hope and despair. These supplied the real plots of the semi-autobiographical romances of his main career. In *Billy Budd*, which has been called his "final testament," this cumulative pessimism has mellowed towards a mature and calm acceptance of the tragedy implicit in human nature, not as unmixed evil but as the opportunity for men to call on the deep reserves of character to make of defeat and death a triumphant assertion of quiet dignity and of the nobility possible to man. The tragic events here, pictured with numerous analogies to the Crucifixion of Christ, are stronger as an argument for a faith in human potentials than as a basis for despair. In this attempt "to justify the ways of God to men," Herman Melville's final message is a touching affirmation of faith in the persistence of good: manly comradeship, gentleness allied to strength, ethical probity both unlettered and schooled, and a conviction that what good men do—and are—is not always interred with their bones.

Recommended reading:

F. Barron Freeman, *Melville's "Billy Budd,"* Cambridge, Harvard University Press, 1948. Valuable critical introduction and textual study.

William Ellery Sedgwick, *Herman Melville, The Tragedy of Mind,* Cambridge, Harvard University Press, 1945. Excellent study of Herman Melville with a chapter on *Billy Budd*.

Raymond Weaver, *Shorter Novels of Herman Melville,* New York, Horace Liveright, 1928. Introduction has an early discussion of *Billy Budd*.

ROMANTIC PAINTING

FRANCISCO GOYA (1746-1828)[1]

AT THE AGE OF FIFTY-THREE, Goya remarked that the censoring of human errors and vices can be an appropriate subject for painting and that he had selected his subjects from the extravagant wrongs common in society and from the vulgar lies sanctioned by custom, ignorance, and interest. This remark was made a short time after the American and French Revolutions had been accomplished. The center of painting had passed to France, but painting had been unable to maintain the standard it had set in the Baroque period, so that the lustiness of a Rubens had faded in the 18th century into the nostalgic and delicate melancholy of a Watteau, the boudoir art of a Boucher, and the eroticism of a Fragonard. The style of these painters was called Rococo. Gay and artificial, delicate and sprightly or melancholy, it was the feminine counterpart of the Baroque. In contrast to the sweep and grandiloquence of the Baroque, its forms were without movement. Movement was restricted to the sliding of lights over sensuous surfaces, over satins or silks or velvety landscapes. At the advent of the French Revolution there had been an abrupt return to Classicism with its accompanying restraint of emotion and its attempt to restore man to heroic stature. This reaction, called Neo-Classicism, failed eventually, but it left behind it a reinforced Academy which, up to our own day, under the name of the *École des Beaux Arts,* has consistently fought all artists who have attempted to move beyond the rigid rules for painting that it had set up. The Academy had the official approval of society, and every artist who dared to be original was to some degree thus alienated from society.

Goya was to begin his career in the manner of court artists such as Fragonard and Boucher in the Rococo style. He executed a series of paintings that were to serve as designs for the Royal Tapestry Works in Spain. They represented popular pastimes in light, flat areas of color that gave a hint of the rich color Goya was to use in his best work. If he had gone no further, he would have remained a highly competent painter in a style that was about to succumb to new forces. He did not remain a Rococo painter, but neither did he return to the Classical. Instead, he plunged directly into the world around him, caustically depicted contemporary events, and was able to suffuse his work with a strong emotionalism. Through this approach he anticipated the turn of French painting to Romanticism by at least a quarter of a century. He found himself in a society and nation that were degenerate. He abounded in animal vigor, tempered by two other and opposing qualities which are revealed in his self-portraits, in a soft and sensual mouth and a sharply penetrating eye. This contrast may assist partially in explaining the range of his style—now rich and almost feminine in its nuances of color, now monochromatic and slashing—and of content—now sensual, now scathing and satiric. Sometimes the presence of one suggests the other, as in his portrait of *Queen Maria Luisa,* where the glittering jewels and rich material make coarse and repugnant the heavy body of the woman. Piero della Francesca in the Italian Renaissance could paint the detestable Sigismondo Malatesta like a youthful saint, but Goya, two centuries later, could neither forget nor ignore the personality of his royal sitters. Their weak and dissolute faces lie forever imbedded in a sumptuous garden of color. The costumes alone are beautifully brushed with strokes that appear sketchy and spontaneous.

The portraits of the Renaissance exhibit a relaxed posture, a sense of stability and poise, and an unshakable self-confidence. The figures exist as self-contained, monumental units in a carefully delimited space. They are meant to be contemplated and admired by the specta-

[1] Programs A and B.

ROMANTIC PAINTING

Fig. 74. Goya, *Senora Sabasa Garcia, ca.* 1808, National Gallery of Art, Washington, D. C. (Mellon Collection)

tor. Goya's portraits, on the contrary, seem to reverse the positions of spectator and subject. Through some means it is the portrait that becomes the active agent; it is the portrait that looks at the spectator and, in looking, judges. The single element that does most to effect this reversal is the eyes. In a characteristic portrait, such as that of *Señora Sabasa Garcia* (Fig. 74), the eyes are large and intensely dark in a pale and flattened face. They stare at the spectator with arrogance and disdain. Goya had greatly reduced the shadows on the face, removing them from the eye cavity and thus heightening the projection of the pupil, and limiting them in most cases to the contours of the face. The figure is also erect and rigid in posture, as a result of which it emanates a feeling of unrest and uneasiness. Unlike the Renaissance figure, that of Goya has become aggressive. It seems to imply that its position in society is precarious and can be maintained only by wit and ingenuity.

The impressionistic handling, particularly noticeable in the veil, derives originally from Velasquez who, more than a century earlier, had experimented with optical realism: the rendition of what one sees before one's eyes as against what one knows. The result in Velasquez was an extraordinarily subtle observation of the innumerable changes in light and tonality (Fig. 73). But, while Velasquez remained purely objective, Goya was to color his impression with his own personality and thus give to his portraits a vigor and vitality that Velasquez's lacked.

One of Goya's greatest paintings is the *Execution of May 3* (Fig. 75), completed in 1814. It depicts a group of Spanish persons being slaughtered by the French soldiers of Napoleon I on May 3, 1808. Its greatness resides in its rising above the merely topical and becoming a universalized comment upon the bestiality of war. The soldiers are represented as a machine in contrast with the disorganized mass of humanity. The treatment of the figures is impressionistic, but the color is far removed from the optical realism of Velasquez. It is expressionistic or emotional in the manner of Grünewald, with off-yellows, brick reds, and whites spotted against a murky and ominous background of deadened greys, all of which accentuate the pitilessness of the murder. The figure with upflung arms, maddened with hatred but resolute, recalls a crucified Christ in his posture. Certainly he is the only one of the group who confronts the machine of war without quailing. Most of the others represent a peasantry terror-stricken and filled with despair. Goya's attitude toward the corrupt Church of his period is strongly stated in the weak and flinching monk with his dissolute face and fear-ridden eyes. There is satiric comment in the fact that it is the simple peasant who faces death while the representative of the Church quails before it. (Goya was to make many other attacks upon the clerics, depicting them as monsters sucking the blood of the country, preaching as parrots, or blessing the death of Truth.)

Goya at one time during his life expressed an indebtedness to Rembrandt. Without doubt the spotlighting of the figures in this and other compositions and his occasional use of backlighting with forms silhouetted against it recall the work of Rembrandt, but the influence is only superficial. Goya was never interested in the study of atmosphere. The darks that surround his spots of light are always without depth; they never suggest the unlimited space that Rembrandt's richly vibrant darks achieve. His light also flattens rather than models or projects. In general, the limitless space of Rembrandt or the deep and limpid space of Poussin have here been flattened. From Goya's time onward, the space enclosed in the picture frame will become increasingly shallow until, in the 20th century, many artists will construct their pictures in flat planes upon the surface of the canvas.

The *Execution of May 3* has been called Romantic. Technically, the term may mean the coloristic tendencies already noted in the Renaissance, especially in the north of Italy, in contrast to the serene and evenly lighted surfaces of Classicism. As a term applying to one period in European art in the 19th century, it implies an escape from the industrialized present either backward into the past or forward into a better future. Such a definition, however, is far from complete. The *Execution of May 3* is neither the one nor the other. In more general terms, Romanticism means a return to a strong individualism and an insistence upon the right of the artist to express his emotions and feelings with respect to his subject matter. It involves a retreat of man into himself, and, since this was a period of tensions and rebellions, the work of Romanticism was frequently preoccupied with death and despair. The retreat of man into himself was to be given a scientific basis in the 20th century in the psychoanalysis of Freud. Goya's *Execution* contains many of these qualities considerably before such a mood became explicit in France and eventually spread through other European countries and the United States. It is a contemporary scene of tragedy commented upon by the artist; it is this element of social criticism which removes it from a strictly realistic representation. Other comments upon war are to be found in Goya's series of etchings called the *Disasters of War*, among which are some of the most vivid and forceful illuminations of war's depravity.

Simultaneously Goya was to explore other avenues which would not be well trod until the late 19th and early 20th centuries. One of these, to be called "Expressionism," was concerned mainly with the emotional aspects of a subject. There are expressionistic elements in the *Execution,* but a discharge of emotion does not sweep all parts of the picture together until later in his life in such a painting as *Old People Eating Their Porridge,* where the darks swallow the lights, the color is reduced to a rich monochrome, and the application of the paint becomes broad and slashing. The concentration here is upon an expression of the absolute futility of old age, and, to retain the full force of that expression, no concession is made to nuances and subtleties.

Another of these avenues, to be called "Surrealism," was the attempt to depict the subconscious as manifested through dreams. Goya was one of the first artists to delve beneath the crust of civilized society and expose its hidden lusts and brutalities. These were the subject of many of his etchings in two other series that he printed toward the end of his life: the *Caprichios* (Caprices) and the *Proverbios* (Proverbs), which have fallen under the scrutiny of present-day psychoanalysts with, as yet, no final interpretations. In these, also, he attacked the superstitions and hypocrisies of his day. The etching, *On a Dry Branch* (Fig. 76), is but a minor illustration of the devastating forcefulness of his attacks. Goya left no written explanation of his themes, partly because it would have been unsafe for him to do so. It has been suggested that *On a Dry Branch* represents one of the cults then active in Spain. Goya here warns us to beware of small groups who remove themselves from society in the belief that they alone have an answer. The foundations upon which they rest are rotten. The hidden hands of the participants suggest idleness. The character of the leader (in the plaid robe) as

ROMANTIC PAINTING

an impostor is pointed up by his partially obscured companion, whose shadowed face turns away from the group in boredom. It is of interest to observe that the women strongly outnumber the men in the audience.

The three works that have been illustrated give only facets of Goya's career. The complexity of his work may be realized in a few examples from the twenty-eight years between 1800 and his death in 1828. During this time he produced the *Maja Desnuda,* one of the most luscious and seductive nudes that can be found in the history of art; the *Execution of May 3,* a bitter diatribe against war; *Esto es Peor* (This is Worse), one of his etchings in the *Disasters of War,* which gives a realistic portrayal of a dismembered nude male spitted upon the sharp branch of a tree; certain group scenes recalling his first sketch for the Royal Tapestry Works; and a painting, *Saturn Devouring His Sons,* where the horror is increased by the thick and shaggy technique and the violent contrasts of light and dark. These represent a movement back and forth between eroticism and satire and a fluctuation in style in a brief span of years that we have not before encountered in any single artist.

The delight in surface and texture, the viciousness of attack, the mixture of styles, and the expressed idea of the nothingness of life, all apparent in the work of Goya, will take on added interest when Picasso is studied later. On occasion, although all belong to the field of Western art, the nationality of an artist has peculiar relevance. Goya and Picasso, both Spaniards, returned frequently to tradition; both have a decided unevenness in their work, with moments of extraordinary brilliance and moments of deadness and lacklustre; both on occasion returned to their earlier styles and sometimes used several styles simultaneously. In this respect, one is made aware of the fact that the Spaniard is a man of passion rather than of intellect. He is thus spontaneous and closer to nature. His reaction is likely to be immediate and explosive. His work is not tempered by thought and tends therefore to be fitful. He is concerned more with the raw materials of art than with their refinement. The abstractions of Braque, a Frenchman, are ordered, calm, and intellectual; those of Picasso, a Spaniard, may be often violent, distorted, and emotional.

Fig. 75. Goya, *Execution of May 3, 1808* (1814), Prado, Madrid (*Anderson*)

Fig. 76. Goya, *On a Dry Branch, ca.* 1820–1824.

Both Goya and Picasso tend to assimilate life by their own being. The very presence of this wholeness permits conflicting tendencies to coexist and may explain in each the existence of both hardness and humanity, of both conservatism and rebellion. It is in keeping with the Spanish temperament that Goya should remark that there are only light and shade, and that painting consists wholly in sacrifices and in accents. Color is the primary element for the simple reason that it is the spontaneous gift of nature to the artist, whereas line and composition are later elements requiring cogitation and therefore interfering with the first impact of nature. There is, as a result, in both artists a rawness that offends those who have been trained in the intellectualities of the Renaissance.

Recommended reading:
Benno Fleischmann, *Francisco Goya,* Vienna, Otto Lorenz Verlag, n.d.
Jean Adhémar, *Les Caprices de Goya,* Paris, Fernand Hazan, 1948. Vol. II of Bibliothèque Aldine des Arts.
Harry B. Wehle, *Fifty Drawings by Francisco Goya,* New York, Metropolitan Museum of Art, 1941.

VII

CONTEMPORARY ART

THE TWENTIETH CENTURY AND ITS ANTECEDENTS[1]

THE GREAT PERIODS OF CULTURAL HISTORY do not readily conform to the arbitrary divisions of our calendars. It is an easy error to assume that cultural periods follow each other in the same fashion as days and years, and that various movements can be said to have begun at an exact time in history. As a matter of fact, the process of cultural change can best be understood as a continuous one in which older ideas gradually transform themselves into new concepts and develop into new ways and forms.

When this gradual process has developed to a certain point, it often happens that great monuments are created which summarize the age, and later on, when the passage of time has permitted us to view the past with a measure of objectivity, we may find it possible and useful to make certain general statements about a period. But when we do so, when we say, for example, that the early 19th century is "Romantic," or that man in the Middle Ages was "other-worldly," we must always bear in mind that what we say is true only to a limited extent. What we really mean when we make such general statements is that at a particular time in history certain tendencies are so widespread and influential that they may be said to characterize that time. It is important, however, that we not lose sight of the fact that these widespread tendencies are themselves in the process of transformations which may later on characterize another age, and that no period in history is exclusively one thing or another.

Now, it is through the medium of art that man has tried in all his history to give expression to what we may call problems of the human condition. For art, in the last analysis, is an affirmation of a point of view and a statement of a philosophy of living. We know something, for example, of what the Greeks thought about the relationship of man to his world from the buildings they erected, the statues they carved, and the books they wrote. The attitudes of Renaissance man are expressed not only in his direct statements but in his painting and his architecture as well. For all men are part and parcel of the times in which they live: their ideas, their feelings, their values, are products of the culture they have inherited, modified by the transmission of this culture through the individual. It is in this fashion that the continuous movement of culture progresses: each man modifies, to a greater or lesser extent, what he has inherited from the past, and in his modification he adds a part of himself. Ultimately the modifications and additions become so marked that we can say that a new period, or a new movement, has been born.

If we attempt to come to some conclusions about what the art of man has in common, without regard to the particular age which produced it or to the particular form which it took, we will see that all of it represents, above all else, an expression of an attitude towards man. For man has always been the overwhelmingly interesting subject to man, and it is himself whom man has always tried to understand. When he has explored the nature of the physical universe, it has been to gain understanding of himself. When he has devoted himself to understanding the nature of God, it has been to gain knowledge of his origin and of his destination. For of all the forms of earthly life, man alone has consciousness of self, and it is a very lonely and very terrifying position which he thereby occupies. He finds himself unable, because of his nature, to be content with mere survival; he needs desperately to know

[1]Programs A and B.

who he is, where he comes from, and where he is going. Man is singularly alone on this earth, conscious of his difference and conscious of his similarity to other forms of life, possessed of a faculty which demands answers because it is equipped to handle answers. Not knowing who he is, nor why he is here, nor where he is going, man has always tried to define himself, which is another way of saying that he has always tried to understand himself. The artistic expressions of man represent above all these definitions of himself, his beliefs, and his attitudes. It is for this reason that when we see the symmetry of a Greek statue we may know that Greek man conceived himself in this way, just as the representations of the Last Judgment by the medieval artists give us yet another definition.

Now, in the 19th century a number of major attitudes came to full development which from that time on strongly influenced the ways in which men tried to achieve understanding of their own behavior. In the first place, the continuity of 18th-century culture had been violently interrupted by the French Revolution, which had turned the major attention and energies of men to social and political ideals. The period of the Revolution itself had been so stormy that there was little time for other than political action, and the energies of the artists were often devoted to the promotion of social causes. But even after the actual strife was over, the effects of the Revolution upon men's attitudes remained strong and gave rise to the fundamental assumption that answers to human problems were to be found in the realm of concrete social and political action and theory. There were partisans in the early 19th century of all shades of political theory: monarchists who wanted a restoration of the deposed Bourbon kings, republicans who fought for a type of social democracy with representative government, adherents of the Bonaparte rule of authority, advocates of a return to churchly government. But all of them, no matter how violently they opposed each other, were making in effect an assumption about the nature of good and evil: that the answers to problems were to be found in the social and political fields.

At the same time, the 19th century saw the development of what has come to be known as the Industrial Revolution and the technological civilization which it brought in its train. It is quite true that more goods could be produced by fewer workers, but it had the unfortunate effect of destroying the guild system and the organizations of craftsmen which had until then served as an effective link with the cultural past. For craftsmen, regardless of the field in which they work, are artisans who create, and their ideas and attitudes are embodied in their creations. From generation to generation there is more than skill and dexterity which is transmitted; there is the sense of individual and qualitative sensitivity which is the supreme gift of the artist and which enables him to put into his work something of himself as well as something of his past. For this reason the minor arts of human culture—the vases and tapestries and bowls and rings and tables—had been until the French Revolution affirmations of human attitudes as important and significant as the buildings, paintings, and writings. The organized guilds, with their traditions of craftsmanship, had served as the medium of transmission for the culture of the past: when the artisans, as a result of the Industrial Revolution, became mere tenders of machines on piecework, isolated laborers with nothing but their time to sell, engaged in producing not individual expressions but stereotyped, standardized products, the isolation of the artist from the past, which had occurred with such explosion during the French Revolution, was confirmed.

Thus, in terms of the two great revolutions, the political French Revolution and the economic Industrial Revolution, the 19th century saw the beginnings of the alienation of the artist, not only from his cultural heritage but from his own contemporaries. He became a disoriented individual, working quite alone, not of this time nor of this place. And more important, he worked in a society which was not interested in him, which considered him as an eccentric, which in all its values and in all its aims tended to repudiate not only what he was doing but his very profession of artist as well. For the 19th century was, in general, most interested in finding answers to human problems in terms of the biological and social sciences, which seemed to offer, if only they were pursued with sufficient energy, the solution to everything.

The artist did not fail to react to his new position in the world, and it is only natural that, finding himself in a state of cultural chaos where the older values had been disrupted and no new ones born to replace them, he should feel a deep need for some sense of authority and for some connection with the past. During the early part of the 19th century the artist had suffered deeply and poignantly: he had retired and nursed his wounds, he had lamented his position, he had bewailed his state and "troubled deaf Heaven with his bootless cries." He had sought solace in nature, in the primitive virtues of simple people, in the unspoiled simplicity of the desert island, in the contemplation of human beauty. His heroes had, like Atala, found peace among the Indians or, like Paul and Virginia, in the sweet innocence of the natural life. He had spoken in lovely lines to his loves; he had, like De Lamartine and De Musset, sung the haunting beauty of the seasons. But his need for belonging, his need for ending his personal frustration, led him to look for authority in the past and to set up his own authority in the present.

The search for authority in the past found expression in the 19th century in the revivals of the Classical and medieval styles, which were used as general models. Now, just as it is true that the art forms of a period are expressions of the affirmations and attitudes of that period, it is equally true that they cannot be expressions of the attitudes of another time. The *Parthenon* represents an integral harmony between the architect and the Greek culture which produced him, and as such it is eternally beautiful and forever gratifying to the beholder. But the *Parthenon,* set down, let us say, between two office buildings in New York, or on the main street of Lansing, would be offensive in its disharmony with its surroundings, and it would represent nothing of the contemporary times. Thus in the 19th century the Classical and medieval revivals were only attempts to find authority in the past which resulted in many instances in disharmonious jumbles and mixtures which were neither one thing nor the other, and which were certainly not expressive of the 19th century except insofar as they exemplified the alienation of the century from its past and from itself.

The effort to bring order out of chaos also found expression in the growth and development of the Academies, bodies of men charged with laying down certain rules which were to govern the production of art. It was felt that in these Academies would be found the stability which was lacking, and that in obeying the rules the artists would in effect be following meaningful precepts. But the Academies made of the artist at best a slavish follower of rules, no longer an individual but a mass-produced technician whose products lacked meaning and significance. Painters were advised, for example, to consult nature with caution, to treat only noble subjects, preferably from the Classics, to emphasize linear drawing rather than color. It is not that such rules, or even their opposites, are in themselves right or wrong: it is that the artistic function is stifled and suppressed by rules which do not arise from the nature of the special problem but are laid down to be followed by everybody, presumably without change.

Thus the artist in the 19th century was in need of stability in a disordered world of tremendous change. Many found it in revivals, many in academies and formal regulation; still others took over in their work the attitudes which the social and biological sciences had developed.

From the development of the biological sciences had sprung a conception of man as the product of his heredity, of his genes, chromosomes, and eugenic history. In terms of this conception man is the sum total of his physical make-up. This view has an important corollary in philosophy: if man is the product of his hereditary composition, he is not responsible for his own conduct. If he be morally reprehensible or a virtual idiot, it is because of the stock from which he springs and not because of any moral or spiritual flaw. In such a view man tends to have no control over his own destiny, and while he may gain some advantage from his biological irresponsibility, by the same token he loses any right to achieve that human dignity which stems from the choice of one's own condition.

On the other hand, the social scientists, men such as Proudhon, Saint-Simon, Engels, and Marx, saw man as the product not so much of his physical as of his social and economic environment, and tended to understand his behavior in these terms. Emma Bovary, the heroine of Flaubert's novel *Madame Bovary,* is an example from fiction of this point of view. Her moral downfall, the breaking up of her family, her ultimate degradation and death, are conceived by Flaubert as having been brought about by the nature of her society, and while he does not in any sense condone her conduct, he none the less asks his reader in effect to understand and to sympathize with Emma, as the unfortunate victim of a social order to which she could not adjust.

These attitudes have in common the conception of man as the strengthless pawn of some larger force, the existence of which is implicit in them. The force may be the social order, the biological structure, the physical world, or any combination of these, which moves men and which men can neither escape nor resist. A tendency arises to conceive the world in terms of large, orderly systems: the economic pattern which Marx outlined, the evolutionary pattern which Darwin noted, the hereditary pattern which forms the basis for most of Zola's novels. In criticism the 19th century produces men like Taine, who understand art as a product of certain fixed forces coming together at particular times. In all the fields of human thought, the 19th century sees the application of systematic principles to human effort and to the problem of understanding man. The systems are different, often opposite and contradictory, but they are for all their many points of difference systems none the less, and it is not hard to understand why such systematization should have been attractive to men without direction, from whom the sense of belonging and the stability of tradition had been stripped with such explosive force.

If at the early part of the 19th century the artist felt himself to be alone and disconnected from meaningful tradition, if he sought a way out by having recourse to the past or by taking comfort from the social and physical sciences, in the latter part of the century a reaction once again set in. The scientific and systematic mind was seemingly able to explain everything: as Huxley pointed out, all that was wrong in society was ascribable only to the imperfect application of the scientific method. Progress was inevitable through the knowledge which the physical sciences could provide. But this attitude tended to leave out something which was of paramount and supreme significance, the nature not of man in general but of man in particular. Men asked themselves whether it was really possible to explain the genius of Shakespeare in any systematic way; whether one could really learn anything about the beauty of a Mozart sonata by tearing the piano apart and learning everything about how it was made. For it came to strike men that useful as systematic knowledge was, it shed much light upon the things which men had in common and little upon the things that set men apart from one another.

This reaction led to important developments in the arts. In painting, for example, there developed an emphasis upon the transmission through the medium of color and form of the impact of the subject upon the artist, of the way in which the artist saw his subject at a given instant, as if he suddenly opened his eyes and transmitted that first blinding view, full of color and form and feeling, which precedes careful analysis. Art of this nature is an art of the senses rather than of the intellect, of feelings rather than of ideas, and it is significant because in choosing to transmit his impression the artist is in reality making a choice of values and is saying that what is important is that the viewer, instead of merely observing the reaction of the artist, must become a participant in the artist's feeling as well. In short, in this fashion the artist re-establishes his integrity and his importance as an individual man and, in addition, re-establishes the importance and integrity of the observer, who has an active, meaningful role to play in the total effect of the work. The poems of Baudelaire, for example, are devoted to the reproduction in words of the most subtle sensory and highly personal reactions, and the same tendencies may be found in the music of Debussy or in the symbolic works of Mallarmé, whose verse can only be understood in terms of himself.

In the sciences this reaction towards subjectivity found a counterpart in the work of Freud and Jung, whose researches form the base for the modern psychiatric sciences. These men, not artists in our sense of the word, attempted in their work to find an answer to human problems in terms of the individual himself, of his *own* history even to his prenatal days. They developed a vast field of learning in which much was found out that had not been suspected before about the nature of the mind, the influences of symbols, the needs, drives, and motives of human conduct. But instead of considering the individual as the product of one thing or another, the psychiatric sciences chose to understand the individual as the product of himself and went to him as the source of information and knowledge.

Thus the 20th century opened upon a reaction to a complex of forces which had characterized the 19th, and it is not surprising that in the arts the reflection of this reaction should be immediately evident. It took two major forms: the emphasis of the interior subjective study of man, and the breakdown of form. The two are not entirely separate.

If man is to be understood in terms of himself, it is clear that the position of the author with respect to his material must radically alter. He can no longer stand *outside* the narrative, directing it, commenting upon it, entering from time to time to make an observation. In the traditional narrative there was an effort to re-create reality, but reality was understood as external reality, the episodes and happenings of people. The events in fictional lives were perceived from the outside, and took the form they did *because the author so decided*. The reader was in effect an audience seeing something enacted before his eyes but conscious none the less that it was being enacted, that it was apart from him. But it is impossible to see inside a person—the flesh and bone form an impenetrable barrier which the eyes cannot pierce. Yet it was the inner life and the interior man which artists in the early part of our century wished to portray. This end could be accomplished only by going inside the character, by regarding the world not at the direction and discretion of the author, but *as the character himself*. Author merged with character, so that the reader was transformed from a passive viewer of events to an active participant. What the character thought, felt, and suffered was as important as what he did. In fiction this technique is known as "stream-of-consciousness" or sometimes as "interior monologue"; its net effect, however, is to view the world through the mind and eyes of another individual, so that it is once again the individual who becomes important.

In painting, this transformation of emphasis is in one sense easier to see, for it is accompanied for the most part by a serious change of form and design. Much of modern painting is of an abstract character in the sense that the painter wishes to abstract from the world around him certain qualities and attitudes and to place them into meaningful patterns. His aim is to represent the world of internal reality rather than the world of external reality—to paint in effect what is within an individual, either his tensions, hopes, and fears or the ideal order to which he aspires.

With the change in emphasis from the objective to the subjective there came a breakdown in form. This breakdown of the older patterns is quite apparent in the work of Schoenberg in music, Feininger in painting, Joyce in literature, to name but a few. It has in the main two causes. The first is the tendency we all have to confuse form with content, so that when we have something vitally new and different to express we have a strong need to express it in new formal patterns. It is a tendency which operates with extraordinary vigor. It operates also in the reverse way, as when, in wishing to recapture a dead era, as the 16th century tried to recapture the Classical age, we try to do it by copying the form, as if in so doing we could make it live again. It is much like going back to a house where we were once happy and trying to recapture our happiness by living in it again. There is perhaps no greater sadness than the sadness of this futile and poignant quest.

There is, however, a much more valid reason for this breakdown of form, that of necessity. Words in their usual, formal patterns; lines in the traditional shapes and forms; notes in the ordinary scales, represent an imposition of rational order and sequence upon the chaos of the mind. We do not think in grammar, nor do we formulate our ideas in groups of fourteen lines; we do not feel in the whole- and half-steps of the major and minor scales nor see in our minds only the regular patterns of the man-made and natural worlds. Quite to the contrary, our thoughts come in a fantastic jumble, out of sequence, jumping from now to last year to next week to when we were three to when we will be dead; our emotions and feelings run a scale of an infinity of steps, and we see shapes and patterns and ideas and relationships which we alone see and which are not perhaps in the world outside us at all. If we are to give expression to these, we may well feel cramped and imposed upon by the exigencies of formal order; we may want twelve tones rather than eight, six words run together rather than six orderly parts of speech, shapes and forms on our canvas which are not representative of external reality at all. We may rebel against the accepted and orderly pattern because we say that this is not the order to be imposed upon the chaos we wish to represent.

So the 20th century is the century of experimentation in form, of the search for satisfactory media. Some painters have used "collage," for example, which is a word derived from the French word "coller," to paste. They have literally pasted pieces of newspaper and colored cloth, in various shapes, upon their canvases, and produced compositions which were at once paintings and bits of reality cut to the painter's concept of the world. Some artists have used twisted wires instead of marble to create figures, others have worked in new musical materials, making use of all manner of sounds which earlier composers would have rejected out of hand. Photographers have tried new techniques, writers like Joyce invented almost a new language, and there have been efforts to combine different media: words and pictures, painting and objects, the tangible with the intangible, voices with instruments in new combinations. Some of the experimentation has been successful, some of it has not been, but the underlying purpose was the same, to give expression to the interior, personal man and to represent *his* world rather than that of objective reality.

It has been remarked earlier that in the 19th century the artist became separated not only from his culture but from his own times as well. This process, despite the efforts made to seek authority here and stability there, despite the great promise of progress which lent so much optimism to much of the 19th century, has continued even farther in the 20th century. The artist of our own day is alienated not only from a traditional past, but he is no longer writing for his own fellow-men. His loneliness has caused him not only to seek answers in a withdrawal from his own times into the realm of myth, fantasy, and, often enough, nightmare, but in so doing he has arrived at a point where what he is doing is no longer comprehensible to any but a very few who are for the most part of his own ilk. It is as well to face the truth; that when we mention the great names of the 20th century, Joyce, Kafka, Schoenberg, Picasso, Proust, we are mentioning men whose work is not easily understandable to us, whose productions we must study with exceeding care if we are to grasp them. They are at once representative of the century and, in their isolation, representative of the enormous gap which has come to exist between the artist and the people for whom he speaks. It was not always so—in the 17th century, for example, there was congruence of writer and reader: the one wrote for the other who was of his class and viewpoint. But today the men who speak of our century best speak of it obscurely—that is, they are above us and away from us and apart from us. It is not of their doing so much as it is of the nature of the times, in which the artist, repudiated for the most part in the past hundred and fifty years, has been compelled to take refuge among his own kind and to hope that in time we will get to be closer to him again.

The lonely isolation of the modern artist is merely an extreme form of the lonely isolation of all of us. Ours is a much-troubled world in which man is alone as he never was before, an individual of startling perception and self-understanding who none the less may be on the brink of causing his own destruction. In the rise of science, in the placing of all his faith in empirical values, in his belief that happiness is to be achieved in factual knowledge, modern man has isolated himself from his fellows more completely than ever before. It is true that in the first blush of discovery the 19th century tended to overlook the individual, who with justification tried to re-establish himself as the supreme entity. But in delving as far as we have into ourselves, there is the danger that we may have lost sight of other men. Aware of this isolation and of the growing loneliness of man, many modern artists are devoting themselves to finding a satisfactory answer, to finding a means of climbing back once again to the safety of humanity. There is a hunger in man for man, and while many artists have not succeeded in their quests, our century, even at its midpoint, can be said to be one of growing concern with the problems of the moral order of the universe, of faith, of the definition of man as part of a meaningful and significant whole. We will in our search lean heavily upon science, but ultimately the atomic physicist, uniquely in control of the secrets of the universe out of all proportion to the ordinary run of men, will have to come to the artist and to the men who have not forgotten to treasure the humanities and ask them what to do with his knowledge. All the development of culture and civilization, and all the suffering man has undergone in his search for knowledge, will certainly have been in vain if, when the atomic physicist comes, he finds no men who know or remember art; or if they do not tell him to throw the bomb away and use his knowledge to broaden the understanding of man and to make more meaningful his strange, bizarre adventure on earth. If this should happen our century would be perhaps the most wonderful century of all, and that, when we get down to it, is what we would like to be able to think.

Recommended reading:

Lewis Mumford, *Sticks and Stones, a Study of American Architecture and Civilization,* New York, Boni and Liveright, 1924.
Joseph Wood Krutch, *The Modern Temper,* New York, Harcourt, Brace, 1929.
T. S. Eliot, *After Strange Gods,* London, Faber, 1934.
Harold V. Routh, *Towards the Twentieth Century,* New York, Macmillan, 1937.
John H. Randall, *The Making of the Modern Mind,* Boston, Houghton, Mifflin, 1926, Book IV.
Wyndham Lewis, *Time and Western Man,* New York, Harcourt, Brace, 1928.

CONTEMPORARY PAINTING AND ARCHITECTURE

IMPRESSIONISM[1]

BY THE MIDDLE OF THE 19TH CENTURY the inspiration of the Romantic movement had played itself out in painting. Nothing remained but academic repetition of exotic motifs, which had once been fresh and original but which were now stale and tinctured with the sentimental vulgarity of the age. The 19th century had witnessed long since the triumph of the Industrial Revolution and was now complacently subsiding into the spiritual coma of Victorian morality. Certain artists, notably Gustave Courbet and Honoré Daumier in France, reacted against this state of affairs and proclaimed the new doctrine of Realism. It was as an outgrowth of this Realism that the important movement in art known as Impressionism made its appearance.

Realism had already been foreshadowed in some of the later works of Goya. In the hands of Courbet and Daumier it became an art that discarded much of traditional subject matter —not only the lyrical and exotic iconography of Romanticism, but also the major religious and humanist themes, which had become meaningless to a class of art patrons who reckoned vice and virtue in terms of profit and loss, and for whom scientific discoveries had appeared to turn the supernatural into mere superstition. According to the Realists, the job of the artist was to represent reality—social as well as visual reality, the ugly along with the beautiful. "Show me an angel, and I will paint one," declared Courbet. All things were equally worthy of artistic representation, so long as they existed in the real world.

Such a doctrine was bound to be unpalatable at a time when the new industrial squalor was making the real world a less and less attractive place, and when people looked to art for an escape from reality rather than a reminder of it. Moreover, by its insistence on the poverty attendant upon the existing social order, Realism carried with it the insidious connotation that all might not be well with the world, a connotation bound to offend the susceptibilities of the dominant classes.

During the 1870's a group of young artists seceded from Realism to found a new movement in painting known as Impressionism, which to a certain extent avoided these difficulties, although at first it provoked as much opposition as anything that had preceded it. From the conceptual standpoint, the Impressionists differed from the Realists in two important respects. First, though they adhered to the belief that the content of art could be derived from anything existing in the real world, their attitude towards subject matter was totally negative, in that they considered it to play no part whatever in achieving an artistic result. All depended on the way in which the picture was painted; the original subject was a matter of complete indifference. In practice, however, they tended to choose just those types of subjects that the Realists had avoided—sunny landscapes, comfortable scenes of well-fed bourgeois domesticity, the pleasures and dissipations of the Parisian man-about-town.

Secondly, they professed to represent the randomness of things seen in casual vision. The artist had to record exactly what he saw at a given moment, and nothing else. Consequently, many Impressionist works seem to lack the "composed" look to be found in most earlier paintings. They have about them a casual, almost accidental quality, as though the artist had chosen quite arbitrarily to reproduce a particular segment of reality. Sometimes, in fact, the borders of the painting seem to cut off the scene at willfully inauspicious places, with one

[1] Programs A and B.

part of a figure or object inside the picture and the rest omitted. The effect of randomness, however, is perfectly deliberate, and is actually obtained by an arrangement of parts as fastidious as may be found in any other painting.

Implicit in this type of composition is an entirely new attitude towards art, an attitude that has come to be known as "art for art's sake." For the apparently indiscriminate demarcation of the boundaries of the picture tends to deny its referential significance within the world from which it is abstracted. If the edge of the picture cuts off half the figure of a man, whatever meaning may have been attached to the figure as a *man,* as a meaningful unit in a real world, is suppressed, and the half-man becomes little more than an arrangement of shapes and colors.

Hence the value set upon the painting is to be assessed solely in terms of its aesthetic qualities, regardless of the significance of whatever real objects may have occasioned them. The indifference to subject matter is merely another aspect of this same, self-consciously aesthetic attitude.

In sum, what started out to be a realistic description of nature or humanity has ended up as something very different, a picture whose merit depends entirely on its beauty, not on what it depicts.

The Impressionists were not unmindful of the role played by the artist's own sensibility in achieving the desired beauty. Émile Zola, their friend and champion, defined a work of art as "a corner of nature seen through a temperament," and this meant that the artist had to paint a scene not necessarily as it really was, but *as he himself saw it.* That is to say, the Impressionist painter concerned himself less with objective realities than with subjective *appearances,* and set himself to study the means of reproducing such appearances in paint in a spirit of almost scientific rigor. This endeavor is related to the positivist philosophy which flourished during the same period, according to which all true knowledge is based upon the observation of natural phenomena.

Many of the most salient characteristics of Impressionism may be traced to this desire to reproduce appearances. The Impressionists literally record *impressions,* and consequently they tend to endow a painting with the spontaneous qualities of a sketch. Details are either omitted altogether or else rigidly subordinated to the main elements of the design, which are themselves sketched in with broad, carefree touches of color.

As everything, in theory, depends on fleeting visual impressions, it follows that landscapes (or any other scenes) should be painted on the spot and not executed, as in traditional painting, in the falsifying light of the artist's studio. Actually, however, only the stricter doctrinairians like Monet followed this dictum, and most Impressionist landscapes were in fact painted indoors.

Developing their theory along logical lines, the Impressionists realized that the shapes and colors of objects are visualized only in virtue of the light that illuminates them. Consequently, they tended to paint objects not as they are known to be from previous experience, which includes tactile as well as visual images, but as they are defined by light, and to record the space-relations of objects by aerial rather than by linear perspective. This abstraction of the purely visual aspect of experience, in conjunction with the over-all sketchiness of treatment, accounts for the hazy, atmospheric bath of light that seems to envelop so many Impressionist pictures.

The painting of light, in fact, became almost an obsession for men like Monet, Pissarro, Sisley, and Renoir, and it led them to several important technical innovations that have left their mark on all subsequent painting. They discovered, for instance, that shadows in nature are seldom black, but tend to assume colors complementary to those of the directly lighted portions of the objects in question (*e.g.,* the shadowed parts of a yellow object will be purplish in hue.)[2] Accordingly, they abandoned traditional *chiaroscuro*—the method of obtaining relief by employing different values, from light to dark, of the same color—and instead of this they substituted the complement of the original color in the shaded areas, modelling objects through transitions from warm to cool hues, and thereby achieving a much higher over-all value pattern. The Impressionists were by no means first in discovering this method, for several of the great masters of the past had made good use of it, notably Velasquez, by whom they were very much influenced. Nevertheless, the Impressionists were the first to apply it consciously and consistently.

Another theory conditioning Impressionist practice was the idea that all "impure" colors should be eliminated. That is to say, the painter's palette should be restricted to the colors of the rainbow, which, being the sole components of sunlight, should also constitute the sole means of representing natural light in a painting.

Lastly, and perhaps most important of all, the Impressionists applied the principle known as "optical mixture." Instead of mixing paint on the palette in order to obtain the exact color desired, they placed separate touches of "pure" color side by side on the canvas. At a certain distance from the canvas the eye of the spectator will no longer discriminate the touches as separate. Their fusion, which is performed by the eye of the spectator, results in a higher degree of luminosity than can be obtained by their mixture on the palette. For instance, strokes of yellow and blue would be juxtaposed directly on the canvas in order to produce the color green when combined by the eye of the spectator. And the resulting green would be more luminous and intense than would be that obtained by mixing colors on the palette before application. As a result of this procedure, in many Impressionist paintings flat areas of color disappear entirely and are replaced by shimmering patterns of variegated dots which destroy all sharp contours and contribute to the hazy, atmospheric effect.

Before considering the works of any individual artists, it should be emphasized that the different Impressionists adhered to these principles in varying degrees, and that while some artists practiced Impressionism throughout their careers, with others it was no more than a passing, though highly significant, phase.

Recommended reading:
J. Rewald, *The History of Impressionism,* New York, Museum of Modern Art, 1946.
W. Uhde, *The Impressionists,* London, Phaidon, 1937.

[2]The complement of a color is that which lies diametrically opposite to it on a color wheel obtained by disposing the colors of the spectrum in a circle (Fig. 77). Warm colors, those which are located nearer to yellow than to blue, will have for their complements cool colors, those located nearer to blue than to yellow.

All colors have three main distinguishing qualities: *Hue,* the name of the color, *e.g.,* red, green, etc.; *Value,* the lightness or luminosity in a scale ranging through the intermediate grays from white to black; and *Intensity,* the strength or purity of the color.

Two colors may be the same in hue, *i.e.,* both red, and the same in value—one neither lighter nor darker than the other—yet vary greatly in intensity, one a fire-engine red, the other a weaker greyed red comparable to brick. Thus the intensity of a color can range from a neutral grey to full strength.

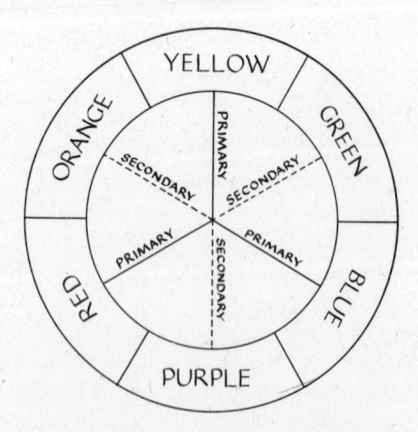

Fig. 77. Standard color wheel showing primary colors and their complements.

CLAUDE MONET (1840-1926)[1]

OF THOSE WHO ESPOUSED IMPRESSIONISM throughout their careers, Claude Oscar Monet must be accounted the most distinguished. He it was who was regarded by the others as the leader of the movement, who exerted the strongest influence in its development, who followed its principles with the most consistent fidelity, and who unwittingly gave it its name (derived from a painting by him entitled *Impression, Sunrise,* exhibited at the first Impressionist show in 1874).

Claude Monet was born in Paris in 1840 but spent most of his early years at the port of Le Havre on the Normandy coast, where his father kept a grocery store. As a schoolboy Monet evinced little interest in his studies. Instead, he attained considerable proficiency in drawing spirited and merciless caricatures of his teachers, some of which came to the notice of Eugène Boudin, a sensitive painter of landscapes and seascapes. Boudin encouraged Monet to become a professional painter, with the result that the young artist decided to pursue his studies seriously in Paris, where he arrived in 1859. Shortly afterwards, however, his work was interrupted by two years of military service, which he spent in Algeria. These years were less unrewarding than might be supposed, for Monet's later preoccupation with color and light undoubtedly sprang to some extent from his early experiences of the hot sun and vivid colors of North Africa. As he himself said, these impressions "contained the germ of my future researches."

On returning to Paris in 1862, Monet entered the studio of Charles Gleyre, whose cold, academic Classicism was hardly likely to commend itself to a young artist already striving for a new freshness of approach towards nature. But it was at Gleyre's studio that Monet met Renoir and other young painters who were groping in the same general direction as himself. Together they formed the nucleus of what was to become the Impressionist movement. Subsequent contact with older artists like Camille Corot, Gustave Courbet, C. F. Daubigny, and Edouard Manet, men who had already revolted against the sterile, machine-like painting of the official Salon, cemented the young men in their determination to create a new art based on direct perception rather than on artifice.

None showed more intransigence in the pursuit of this aim than Monet. Always more partial to pure landscape than his fellows, he soon followed the example of Daubigny in painting directly from nature, executing even the largest canvases in the open air. What is more, having once begun a landscape under given conditions of light, Monet refused to continue his work until these same conditions were duplicated, lest the fidelity of his impression be impaired.

To escape the disturbances of the Franco-Prussian war and the Commune, Monet spent most of the years 1870–1871 abroad, chiefly in England. Here he encountered the works of the English landscapist J. M. W. Turner, who had treated effects of sunlight with a dazzling boldness of color and handling never before attempted in paint. And repelled though he was by Turner's turbulent Romanticism, Monet was nevertheless strongly encouraged and confirmed in the direction which his own art had already assumed—towards a brighter color vocabulary and a heightened perception of fugitive effects of light and atmosphere.

Throughout the sixties and seventies Monet was forced to pay a bitter price for his stead-

[1] Program A.

fast sincerity, suffering neglect, derision, and such extremes of poverty that at times he had not the wherewithal to buy paints or canvas. In 1874 the Impressionists had banded together and held an exhibition of their own, in open competition with the Salon, but their efforts were rewarded only with howls of indignation from both critics and public. Subsequent exhibitions did little to improve the situation, and in the early eighties petty personal quarrels and more serious artistic rifts began to make inroads on the solidarity of the group itself, tending to break up Impressionism as a coherent movement. Henceforth each artist pursued the path of his own choosing.

But by now the opposition of the public was also beginning to disintegrate, and more and more converts among dealers and collectors, on both sides of the Atlantic, joined the small nucleus of those who had remained faithful during the lean years. Monet's later years were blessed with financial affluence and world-wide fame. In 1883 he had moved to a house at Giverny, northeast of Paris, and here he lived quietly, with occasional trips to Holland, London, or Venice as the only interruptions of his work routine, until his death in 1926 at the age of eighty-six. The countryside around Giverny, especially his own delightful garden and its lily-pond, provided the chief artistic inspiration of his later years.

Except for the work of his youth, which still shows traces of the sombre color schemes and muddy shadows of his predecessors, Monet's entire output embodies the characteristics of Impressionism enumerated in the preceding section. In such a work as the *Boats at Argenteuil* at the Boston Museum, done about 1874 (Fig. 78), we see already the Impressionist system of juxtaposing small blobs of pure color, meaningless when looked at closely but forming a spontaneous yet coherent description of appearances when fused by the eye at a distance.

Linear elements, it will be noticed, have practically disappeared from this composition, and even where present, as in the masts of the boats, they are blurred and broken. For lines in nature are actually color transitions, and as they exist only as mental constructs, they cannot figure prominently in an accurate reconstruction of appearances.

Other Impressionist features are equally present in this work. The palette, while not yet completely "pure," is largely confined to rainbow hues. Complementary colors are employed throughout in the shadows, the pinks and yellows of the sunlit houses and trees changing to cool blues and greens in their shaded portions, with the same contrasts repeated in more subtle transitions in the lambent mirroring of these objects in the river. The composition has a carefree, haphazard quality typical of Impressionism; though in actuality Monet and his confrères were seldom as casual as they intended to appear, and the design of the *Boats at Argenteuil* has certain features that tend to recur in their works. The scene is looked down upon from a fairly high vantage point, and the various elements tend to recede into the distance along a diagonal line, in this instance formed by the bank of the river. This method has little in common with the familiar Baroque diagonal, which was used for dramatic purposes. Here we find a flatter, more pattern-forming effect which betrays the influence of Japanese color-prints, imported into France in large quantities in the second half of the 19th century and highly regarded by the Impressionists.

The tranquillity of the scene, its hot, lazy light and atmosphere of summer indolence, is again typical of Impressionism, of an art form that cannot concern itself with narrative or drama but only with those aspects of experience which subsume intrinsically pleasurable or aesthetic qualities. And in the spirit of this work there is something also that is peculiar to Monet's own art, a kind of poetic flavor that can well, though paradoxically, be described as a detached lyricism.

We see more of Monet's personal propensities in a painting of the *Gare St. Lazare* (Fig. 79). He ignores completely the possible social meaning and dramatic potentialities of a mammoth railway station, with its seething bustle of men and machines. Instead he concentrates on the atmosphere of the place, faithfully recording the sunlight that streams in at the glass

Fig. 78. Monet, *Boats at Argenteuil, ca.* 1874, Museum of Fine Arts, Boston (courtesy of Museum of Fine Arts)

panes of the roof and percolates down through clouds of steam and smoke, to form a tracery pattern of light and shade on the ground. The fetid, humid, but impalpable atmosphere is vividly contrasted with the tangible bulk of mechanical contrivances, like the locomotive, that emerge through the haze. Indeed, Monet has cleverly incorporated this contrast into the whole design of the painting, for it will be noticed that the puff of smoke emitted by the locomotive is practically the same shape as the machine itself, except, of course, that it is inverted. Similarly, the strong angle formed by the pitched roof of the station is faintly re-echoed in an inverted angle formed by the skyline beneath it, whose haziness is further contrasted with the locomotive at its apex.

Thus Monet again shows his recurrent interest in a kind of visual counterpoint obtained by contrasting values in objects and their reflections. Here, however, the pattern is more subtle and complex than in the *Boats at Argenteuil,* for it involves not merely contrasts of light but contrasts of atmosphere also. Nor are the reflections simple mirror images, but elements of contrasting identity and texture.

The *Gare St. Lazare* is but one of a number of versions of this subject painted by Monet in 1876–77. It was characteristic of him, especially in his later years, that he should paint numerous versions of the same subject, seen from different viewpoints and under varying conditions of light and atmosphere. Often he would work on several canvases at the same time, moving from one to another as the light changed. The series of *Poplars* (1891), *Haystacks* (1893), *Rouen Cathedral* (1894), and *Waterloo Bridge* (1903–4) are all well known.

As an example of Monet's late style, we may look at one of the many versions of *Rouen Cathedral* (Fig. 80). The subjects of these series are very carefully selected to conform with the painter's visual requirements. It will be noticed that the part of the cathedral painted is an example of *late* French Gothic architecture, with all the flamboyant ornament and complex corrugated surfaces associated with this style. These elaborate surfaces catch the light and break it up into shifting, flickering patterns of great intricacy: a fit challenge for the extraordinary power of observation and manual dexterity which Monet had by now acquired. Color is greyer, less brilliant, and less localized than in his earlier works, but it is also more luminous and more subtly variegated within the limits of a narrow scale of intensity. The texture of the paint is rougher and heavier, the brushwork bolder and more assured.

One no longer feels that Monet is simply painting objects as they are revealed by light. Instead he seems to have taken matter and light and woven them together into a rich, uniform fabric endowed with a kind of substance or texture entirely its own, differing from that of either of its components. This over-all "substance" produces a strange sense of abstract unity, peculiar to certain of Monet's later works. For if the objects depicted appear flimsy (solidity was never a strong point with the Impressionists), the "substance" has power and authority; though the atmosphere is hazier than ever, the conception is crystal clear, and though the composition appears arbitrary, it is nevertheless rhythmical and coherent.

We see some of the same stylistic qualities in the *Waterloo Bridge* of 1903 in the National Gallery at Washington (Fig. 81)—the same bold strokes of the brush and subtle juxtapositions of warm and cool hues of low intensity, giving an over-all greyish tonality. Here, as usual, the landscape is seen from a height, thereby enabling the artist to record varying atmospheric conditions at different distances from the point of vision. In the foreground the air is

Fig. 79. Monet, *Gare St. Lazare,* 1876–1877, Louvre, Paris (*Archives photographiques*)

CONTEMPORARY PAINTING AND ARCHITECTURE

clear, but smoke hovers about the bridge in the middle distance. Beyond the bridge it becomes clear again, while a dense blanket of vapor and mist envelops the background across the river, leading the eye on into the hazy infinity of the horizon. Thus is generated a soft, rhythmical alternation of atmospheric textures which enhances the mood of dreamy introspection pervading this and so many of Monet's other late works. The mood reaches its culmination in his last great series, the *Water Lilies,* in the Orangerie at Paris. His obsession with reflected images at last acquires explicit meaning, for here one cannot but realise that the pond at Giverny has become essentially an introspective mirror of the artist's own soul.

Monet lived long enough to see his own art not only accepted by those who had once scorned it, but outdated by new advances which have revolutionized the form and content of painting. Of late there has consequently been a tendency to belittle him in comparison with those of his contemporaries who forsook Impressionism and anticipated the abstraction or expressionism of modern painting. Monet's art, however, must also be judged on its own merits, and not merely on the merits (or shortcomings) of 20th-century painting. Admittedly his range is narrow, but within the rigorous limits which he set himself, he achieved a purity of expression equalled by very few of his contemporaries. And his is the most authoritative text of an artistic doctrine which dominated a whole chapter of art history.

Fig. 80. Monet, *Rouen Cathedral,* 1894, Metropolitan Museum of Art, New York (courtesy of the Metropolitan Museum of Art)

Fig. 81. Monet, *Waterloo Bridge,* 1903, National Gallery of Art, Washington, D.C. (Chester Dale Collection)

Recommended reading:
Daniel Wildenstein, *A Loan Exhibition of Paintings by Claude Monet,* New York, Wildenstein, 1945.

PIERRE AUGUSTE RENOIR (1841–1919)[1]

NOTHING IN ART HISTORY is more astonishing than that a series of narrow dogmas such as the principles of Impressionism should, instead of stultifying all who had contact with them, beget a variety of major creative talents who between them changed the course of Western painting. Renoir, Degas, Cézanne, Gauguin, Van Gogh, and Seurat all practiced Impressionism at one point or another in their careers, and all, in greater or lesser measures, forsook this type of art later in life in favor of a more subjective approach towards nature. Renoir always remained more faithful than the rest, for he had been one of the original enthusiasts of the movement, and its principles were doubtless more deeply embedded in his consciousness. Yet he too felt in time, what Monet never did, that a close adherence to the movement cramped the full range of his expression.

Pierre Auguste Renoir, son of a tailor, was born at Limoges in 1841. His family moved to Paris, where as a young boy he was apprenticed to a porcelain painter. Later he found employment painting fans, window-shades, screens, etc. It is quite probable that his later love for strong, glistening colors owed something to his experience in these fields, and the almost effeminate charm pervading much of his work, a quality that persistently conjures up memories of 18th-century Rococo art, may perhaps also be traced to his early training in the decorative arts.

Having decided to become a professional painter instead of a decorative craftsman, Renoir entered the studio of Gleyre in 1862. Here he met Monet and other young rebels of his own generation. For several years, however, Renoir, having fallen heavily under the influence of the realist Courbet, lagged behind the others in the progress towards a brighter palette and a more spontaneous view of nature. But at the end of the sixties he turned definitely to the path pioneered by Manet and Monet, and continued to follow it for a dozen years or more, himself contributing notably to the growth of the movement. Probably it was he who first consciously restricted his palette to the colors of the rainbow.

One of his most important pictures of this time is the famous *Moulin de la Galette* ("biscuit-mill"), painted in 1876 (Fig. 82). The Moulin de la Galette was an old mill located in the bohemian quarter of Paris known as Montmartre, which had been turned into a cafe where open-air dances were held for the youth of the neighborhood. In his picture Renoir shows us a happy throng of revellers capering in and out of brilliant sunshine which sparkles through the leafy branches overhead. He painted the scene on the spot; perhaps only by so doing could he have captured its exuberance with such fidelity. This is the quintessence of Impressionism. The composition looks spontaneous as a snapshot, the structure as flimsy as it would have appeared to a casual onlooker; even the brush strokes seem carefree as the merrymakers they describe. Yet cunning entered this picture also, for the design is hardly as haphazard as might be thought on first sight. It is, indeed, a characteristic example of the influence on Impressionism of the Japanese woodcut, whence Renoir almost certainly derived the idea of observing the scene from a height and leading the eye into the distance along diagonal lines. In this instance the diagonal movement starts with the seat lolled upon by the young lady in the foreground and is continued by the disposition of the table and of the figures grouped about it. The pairs of dancers to the left are also placed in such a way as to carry the eye into the distance along a second diagonal which re-echoes the first. Yet, just as in the Japanese woodcut, the effect of this recession is not to provide a powerful illusion of depth,

[1] Program B.

but simply to impose an unfamiliar, and therefore striking, pattern design on what would otherwise appear a rather commonplace scene. Emphasis on depth or configuration was quite foreign to Impressionism, for our apprehension of this quality is only partially ocular and depends to a large extent on previous experience.

The pattern effect is cleverly orchestrated by a color scheme in full accord with Impressionist principles. Though probably black in the originals, the costumes worn by the men and women in the foreground are painted in dark blues and purples which contrast boldly with the white stripes in the dress of the aforementioned seated lady. Shadows cast on the ground by the trees are likewise blue, but of a lighter shade, and these in turn form a softer contrast with the white spots of ground directly lit by the sun. This secondary color contrast parallels the secondary diagonal of the dancers moving in and out of the light. The yellowish green of the trees and small touches of red relieve an otherwise predominantly cool color scheme.

Neither in this nor in many of the other works of the seventies does Renoir evince the disciplined control in the handling of brilliant colors to be found in Monet's works of the same period. On the other hand, Renoir achieves a unique combination of bold execution and feathery lightness of touch. His colors seem to glow with a soft, warm, almost velvety sheen.

These qualities are allied to a yet more fundamental difference manifested in his work. Renoir's view of the world is basically anthropocentric. Though he painted numerous landscapes, he has little of Monet's sympathy for landscape in itself. He is far more concerned with people. In particular, he loved to record the simple pleasures and rituals of everyday bourgeois life, especially those in which woman figured prominently. For by virtue both of his early training and of his innate gifts, Renoir was above all a painter of women, capable of endowing the sex with a mixture of fragile elegance and colorful, sensuous vigor that had hardly been witnessed in art since the 18th century.

It was owing to the possession of these aptitudes that Renoir suffered less neglect than many of his Impressionist colleagues. Rich bourgeois matrons were so allured by the charms of his palette that they were willing to stomach the odium of Impressionism and commission him to paint their portraits. Renoir played his part in return by relinquishing a strict adherence to Impressionist principles in the execution of such commissions.

In his role as society portraitist, Renoir may be seen at his best in such a work as the *Portrait of Mme. Henriot,* in the Levy Collection, New York (Fig. 83). Here the painter has caught with extraordinary skill the essentially feminine charms of his sitter. Ineffable delicacies of form and feature, realized in pastel shades of blue, green, and pink, give the lady an air of aristocratic grace that might well verge on over-refinement were it not offset by her humorously arched eyebrows, her vivacious brown eyes, and the warm, tremulous flicker of a smile that plays across her lips. The clasping movement of the lightly sketched-in hands also contributes to the nervous vitality of the total impression.

Such a work inevitably calls to mind the great portraits of La Tour, Fragonard, Gainsborough, and other 18th-century masters. But none approached Renoir in sheer lightness of touch, nor succeeded in bathing his women in so aromatic a perfume. Mme. Henriot fuses

Fig. 82. Renoir, *Moulin de la Galette,* 1876, John Hay Whitney Collection, New York

into an atmosphere so intimate that its substance seems but a sublimation of her own physical presence. The configurations of her face and body seem wafted on to the canvas with the subtlest juxtapositions of warm and cool tints. No gross modelling, no masculine contour, no violence of light and shade, is allowed to disturb this etherealized apotheosis of the boudoir.

A visit to Italy in 1881–1882 appeared to convince Renoir that his art was deficient in certain qualities revealed to him in the works of Raphael and other great Italian masters. He must have realized that the gains of Impressionism necessarily involved sacrificing much that was of value in the great traditions of Western art. At all events, during the next few years we find him abandoning a strictly Impressionist attitude in favor of more solidly constructed forms, more incisive contours, and more obvious, stable, "Classical" compositions. Assiduously he set himself to learn how to *draw:* an attainment that production of the hazy, luminous effects of Impressionism had scarcely seemed to demand.

The most ambitious result of this new phase of his development is the *Bathers* ("*Les Grandes Baigneuses*") of 1884–7 in the Philadelphia Museum (Fig. 84). The subject of this picture eminently expresses Renoir's natural proclivities. He was ever responsive to the gay, colorful, and sensuous aspects of life, and as time went on, more and more of his efforts were bent towards recording the voluptuous shapes and soft, creamy skins of bathing girls. Here, however, his natural exuberance seems a bit inhibited by the self-consciously monumental design and academic drawing of the figures. The three nude girls frolicking at the bank of a stream are arranged with studied care into a triangular composition of obvious Renaissance derivation. Their attitudes are intended to be spontaneous, but instead their poses seem rigid and frozen by the hard contours they are enclosed within. Certainly, this new linear style yields more perfect drawing and greater solidity than is to be found in any of Renoir's earlier works, but these gains fail to outweigh the accompanying loss of freshness and freedom. The colors, too, have a lacklustre quality alien to the very essence of Renoir's vision.

Happily, this phase did not last very long, for in the nineties Renoir was able to achieve a synthesis of his Impressionist and "Classicist" manners that not only preserved some of the virtues of both but also superadded qualities not previously to be found in his work. This, his last, style is well exemplified by the *Three Bathers* in the Cleveland Museum, painted in 1897 (Fig. 85). It is a work which in virtue of the very similar subject lends itself to com-

Fig. 83. Renoir, *Portrait of Mme. Henriot*, ca. 1877, Levy Collection, New York

Fig. 84. Renoir, *Bathers* [*Les Grandes Baigneuses*], 1884–1887, Philadelphia Museum of Art, Carroll Tyson Collection (by permission)

parison with the Philadelphia *Bathers* of ten years earlier. Both works portray three buxom girls frisking at the water's edge, both are arranged in roughly triangular compositions, and both achieve greater solidity than pure Impressionism permits. Here the resemblance ends, for whereas in the earlier picture the design seems contrived, in the later it appears a natural consequence of the action depicted; whereas in the former the outlines are precise and linear, in the latter they are soft and hazy; and whereas color in the former is dull, in the latter it is strong and high-keyed.

Renoir has indeed reverted to more conventional methods of modeling in chiaroscuro in order to obtain the heavy plasticity of the Cleveland bathers. He has largely discarded "optical mixture" and uses the opposition of warm and cool tones only sparingly. But the strength of internal modeling enables him once more to soften the contours, broaden the brush strokes, and reduce the shapes to a massive simplicity, thus recapturing something of the Impressionist spirit while preserving and even surpassing the monumentality of the Philadelphia picture.

Though individual configurations are modeled in terms of value rather than of color, the over-all lighting is diffused and brilliant. On the ample bodies of the girl bathers its disposition reminds one of the concentric color bands of a contour map, with highlights reserved for the soft, rounded tumuli of breasts and thighs, the values darkening in the descent across dimpled valleys of flesh to the hollows of backs and groins. Similar treatment is accorded other elements like the girls' brazen hair; and since the general color scheme is of quite extraordinary heat, the entire picture appears to vibrate with torrid pulsations of color.

The girls themselves are pure creatures of the senses, playful young animals who transcend mere carnality by virtue of that instinctive grace and enormous vitality which only animals possess. Warm flesh tones dominate the whole scene, challenged only by the red-hot splash of drapery on the right, which is the red of blood.

Renoir continued to paint in this same general manner until his death in 1919, turning out painting after painting peopled with similar voluptuous nudes. In old age his hands became so paralysed with rheumatism that he was unable to hold a paint brush. Yet he continued to paint to the very end, with the help of his nurse, who strapped brushes to his wrist and squeezed out the colors on the palette. These later works often suffer from weak drawing, but the vitality of their color is perhaps greater than ever. Red finally emerges as the dominant color, which all others subserve.

It is a far cry indeed from the delicate features of Mme. Henriot to the lusty loins of Gabrielle, the servant girl who was Renoir's favorite model in his later years. But though its

Fig. 85. Renoir, *Three Bathers*, 1897, Cleveland Museum of Art (by permission)

texture changes, the common thread of muliebrity runs continuously through his work, and to the rendering of each type he brought to bear the just means of plastic expression. We do not look to Renoir for profound intellectual or spiritual values; we do, however, see in him the most persuasive apology for healthy sensualism in art since Rubens.

Recommended reading:
T. Duret, *Renoir,* New York, Crown, 1937.
A. C. Barnes and V. De Mazia, *The Art of Renoir,* New York, Harper, 1935.

POST-IMPRESSIONISM

PAUL CÉZANNE (1839–1906)[1]

TOWARD THE END OF THE 19TH CENTURY, a new artistic style known as Post-Impressionism sprang out from and reacted against the now flourishing Impressionist movement. Like Renoir, the Post-Impressionists founded their art upon the fresh resources of color and light revealed by the Impressionists but rebelled against the flimsy construction and apparently random composition enjoined by Impressionist principles. Unlike Renoir, they were prepared to abandon the Impressionist quest for visual imitation in an effort to increase solidity of structure and clarity of design, to paint the permanent substance rather than the fugitive appearance. Instead of reproducing the extensions of nature by analyzing their apparent components of color and light, they employed these and other components to create new patterns which, based ultimately though they were upon the configurations of nature, reflected a synthesis conceived in the mind of the artist. This mental re-ordering of nature varied widely from painter to painter; in some, like Van Gogh and Munch, it took the form of distortion for expressionistic effect, while in others, like Cézanne and Gauguin, the emphasis lay upon the re-ordering in itself, upon transforming the amorphous and chaotic raw materials provided by nature into a coherent synthetic product endowed with a plastic unity of its own.

These artists never completely shed their allegiance to nature. Yet by disintegrating natural shapes they paved the way for the dominant abstract and expressionist tendencies of early 20th-century art.

Of the Post-Impressionist artists Paul Cézanne was beyond question the most influential. He was born in 1839 at Aix-en-Provence, in southern France. His father, a domineering *nouveau riche* banker, vigorously discouraged his early artistic leanings, compelling him to study for the law. But Paul, supported by his boyhood friend Émile Zola, finally had his own way and abandoned legal studies in favor of an artistic career. He came to Paris in 1861 and there studied at the Académie Suisse, an informal art school. Soon afterwards he became discouraged and returned to Aix, where his father promptly ensconced him in the family bank.

In the following year, however, he resumed his interrupted vocation. He went back to Paris, and was not again to be deflected from the purpose of becoming a painter. Nevertheless, the pattern of conduct established in these early struggles persisted for many years. Cézanne continued to shuttle between Paris and Provence almost until his death in 1906, no sooner settling down in the one place than being stricken with an irresistible urge to move to the other. By temper he was proud, sensitive, and irritable, sometimes subject to fits of explo-

[1] Programs A and B.

sive rage which appeared to derive from feelings of inferiority. He had a morbid dread of social entanglements and constantly feared to be imposed upon. Despite the revolutionary character of his art and the lack of recognition from which he suffered throughout his life, there was a curious streak of conservatism in his nature, a respect for constituted authority that impelled him to submit his paintings to the official Salon time after time, notwithstanding their inevitable rejection and his own underlying contempt for the institution. Similarly, though frequently at odds with parental authority, he continued to stand in almost pathetic awe of his tyrannical father, on whom he depended financially, until the latter's death as late as 1886.

In Paris during the sixties Cézanne became acquainted with the young rebels who later formed the Impressionist group. At first, however, he was not much affected by their doctrines, but painted in a murky, Romantic manner influenced by Tintoretto, Delacroix, and Daumier, among others. His conversion to the Impressionist style took place mainly in the years 1872–1874, when he was living at Auvers-sur-Oise, a village about twenty miles from Paris. Camille Pissarro, the distinguished Impressionist, lived at that time in the nearby village of Pontoise, and under his influence Cézanne modified his art to conform with the new movement. He largely discarded narrative subject matter, took to painting landscapes in the open air, lightened his palette, and in general adopted the characteristic Impressionist methods of increasing luminosity.

For several years subsequently Cézanne was identified as a member of the Impressionist group, but it was not long before his aims and practice began to diverge radically from theirs. The direction in which he was moving may be appreciated by examining the view of *L'Estaque* in the Chicago Art Institute (Fig. 86), a typical landscape of the 1880's, when his personal style was already well developed. L'Estaque, an industrial suburb of Marseilles, was a favorite retreat of Cézanne's, and the present picture is but one of numerous versions of the subject painted by him. Here we see the town with its factory chimneys in the foreground, beyond which stretches the Bay of Marseilles. In the distance, mountains rise from the coast across the bay.

Cézanne's treatment of the landscape has obvious affinities with Impressionism. The lighting is brilliant and diffused, the colors luminous, high in intensity, and "broken" in their

Fig. 86. Cézanne, *L'Estaque,* 1886–1888, Art Institute, Chicago (courtesy of The Art Institute)

application. Instead of chiaroscuro, careful contrasts of warm and cool hues are employed to obtain relief. Equally Impressionist is the general nature of the composition—the scene viewed from a height, with the diagonal shoreline leading the eye into the distance.

But obvious differences may be observed at the outset. Cézanne endows the various elements in the painting with greater solidity than is normal in Impressionism. He is concerned far more with the permanent structure of objects than with their fleeting appearance as revealed by transitory conditions of illumination. In the painting of the houses in the foreground he shows willingness to resort to extreme simplification in order to emphasize their underlying geometrical shapes. Cézanne himself once remarked that the painter's object should be to reduce nature to the cylinder, the sphere, and the cone, and while this dictum cannot be predicated as a literal statement of his actual aims or practice, its relevance may be appreciated from the austerity with which the quasi-cubical volumes of these houses are depicted. Any details which might detract from the clarity of these volumes are eliminated. Nor is any feeling for the textures of natural objects allowed to intrude upon our perception of their orderly interrelationships.

The very application of paint is more methodical and less sensuous than in the typical Impressionist painting. It is laid on quite thinly, in places with almost the transparency of watercolor, and neat parallel strokes of the brush tend to replace the more erratic blobs of Impressionism. Contours are often reinforced with strong, broken lines—another frank subversion of Impressionist principles.

As in most of Cézanne's landscapes, the concise organization of the scene extends not merely to its internal plastic components, but equally to the delimitation of its planes. For instance, if one compares the present picture with Monet's *Waterloo Bridge* (Fig. 81), a typical Impressionist landscape, also viewed from a height, it will be noticed that whereas in the Monet the front and back boundary planes of the pictorial extension are extremely (and probably deliberately) vague, in the Cézanne they are strongly emphasized by solid masses. Instead of constituting the front planes with an indefinite stretch of water, which provides no cogent psychological demarcation between the real space of the spectator and the illusory space of the picture, Cézanne emphasizes this division by placing in the extreme foreground the hard, cubical masses of the houses. Similarly, whereas Monet marks no farthermost boundary plane, one's eye being permitted to rove into an infinite mist about the horizon, Cézanne curtails any such ocular excursions with an impassable backdrop of mountains.

Defining the pictorial extension in this way contributes to another effect besides the obvious one of discrete, box-like space-organization. It aids Cézanne to achieve also a tightly controlled *two-dimensional* pattern, and to co-ordinate this with his three-dimensional space-design. For effects of infinite or overemphasized regression and progression in a landscape are normally extremely destructive of flat pattern values. If the spectator's eye is drawn rapidly and irresistibly into a great depth, there is induced the psychological effect of a "hole" or funnel, which tends to disturb the identification of the scenic illusion with the physical picture plane, *i.e.*, with the painting regarded solely as a flat pattern of colored shapes. Now, Cézanne's greatest concern in painting was to produce a totally unified work of art, by controlling perfectly the chaotic data supplied him as subject matter by nature. Since over-all control predicated not only a space-organization but also a pattern-design integrated with it, it will be understood why he was careful to limit strictly the receding and advancing planes of the landscape.

To achieve the ends described above, Cézanne did not hesitate to distort nature whenever he found it expedient to do so. In *L'Estaque* conventional perspective has been openly flouted, for the scene is viewed simultaneously from two different eye levels. The land and houses in the foreground are only a little below the level of the painter's eye, but the Bay of

Marseilles and that part of the coast beyond the factory chimney on the left are seen as though looked down upon from a great height. That is to say, the angle at which the line of sight intersects the horizontal at sea level is much greater in the area of the middle distance than it would be if the perspective of the foreground prevailed throughout. As a result, the entire area of water appears to be tilted upwards.

What are the consequences of this procedure? In the first place, the background is shifted much nearer to the spectator, and the distant mountains appear magnified. This, of course, results in strengthening the finite, shut-in quality of composition for which Cézanne was aiming. The funnel effect is decisively avoided. But the flat pattern is also affected in a more direct manner, for, by being tilted upwards, the sea impinges upon it as a much greater area, forming a more prominent element in the total design. The pattern of the sea, in fact, stretches now over an area almost as large as that of the foreground land mass, and it will be observed that the two areas are roughly equivalent in shape, only reversed, so that they complement each other in a kind of scenic *contrapposto*. Moreover, the complementary pattern relationship extends to color as well, the dominant warm-toned orange of the land contrasting boldly with the cool deep blue of the sea.

The pulling forward of the mountains across the bay causes their pattern value to be enhanced also. As if to allay any further possible doubt of his intentions, Cézanne calmly violates the most obvious rules of aerial perspective by exorbitantly reinforcing the linear contours of a range of mountains many miles distant, thereby causing them to spring into the foreground and tying them firmly to the picture plane. They thus come to constitute one of four primary pattern-zones into which the painting is divided. Yet aerial perspective is not completely disregarded, for in virtue of their tempered color values and intensities, in relation to the strong tones of the sea and land before them, these mountains have been gradated correctly in accordance with the actual distance at which they are situated. Their internal gradations of tone are just strong enough to emphasize configuration, just mild enough and cool enough to establish their distance, and warm enough to form an effective pattern contrast with the still colder bands of sky above and sea below.

The relationship of mountains to sky, in fact, re-echoes, but in muted intensities, the dominant contrast between foreground and sea. In each case the warm colors of the lower zone are set against the cool of the upper; the broken, variegated colors of the lower against the flatter monochrome blues of the upper; the hard, corrugated shapes of the lower against the smooth plain surfaces of the upper. The four zones become elements of a single motif that receives both vigorous primary statement and subtle reiteration.

The marvel of Cézanne's pattern sense, of his irresoluble fusion of two- and three-dimensional design, cannot be explained away by reference to capricious distortions of shape or perspective. In his greatest works the essence of the pattern lies in the very bones of the landscape he sees laid out before him. Distortions notwithstanding, in the last analysis it is the real, three-dimensional landscape itself, vividly apprehended, and indeed loved, by Cézanne, that dictates the pattern, not the pattern the landscape. Certainly we feel this to be true in the case of *L'Estaque,* where the zonal articulation of the pattern seems to spring inevitably from the natural elements of the scene.

For the most part, distortion in painting is but an accessory to the main objective, which is the transmuting of natural data into pictorial terms. Any such transmutation is bound to be arbitrary—Cézanne's no more so than others'—because it is patently impossible to produce a facsimile of dynamic three-dimensional extension on a static two-dimensional surface. The painter must therefore limit himself to reproducing certain facets of the reality which he sees and *feels* in the world around him, and in making his transcription he must adopt those pictorial instruments or conventions best suited to embody his individual vision. What Cézanne saw most vividly in nature were suggestions of morphological order, such that from a given

Fig. 87. Cézanne, *Still-Life with Fruit Basket,* 1886–1888, Louvre, Paris (*Archives photographiques*)

scene he was enabled, out of a selection of the elements contained therein, to construct in his mind a synthesis suitable for pictorial representation. Any natural elements which fell without this mental distillation were disturbing, chaotic, amorphous, and had consequently to be discarded. Likewise, the desired pictorial interrelationship of those elements retained could not necessarily always be encompassed by depicting the whole scene from any single point of view, *i.e.,* by adherence to traditional, homologous perspective. Hence the use of multiple viewpoints, leading to distortions of shape, to which attention has already been drawn.

Although they are means rather than ends, Cézanne's distortions are nevertheless of great interest, for devices which to him were mere adjuncts in the communication of a transfigured vision of nature became, in succeeding generations, basic implements for attempts to eliminate nature altogether. In his still-life paintings we frequently find distortions far more radical than those noted in *L'Estaque*: Perhaps because still-life subjects lacked the associative values attaching to landscapes, he was led to regard them in a more impersonal, objective manner, and to utilize their design potentialities with greater freedom from conventional modes of visualization. The *Still-Life with Fruit Basket* in the Louvre, Paris, dating from 1886–1888, is an excellent example (Fig. 87). Here the table itself is seen from two distinct eye-levels, the left side being looked down upon from a greater height than the right. This results in a split in the plane of the table top. Its edge appears nearer and lower on the left than on the right, the point of disjunction being masked by the cloth. In this way a quality of unobtrusive tension is set up between the two sides of the table, increasing the animation of the general design. The various objects that go to make up the still-life are seen from a number of different eye levels, all of which, however, approximate one or another of those from which the dichotomized table top is viewed. For instance, although the left part of the table plane is intersected by the line of sight at a large angle, the sugar bowl standing upon it appears as though viewed from a shallower angle, more nearly equivalent to that of the right side of the table. Its contours thus gain a stronger pattern value than they would have were they seen from the same angle as the part of the table on which they are situated. On the other hand, the large ginger jar next to the sugar bowl is seen from a high level. Here the foreshortened view enables the spectator not only to appreciate fully the plastic quality of the object, but again to see a more exciting pattern of line and color. For if the line of sight were low, all that would show at the top would be the lip of the jar, seen as an uninteresting straight line, or at best only as an ellipse with a very narrow minor axis. As it is, the interior is seen in the shape of an ellipse with a broad minor axis, forming a dark area large enough to contrast powerfully with the light values of the exterior of the jar and to assert its value as a pattern motif repeated throughout the painting. Now Cézanne can even paint a strong dash of red as the highlight of the *interior,* a color which repeats the red of one of the pears in the foreground.

Most daring of all is the treatment of the basket of fruit on the right, from which the painting takes its name. The lines of sight along which this single unit is viewed stem from no fewer than three distinct sources. First, the wickerwork body of the basket is seen from a low level, at approximately the same angle as the right table plane, on which it stands. Secondly, the top of the basket is depicted as from the same large angle used for the adjacent ginger jar, the resultant upward tilt affording a view of the contents, with their vivid pattern values, that would otherwise have been denied. Thus far, the multiple perspective noted has been the result of vertical changes of eye level, but in the painting of the handle of the basket Cézanne shifts the *lateral* angle of the line of sight. The other viewpoints, regardless of their angle with the horizontal, are all located in planes roughly at right angles to the picture plane. The basket handle, however, is painted as though seen from a point far to the right, so that although the major axis of the basket lies practically parallel to the picture plane, the axis of the handle appears not at right angles to it but at something like a 60-degree angle. It is not hard to see the pictorial advantage of this manipulation, for instead of appearing as a dull straight line the handle now describes a graceful elliptical curve, harmonizing with similar line-motifs in the ginger jar, fruit, and other objects.

From the above analysis it may be correctly inferred that in his still-life painting Cézanne continually shifts the perspective in such a way that the optimum pattern value is extracted from each object, or part of an object, depicted. At the same time, and this is perhaps a measure of his amazing pictorial genius, he manages to select the multiple simultaneous viewpoints in such a way that the sense of volumetric extension is enhanced rather than diminished. It is in this last respect, among others, that Cézanne's art is richer in pictorial insights than that of the 20th-century Cubists who followed him on the path of distortion for pattern effect.

Similar, and far more elaborate, analyses could be made of almost any of Cézanne's later works. It will suffice for our purpose to examine very briefly a single example of another class of Cézanne's painting, namely portraiture. The *Man with Folded Arms,* dating from *ca.* 1895–1900 (Fig. 88), is a representative example. The peasant who posed for this portrait stands with his back to a wall and his arms folded, and perhaps the first feature that will strike the eye of those who have read the foregoing is the fact that the subject of the portrait hides an obvious disjunction between the sections of the wall moulding to be seen on either side of him. This primary distortion affords a clue to the whole pictorial approach in this painting—a lower eye-level and greater sense of depth on the left, a higher eye-level and more restricted feeling of space on the right. It is interesting to note the way in which Cézanne has subtly emphasized the irrational displacement of the wall moulding by the perfectly rational manner in which the man's arms are folded, with the arm on the left (of the

Fig. 88. Cézanne, *Man with Folded Arms, ca.* 1895–1900 (courtesy of Mr. Carleton Mitchell, Annapolis, Md.)

picture) naturally higher than that on the right, and how the sharp disjunction of the two sleeve ends hints eloquently but elusively at the dubious meeting of the two sections of wall moulding behind the figure.

The double eye-level embodied in the moulding is used to create a feeling of tension between the two sides of the painting, a feeling which results from the suggestion of upward movement from the lower level on the left straining against a downward movement from the upper level on the right. From the lower level, we look up at the man's left eye (*i.e.*, left from the spectator's standpoint); from the upper, we look down at his right. The whole face is distorted in order to produce diagonal accents from upper left to lower right, further reminders of the friction between the opposed movement of the two sides.

It will also be noticed that the entire face is flattened almost to a plane, and that this plane seems to hinge at the left while it rotates outward at the right. The circular movement is increased by the manifestly cross-eyed gaze of the right eye. It is as though the shallow space on the right endowed the wall with a forward movement pushing the face around into the deeper space on the left, where the wall seems to recede into the background, drawing the face along with it with the suction of a vacuum. In other words, Cézanne has locked this figure in the coils of a disjunction of space, of which the split pattern elements noted previously are but the projection to a plane.

Enough has been said to indicate that for Cézanne the art of portraiture suggested problems of pictorial organization identical with those that absorbed him in the delineation of inanimate nature. It has indeed been suggested that these problems formed his exclusive concern as a portraitist, that he regarded a human being in identically the same light as an apple or other object whose shape and color stimulated his pictorial instincts. While this view is perhaps borne out in certain of his portraits, it is unquestionably erroneous in the case of the majority. No one could fail to be impressed by the way Cézanne has seized upon the dour independence of his peasant model in the *Man with Folded Arms*. To be sure, his attitude is calm and impersonal compared with that of a Rembrandt, but it cannot be gainsaid that in this and other examples the pictorial manipulations serve not merely to create a pattern but also to extract something of the essence of the sitter's character.

Because Cézanne more than any other 19th-century painter focused his attention on what may be termed the formal aspects of his art, it is very easy to exaggerate these aspects at the expense of others which are equally present. His genuine love for nature, and the ultimate dependence of his art upon it, has already been alluded to. We have also drawn attention to the fact that realism as applied to art is of necessity a somewhat arbitrary conception. It could readily be maintained, for instance, that Cézanne's painting is *more* realistic than any that preceded it. For while the use of shifting perspectives denies a rational recording of instantaneous appearances such as the Impressionists strove to produce, it involves implied elements of time and motion, which are conditions of real observation neglected in conventional perspective; and it may also be said, by offering changing views of the different parts of a scene, to provide a more comprehensive and dynamic *knowledge* of the subject matter as a whole.

Bearing these reservations in mind, it may be affirmed that Cézanne's major bent was undoubtedly towards formalism, that he was more concerned with abstract pictorial relations between objects than with the significance of the objects themselves. Except for his love of certain landscape subjects like Mt. Ste. Victoire and L'Estaque, he seemed comparatively indifferent to the content of his subject matter and tended to paint whatever happened to be conveniently at hand (which probably explains the large number of self-portraits). Even the Impressionists, for all their apparent repudiation of value judgments, selected subjects connoting the aesthetic aspects of a definite way of life, the life of the Paris bourgeois. They were incapable of painting a subject like the *Man with Folded Arms* without sentimentalizing, for sentimentality was the normal bourgeois attitude towards matters rural. Cézanne, on the other hand, never sentimentalizes, and he ignores completely the urban sophistication beloved by the Impressionists.

It is as though in his art Cézanne were turning his back against the world with which in real life he was so ill-equipped to cope, and retreating into a mental world of his own construction. Probably his quest for power and lucidity of design in art may be explained partly as a compensation for feelings of inferiority and insecurity which he experienced in real life. His neurotic personality was perpetually exasperated by conflicts with a *parvenu* father and other exponents of commercialized values he was loath to accept.

But it is well to remember that others among the Post-Impressionists were also maladjusted psychologically and that their art does not necessarily show the same craving for organization. However, it does exhibit an identical desire to escape from the artistic categories of the past. Therefore, although Cézanne's individual personality is of importance for the understanding of his art, it is perhaps more signifrcant to conclude generally that during the last years of the 19th century the tension between the *most sensitive* artists and the inimical values of a cancerous civilization increased to a point where Impressionist complacence no longer satisfied, and the artist was obliged to resort to an active retreat into the recesses of his own mind, whether in the form of the logical abstract synthesis of a Cézanne or a Seurat, the tortured expressionism of a Van Gogh or a Munch, the fantasy of a Redon or an Ensor, or the escape to the primitive of a Gauguin.

Conditions of cultural, social, and economic strain which were beginning to be felt by artists in the 19th century have become vastly aggravated in the course of the upheavals of the 20th, and the new pictorial modes devised by the Post-Impressionists are in consequence firmly established as a basis for the accepted vocabulary of the modern abstract and expressionist painter. In the 19th century only the most acutely sensitive artists were capable of a response at once so refined and so radical to the world in which they found themselves. That Cézanne and the other Post-Impressionists were able to discover and explore so profoundly the true paths of a future cultural development is a measure of their greatness. In the 20th century, when social chaos and disintegration have become overt and not merely incipient, no unusual powers of discrimination have been required to sense and to reject the diseased fabric of accepted values, and countless modern artists have done just this. No wonder the Post-Impressionists were sometimes extremely eccentric individuals—the borderline between the hypersensitive and the psychotic is not always clear-cut. The modern artist, on the other hand, despite opinions to the contrary, is neither mad nor necessarily a genius. He communicates what can only be considered an entirely normal and characteristic reaction to the conditions of 20th-century life.

Recommended reading:
Roger Fry, *Cézanne: A Study of His Development,* London, Leonard & Woolf, 2nd edition, 1932.
Fritz Novotny, *Cézanne,* New York, Oxford University Press, 1948.
Erle Loran, *Cézanne's Composition; an Analysis of His Form with Diagrams and Photographs of His Motifs,* Berkeley and Los Angeles, University of California Press, 1943.

PABLO PICASSO (1881–   )[1]

WHATEVER THE ULTIMATE JUDGMENT of posterity may be, there can be no doubt that in his own time Pablo Picasso has been the best-known and the most influential artist of his generation. Today a man close to seventy, his creative activity extending over five decades is one of the most prolific and remarkable in the history of painting. Others may have achieved works of greater formal perfection or greater sensitivity, but Picasso has given moving expression to the chaotic and violent spirit of the 20th century. Like James Joyce in literature and Stravinsky in music, Picasso has experimented with all sorts of new forms and shows a variety and originality which is impressive indeed. No better introduction to contemporary painting could be found than the study of Picasso's work, for its complexity and experimental character is most typical of our troubled age.

Pablo Picasso was born in Malaga, Spain, in 1881, the son of an Academic painter who taught at the Barcelona Academy of Fine Arts. While still a boy the young painter showed remarkable talent and was able to pass the entrance examination to the Academy at an age when others were just beginning to learn their craft. Soon, however, he found the sterile atmosphere of the Academy not to his liking and set himself up as an independent artist. His early work is strongly under the influence of the great 17th-century painters of Spain, notably Velasquez and Zurbaran. But Spain and her tradition could not hold the young painter; in

[1] Programs A and B.

Fig. 89. Picasso, *Old Guitarist,* 1903, Art Institute, Chicago (courtesy of the Art Institute, Helen Birch Bartlett Memorial Collection)

1900 he went to Paris, which for over a century had been the artistic center of the Western world. Although Picasso returned to Madrid after a few months, he settled in Paris in 1901 and has remained there with only short interruptions ever since.

In Paris he came into contact with the work of the *avantgarde* artists such as Gauguin, Van Gogh and, above all, Toulouse-Lautrec, whose work influenced the young painter greatly. He soon found his own style of painting, which was to be expressive of the sadness and poverty of those early years of his career. This period, which lasted from 1901 to 1904, is known as the Blue Period because of the dominant blue tonality of his paintings. The subject matter consists of blind beggars, poverty-stricken mothers, and melancholy drinkers, a subject matter indicative of the mood which was characteristic of the end of the century, the so-called *fin de siècle* spirit.

One of the outstanding paintings of Picasso's Blue Period is the *Old Guitarist* of 1903, in the Art Institute of Chicago (Fig. 89). Painted when the artist was twenty-two years old, it is an excellent example of his early style. Continuing the Expressionistic tradition of Grünewald and El Greco, Picasso here used distortion and exaggeration for the sake of greater emotional intensity, except that the earlier masters used these Expressionist means for the sake of bringing out the religious intensity of the scenes portrayed, while the modern artist portrays the poverty and despair of the blind beggar. The angular pattern of the bodily forms, the elongation of the limbs, the overhanging head, the emaciated face, the chalk-white and blue tonality, all reinforce the tragic mood. At the same time, the highly formalized pattern of the lines and the shallow space already foreshadow the artist's abstract style of the following years.

Following the Blue Period there is a brief interval, extending through 1904 and 1905, known as the Rose Period from the dominant tonality of his painting. During this period the painter portrayed subjects taken from the life of circus people, harlequins, and actors. Here again it is the sadness and loneliness of their lives which attracts him, for he seems to see a kinship between the sad clowns and the modern artists. Both —artist and harlequin—stand aloof from the industrial and commercial society of our age, which considers them as ambiguous people who are merely tolerated for their entertainment value.

In 1906 Picasso, now twenty-five years old, began to explore completely new directions. Under the influence of Cézanne, whose work was now beginning to be shown widely in Paris, and the carvings of primitive peoples, especially the African Negroes and the ancient Iberians of Spain, Picasso completely changed his style. A work like the famous *Les Demoiselles d'Avignon* of 1907, now in the Museum of Modern Art, shows

Fig. 90. Picasso, *Three Musicians,* 1921, Museum of Modern Art, New York, Mrs. Simon Guggenheim Fund

these influences clearly. From Cézanne and the primitives Picasso had taken over a new interest in formal design and abstract geometrical shapes, so that the visual reality is no longer represented in the way we see it but subordinated to the formal pattern the artist is trying to create. At the same time, the savage vitality and expressive power of the primitive works has been influential in giving his work a vigor which is far removed from the refinement and decadent spirit of his earlier paintings. This period is usually referred to as his African Period and extends from 1906 to 1908.

During the latter year Picasso began placing more and more emphasis upon the purely formal elements. A style resulted which is called Cubist and which lasted from 1909 to 1912. This first phase of his Cubist style is usually referred to as analytical, because the artist in these works attempted to break down the natural forms into their geometric components in accordance with Cézanne's dictum: "Everything in nature adheres to the cylinder, the sphere, and the cone." Under the impact of this development the appearances as we see them in nature give way more and more to an abstract formal pattern which, in a work like *Ma Jolie* (1911) in the Museum of Modern Art, no longer bears much resemblance to the subject which inspired it. At the same time, Picasso and the other Cubists always use nature as their point of departure and are never pure abstractionists like the Non-Objective painters. In these analytical Cubist works olive greens, grays, and browns are used almost to the exclusion of bright colors. Space is indicated only by the darker tones which recede and the warmer ones which come forward; otherwise the forms are flat and abstract. It is the severe beauty of the abstract, geometrical shapes which gives these paintings their particular quality. There can be no doubt that the mature Cubist works, which were painted when the artist was thirty, have been among the most influential paintings of the 20th century.

However, the severity of the pure Cubist paintings of these years is soon abandoned. A reintroduction of bright colors and more representational forms leads to a period known as Synthetic Cubism, a style lasting from about 1912 to 1921 and finding its climax in the famous *Three Musicians* (Fig. 90), now in the Museum of Modern Art. The three figures forming this group are shown seated at a table playing musical instruments. The one on the left, playing a clarinet, is a Pierrot; the one at the center, playing a guitar, a Harlequin; the figure on the right, holding a sheet of music, a monk. All of them are wearing masks which give them a mysterious and strange expression. The forms employed are simple and abstract, consisting largely of geometrical, angular shapes in keeping with the tenets of Cubism. The colors, in contrast to the subdued ones of the Analytical Cubist period, are bright and decorative, further adding to the gaiety of the mood. The rendition of space is deliberately ambiguous, a witty playing on the tension between linear perspective and flat two-dimensional pattern. In contrast to the expressionistic intensity of the *Old Guitarist,* the emphasis is here upon the abstract, formal beauty of design.

During these years Picasso also became interested in the rendering of textures: in a technique called *collage* he actually introduces into his paintings materials such as wood, paper, and cloth. An aftermath of this period may be found in the abstract still lifes of 1924 to 1926, in which the geometrical beauty of his earlier Cubist works is combined with a greater variety of form and color.

During the very same years Picasso was also working in a far different style which, because of its dependence upon the work of the ancients, is referred to as his Classical style. As early as 1917, while travelling in Italy, Picasso had come under the influence of Italian and Greek art and had done some traditional drawings which recalled the work of Ingres rather than the Cubists. From 1920 until about 1925 Picasso employed the Classical style alongside of the Synthetic Cubist style. The masterpiece of this period is probably the *Woman in White* of 1923, in the Museum of Modern Art. Here the serene beauty and formal perfection of Greek art is recaptured in terms which are at the same time wholly modern in their economy and

CONTEMPORARY PAINTING AND ARCHITECTURE

abstract beauty. The result is an art which is not as revolutionary or influential as his Cubist art but nevertheless has a great appeal, especially for those who find the master's bolder and more experimental works difficult to accept.

The decade between 1927 and 1937 was for Picasso one of uncertainty and transition. One style follows another, none of them lasting very long. The works of these years, although often interesting, are on the whole inferior to his earlier and his later productions. Probably the two most important phases of these years are his Bone Period of 1928 and 1929, in which he uses abstract shapes resembling bones and primitive carvings for his inspiration, and his Stained Glass Period of 1931 and 1932. The masterpiece of the latter period is his well-known *Girl Before the Mirror* of 1932, in the Museum of Modern Art. The style employed resembles that of the stained-glass windows of medieval cathedrals in its flat areas of glowing color and its heavy black outlines, which take the place of the lead ribs in the church windows. The content of the work is characteristic of the 20th century in its rendering of the sexual awakening of a young girl as she looks into the mirror and sees herself a young woman. Here, as in other works of this period, the teachings of Freud about our unconscious have had a marked influence on Picasso, as they have had on the Surrealist painters of our age.

The next truly great period of Picasso's artistic career starts with 1937, when the Loyalist Government of Spain, fighting for its life in civil war, commissioned him to paint a mural for the Paris World Exposition. The result was Picasso's famous *Guernica* (Fig. 91), which

Fig. 91. Picasso, *Guernica*, 1937 (courtesy Museum of Modern Art, New York). Owned by the artist.

is probably the artist's best-known and, in the opinion of some critics, his finest work. The subject was inspired by the destruction of the ancient Basque city of Guernica by German Nazi bombers. As Picasso once said, this painting was his contribution to the struggle between the forces of barbarism and civilization. The simple geometry of many of the forms and the flat, abstract space are employed side by side with expressionistic distortion. In the center of the composition, portraying the tragedy and destruction of war, is the horse pierced by a spear, the symbol of the forces of the Republic which are being vanquished. Behind the horse, calm and triumphant amidst this scene of carnage and chaos, is the bull, symbol of the forces of evil and Fascism. Above the horse, illuminating the scene, is an electric light bulb. To the right is a burning house with one woman perishing in the flames, another rushing out of the building, and a third leaning out of the window holding a lamp as if to illuminate the darkness. At the left, in the foreground, are a dead warrior with a broken sword, symbol of the valiant struggle of the Spanish people, and behind him, a mother crying out in agony, holding her dead child in her lap. The composition formed by the figures is triangular. The onlooker's eye is led from the lower right-hand corner through the leg and body of the woman to the bulb, then down again on the left side across the tail of the horse to the head and arm of the warrior. The color scheme is sombre, in keeping with the character of the scene portrayed; it consists wholly of blacks, grays, and whites. The abstract, symbolical nature of the painting makes it a universal symbol of the horror and tragedy of the war years. Other works of our age may be more pleasing, and some even aesthetically more successful; this painting, however, sums up in tremendously expressive and powerful terms the tragedy and chaos of the period in which we live.

The same theme is also treated on a far less ambitious scale in the *Girl with a Cock* of 1938 (Callery Collection), in which the sadism of our age is mirrored in the cruel expression of the girl about to kill the bird. Once again distortion and abstraction are employed in order to reinforce the emotional impact of the scene portrayed. Equally forceful are many of Picasso's paintings of the war years, for they too mirror in very expressive terms the chaos and tragedy of our terrible age. Remaining in Paris during the whole of this time, Picasso became a symbol of the forces of resistance who, in spite of all hardships and dangers, did not yield to the foreign intruder. In the output of these years may be observed the same merging of abstract and expressionistic tendencies which was characteristic of *Guernica*.

Since the war Picasso has turned to a different type of subject matter and less tense and distorted forms. In fact, the paintings and drawings of his most recent years are light-hearted and gay. They represent centaurs and fauns, rendered with a freedom and abandon which is quite unlike the powerful and tortured forms of his earlier work. Possibly the joy over the end of the war and the defeat of Fascism or happiness over his personal life changed his entire attitude. At all events, his current work reveals him once again as a highly creative and original artist.

Recommended readings:
A. Barr, *Picasso, Fifty Years of His Art*, New York, Museum of Modern Art, 1946.
S. Janis, *Picasso, the Recent Years*, New York, Doubleday, 1946.
J. Sabartes, *Picasso*, New York, Braun, 1946.

CONTEMPORARY ARCHITECTURE

FRANK LLOYD WRIGHT AND THE INTERNATIONALISTS[1]

I. THE QUAKER MEETING HOUSES of Pennsylvania are among the most distinguished works of architecture which America has produced. They represent in architecture the extremest departure imaginable from the solemn majesty of a Gothic cathedral. Unpretentious buildings in brick or local stone, totally unadorned except by the honest timbers in their roofs and the rectangles of their window openings, they are matched in their plainness only by the rude wooden benches which make up the furniture of their interiors. Everywhere they represent the same terse simplicity and frankness, the brief accommodation of a religious inwardness which employs no altar and which depends on no external rite. Quaker meeting house and Gothic cathedral stand a world removed from each other, though each is equally a church and each is dedicated to the worship of the self-same God. Catholic rite and Quaker meeting are served in their several ways. As the rite has altered, the buildings have altered with it: the difference, to Catholic and Quaker, is vital and real. The architecture is therefore an honest document of a difference among men.

The contrast of Gothic cathedral and Quaker meeting house illustrates the recurrent task to which every culture must address itself. For it is the business of a culture to guarantee that its forms—of art, of morals, of politics, of society—remain consonant with the actual lives which men lead and with the values after which they aspire. If human beliefs and human needs were subject to no change, it would be possible for each generation of men simply to inherit the accomplishment of its predecessor and reduplicate it; nor would any historical period be required, by a creative act of its own, to fashion the distinctive forms in which the content of its existence might be sufficiently held. No institution, no form, whether of art or morals or politics, is in fact self-justifying. The only legitimate conservatism is grounded in a respect for the dignity not of forms or institutions, but of men. It is the function of human institutions to sustain this dignity, of forms to communicate it. If they fail, they constrain and stifle it; if they succeed, they vary with the needs and beliefs which find free expression in them.

The forms of a culture can never therefore be acquired by simple inheritance, as a natural specimen inherits the character of its species. I am man by no choice of my own, but simply by being born of man. But I shall be Christian—Catholic or Quaker—by choice alone, namely by actively consecrating myself, by appropriating a character which being born is not sufficient to guarantee. Neither can I have my Christianity by simple gift of church or society, for from these I have only its empty form which I may take up or put off without cost to what I am. I shall be Christian only by a deliberate exclusion of other things which it is equally possible for me to be—worldling, seducer, sensualist, swine. The form of Christianity may exist for me as the actual vehicle of a meaning only by my own act: church and society may supply its forms; I alone can regenerate its meanings. If I have it otherwise than by my own act, my having it is a sham in which I piously attitudinize and lie.

As the form of Christianity may retain its external character but lose its meaning, so an architectural form may lose its connection with the affirmations of society which alone can justify it. In the North-Central part of the United States, wherever immigrants of Dutch stock have settled, there appears a characteristic curved roof-line giving to the planes of a gable roof a concave slope downward. The feature is an imitation in wood of the thatched

[1] Programs A and B.

roof of Dutch houses in the Netherlands. There, the roof at its lower edge flattens toward a horizontal plane in order that the downward pressure of the thatch above might be met and held in place by the inertia of the thatch below. The curved contour, which in a thatched roof is physically indispensable, has in a roof of wooden shingles only the quaintness of a reminiscence. Structurally, it is without meaning. Architecturally, it is frivolous, especially where its original sense has been lost or obscured, so that it no longer serves to sustain a recollection of the old world or to sharpen a perception of the new. The example is homely, but it contains a principle. The form has been dislocated from the context in which alone it had a meaning. Since its vitality consists in being the vehicle of a meaning, in the moment that its meaning is lost so that only an empty form is preserved, it is architecturally, and quite literally, dead.

This principle disqualifies the majority of works—dwellings as well as public buildings—which have professed the character of architecture in the 19th and 20th centuries. The 19th century was the scene of what is known in the history of architecture as the "Battle of Styles." A whole series of revivals of the historical styles followed in swift succession one upon another. At the end of the century Roman, Gothic, Greek, Romanesque existed side by side in a mixture of loosely imitated idioms, each claiming to itself the dignity of its once authentic source. Learned and serious theorists expounded the architecture of Greece and Rome as the model for intellectual and republican ideals; John Ruskin regarded the Gothic architecture of the Middle Ages as a means for the moral and social regeneration of man. The effect upon the practitioners of the art of building was disastrous. The result is known as eclecticism, a tendency to employ the external detail of the several historical styles in an indiscriminate medley of borrowings which had neither the originality of authentic art nor the humility of true imitation.

The real issue of the Battle of Styles has been to call in question not the superiority of any historical style, but the meaning of style itself. The stylistic character of the *Parthenon* (Fig. 5) or of *Amiens Cathedral* (Fig. 26) is not a matter of the external ornament and detail which an imitator may copy; it is the inevitable consequence of the use which each of these buildings served and of the philosophic and spiritual awareness which each communicates. A form which is unrelated to the special uses or aspirations of men is empty and meaningless; architecturally it is dead. The real criterion of style in architecture, the measure of its vitality, is the fitness of form to function. What really matters in a building, what therefore constitutes the art of building, is the adjustment of its form to the living needs, ideal as well as utilitarian, which it must serve.

II. In 1901, at Hull House in Chicago, Frank Lloyd Wright delivered a lecture which he entitled "The Art and Craft of the Machine." Wright was speaking to an order of society in which the Industrial Revolution had irrevocably destroyed the craft traditions. It is the disappearance of these traditions which has given to the 19th- and 20th-century city its aspect of nondescript ugliness in detail, even while its major shapes spring huge and angular, in a profoundly moving image, against the sky. For it came shortly to be known to those who professed to imitate the historical styles that the fashioning of a Greek egg-and-dart motive in a Classical capital, or a leaf motive in a Gothic stringcourse, required more than the learning of the erudite. It demanded a technical craft which society had ceased to nurture except in certain isolated spirits, professional artists, who were unwilling to dispose their gifts on a task so limited. Attempts were made to revive the crafts. The finest and most influential attempt was William Morris' Arts and Crafts Movement, which survived his death in 1896. No one had perceived so clearly the costs at which the benefits of an industrial society had been bought. But the Arts and Crafts Movement, which rejected the moral insobrieties of the machine-age, was unable to alter its character or to stop the monotony of its revolutions. The title of Wright's lecture was therefore to be pondered on, for here was an attempt not to reject the machine, but to employ and exploit its authentic virtues in 20th-century society.

There is no more important work before the architect now than to use this normal tool of civilization to the best advantage, instead of prostituting it as he has hitherto done in reproducing with murderous ubiquity forms born of other times and other conditions . . . which it can only serve to destroy.[2]

Wright is the Jeremiah of modern artists. He is not, and has never conceived himself to be, the mere critic of architects. His reflections on architecture have an ineradicable moral flavor. Even in a discourse on the nature of materials—on the properties of wood or stone or brick, on the possibilities available in steel and glass and reinforced concrete—the reflection is incidental to a reflection on the moral condition of society. For a building, whatever else it is, is in the first instance a thing of utility. It exists, as any tool exists, for use, as a means of serving some need which men regard as significant. The needs of society are, for better or worse, prescribed to architects, not by them. They consist of gross wants, to which the environment must be shaped and adjusted, to which, therefore, architectural designs must conform. It is in reference to these needs, against the web of human purposes which the architect has not himself chosen, that the distinction of his work can be judged. Architecture can never have, therefore, either the purity or the absoluteness of free art. Its formal character is the result of no caprice or abstract aesthetic, but of radical subordination to the ends and purposes which men hold. Since the ends of society are not of his choosing, but only the means, it falls to the architect to civilize by means alone. His function as engineer is merely to build and in building to accommodate a need; his function as architect and artist is to guarantee that what is built shall be the perfect complement of what man is, the genius of sovereign rationality in society, enabling it to be as free as it is historically capable of becoming.

No one has discerned more clearly than Wright the necessity of restoring art to a position of moral relevance in the modern world, nor has any writer on the arts exercised so profoundly disturbing an influence on the modern dogma, that it is the business of art to be free, to exist for its own sake, insubordinate even to life.

III. As Classical architecture rests upon the principle of the post and lintel, and medieval architecture on the principle of the arch, contemporary architecture is engaged in exploiting the resources of a third principle of construction, the principle of the cantilever.

The principle consists in the use of a horizontal member, called a cantilever, as a means of carrying a load in projection from a vertical support. In effect, it is a beam supported only at one end so as to form, by its rigidity, a bracket. The overhang of a projecting cornice is the most familiar illustration in stone or wood.

The major part of a modern steel structure employs an ordinary post and lintel principle. It is contrived upon a rigid steel frame, composed of vertical piers and horizontal beams.

[2]*Frank Lloyd Wright on Architecture, Selected Writings 1894–1940,* ed. F. Gutheim (New York, Duell, Sloan and Pearce, 1941), p. 24.

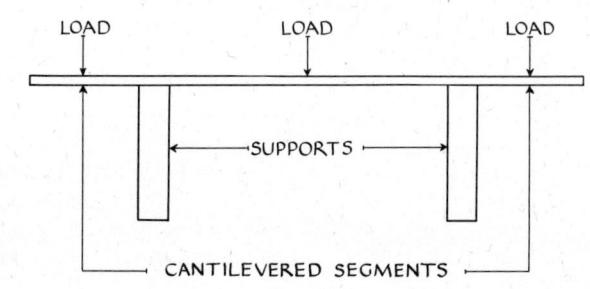

Fig. 92. Cantilever Construction (reproduced from *Humanities 1 Handbook,* Second Edition, October, 1946, by permission of the University of Chicago Press)

CONTEMPORARY ART

The cantilevers are those segments of the beams which extend beyond the outer limits of the building as defined by its vertical supports (Fig. 92).

This steel frame, together with its cantilevers, defines the volume which is to be enclosed by walls. In traditional masonry construction a wall has a dual-function: it acts as a screen, separating interior from exterior; it carries a load, each lower course of masonry supporting the weight of the wall above it. In steel construction the wall is preserved only in its function as a screen. The wall supports nothing; on the contrary, it is suspended from the steel frame, literally hung from it, precisely in the manner in which the clapboards of a Cape Cod cottage are applied to a wooden frame, which performs the function of sustaining the structure independently of them. For this reason a horizontal strip of wall may in steel construction alternate with a continuous horizontal strip of window glass. Both are screens which together form the enclosing shell of the building. The two are unrelated in the way of support and load (Fig. 93).

The principle of the cantilever exploits the property of tensile strength in materials. The materials of construction which have made possible its extended use in architecture are steel and ferro-concrete.

Concrete has two properties which make it serviceable as a constructive material. The first of these, a property realized and exploited by the Romans, is its character as a plastic: poured into a wooden form of any desired shape, it hardens as a monolith of a strength and durability comparable to stone. Its second property, one which it shares with stone, is its resistance to compression: it is capable of bearing great weight so long as the downward thrust of its load may be transmitted directly, as in a pier, to the earth. When this condition is not realized, as in a lintel, concrete like stone is liable to fracture. For in this instance, where the thrust of the load in the space between supports cannot be directly transmitted to the earth, the active stresses are not merely stresses of compression but stresses of tension as well (Fig. 94). The weakness of a concrete lintel is on its lower side, where the stress of the load does not compress the particles but on the contrary works to draw them apart.

The use of steel as a reinforcement for concrete supplies at points of stress the strength under tension which concrete by itself lacks. Steel rods, wire-mesh, etc., are introduced into the form before the concrete is poured, and are so disposed as to take the tensile stresses, which may be predicted in advance. Ferro-concrete, as the combination of the two materials is called, is not only a less costly material of construction than steel alone; it is fireproof as steel is not.

With steel and reinforced concrete the uses of the principle of the cantilever are inexhaustibly various. It exhibits itself

Fig. 93. Howe and Lescaze, *Philadelphia Savings Fund Society Building,* 1932-1934 (by permission of Mr. Lescaze, photograph courtesy of Museum of Modern Art, New York)

Fig. 94. *Principles of Reinforced Concrete Construction* (reproduced from *Humanities 1 Handbook,* Second Edition, October, 1946, by permission of the University of Chicago Press)

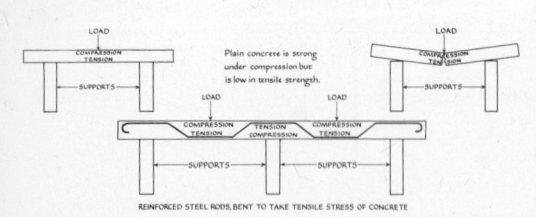

wherever steel is used with understanding—in bridges, houses, ships, skyscrapers, arenas, railway terminals. Its vividest illustration in light metal is the airplane wing. It has placed in the hands of the modern architect who will master its architectural use the means of a new imaginative conquest of space.

IV. The most important fact about any space which is calculated for human use is the plan which disposes its volumes. The vertical planes which contain these volumes perform the function of screens: they ensure privacy where it is wanted, they provide shelter. Beyond this they are the simple logical consequence of the plan.

The predominance of the plan is the primary article of Wright's architecture. It remains the basis upon which he has exercised the decisive influence on the architecture of all of his contemporaries in the modern movement without exception. Elevations of modern buildings vary widely enough. It is mainly with respect to elevations that Wright is distinguished from the group of architects who practice what is called the International Style. There is, however, not a single architect of distinction in the world today in whose work Wright's planning is not spontaneously declared.

The plan is, in Wright's practice, the initial act of legislation from which every later decision of the architect in regard to the elevation of his building must consistently follow. For with the plan which distributes and apportions the space of the building, he exercises the eminent rationality which serves needs by discovering the order among them. Roof and wall and window may complement a plan; they may sustain or muddy it. They will never compensate for its defects, since everywhere they simply execute its enactments, as the chords of music subserve themselves to a melodic pattern which marks the cadences.

The plan of a building, which lays out in two dimensions the divisions of the space to be enclosed, already implies the dimension which it omits. It conceives the space as a compound volume, the parts of which it proceeds to distribute for special uses. Wright's distinctive type of planning is called "open planning" (Fig. 95). In a traditional closed plan the space is not merely compound, but composite; it is formed of a series of insulated boxes which open incidentally into one another. The phrase "open planning" means, on the contrary, that the compound space which the building encloses is regarded as a continuous ordered unit. The unity of the interior space is preserved by order, not by partitions. To segment the space without respect to actual needs is necessarily, therefore, to violate it. If the interior volumes are properly distributed and apportioned, an interior partition can have only the single function of ensuring personal privacy among individuals. Except for this, the interior spaces are continuous; they flow into each other and interpenetrate. In a dwelling, only the service quarters, the bedrooms, and baths are screened; the remaining space is one and undivided. The result is a sense of ordered freedom, resilient and uninhibited.

Fig. 95. Wright, *Falling Water House*, 1936, Bear Run, Pa., owned by E. J. Kaufmann; plan of first floor (by permission of the architect, photograph courtesy of Museum of Modern Art, New York)

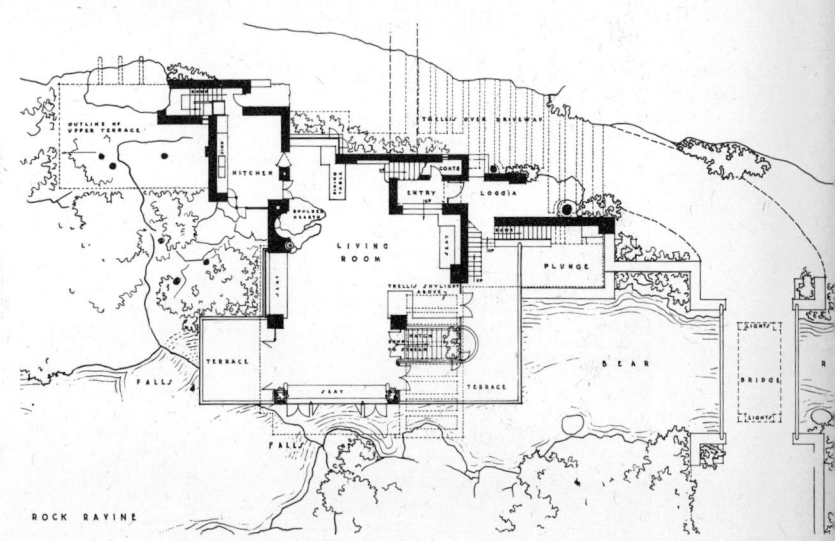

V. Architectural forms have the virtue of symbolizing the way in which men spontaneously conceive themselves to be related to their world. The distinctive feature of an American house, its special and characteristic appurtenance, is the stoop. Classical buildings are fitted with porticoes; an American dwelling has its porch. The difference between porch and portico is a veritable difference of worlds. For it is the business of a portico to delimit a man-made space; it emphasizes the difference between the measured space which belongs to the building and the natural space beyond. The function of the American porch is precisely the opposite. It extends the space of the house into nature, invites nature indoors, and affirms the identity of both. Between man and nature the opposition is suppressed. Man is a parcel of the universal nature which includes him and extends beyond him and forms the stage of his life.

Wright's conception of the human dwelling has transformed the features of the old stoop; he has preserved in his buildings the fundamental sympathy with nature which it represents. Whether it is better to say that the porch has been eliminated from the house, or simply that it has absorbed the house, so that the house becomes a porch upon the world, is difficult to decide. The sympathy with nature which it expresses is the same in either manner of speaking. It is the element of Wright's work which has caused him to be described as a Romantic artist. It is stated, in terms of design, in the importance which is given to the site of buildings and in the insistence upon preserving a continuity between interior and exterior space (Fig. 96).

When, in cities, a dwelling requires to be screened from the noises of the street, the site acts as a negative condition upon any design which an architect may produce. It simply eliminates possibilities without determining in a positive sense what the character of the design shall be. The effect of Wright's respect for site is to make the site of a building an integral part of his design. It is a commodity for use, which may be exploited as well as endured. The imaginative use of space provides not merely shelter, but light and air, the patterned animate moving shapes of cityscape, the geniality of natural settings. Building and site are organically related, each the complement of the other. As a living form exists in perfect adjustment to its environment or else perishes, so should buildings. They belong to their landscape, they stand rooted in it, they are even apt to repeat its motives in the textures of woods and of local stone, in the low-lying hipped roofs of the prairie states or the expanded horizontals of the desert.

By the same principle which takes site and building together as a unit, the man-made space of the building opens freely outward upon natural space. The separation between interior

Fig. 96. Wright, *Falling Water House*, 1936, Bear Run, Pa., owned by E. J. Kaufmann
(*Bill Hedrich, Hedrich-Blessing*)

Fig. 97. Wright, *Falling Water House*, 1936, Bear Run, Pa., owned by E. J. Kaufmann
(*Bill Hedrich, Hedrich-Blessing*)

and exterior is maintained only so far as the purposes of shelter are served by it. For the rest, opaque walls are replaced by translucent glass screens; natural forms are imported indoors in the rough-hewn textures of natural stone hearths or in indoor plant-life; verandahs extend outward under the openness of the sky, searching out the sound of birdcall and the falling waters of streams.

As Romanticism in poetry invariably gains in concentration and poignancy by discipline to the sonnet form, the special quality of its freedom emerging in its act of servitude, so Wright's best work is invariably the sparsest in its means. Its characteristic quality is the sheer geometric lucidity with which space is molded (Fig. 97). The composition works in horizontals, disposing volumes about the chimney's mass. Cantilevered segments free the several levels from the dominion of the ground plan, generating a new plan of their own at a loftier story. The contrasted levels remain nevertheless related in an abstract design of line and plane and volume, as inevitable as geometry, as incalculable as the flight of a bird.

VI. It is customary to describe modern architecture by a negative characteristic, namely, the absence of ornament. The description has gained currency from the circumstance that contemporary architecture represents a conscious revolt against the imitation of the historical styles, and further, that it has a marked character of severity and simplicity.

The fundamental principle of all ornament is the repetition of identical elements. The principle is as old as art itself: it realizes itself in the purely abstract iteration of the polka dot or checker, or in the patternized repetition of natural forms such as the Greek honeysuckle or egg-and-dart. Modern architecture, far from rejecting the principle, precisely illustrates it. What it rejects is alone the use of applied ornament, that is, of ornament which is not authentically realized from architectural forms themselves. Its major ornamental features consist in the distribution of windows and spandrels, piers and planes, each identical with the last, forming a pattern of the elements cognate to architecture itself (Fig. 93). Occasionally, the principle is exhibited in its austerest generality, divorced even from the repetition of shape. Traditionally, the unit of an ornamental pattern is an individual shape of specific texture; in modern architecture, the repetition may illustrate itself in the repetition of texture alone, exploiting the nature of the materials employed, either the grain of natural woods, the machine precision of glass or metal, the rusticated texture of stone, or the rough plank-texture of the wooden molds for poured concrete.

VII. The name given to architecture of the 19th and 20th centuries, which employs frank construction and subordinates design to human needs, is functionalism. Functionalism is in fact a general movement which has involved the work of a considerable number of architects in Europe as well as America. Wright's influence has been decisively felt by them all, though with his usual acerbity he has refused to acknowledge any one of them as his lawful progeny Wright's own work has been uneven, but the powerful bold idiom which he has practiced for more than fifty years is inexhaustibly rich. His assurance in his old age has suffered as little decrepitude as Titian's. At his worst, he is simply undisciplined; he is, at his best, inimitable. By contrast to him, the functionalists have the doctrinaire tameness of persons incapable of sinning magnificently. They have suffered the misadventure of being too early classified, which is a fault of their own. In 1932 the functionalism which had occupied the period since the first World War was given a name. It was called the International Style, and four architects were signalized as its major exponents—Walter Gropius and Mies van der Rohe in Germany, Le Corbusier in France, J. J. P. Oud in Holland. The International Style originates no new principle of architecture which is not to be found in Wright's work. Its positive significance has been to discover the uses of restraint and discipline, which Wright's example has only incidentally afforded. The consequence has been that Wright remains to this day a solitary spirit, uneasy even with the servitude of apprentices whom he himself has trained; the architects of the International Style have meanwhile consolidated the advance which they have together made. The conception of buildings as volume rather than mass, of walls as screens rather than supports, of space as continuous rather than discrete no longer depends so abjectly on the work of a single man and will not be extinguished with him. The International Style has produced results as distinguished as Oud's *Workers' Houses,* Hook of Holland, 1924–27; Mies van der Rohe's *Tugendhat House,* Brno, Czechoslovakia, 1930: Erich Mendelsohn's *Schocken Department Store,* Chemnitz, Germany, 1928–30; Howe and Lescaze's *Philadelphia Savings Fund Society Building,* Philadelphia, 1932–34. The style of such buildings resides rather in their self-consistency and relevance than in an external idiom which architects and builders may now begin, as indeed they have already begun, to exploit with the complacency of carpenter's Gothic. Le Corbusier's conception of the human dwelling as a machine for living (*machine à habiter*) contains a truth; it contains also a peril in the moment that it becomes a dogma of easy currency. Slab roof and cantilevered porch, ribbon window and ceramic spandrel, stilted volume and free partition, have become already worn, not because they have been repeated, but because they have been repeated inhumanely without imagination. The work of the architects is nevertheless the most positive art which the 20th century has produced. Its direction is known, its primitives are present, its possibilities have been barely touched upon.

Recommended reading:

J. M. Richards and E. Mock, *An Introduction to Modern Architecture,* New York, Penguin, 1940: an excellent introduction published at very low cost.

H. R. Hitchcock and P. Johnson, *The International Style: Architecture Since 1922,* New York, Norton, 1932: a formulation of the principles of the International Style with illustrations of works by Gropius, Le Corbusier, Oud, Mies, and others.

H. R. Hitchcock, *In the Nature of Materials: The Buildings of Frank Lloyd Wright, 1887–1941.* New York, Duell Sloan and Pierce, 1942.

Museum of Modern Art, *What is Modern Architecture?* 2nd ed., New York, 1946.

CONTEMPORARY LITERATURE

THOMAS STEARNS ELIOT (1888–   ): *Gerontion*[1]

Gerontion is at first a puzzling and difficult poem because, like abstract painting, it is hard to see what it is *about*. The form is clear, and there seems to be a plot or action. Characters appear and disappear, a situation is presented, or perhaps merely suggested, and reflections and conclusions are drawn. But everything is so oblique, and the literary and historical references with which the poem abounds so subtle or erudite, that it is not surprising that *Gerontion* should have been appreciated as great poetry before its complete meaning had been rightly or widely understood. It was felt at once that the loose blank verse in which the poem is written was handled with a mastery of style that recalled the distinction of the late Elizabethan dramatists and, indeed, of Shakespeare himself. And, further, it was clear in a general way that the poem (written in 1920) was about history, that it concerned itself with the breakdown of civilization, culture, and religion in Europe, and that it was an expression of emotional attitudes about the contemporary chaos—and perhaps also that it was an intensely religious poem. But beyond this nothing was certain. The abstract and apparently disconnected method of development, the unfamiliar allusions, and the fact that the poem, like some modern painting (Picasso) and some modern music (Stravinsky) was breaking sharply away from the superficial verisimilitude of 19th-century realism and, in Eliot's case, returning to something like the complex traditionalism of Milton's *Lycidas*—all this made the detailed significance of the poem hard to perceive. Not until the poem has been analysed in detail is it possible to grasp its full significance.

To begin with, the title, *Gerontion,* means "oldness," and the poem is a soliloquy or an abstract dramatic monologue, the reverie of an old man, who stands as a symbol of the spiritual decrepitude of our age of collapsing values and of religious and cultural confusion. The epigraph,

> Thou hast nor youth nor age
> But as it were an after dinner sleep
> Dreaming of both,

is from the Duke's speech in Shakespeare's *Measure for Measure* (III, i); it asserts the emptiness of a life divorced from significant action and, by implication from the situation in the play, the superiority of death to such a life.

The poem is an impersonal and dramatic one, and the action takes place in an old man's consciousness—an old man who is himself the symbol of an age, a civilization, a period of history—and the poem as it develops is a meditation on history, its present stage and the lessons that can or cannot be drawn from it.

The opening lines give a vivid impressionistic picture of decay and weariness, of a time of regret for the heroism and certainty of a period of action far in the past. Rain, the sea, water, are symbols in this poem of spiritual vitality, and conversely dryness ("a dry month"), sand, rock, and stone, of spiritual deadness and insensitivity.

The "hot gates" is a reference to Thermopylae (which means literally "the hot gates"), the most heroic episode in the Greek wars for freedom against the invading Persians. The reference to heroic action in the distant past of the race only emphasizes more forcefully the present age of meaningless, tired routine in which there is no incitement to significant heroic action.

[1] Programs A and B.

As the nightmare-like picture develops, we get a view of modern Europe as a bankrupt, decadent, and wasted land, the fitting symbol for which is an old man,

> A dull head among windy spaces,

in a patched and tumble-down house in a refuse-laden stony field. Suddenly a suggestion is made as to the cause of the break-down. It is the absence or corruption of the religious spirit in the modern world, and particularly the decay of faith in Christianity, that has robbed our culture of significance and meaning. This is suggested indirectly in the phantasmagoric pictures and bitter prophetic words which follow the lines beginning "Signs are taken for wonders." "We would see a sign!" is the scornful and dubious cry of the Pharisees demanding of Christ that he perform a miracle to prove his divinity.

> The word within a word, unable to speak a word,
> Swaddled with darkness

is an allusion to a Christmas sermon preached by Bishop Lancelot Andrewes at the Court of King James I. The preacher is referring to the divine mystery of the infant Christ in the manger—himself the Word, that is, God, and yet at the same time a human infant in swaddling clothes, unable to speak a word. The effect of this modified quotation is to suggest in the most concentrated way the modern rejection of belief, our Pharisaical demand to be shown proof before we believe and the inability of Jesus to speak to us today. How different in an earlier, fresher age, "the juvescence of the year!" Then Christ came with the power and beauty of a tiger, with the godlike energy and glory that Blake's tiger symbolizes. There is here a conscious, if oblique, reference to Blake's famous lyric,

> Tyger, tyger, burning bright
> In the forests of the night.

Now Spring is simply the spawning rebirth of vegetable and animal matter, not a renewal of spiritual strength or a resurrection of the crucified Christ. Hence May is "depraved," and it is the flowering judas, recalling not Christ but Christ's betrayer, which is eaten, divided, and drunk "among whispers" in a sinister and blasphemous celebration of the Mass. Who are the celebrants of the unholy service? They are figures briefly but vividly etched as the empty, slightly decadent, and neurotic denizens of a chaotic cosmopolitan world, shadows in the mind of the symbolic old man whose reverie is the substance of the poem.

Now the nightmare-like reverie, filled with sudden glimpses and half-remembered figures, is replaced by a passage of controlled meditation. The protagonist of the poem, this old man in a dry month, who is filled with the knowledge of evil, if not of good, considers the possibility of redemption: "After such knowledge, what forgiveness?" Can we not from the knowledge of the past and the intelligent study of history learn how to recover faith and wholeness and the human perfection that comes from spiritual health? But alas, vanity, distraction, and confusion subtly distort the lessons of history. Indeed, good and evil, virtue and vice, honesty and hypocrisy are so inextricably mixed that we have lost the means and the power (and perhaps the will) to win forgiveness and return to the life-giving springs of faith.

> The tiger springs in the new year. Us he devours.

This completes the cycle of the Christian year, the Great Year of two thousand years of Christianity. Originally ("in the juvescence of the year") Christ came with the power and the beauty of the tiger. He came, as Mr. Mankowitz declares in his *Notes on Gerontion*, "gently, in our interest." But now after the "impudent crimes" and "unnatural vices" he comes again in the new year as a devouring, destroying, punitive force.

Already the destruction has been partially accomplished, and before we can reach any conclusion to our effort to examine the meaning of history, we "stiffen in a rented house"—that is, we grow insensitive, old, unsubtle, and unresponsive, stagnating in a culture we live in but cannot make our own. In this phrase there is a suggestion, too, of the brevity of life. The end of the materialist is to stiffen in death in the coffin he occupies but does not own.

After protesting his sincerity in making these bitter and despairing judgments, the protagonist continues to develop his awareness of the consequences of our condition. Human contact, the life-giving sense of oneness that was once possible in passionate love, has been transformed from beauty to terror, and at last has been adulterated by nervous, destructive probing, until finally the senses themselves have been weakened, distorted, and intellectualized almost out of existence, so that not even these can be used to draw human beings together.

> I that was near your heart was removed therefrom
> To lose beauty in terror, terror in inquisition.
> I have lost my passion: why should I need to keep it
> Since what is kept must be adulterated?
> I have lost my sight, smell, hearing, taste, and touch:
> How should I use them for your closer contact?

It is significant that in this passage T. S. Eliot has drawn upon the versification of some of the late Elizabethan dramatists, who were expressing a similar disillusionment with the enthusiasm and sensuous excitement of the earlier Renaissance. Eliot's paragraph beginning, "I that was near your heart," recalls in its cadence at least three passages from the Elizabethan dramatists that the modern poet has written about in his critical essays. The first is from Middleton's *The Changeling* (V, iii):

> O come not near me, Sir, I shall defile you!
> I that am of your blood was taken from you
> For your better health· look no more upon 't,
> But cast it to the ground regardlessly,
> Let the common sewer take it from distinction.

The second is from Chapman's *Tragedy of Charles, Duke of Byron* (V):

> Why should I keep my soul in this dark light,
> Whose black beams lighted me to lose myself?
> When I have lost my arms, my fame, my wind,
> Friends, brothers, hopes, fortunes, and even my fury?

And the third is from *Hamlet* (III, iii):

> Eyes without feeling, feeling without sight,
> Ears without hands or eyes, smelling sans all,
> Or but a sickly part of one true sense.

What all these passages have in common is a tone of bitter and disillusioned self-contempt, and in echoing them (not literally, but in cadence and rhythm) the modern poet is suggesting a comparison between the complexity and corrupting weariness of the modern intellect and the bitterness and horror with which the late Elizabethan and Jacobean dramatists expressed *their* sense of the spiritual corruption of the later Renaissance.

In the stanza that follows we have a concentrated and very vivid analysis of modern decadence. Indeed, it is almost a definition of our decadence:

> Excite the membrane when the sense has cooled,
> With pungent sauces, multiply variety
> In a wilderness of mirrors.

Then comes an ominous note. Do we imagine that such a civilization and such a culture will live forever? Already the spider and the weevil are preparing themselves. The time will come when all the frail and empty characters such as those glimpsed for a moment in the early part of the poem will be whirled into existlessness. Other names are mentioned, De

Bailhache, Fresca, Mrs. Cammel, but they take their place in the slightly sinister cosmopolitan society inhabited by Fräulein Von Kulp, Madame de Tornquist, Mr. Silvero and the rest.

In this passage too there is another oblique reference to the Elizabethans. The lines

>   ... whirled
> Beyond the circuit of the shuddering Bear
> In fractured atoms. . . .
> White feathers in the snow. . . .

are a reminiscence of a passage in Chapman's tragedy *Bussy D'Ambois* (V, i):

>   ... fly where men feel
> The burning axletree, and those that suffer
> Beneath the chariot of the snowy Bear. . . .

And now by a process of free association that anticipates the technique of the psychological novel and the movie the poem is filled with images of the open sea, the salt stinging spray, and the untrammeled wind. These are symbols of spiritual vitality in sharply ironic contrast to the symbols of spiritual torpor with which the poem is mainly filled, and to which it returns in the final dispirited look at himself with which the tired old man concludes his reverie. The last line of all is a critical summing up of the poem itself.

> Tenants of the house,
> Thoughts of a dry brain in a dry season.

This is the humiliating truth of what the poem is and what it is about.

But humility is the beginning of wisdom and the beginning of holiness. Perhaps there is hope of grace and salvation. This is not suggested here, but in the later religious poems of T. S. Eliot, *Ash Wednesday* (1930) and the *Four Quartets* (1935–1944), the positive rather than the negative aspect of the modern search for faith is explored. In the light of these *Gerontion* appears as a confessional poem. It is based on the assumption (as is also the more ambitious treatment of the same theme in the epoch-making *The Waste Land*, 1922) that the healing waters of God's grace have been dried up within us and that the modern task is to discover the way to make them flow again.

Recommended reading:

F. O. Matthiessen, *The Achievement of T. S. Eliot*, New York, Oxford University Press, 1935, revised edition, 1947.

B. Rajan, *T. S. Eliot, A Study of his Writings by Various Hands,* London, Dobson, 1947. (Includes W. Mankowitz, "Notes on 'Gerontion.'")

Theodore Spencer, "The Poetry of T. S. Eliot," *The Atlantic Monthly*, LI, 60–68.

Leonard Unger, *T. S. Eliot, A Selected Critique*, New York, Rinehart, 1948.

JAMES JOYCE (1882–1941): *A Portrait of the Artist as a Young Man*[1]

THE POSITION OF THE ARTIST IN THE 20TH CENTURY presents a peculiarly difficult problem. The traditional values of the past seem insufficient, and yet they have not been replaced by newer ideas to which he may cling without fear or doubt. The artist of the 20th century is not a part of an orderly and systematic world whose basic assumptions he need only express in order to fulfill his role in society. On the contrary, he is obliged by the nature of his times to seek new values and to try through this search to point an orderly way to his contemporaries.

It is not unnatural that at a time when the world is chaotic the search for certainty should involve turning back upon oneself. The individual becomes, when all else is confused, the one fixed point from which a new beginning can be made. The problem of seeking truth is thus in our modern world the problem of discovering one's own relationship to the universe. For this reason the most significant literature of the 20th century is subjective, a literature which attempts, in its careful exploration of the individual personality, to arrive at a more inclusive understanding. The artist is the subject matter of his own work, and it is in his examination of his own problems and personality that he defines and illuminates the problems of his times.

A Portrait of the Artist as a Young Man (1916), based as it is almost exactly upon the first twenty years of Joyce's life, is typical of the subjective, autobiographical literature of the 20th century. The hero of the novel, Stephen Dedalus, is Joyce himself, and the work revolves around three major crises in his life. The story of the development of Stephen from childhood to young manhood is the story of Joyce, but it is, of course, much more than that. It is the larger story of the growth, under the particular conditions of our modern world, of the artist, of the sensitive, expressive man, and it sheds light upon the strength and the weakness of his efforts to find a meaningful definition of the universal order.

In general, the first portion of the novel is concerned with Stephen's infancy and with his growing consciousness of religion. His religious awareness is followed by an awakening of his sexual instincts which culminates in a sinful affair at the age of sixteen. The second section of the work is concerned with Stephen's efforts to reconcile his religious beliefs with the sin he has committed: he is tortured by a deep sense of guilt, and yet he rebels against the restraints of his orthodoxy. The last part of the novel treats of Stephen's college days and brings him to the point of leaving Ireland forever, a lonely exile devoted to art.

At the end of the novel Stephen is about to leave upon a journey which will take him forever from his past life and associations. It is at once an actual and a symbolic journey upon which he is about to embark, and we can understand it when we recall that Joyce, in young manhood, left Ireland and never came home again except for a brief visit to his mother's deathbed some years later. Joyce, or Stephen, knew that above all it was necessary to break completely with the past, that expression and self-understanding, if they were ever to be achieved, could come only in new terms which would have to be fashioned out of different experience. The leaving of the homeland is thus symbolic of the rejection of the traditional values and of the recognition that new values would have to be sought elsewhere. The problem of the artist is by no means solved in the scope of Stephen's early life, but its terms are set: the past is not meaningful, the artist cannot remain in peace and comfort where he is, it is necessary to accept the lonely, bitter, and self-contained role of the wanderer and exile, not of this time or that place, looking in a sense for a home and for meaning. Joyce's later life and work represent a continuation of the life of Stephen. He travelled extensively on the

[1] Program A.

European continent, living variously in Italy, Switzerland, and France, and died far from his native Dublin, having created two monumental works, *Ulysses* (1922) and *Finnegan's Wake* (1939), which are sagas of the voyage of modern man. In these later works Joyce develops the techniques which he started in the *Portrait* and carries them out to their ultimate conclusion of what is virtually a new language called into existence in his effort to give expression to the complexity of man's inner thoughts and motivations. Stephen reappears in *Ulysses,* not as the central character, but still as the searching artist: this time the nature of the problems is more mature, more complex, but essentially the body of Joyce's work is the reflection under innumerable forms, in a style which will never be equalled or even imitated, of the journey from infancy to death of the artistic individual in modern times. Joyce is without question one of the greatest writers of all time and the man who has given what is perhaps the most significant expression to his own generation. In reading the *Portrait,* we start at the beginning of his work and life, and we should remember that both the work and the life go on to great heights of literary excellence and to depths of personal tragedy and loneliness.

The novel can best be understood and appreciated if we remember that its purpose is to make us participate in the feelings and thoughts of Stephen. What is important is not *what* happens to Stephen but what Stephen *thinks* and *feels* about what happens to him. Joyce takes us into the very consciousness of the character himself, so that we view the world through Stephen's eyes. At the beginning of the novel, in the episode on the playing field, we feel his sense of having been unjustly treated, his need to justify himself. The entire episode is told from Stephen's point of view, including the thoughts as well as the words:

> Rody Kickham was a decent fellow but Nasty Roche was a stink. Rody Kickham had greaves in his number and a hamper in the refectory. Nasty Roche had big hands.

These are Stephen's thoughts, induced by his feeling that he is small and weak and then recalling that Rody Kickham is not small or weak, which in turn brings Nasty Roche to his mind. There is a constant association of ideas, and what we learn of Stephen we learn by seeing and feeling as Stephen does, rather than through the explanations of an outside narrator. In this technique, Joyce's novel differs from the novels of traditional form. It is an example of the technique of "interior monologue" which is a characteristic of much of 20th-century writing.[2]

In Chapter II Stephen is older and is coming to be affected by literature, beauty, and abstract ideas which he could not have understood earlier. He is near adolescence, and, like many of that trying age, he imagines himself in many different roles. In particular he conceives himself as a sort of Byronic hero—dashing, idealistic, and sensitive—and when an essay he has submitted to an English class is branded as heresy, he takes refuge in his part. Further, Stephen is at an age when he is becoming increasingly aware of sexual desires, to which he gives expression in an extremely romanticized and complicated affair. His attitude, half-mature, half-childish, compounded of basic feelings and intellectualized rationalizations, is wonderfully brought out by the nature of the prose in which the affair is described:

> He had tried to build a breakwater of order and elegance against the sordid tide of life without him and to dam up, by rules of conduct and active interests and new filial relations, the powerful recurrence of the tides within him.

This overwritten rhetoric is not Joyce's style but Stephen's: it is in this fashion that Stephen conceives himself and his desires. For since the reader is within the consciousness of Stephen, it is in Stephen's own terms that he must see and feel.

Chapter III is the story of Stephen's remorse and of the battle within him against his con-

---

[2] See, above, p. 317.

sciousness of mortal sin. In the earlier chapters of the book, especially in Chapter I, where Stephen is a very young boy, he has been exposed to the teachings of the Church in the normal course of his upbringing and education. As a young child, he cannot comprehend theological doctrine. His religious beliefs come to him from his tutors in sermons, words, and admonitions. He builds up, with the vivid imagination of the young, a concept of the nature of Heaven, of damnation, and of sin. The idea of sin, with its concomitant idea of terrible retribution, is ingrained in him before he is old enough to understand intellectually what sin is and why it is punished. In his adolescence he carries in him the deep and fundamental consciousness of sin which stems from his early training, and when he does commit a wrongful act he reacts to it as he once reacted to the abstract idea. He is still enough of an adolescent to find and repeat to himself a verse which seems at the time to have been written only for him:

> O grave, where is thy victory?
> O death, where is thy sting?

In this chapter we go through the torments of Stephen's guilty repentance. Again, the language in which this section is written is not Joyce's prose but that of Stephen: the words, the concepts, the very syntax and form of the phrases, constitute Stephen's own definition of himself. He casts his thoughts in a mold which explains those thoughts; Joyce does not need to tell us anything, for we are within Stephen's mind and thinking along with him:

Every word of it was for him. Against his sin, foul and secret, the whole wrath of God was aimed. The preacher's knife had probed deeply into his disclosed conscience and he felt now that his soul was festering in sin. Yes, the preacher was right. God's turn had come. Like a beast in his lair his soul had lain down in its own filth but the blasts of the angel's trumpet had driven him forth from the darkness of sin into the light.

The words "foul," "festering," and "filth" are not words we would ordinarily use, but rather words from a sermon or from some book. And the concepts of the "beast in his lair," the "blasts of the angel's trumpet," and the "wrath of God" are phrased in purple prose, certainly not in the language of a young boy. But Stephen is reacting not so much to what he has done as to all the religious experiences he has had beforehand, in which sin and the punishment for sin were painted in just such terms.

Chapter IV is a sort of peaceful interlude in which, his torment having been appeased by his confession and absolution, Stephen has time to resume the more normal concerns of a young lad. He contemplates college and for the first time, in thinking about what he is going to become and do with his life, he realizes that his real purpose is that of being an artist. He discovers that within himself are ideas and attitudes which demand expression; more important, he discovers that who he is and what he is feeling are matters of supreme interest and importance to him. It can perhaps be said that in this chapter he becomes aware of the fact that he is different from other young men and that in the future he must go his own way unencumbered by the torments and doubts which spring from trying to force his own personality into the general pattern. He does not know specifically what he wants, but he is beginning to understand that he will have to discover it for himself and through himself, and not elsewhere. The broad outline of his future life becomes clear to him, and this section of the novel is one of self-realization, tranquillity, and sensitive development.

Chapter V is the story, finally, of Stephen's rebellion against the churchly doctrines. It is principally an intellectual rebellion in which he cannot bring himself to worship symbols which he has come to consider false, and yet cannot bring himself to deny the godly aspects of his theology. It is a revolt more against the observances of the Church than against its fundamental tenets, but it is more than that. All his life Stephen has been inextricably bound up in the Church, the family, the school, and Ireland. Consider that his teachers are priests, his priests are teachers, his family is rabidly patriotic, his country is Catholic, his parents represent authority, the Church represents his parents, the country and his parents and the teachers and the Church are all bound up in one. Where one begins and the other ends, it is impossible to say. The wonderful Christmas dinner in Chapter I demonstrates this: the little boy is home for a religious holiday—it is also an occasion for a family reunion (he goes home on two levels, to observe the birth of Christ and to see his parents)—and the conversation at table turns to the priests and the Church as well as to family matters and turkey. But the family is also Irish, and so are the priests, and they are all concerned with Irish politics and history. In the ensuing discussion, heated things are said about priests in politics which are angrily refuted on purely religious grounds. The argument proceeds on these two levels, the religious and the political-national, because in the minds of Stephen's family there is no clear distinction: they talk in the same sentence as Catholics, Irishmen, parents, and political partisans. In his rebellion against the practices of the Church, Stephen is by the same token rebelling symbolically against his whole previous life—he is rejecting authority from whatever source—his family, his country, and his Church. He cannot remain in Ireland without remaining with the Church and his family. When one is rejected, the others must also be, because they are all aspects of the same thing, only taking on slightly different external forms and emphases. When the one is gone, all are gone, and nothing remains but for Stephen to start upon his solitary journey into exile.

In this separation of the young man from the entire complex of his background, there is the symbol of the alienation which has affected the 20th-century artist. Repudiating the traditions of his past, emancipating himself from all that has come before, the 20th-century artist, like Stephen, sets out on a lonely voyage. His heroes, too, reflecting as they do his own problems, are lonely heroes. They must find strength in themselves and discover a means of surviving in a world which they consider hostile, unfriendly, and apart from them. They are men who take matters into their own hands because they find other hands unwilling or unable to help them. They are strong in the sense that they manage to find a way of living that helps them to survive; they are weak, perhaps, in the sense that they are separated from other men with whom they can find no contact, from whom they can derive no comfort. The modern hero is often sensitive, often understanding, often brave and courageous, often moral and just, but he is terrifyingly alone. In this final chapter of the *Portrait,* Joyce has succeeded in making one of the most penetrating analyses of the growth of separation that has ever been written.

It is clear that throughout the novel we are participating directly in the growth of a young man to a decisive point in his life. The action is minor, and the substance of the novel is not what Stephen does, or what happens to Stephen in the way of incident, so much as it is the development which he undergoes. This development is in many ways a curious one. For example, quite early in his life, the young Stephen plays with words:

> O, the green wothe botheth

he sings in place of

> O, the wild rose blossoms
> On the little green place.

He seizes the rhythm and the metre and the form of the words and substitutes other sounds which do quite as well. Later on in the same chapter he thinks of the belt on his coat:

That was a belt round his pocket. And belt was also to give another fellow a belt.

Here, in his mind, starting with ordinary and concrete meaning of "belt," he passes on to another usage of the same sound: he awakens to the fact that a belt is not always a belt, but that a belt is what you make it at the time you use the word. His reaction is a young one, of the same order as that of a baby who has a hard time learning that "Mama" is not only his own mother but the name of his playmate's mother too; but it demonstrates an early sensitivity to words and verbalization which becomes in his later life (as so clearly it became in the later work of Joyce) a method for arranging experience. Stephen (and for "Stephen" read "Joyce" throughout) tends to understand his problems in verbal forms and to handle his problems on the verbal level. His emotions are tied up with words, and it becomes difficult for him to determine in later life, when his experiences are more complex, where reality ends and verbalization begins. Stephen feels that by naming something you gain a certain power over it, and this almost magical worship of the word as a source of power is here exposed on the most subtle and complex level of our culture, although it is a common phenomenon among primitive tribes.

Ultimately, the novel achieves its result through words. Feelings are associated with phrases, emotions are conceived in rhetorical forms, and Stephen's own reactions are often literary. In his later work, *Ulysses* and *Finnegan's Wake,* Joyce carries to the greatest possible extreme this handling of words, with a richness of association that makes these books a continuous, though difficult, pleasure.

Certainly, if Stephen is the archetypical modern artist, he stands for two aspects of the modern artist which are of paramount importance: his isolation from his culture and his flight from reality. It is not impossible to conclude that in Joyce the artist has finally reached the last *impasse* of the age, a concern for self, an egocentric view and a preoccupation with form for the sake of form. On the other hand, Joyce paints with a subtlety that may never have been equalled, a sensitivity and an understanding which few writers have had. It is perhaps up to us to see to it that the intellectual and sensitive qualities of Stephen do not fritter themselves away in loneliness: one thing we can do is to understand him in all his complexity. By doing so we will be understanding ourselves and our times, and we can come no closer to what Joyce wanted the reader to do than to understand Stephen. For Stephen is the book, and the book is Stephen and Joyce is Stephen and he is writing for us.

Recommended reading:
Harry Levin, *James Joyce: A Critical Introduction,* New York, New Directions, 1941.
Herbert Gorman, *James Joyce,* New York, Farrar and Rinehart, 1939. A biography.
Theodore Spencer, ed., *Stephen Hero, a Part of the First Draft of "A Portrait of the Artist as a Young Man" by James Joyce,* New York, New Directions, 1944. Introduction also in *Southern Review,* Summer, 1941.
Seon Givens, ed. *James Joyce, Two Decades of Criticism,* New York, Vanguard, 1948. Especially see "The Portrait in Perspective," by Hugh Kenner, pp. 132–174, and the article by James T. Farrell, "Joyce's *A Portrait of the Artist,*" pp. 175–197.

JOSEPH CONRAD (1857–1924): *Victory*[1]

I. JOSEPH CONRAD is one of the most remarkable figures in the whole range of English literature. He was born in Poland in 1857, the son of well-to-do parents of the land-owning class. His full name was Teodor Jozef Konrad Korzeniowski. His parents died as a result of the hardships suffered in exile to northern Russia for the part they had played in the Polish nationalist movement, and Conrad was left an orphan at the age of ten under the care of a maternal uncle. In boyhood Conrad developed an overpowering desire to go to sea, and in 1874 he travelled to Marseilles and gained experience as a seaman on French sailing vessels. He took part in some dangerous gun-running expeditions to Spain, visited England, sailed before the mast to Australia and back, learned English, passed his examinations as Third Mate, and then served as an officer on ships sailing to the Dutch East Indies and the Malay Archipelago. His personal experiences on these voyages gave him the material for some of his best-known novels and stories, *Almayer's Folly* (1895), *The Nigger of the 'Narcissus'* (1897), *Lord Jim* (1900), *Youth* (1902), and *Victory* (1915). In 1886 he passed his examinations and became a Master Mariner. The same year he became a British subject. In 1890 he went to the Belgian Congo and encountered the experiences that are retold in the finest of his long short stories, *The Heart of Darkness* (1902). At this time he was beginning to set down his experiences in the form of fiction and was at work on his first book, *Almayer's Folly*, which was published five years later. His last ship was a famous sailing-ship, the *Torrens*, and among the passengers on the voyage from Australia to England in 1893 was John Galsworthy, not then yet a famous novelist. But Galsworthy read the manuscript of Conrad's first novel and encouraged the Anglo-Polish sailor to devote himself seriously and exclusively to writing.

In 1896 Conrad gave up the sea, married, and settled down in Kent. Here in the latter half of a life that until then had been spent in adventurous action on the seven seas and in the Far East he devoted himself to writing in a language that was not his native one a series of novels that won him recognition before his death in 1924 as one of the finest English novelists of the 20th century.[2]

II. *Victory* is subtitled "An Island Tale," and that is what on the surface it is—an exciting story of love, adventure, and self-sacrifice in the South Seas. The central figure is romantic enough. He is the aristocratic Axel Heyst, a self-exiled and disillusioned wanderer who believes that the only way to escape the cruelty and futility of life is to look on the spectacle with a mixture of pity and ironic detachment, studiously refraining from involvement in action. But he has failed to take into account his human sympathies and the strength of the appeals of decency and justice; and on two occasions—one preliminary to the main action but subtly and fatally connected with it, and the other the main action itself—Heyst is drawn into active participation in life. The results are not fortunate. The best intentions go awry, and the noblest motives lead to disastrous conclusions. Heyst's pessimistic view of humanity as a pitiful mixture of folly and knavery might well seem to be justified by the concatenation of events which brings a tragic end to his humane and quixotic involvement in the life of a human being who is described as "cornered"—the girl Lena. Certainly in the gross imbecility and malicious cowardice of the Teutonic innkeeper Schomberg, in the devilish concentration

---

[1] Program B.

[2] Besides the novels already named Conrad wrote *Nostromo* (1904), his longest and finest work; *The Secret Agent* (1907); *Under Western Eyes* (1911); *Chance* (1913); *The Shadow Line* (1917); *The Rescue* (1920); and *The Rover* (1923).

upon murder of the sinister Mr. Jones and his feline "secretary," Ricardo,—to say nothing of the subhuman savagery of their dog-like servant Pedro and the inscrutable self-interest of Mr. Wang, Heyst's Chinese servant—there are wickedness and folly enough. But Heyst, who has the dignity and the noble intentions of a genuine tragic hero, has the fatal weakness too. And it is this, as much as any external agency, that brings about his downfall. His pride and the very philosophy of withdrawal, rooted in pity and sympathy though they are, have unfitted him to defend himself and the girl whose fate he has become responsible for. This indeed is one of the fundamental ironies in a book that is drenched in irony. Heyst at the last, in a tragic dénouement that recalls the corpse-littered end of *Hamlet,* realizes his own responsibility. "Ah, Davidson," he cries, "woe to the man whose heart has not learned while young to hope, to love,—and to put its trust in life."

Heyst has realized too late that his philosophy of sceptical detachment based on a disillusioned underestimate of the worth of life itself had been responsible for his failure to know and have faith in either Lena or himself and was the prime cause, too, of his inability, both practical and moral, to deal effectively and certainly with the threat launched by evil forces from outside. This is his tragedy, and he recognizes its consequences as clearly at the end as did the great exemplar of the paralysing effect of scepticism upon action, Hamlet himself.

III. Conrad was an extremely self-conscious artist, and his experiments in the technique of the novel, his attempts to heighten suspense, enhance reality, and drive home the point of his story by the artful and gradual revelation of varying partial points of view, link him with the great master of modern fiction, Henry James, whose disciple, indeed, he was in *Victory* and certain other of his later novels. The structure of *Victory* is well worth examining by the reader who wishes to get the maximum enjoyment from the book. Such a reader should keep his attention alert to catch the many subtle and significant shifts in the point of view from which events are perceived and comprehended, a challenge all the more stimulating because these shifts may occur several times within a chapter and sometimes within a paragraph or even a single sentence.

The novel is divided into four parts, the first two of them being a necessary preliminary to the main action, which, although it has been set in motion, is not presented directly nor its consequences worked out until Parts III and IV.

The first part introduces the protagonist of the tragedy, Axel Heyst—"enchanted Heyst" as the traders and business men in the islands of the Dutch East Indies call him. The whole of Part I is presented from the point of view of an unnamed narrator, a disinterested but well-meaning representative of the local white traders. From the disjointed and fragmentary knowledge of this observer we learn the local gossip about the uprooted Heyst, about his rescue of the grateful Morrison, a trader and shipowner whom Heyst is able to save from financial ruin and who promptly showers upon his somewhat embarrassed benefactor a load of gratitude that threatens to destroy Heyst's carefully cherished independence. We learn, too, of the stupid and malicious hotel-keeper Schomberg, whose jealous hatred of the unconscious Heyst sets in motion a flood of malicious gossip, which, when Morrison on furlough in England catches pneumonia and dies, goes so far as to accuse Heyst of swindling his friend and sending him home to die. Of course, no one believes Schomberg's fantastic interpretation of events, but later the calumny is to rise up before Heyst, whose high-minded disgust poisons the very sources of action at the moment when he most needs energy and decision.

The affair of Morrison is preliminary to the main action. This concerns itself with Heyst's chivalrous and well-meaning "rescue" of the girl Lena, whom he saves from brutal mistreatment and from the unwanted attentions of Schomberg, by taking her away from her place in a touring ladies' orchestra and eloping with her to his solitary island of Samburan. Lena is a charming and pathetic figure, and Heyst's impulse to save her is honorable and generous. The action that follows is concerned with what results from this decisive action, a second and much more hazardous departure from Heyst's philosophy of aloofness.

The crucial event itself is presented in Part I only indirectly and inconclusively, from the point of view of an observer who picks up the story from gossip and hearsay, and it is not until Part II that the action backtracks upon itself to present, mainly from the point of view of Heyst himself, the significant and eagerly awaited details of Heyst's meeting with Lena and his determination to become responsible for her fate and take her with him to his island.

The first two books are a preliminary starting of the action and in the dramatic structure of the novel correspond to Act I of *Othello*. Just as the scene shifts to Cyprus where Othello and Desdemona have been transported, so too in *Victory*, Book III (the beginning of Act II), the scene shifts to the solitary island, and Heyst and Lena take the center of the stage.

At this point in the action Heyst might have echoed Othello's unconscious irony: "If it were now to die, 'twere now to be most happy."

Heyst and Lena are two innocent beings in what seems to be a paradise. But already Heyst has partaken of the apple of involvement, and, though he does not know it, evil is already preparing itself to descend upon him and destroy him.[3] Heyst is ignorant of what the reader already knows from the closing chapters of Part II. The deadly and irresponsible forces of chaos in the persons of Mr. Jones and his follower Ricardo having been excited by Schomberg's fantastic tale of Heyst's wealth hidden on the island, are already on their way to break in upon their unsuspecting and easily disarmed victim.

From this point on, the movement of the story is filled with suspense and a cumulatively mounting horror. We watch the "doomed man" as Jones and Ricardo call Heyst, play out with delicate irony and magnificent courage a losing battle with opponents whose ruthlessness, singleness of purpose, and weapons he cannot match. It is Lena, whose life of suffering and exploitation has given her knowledge, courage, and determination, who takes the risk of losing Heyst's love—his full comprehension she has never had—by entering into a deceptive compact with the enemy, stealing a weapon, and opening a breach between Jones and Ricardo that might, but for a misdirected bullet, have ended in a real instead of a quixotic and ambiguous victory.

IV. Conrad differs from such contemporaries among the Edwardian novelists as John Galsworthy, Arnold Bennett, and H. G. Wells in that his interests are not sociological or humanitarian but aesthetic and philosophical. He was a disciple of the great Russian masters Turgeniev and Dostoievsky and of the Europeanised American, Henry James. In widening the scope of the novel and developing its technique, it may be said that he applied the methods of impressionism to romantic or exotic subjects and that he carried forward (along with Henry James) fruitful experiments in the form and structure of the novel, and anticipated the experimental novel of Virginia Woolf, William Faulkner, and James Joyce.

His work is an important stage in the development of a subjective or inner realism that sought to apply to the mental processes of his characters the same sort of minute and dispassionate analysis that the great French realists (Balzac, Flaubert, Zola) had applied to external objects and events. He does not plunge directly into the stream of consciousness as the brilliant Freudian novelists do, but he is as subtle and accurate as any of them in his analysis of the way in which sense impressions affect the consciousness. What is even more remarkable is the fact that he makes intensely thrilling drama out of the way in which mental processes are resolved into action and then out of the way in which those actions are evaluated in moral or ethical terms. Conrad is at once an impressionist, a dramatist, and a moralist, and all three aspects are woven together to form an integral part of his work as an artist.

[3]The metaphor of Eden and the sinister suggestion of its loss is developed by Conrad with great subtlety and skill on the first page of Part III.

He has stated his concept of the function of the novel and of the responsibility of the novelist in the Preface to one of the earliest of his masterpieces, *The Nigger of the 'Narcissus'* (1897), a short novel devoted entirely to the subject that Conrad knew most intimately—sailing ships, the men who manned them, and the sea itself. The novel as a work of art, he declared, makes its appeal to temperament. It must be an impression conveyed through the senses, and it must carry conviction to the hidden springs of responsive emotion. The artist, Conrad declared, descends into himself—nearly all Conrad's own fiction is autobiographical—and makes an appeal to that part of our being that is not dependent on knowledge or wisdom. He speaks to our capacity for delight, wonder, and sympathy. "My task is," Conrad continued, "by the power of the written word to make you hear, to make you feel—it is, before all, to make you see. . . ."

The object of the artist he describes in terms of impressionism and humanity. It is "to snatch, in a moment of courage, from the remorseless rush of time a passing phase of life." But this is only the beginning. "The task approached in tenderness and faith is to hold up unquestioningly, without choice and without fear, the rescued fragment before all eyes in the light of a sincere mood. It is to show its vibration, its color, its form . . . reveal the substance of its truth . . . the stress and passion within the core of each convincing moment. . . .

"To arrest, for the space of a breath, the hands busy about the work of the earth, and compel men entranced by the sight of distant goals to glance for a moment at the surrounding vision of form and colour . . . and to give them the understanding of these forms and colours that shall induce pity and sympathy . . . this is the aim of the sincere artist."

In these sentences from what amounts to a formal statement of Conrad's creed as an artist, the reader can hardly fail to detect the emphasis upon clarity of vision, personal integrity, and an attitude towards humanity that is composed of about equal parts of sympathy and of pity. It is at once sceptical and strongly ethical, and it is not difficult to see in it the germ of the attitudes that were later to crystallize in the figure of Axel Heyst.

The mixture of scepticism and faith, of pity and sympathy, which is so fundamental a part of the temperament with which Conrad looks at life, is given an even more direct expression in another important document, "A Familiar Preface" to an autobiographical work entitled *A Personal Record,* published in 1912. Here, after developing along somewhat similar lines his theory of impressionism and artistic sincerity, he begins to speak of the spirit in which he is compelled to regard human life. The sight of human affairs, he says, deserves Admiration and Pity. And Respect. "Conscious resignation informed by love" he declares to be the only possible attitude in the face of the spectacle of human life and the problem of evil. Again the reader will be reminded of Heyst, or perhaps of Heyst's philosophical father. "Resignation," he goes on to say, "is not the last word of wisdom. I am too much a creature of my time for that. But I think the proper wisdom is to will what the gods will without perhaps being certain what their will is—or even if they have a will of their own."

In spite of this apparent scepticism, Conrad's work testifies to the presence of an underlying faith, a faith, he has said, which holds that "the temporal world rests on a few very simple ideas. . . . It rests notably, among others, on the idea of Fidelity. . . ." It is this faith that Conrad's most striking characters uphold, or just fail to hold on to, or illustrate by denying it. With the case of *Victory* before us it is not necessary to mention such figures as Lord Jim, Nostromo, or Captain MacWhirr (in *Typhoon*); Axel Heyst and Lena and Captain Davidson live in it, and two of them die in it, while Jones, Ricardo, and the unspeakable Schomberg are faithful to nothing but themselves and consequently move about in a Hell of their own making.

The union of psychological insight and moral seriousness makes Conrad an important modern novelist, and *Victory* is an important modern novel because it is a prophecy of one of the great tragic paradoxes of our time: that man's best qualities often make him powerless to resist irrational force, ruthless cunning, and the accident of surprise. In the face of the modern world-dilemma, which Conrad prophetically foreknew, he places before us a pattern of what it means to be a free man. He is sceptical without being disillusioned, and detached without being unsympathetic; and he has been able to endow the heroic virtues of fidelity and courage with an almost religious significance without having recourse to the supernatural.

Recommended reading:
F. R. Leavis, *The Great Tradition,* New York, George Stewart, n.d. [1948?]
R. L. Mégroz, *Joseph Conrad's Mind and Method,* London, Faber, 1931.
Edward Crankshaw, *Joseph Conrad, Some Aspects of the Art of the Novel,* London, John Lane, 1936.
Virginia Woolf, *The Common Reader,* New York, Harcourt, Brace, 1925.
H. L. Mencken, *A Book of Prefaces,* New York, Knopf, 1917.
James Huneker, *Ivory Apes and Peacocks,* New York, Scribner's, n.d.

CONTEMPORARY MUSIC

PAUL HINDEMITH (1895–): *Quintet for Wind Instruments*[1]

PAUL HINDEMITH was born near Frankfurt, Germany, in 1895. Political developments within Germany during the 1930's made it necessary for him to leave the country, and for a time thereafter he was musical adviser to the Turkish government. Later he came to the United States, of which country he is now a citizen, and for a number of years has taught music composition and theory at Yale University. Active as composer, theorist, performer, and teacher, he is one of the leading figures of 20th-century music.

Hindemith was schooled in the style of late German Romantic music, but quickly abandoned the style because it was not congenial to him nor to what he wished to express in music. Thus he belongs to that large group of 20th-century composers who rejected the musical tradition in which they had been nurtured and who experimented freely with the language of music. Younger than his contemporaries Igor Stravinsky and Arnold Schoenberg, Hindemith was less tied to the Romantic tradition; he was only seventeen when Schoenberg's song-cycle *Pierrot Lunaire* ("Moonstruck Pierrot") caused a riot in Vienna, and only eighteen when Stravinsky's equally revolutionary ballet *The Rite of Spring* created a scandal in Paris. The extreme dissonance, melodic angularity, and jagged rhythms of early 20th-century music were already well established while Hindemith was still a student; in his first mature works he began to exploit all of these "new resources" freely.

With the new style came a new attitude toward music. Hindemith expressed it thus:

It is to be regretted that in general so little relationship exists today between the producers and consumers of music. . . . The demand for music is so great that composer and consumer ought most emphatically to come at least to an understanding.

and

A composer should never write unless he is acquainted with the demand for his work. The time of consistent composing for one's own satisfaction is probably gone for ever.

In the light of these statements should be judged the movement called "Workaday Music,"

[1] Program A.

which appeared in Germany during the 1920's. For a time Hindemith was spiritual leader of a group of composers who wrote music on order—whether for the birthday celebration of a symphony orchestra, an opera for children, or marching music for a political group. Whatever the merits of such an aesthetic program—and it is significant that the movement was short-lived—nothing could better illustrate the difference between 19th- and 20th-century music and musicians.

In the 19th century Beethoven and the Romantic composers after him wrote first of all to satisfy and to express themselves; the work created the demand. At an earlier time both Bach and Mozart had written works "on order"; however, the societies in which they lived used new music, and writing to specification was a normal part of the composer's professional life. Originating as it did with an individual and not with society, Hindemith's attempt to return to the earlier system of "music for use," was artificial in origin and doomed to failure from the start. It is only necessary to ask what "use" the 20th century makes of music. The answer is implicit in the ensuing pages, in which Hindemith's *Quintet for Wind Instruments* is studied, not as a thing of everyday utility, but as a work of art, unique unto itself, communicating musical ideas of significance.

Hindemith's *Quintet,* though written during the terrible post-war year 1922, reflects little of contemporary Germany in the music unless it be found in the sharpness of the melodic line and in the prevailing melancholy of the third movement. Written without program or extra-musical association, the *Quintet* is an abstract chamber work for five instruments—flute (the piccolo substituting in one movement), oboe, clarinet, French horn, and bassoon. The instruments were apparently chosen for their contrasting *timbres* (tone colors), since the five are rarely blended into a composite sound. In this detail the *Quintet* recalls the Baroque orchestration of Bach.

Tonality is treated with the greatest freedom, and the combination of two or more different keys *(polytonality)* occurs in several sections. Indeed, so free is Hindemith's treatment of key that only one of five movements ends on the "tonic" with which it began. Coupled with this freedom from the major-minor tonal system is a free use of dissonance. Note, for example, the first chord of the *Quintet,* which reduced to its tonal elements consists of two superimposed seconds (C-D-E). It is characteristic not only of Hindemith's music but of 20th-century music in general that dissonance is no longer subservient to consonance. The bite of a dissonance, cultivated for its own sake and for its expressive character, is infrequently softened by a resolution to a consonance.

Though less experimental in his treatment of rhythm than other contemporary composers, Hindemith writes melodic lines of tremendous drive. Each musical idea is clearly defined, and a Classical conciseness marks all sections of the *Quintet*. In addition, there is little change of dynamic level within a movement. The type of *crescendo-decrescendo* so characteristic of Beethoven's music is rarely encountered. Instead, sections of quiet music are followed by sections of loud music, or vice versa; a change of dynamics is most frequently achieved by a change in the number of instruments playing.

The formal plan of each movement of the *Quintet* is of the greatest simplicity, allowing the listener to concentrate on the more complex aspects of the music—texture, harmony, melody. Nothing could contrast more with the first movement of Beethoven's *Violin Concerto* than the opening movement of the *Quintet,* which is also in sonata-form, though in miniature. Hindemith's themes, albeit individual and characteristic, are not imbued with any particular dramatic significance, nor are they placed in conflict with each other; the mood of the music remains relatively the same throughout the movement, and the development of a theme is by repetition and extension rather than the thrust and counter-thrust of a typical 19th-century sonata Development section.

368 CONTEMPORARY ART

FIRST MOVEMENT: Playful, moderately fast.

Form: Sonata-form.

Exposition (mm. 1–36). The first subject, a six-measure melody of extraordinary vigor and range (two octaves plus a sixth), begins immediately in the clarinet (Ex. 99)[2]. With slight variation of the last half, it is instantly repeated by the oboe (mm. 7–12). The accom-

Example 99

paniment, played by the French horn and bassoon, later joined by the oboe, is basically consonant in itself but combines dissonantly with the melody. Characteristic of the accompaniment is the rhythmic figure, ♫ ♫ , which permeates the first movement.

Precisely where the *Transition* begins is difficult to determine, since Hindemith, instead of introducing the usual new "transitional" material, develops the first subject (mm. 13–23). At letter B of the score the oboe states the second subject (mm. 24–27), a melody more lyrical and less athletic than the first subject (Ex. 100). It is immediately repeated by the flute and oboe (mm. 28–31), playing, not in unison, but a third apart. Note the many cross-

Example 100

[2] Both the clarinet and French horn are transposing instruments (*i.e.,* they do not play the pitches that are notated). In the examples that follow, the music is rendered *as it sounds.* Examples 99-105, from Hindemith's *Quintet for Wind Instruments,* are reprinted by permission of the copyright owners, Associated Music Publishers, Inc.

CONTEMPORARY MUSIC

relations (*i.e.,* mutually incompatible tones, such as C-natural in one voice followed by C-sharp in another) which occur in this second statement of the melody.

The *Codetta* (mm. 32–36) begins with a one-measure motive (characterized by the leap of a ninth, B to C) first stated by the clarinet (Ex. 101). This is bandied about by flute, oboe,

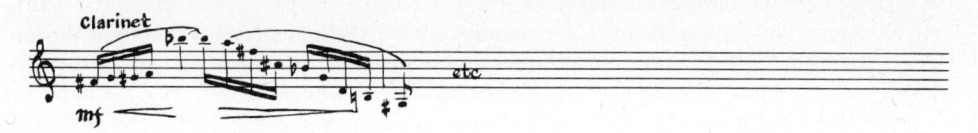

Example 101

and clarinet. Without pause or cadence the intensity of the music suddenly increases and the—

Development section (mm. 37–53) begins. Against the repetition of the ♩♫ ♩♫ rhythmic figure in the other instruments, the clarinet "discusses" the second subject, twisting and turning it about until the subject is exhausted. At this the bassoon rushes in (letter D) with the codetta motive, and the clarinet promptly begins the—

Recapitulation (mm. 48–75) with a statement of the first subject, with the first phrase of the melody altered, and the last half taken over by the flute. The original first phrase is now repeated by the oboe (mm. 53–58), but the last half is modified. Three times the flute plays a fragment of the first subject, the third time adding the one-measure codetta motive, whereupon the oboe repeats the first phrase of the first subject twice. The instruments pause (m. 69). Unaccompanied, the bassoon enters with the initial phrase of the second subject; however, instead of continuing with the remainder of the subject, the bassoon introduces the codetta motive. This is promptly repeated by the clarinet, and the movement is finished as abruptly as it began.

Since the Classical major-minor tonal system is almost meaningless for this music, the sonata-form is not determined by key-areas. Instead, it is the relationship of themes, their development and reappearances, that declare the form. To be sure, the first subject appears in both Exposition and Recapitulation with the same pitches, but so does the second subject (or as much of it as is given).

SECOND MOVEMENT: Waltz, very soft throughout.

This movement, a rather fast waltz, is built on the following simple plan (each letter representing a full section of music): A A² B C B² A³ Coda.

Section A (mm. 1–14). Bassoon and French horn establish the triple waltz meter, and in measure 5 the clarinet enters with an elegant melody arranged in two five-measure phrases.

Section A² (mm. 15–24). The clarinet's melody is promptly repeated by the piccolo (a higher instrument which substitutes for the flute in this movement[3]) to a slightly more animated accompaniment.

Section B (mm. 25–31). A new, contrasting melody is introduced by the oboe (Ex. 102). The nasal tone of the oboe and the *staccato* (detached) repeated notes of this short melodic

Example 102

idea (♫♫ ♩♩ ♫ ♩♩) offer sharp contrast to Section A² as well as to—

Section C (mm. 32–51). Against an accompaniment which develops the repeated-note figure of Section B, the French horn plays a graceful, syncopated melody eight measures in

---
[3] It sounds an octave higher than the written notes.

length. An intrusion (mm. 39–43), which interrupts the flow of the melody, is followed by a repetition of the first eight measures.

Section B² (mm. 52–57). This is an exact repetition of mm. 25–31, and is followed by—

Section A³ (mm. 58–67), an almost exact repetition of A². After this section the *tempo* changes to "Somewhat slower" and the—

Coda (mm. 68–90) begins. First, the clarinet follows the bassoon, each imitating the latter's one-measure motive. Then the oboe recalls the repeated-note motive of Section B. The bassoon, solo, muses rather seriously; the oboe repeats its *staccato* motive; this is echoed by the piccolo, bringing the movement to a close.

THIRD MOVEMENT: Placid and simple.

This, the slow movement of the *Quintet,* falls into four clearly defined sections: A (ternary form), an episode B (melody with *ostinato*), A² (a free repetition of A), and Coda.

Section A (mm. 1–29). A placid melody is played by the flute accompanied a third lower by the clarinet and joined at phrase-endings by oboe and bassoon (Ex. 103). Cross-relations (*e.g.,* measure 2: B and B-flat), bits of *chromaticism* (*e.g.,* measures 6–7: oboe), and dissonances, though also found in the first two movements, have an added expressiveness in this movement because the *tempo* is slower and thus their effect is prolonged.

Example 103

In the middle section of this ternary form the flute continues to spin out a melody in short phrases. One by one the other instruments enter, first imitating the flute's melody, then continuing more or less independently. As the polyphonic texture increases in density, so the character of the music grows more intense, leading to the return of the music heard at the beginning of the movement. This time, however, the melody is played by the oboe with full, rich accompaniment by all the other instruments.

Section B (mm. 30–54). In sharp contrast to the polyphonic texture of Section A, the *episode* begins with a two-measure *ostinato* (Ex. 104) played by flute, French horn, and bassoon. This muffled, repeated figure (mm. 30–31) occurs ten times in the next twenty measures.

Example 104

Against the *ostinato*, the oboe plays a long, elegiac melody (mm. 33–42) which, in its first phrase, is an obvious variation of the flute melody heard at the beginning of this movement (*cf.* mm. 1–4). It is repeated (mm. 43–50), slightly abridged, by the oboe doubled two octaves lower by the bassoon. The doubling of two such different instrumental *timbres* (tone colors) gives to the melody an extraordinary character. Note the new dimension introduced when the bassoon drops an additional octave lower (m. 46). The *ostinato* and oboe-bassoon melody stop abruptly, and the flute enters, anticipating the return of Section A by repeating three times the first two pitches of the beginning (mm. 52–54). A solo phrase, *ritenuto* (held back), by the flute leads to a return of the melodic material of —

CONTEMPORARY MUSIC

Section A² (mm. 55–70). The following eight measures (mm. 56–63) are an exact repetition of the first eight measures of the movement (see Ex. 103). Then the last eight measures of Section A are repeated, but in reverse order. Note that the middle part of the original ternary form has been suppressed, so that only the first and last sections remain. There is a measure's silence, and then the—

Coda (mm. 71–88) begins. The first three measures of Section A, played by clarinet and oboe, then clarinet and flute, are superimposed on part of the *ostinato* figure of Section B, played by the French horn. Next the upward leap of the minor third, characteristic of the melodies throughout this movement, is repeated. A quiet phrase played by the flute alone is followed by a final reminiscence of the leap of the minor third.

FOURTH MOVEMENT: In rapid quarters.
                      Cadenzas.

This movement, a kind of intermission, affords each instrument the opportunity of exhibiting its virtuosity. The cadenzas are short, only one exceeding two measures, and each is prefaced by a little *ritornello,* or "returning" passage, played by four of the five instruments.

FIFTH MOVEMENT: Very lively.

This movement, like the second and third, falls into several well-defined sections: A B C D B² A² Coda.

Section A (mm. 1–13). For the first time all five instruments begin a movement together. The theme, a boisterous one, is harmonized with many "hollow" fifths (Ex. 105) and there is considerable note-against-note movement (*e.g.,* measures 6–9). Within the simple texture

Example 105

the rhythmic juggling of duple and triple measures (*e.g.,* measures 3–5, 8–10, etc.) and irregular melodic phrasing is quite evident, as is the syncopation which follows in—

Section B (mm. 14–51). Against the bassoon's equal-note movement and a series of short *ostinato* figures played by the clarinet (mm. 14–19, 20–25, 26–31), the oboe, joined by the flute, plays a consistently off-the-beat motive. This hurried figure is played three times, each time at a higher pitch level. Then only the last part of the theme is repeated, and finally only the clarinet is left repeating five descending chromatic notes five times, in such a way that with each repetition a different pitch appears on the first (accented) beat of the measure. A subsequent development of this off-beat melody (mm. 40–51) is interrupted by—

Section C (mm. 52–65). A new melody, played by the oboe, is instantly taken by the flute, and later in part by the bassoon. The strong duple meter of this sprightly melody contrasts sharply with the basically triple meter of the preceding section and with that of—

Section D (mm. 66–97). The flute plays a jaunty melody in triple meter to an active accompaniment provided by the other instruments. For a moment (mm. 77–83) the lower instruments break the smooth flow of the music with a bit of polyphonic interplay. The flute melody returns (m. 84), but once again the various instruments assert melodic independence (mm. 90–96), this time creating a host of sharp dissonances.

Section B² (mm. 98–117), its ending slightly altered, leads in turn to a repetition of the first 13 measures of—

Section A² (mm. 118–130). At measure 130 the oboe suddenly repeats the brittle melody of Section A and with this the—

Coda (mm. 131–164) begins. The clarinet plays part of the melody begun by the oboe. Then three measures of the opening of the movement (see Ex. 105) occur, followed by the syncopated melody of Section B, its last phrase repeated several times by three, then four, instruments. Two flourishes and three repetitions of the original "hollow" fifth E–B, and the movement is finished.

Recommended reading:
Constant Lambert, *Music Ho! A Study of Music in Decline,* New York, Scribner's, 1934, pp. 246–274.
Adolfo Salazar, *Music in Our Time,* tr. Isabel Pope, New York, W. W. Norton, 1946, pp. 248–255.

IGOR STRAVINSKY (1882–   ): *Octet for Wind Instruments*[1]

IGOR STRAVINSKY was born near St. Petersburg (now Leningrad), Russia, in 1882. As is the case of so many contemporary artists and musicians, the political turmoil of the 20th century has made of him an exile. Being *persona non grata* in his native land, where Soviet critics find his music "decadent," he has lived in many parts of Europe and finally in the United States, of which country he is now a citizen. Even in those countries which do not subordinate art to social uses, Stravinsky has not always found ready acceptance for his music; for Stravinsky is a "modern" composer, as unorthodox in his art as the painter Picasso and the writer James Joyce are in theirs. Indeed, all three of the artists named are key figures in the artistic revolution of the first two decades of the 20th century.

The precise nature of this or any artistic revolt is difficult to define, since in every instance it is part of an evolving pattern. The most radical of 20th-century artists were not born rebelling. Legitimate heirs to the achievements of the past, they learned from those they later repudiated, took from them their cue for revolt. Nor did this recent artistic revolution take place quickly. The musical style characteristic of the 20th century was created during the years between 1860, when Richard Wagner composed his opera *Tristan und Isolde,* and the first decade of the new century, when such "modern" works as Stravinsky's ballet *The Rite of Spring* and Arnold Schoenberg's song-cycle *Pierrot Lunaire* ("Moon-struck Pierrot") shocked the musical world. Within this post-Romantic period the search for ever more extraordinary means of expression changed the very complexion of music.

As a result of his studies with Nicolas Rimsky-Korsakov, Stravinsky's first compositions are written in the opulent, late-19th-century post-Romantic manner of his teacher. *The Rite of Spring* (1913), the major work of Stravinsky's first or "Russian" period, is a direct descendant of Rimsky-Korsakov's *Sheherazade* (1888). Both works are programmatic, illustrating non-musical ideas and scenes; both are written in a nationalistic idiom with borrowings from or imitations of Russian folk-song; and both employ the orchestra in a highly coloristic manner. Stravinsky's ballet differs from the genial, fairy-tale tone-poem of his teacher in its frenzied rhythms, extreme dissonance, and emphasis on the harshest, most

[1]Program B.

barbaric of orchestral colors. Within the framework of late-19th-century program music Stravinsky contrived an anti-Romantic musical language of the greatest significance for what is considered the 20th-century idiom.

Unlike his teacher, who was content to exploit program music all his life, Stravinsky abandoned the form as soon as he had mastered it. At the time of World War I and the Russian Revolution, he began to write "abstract," non-programmatic music for chamber groups. Instead of using loosely connected sections as he had in his earlier ballets, Stravinsky experimented with earlier musical forms, both polyphonic and homophonic. Instead of fashioning melodies after Russian folk-song, he now modeled his melodies on formulas and styles of earlier periods, though stamping them with an imprint of his own. And instead of using an essentially homophonic texture, he employed polyphony to a greater extent. Carried over from the earlier ballet scores were the strong rhythmic element, the free use of dissonance, and an extraordinary feeling for instrumental color.

Intimately associated with this change of style was Stravinsky's new attitude toward music, particularly toward his own. It is best expressed in the composer's own words:

The phenomenon of music is given to us with the sole purpose of establishing an order in things, including, and particularly, the coordination between *man* and *time*. To be put into practice, its indispensable and single requirement is construction. Construction once completed, this order has been attained, and there is nothing more to be said. It would be futile to look for, or expect anything else from it. It is precisely this construction, this achieved order, which produces in us a unique emotion having nothing in common with our ordinary sensations and our responses to the impressions of daily life. One could not better define the sensation produced by music than by saying that it is identical with that evoked by contemplation of the interplay of architectural forms. Goethe thoroughly understood that when he called architecture petrified music.[2]

There is in Stravinsky's radical change of style a sign of the dilemma faced by many creative artists in the 20th century. None of the composers already encountered in this volume found it necessary to discard one style of composition and adopt another; each worked within a style, developing what he had inherited. But Stravinsky, as well as other 20th-century composers, began to write in the style of his immediate predecessors, only to find himself so out of sympathy with this style that it was necessary for him to make a complete break with it. As the youth, no longer able to accept and submit to the ideas of his parents, rebels, so Stravinsky and many of his contemporaries rejected the tradition in which they had been nurtured. Turning to earlier periods—the Baroque, the Classical, the Rococo—each artist selected what most appealed to him and fashioned his music in the light of these earlier styles.

Not tradition but choice became the basis on which the composer rested his art. As a result the music of the early 20th century presents almost as many different styles as there are composers active. To appreciate the cultural significance of this diversity it is necessary only to contrast the early 20th century with such a period as the late 18th, in which all composers shared the same musical language, but differed in the way in which they used it.

It is from the point of view expressed in the quotation above that Stravinsky wishes the listener to approach his *Octet for Wind Instruments*. This work, written in 1923, ten years after his programmatic ballet *The Rite of Spring,* is the very antithesis of the earlier work. First, the *Octet* is a chamber work for eight wind instruments: flute, clarinet, two bassoons, two trumpets, and two trombones. There is no program or extra-musical association; the work, like the chamber music of Mozart, is abstract in nature. In the prevailing polyphonic texture each instrument preserves a good part of its individuality. Only rarely are the eight instruments blended as Beethoven combined various instruments for a homogeneous, composite

[2]*Stravinsky: An Autobiography* (New York, Simon and Schuster: 1936), pp. 84–85.

sound. Tonality is treated with the greatest freedom. Coupled with this freedom from the major-minor tonal system is a free use of dissonance. It is characteristic not only of Stravinsky's music but of 20th-century music that dissonance is no longer subservient to consonance.[3] The bite of a dissonance, cultivated for its own sake and for its expressive character, is infrequently softened by a resolution to a consonance. In addition, meter and rhythm are of the greatest importance, though both are dealt with in a quite unorthodox manner. Within a single movement measures of duple and triple are freely mixed, the counting unit (*e.g.*, 3/4, 2/16, 2/4, 3/8, etc.) changes, and unusual meters, such as 5/8, are not uncommon. As a result, the metric continuity present in compositions which have a duple or triple meter throughout is lacking. In place of metric continuity in Stravinsky's music, there is a new freedom of rhythmic design. Quickly changing accents (*e.g.*, ONE-two, ONE-two-three, ONE-two-three, ONE-two-THREE-four-five, ONE-two, etc.), not to be found in the music of Bach or Mozart or Beethoven, give the music a new kind of rhythmic excitement.

The forms employed by Stravinsky are free. Instead of the fixed patterns of Classical music (*e.g.*, sonata-form, simple episodic form, etc.), Stravinsky approaches the evolving type of organization found in much of Bach's music. Better yet, one might liken Stravinsky's music to a development section of a sonata-form movement: themes are taken up, developed freely, and discarded, and new themes appear, to be treated in like manner. Balance is achieved by consistency of texture and by the eventual return of the initial theme or themes. However, instead of an exact A B A² type of repetition, the return of the first theme or themes usually occurs in a new context. By these means Stravinsky achieves balance in his music even while preserving freedom.

FIRST MOVEMENT

Sinfonia (mm. 1–41): *Lento*. Like the prologue to a play, the slow (*Lento*) Sinfonia to the first movement excites the listener's curiosity without precisely satisfying it. A twice-stated two-measure phrase, begun by trumpet and continued by bassoons, clarinet, and flute, sets the stage. Then a quiet three- (later four-) part polyphony begins in the woodwinds. The lack of profile in the melodic strands and their ceaseless searching (which is to be seen in the many note-repetitions and in the frequent breaking off of phrases), the avoidance of clear-cut tonality by the use of chromaticism (*e.g.*, mm. 14–18, flute: C B C B C B-flat), and the frequent change of meter all contribute to the "prefatory" character of the first 41 measures.

This air of indecision is finally concentrated in the melodic line of the flute (mm. 20–30), with the repetition of a slightly changing phrase. Increasing activity, signalized by the entrance of the other instruments, leads to a return of the opening "curtain" motive (m. 37), and the Sinfonia ends with a resounding dominant-seventh chord. Lack of tonal focus, which characterizes the Sinfonia, ends with the firm resolution of the dominant-seventh on the tonic of E-flat major at the beginning of the—

Allegro Moderato (mm. 42–175): The first movement proper begins with a brilliant seven-measure theme played by trumpet I (Ex. 106). While all of the instruments enter in unison with the trumpet, they quickly assert their independence by surrounding the theme with a

Example 106[4]

---

[3]See Chapter VIII, p. 390.
[4]Examples 106–114, from Stravinsky's *Octet for Wind Instruments*, are reprinted by permission of the copyright owners, Boosey and Hawkes, Inc.

polyphonic web. Trumpet I immediately repeats its theme, imitated by trumpet II and flute. Against an active bass line played by bassoons and trombones, the trumpet begins the theme a third time, playing only the first three measures but repeating them three times, each time a tone lower.

The texture of the music suddenly thins; the bassoons play an ascending scale-like figure, and a new theme (Ex. 107) is introduced by trumpet I (mm. 70–75), trumpet II adding sev-

Example 107

eral "curlicues" (mm. 76–79). The first half of the theme is repeated by flute, clarinet, and trombone I, and then disappears while the figures introduced in the accompaniment are developed.

A third theme (Ex. 108) is introduced by the clarinet, playing in its lowest register (mm. 95–97). This theme is completed by the bassoon (mm. 98–100), and developed by the flute

Example 108

and clarinet. Still another melodic idea (Ex. 109), played by the clarinet (mm. 111–117), appears for a moment, followed by a return of the "curlicue" phrase of the second theme, and then by a new development of the first half of this theme (mm. 122–138).

Example 109

The bassoon, soon joined by the trumpet, then by flute and clarinet, begins an extended anticipation of the first trumpet theme, which finally returns in its entirety in the trumpets (mm. 152–157). It is immediately taken up by trumpet II, then in imitation by trombone I. A tremendous burst of energy in all the instruments leads to a final, triumphant statement of the first theme, and the First Movement is over.

SECOND MOVEMENT: Theme and five variations.[5]

Theme (mm. 1–14): The seven-phrase Theme (Ex. 110: the phrases are numbered) is begun by the flute and clarinet in unison (mm. 1–8), continued by trumpet I (mm. 9–11), and completed by trombone I (mm. 12–14). Though basically in D minor, the frequent half-

Example 110

step movement (*e.g.,* C, C-sharp; B, B-flat) gives the melody a *chromatic* character, making it difficult to determine with certainty whether, at any given moment, it is in major or minor. The accompaniment, which consists of *staccato* (detached) chords played off-the-beat,

[5] See Chapter VIII, pp. 404–5.

changes from D minor to D major. Occasionally the melody and its accompaniment are clearly in conflict (*e.g.,* measure 1: D-natural in the accompaniment, C-sharp in the melody). In spite of this seeming tonal anarchy, the theme and its accompaniment unite in an expressive, logical music in which the many dissonances become, upon acquaintance, an essential part of the design.

That the Theme in its entirety is never stated by a single instrument is characteristic of Stravinsky's music. Instead the individual phrases are allotted to contrasting instruments. In this way the composer achieves an interesting succession of instrumental *timbres* (tone colors) and at the same time avoids the continuous, "singing" melodic line so closely associated with the music of the 19th century.

In the five variations which follow, the Theme, nebulous in itself, is frequently so altered that its recognition by the ear alone is impossible. Sometimes two phrases of the melody occur simultaneously; sometimes a long interval intervenes between phrases consecutive in the original Theme, so that the continuity of the original is lost. In some variations phrases of the theme fail to appear. Often the music surrounding the Theme, the "accompaniment," is of greater immediate interest to the ear than the Theme. Such treatment of a Theme is similar to the use of the plainsong in Josquin des Prez's *Pange Lingua Mass*.

Variation 1 (mm. 15–26): Against a rushing, scale-like accompaniment in the other instruments, the trombones proclaim the first two phrases of the Theme in quarter notes. Phrases 3 and 4 are played off-the-beat in *staccato* eighth notes by trumpets, clarinet, and flute in unison, while the bassoons repeat a short, *ostinato* scale. Phrase 5 is intoned by trumpets, while at the same time the trombones play phrase 6. Bassoon II repeats phrase 6, which is immediately imitated by bassoon I and clarinet. The entire variation is in triple meter.

Variation 2 (mm. 27–56): The meter momentarily changes to duple, and the bassoons and trombones play a march-like accompaniment against which trumpet II plays phrase 1 of the Theme, now considerably altered and in a dotted-note rhythm (Ex. 111). Phrase 2 is inserted

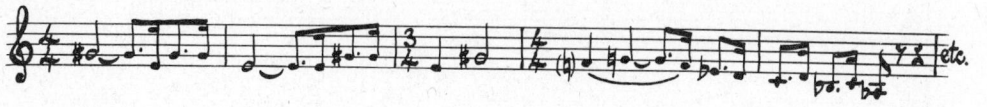

Example 111

by trumpet I joined by the flute. While the clarinet plays phrase 3, the flute develops a bit of trumpet II's variation of phrase 1, especially the dotted-note rhythm. The clarinet joins in this development, and, as the music grows in intensity, trumpet I quietly repeats phrase 3 and continues with a variant of phrase 4. There is a return to the initial march-like accompaniment of *staccato* notes, and trumpets I and II play phrase 5. The last two phrases of the Theme are obscured by short cadence figures.

Ritornello (mm. 56–67): A repetition of the first variation, with slight alteration of the final cadence, serves as a *ritornello* or section of "returning" music.

Variation 3 (mm. 68–122): A graceful waltz melody, played by the flute and set to a simple accompaniment, serves to draw the listener's attention away from the Theme, which occurs in scattered phrases played by trumpet II. The flute's melody, which recalls Stravinsky's ballet music because of its poised, finely etched line and the precision of the ONE-two-three accompaniment, is later shared by the clarinet. At the end of the variation there is a quickening of the tempo and a change to duple meter, and without cadence or pause Variation 4 begins.

Variation 4 (mm. 123–208): Against an active, wiry clarinet and bassoon accompaniment, the trumpets intone the Theme phrase by phrase. The accompaniment gradually becomes more melodic in character, and as its material is developed, the original Theme becomes less significant; all attention centers on the accompanying activity of the flute, clarinet, and bassoons. Only towards the end of the variation (mm. 192–208) does the character of the beginning return and the listener's attention again center on the trumpet statement of the Theme.

Ritornello (mm. 209–219): This is the third appearance of the first variation. In a movement dedicated to variation, in which each section is different in character, the repetition of the first variation serves as an important integrating element.

Variation 5 (mm. 220–251): This variation, designated "Fugato," has some of the characteristics of a *fugue*, a type of polyphonic composition based on the imitation of a single melodic idea.[6] However, Stravinsky treats his material so freely that only the "atmosphere," not the actual structure, of a *fugue* is present. An abbreviated form of the Theme, in slow tempo and 5/8 meter, is presented by the bassoons. It is immediately imitated by the clarinet, while the bassoons continue with independent melodic lines. Next the same abbreviated form of the Theme occurs in trumpet I (mm. 230–233), and then in flute and clarinet in unison (mm. 234–239). The polyphonic web grows in complexity, as each part moves with some independence of the others. Then flute and clarinet alone recall the *fugato* theme, the texture lightens, and at measure 251 the tempo accelerates.

Coda and Link (mm. 252–263): The solo flute begins ruminating on the angular intervals of the *fugato* theme, bringing the fifth variation to a close. Without cadential ceremony the music is turned over to the bassoons, whose prefatory remarks lead directly to the Third Movement.

THIRD MOVEMENT: Finale.

A bumptious, good-natured theme is announced by the first bassoon (mm. 1–10) accompanied by the second bassoon (Ex. 112). With the addition of a faster clarinet figure, the first bassoon repeats its melody (mm. 11–19), adding a few measures of new material. But the first bassoon will not have done and proceeds to repeat its initial melody (mm. 30–37).

Example 112

This self-absorption of the bassoon is now challenged by the other instruments, led by trumpet II, which introduces a new theme (Ex. 113). The other instruments, especially

Example 113

[6]See Chapter VIII, pp. 394–95.

CONTEMPORARY MUSIC

flute and clarinet, join in with bright, ornamental phrases. A second statement of the new trumpet melody is partially imitated by trombone I.

But the bassoon is not yet finished. It returns to its original melody (a literal repetition of measures 13–28). However, the bassoon melody, together with its original accompaniment, is taken over by the trumpets (mm. 64–75), which brilliantly develop the first two measures of the theme. Next the flute, supported by clarinet and bassoon I, develops the rest of the original bassoon theme (mm. 76–92). This is followed by a development of the trumpets' theme (mm. 93–111). The trombone begins a parody of the bassoon's melody (mm. 94–119), and this is taken up by the trumpet II (mm. 119–127). The music, constantly rising in pitch, grows in intensity. Syncopations occur more frequently, until there is a sudden pause followed by the—

Coda (mm. 144–170): The instruments, moving note-against-note and quietly, introduce a last transformation of the original bassoon theme. Note that the consistent syncopation (Ex. 114) avoids the strong accent which would normally occur at the beginning of the second measure and creates a rhythmic phrase of two-bar length. Such juggling with the barline and the normal metric accent, so characteristic of 20th-century music, gives to the Coda a curious "off balance" character which adds to the general mood of exhilaration. The ending occurs suddenly—due to the fact that the final chord is on a weak (hence, unaccented) beat of the measure—and thus surprises the listener.

Example 114

Recommended reading:
Igor Stravinsky, *Stravinsky: An Autobiography,* New York, Simon and Schuster, 1936.
Igor Stravinsky, *Poetics of Music in the Form of Six Lessons,* tr. A. Knodel and I. Dahl, Cambridge, Harvard University Press, 1947.
Constant Lambert, *Music Ho! A Study of Music in Decline,* New York, Scribner's, 1934, pp. 63–97.

		Gb/F#	Ab/G#	Bb/A#		Db/C#	Eb/D#		Gb/F#	Ab/G#	Bb/A#		Db/C#	Eb/D#

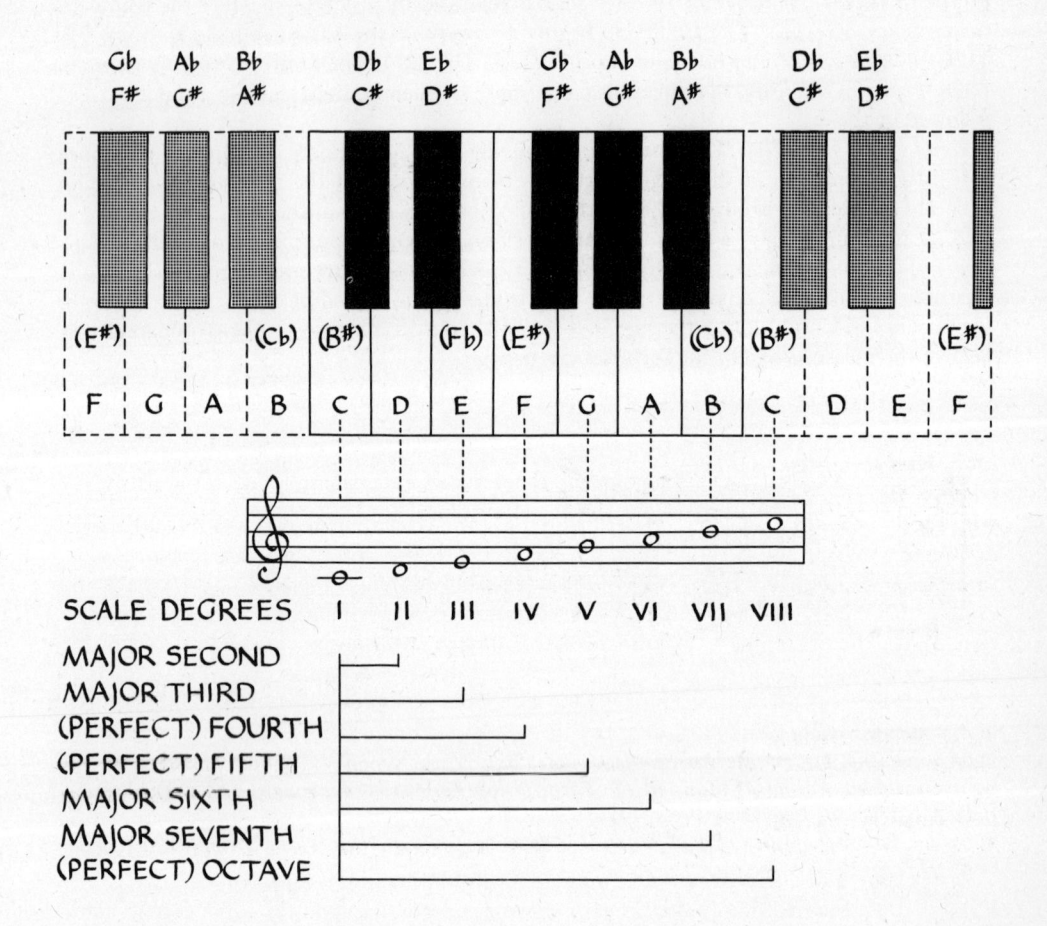

(E#) (Cb) (B#) (Fb) (E#) (Cb) (B#) (E#)

F G A B C D E F G A B C D E F

SCALE DEGREES I II III IV V VI VII VIII

MAJOR SECOND
MAJOR THIRD
(PERFECT) FOURTH
(PERFECT) FIFTH
MAJOR SIXTH
MAJOR SEVENTH
(PERFECT) OCTAVE

VIII

RHYTHM, TONALITY, AND FORM IN MUSIC

ELEMENTS

THIS DISCUSSION OF THE ELEMENTS OF MUSIC will fall under two main headings: (I) Rhythm, and (II) Tonality. Under the first we shall discuss: (A) *Basic rhythm, i.e., time* or *meter;* (B) *Secondary rhythm;* and (C) *Periodic or structural rhythm, i.e.,* phrases and other rhythmic periods. Under II will fall: (A) *Scales* and *modes;* (B) *Harmony;* and (C) *Modulation.* There will be no discussion of *melody* in the abstract.

I. *Rhythm.*

The root meaning of the word "rhythm" is *flow*. (The Greek verb *rhéo*, from which the noun *rhythmós* derives, is cognate with the English word *stream*). In music the term is used in a variety of senses; all of them, however, can be connected with the idea of *onward* movement or flow, of one sort or another. The three usages commonly distinguished are:

(A). *Basic rhythm,* which is technically called *time* or *meter* and should be referred to as such. Music being a temporal art, its fundamental rhythmic feature is the *beat* or *pulse* which, whether fast or slow, is felt from the beginning of a movement to the end, underlying the whole tonal structure. In some types of unisonic (one-voiced) unaccompanied music, such as Gregorian chant and natural folk song, the beat is treated with a certain freedom; that is to say, it is not a *regular* pulsation, but subtly variable. In music of more than one voice, however (which means, in the vast majority of pieces), the beat is regular, and the series of pulsations is like the ticking of a clock, marking off time as mechanically as the lines of graph-paper mark off space.

Now, it happens that any series of regular pulsations is apprehended by the human mind in one of two ways—either in units of two or in units of three. Thus in music the underlying pulse is felt *either* as an alternation of stressed and unstressed beats *or* as one stressed followed by two unstressed beats. The former is called *duple time* (or *duple meter*), the latter *triple time* (or *triple meter*).

        DUPLE: > ∪ > ∪ > ∪ *heavy* light *heavy* light, etc.
        TRIPLE: > ∪ ∪ > ∪ ∪ *heavy* light light *heavy* light light, etc.

Each of these may be complicated in various ways, depending upon the subdividing of the basic beat. In writing music, it is customary to mark off the units of the time-pattern by vertical *bar-lines,* and to write at the beginning of the movement a *time-signature* consisting of two superimposed figures ($\frac{2}{4}$, $\frac{3}{2}$, $\frac{6}{8}$, etc.), the upper of which indicates the number of beats between two bar-lines (*i.e.,* the number of beats per *bar* or *measure*) and the lower of which indicates the kind of note used as the beat (1=whole note ○ ; 2=half note ♩ ; 4=quarter note ♩ ; 8=eighth note ♪ ; 16=sixteenth note ♬ ; 32=thirty-second note ♬ ; each of these, in any given movement, being half the duration of the preceding one, as the terminology indicates). However many beats there may be in a measure, the basic time-scheme will be either duple or triple (or, in irregular rhythms, some combination of these). Thus, if the upper figure of the time-signature is 2, 4, 6, or 12, the time is basically duple, and the piece may conceivably be *marched to* (*left—*right*—left—*right; but the "march" will be at a rate or *tempo* ranging from break-neck to funereal); while if the upper figure of the time-signature is 3 or 9, the time is basically *triple,* and the piece may conceivably be *waltzed to* (again with tremendous variations of tempo). The special time-signatures **C** and **¢** represent $\frac{4}{4}$ and $\frac{2}{2}$ meters respectively.

(B). *Secondary rhythm.* Normally, the notes of a piece of music vary in length or duration. The longer notes, simply because they are longer, are felt to be weightier or more heavily accented, whether they coincide with a basic time-stress (as they often do) or not; and the shorter notes, of lesser weight, are felt to lead forward to the longer ones. This sets up, within the basic and continuous time-flow, a series of shorter but more dynamic flows, the varying energies of which depend on the particular dispositions of longer and shorter notes. There is a strong tendency to repeat throughout a movement a particular rhythmic pattern, once it has been introduced, or to repeat more than one such pattern. This tendency is illustrated by movements as diverse in type and scope as *My Country, 'Tis of Thee* and Beethoven's *Fifth Symphony* (first movement). In such cases, the patterns are technically called *figures* or *motives.* Whether there is obvious *figure-development* of this sort or not, the character of the music will be greatly affected by the arrangement of note-values within it. This is what is meant when one says that the *rhythm* of a piece is energetic or placid, angular or smooth, nervous or restful, etc.; and it is in this sense that one refers to the *rhythm* of a particular bar of a piece, and observes that it is the same as, or different from, the *rhythm* of some other bar.

Note that both the above types of rhythm (basic and secondary) may be considered apart from musical *pitch* or tone. One may tap out duple or triple time, or the rhythm of *Old Black Joe,* without pitch-variations, and make the patterns clearly recognizable. Note further that basic rhythm and secondary rhythm often reinforce each other (longer or "weightier" notes coinciding with metrical accents), but just as often are at variance, thereby creating rhythmic tensions, nuances, and interplays which add to the complexity and interest of the music.

(C). *Periodic or structural rhythm.* Just as, in the figure or motive, there is a flow towards the long or weighty note, so in the structure of a movement as a whole one is aware of larger rhythmic flows, extending through several bars and "aiming at" weightier climaxes (followed by momentary relaxation). As in the preceding types of rhythm, this too can be felt apart from musical pitch or tone. If one taps out Example 115 (which is the pattern of the

Example 115

opening of Ravel's *Bolero*), one feels not merely the flows indicated by the shortest arrows (*i.e.,* the *figures*), but also the flow of bar 1 to the first beat of bar 2, and the larger flow of bars 1 and 2 to the first beat of bar 3, which is the climax of this whole example. Much primitive drum-music, and some sophisticated Oriental and modern music, consists of nothing but this type of "pure" rhythm (highly complicated, of course). But in most music the tonal elements—*melody* and *harmony*—reinforce the rhythmic, the former by its rising and falling inflections, the latter by its orderly sequence of chords; and we may in general describe *periodic* or *structural rhythm* as the flow, tendency, or drive of a series of sounds towards points of climax (and consequent relaxation) called *cadences,* which are as much melodic and harmonic as they are rhythmic features.

To avoid digressing, let us for the moment consider cadences as the musical equivalents of punctuation-points in speech or writing. Just as the sense of a phrase or a sentence flows forward to the comma-point, semicolon-point, or period-point, so the "sense" of a melody and of the chords which support it flows forward to cadence-points, some of which are more conclusive than others.[1] Borrowing our terminology from literature, we speak of these sense-flows as *phrases* and *sentences* (or *periods*); the *figures* or *motives* already discussed are lesser sense-flows within the phrase, as can readily be seen from Example 115. And just as an essay or a poem is a structure composed of phrases and sentences, organized into larger paragraphs or stanzas and adding up to a complete whole, so a piece of music is an aggregate of well-organized, balanced phrases, sentences, and larger rhythmic periods. The chief distinction between literary and musical phrases is that while the former are of no set length, the latter show a distinct tendency, at least in music of certain styles, to be standardized at a certain number of bars' length. The four-bar phrase is so common as to be spoken of as the "regular" phrase-length; but it is inaccurate to regard any particular rhythmic flow as regular for all music.

"Rhythm" in this sense is always at variance with time or meter, precisely as the sense-flows of poetry are at variance with the metrical scheme. Rhythm *mitigates* the strictness of time, robs it of its squareness and mechanical exactitude. On the other hand, time *disciplines* rhythm, keeps the flow within due bounds, and permits no *"over*-flow." In the performance of music, that interpreter will be the best who best understands the structural rhythm of the piece, and makes the nicest adjustment between it and the time.

II. *Tonality*.

The concept of tonality, or "key-feeling," in music arises from the artistic necessity of selecting, from all the possible pitches or tones available, a limited number which are intelligibly related, and organizing them around some one central tone called *the* tone, or technically *the tonic*. Except for some styles of modern music in which tonality is intentionally avoided, it is a fact that any meaningful succession or combination of pitches will gravitate to some fixed point or tonic, which not only provides a satisfactory, conclusive resting point in the series, but also serves as a center towards which all the other tones of the series are oriented. An "intelligible relationship" of pitches around a tonic—a definite tonal pattern of any kind—can be systematized into a series known as a *scale* (or *mode*); and melodies and harmonies based on one particular scale are said to be in a particular *key* (or mode).

(A). *Scales and modes*. Now, the number of totally different pitches available for music-making is not infinite. If one takes any single pitch and proceeds gradually higher or lower, one comes eventually to another pitch which accords with it so perfectly as to seem to be a duplicate of it at a higher or lower tonal level. This second pitch is called the *octave* of the first; the tonal "distance" between the two pitches is called the *interval* of an octave. In the music of the Western world, the *smallest* interval used is called a *semitone* or *half-tone;* and it will be found by reference to the piano keyboard (where the interval between any note and the *immediately* next note, whether black or white key, is a semitone) that there are *twelve* semitones between any given pitch and its octave: see page 380.

Differences between scale-types reside in the different selections made from these twelve possible pitches within the octave. To illustrate forcibly the great differences of character which differing scales will effect in the music based upon them, consider the *pentatonic* (or five-note) scale and the *whole-tone* scale (Exs. 116 and 117). The former uses (of the twelve possible pitches within the octave) only numbers 1, 3, 5, 8, 10; expressing it in musical language, the intervals from tonic to tonic consist of a (whole) tone, another (whole) tone, a tone-and-a-half, a (whole) tone, and a tone-and-a-half (to the upper tonic); *i.e.,* 1-1-1½-1-1½. Music based on this scale—*e.g.,* the melodies *Swing Low, Sweet Chariot* and *Deep River*—has a warm, gentle, comforting character, often enhanced by a special cadence-formula (*sol, la, do,* or *la, sol, do*). The whole-tone scale, consisting entirely of whole-tone

[1] See, below, under *Harmony,* pp. 386–88.

Pentatonic scale *Deep River*

Example 116

Whole tone scale *Debussy: Fêtes*

Example 117

intervals, produces a vastly different effect. Music based on this scale sounds exotic, colorful, and somewhat Oriental. In spite of its masterly use by Debussy in the early 20th century, it "wears" poorly, and has not been generally adopted (though its influence can be seen in popular music of the dance-band, juke-box, and Hollywood sound-track variety).

The various *church modes* of medieval (and Renaissance) days utilized other arrangements of tones and semitones within the octave. They are called *modes* and not *scales* because, unlike the latter, they were originally "not transferable"; that is to say, they were associated with certain fixed *tonics* or *finals,* whereas any scale may start on any one of twelve notes (see below). It is beyond the scope of this article to discuss modes in detail[2]; two of them—the *Dorian* on D and *Phrygian* on E—are shown, with melodies founded on them, in Examples 118 and 119. The plainsong melody *Pange Lingua* (Ex. 3) is another Phrygian

Dorian mode English Folksong: *Brigg Fair*

Example 118

---

[2] But see the article on Plainsong, pp. 54–60.

ELEMENTS

Phrygian mode   Tallis: *Psalm-melody*

Example 119

[*Note the frequent changes from duple to triple measures in this melody*]

example; the *Kyrie* (Ex. 1) is another Dorian example. The peculiar "flavor," the archaic sound and "atmosphere" of these Gregorian (and folksong) melodies, are due largely to their *modal* character, which was preserved fairly pure as long as music was unisonic (one-voiced) and unaccompanied by chords. Composers of the 20th century have availed themselves of this ancient resource, among many others, in an attempt to vary their tonal palettes; but from about 1550 to 1900 Western music has been almost entirely based upon the two modes which (with slight modifications) became known as the *major* and *minor scales,* of which examples are given (Exs. 120 and 121). The MAJOR scale has the following sequence

Major scale of C

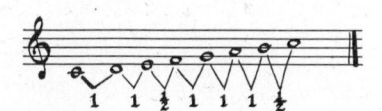

Example 120

Minor scale of C

Example 121

of intervals: 1-1-½-1-1-1-½. The MINOR scale has: 1-½-1-1-½-1½-½. As in former instances, the *character* of music based on a major scale differs tremendously from that of music based on a minor scale; the former sounds "open," and the latter "closed." These words, however, convey little by way of description; the quickest way to appreciate the vast distinction is to take a familiar *major* melody like *The Star-Spangled Banner* and change it into minor, or take a *minor* melody like *Go Down, Moses* and change it to major.

To determine whether a piece is in major or minor, first find *and sing* the tonic or key-note, then sing the major pattern *do-re-mi* and prolong the *mi*. If this "fits" the tonality, the piece is major; if it produces a dissonance (clash), the piece is minor.

Since, as we have seen, there are twelve different pitches (a semitone apart) within an octave, it follows that a major scale or a minor scale can be based on any one of twelve different tonics. There are thus twelve different keys, each with its major and minor form. By referring to the piano keyboard (Fig. 98), and remembering the two basic patterns—major and minor—one can name the notes of any of the twelve major and twelve minor scales. It will be found that only one of these twenty-four—*viz.*, the C major scale—can be constructed without using *sharps* and *flats,* the former (♯) indicating the *raising* of a note by one half-tone, the latter (♭) indicating the *lowering* of a note by one half-tone. In constructing scales, remember that the different pitches *always have different letter-names;* this will decide whether a sharp or a flat has to be used at any given point. (*E.g.*, the scale of F major will run F-G-A-B♭-C-D-E-F, not F-G-A-A♯-etc.).

The pitches of scales are given generic names. Learn the following three: The first pitch (the *key-note*) is called the *tonic;* the fifth (counting upwards) is called the *dominant;* the fourth is called the *subdominant.*

The *interval* (tonal distance) between tonic and tonic is called an octave, as we have seen. The interval between tonic and dominant (upwards) is called a *perfect fifth*. The interval between tonic and subdominant is called a *perfect fourth*. These three will be constant in major and minor scales. The interval between tonic and the third note of the scale is called a *major third* when the scale is major, and a *minor third* when the scale is minor.[3]

(B). *Harmony*. Tonality is greatly emphasized by the use of pitches in combination—*i.e.*, sounded simultaneously. Such combinations are called *chords;* their systematic use produces *harmony*. The simplest chord-type is the *triad* (Ex. 122), consisting of two superimposed in-

Example 122

Principal triads
C major   C minor

I - Tonic   V - dominant   IV - subdominant   I - tonic   V - dominant   IV - subdominant

tervals of the third (*e.g.*, C-E-G; C to E is a major third, E to G a minor third). There is a triad for every note of the scale. Learn the three *principal triads* based on the tonic (I), dominant (V) and subdominant (IV). In a *major* tonality, these three are all *major* ("open-sounding") triads, since the lower of the two thirds they contain is major. In a *minor* tonality V is still a major triad, but I and IV are *minor* ("closed-sounding") triads, the lower third being minor in each case (see Ex. 122).

The importance of these three principal triads is tremendous. To begin with, these three alone are sufficient to *establish* (technical term) a particular tonality (key), since among them they contain all the notes of a particular scale. Thus if we play (I)-IV-V-I in D major (Ex. 123) we have at once established D major, *and no other,* as our tonal center or key; if

Example 123

Key-establishment

I   IV   V   I   I   IV   V   I
  D major   A minor

---

[3] All these interval-names, and others we have not mentioned, are used generically to describe the various intervals whenever they occur; *e.g.*, in a major scale, not only is the interval between the first note and the third a major third but also the interval between the fourth and the sixth notes is a major third, and the interval between the fifth and the seventh notes likewise, since all these contain the same number of semitones (4). The interval between the second and fourth notes of a major scale, however, is a *minor* third, as also are the intervals between the third and fifth notes and between the sixth and eighth notes; since all these contain the same number of semitones (3) as the original minor third in a minor scale (first to third notes).

ELEMENTS

we play (I)-IV-V-I in A minor, we establish A minor, *and no other,* as our key. (Note that we play them in the order IV-V-I, ending with I, since all the chords of a key gravitate towards the tonic chord, just as the individual pitches gravitate towards the tonic note.)

Secondly, these three chords alone are sufficient to provide a basic accompaniment to many simple melodies; or putting it the other way round, many simple melodies are based on these three chords (*e.g., Auld Lang Syne; Old Folks at Home; Dixie*). Harmonizations using only three different chords will, of course, be extremely simple (not to say monotonous); but the fact that such harmonizations can be made at all illustrates the fundamental nature of the three principal triads (Ex. 124).

Principal triads as fundamental harmony   Beethoven: *Clarinet trio, op. 11; last movement*

Example 124

Thirdly, these three are the chief chords used to form *cadences* (Ex. 125) in music from 1600–1900 (approximately). When they occur (in certain specific formulas) at points of

Cadences

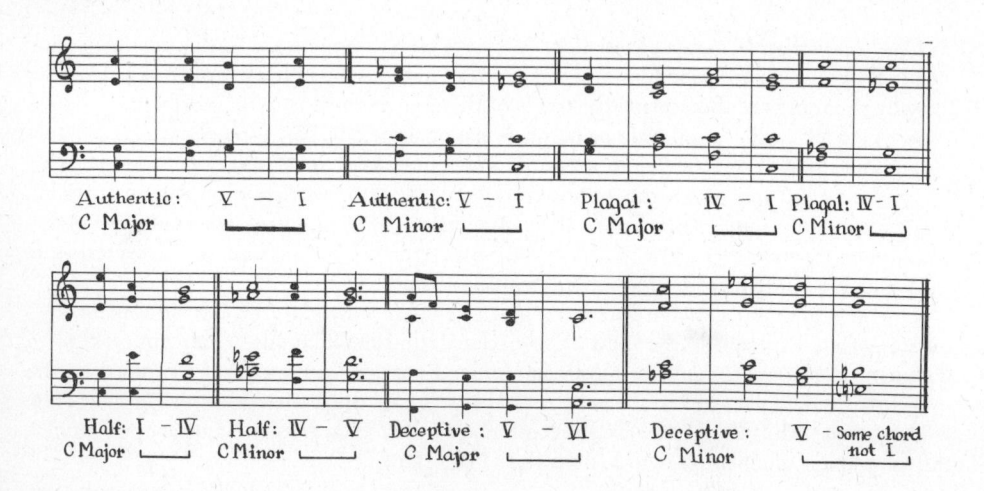

Example 125

climax in the structural rhythm, they provide harmonic reinforcement of the melodic and rhythmic "breathing-points" already discussed (see *Rhythm* C.). So powerful is this harmonic reinforcement that we generally speak of cadences in terms of the chords which are associated with them. Thus we call the progression V-I the *authentic cadence;* this is the most conclusive cadence of all—the musical period-point. The progression IV-I is called the *plagal cadence;* it is the common "Amen" formula, likewise conclusive but more restricted in its use. The *half-cadence* (*semicadence*) is an intermediate cadence, less conclusive than the foregoing—the musical comma or semicolon. It consists of V preceded by any other chord; I-V is one common form. The *deceptive* or *interrupted cadence* is a special progression, which interrupts an authentic cadence (V-I) by substituting some other chord for the expected tonic; V-VI is one common form. All these patterns become "cadences" *only* when they occur *at the ends of rhythmic "flows."* Even V-I, the most conclusive progression of all when it occurs *at the end* of a phrase or sentence, is not in itself a cadence, as we may see from the opening harmonies to many a melody that begins *sol | do* (dominant tonic).

Even simple harmony does not consist in a succession of triads as such, but of chords of more than three notes combined in all sorts of arrangements. The tonic chord of C major, for instance, in a simple arrangement for four voices (bass, tenor, alto, soprano) may be spread over two octaves, as in the first chord of Example 125. Observe that one note (the tonic, in this case) is *doubled, i.e.,* used twice. The same chord arranged for full orchestra might spread over six or seven octaves, and every note of the basic triad would then be "doubled" many times over, so that the chord would be written (from double-bass to piccolo) something like this: C C G E G C E G C E G C E G C C. Furthermore, the bass note of a chord need not always be the *root—i.e.,* the note on which the simple triad is built (C is the root of the triad C-E-G); quite as frequently one of the other constituent notes is in the bass, and we then have chords like E-C-G-C and G-E-G-C which have different effects from that of the "root-position" chord. But whatever the particular arrangement, and however much doubling occurs, the chord is always reducible to the basic triad and is called by the root-name of that triad.

We have thus far discussed only triads and their possible arrangements. It should be added that there are also more complicated basic combinations called *seventh-chords, ninth-chords, etc.,* which contain four, five, or more different pitches, and which are constructed by superimposing additional thirds on top of the triad. A very common seventh-chord is the *dominant seventh* (in C major or minor, G-B-D-F), the sound of which is familiar to everyone. Another third added to this (G-B-D-F-*A*) would produce the *dominant ninth,* likewise a fairly familiar sound to 20th-century ears. For our present purposes, it will be sufficient if we learn to identify the simple triads I, V, and IV, and the cadences which utilize them, leaving the consideration of ninth-chords and more complicated combinations until we come to the kind of music in which they are used (Wagner and post-Wagnerian composers).

(C). *Modulation* (Change of tonality). We have seen that there are twelve possible major tonalities, with their corresponding minors; and we have learned how to *establish* any one of these by sounding the three principal triads of that key. Now it is quite possible to produce a short piece of music (a folksong or hymn or national melody, for instance) which remains throughout in one key; *My Country, 'Tis of Thee* and *Drink to Me Only with Thine Eyes* are examples. But for movements of any considerable length, restriction of the music to one tonality would be intolerable; tonal variety is achieved by *modulating* from one key to another, or to several others, always, however, with reference to one basic tonal center—one particular key—in which the movement begins and ends.

Some keys are more closely related to a given key than others. In the case of a major key, the key of its dominant is the most closely related, and modulations "from tonic [key] to dominant [key]" are among the most common and natural. In the case of a minor key, the most natural modulation is to the *major* key based on its third scale-note; this is called the *relative major.* Thus from *C major,* the commonest modulation is to G major; from *C minor,* the commonest modulation is to E flat *major* (Ex. 126).

ELEMENTS

[Musical example 126: excerpts from Beethoven (C Major → G Major, dominant key), Bach (C Minor), and Eb Major (relative major key)]

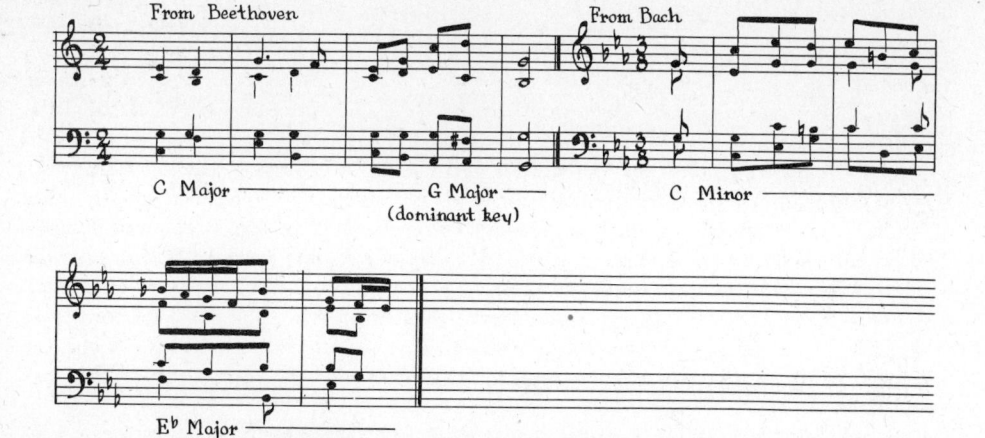

Example 126

What happens when one modulates from one key to another is that the "center of gravity" shifts, and a note which was originally dependent upon the old tonic becomes itself a new tonic, the basis of a new scale, and the center of attraction of a new series of triads. Thus in the key of C major, the dominant G and its triad G-B-D lead naturally to the tonic C and its triad C-E-G (as in the authentic cadence). A shift of tonality—a modulation to the key of G major—means simply that G is now taken as tonic and its triad G-B-D as the tonic triad; which involves a reorientation of pitches and triads around G and G-B-D as centers. The original tonic triad C-E-G now becomes *subdominant* of the new key, and a new dominant triad D-F♯-A, introducing one new pitch (F♯), comes into being; both these triads leading to, or leaning towards, G-B-D as tonic triad. Modulation thus produces a deflection of the original melodic and harmonic flow. If the keys concerned are closely related, the deflection is so slight as to be easily accepted by the ear, and correspondingly hard to spot. If the keys are not related (*i.e.,* if there are in the new key several pitches not found in the original key), the deflection is greater and strikes the ear more forcibly, thus being easier to spot. A modulation from C major to G major (Ex. 126), especially if transient, may pass unnoticed by the untrained ear; a modulation from C major to D♭ major (Ex. 127) would be spotted by everyone.

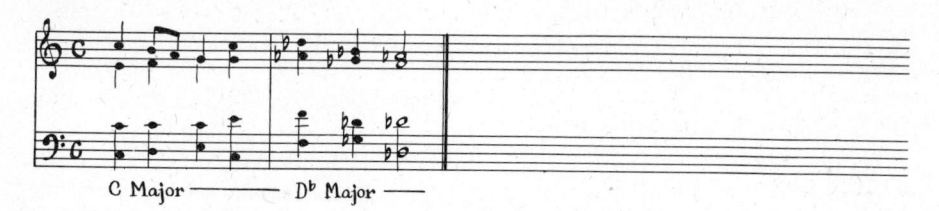

[Musical example 127: C Major → D♭ Major]

Example 127

As suggested in the preceding sentence, modulations may be *transient* (a new key being briefly hinted at in passing) or *confirmed* (the music passing definitely over to the new key, and remaining there at least long enough to establish a new tonal atmosphere). The first phrase of *The Star-Spangled Banner* contains two transient modulations; they are both such brief excursions from the tonic key as not to upset the basic tonic feeling of the opening. By contrast, the first phrase of Boccherini's popular *Minuet in A major* is squarely in the tonic key, and the second phrase just as squarely in the dominant key (E major); we have a definite sensation of starting in one tonal area and crossing over to another for a while. The latter, incidentally, is the more usual procedure; first *establish* your tonic (your "home base"), then make excursions away from it. We shall discover, when we come to consider the larger forms of music such as the *fugue* and the *sonata,* that such excursions may be quite lengthy; but they all depend for their intelligibility upon the firm establishment of an original tonic key as "home base." An excellent and familiar example is the opening of the first movement of Beethoven's *Fifth Symphony,* where the principal triads of C minor form the basis of the first 52 bars, after which a modulation to the relative major (E♭ major) is recognizable by everyone.

POLYPHONY

I. *The Nature of Polyphony.*

A. *Definition.* If two or more melodies are played together the result is *polyphony* or multiple melody. Each of the superimposed melodies retains much of its individuality, though at the same time each relinquishes some of its independence in order to combine harmoniously with the other melodies.

Since in many periods polyphonic music has been performed by human voices, it is customary to refer to each of the superimposed melodies, whether they are played by instruments or sung, as *voice-parts*. The term *voice-part* in the present context will have the meaning *one of the superimposed melodies in a polyphonic composition.*

One of the results of polyphony is the simultaneous sounding of two or more pitches resulting from the combination of two or more melodies; this composite sound is called *harmony*. With the term *harmony* two factors of considerable importance are introduced. The first of these is the "vertical" relationship of simultaneously sounding pitches (*i.e.,* consonance and dissonance); the second is the "horizontal" relationship in time of successive pitch combinations (*i.e.,* polyphony and homophony).

B. *Consonance and dissonance.* Two pitches sounded together either duplicate each other (*i.e.,* sound the same pitch), or differ from each other (*i.e.,* sound different pitches). In the first instance the two pitches form a *unison;* in the second instance they form an *interval*. If the interval formed is a third, fifth, sixth, or octave, it is a *consonance* and pleasing to the ear. If the interval formed is a second, fourth, or seventh, it is a *dissonance;* the two pitches will "clash," and the result is displeasing to the ear. Unrelieved consonance palls while unrelieved dissonance disquiets. All harmony proceeds on the principle of contrast: a judicious intermingling of consonance and dissonance.

Since a dissonance creates a tonal tension which demands *resolution* (*i.e.,* "relaxation"), the treatment of dissonance is important as a criterion of style. Music of the Renaissance is characterized by a restricted use of dissonance. Each dissonance is *prepared* (*i.e.,* preceded by a consonant interval) and carefully *resolved* (*i.e.,* followed by a consonant interval). The result is a basically consonant music of great restraint and balance. Baroque music is characterized by a freer and more frequent use of dissonance; the *preparation* is often slighted or even omitted, and the *resolution* often so delayed that the tension produced by the dissonance is prolonged. The result is a music of strong contrasts and less restraint. In 20th-century music few of the earlier prohibitions and restrictions placed on the use of dissonance are observed: consonance and dissonance are on an equal footing. As a result, music of the present century is frequently characterized by its lack of restraint.

POLYPHONY

The following examples of dissonance treatment in (a) the Renaissance, (b) the Baroque, and (c) the 20th century, will illustrate what has been said in the preceding paragraph. The *preparation* is marked "p," the *dissonance* "d," and the *resolution* "r." (Ex. 128)

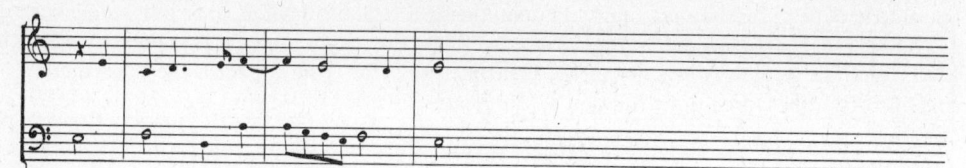

Example 128

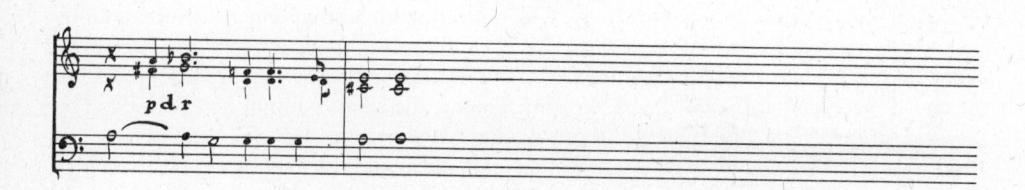

C. *Polyphony and homophony.* The second factor introduced by harmony is the treatment of successive pitch combinations or *chords*. Music conceived primarily in terms of superimposed melodies is called *polyphonic* or *contrapuntal* (noun: *counterpoint*). Music conceived primarily in terms of chords is called *homophonic* or *chordal*.

Since both polyphonic and homophonic music consist of the sounding together of different pitches (*i.e., harmony*), the difference between the two is one of emphasis. Polyphony is composed of relatively unfettered melodic strands governed only by the consonant-dissonant relationship between pitches. Chords resulting from the superimposed melodies are by-products of an essentially linear (*i.e.,* "horizontal") music. Homophony, on the other hand, consists of a consciously ordered succession of chords which supports a single melody. Presented diagrammatically, the difference can be expressed as follows:

POLYPHONY   HOMOPHONY

The following music examples will illustrate what has been said above. Example 129 is taken from the final section of a polyphonic composition for four voice-parts. Reduced to a bare chord succession as it is in the example, the music appears to be a dull repetition of three triads: C-E-G, D-F-A, E-G-B. Yet this is the climax of the piece. To realize the composer's original intention, each voice-part must be performed by an individual voice or instrument. When this is done, the interplay of the several superimposed melodies will become apparent and the vitality of the music will assert itself.

Example 129

Example 130 is taken from the beginning of a composition, but in this instance the music is homophonic. The predominant melody, which is in the highest voice-part, is supported by a carefully-selected succession of chords. Each chord seems to issue from the preceding chord and to lead naturally to the next. If, however, the individual voice-parts producing the chord succession are isolated and performed alone, the result will not be a melody. The demands of the chord succession will force the individual voice-parts—*e.g.*, bass, or tenor, or alto—to proceed at times arbitrarily, without regard to smoothness, continuity, logic. There is only one melody, in homophonic music, which is supported by the chords. Both melody and chordal support must be performed together if the composer's intentions are to be realized and the music made meaningful.

Example 130

Whereas the composer of polyphonic music is more concerned with the melodic movement of each superimposed melody, the composer of homophonic music reveals a greater concern for the logic with which the chordal movement supports and enriches the predominant melody. To be sure, the examples given above present extremes. Most music in varying degree is polyphonic *and* homophonic: the emphasis given to one or the other determines whether a piece of music is said to have a polyphonic *texture* or homophonic *texture*.

II. *Polyphonic Formal Procedures.*

A. *Form in music*. Unlike a painting, which exists complete in space before the spectator, a musical composition exists in time. Its total quality, therefore, can be apprehended by the listener only in retrospect, after hearing the entire composition. Nor does music, except by an artificial association, share literature's ability to express specific and detailed ideas through word and image. Music is a language of sounds expressing abstract ideas which will not suffer precise translation. For these reasons perception of formal organization in music presents problems not found in the other arts.

B. *Relationships between superimposed melodies*. Polyphony has been defined above as "two or more melodies played together." If the several melodies are dissimilar, the composer need only fit them together so that their simultaneous unfolding is smooth and meaningful.

The exact opposite of this may also hold: two or more voice-parts can have the same melody. In this instance the melodies, though duplicating each other, are not begun simultaneously but in overlapping succession. In other words, polyphony results because each voice-part enters with the melody at a different time. Presented diagrammatically the staggered entrances appear as follows (each letter representing a musical phrase):

```
a b c d e f g h i . . j
a b c d e f g h i . j
a b c d e f g h i j
```

As seen in the diagram, a discontinuance of exact imitation occurs near the end of the composition so that the voice-parts can finish together.

Most polyphonic music consists of superimposed melodies which are neither completely different nor completely the same. A polyphonic composition in which the voice-parts share some phrases of melody and also have unique phrases is most common. The technique employed is that of *imitative polyphony*. As expressed by a 16th-century theorist:

> He who wishes to play polyphony . . . has to imagine that the four voices are four rational men, each of whom speaks separately, if he has something to say, and is quiet when he should be quiet, and answers when he should answer, and always keeps his relationship to the others according to the rules of reason.

In the following diagram of a typical passage written in imitative polyphony the letter "x" represents unshared phrases and the other letters of the alphabet represent shared material; the blank spaces stand for *rests* (silences).

```
A x    B x x x              C x
A    x B x x x x B    C x x
  x A x    B x x x C x x    C etc.
A x x x              B x x  C x x
```

The time interval between a melodic statement and its imitation in another voice-part determines the psychological effect of the imitation. If the time interval is short and the voice-parts follow each other in quick succession (called *stretto*), intensity results. If, on the contrary, the time interval is great, the intensity is less. A composer of polyphonic music employs time intervals of varying length between statements and imitations to create contrasts of activity and repose.

C. *Relationships between polyphonic sections*. In addition to the relationship which exists between the superimposed melodies of a polyphonic work, there is the larger relationship of one section to another. Unlike the music of the Classical and later periods,[1] polyphonic works are found to have no set formal pattern, to fit no set molds. Instead, they follow certain formal procedures. Some of these will be discussed under the following headings: 1) sectionalization without repetition, 2) sectionalization with repetition, and 3) use of a recurrent melody.

1. *Sectionalization without repetition*. A vocal polyphonic composition of the 16th century can be separated into several more or less well-defined sections. Usually each section contains a single fragment of the total text and each text fragment is associated with its own characteristic musical phrase. Within a single section the same text fragment will occur in all voice-parts, and the musical phrase to which it is set will be passed from one voice-part to another in imitative polyphony. Change of text is accompanied by a change of musical phrase. The entire composition therefore consists of a series of autonomous sections. Usually neither the text fragment nor its musical phrase occurs in more than one section. It must be emphasized that this is a norm from which composers frequently deviate. Deviation, however, will never be so great as to destroy the basic plan.

It will be seen from what has just been said that polyphonic formal procedure is by its nature dynamic, evolving, a "becoming." A melody is taken up by the several voice-parts, imitated and developed, and then discarded when a new melody enters. Integration is achieved by such means as homogeneity of texture (imitative polyphony), the strong family resemblance which usually exists between the musical motives of sections, and continuity of text

---

[1] See, below, pp. 395–410.

and mood. Diversity is achieved by varying the number of voices active at any one time (*e.g.,* Josquin des Prez's use of several voice-parts in pairs as well as in combination), by varying the interval between imitative entries, and by an occasional use of homophonic sections. Intensity is achieved by increased melodic activity in the voice-parts and by the use of such devices as *stretto.*

2. *Sectionalization with repetition.* In the course of a polyphonic work a section is sometimes repeated. The repetitions are rarely "enclosing" (*i.e.,* A B C .. F A^2, each letter representing a polyphonic section such as that described above[2]). Rather they follow one of the following plans: A A^2 B C D, or A B C D D^2, etc., and thus do not alter the dynamic (evolving) quality of the polyphonic composition by fencing it in (A B ... F A^2).

In Wilbye's madrigal, "Sweet Honey-Sucking Bees" (Prográm A) repetition of the final section (A B ... E F F^2), occurs in both parts of the work. In the madrigal by Henry Farmer, "Fair Phyllis I Saw Sitting All Alone" (Program B), both the first and last sections are repeated (A A^2 B ... E F F^2). Though in each instance cited both text and music are repeated, it may happen that the music is repeated to new text, as in Orlando Gibbons' madrigal "The Silver Swan" (Program B), which follows the plan: A B B^2.

3. *Use of a recurrent melody.* Another type of polyphonic organization, usually associated with the *fugue,* is the use of a recurrent melody. Within a constantly evolving polyphonic web this one melody returns repeatedly, frequently after long absence. Repetition of polyphonic *sections,* however, is avoided. The integration of the whole work resides in the "development" of each melodic strand and the frequent return of the recurrent melody, *always in a new context.*

The formal plan of a *fugue* is simple. Voice-part 1, unaccompanied, states the *subject,* the recurrent melody which all voice-parts will share. When this voice-part has stated the subject in its entirety, Voice-part 2 enters with the same subject in a different key, while Voice-part 1 continues with a new melody called the *counter-subject.* When Voice-part 2 has completed the subject, it begins the counter-subject, while Voice-part 3 begins the subject. And so the music continues until all voice-parts have entered with the subject. This much of the fugue is called the *Exposition* (*i.e.,* that section in which each voice-part *expounds* the subject at least once). The number of voice-parts engaged in the fugue is usually three, four, or five. Whatever the number chosen by the composer, it will remain constant for the entire fugue.

Throughout the fugue both the subject and the counter-subject remain melodically unchanged, though appearing in different tonalities. Having stated both, a voice-part may be temporarily silent or continue with *free material* which need not be used in the other voice-parts. The following diagram shows a possible, *not a fixed,* pattern of Expositional entrances. The voice-parts may enter in any order chosen by the composer.

```
1st voice:     SUBJECT...counter-subject.....free material................
2nd voice:               SUBJECT......counter-subject....free material
3rd voice:                         SUBJECT......counter-subject
4th voice:                                   SUBJECT...
```

After the Exposition the fugue continues with an alternation of *episodes* and *entries.* A section of the fugue in which no voice-part states the subject is called an *episode.* Such a section may contain imitation between voice-parts, but the shared material will be new melodic ideas and/or *fragments* of the counter-subject or subject.

A return of the *full* subject in one of the voice-parts is called an *entry.* Usually the subject is accompanied by the counter-subject in another voice-part, though this is not a hard-and-fast rule. Those voice-parts not stating the subject will continue with the type of imitation found in the episode, or they may have free material.

The remainder of the fugue consists of a series of episodes and entries, the exact number

[2] The figure 2 means simply "for the second time."

depending on the ingenuity of the composer. Towards the end, at the climax of the fugue, all voice-parts may enter with the subject in close succession (*stretto*). Frequently the final entry is in the lowest voice-part, since the sonority of this voice-part gives added weight to the last section of the fugue.

Presented in diagram, the main body of the fugue (*i.e.,* all that follows the Exposition) *might* follow the following plan. Free material is represented by "–", shared material by "x". It is important to note that the nature and length of the episodes and entries is not fixed. No two fugues are exactly alike, though in basic plan they follow the outline given above.

```
EPISODE  ENTRY              EPISODE  ENTRY                    ENTRY (stretto)

   x--x--x---SUBJECT                    ct.-sub.                   SUBJECT
   x--x--x ct.-sub.       x-x-x-x-x-x-x-x-SUBJECT                  SUBJECT–
   . . . . . . . . . .      x-x-x-x-x-x-x-x-x------ etc.           SUBJECT--- etc.
   x--x--x-------                                                   SUBJECT----
```

THE FORMS OF HOMOPHONIC MUSIC

THE PRECEDING SECTION was concerned with formal procedures in polyphonic music. As was pointed out, polyphonic form is in general fluid or evolving; the *procedures* followed in a Mass-section or a fugue may be described, but to give a *scheme* or set pattern applicable to all Mass-sections or all fugues is impossible. With the swing from polyphonic to homophonic styles of writing which occurred (roughly speaking) around the year 1600, there developed an interest in formal patterns of a more static or "closed" type, such as were more suitable for the *instrumental* music which now came to the fore. For it must be realized that when music is divorced from words it has to adopt a tighter, more clear-cut formal organization than is obligatory when there is a text to supply a large part of the "sense" of the piece. Added to this fact is another of equal importance: after about 1600 the free and subtle interplays of vocal polyphonic rhythms were abandoned in favor of the *metrical* rhythm of the bar or measure; with homophony came "the tyranny of the bar-line," the *beating of time* which we associate with most music of the period 1600–1900. This again made for greater crispness in musical forms—more balanced periods, and clearer patterns. Finally, the Age of Reason in the 18th century brought Classicism in music; and one of the prime qualities of the Classical in art is its love of precision and formal regularity. We find, therefore, a gradual crystallization of forms through the Baroque period (1600–1750, roughly) culminating in the fixed patterns of the homophonic Classical composers (1750–1800) with which this section is mainly concerned. It remains only to say that the next style-period (the Romantic, 1800–1900) proceeded once again to modify the Classical forms in the interests of expression; but it did this, in general, by expansion of the forms rather than by rejection of them, so that the basic patterns often remained the same. Indeed, even 20th-century composers have found the forms here to be described suitable for further exploitation, though it is a far cry from, for instance, the Classical sonata of Mozart to the latest symphony of Stravinsky.

We shall discuss the forms of homophonic music under two main headings: (I) *One-Movement Forms,* (II) *The Sonata* (a Cyclic Form). The particular choice of the single-movement forms under (I) is governed by the fact that all of them, in addition to being the structural types of innumerable separate, independent pieces, are to be found in the various movements of the cyclic form discussed under (II). In other words, we have to understand the forms headed (I) in order to grasp the structural scheme of a *sonata,* of which our study contains several examples.

I. *One-Movement Forms.*

(A). Binary
(B). Ternary
(C). Simple Episodic } *Episodic forms*
(D). Rondo
(E). Variation
(F). Sonata-Form
(G). Sonata-Rondo

(A). *Binary Form.* This is a bipartite (two-part) form, based on the extremely simple, logical plan of *statement and response,* or *thesis and antithesis* (*cf. parallelism* in literature: "The Lord is my shepherd: I shall not want"). An example familiar to everyone is the national air *My Country, 'Tis of Thee;* the first part extends to the authentic cadence at "Of thee I sing," the second part completes and balances this. For analytical convenience, the parts are labelled "A" and "B" respectively. Note the following features:

1. Since balance in the arts is not a "mathematical" concept, Part B is often longer than Part A, especially in the more developed examples of the form (Exs. 131, 132, and *My Country, 'Tis of Thee*).

Binary Form   *English Morris-dance*

Example 131

Binary Form   Mozart: *Piano Sonata in C Major [K.330], 2nd movement*

Example 132

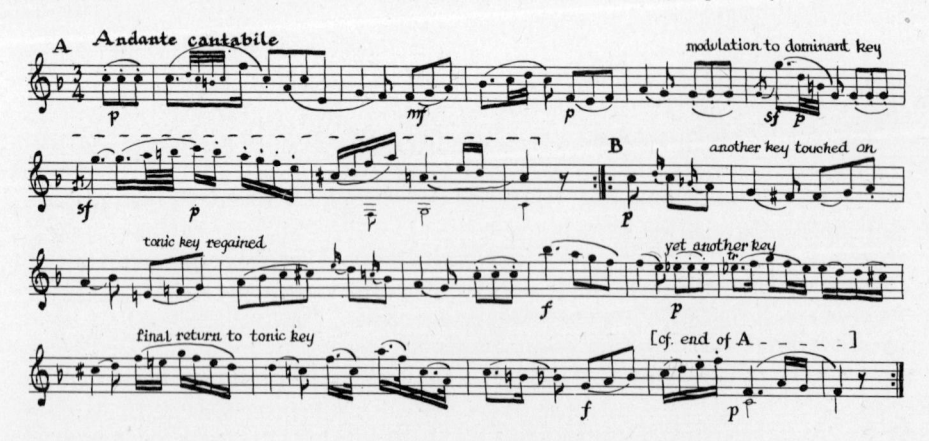

2. Each part may be repeated (A-A:B-B), especially in instrumental music without words. This is called *sectional repetition,* a kind of exact restatement peculiar to music. In writing,

THE FORMS OF HOMOPHONIC MUSIC

sections to be repeated are enclosed within double-bars and double-dots. Binary form, therefore, is schematically represented:

$$\|: A :\|: B :\|$$

The repetition is referred to as the *repeat* (Ex. 131).

3. Part A often modulates (changes key) at its end, generally to the nearest related key (*i.e.*, to the *dominant* when the tonic key is *major*, to the *relative major* when the tonic key is *minor*)[1]; Part B returns to the home key (the tonic), frequently via other tonalities (Ex. 132).

4. There is a tendency, especially in instrumental music, to revert *at the end* of Part B to *the end* of Part A, by repeating the cadence-bars of the first part exactly or with necessary changes, and thereby integrating the composition through *thematic repetition* (Ex. 131).

5. Part B is often, especially in instrumental music, a *development* of the musical idea propounded in Part A. In *My Country, 'Tis of Thee* the musical figure set to these opening words dominates the whole composition. Example 132 shows the same kind of thing more subtly handled.

Binary form has the merits of balance, simplicity, and compactness. It is found in folksongs, national airs, hymns, etc.; in "art music" it occurs repeatedly in the *suites* (sets of short dance-movements) of the 17th- and 18th-century composers, as well as in sub-sections of longer movements of later date. But it is not capable of great expansion; the two parts can be just so long and no longer. (The given examples by no means show the limits of size, but the statement just made is none the less true.) We do not find binary form, therefore, as the basis of movements of any considerable complexity; and in this respect it must be contrasted with the form next to be discussed.

(B). *Ternary Form.* This is a tripartite (three-part) form, based on the principle of *statement, digression* or *development*, and *restatement*. The form is thus represented schematically, the double-bars and double-dots indicating the usual repeats, and the figure 2 meaning simply "for the second time":

$$\|: A :\|: B\text{-}A^2 :\|$$

Note the following features:

1. The critical point—the point that decides whether the form is ternary—is the point of *return to the beginning*, after digression or development. Provided this is clearly established (not merely by repeating the opening passage, but—what is equally important—by making the end of Part B *lead up to* and *prepare for* the return), then—

2. —the restatement ("A^2") need not be exact. In simple cases it is (Ex. 133); in more

Ternary Form · Mozart: *Clarinet Quintet, 3rd movement*

Example 133

[1]See, above, "Modulation," pp. 388–90.

complicated music, especially instrumental, the restatement may be much modified (Ex. 134);

Ternary Form Beethoven: *String Quartet in C Minor [Op. 18, No. 4], 3rd movement*

Example 134

and in the cases referred to in the next note it *has* to be modified, at least in tonality.

3. As in binary form, Part A often modulates, towards its end, to the nearest related key (see above). When "A" is restated as "A²," its ending will have to be changed, otherwise the piece would close in a different key from that in which it began (Ex. 135).

Ternary Form Haydn: *Piano Sonata in E Flat, 3rd movement*

Example 135

4. *Nature of Part B:* Sometimes, as in the familiar song *Drink to Me Only with Thine Eyes,* Part B is a digression—a turning away from the subject matter of Part A to something different (though not irrelevant). Far more often, however, Part B is a *development* or "discussion" of an idea introduced in Part A—an unfolding of its inherent musical possibilities, an elaboration of the theme, as in a well-constructed speech or essay. Especially is this true in instrumental music, where there are no words to continue the "sense" of Part A (Exs. 133, 134, and 135).

5. Whether simple digression or development, Part B frequently modulates through other tonalities than those (or that) of Part A. The return to the tonic key is made just before the beginning of "A²"; usually Part B is brought round to a half-cadence in the tonic key, or to a modulation to the dominant key—in either case ending with the "V" chord which leads naturally to the "I" of the opening of "A²" (Exs. 133, 134, and 135).

6. As to the sectional repeats, note that "B-A²" are repeated *together,* not separately. The only variant of the repeat-scheme given above that we need mention is found in ternary form with words (folksongs, national airs, juke-box tunes), where the *first part only* is repeated—obviously to accommodate the text. *Drink to Me Only with Thine Eyes* shows this pattern, which may be represented: A-A | B-A².

Ternary form exhibits the qualities of unity ("A-A²") and variety ("B"). Unlike binary form, it has been found capable of tremendous expansion, so that compositions ranging in scope from simple folksongs and popular jingles all the way to complex symphonic movements have been based on this highly adaptable scheme. The pleasure of returning, after digression or elaboration, to a more or less straightforward restatement of the matter first raised, seems to fulfill a fundamental psychological need; which explains the continued and apparently inexhaustible interest in the form.

Special Features. Two features illustrated in the examples—the *coda* (Ex. 134) and the *link* (Ex. 133) are not basic to binary or ternary (or any other) forms, but are of vital significance, especially in the longer movements later to be discussed.

1. The *coda* (literally, "tail") consists of additional material at the end of a movement, carrying it beyond the expected conclusion, with the object of intensifying or adding weight to the close (Ex. 134). In simple cases it involves little more than repetition of the final cadence, exactly or with slight modifications of melody (*e.g.,* the sentimental ditty *Just a Song at Twilight*). More often (as in Ex. 134) it rounds off an ending which would otherwise be too abrupt, or supplies a climax to the whole piece (especially in long movements). Though illustrated here in connection with ternary form, *the coda is not confined to that form;* it is a common feature in all types of structure (binary, ternary, episodic, rondo, variation, and especially *sonata-form,* which is found in sonatas; see below).

2. The *link,* as here described, is a feature of ternary form and its correlatives; it is not found in binary form. It consists of material inserted between the end of Part B and the beginning of "A²," with the object of intensifying the critical point of return by *building up to* or *driving into* it. It is very frequently based on the dominant chord of the home key, a chord which, the more it is repeated or prolonged, creates the more urgent necessity of *resolving* onto the tonic chord at the beginning of "A²".[2] Such links are also found between the longer divisions of larger forms, where they frequently have the additional function of modulating from one section in one key to another section in another key (Ex. 136).

(C). *Simple Episodic Form.* We have seen that in both binary and ternary forms *development of theme* plays an important part; that is to say, the whole composition—whether binary or ternary—is *generally* concerned with discussion of a musical idea propounded in Part A (though it is *possible* to have something different in Part B). The principle of development,

[2] See note 5 under *Ternary Form,* and Ex. 133.

however, is not the only one available in music; of equal importance is the principle of *contrast*, which finds its clearest expression in two types of structure called *episodic*— the *simple episodic form* and the *rondo form*. These two forms illustrate a very obvious way of building up a longer movement than those we have been considering, for both of them depend upon the association, within a larger unity, of two or more binary or ternary movements in certain relationships.

Schematically, *simple episodic form* may be represented thus:

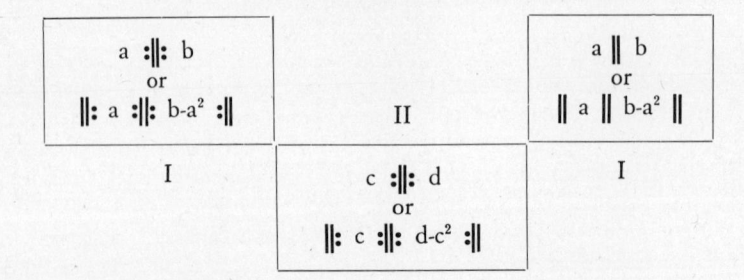

a :‖: b or ‖: a :‖: b-a² :‖	II	a ‖ b or ‖ a ‖ b-a² ‖
I	c :‖: d or ‖: c :‖: d-c² :‖	I

It will be seen at a glance that this is a correlative of ternary form, in that it consists of a first part (I), a middle part (II), and the first part (I) repeated. Equally obvious is one of the big differences between episodic and ternary forms, *viz.*, that in the episodic scheme each of the three main parts is itself a complete, self-contained binary or ternary form, which "makes sense" on its own. (All of the ternary examples quoted under (B) above are, in fact, *the first parts* of simple episodic movements.)

But there are other important respects, not shown in the scheme, in which episodic form differs from ternary; all are concerned with *the nature of the middle part (II)*. Whereas in ternary form Part B, even if a digression, is only in *relative* contrast to the "A-A²" parts, in episodic form the contrast between I and II is *absolute,* within the limits of congruity. For in episodic form (the underlying principle of which is not development but contrast) the middle part

(1) introduces an entirely new theme,
(2) is of a markedly different character or "mood,"
(3) is generally (though not invariably) in a new tonality.

These three factors make the middle part an *episode,* which may be defined as a section, enclosed within a larger movement, whose function is to act as a *foil* or *relief* to the surrounding material. Hence the name of the form.

The simplest, most clear-cut example of this type of structure is the *minuet-and-trio* (since Beethoven, the *scherzo-and-trio*), one of the few original dance-forms to retain a place in the sonata and symphony.[3] As can be seen from Example 136, the minuet (here in binary form) is bold in character, the trio (here in ternary form) is lyrical and flowing; then the bold minuet is repeated, the only change being the omission of sectional repeats within the minuet the second time over. So formalized is the scheme that the repeat of the minuet (after the trio) is never written out; the sign *Menuetto da capo* or simply *Da capo* (abbreviation: *D.C.*) is written at the end of the trio, directing the performer to repeat "from the beginning." it should be noted in passing that the character-sequence here illustrated (*bold—lyrical—bold*) is the typical sequence in simple episodic forms, whether in the stereotyped minuet-and-trio or in the freer adaptations of the scheme mentioned below. (There are, however, plenty of exceptions, in which the *episode* is made of sterner stuff than the first and third parts, and the character-sequence then becomes *lyrical—bold—lyrical.*)

[3] See below: *The Sonata*, pp. 410–13.

THE FORMS OF HOMOPHONIC MUSIC

Simple Episodic Form — Mozart: *Eine Kleine Nachtmusik,* 3rd movement

Example 136

The *da capo aria* of Baroque vocal music is another stereotyped example of simple episodic form. In this case, however, some of the episodic criteria above mentioned (*e.g.,* new theme, new character) may be lacking; in fact, a certain amount of *development* of Part I may be found in Part II, which makes one hesitate to call Part II an "episode." On the other hand, the three main divisions of a *da capo aria* are always separable and complete in themselves (contrast ternary form)—so much so that in modern performances of Baroque arias it is not uncommon to sing the first part only, omitting Part II and the consequent repeat of Part I (*e.g.,* the contralto aria "He was despised" in Handel's *Messiah*); and Part II is almost invariably in a new key, or keys.

Other pre-Classical uses of episodic form, quite as "formalized" as the minuet-and-trio, are found in the 17th- and 18th-century suites, where we see such movements as Bourrée I—Bourrée II —Bourrée I *da capo,* Gavotte I—Gavotte II—Gavotte I *da capo.* In these cases the component movements are almost invariably binary in form, as mentioned above (see *Binary Form,* end note).

Lest it be thought that simple episodic form is always thus clear-cut and sectionalized, we must point out that the same basic principle of *episodic contrast* has served for movements far removed in spirit from the dance, and far freer in structure than the minuet-and-trio. Such movements may occur, for instance, as the slow, expressive second movements of sonatas (see below), or as independent pieces (Rachmaninoff's famous *Prelude in C sharp Minor* is one). In these cases it is common to find modifications in the directions of (1) greater continuity throughout, the several parts being made to flow one into another without the definite sectionalization of the dance-form; and (2) variety in the third main division, the repeat of Part I being written out and considerably altered, often with the addition of a coda. The Romantic composers, in particular, were experts at ringing the changes on this simple basic scheme; a striking example can be found in Chopin's piano *Prelude in D flat Major* (the so-called "Raindrop Prelude"), which incidentally shows the *lyrical—stern—lyrical* sequence of moods.

(D). *Rondo Form.* This is the other episodic form mentioned in the opening paragraph of (C), above. It represents an expansion of the idea of simple episodic form, by the addition of further episodes (each complete in itself, and each with its own theme, character, and—generally—key), separated by further repetitions of the opening part (I), which thus keeps "coming round"; hence the name of the form. Theoretically there is no limit to the number of episodes which may be included in a rondo scheme; in fact, there is some historical evidence for assuming that the form derives from the folk-music custom of alternating chorus- and solo-singing in such a way that the chorus remains constant (the *refrain*) while the solo-passages (extemporized) vary—this alternation being kept up as long as the singers wish, or until the text of the song is completed. But the Classical composers (and later writers) found that practical considerations limited the number of episodes to *two;* and we may present the scheme of *Classical rondo form* thus:

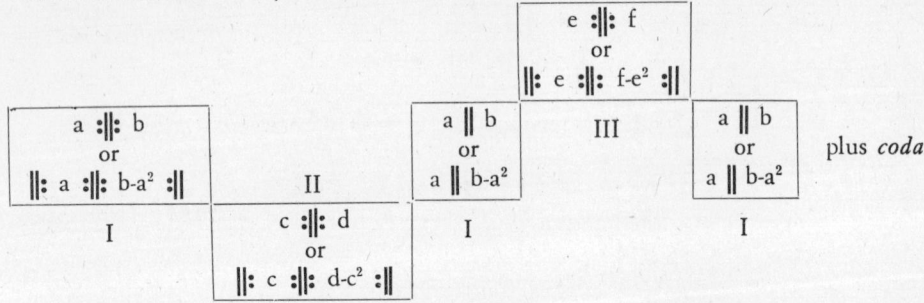

$$\begin{array}{ccccc}
& & & \boxed{\begin{array}{c} e \;:\|: f \\ \text{or} \\ \|: e \;:\|: f\text{-}e^2 \;:\| \end{array}} & \\
\boxed{\begin{array}{c} a \;:\|: b \\ \text{or} \\ \|: a \;:\|: b\text{-}a^2 \;:\| \end{array}} & & \boxed{\begin{array}{c} a \;\|\; b \\ \text{or} \\ a \;\|\; b\text{-}a^2 \end{array}} & \text{III} & \boxed{\begin{array}{c} a \;\|\; b \\ \text{or} \\ a \;\|\; b\text{-}a^2 \end{array}} \quad \text{plus } coda \\
\text{I} & \text{II} & \text{I} & & \text{I} \\
& \boxed{\begin{array}{c} c \;:\|: d \\ \text{or} \\ \|: c \;:\|: d\text{-}c^2 \;:\| \end{array}} & & &
\end{array}$$

The episodes contrast in key, character and theme not only with the main, recurring part (I) but also with each other, as may be seen from the example quoted from Haydn (Ex. 137). Note that the parts are all self-contained, complete binary or ternary forms, which "make sense" separately as well as in conjunction. In rondo form these individual parts tend to be

Rondo Form   Haydn: *Piano Sonata in D Major, 3rd movement*

Example 137

Example 137

[musical score with annotations: "followed by 2nd episode (ternary) G major throughout. B 8va— A² exact restatement of A Link (an 'extra', not basic to rondo form) leading back to the key of the main theme, and enhancing its 3rd entrance by withholding it till HERE! Tonic key (D maj.) Main theme A etc, as before, but with an embellished accompaniment, and a two chord CODA at the end."]

shorter than in simple episodic form, since the whole movement must be kept within certain bounds. Indeed, there are not lacking examples in which the individual members are less than complete binary or ternary forms—in which they are, in other words, a phrase or two long and no more. But such examples are mostly pre-Classical, and do not invalidate the given scheme.

Just as, when we say "minuet," we think of a dance *style* as well as of a form, so when we say "rondo" we associate the word with something gay, spirited, and witty, in fast tempo. This is because the form was often used by the Classical composers for the fast final movements of sonatas and symphonies, wherein high spirits and jollity are typical (the Haydn example is the final movement of a pianoforte sonata in D major). But just as we have seen that episodic form was used for movements quite un-minuet-like, so we must observe that the rondo *form* has been extensively used for pieces far different in spirit from the gay rondos of Classical *finales*. The expressive slow movement of Beethoven's *Pathétique* pianoforte sonata is in rondo form, as also are the slow movements of both Mozart's and Beethoven's quintets in E flat major for piano and wind instruments. In such cases in particular we are likely to find the same modifications as were commented on in connection with the "freer" types of simple episodic form—to wit, greater continuity between sections (by the inclusion of links, or by the avoidance of full stops at the ends of parts), and variation of the main division (I) at its later appearances. In *slow* rondo-forms the latter modification is almost a necessity, as the exact repetition (twice) of Part I in slow tempo would be tedious.

It is most necessary to grasp the distinction between *a rondo*—of the fast, jolly type—and rondo *form,* which is an episodic principle, divorced from style. It happens that in this volume we have an example of a *minuet with two trios* (Mozart's *Clarinet Quintet,* third movement), which is in rondo *form* but which is decidedly not *a rondo.* The minuet-with-two-trios is a comparative rarity; one of the big points against it is precisely what was mentioned at the end of the preceding paragraph—the tedium which is apt to be felt at the exact repetition, twice, of the minuet. Mozart overcomes this by making both his trios (the episodes) longer than the minuet; but the inherent disadvantages of the procedure prevented its frequent adoption.

(E). *Variation Form.* Development of an idea by presenting it in varying guises is of the essence of musical expression. One might almost say that there can be no musical "sense" without variation of one sort or another, whether the musical idea be Gregorian, Beethovenian, or juke-box. What happens in the special form known as *variation-form* (or *theme-and-variations*) is that attention is directed to the process of variation exclusively, and a complete movement is built up simply by progressive mutation or elaboration of *one* musical theme, unsupported by contrasting themes. In Classical and Romantic music, this theme is always a compact, clear-cut binary or ternary form, purposely simplified in structure so as to be easily remembered. This is repeated over and over again with increasingly complicated permutations (variations), until a *set* of from five to forty repetitions is built up. The modifications may be anything from simple melodic or harmonic *figuration* ("playing around" the basic melody or harmony) to drastic changes of *tempo* (slower rate changed to faster, or *vice versa*), of *time* (duple meter changed to triple, or *vice versa*), of *tonality* (major key changed to minor, or *vice versa*), of *texture* (homophonic changed to polyphonic, or *vice versa*), etc. Often, too, a larger form is superimposed on the set of variations by grouping the latter in such a way as to make them appear in contrasting "blocks." If, for instance, the theme is in fast tempo and major key, and Variations 1-3 are of the same general nature, the interposing of a slow Variation 4 in minor key before fast, major-key Variations 5-8 would give a kind of "episodic" feeling to the whole set (though of course Variation 4 would not be an episode in the strict sense of the term). This kind of contrast is, in fact, carefully planned by the writers of variations, since there is no other relief from the repetitiousness inherent in the form.

As to the number of variations, this depends upon the nature of the movement. When variation-form is used in the slow movements of sonatas (see below), there are usually no more than four or five variations, for reasons of duration. In fast final movements of sonatas there may be more (seven to ten), the last often being worked up into a brilliant coda. In independent sets—not in sonatas—the number may be much larger (*e.g.,* Beethoven's *Thirty-Two Variations in C Minor,* for pianoforte). In the longer sets, in particular, the connection of some of the variations with the theme may be hard to grasp; but one factor will remain constant—the basic binary or ternary form in which the theme was written. This will rarely be impaired, since the phrase-structure, cadence-scheme, and architectural plan are sufficient, after a certain number of repetitions, to bind a variation to the theme when all else is different. The only common departure from the theme-structure is in the final variation, which, as stated above, may "cut loose" and build up into a coda of sizable dimensions.

No example of variation form is given here, for reasons of space. Students are referred to the last movement of Mozart's *Clarinet Quintet*[4] for a delightful instance, which, however, gives little idea of the tremendous possibilities of this form as a vehicle of musical expression. For the latter, play Brahms's orchestral *Variations on a Theme by Haydn,* or the last movement of Beethoven's *Eroica Symphony* (No. 3).

(F). *Sonata-Form.* It was mentioned above (under *Ternary Form*) that the scheme of tonal organization based upon *statement—digression* or *development—restatement* proved capable of vast expansion. Such an expansion of the basic ternary principle is *sonata-form,* the most complex and yet logically clearest of all instrumental forms (with the possible exception of the fugue, which is in any case a polyphonic form, and vocal as well as instrumental). As the name implies, sonata-form is found most often in sonatas (see below). It is so typically the scheme of *first movements* of sonatas (though it may also occur in other movements) that an alternative name for it is "first-movement form"; and since these first movements are generally *allegro* (fast), a third name used is "sonata-allegro form." We shall use here the first name—*sonata-form;* but the others are worth mentioning if only to make it clear that we are talking about the form of *one of the movements* of a sonata, not of the sonata as a whole. Also to be borne in mind is the fact that sonata-form, like all the other one-movement forms here discussed, may occur in independent pieces—*e.g.,* operatic overtures—not connected in any way with the cyclic form of the sonata.

[4] See, above, pp. 256–59.

It is beyond the scope of this article to discuss the steps by which simple ternary form was gradually expanded into sonata-form. We need hardly point out that there were many intervening stages; but it is the peculiar glory of the Classical composers—particularly Haydn and Mozart—that they carried the development of the scheme to a point of highest perfection, by using it over and over again for the expression of their greatest musical thoughts. When Beethoven came along, with his strong Romantic leanings, he found ready to hand a form which needed only broadening and deepening to make it capable of carrying *his* mighty affirmations and poetic imaginings, too; and after him a whole century of composers found in this scheme a frame for their larger, more "abstract" ideas, even though they turned from it to other forms for their intimate, more typically Romantic communications. The plan here given, then, is applicable (with adaptations) to sonata-form movements from Haydn and Mozart down to Brahms and Tschaikovsky, and even (with still further adaptations) to 20th-century sonata-form writers; but as it stands it is the Classical scheme of sonata-form.

A EXPOSITION (statement)	B DEVELOPMENT (rarely digression)	A^2 RECAPITULATION (restatement)
I. 1st subject, in tonic key. Transition, leading to — II. 2nd subject in contrasted key (*dominant*, for major tonics; *relative major*, for minor tonics). One or more distinct themes. Codetta	"Discussion" of thematic material of Exposition (or part of it) in various keys and diverse ways; an "unfolding" of its inherent musical possibilities. Works back to half-cadence in tonic key. Link	I. 1st subject, in tonic key. Transition, altered so as to lead to — II. 2nd subject, *in tonic key* (themes as in Exposition). Coda

1. Repeats, if made at all, are as in simple ternary form, *viz.*:

$$\|: \text{Exposition} :\|: \text{Development—Recapitulation} :\|$$

As the form kept expanding, these repeats were omitted; but in the performance of 18th-century sonata-form movements it is still customary to repeat the Exposition (only), as also is done in the case of 19th-century movements whenever the Exposition is short (*e.g.*, Schumann's *Symphony No. 2* in C major, first movement), or the composer specifically calls for the repeat (*e.g.*, Beethoven's *Eroica Symphony*, first movement).

2. Distinguish between *"subject"* (=one of the two main tonal "blocks" in Exposition and Recapitulation) and *"theme"* (=a distinctly recognizable musical "idea," with a character of its own). Where there is only one theme to a subject (as frequently happens in the case of first subjects), the terms become synonymous; even so, it avoids confusion to refer to the "first subject" rather than the "first theme," because *second subjects* typically contain several themes, which have to be referred to as "second subject, *first theme*," "second subject, *second theme*," etc. (Convenient abbreviations for these are II(1), II(2), etc.) In sonatas, a theme is generally regarded as having a certain scope and completeness; it may contain contrasting elements (which are referred to as motives, figures, sections, or simply parts of the theme), but inasmuch as these are felt to be contributory to one complex musical "idea," they are not themselves called "themes."

In Classical music, the first subject generally ends with a definite authentic cadence, or a half-cadence followed by rests. Sometimes, however, it merges with the beginning of the transition; and this is common in Beethoven and the later Romantics.

3. The *transition* is a connective passage, its chief function being to negotiate the change from the first subject to the second subject. Generally it contains the necessary modulation (key-change) from tonic key to dominant (or, for minor tonics, relative major); in which case it has to be rewritten in the Recapitulation to avoid such modulation.[5] In some cases[6] the transition itself does not modulate, but simply brings the music "into position" for the second subject to take off in the new key (in the Exposition) or continue in the same key (in the Recapitulation). In any case, it may be constructed out of (a) new material, (b) first-subject or (if there is one) Introduction material, (c) a combination of new and previously-heard material. In 18th-century sonatas, transitions are generally well-defined and conventional; they often feature scale-passages and *arpeggios* ("broken-chord" patterns) of a brilliant but not very pertinent nature, and end with emphatic cadence-repetitions followed by a rest; which makes the beginning of the second subject stand out obviously. Later sonata-writers (from Beethoven on) tend to make their transitions grow out of the first subject and lead right into the second subject; so that in some cases it is doubtful where the first subject ends and the transition begins, or indeed whether there is a separable transition at all.[7]

4. The *second subject,* or at least its first theme, generally contrasts with the first subject not only in key but also in character. First subjects tend to be bold, succinct, arresting, frequently based on one terse figure or two sharply contrasting figures; second subjects, on the other hand, characteristically begin with a lyrical, melodious, "feminine" theme, after which subsequent themes may again be assertive.

In 18th-century sonata-form movements one sometimes finds the second subject beginning with the same theme as was used in the first subject. An instance occurs in the first movement of Mozart's *Pianoforte Quartet in G Minor,* discussed in this volume on page 237. This is not, however, the normal procedure even in the earlier sonata-writers (Mozart and Haydn), and one never finds it in Beethoven or his successors. The new key was felt to demand a new theme or themes; once such new material had been brought in, a reverting to first-subject material in the form of a closing section or a codetta (see below) was quite common.

5. The *codetta* (diminutive form of *coda*) is the final section of the second subject, confirming the end of the Exposition (in the contrasted key) and marking the point beyond which, normally, no new themes will be introduced. In 18th-century music, codettas tend to be conventional cadence-repetitions, featuring scales and *arpeggios;* later this section was tied up thematically with material previously set forth (especially first-subject ideas), thus rounding off the whole Exposition. Also the codetta may have a new and perfectly legitimate theme of its own, constructed, however, with definite cadential purpose and "end feeling."

Sometimes a *link* follows the codetta, leading back to the tonic key for the repeat of the Exposition. This link is often supplied with first and second "endings," so that the second time over it leads on into the Development. It generally uses first-subject material.

6. The *Development* is, in a sense, the most important part of a sonata-form movement. Here the composer, having presented for our consideration certain musical ideas (themes), proceeds to "discuss" or "analyze" them, and to draw out of them, according to his desire and skill, their many implications and inherent qualities. If the Exposition be likened to the opening part of a speech, in which the topic is introduced and delimited, the Development may be likened to the argument, in which the original propositions are analyzed and elaborated logically and convincingly. No one plan of development can be given; no two Development sections are alike. The following are some of the means most frequently utilized:

a. *Change of tonality, i.e.,* presentation of themes in keys other than those of the Exposition.
b. *Change of mode, i.e.,* presentation of major themes in minor, or *vice versa.*
c. *Change of register, i.e.,* presentation of themes higher or lower than their original range.

[5]*Cf.* Note 3 on *Ternary Form* above (section B).
[6]*E.g.,* the Overture to *The Marriage of Figaro,* by Mozart.
[7]See the first movement of Beethoven's *Fifth Symphony.*

d. *Change of dynamics*, from loud to soft, or *vice versa;* or loudening or softening single notes of themes originally even-toned, or *vice versa;* or other variations of loudness and softness.

e. *Change of harmony* or of *accompaniment, i.e.*, resetting themes so that their originally simple harmonies are enriched, or *vice versa;* or so that an original accompaniment which was quiet and subdued becomes energetic and restless, or *vice versa*.

f. *Change of rhythm*, either basic rhythm (time) or structural rhythm (phrase-structure); *i.e.*, presentation of duple-time themes in triple time, or *vice versa;* or lengthening or shortening the original phrase-structure of themes.

g. *Contrapuntal treatment, i.e.*, taking themes (or fragments of themes) and tossing them around among various *voices* or *parts* of the harmony, so that the themes appear "against" themselves; especially in a kind of writing called *fugato* ("fugal," *i.e.*, in the style of a fugue), which is a favorite developmental device.

h. *Combination of themes, i.e.*, the association of two or more distinct themes in a complex texture; or the addition to themes of new counter-melodies not heard before. (This would also be "contrapuntal treatment.")

i. *Figure-development, i.e.*, the "driving in" of characteristic figures (motives) of themes, by repeating them over and over, not exactly but with infinite variations, and with cumulative effect. Though listed last, this is perhaps the most cogent and certainly the most common means of thematic development.

It should not be assumed that all of the above procedures occur in the same Development. Moreover, a composer's genius and the quality of his thematic ideas will alone dictate the degree to which he subjects those ideas to analysis and "discussion." There is a great difference, for instance, between the Developments of Mozart and those of Beethoven, principally because Mozart's themes are different from Beethoven's. In Mozart, the themes are almost always perfectly finished melodies at their first presentation (in the Exposition); he therefore, quite properly, tends to repeat rather than develop them in his Development sections, especially by a kind of chain-repetition called *sequence*. Beethoven, on the other hand, often writes themes which, in themselves and on first presentation, are terse, abrupt, non-melodious; mere pegs, in fact, on which to hang a masterly Development. Mozart is the great melodist of music; Beethoven and Bach, the supreme masters of thematic development.

As to the phrase "rarely digression" which appears under the heading *Development* in our outline-scheme above (p. 405), it will be seen from the foregoing notes that the function of the Development is to "discuss" themes already presented, not to digress to new ideas. It happens, however, that in the course of some Development sections a composer may feel the need of introducing an entirely new theme, to serve as a foil to the ideas he is discussing; much as a skilled orator, after hammering away on a certain idea, may refresh his audience's attention by the introduction of an anecdote or some other parenthetical matter, after which he returns to his main theme with greater effect. Such a "parenthesis" in a Development section is called an *episode*.[8] Episodes are generally short, and usually occur only once in a Development.

7. The *link* from Development to Recapitulation is a much-magnified form of the link discussed above under *Ternary Form*.[9] It serves the same purpose of *driving into* the return to the beginning, thus emphasizing this structurally vital point. It is often constructed over a sustained or reiterated bass note, called a *pedal* (usually a *dominant* pedal, *i.e.*, the "V" of the "I" which almost always opens the Recapitulation).

8. Of the *Recapitulation* little need be said, other than that it restates the themes of the Exposition, in the order in which they appear in the Exposition, but now *all in the tonic*

---
[8]See definition above, under *Simple Episodic Form*, p. 399.
[9]*Special Features*, p. 399.

key (*i.e.*, the second subject is now in the same key as the first subject). In many cases this restatement is exact, except for the necessary alteration of the original transition;[10] in some cases, however, alterations not structurally called for are made, simply because the composer does not choose to repeat himself exactly.[11] Whatever alterations may be made will be merely incidental, not basic; for the function of the Recapitulation is restatement, not development. The Exposition states; the Development analyzes; the Recapitulation re-synthesizes.

9. The *coda* is, of course, vastly extended in sonata-form, as compared with the simple codas of ternary (or other) forms.[12] It rounds off the whole movement, bringing the music to an effective and clinching close. Eighteenth-century codas tend to be brilliant displays of musical pyrotechnics, composed of flashing scale-passages and arpeggio-work, all emphasizing the tonic key and chord. From Beethoven on, the coda assumes the importance and function of the dénouement of a drama, or of the peroration of a good piece of oratory. In it the composer says his final words about his themes, drawing them together and building up to a dramatic climax. Beethoven, in particular, expands his codas until they become almost second Development sections. He will even (*though rarely*) introduce a new theme at this late stage; but generally he forges preceding themes, especially the first subject, into their final crashing forms, ending forcibly and abruptly.

10. Last in order of comment, because it is a feature found only with some, not with all, sonata-form movements, is the *Introduction*. This is "outside the form," being typically a slow, dignified prelude to an *allegro* (fast) movement, not a part of it. It is more common in symphonies (sonatas for orchestra; see below) than in solo or small-ensemble sonatas. Eighteenth-century Introductions tend to be little more than pompous, dignified summons to attention, establishing the key of the movement and ending with an unmistakable, forward-pointing cadence and rests.[13] Beethoven was the first to realize the possibilities of the Introduction as a vital, integral dramatic device. He uses it in many ways: (1) to demand, not beg, attention; (2) to establish a dramatic or "moody" atmosphere; (3) to propound a basic "text" (*i.e.*, figure, motive) which is worked into the *allegro* following.

Examples of sonata-form are found in works discussed in this volume. Since they are all analyzed in detail there, it is unnecessary to quote an example here. The above notes are general explanations of features found in some or all of the sonata-form movements studied. Note 10 on the *Introduction* is included for the sake of completeness, though it happens that no example occurs in the works chosen for our study. For a good 18th-century (Classical) Introduction, see Mozart's *Symphony No. 39*, in E flat major, first movement. For typical Beethovenian Introductions, see the *Pathétique* pianoforte sonata and the *Third, Fourth,* and *Seventh Symphonies* (first movements in all cases).

(G). *Sonata-Rondo Form.* This is a hybrid, resulting from the "cross-breeding" of sonata-form and the older rondo form. We find the first examples in the Classical composers,[14] but it was Beethoven who adopted the form regularly, in the final movements of his sonatas, to replace the older or simple rondo. Since Beethoven, "rondo" in these movements almost invariably means "sonata-rondo," though the composers themselves never used the term.

To make the connection between older rondo, sonata-form, and sonata-rondo clear, let us represent the *component parts* (the main theme and episodes) of older rondo by Roman numerals, and the *subjects* of sonata-form by the same Roman numerals. The first two columns in the figure below may then be compared with the third column, which is the scheme of sonata-rondo.

[10]See Note 3 above, p. 406.
[11]See Recapitulation of first movement of Mozart's *Clarinet Quintet*, p. 252.
[12]See above, under *Special Features*, p. 399.
[13]*Cf.* Note 3 above on the 18-century *transition*, p. 406.
[14]See the last movement of Mozart's *Pianoforte Quartet in G Minor*, p. 245.

THE FORMS OF HOMOPHONIC MUSIC

Older rondo	*Sonata-form*	*Sonata-Rondo*
I tonic key	⎡I tonic key	⎡I tonic key
	⎢ Transition	⎢ [Transition]
II new key	⎣II new key	⎢II new key
I tonic key		⎣I tonic key
III another key	Development—other keys	III or Development—other keys
I tonic key	⎡I tonic key	⎡I tonic key
	⎢ Transition altered	⎢ [Transition altered]
	⎣II tonic key	⎢II tonic key
Coda	Coda	⎣I and/or Coda

It will be seen that the old "first episode" (the II) of simple rondo form has become a "second subject" in sonata-rondo form, by virtue of its repetition at the end of the movement *in the tonic key,* exactly as the second subject of sonata-form is treated. It will be seen, further, that whereas the sonata-rondo *may* contain a "second episode" (the III) just like simple rondo form, it is just as likely to replace this with a Development section, such as is found in sonata-form. On the other hand, sonata-rondo diverges from sonata-form in having, in its "Exposition," *a return to the main theme (I) in the tonic key,* exactly as simple rondo returns to I in the tonic after its first episode.

Further comparisons and contrasts are involved, which cannot be shown schematically. Most important of these is the fact that, whereas the component parts of simple rondo form are generally complete little binary or ternary forms in themselves,[15] the component parts of sonata-rondo are often *not* complete forms, but may be more freely constructed after the fashion of the subjects and themes of sonata-form. (Note that we do not say that they are *always* thus constructed, but simply that they *may be*.) The effect is to make the various parts of the sonata-rondo movement *flow into* or *merge with* each other in a way not typical of older rondo form, but eminently typical of sonata-form. This greater cohesion is aided by the frequent (but not invariable) use of the *transition* in sonata-rondo form, for the same purposes as in sonata-form, *viz.,* to negotiate the key-change more smoothly in the Exposition, and to ease the change of mood between contrasting thematic ideas.

For all these reasons—and others not mentioned—we use the terminology of sonata-form in describing sonata-rondo form. Thus we speak of its Exposition (I–II–I), its Development (if there is one), and its Recapitulation and Coda; and likewise of its first (I) and second (II) *subjects*. The only term taken from the older rondo form is *the* Episode (not, now, the *second* episode), if that feature (III) occurs instead of a Development.

Three examples of sonata-rondo form occur in works discussed in this volume (Mozart's *Pianoforte Quartet in G Minor,* p. 245; Beethoven's *Pianoforte Concerto No. 4,* p. 296; Beethoven's *Violin Concerto,* p. 285; final movements in each case). None of these examples conforms *exactly* to the scheme given above; but to understand their particular divergencies the above "normal" outline must be kept in mind. For an example of complete adherence to the given scheme we refer the student to the last movement of Beethoven's *String Quartet in C Minor,* Opus 18, No. 4, which is remarkable for the strictness with which the "sectionalization" of older rondo is preserved (each component part being a complete binary or ternary form in itself, with the usual "double-bar and repeat" signs).

[15] See scheme above under *Rondo Form,* p. 402.

II. *The Sonata.*
(A Cyclic Form).

(A). Definition
(B). Nomenclature
(C). Tempo-Scheme and Internal Forms
(D). Key-Scheme
(E). Character-Sequence of Movements

(A). *Definition.* A sonata is an instrumental composition, varying in length from about eight or ten minutes to as much as an hour and a half; and comprising either three or else four distinct movements in related keys but different *tempi* (speeds), one of the movements at least (usually the first) being in sonata-form.

This definition covers four points which are worth additional comment.

(1) A sonata is a composition *for an instrument or instruments.* The very word *sonata* means "sounded" or "played," as opposed to *cantata,* which means "sung." In the 17th and early 18th centuries the name was used for instrumental pieces of many different types; but since the Classical period, *sonata* has been reserved for compositions which meet the terms of the above definition.

(2) The sonata is *tremendously variable in size.* The variability is noted above with reference to duration, since music is a temporal art. It is impossible to be precise about the lower or upper limits, but they are approximately as stated. Sonatas shorter than about eight minutes would probably be called *sonatinas* (a diminutive form of *sonata*). Sonatas as long as an hour and a half would occur only as out-sized *symphonies* (see B. below).

(3) A sonata has *either* three *or else* four distinct, separable movements. These are complete in themselves, both in form and in content; so much so that some one movement of a sonata may gain popularity and be performed in isolation without the layman's knowing or caring about its context. (Such cases are the first movement of Beethoven's *Pianoforte Sonata in C Sharp Minor,* doubly misnamed the "Moonlight Sonata," and the slow movement of Chopin's *B Flat Minor Pianoforte Sonata,* known as "Chopin's Funeral March"; also the first movement of Beethoven's *Fifth Symphony,* in C minor, known as *"The* Fifth Symphony"). Heard in context, however, the movements are found to be related tonally (see D. below), complementary in character (see E. below), and contrasting in tempo or speed (see C. below); and it is precisely by virtue of these relationships that they form a larger unity or "cycle" which we describe by a singular noun—*sonata.*

Sonatas do exist which have less than three or more than four movements; but they are comparatively rare. As to the choice of three as against four movements, this is largely a matter of historical period and the particular medium for which the sonata is written, though the character of the composition as a whole enters into the choice also We need not digress into these considerations, but simply state that a sonata will have sometimes three, sometimes four movements, depending on when it was written (Haydn? Beethoven?), what instruments are involved (solo pianoforte? orchestra?), and what its general mood is (intimate? heroic? impassioned? rhapsodic?).

(4) *At least* one movement of a sonata is in sonata-form (which we have discussed in detail under *One-Movement Forms,* section F). There may be more than one sonata-form movement; there are often two (first and last movements) and sometimes three (first, second and fourth in a four-movement sonata); but very rarely will sonata-form fail to appear at all. So regularly is it found in first movements (which are generally *allegro, i.e.,* in fast tempo) that it has acquired the alternative names "first-movement form" and "sonata-allegro form."

(B). *Nomenclature.* When a composition of the type defined above is written for a solo instrument (*e.g.,* pianoforte) or for two instruments combined (*e.g.,* piano and violin), it is called by its proper formal name, *sonata.* When, however, it is written for more than two instruments, it is (illogically) named *trio, quartet, quintet, sextet, septet,* or *octet* according to the *number of instruments* involved. Additional adjectives indicate the particular medium (the *kind* of instruments) in some cases; a *string quartet* is a sonata for four stringed instruments (two violins, viola, 'cello), whereas a *pianoforte quartet* is a sonata for pianoforte and three stringed instruments (violin, viola, 'cello). All sorts of instruments may be brough into combination, and in odd cases these are named by name (*e.g.,* quintet for oboe, clarinet, bassoon, horn, and pianoforte). A sonata for orchestra has the special name *symphony* (which literally means nothing more than "a sounding together"). A sonata for orchestra with solo player or players is called a *concerto,* the name of the solo instrument being added to specify the medium (*e.g.,* violin concerto, pianoforte concerto).

The single fact which must be grasped about all these confusing terms is that, whatever the medium and however many instruments are involved, *these compositions are the same in basic structure;* they are all *sonatas,* and what we say about the sonata will apply equally to them. Since, in the past two hundred years, thousands upon thousands of such compositions have been produced, of which hundreds of great ones have survived, it will be seen that discussion of the sonata covers an immense range of solo instrumental music, small-ensemble or "chamber" music, and symphonic music, from Haydn to Hindemith.

(C). *Tempo-Scheme and Internal Forms.* These can best be shown together, in table form.

Three-movement sonata

First movement: *Allegro* (fast, but generally not *very* fast).
                   Form: Sonata-form.
Second movement: *Andante* (slowish, easy-going) or *Adagio, Largo,* etc. (slow).
                   Form: Episodic; expanded ternary; variation; older rondo; sonata-form (the last comparatively rarely, and when used, compressed—either by omitting the Development or by using only one theme per subject, or by both of these methods).
Last movement: *Allegro* (fast) or *Presto* (very fast).
                   Form: Sonata-form (frequently); older rondo; sonata-rondo; variation.

Four-movement sonata.

To the above table add, between the second and last movements, a minuet-and-trio or (since Beethoven) a scherzo-and-trio, as a third movement. Tempo: *Allegretto* (somewhat fast) for the typical minuet-and-trio, *Allegro* (fast) for the typical scherzo-and-trio. Form (in either case): Simple episodic, of the strictest, most stereotyped kind.

Sometimes the minuet or scherzo appears between the first and the slow movements; but this is rather uncommon, and done for some special reason. Sometimes, too, the tempo-scheme of a sonata is different from the above. A composer may choose to begin with a slow or slowish first movement (perhaps in some form other than sonata-form) and follow this with a faster second movement; or the final movement may, in a few rare cases, be slow. The Classical composers, and Beethoven in his early days, were careful to acknowledge such departures by the use of the term *fantasia* (fantasy, fanciful composition) or the like; the popular "Moonlight Sonata" is in fact the (irregular) slow first movement of just such a sonata, specifically entitled by Beethoven *Sonata quasi una fantasia, i.e.,* "fantasy-sonata" or "sonata in free form." Later, however, when Beethoven in his last works molded the sonata to his own philosophical needs, he would vary the order (and number) of the movements without apology; and in this he was followed by the Romantic composers, in certain specific examples. Nevertheless, it is clearly demonstrable that the vast majority of sonatas, whether by the Classical composers, by Beethoven, or by the later Romantics, hew to the above line, which has about it a certain aesthetic logic and formal perfection (see E. below).

(D). *Key-scheme.* For present purposes it is enough to say that the first, the third, and (if there is one) the fourth movements will be in the same key; the sonata is identified thereby (plus *opus number, i.e.,* the sonata's number in the complete list of the composer's works; *e.g., Pianoforte Sonata in F Minor,* op. 57). The slow movement (the second) will almost always be in a different but related key. As time went on, composers began to widen the range of tonalities of the movements of their sonatas; the well-known *Largo* (slow movement) of Dvořák's *Symphony No. 4,* in E Minor ("From the New World"), for instance, is in D flat major—a key so remote from the E minor of movements 1, 3, and 4 that the composer feels it necessary to begin the slow movement with a modulatory introduction bridging the wide tonal gap. The majority of sonatas, however, have a quite obvious key-relationship between movements. The only special case we need mention is that in which a sonata in a *minor* tonality changes to the *major* of the same tonic (the "parallel major") for its final movement. This is quite common even in Classical writers; the *G Minor Pianoforte Quartet* by Mozart included in this volume (p. 236) has a third (last) movement in *G major;* and the keys of Beethoven's *Fifth Symphony,* in C minor, are: First movement in C minor, second movement in A flat major, third movement in C minor, last movement in C *major.*

Note well! When we say that a movement (or any sizable section of music) is "in" a certain key, we do not mean that the music remains in that key throughout, but simply that that key is its tonic, tonal center, or "home key," in which it begins, to which it returns. and in which it ends.

(E). *Character-Sequence of Movements.* The wide range of mood, or (better) of *character,* embraced by the sonata—especially the four-movement sonata—explains why this form has continued to attract composers and listeners for more than two centuries, providing as it does a "cycle" of musical experiences (hence "cyclic form"), a closely-related sequence of intellectual-emotional-kinesthetic appeals, which add up to something like a psychological drama.

(1) The first movement is generally the most imposing and brilliant, and the longest in number of bars (though its *allegro* tempo may make it shorter than the slow movement in duration). Coming when the attention of the listener is keenest, it uses the most complex and logical structure (sonata-form) for its closely reasoned "argument" or dialectic. Though it has "feeling" in plenty, its appeal is primarily to the reason (*intellectual appeal*).

(2) The second movement, in slower tempo, is typically lyrical, song-like, warmly or pathetically expressive. After the intellectual concentration of the first movement it comes as a foil or relief, its basic structure being in general quite simple (see C. above). Its appeal is to the heart (*emotional appeal*).

(3) The minuet or scherzo (generally the third movement of a four-movement sonata) is in essence a compensatory or mediatory movement, easing what might otherwise be too sudden a change from the lyricism or pathos of the slow movement to the high spirits of the final movement. This statement may appear questionable, when one remembers that there are thousands of three-movement sonatas which manage to get along quite well without a minuet or scherzo. But the fact is that Haydn, who did more than anyone to establish the pattern of the Classical sonata, evidently felt the need of this intervening movement, since it was he who added the minuet to the three-movement scheme he inherited from previous writers. Once added, it proved to be a welcome resource of which composers could avail themselves in sonatas whose general character called for this particular type of mood between slow and final movements. It must also be admitted that custom played its part in the matter. Haydn's quartets and symphonies generally were in four movements, while his solo sonatas and concertos generally had only three; Mozart, who learned from Haydn, followed the same habit; and even Beethoven, who never wrote a three-movement quartet or sym-

phony, always wrote three-movement concertos and sometimes three-movement solo-sonatas. (So firm is tradition that even today *concertos* are generally in three movements.)

The courtly minuet-and-trio of the 18th century was a graceful, rhythmic dance—an appeal to the motor mechanisms of the body, an invitation to physical motion. Its appeal was therefore *kinesthetic*. In the hands of the sonata-writers its tempo was quickened and its content enlarged, so that one cannot literally "dance the minuet" to a minuet by Haydn or Mozart. Beethoven further quickened the tempo, and used the form for expressing moods totally un-minuet-like; aware of what he was doing, he changed the name to *scherzo* (which literally means "a joke" or "a playful movement")—taking his cue from Haydn, who once or twice had used this term. Since Beethoven, *scherzi* have been written in a large variety of moods, many of them far from "joking." But whatever the mood, and however variable the speed, the rhythmic quality and compensatory function of the movement remained, whether it mediated between slow and final movements or (as often in 19th-century sonatas) between *lyrical* first movements and slow ones.

(4) The fourth movement (or, in a three-movement sonata, the third) is characteristically a hearty, spirited, fast, and even furious-fast affair, whose function is to round off the cycle of moods with an exciting, brilliant, often humorous "last act"; or if not that, then with a note of optimism and joy. Its favorite forms are not complicated (see C. above); when sonata-form (or sonata-rondo) is used, the prevailing character generally dictates an avoidance of lengthy development or "argument," such as is found in first-movement sonata-forms. The *finale,* we may fairly say, is *an appeal to the "high spirits"* of the listener; and as such it frequently has kinesthetic appeal as well.

INDEX

Academies, 234, 308, 315
Acropolis, Athens, 2, 11, 19
Adoration of the Magi (Bruegel), 98
Aeschylus, 2, 11, 17, 111, 261
Agnus Dei, 56, 58, 119–20
Alba Madonna (Raphael), 180
Alexander of Macedon, 3
Alla breve, 215
Almayer's Folly (Conrad), 362
Altarpiece, 73–77
Ambitus, 54, 56, 57, 59, 133
Ancients and Moderns, quarrel of, 145
Andrewes, Bishop Lancelot, 354
Anthropomorphism, Greek, 18
Antigone (Sophocles), 4–6, 12–17
Antony and Cleopatra (Shakespeare), 102–03, 106–13
Apollo and Daphne (Bernini), 173
Arcadia (Sidney), 136
Arch, 45–49
Archaic period, Greek sculpture, 29
Archimedes, 147
Arena Chapel (Giotto), 65–70
Areopagitica (Milton), 131
Aria, 220
Aristophanes, 11
Aristotle, 3–5, 35, 306
Arpeggio, 238, (n. 7)
Ars Poetica (Horace), 233
Art, as historical revelation, 33; relation to nature in classical and medieval styles, 36–37
Artist, condition of the, Medieval, 37–39; Renaissance, 65; Baroque, 151; 19th century, 302, 314; 20th century, 37, 314, 357–58, 360–61
Ash Wednesday (Eliot), 356
Assumption of the Virgin (El Greco), 165
Athena Parthenos (Pheidias), 20, 30
Athena Promachos (Pheidias), 19

Bacchus and Ariadne (Titian), 158
Bach, Johann Sebastian, 54, 146, 148, 150, 191, 193, 194–224, 367, 374, 407
Bacon, Francis, 145, 147–48, 231
Ballad, 271
Ballet music, 372, 377
Baptistery, Florence, 79
Baroque, contradictory tendencies of, 146, 148; contrasts in art, 151; emotionalism, 149, 151, 167, 229; fusion of the arts, 172; metaphor, 151; music characteristics, 191–93; nationalism, 147–48; painterly naturalism, 173; relation to Renaissance, 145–46, 151; religious conflicts, 148; scientific inquiry, 146–47; secularization of art, 150–2; sensuality, 172; sig-

nification of term, 146; sceptical rationalism, 146–47, 150; theatricality, 149, 174, 191
Basso continuo (through bass), 192–93, 197 *passim,* 213 *passim*
Basso ostinato 193, 201–02, 204, 207–08, 216
Bathers (Renoir), 330
Batter My Heart (Donne), 225–27, 229
"*Beau Dieu*" (Amiens), 44, 53
Bide, 38
Beethoven, 367, 373, 405, 411–13; characteristic procedures, 286, 292, 406; contrasted with Mozart, 276–79, 290, 293, 407; expansion of instrumental development, 278; life, 277; musical style, 277, 288–89; orchestra, 278, 284; symphony no. 3 ("Eroica"), 289, 405–06, 409; no. 5, 237, 277, 279, 289, 382, 390, 410, 412; no. 9, 301
Bernini, Gian Lorenzo, 149, 172–75
Billy Budd, Foretopman (Melville), 304–07
Binary form, 193 *passim;* discussion and illustration 396–97; examples in works studied, 257, 287; sectional repetition, 396; thematic development in, 397
Blind Leading the Blind (Bruegel), 98
Boats at Argenteuil (Monet), 324
Bolero (Ravel), 382
Bosch, Jerome, 96–7
Botticelli, 64
Brandenburg Concertos (Bach), 54, 194
Bruegel, Pieter, 67, 97–100
Brunellesco, 79
Burial of Count Orgaz (El Greco), 162–66
Bussy D'Ambois (Chapman), 356
Byzantine art, 68, 164

Cadence, 136, 191, 382, 387–88; authentic, 388; deceptive, 388; half, 388; plagal, 388
Cadenza, *see* Concerto
Callicrates, 19
Campion, Thomas, 228
Candide (Voltaire), 231, 263–68
Canonic imitation, *see* Polyphony
Cantata, Baroque, 212–24, 410
Cantata No. 4 (Bach), *see Christ Lag in Todesbanden*
Cantilever principle, 347–49
Cantus firmus, 120, 195
Cardinal Fernando Niño de Guevara (El Greco), 165–67, 189
Cardinal Scipione Borghese (Bernini), 174

Carpe diem, 228
Carpenter's Family (Rembrandt), 180
Castle of Otranto, The (Walpole), 234
Catharsis, 14
Cathedral, Medieval, 40–2; construction, 45–53; design, 49–53; elevation, 41, 44; expression, 43, 50; interior, 49; orchestration of arts, 51; plan, 40; program, 43, 52; sculpture, 52
Catholic Church, 35, 54, 65
Catholic reaction, *see* Counter Reformation
Catullus, 228
Cézanne, Paul, 332–39
"Chamber," *see* Elizabethan stage
Chamber-music, 236 (n.2), 367, 373, 411
Changeling, The (Middleton), 355
Chapman, George, 355–56
Characteristics (Shaftesbury), 275–76
Chiaroscuro, 77, 80, 90, 162–66, 182
Chopin, 288
Chorale, 193, 207, 212 *passim,* 224; arrangement, 207, 214; variations, 193, 213
Chord, 119, 133, 191, 386–90
Chordal style, 134, 135, 137, 139, 143, 192
Christ before Pilate (Tintoretto), 154
Christ Crowned with Thorns (Titian), 91
Christ Lag in Todesbanden (Bach), 212–24
Christianity, 1, 9, 33–39, 61–68, 267, 354
Chromaticism, 203, 221, 370, 374, 376
Cicero, 38, 62
City State, Greek, 3–4
Clarinet Quintet (Mozart), 236, 249–59, 404–05
Classical style in art, 36, 176–79
Classical style in literature, 14, 229, 261–62, 301–02
Classical style in music, 235–36
Classicism in art, 160
Classicism and the enlightenment, 231–59
Coda, 56, 399
Codetta, 407
Collage, 318–42
Color, complementary, 322 (n. 2); Impressionist use of, 321–32; in Flemish painting, 277; Italian Renaissance, use of, 90
Colorism, 90
Composition, geometric, 78
Conceit, 227, 230

Concertato style, 193
Concerto, 278–301; cadenza, 278, 283, 294, 371; double exposition, 278, 279–81, 289–94
Concerto grosso, 204
Confessions (St. Augustine), 55, 62, 64
Conjunct motion (movement), 54, 56, 57, 59
Conrad, Joseph, 362–66
Consonance, 119, 121, 390
Constantine, 35
Contemporary art, 313–45
Contemporary architecture, 345–52
Contrapposto, 87, 169
Corpus Christi, Feast of, 58
Counter-melody, 120
Counterpoint, 390
Counter Reformation, 146, 148–49, 160–61
Couperin, Francois, 148, 191
Courtly love poetry, Renaissance, 114–15, 131, 225, 229
Crescendo, 238 (n. 8)
Cross-relations, 368–69, 370
Crucifixion (Grünewald), 95–97
Cubism, 342

Da capo, 400–01
Daily Hours of Divine Service, 55
Dante, Alighieri, 61, 64–65
Darwin, Charles, 316
Dawn (Michelangelo); 87, 146
Day (Michelangelo), 86
Death of St. Francis (Giotto), 72
Decay of faith (20th century), 354
Defence of Poetry, A (Shelley), 273
Deism, 232, 264
Delian naval league, 2
Delphic Sibyl (Michelangelo), 86
Deluge (Poussin), 179
Demoiselles d'Avignon, Les (Picasso), 341
Descartes, René, 147–48
Descent from the Cross (Rubens), 168–70
Descent of the Holy Ghost (El Greco), 165
Description of the Contrarious Passions in a Lover (Petrarch, Wyatt), 114–15
Deserted Village, The (Goldsmith), 234
Dialogues (Plato), 3, 7
Diderot, 265–66
Dionysus, 2, 10–11
Dissonance, 119, 121–22, 133, 142–43, 192, 208, 217, 370, 390; preparation of a, 119, 390; resolution of a, 119, 390; suspension, 119, 121, 133, 134, 135, 192; unprepared, 192; free, 367, 373, 390
Divine Comedy (Dante), 61, 65
Dominant, 386
Dominican Order, 149
Donne, John, 149–51, 224–27, 230, 303
Dorian Conquests, 1
Dorian mode, 56, 59, 384–85
Double exposition, *see* Concerto
Drink to Me Only with Thine Eyes (Jonson), 399
Duccio, 69

Duple time, 381
Dürer, Albrecht, 64, 66

Eclogues (Virgil), 136
Ecstasy of Santa Teresa (Bernini), 149, 174
Edict of Milan, 35
Eleazar and Rebecca (Poussin), *see* Meeting of
Elegy Written in a Country Church-Yard (Gray), 260–62, 301–02
El Greco, 148, 152, 161, 167
Eliot, Thomas Stearns, 227, 229, 353–56
Elizabethan England, 131
Elizabethan playhouse, 100–05; admission fees, 101; entrances, 101; galleries, 100–01; pit, 100–01; reconstruction of Globe, 100–05; tiring house, 101; *see* Elizabethan Stage
Elizabethan poetry, 114–16, 131
Elizabethan stage, 101–05; costumes, 105; doors, 103; "heavens" (canopy), 102; "hut," 102; inner stages: "music room," 102–03, "study," 102–03, "chamber," 102–03; platform, 101–03; "properties," 103; scenery, 103; sound effects on, 102; trap doors on, 102; window balconies, 104–05
Elizabethan Tragedy, 106–13; characterization, 109–13; dramatic unities in, 106–07; moral content, 111–13; nature of, 106–08; structure of, 106–11; tragic hero in, 107, 112–13
Enlightenment, 146, 231–59, 260, 263, 267
Entry, *see* Fugue
Episode, *see* Episodic form, Fugue
Epithalamium (Spenser), 115–16
Erasmus, 63–64
Erechtheum, 2, 19, 24 (n. 6)
"Eroica" symphony, *see* Beethoven
Essay on Criticism (Pope), 233
Essay on Man (Pope), 233
Esto es Peor (Goya), 311
Et in Arcadia Ego (Poussin), 179
Etching process, 183–84
Eucharist, 58
Euripides, 11, 17
Execution of May 3 (Goya), 309
Exposition, *see* Sonata-form, Fugue, Concerto
Expressionism, 162, 310

Faerie Queene, The (Spenser), 115
Fair Phylis (Farmer), 136–40, 143, 394
Fall of Icarus (Bruegel), 98
Farmer, John, 131, 136–40, 394
Ferney, 266–67
Ficinus, Marsilius, 63
Fifth Symphony, see Beethoven
Figures (music), 382–83
Finalis, 55-56, 57, 59, 384
Fingal (Macpherson), 275
Finnegan's Wake (Joyce), 358, 361
Flaubert, Gustave, 316
Folk-song, 54, 137, 372–73, 381
Fontenelle, 264
Form, and function, breakdown of, 317; in music, 392–413

Four Quartets (Eliot), 356
Fourth Pianoforte Concerto (Beethoven), 277–78, 289–301
Free association, 356, 358
French Revolution, 302, 314
Fresco, 70
Fugato, 378, 407
Fugue, 193, 208, 378, 390, 394–95; counter subject, 208, 210, 394–95; entry, 394–95; episode, 208, 210, 394–95; exposition, 208, 209, 394; subject, 208–10, 394–95
Functionalism, 352

Galsworthy, John, 362, 364
Gare St. Lazare (Monet), 325
Gerontion (Eliot), 353–56
Ghent Altarpiece (Van Eyck), 73
Ghiberti, 64
Gibbons, Orlando, 131–32, 140–43, 394
Gide, André, 265
Giotto di Bondone, 61, 64, 65, 68
Giovanni Arnolfini and His Wife (Van Eyck), 77
Girl Before the Mirror (Picasso), 343
Girl with a Cock (Picasso), 344
Giuliano (Michelangelo), 86–88
Glaze, 91
Glissando, 247
Globe Playhouse, *see* Elizabethan playhouse
"Golden Age" of Greece, 1–3, 11
Goldsmith, Oliver, 234
Gothic, 41–44
Gothic Revival, 234
Goya, Francisco, 308–12
Grace-notes, 250 (n. 3)
Gray, Thomas, 260–63, 301–02
Great Year, The, 354
Greek art, contrasted with Medieval, 36–37; generalization in, 6, 36
Greek communities, dispersion of, 3
Greek theater, 2, 11
Greek theory of individual and the state, 3–4, 14
Greek tragedy, characters, 17, 111, 113; chorus, 10–12; dramatic unities in, 13; manner of presentation, 11–12; moral content, 4–5, 9, 14–15, 111; nature of, 15–16; origin and development, 2, 10–11; structure of, 12–14; tragic hero in, 12, 16–17
"Gregorian Chant," *see* Plainsong
Grisaille, 74
Grünewald, Matthias, 67, 94–97
Guernica (Picasso), 343
Gulliver's Travels (Swift), 231

Hagenau, Nicolas von, 95
Hals, Franz, 152
Hamlet (Shakespeare), 102–03, 107, 109, 112, 229, 355, 363
Handel, George Frederick, 148, 191, 193, 401
Harmony, 54 (n. 2), 132, 140, 143, 191–92, 206, 386–88, 390
Harpsichord, 192
Harvesters (Bruegel), 67, 98

415

Hawthorne, Nathaniel, 51
Haydn, Franz Josef, 236, 288, 402, 405-06, 410-11, 412-13
Haymo letter, 42
Heart of Darkness, The (Conrad), 362
Hebraism, 33
Hegeso Stele, 6
"Hellas," 1
Henri IV Presented with the Portrait of Marie de Medicis (Rubens), 170-72
Heraclitus, 7
Herodotus, 2-3
Herrick, 148, 228
Hindemith, Paul, 54, 366-72, 411
History of the Peloponnesian Wars (Thucydides), 3
History of the Persian Wars (Herodotus), 3
Hobbes, 148
Holbein, 64
Holy Sonnet XIV (Donne), 225-27, 229
Homer, 1, 18
Homophonic forms, 395-413
Homophony, 193, 390-92
Homophonic texture, 193, 392
Horace, 151, 233
Humanism, 61-65, 67, 114-15, 146, 160
Humanities, 64
Huxley, Thomas Henry, 316
Hybris, 5, 15
Hymn to Adversity (Gray), 261
Hymn to Earth the Mother of All (Homeric), 18-19

I-beams, 21
Iconography, 38-39
Ictinos, 2, 19
Idealism, Greek, in art, 6; in philosophy, 6-9
Ideas, theory of (Plato), 7-9, 63
Idylls (Theocritus), 136
Imagery, 116-17, 226-27, 262, 353-56
Impressionism, 316, 320-26, 333
Impressionistic painting, 189, 309
Individualism, Renaissance, *see* Protestant Reformation, Renaissance, Romanticism
Industrial Revolution, 302, 314
Innocent X (Velasquez), 188
Interior monologue, technique of, 358
International style of architecture, 345-57
Interval, 119, 133, 192, 383, 386, 390; augmented, 199; octave, 54, 122, 142, 383
Ionian Confederacy, 2
Isenheim Altarpiece (Grüenwald), 67, 94-97

Jacob Harring (Rembrandt), 184
James, Henry, 363-64
Jefferson, Thomas, 233
Jesuits, 149, 226
Job, 33-34
Johnson, Samuel, 227-28, 260-61
Jonson, Ben, 224, 228
Joyce, James, 372, 357-61, 364

Jubilate Deo, 59-60
Judgment of Paris (Rubens), 171
Julius Caesar (Shakespeare), 103, 112
July (Bruegel), 98

Keats, John, 271-72, 274, 302-04
King Lear (Shakespeare), 112
King Oedipus (Sophocles), 6, 9, 12-17, 33-34
Kouroi, 29
Kyrie, 56, 58, 119-26

Lamentation (Giotto), 70-73
Lamia (Keats), 271
Landscape, 91, 97, 166, 178, 184
Landscape with Stone Bridge (Rembrandt), 185
Laocoön and His Sons, 89
Lapiths and Centaurs, 31
Last Supper (Leonardo), 81
Last Supper (Tintoretto), 156
Le Corbusier, 352
Leibniz, 263-64
Leonardo da Vinci, 64-66, 78-83, 158
L'Estaque (Cézanne), 333
Lichfield Cathedral, 51
Light, treatment of, 77
Lines Written a Few Miles above Tintern Abbey (Wordsworth), 270, 274
Link, 399, 407
Lippo, Lippi, Fra, 64
Lisbon Earthquake, The (Voltaire), 263-64
Locke, 148, 266
Lord Jim (Conrad), 362, 365
Lorenzo (Michelangelo), 65, 85-88
Love, Platonic, 91, 115
Luther, Martin, 194, 207, 212
Lydian mode, 57, 59
Lyric poetry, 114-17, 224-30, 260-63, 301-04, 353-56
Lyrical Ballads (Wordsworth), 272, 275

Macbeth (Shakespeare), 105, 107 112
Macpherson, James, 275
Madame Bovary (Flaubert), 316
Madonna and Child Enthroned (Giotto), 70
Madonna of the Rocks (Leonardo), 79-80
Madrigal 131-43; English, 131-43; Italian, 131; style, 131-32; text, 131-32; *see* word-painting
Magnificat, The (Bach), 192, 194-212
Maids of Honor, The (Velasquez), 188
Maja Desnuda (Goya), 311
Majestas (Giotto), 70
Ma Jolie (Picasso), 342
Major, *see* scales
Man with Folded Arms (Cézanne), 337
Mannerism, 152-53, 165
Mardi (Melville), 305-06
Marvell, Andrew, 228-30, 303
Marx, Karl, 316
Mass, 55, 118-21
Mean, doctrine of the (Greek), 5-6

Measure for Measure (Shakespeare), 353
Medici Chapel (Michelangelo), 83-88
Medieval art, contrasted with Greek art, 36-37; generalization in, 37; other worldliness, 37; moral purpose, 38
Medieval philosophy, immortality as justification for pursuit of knowledge, 35; reason and faith, 35-36
Medieval view of man and the world, 62-63, 108
Meditations (Descartes), 147
Meeting of Eleazer and Rebecca (Poussin), 176
Melismatic style, 60, 132, 135
Melville, Herman, 304-07
Metaphysical poetry, 227-28
Meter (in music), 59, 192, 381-82; irregular, 55, 371, 374; subordination to text, 55, 121; *see also* Rhythm
Michelangelo Buonarotti, 63-66, 83-84, 145-46, 169, 172
Middle Ages, 33-60
Middleton, Thomas, 355
Midsummer Night's Dream, A (Shakespeare), 105
Mies van der Rohe, 352
Mill, The (Rembrandt), 185
Milton, John, 131, 148, 150, 224, 353
Minuet in A Major (Boccherini), 389
Minuet and trio, 400, 403, 411-12; with two trios, 254-56
Miracle of St. Mark (Tintoretto), 153
Moby Dick (Melville), 304
Modes, 55, 191, 383-86; in polyphonic music, 121, 132
Modulation 59, 191, 197, 388-390, 397-98; in sonata form, 406
Monet, Claude Oscar, 323-27
Morley, Thomas, 131-32
Motives, 382-83
Moulin de la Galette (Renoir), 328
Mt. Olympus (Pheidias), 31, 89
Mozart, Wolfgang Amadeus, 235-59, 249, 265, 278, 367, 373, 395, 405, 413; contrast with Beethoven, 276-79, 288, 407; elegance in phrasing, 238-39, 246, 257; life, 235-36; lyricism in slow movements, 242, 252-56; mastery of clarinet-writing, 249; musical style, 235-36; typical development techniques, 240
My Country 'Tis of Thee, 382, 396-97

Nature, 302
Neo-Classicism, 146, 232, 302; in literature, 233; in architecture, 233; in music, 234
Neo-Platonism, 63, 84-88, 91
Nicaea, Second Council of, 38
Nicomachean Ethics (Aristotle), 4
Nigger of the 'Narcissus,' The (Conrad), 362, 365
Night (Michelangelo), 86
Ninth Symphony, see Beethoven

416